INDEX TO THE
1820 CENSUS OF
MARYLAND
and Washington, D.C.

I0105283

Compiled by
GARY W. PARKS

CLEARFIELD

Reprinted for
Clearfield Company, Inc. by
Genealogical Publishing Co., Inc.
Baltimore, Maryland
1999

NOTE TO THE READER

This is an index to the 1820 census of Maryland and the District of Columbia, in effect a complete register of the heads of households living in Maryland and Washington, D.C. at the time of the fourth census of the United States. The data furnished in this index was taken from a mircofilm copy of the original census schedules (M33, nos. 40-46 and no. 5), then arranged in alphabetical order by head of household.

Legibility of the original entries varies from poor to excellent, depending on the handwriting of the census enumerator and the quality of the microfilm. Nevertheless, every effort has been made in this work to provide the researcher with the most accurate transcription possible. Alternative and questionable entries have been marked thus: question mark in parenthesis (?) - - *surname questionable*, or question mark without parenthesis ? - - *given name questionable*.

Researchers are cautioned that standard spellings were the exception rather than the rule, particularly with surnames. Thus, vowels were freely interchanged, consonants doubled or deleted, and names spelled phonetically. Note, for example, the name Marey FRONSWA (Baltimore City, p. 395)—a plausible spelling for Mary FRANCOIS. Readers are encouraged to apply their research skills as well as their imagination.

This book would not have been possible without the aid of Sis and Pete Parks, who spent countless hours arranging the entries in alphabetical order, and Michael Tepper and Eileen Perkins of the Genealogical Publishing Company. A special note of thanks goes to Bob Barnes for providing the seed of this project—a transcription of portions of Baltimore County's 1820 census.

Gary W. Parks
Abingdon, Maryland

FOR MY GRANDMOTHER,

EMMA

TABLE I

County	Abbreviation	Roll no.
ALLEGANY COUNTY	ALL	40
ANNE ARUNDEL COUNTY	ANN	41
BALTIMORE COUNTY	BAL	41
BALTIMORE CITY	BCI	42
CALVERT COUNTY	CAL	40
CAROLINE COUNTY	CLN	40
CECIL COUNTY	CEC	40
CHARLES COUNTY	CHA	40
DORCHESTER COUNTY	DOR	43
FREDERICK COUNTY	FRE	43
HARFORD COUNTY	HAR	44
KENT COUNTY	KEN	44
MONTGOMERY COUNTY	MON	44
PRINCE GEORGE'S COUNTY	PRI	44
QUEEN ANNE'S COUNTY	QUE	45
SAINT MARY'S COUNTY	SAI	45
SOMERSET COUNTY	SOM	45
TALBOT COUNTY	TAL	46
WASHINGTON COUNTY	WAS	46
WORCESTER COUNTY	WOR	46
WASHINGTON, D.C.	D.C.	5

TABLE II

ALLEGANY COUNTY (Roll #40), pp. 2-39. Machine stamped and handwritten numbers, left margin. Page number generally refers to numbered page and page immediately following. 1st Election District, pp. 2-5; 2nd Election District, pp. 5A-8; 3rd Election District, pp. 8A-10; 4th Election District, pp. 10A-14, inc. Town of Western Port, p. 14; 5th Election District, pp. 14A-19; 6th Election District, pp. 20A-30, inc. Town of Cumberland, pp. 26-30; 7th Election District, pp. 31-37, inc. Village of Old Town, p. 36; 8th Election District, pp. 37-39.

ANNE ARUNDEL COUNTY (Roll #41), pp. 253-405. Machine stamped numbers, left margin. Page number generally refers to numbered page only. 1st Election District, pp. 253-282; 2nd Election District, pp. 283-293; 3rd Election District, pp. 296-313; 4th Election District, pp. 315-348; 5th Election District, pp. 349-384 (pp. 383 & 384 were photographed twice); 6th Election District, "City of Annapolis being the 6" election district", pp. 388-404; ends page 405.

BALTIMORE COUNTY (Roll #41), pp. 2-251. Handwritten numbers, left margin. Page number generally refers to numbered page only. 7th Election District, pp. 2-31 (pp. 22 & 23 were photographed twice); 6th Election District, pp. 36-73; 5th Election District, pp. 76-102; 4th Election District, pp. 105-134; 3rd Election District, pp. 138-168; 1st Election District, pp. 173-211; 2nd Election District, pp. 214-251.

BALTIMORE CITY (Roll #42), pp. 2-540. Handwritten numbers, left margin. Page number generally refers to numbered page only. 1st Ward, pp. 2-42; 2nd Ward, pp. 45-104, inc. 1st Division "being all South of the Centre of Allisanna Stt. (pp. 45-61), 2nd Division "from the N. side of Allisanna St. to S. Side of Wilk St. (pp. 61-75), 3rd Division "being fr. the N. side of Wilk to the S. side of Dulany Sts. (pp. 75-96), 4th Division "from the N. Side of Dulany St. to Harford road (pp. 96-103); 3rd Ward, pp. 109-163A (note that p. 161 immediately follows p. 162); 4th Ward, pp. 166-204; 5th Ward, pp. 207-234; 6th Ward, pp. 239-260; 7th Ward, pp. 265-288; 8th Ward, pp. 293-328; 9th Ward, pp. 333-362; 10th Ward, pp. 367-420; 11th Ward, pp. 425-468; 12th Ward, pp. 473-540.

CALVERT COUNTY (Roll #40), pp. 40-70. Machine stamped and handwritten numbers, left margin. Page number generally refers to numbered page and page immediately following. 1st District, pp. 41A-46, inc. "St. Leonards Creek Town," p. 44A; 2nd District, pp. 47-56, 66A-70; 3rd District, pp. 58A-65; ends page 70.

CAROLINE COUNTY (Roll #40), pp. 71-117. Machine stamped and handwritten numbers, left margin. Page number generally refers to numbered page and page immediately following. 1st Election District, pp. 72-83; 2nd Election District, pp. 85-101; 3rd Election District, pp. 104A-117.

CECIL COUNTY (Roll #40), pp. 119-188. Machine stamped and handwritten numbers, left margin. Page number generally refers to numbered page and page immediately following. 1st Election District, pp. 119-130; 2nd Election District (inc. Elkton), pp. 131-149; 3rd Election District, pp. 151-169; 4th Election District, pp. 171A-188; recap. of 3rd & 4th Election District statistics, p. 188; ends page 188.

CHARLES COUNTY (Roll #40), pp. 189-229. Machine stamped and handwritten numbers, left margin. Page number generally refers to numbered page and page immediately following. 1st Election District, pp. 189A-198; 2nd Election District, pp. 200A-208A; 3rd Election District, pp. 210A-219; 4th Election District, pp. 220A-229.

DORCHESTER COUNTY (Roll #43), pp. 3-65. Machine stamped numbers, left margin. Page number generally refers to numbered page and page immediately following. 5th Election District, pp. 3-16; 3rd Election District, pp. 18-26 (page 26 was photographed twice); 4th Election District, pp. 27-37 (page 32 was photographed twice); 2nd Election District, pp. 39-46, inc. Elliotts Island, pp. 42-(46?); 1st Election District, pp. 49-65 (page 54 was photographed twice); ends page 65.

FREDERICK COUNTY (Roll #43), pp. 66-234. Machine stamped and handwritten numbers, left margin. Page number generally refers to numbered page and page immediately following. 9th Election District, pp. 68-79; 1st Election District, pp. 79A-88; recap. of 9th & 1st Election District statistics, pp. 88-91; 2nd Election District (Frederick Town), pp. 93-108; 2nd Election District ("outside town"), pp. 109-118A; 3rd Election District, pp. 122-138; 5th Election District, pp. 140-153, inc. Emmittsburg, pp. 140-142; 4th Election District, pp. 154-166, inc. Graceham, p. 154, Mechanics Town, pp. 154-155, Creegers Town, p. 155, & Lewis Town, p. 156; Taney Town Election District, pp. 168-184; 7th Election District (Westminster), pp. 186-206; 8th Election District, pp. 209-232, 234 (page 218 was photographed twice), inc. Liberty Town, pp. 219A-(230?); ends page 234.

HARFORD COUNTY (Roll #44), pp. 4-82. Machine stamped numbers, left margin. Page number generally refers to numbered page and page immediately following. 1st Election District, pp. 4-13; 2nd Election District, pp. 18-33; 3rd Election District, pp. 37-51; 4th Election District, pp. 55-66; 5th Election District, pp. 70-82.

KENT COUNTY (Roll #44), pp. 85-126. Machine stamped and handwritten numbers, left margin. Page number generally refers to numbered page and page immediately following. 1st Election District, pp. 85-96; 2nd Election District, pp. 100-111, inc. Chester Town, pp. 100-(109?); [3rd Election District], pp. 115-126, inc. Town of the Hd. of Chester, pp. 114-115; ends page 126.

MONTGOMERY COUNTY (Roll #44), pp. 129-178A. Machine stamped and handwritten numbers, left margin. Page number generally refers to numbered page and page immediately following. 2nd Election District (Medley's District), pp. 129-146; 4th Election District, pp. 147A-157; 3rd Election District, pp. 158A-169; 1st Election District (Goshen District), pp. 170-178A.

PRINCE GEORGE'S COUNTY (Roll #44), pp. 180A-242. Machine stamped and handwritten numbers, left margin. Page number generally refers to numbered page and page immediately following. 1st Election District (Vans Ville Election District), pp. 180A-188; 2nd Election District (Bladensburg Election District), pp. 191A-[200], unnumbered page immediately following page 199 has been assigned the page number PRI [200]; 3rd Election District, pp. 201-209, inc. Queen Anne, p. 206, (pps. 208-209 were photographed twice); [4th] Election District (Nottingham Election District), pp. 211-220, inc. Nottingham, p. 219; 5th Election District (Piscataway District), pp. 221A-233, inc. Town of Piscataway, pp. 222, 226, 232, (pp. 229, 232-233 were photographed twice); 6th Election District (Spaulding's District), pp. 235-242.

QUEEN ANNE'S COUNTY (Roll #45), pp. 1-50. Machine stamped and handwritten numbers, right margin. Page number generally refers to numbered page and page immediately following. 1st Election District, pp. 2A-22; 2nd Election District, pp. 23-43; 3rd Election District, pp. 45-50.

SAINT MARY'S COUNTY (Roll #45), pp. 51-100. Machine stamped and handwritten numbers, right margin. Page number generally refers to numbered page and page immediately following. 1st Election District, pp. 53A-59; 2nd Election District, pp. 62A-71; 3rd Election District, pp. 73A-84; 4th Election District, pp. 86A-100.

SOMERSET COUNTY (Roll #45), pp. 101-158. Machine stamped and handwritten numbers, right margin. Page number generally refers to numbered page and page immediately following. 1st Election District, pp. 101A, 103-121; 2nd Election District, pp. 122-141, inc. Dames Quarter, Menokin, Poquoson, Trappe, Pocomoke, Monie, & Princess Anne; 3rd Election District, pp. 142A, 144-158.

TALBOT COUNTY (Roll #46), pp. 2-53. Machine stamped and handwritten numbers, left margin. Page number generally refers to numbered page and page immediately following. Easton District No. #1, pp. 2-16, inc. Easton, pp. 8A-14, & "The begining of Eston Point", p. 14; Saint Michael's District No. #2, pp. 19-29; Trappe District No. #3, pp. 31-42, inc. Trapp Town, pp. 34A-35; Chappel District No. #4, pp. 45-53.

WASHINGTON COUNTY (Roll #46), pp. 55A-151. Machine stamped and handwritten numbers, left margin. Page number generally refers to numbered page and page immediately following. 1st Election District, pp. 55A-75, inc. Sharpsburgh, pp. 55A-58 & Boonsborough, pp. 58A-74; 2nd Election District, pp. 76-91, inc. Williams Port, pp. 77-90; 3rd Election District, pp. 93-130, inc. Hagerstown, pp. 113A-123, Funcks Town, pp. 124A-126, Smith Burgh, pp. 127A-128, Cavetown, p. 128A; 4th Election District, pp. 132-142, unnumbered page-second leaf after numbered page 134 has been assigned the page number WAS 134 [A], WAS 134 [A] also refers to the third, unnumbered leaf after numbered page 134; 5th Election District, pp. 144-151, inc. Hancock Town, pp. 145-146; ends page 151.

WORCESTER COUNTY (Roll #46), pp. 153-220. Machine stamped numbers, left margin. Page number generally refers to numbered page and page immediately following. 1st Election District, pp. 153-164; 2nd Election District (Snowhill Town), pp. 169-181; 3rd Election District, pp. 184-198; 4th Election District, pp. 199A-207; 5th Election District, pp. 209-220.

WASHINGTON, D.C. (Roll #5), pp. 1-222. Typewritten numbers on attached slips of paper, upper right corner. Page number generally refers to numbered page only. 1st Ward, pp. 3-19; Georgetown, pp. 20-61; Washington County, "West of the road leading from 14th Street West by Rock Creek Church to the North line", pp. 62-68; 2nd Ward, pp. 71-84; 3rd Ward, pp. 85-99; 4th Ward, pp. 100-109; 5th Ward, pp. 111-119; 6th Ward, pp. 120-133; Washington Co. (D.C.) South of Eastern Branch (Branck) Potomack, pp. 134-139, inc. "Dist. South of the Eastern Branch, & Dist. North of the Eastern Branch, East of 15th Street west, and out of the limits of the City", pp. 137-139; Town of Alexandria, pp. 143-219 (pages 195 & 197 duplicate one another); recap. of Washington, D.C. statistics, p. 222.

INDEX TO THE 1820 CENSUS
OF MARYLAND
and Washington, D.C.

INDEX TO THE 1820 CENSUS OF
MARYLAND AND WASHINGTON, D.C.

INDEX TO THE 1820 CENSUS OF MARYLAND AND WASHINGTON, D.C.

ABIGALL, Richard	PRI 208	ADAMS (continued),		ADAMS (continued),	
Thomas	PRI 206	Charlotte	SOM 141	Margarett	BCI 305
ABILL, Francis-overseer,		Chloe	CHA 191	Margt.	D.C.112
poore House	SAI 76	Christina	FRE 160	Mary	SOM 153
Julet	SAI 76	Clinton	D.C.13	Milley	SOM 153
ABLE, Christian	BCI 528	Cornelious	SAI 76	Minor	DOR 62
John S.	BCI 479	Edward	TAL 35	Nancy (of Saml.)	SOM 157
Mary (Miss)	CAL 43	Elizabeth	D.C.47	Nathan	D.C.5
Samuel	WAS 121	Elizebeth	DOR 31	Nathan	SOM 146
ABOTT, John H.	FRE 94	Emily	D.C.95	Nathinel	DOR 21
ABRAHAM, Moses	BCI 148	Fortin	DOR 11	Nehemiah	SOM 135
ABRAHAMS, Jacob	BCI 154	Frans., Jr.	D.C.175	Philip	WAS 102
ABRAM, John	ANN 360	Geo.	D.C.125	Philip C.	SOM 127
John	BCI 58	Geo.	D.C.130	Posey	CHA 191
ABRAMS, Abraham	BCI 137	George	ANN 300	Rachel-f.c.p.	HAR 11
Eleanor	CEC 153A	George	CLN 110	Raymond	SOM 148
Jacob	BCI 48	George	D.C.48	Richard	D.C.60
Peter	CEC 153A	George	DOR 7	Richard	FRE 201
Woodward	CEC 153A	George	FRE 179	Rumford	CLN 105
ABRECHT, George	FRE 94	George	SAI 68	Sally	SOM 141
ABREICHT, William	WAS 111	George	WAS 108	Sally (H)	SOM 156
ABSLEY, Delany	KEN 91	Gustavus	CHA 196A	Sally (of H.G.)	SOM 156
ABY, Barbary	BCI 319	Hannah	CLN 115	Sally (of W.)	SOM 156
Christopher	BCI 53	Henry	CLN 113	Sam-f.c.p.	HAR 10
Jacob	BCI 319	Henry	D.C.31	Samuel	CHA 225
ACHABARGER, Peter	WAS 104	Henry	WAS 114	Samuel	SOM 149
ACHREMAN, John	D.C.8	Henry	WAS 117	Samuel	TAL 12
ACKLAND, Jams.	BCI 230	Hope	SOM 113	Sarah	BCI 5
ACKLEY, Julius	BCI 459	Ignatius	PRI 207	Sarah	BCI 301
ACKNER, Philip	WAS 100	Isaac M.	SOM 123	Stephen	SAI 75
ACKWORTH, Stephen	BCI 78	Jacab	DOR 25	Stephen	SOM 156
ACLE, Amos	WAS 67	Jacob?	DOR 25	Stephen (of Abrm.)	
George	WAS 102	Jacob	FRE 162		SAI 68
George	WAS 128A	Jacob	WAS 94	Thomas	CLN 112
Henry, Senr.	WAS 68	James	BCI 53	Thomas	D.C.36
Jacob	WAS 85	James	CHA 203	Thomas	DOR 29
John	WAS 61	James	D.C.71	Thomas	DOR 31
John	WAS 68	James	FRE 74	Thomas	FRE 172
John	WAS 85	James	PRI 224	Thomas	PRI 213
Judy	WAS 60	James	SOM 154	Thomas	SOM 148
ACTON, Elizabeth	CHA 221	James	WAS 62	Thomas	SOM 153
George	CHA 218	James	WAS 109	Walker	HAR 79
Henry	CHA 215	Jane	CHA 207B	Washington	CLN 105
Randolph	CHA 226	Jesse	SOM 147	Whopping	BAL 246
Samuel (?)	WAS 119	John	BCI 300	Will.	D.C.106
Theodore	CHA 217	John	BCI 476	Will	D.C.113
Verlinda	CHA 215	John	CEC 153A	William	ALL 14
William	CHA 215	John	CHA 192	William	CHA 224
Wood	CHA 224	John	D.C.198	William	HAR 28
ACTOR, Samuel (?)	WAS 119	John	HAR 75	William	HAR 7:
ACWORTH, Beacham	SOM 103	John	MON 158A	William	SOM 1:"
Samuel	SOM 109	John	MON 177	William	SOM 153
ADAIR, John	FRE 151	John	PRI 224	William	TAL 9
ADAM, John	D.C.170	John	SOM 132	William (Capt.)	WOR 212
Wm.	BCI 344	John	SOM 141	Wm.	BCI 224
ADAMS, Aaron	ANN 333	John	SOM 156	ADAMSON, John	MON 167
Abenigo	D.C.203	John	WAS 58A	John, Jur.	MON 158A
Abraham	SAI 62A	John	WAS 88	Lloyd	MON 147A
Absolum	BAL 185	John (of George)	CHA 227	ADDAM, James	SAI 97
Adam	TAL 10	John (of John)	CHA 224	ADDAMS, Ann	SAI 97
Alexander	BCI 21	John Q.	D.C.97	William H.	QUE 46
Amey	DOR 32	John S.	BCI 321	ADDERTON, James	SAI 97
Ann	CHA 192	Joseph	BCI 22	Joseph	CHA 202
Beauchamp D.	SOM 106	Joseph M.	CHA 189	Judeth A.	SAI 57
Benedict L.	MON 165	Joshua	CLN 105	ADDINGTON, Richard	
Benjamin	ANN 280	Joshua	TAL 34A		CAL 64
Benjamin	CLN 87	Judah (f.n.)	SOM 120	ADDISON, Anna	BCI 267
Benjamin	CHA 216	Lazarus	SOM 149	Catherine	CAL 42
Benjamin	MON 147A	Leonard	D.C.150	Edwd.	D.C.138
Benjamin	MON 147A	Levin	DOR 29	Henry	D.C.103
Caleb	HAR 75	Levin	DOR 32	Isaac	BCI 509
Caleb	MON 147A	Lila	DOR 31	Jacob	FRE 106
Cato	FRE 118	Lydia	PRI 224	John	BCI 26
Charles	D.C.30	M.	BCI 211	John	PRI 238
Charles J. (I.?)	DOR 21	Maclemar	SOM 135	Nancy	BCI 483

3

ADDISON (continued),		
Nathaniel	PRI	211
Polaskey	FRE	110
Thos. G.	D.C.	135
ADEEAR, Mudan (?)	BCI	220
ADELSPERGER, Thomas		
	FRE	187
ADER, Abraham	FRE	73
Susa	FRE	220
ADISON, Anthony	D.C.	60
Thomas B.	D.C.	51
Walter (Rev.)	D.C.	58
ADKEY, Jo	QUE	7
Thomas	KEN	85
ADKINS, Azeriah	WOR	219
Bart(z)illa	WOR	201
Barzilla?	WOR	201
David	WOR	205
Elijah	WOR	200
Henry	WOR	216
John, J.	WOR	200
Jonithin	WOR	201
Jonithin	WOR	202
Josiah	WOR	200
Mary	FRE	109
Middleton	WOR	200
Middleton	WOR	204
Milby	WOR	200
Nimrod	WOR	200
Precilla	WOR	199A
Precilla, W.	WOR	207
Sampson	WOR	200
Samuel	DOR	8
Stephen	WOR	188
Stephin	WOR	199A
Stevin	WOR	199A
William; S.	WOR	200
William, of N.	WOR	200
Wm.	BCI	531
ADKINSON, John	BAL	180
Joseph (?)	BAL	206
Thomas	DOR	44
ADKISON, Joseph	BAL	206
ADLESPARGER, Joshua		
	FRE	170
ADLESPERGER, John	FRE	173
ADLEY, James	WAS	63
Tom (negro)	TAL	21
ADLUM, John	D.C.	65
John	MON	134
Joseph	FRE	109
Margaret	FRE	96
ADOMS, Edward	TAL	3
ADOR, John	FRE	73
ADREON, Mathias	BAL	26
ADRIAN, Christ.	BCI	527
George	BCI	528
William	BCI	49
ADUMS, Peter	SOM	137
ADY, James	HAR	39
Samuel	HAR	38
Solomon	HAR	38
AERES, Joseph (?)	KEN	88
AESTERLINE (See also		
HESTERLINE),		
Catharine	FRE	189
AFFARRUGS, John	BCI	150
AFTY, Abraham	D.C.	206
AGAIN, Elijah	BAL	244
AGAN, William	BCI	437
AGENENE, William (?)	BCI	37
AGENEW, William	BCI	37
AGNEW, John	FRE	140
Robert	WOR	159
Samuel	FRE	141

AGRY, Samuel	D.C.	210
AHALT, Henry	FRE	131
Jacob	FRE	130
AIKEN, Prudence (?)		
	D.C.	90
AIKENS, William	HAR	74
AIKIN, Prudence	D.C.	90
AIKMAN, Robert	SOM	133
AILER (See also OILER),		
Amon	BAL	13
George	BAL	20
George	BAL	21
Mathias	BAL	19
William	BAL	24
AILES, Samuel	HAR	70
AIMES, Tilman	BCI	509
AINSWORTH, Elizabeth		
	WAS	65
Robert	WAS	62
AIRBOUGH, John	BAL	53
Peter	BAL	52
AIRES, Joseph	KEN	88
AIREY, Francis A.	DOR	51
Richard	BCI	313
AIRS, Abraham	BAL	112
Archibald	SOM	109
George	SOM	115
Jacob	BCI	217
James	BAL	233
Littleton	SOM	116
Mary	ANN	366
AISQUITH, John,		
Esqr.	BCI	282
AITKEN, Geo.	BCI	251
Robt.	BCI	248
AKERS, Charles,		
Ovsr.	TAL	40
Sarah	DOR	63
AKIN, Samuel	CEC	153A
AKINS, George	HAR	31
ALAWAY, William	QUE	34
ALBA, Wm.	MON	167
ALBAUGH, Absolum	FRE	99
Daniel	ALL	34
David	FRE	99
Margrate	BAL	154
Solomon	FRE	99
ALBAUGHS, John	FRE	221
ALBERG, Christian	BCI	100
ALBERGER, Jacob	QUE	25
Samuel	BCI	97
ALBERS, Solo. G.	BCI	221
ALBERT, Elizabeth	HAR	75
Elizabeth	WAS	87
Ereve P.	BCI	128
George	WAS	111
Jacob	BCI	441
Jacob	WAS	89
John	WAS	118
Martin	WAS	94
Philip	HAR	72
William	HAR	72
William	WAS	79
William	WAS	88
ALBERTS, Lodman	BCI	13
ALBERTSON, Jonathan		
	CEC	171A
ALBRICHT, Jacob	WAS	137
ALBRIGHT, Charles	FRE	117
John	BCI	492
Joseph	BCI	492
ALBRITON, James	CHA	223
ALBURN, George	BAL	143
Zacharias	BAL	151

ALCOCK, Robert	ANN	318
William J.	BCI	448
William K.	BCI	433
ALDEN, Mary	BCI	228
Semeon	BCI	228
ALDER, Ebenezer	CEC	132
Michal	BAL	2
Robert	BAL	2
ALDERFRITZ, Catherine		
	BCI	93
ALDERSON, Abel	HAR	62
George	BAL	106
ALDRIDGE, Charles	CLN	107
James	PRI	181
John	DOR	60
John	DOR	65
John	MON	136
Leonard	BAL	67
Martha	PRI	185
Rebecca	CEC	131A
ALDRICE, John	QUE	26
ALEBAUGH, John	WAS	59
ALER, Thomas	FRE	192
ALEXANDER, --- (?)		
	BCI	414
Adam	BCI	126
Amos	D.C.	196
Andrew	CEC	132
Andrew	CEC	154
Andrew	HAR	73
Arthur	ALL	24
Austin	D.C.	213
Charles	D.C.	73
Edward	CEC	153A
Elijah	BCI	306
Eliza.	BCI	215
Eliza	BCI	249
Ephraim	CEC	153A
Ezebeld	BCI	267
Francis	D.C.	213
Geo.	FRE	127
George	CEC	171A
Grace	CEC	154
Henry	FRE	131
Israel	CEC	131A
Jacob	FRE	134
James	CEC	154
James	HAR	73
Jeremiah	HAR	21
John	CEC	131A
John	HAR	73
John	QUE	33
Joseph	CEC	132
Josiah	CEC	131A
Margaret	CEC	153A
Mary	FRE	134
Matthew	CEC	153A
Robert	BAL	180
Sarah	DOR	5
Thomas	BAL	228
Thomas	BCI	18
Val.	FRE	133
Waltr. S.	D.C.	213
William	ANN	400
William	BAL	226
William	CEC	153A
William	CEC	153A
William	HAR	74
William, Esqr.	CEC	131A
William B.	CHA	212
ALEXANDR., R		
(See Thos. BARR,		
Overseer of R.		
ALEXANDR.)		

4

ALEXANDRIA, Richard		
	CEC	119
ALEXANDRIA JAIL	D.C.	147
ALFERD, Elisabeth	KEN	105
ALFORD, Jacob	BCI	184
Martin	TAL	34A
Matthias	CLN	106
ALFRED, Jeremiah	BCI	70
ALGIER, George	BAL	148
ALHAUSEN, John E.	BCI	335
ALL, Cannon	BCI	514
James	BAL	223
John	ANN	356
John	BCI	510
ALLBRITON, John	D.C.	212
ALLCOCK, Elizabeth		
(Miss)	BCI	268
ALLCORN, Margaret	BCI	145
ALLDER, Darkey	PRI	222
James L.	PRI	222
ALLDRIDGE, Samuel	CEC	153A
ALLEGRE, Joh. B.	BCI	350
ALLEN, --- (Capn.)	BCI	150
Aaron (Mr. Dorsey)		
	D.C.	67
Adam	D.C.	42
Adam P.?	ANN	281
Adam T.	ANN	281
Annas	CHA	197
Benjamin	PRI	[200]
Caesar	BCI	88
Carrel	D.C.	147
Casander	ANN	254
Catherine	BAL	195
Chloe	CHA	194
David	BCI	153
David	BCI	228
David	CHA	195
Dennis	D.C.	214
Dinah, free	CAL	64
Dorcas	BCI	63
Ebenezer N.	HAR	7
Edward	BCI	66
Eliel	BAL	230
Elizabeth	ANN	272
Elizh.	BCI	174
Frank-ng.	CEC	119
George	ANN	275
George	BAL	226
Hazel	ANN	297
Henry	MON	159
Henry-ng.	CEC	119
Hleazer	PRI	237
Hugh	BCI	173
Igns.	D.C.	113
Isaac	BCI	112
Isaac	HAR	48
Jacob	BCI	66
James	ANN	321
James	ANN	375
James	BCI	7
James	BCI	200
James	CEC	119
James	HAR	74
Jas.	FRE	135
Jemima	PRI	236
Job	SOM	103
John	ANN	382
John	BAL	44
John	BAL	120
John	BCI	45
John	BCI	278
John	BCI	385
John	BCI	481
John	D.C.	79
John	D.C.	88

ALLEN (continued),		
John	HAR	47
John	PRI	193
John	PRI	237
John	PRI	240
John, Junr.	PRI	237
John (of Joshua)	WOR	157
John (of Stephen)	WOR	155
John-overseer poor		
	CAL	46
John (Ser)	SOM	106
John H.	BCI	456
John W.	BAL	230
Levin	WOR	178
Lissey	D.C.	180
Lucy	PRI	236
Margt.	BCI	200
Mary	BCI	126
Mary	SAI	57
Mordica J.	CEC	119
Nancy	D.C.	21
Nathan	ANN	286
Nathan	ANN	302
Nathan	QUE	31
Owen	BAL	220
Peter	WOR	155
Pheby	BAL	209
Reuben	BCI	322
Reuben	DOR	51
Rewben?	DOR	51
Richard	BAL	37
Robert	BCI	22
Robert	D.C.	67
Robert, M.D.	CEC	171A
Robert D.	BCI	94
Samuel	BCI	89
Samuel	MON	147A
Sarah	TAL	3
Soloman	BAL	43
Solomon	HAR	26
Thomas	HAR	26
Thomas	KEN	106A
Thomas	PRI	236
Thomas (Col'd. Man)		
	BAL	224
Thos.	D.C.	112
William	BAL	230
William	HAR	9
William	HAR	26
William	SOM	125
William H.	HAR	48
Zadock	WOR	176
ALLENDAR, John	BCI	136
ALLENDER, Edward	BAL	237
John	HAR	38
Joseph	BCI	45
Nicholas	HAR	44
Nicholas	HAR	75
Sarah	BAL	127
William	BAL	122
William	BAL	239
William	BAL	239
ALLENDORFER, Henry		
	D.C.	89
ALLERE, John (?)	BCI	278
ALLERFREAT, Peter	BCI	534
ALLEX, Michael	FRE	97
ALLEXD., Hester	BCI	338
ALLEY, Ignatius	CHA	220A
Micajah	BCI	251
Wm.	KEN	123
ALLGIER, Elizabeth	BAL	158
Henry	BAL	158
John	BAL	158
ALLIN, Henry	TAL	47
John	TAL	48

ALLINDER, James	WAS	63
William	WAS	128A
ALLISAN, George (?)	D.C.	30
ALLISON, Andrew	WAS	123
Daniel	WAS	84
Elijah	MON	164
Francis	D.C.	106
George	D.C.	30
James	ANN	402
John	SAI	69
Mary	BCI	252
Peter	CEC	171A
Robert	BCI	384
Will.	D.C.	104
William	CHA	193
ALLISSON, Ann	D.C.	154
James	D.C.	176
ALLISTER, James	FRE	156
ALLMAN, Jacob	BCI	200
ALLNUTT, Elizabeth	CAL	58A
John	MON	137
Laurence	MON	135
Thomas	CAL	59
Thos.	CAL	49
Thos.	MON	136
Wm.	CAL	49
ALLOWAY, Gabrial	KEN	103
ALLRICKS, Hermanus	BCI	134
ALLRIGHT, Joseph	D.C.	123
ALLSIP, Hosley	ANN	277
Jacob	WAS	73
Thomas	ANN	277
ALLSTAN, Henry	SAI	97
Thomas, Sen.	SAI	97
ALLTRITON, William	CHA	204
ALLUM & COPPERAS		
COMPANY	ANN	311
ALLWELL, John	ANN	307
ALLWOOD, John	WAS	96
ALMANY, John	HAR	61
ALMEDA, Joseph	BCI	412
ALMEIDA, Joseph	BCI	117
ALMOND, Richd.	D.C.	82
ALMONY, Abraham	HAR	58
Benjamin	BAL	79
Elija	BAL	79
James	BAL	79
Wm.	BAL	79
ALMS & WORK HOUSE		
	D.C.	211
ALMS HOUSE	HAR	48
ALMS HOUSE, BALTI-		
MORE	BCI	464
ALMS HOUSE-W. COUNTY		
	WOR	174
ALMYR, Lewis	BCI	86
ALNUTT, Aden	MON	143
Edmon	CAL	53A
James	BCI	369
James	MON	129
ALPHA, Mitchel	SOM	108
ALPHART, Jno.	BCI	190
ALSOUP, Joseph	FRE	124
ALT, James (?)	BAL	223
ALTER, --- (Widaw)	BCI	395
George	WAS	94
Susanah	WAS	113A
ALTFATHER, Henry	BCI	398
ALTHOFF, Henry	FRE	171
ALTICK, Michael	WAS	96
ALTIER, Jacob	BAL	223
ALTON, Susanna (Mrs.)		
	CAL	51
ALVEY, Bassil	SAI	87
Darcus	SAI	93
George W.	SAI	87

ALVEY (continued),			AMOSS (continued),			ANDERSON (continued),	
Jeremiah	SAI	95	Martha	HAR	62	Isaac	KEN 100
John	SAI	89	Mary	HAR	64	Isaac	KEN 110
Josias	SAI	86A	Mordecai, Senr.	HAR	58	Isaac	KEN 125
Sary	SAI	87	Robert	HAR	63	Isaac	SOM 103
ALVIS, Peter	BCI	528	Sarah	HAR	64	Jacob	ALL 17
ALWILL, John	TAL	51	Susannah	HAR	62	Jacob	CEC 131A
AMAIMAL, Augustus	BAL	231	Thomas	HAR	63	Jacob	FRE 148
AMANNAL, Augustus	(?)		William	HAR	43	Jacob	KEN 105
	BAL	231	William, Junr.	HAR	63	James	ANN 342
AMANUAL, Augustus	(?)		William S.	HAR	63	James	ANN 342
	BAL	231	Wm. of Mord.	HAR	59	James	ANN 343
AMBEY, Henry	DOR	15	Wm. of Thos.	HAR	63	James	ANN 353
AMBROSE, Charles	BAL	28	AMOUR, Hugh	CEC	131A	James	BAL 222
Didamus	BAL	23	AMOUS, James	WAS	134[A]	James	CLN 89
Henry	FRE	130	AMROSE, Henry	WAS	73	James	D.C.178
Henry	FRE	151	AMUS, Bina	KEN	119	James	SAI 70
John	BCI	222	AMY, Philip	BCI	506	James	SOM 155
Nathan	ANN	297	ANCHORS, Francis	ANN	368	James-Negro	HAR 49
Peter	WAS	60	AND (See also ENT),			James, Junr.	MON 158A
Robert	BAL	15	Asa	FRE	85	James M.	KEN 104
Solomon	ALL	29	ANDAY, Paul	HAR	44	James M., Sen.	KEN 93
William	BAL	16	ANDERS, Henry	FRE	176	Jane	QUE 46
William	BAL	28	Jacob	FRE	175	Jas.	D.C.106
AMBUSH, Yorick	D.C.	136	John	FRE	178	Jesse	PRI 238
AME, --- (Mr.) (?)			Mary-ng.	CEC	119	Jno.	QUE 3
(at Hy. THOMPSON)			William	FRE	174	John	BAL 246
	BAL	227	ANDERSAN, Esau	DOR	34	John	BCI 25
AMELUNG, F.L.E.	BAL	195	Hannah	DOR	34	John	BCI 119
AMER, Nicholas	QUE	37	William	DOR	33	John	BCI 411
AMERICA (See also			ANDERSEN, Benja.	BCI	408	John	CEC 132
MARICA, MERICAN,			ANDERSON (See also			John	DOR 32
MERICHA, MERRICA),			ENDERSON),			John	DOR 60
Daniel	WOR	180	--- (Mr.)	BAL	244	John	HAR 43
George	WOR	175	--- (Mrs.)	D.C.	19	John	KEN 88
John	BCI	321	Abraham-ng.	CEC	119	John	PRI 191A
AMEY, Daniel	BCI	431	Abram. G.	HAR	60	John	WAS 116
Henry	BCI	435	Absalom	ANN	332	John, Senr.	CEC 131A
AMI, --- (Mr.) (at Hy.			Adam	CEC	171A	John, Junior	CEC 131A
THOMPSON)	BAL	227	Alexander	SOM	113	John H.	SOM 139
AMICH, George	FRE	159	Andrew	ANN	379	Jordan	HAR 28
Mary	BCI	486	Ann	CHA	223	Jos.	MON 173
AMILONG, Joseph	BCI	396	Ann (See Eliza. &			Joseph	BCI 435
AMMON, James	HAR	77	Ann ANDERSON)	HAR	59	Joseph	D.C.91
John	HAR	77	Aquila	BAL	89	Joseph	SAI 86A
AMOLD, Joseph (?)	BAL	52	Ben-Negro	HAR	65	Joseph-ngro.	CEC 119
William (?)	BAL	58	Benjamin	CHA	205	Joshua	BAL 87
AMON, John	WAS	57	Benjamin	HAR	63	Lenard	BAL 95
AMOS, Benjamin	BCI	148	Charity	D.C.	177	Martha	CEC 153A
Benjn. of Wm.	HAR	42	Clarissa	FRE	100	Mary	BCI 245
Frederick	BAL	241	Daniel	SOM	105	Mary	BCI 249
Isaac	BAL	237	Deborah	TAL	36	Mary	FRE 76A
James	ALL	30	Desire Rosette	BCI	67	Mary	QUE 37
James of Mord.	HAR	58	Dickerson	BAL	249	Marya	BCI 483
James of Wm.	HAR	43	Edward	DOR	36	Nathan	BAL 246
Jas.	BCI	227	Edward	KEN	102	Nathaniel	BAL 188
John	BCI	186	Edward E.	ANN	344	Peter	QUE 18
Lemuel	HAR	42	Elenor	PRI	230	Peter	SOM 124
Mordecai of Js.	HAR	58	Elenora	BCI	153	Phillis	KEN 103
Tobias	BCI	304	Eliza. (See Eliza. &			Philm.	MON 172
William	BCI	54	Ann ANDERSON)	HAR	59	Ricaud	BAL 110
William	BCI	127	Frank	PRI	182	Richard	ANN 318
AMOSS, Abraham	HAR	63	George	HAR	43	Richard	BAL 236
Aquila	HAR	72	George	KEN	109	Richd.	MON 163
Benjamin L.	HAR	60	George	SOM	113	Robert	CEC 153A
Catherine	HAR	46	Gustavus	BCI	61	Robt.	D.C.165
Daniel	HAR	62	Henry	BCI	188	Sam	QUE 7
Daniel, of Wm.	HAR	63	Henry	MON	152	Sam	QUE 20
Elizabeth	HAR	63	Henry	SOM	108	Samuel	ANN 332
George	HAR	71	Henry	TAL	8A	Samuel	ANN 338
Henry R.	HAR	58	Henry	TAL	33	Samuel	BCI 429
James	HAR	40	Henry U.	PRI	225	Samuel	CEC 131A
James B.	HAR	64	Hetty	BCI	463	Sandford	D.C.147
John T.	HAR	59	Hezekh.	D.C.	126	Sarah	SOM 110
Joshua of Robt.	HAR	64	Hugh	BCI	296	Simon	KEN 102
Luke	HAR	43	Ira	BAL	79	Solomon	BCI 489

6

ANDERSON, (continued)		ANDREWS (continued),		APPLEMAN, Philip	FRE 134
Stephen	MON 173	William	HAR 45	APPLER, David	D.C.79
Stephen	WOR 187	William	PRI 192	Jonathan	D.C.79
Thomas	ANN 352	William H.	BAL 131	APPLETON, Charles H.	
Thomas	BAL 78	ANDRU, Justis	WOR 217		BAL 2
Thomas	BCI 54	ANDRW, Justis (?)	WOR 217	William G.	BCI 272
Thomas	BCI 74	ANGEL, Andrew	FRE 193	APPOLD, Frederick	TAL 10
Thomas	CLN 108	Ellen	D.C.150	Geo.	BCI 185
Thomas	KEN 102	Isaac	FRE 218	APRON (See also EPRON),	
Thos.	MON 175	Jacob	FRE 198	M.	BCI 211
William	D.C.7	Jacob	FRE 219	APSLEY, William	KEN 102
William	D.C.33	John	BAL 249	William	KEN 110
William	HAR 63	Thomas	MON 166	ARA, Samuel	ANN 345
William	KEN 118	ANGER, Unit	KEN 109	ARAMBEL, --- (Mrs.)	
William J.	BCI 48	ANGLE, David	WAS 134[A]		BCI 399
Wm., ju.	KEN 117	ANHELBERGER, George		ARBAUGH, Balser	BAL 150
Wright	CLN 100		FRE 117	Jacob	FRE 188
ANDES, Adam	FRE 228	Jacob	FRE 115	ARBISHOB, of Balti-	
ANDRE, John	D.C.95	Philip	FRE 115	more	BCI 391
ANDREW, Abraham	CLN 110	ANIBA, William	WAS 122	ARBISHOP, of Balti-	
Beacham	DOR 63	ANICE, Rachel	BCI 133	more (?)	BCI 391
Curtis	CLN 110	ANKNEY, David	WAS 136	ARBUCCLE, Thomas	D.C.16
David	CLN 115	Henry	WAS 136	ARCHANIAN, James	BCI 133
Edmond	CLN 115	ANNAN, Robert L.		ARCHER, John	HAR 78
Elijah	DOR 50	(Doctor)	FRE 141	Robert H.	CEC 153A
Elijah	DOR 58	ANNER, John	QUE 26	Stevenson	HAR 43
George	CLN 114	ANNICE, Moses	BCI 14	Thomas	HAR 8
Isaac	CLN 106	ANNIS, Gregory	D.C.102	ARCHEY, James	WAS 59
Jacob	CLN 114	ANNISS, Saml.	BCI 244	ARCHIBALD, David	CEC 171A
John	CLN 112	ANSERT, M. L.	PRI 230	ARDINGER, Christian	
John	HAR 23	ANSLEY, George	SOM 112		WAS 78
Luke	CLN 114	Matthias	DOR 8	Peter	WAS 80
Mary	CLN 115	ANSPACH, Frederick	BCI 443	Philip	WAS 79
Medford	DOR 50	ANSPERGER, Christian		ARDRAY, Robert	D.C.6
Melvik	CLN 108		FRE 111	ARDREY, William	DOR 11
Michael	CLN 115	ANTHER, Michal (?)	BAL 8	ARES, Thomas	FRE 88
Newton	CLN 106	ANTHONEY, --- (?)	BCI 404	ARISSE, Charles	BCI 446
Newton	CLN 114	Robert	BCI 33	ARKISIMER, Joseph	FRE 134
Nimrod	CLN 107	ANTHONY, Daniel	HAR 22	ARLESTON, Mary	BCI 69
Noble	DOR 61	Francis	BCI 82	ARLETT, Francis	QUE 23
Peter	CLN 113	Henny	QUE 6	ARMACOST, Michael	BAL 151
Richard	CLN 111	Henry	FRE 141	ARMAGER, John, of	
Richard	CLN 113	Henry, Sen.	QUE 7	Wm.	ANN 268
Richard, Jr.	CLN 92	Henry, Ju.	QUE 7	Thomas	ANN 274
Richard, Jr.	CLN 115	Joseph	CLN 88	ARMAGOSH, Adam	BAL 18
Samuel	CLN 107	Joseph, Jr.	CLN 80	ARMAN, John	ALL 16
Samuel	DOR 55	Lydia	CLN 99	Michael E.	FRE 77
Thomas	TAL 7	Robert	BCI 95	ARMAT, Christopher	BAL 223
Thomas, Sr.	CLN 114	Robert	FRE 220	ARMATAGE, Frances	BAL 105
Tilghman	DOR 58	Saml.	DOR 11	William	BAL 105
Tilghman	DOR 65	Samuel	DOR 12	ARMEGER, Jose	BCI 333
William	CLN 111	Stephen	FRE 220	ARMELONG, Fred.	BCI 476
William	DOR 62	ANTONEY, Wm.	BCI 193	ARMEY, M.	BCI 403
ANDREWS, Abraham	HAR 45	ANTONY, Isaac	BCI 303	ARMIGER, Benjamin	ANN 297
Chapman	DOR 9	John	KEN 119	Samuel	ANN 312
Chas. R.	MON 172	ANTROVUS, --- (Mr.)		ARMINGTON, Martin	KEN 121
Christr.	D.C.81		D.C.12	ARMITAGE (See also	
Elizabeth	D.C.22	ANVELLAR, Joseph	WAS 149	HARMITAGE),	
George	ANN 316	APLER, Abraham	FRE 200	Benjamin	BCI 446
Henry	CEC 131A	Jacob	FRE 202	James	BCI 109
Jacob	D.C.172	APPELBY, Resin?	BAL 208	ARMOCOST, Adam	BAL 154
Jacob	FRE 224	Rezin	BAL 208	Christopher	BAL 144
James	TAL 14A	APPELHOUSE, Leonard		John	BAL 154
John	CEC 131A		WAS 146	ARMOND, Jane	SOM 128
John	FRE 223	APPLEBY, Emanuel	BCI 310	Willm.	D.C.192
Joseph	DOR 35	James	BCI 319	ARMONS, James	BCI 127
Nancy	D.C.9	John	MON 173	ARMOTT, Wm.	BCI 391
Nathaniel	DOR 37	Thomas	BCI 240	ARMOUR, Mary	BCI 241
Nethn.	BCI 174	Thos.	MON 137	Samuel	CEC 119
Richd.	MON 172	Thos.	MON 142	William	WAS 121
Robert	PRI 229	William	BAL 231	ARMSEY, Mary	D.C.194
Sarah	DOR 59	APPLEGERTH, Thomas		ARMSTEAD, --- (Col.)	
Sovern	TAL 12	(of G.)	DOR 13		D.C.60
T.P.	D.C.88	APPLEGIRTH, Nathaniel		--- (Mr.)	BCI 265
Thos.	MON 172		DOR 6	Louisa	BCI 324
W. (Revd.)	D.C.148	William	DOR 6		
		APPLEGITH, Thomas	DOR 10		

ARMSTEAD (continued),		ARNOLD (continued),		ARVIN, Edward, Senr.	
Robt.	D.C.130	Henry	FRE 85		CHA 215
ARMSTRONG, Andrew		Henry	WAS 136	Edward, Junr.	CHA 215
	BCI 58	Hester	BAL 53	ASBY, John	BCI 324
Andw.	D.C.125	James	BCI 243	ASCHOME, Thomas	QUE 24
Betsey	WOR 180	James	PRI 239	ASCUM, Alexander	SAI 68
Betty	WOR 170	Jarrett	D.C.191	ASH, Curtis	BCI 211
Easter	WOR 178	John	ALL 4	George	BCI 91
Elizabeth	SAI 63	John	ANN 312	Jacob	CEC 131A
Francis	BAL 182	John	BCI 215	Jesse	CEC 131A
George	BCI 358	John	FRE 127	John	ALL 31
George	WOR 179	John	PRI 206	John	BAL 196
Harlet	WOR 179	John C.	ALL 16	John	BCI 90
Henry	BCI 155	Jonathan	ALL 16	John	WAS 132
Isaac	BCI 319	Joseph	BAL 52	Joseph	CEC 131A
Jacob	WOR 212	Joseph	FRE 191	Perre	CLN 73
Jacob; J.	WOR 217	Joseph	PRI 206	Sarrah	CEC 131A
James	BCI 220	Margt.	BCI 240	Susan	CLN 74
James	BCI 278	Mary	BAL 129	ASHBURNER, John	SOM 116
James	SAI 69	Peter	BAL 207	ASHBURRY, Ann	WAS 86
James C.	BCI 155	Polly	D.C.22	ASHBY, William	ALL 4
Jas.	BCI 225	Rachael	BAL 53	ASHCOM, John C.	SAI 87
John	BAL 189	Rezin	D.C.136	ASHCRAFT, Thomas	BCI 27
John	BCI 49	Ricd.	D.C.135	ASHEN, Francis	D.C.42
John	BCI 87	Samuel	ANN 339	ASHER, Averilla	BAL 131
John	CEC 132	Thomas	ANN 347	Cloe	BCI 157
John	FRE 100	Thomas	BCI 87	Isaac	BAL 131
John	FRE 143	Thomas	DOR 23	Thomas	ALL 7
John	KEN 121	Thomas	PRI 239	William	BAL 107
John, Senr.	BCI 280	William	ANN 330	ASHFORD, Juda	D.C.212
John D.	HAR 61	William	BAL 58	ASHKITLLE, James	WAS [135]
Peter	BCI 318	William	FRE 193	ASHLEY, Isaiah	KEN 87
Peter	WOR 212	William	HAR 19	John	HAR 24
Rachel	HAR 28	ARNOLL, Clement	DOR 11	John	KEN 105
Ralp	WAS 85	ARNSPERGER, Lawrence		Robt.	QUE 12
Rob	BCI 507		FRE 150	Sarah	KEN 105
Robert	ALL 22	ARP, James	D.C.33	William	KEN 89
Russell	CLN 74	ARQUIT, Eli	BCI 6	ASHMAN, Wm.	BCI 511
Saml.	D.C.173	ARRANDT, George	WAS 112	ASHMEED, Geo.	BCI 402
Samuel	FRE 94	ARRANTS, James	CEC 154	ASHMERE, John	BCI 226
Solomon	BCI 87	Johannos	CEC 153A	ASHMORE, John	HAR 76
Thomas	BCI 316	John	CEC 154	ASHPAUGH, John	ANN 304
Thomas	HAR 28	William	CEC 154	ASHTON, Daniel	D.C.63
Thos.	BCI 225	ARRER, Benjn.	KEN 118	Edward	HAR 64
Thos.	D.C.129	ARRINGDALE, John	TAL 3	Henry	D.C.83
Walter	BCI 323	Thomas	TAL 48	John	BAL 189
William	ALL 2	ARROW, Henney	TAL 40	Joseph	HAR 56
William	CEC 132	William	BAL 222	Margt.	D.C.164
William	WOR 206	ARSCOT, Richd.	QUE 13	Richard	HAR 59
Willm.	D.C.126	ARSCOTT, Joseph	QUE 36	Rosmus	D.C.62
Willm.	D.C.204	ARSENAL, UNITED		West	D.C.182
Wm.	KEN 125	STATES	BAL 210	ASHWELL, Mary	BCI 210
ARMSWORTHY, Bennett		ARSKUM, Alexander	BCI 24	ASKER, Cloe (?)	BCI 157
	SAI 68	ARTER, Peter	FRE 182	ASKEW, John	CAL 43
James	SAI 63	ARTHUR, --- (Mrs.)	BCI 128	Mary	BCI 127
William	SAI 54	Charles	FRE 156	Mihael	CAL 43
ARMWOOD, Daniel	SOM 124	Daniel	FRE 218	Peter	CEC 171A
Danl.	SOM 127	David	KEN 102	ASKEY, Joseph	BCI 26
Jas.	WOR 176	Elizabeth	KEN 100	Robert	HAR 38
ARNALD, Quilla	D.C.59	Frederick	FRE 193	William	BCI 31
Sarah	BCI 530	George	ALL 17	ASKINS, Vincent	D.C.209
ARNET, Henry	DOR 60	John	HAR 60	ASKRIDGE, John	DOR 19
ARNETT, John	CLN 115	Joseph	FRE 193	ASLIN, Jos.	MON 136
ARNEY, Joseph	D.C.35	Solomon	FRE 189	ASQUITH, Charles	ANN 270
ARNISTEAD, Robt. (?)		William	BAL 179	ASQUITH, Rob. C.	BCI 349
	D.C.130	ARTHURS, Mark	CEC 154	ASTERFIELD, Caleb	BCI 147
ARNOL, Edmond	SAI 97	ARTIS, Jeremiah	SAI 56	ATCHERSON, Gustavus	
Jane	ANN 256	ARTZ, Catherine	WAS 81		CHA 213
Robert	ANN 256	Christian	WAS 59	Sarah	CHA 212
ARNOLD, Anthony	ALL 16	David	WAS 115	William	CHA 214
Anthony	BAL 53	Henry	WAS 85	ATCHISON, Henry	PRI 223
David	FRE 128	Peter	WAS 81	Ignatius, (Overs.)	
Elizabeth	ALL 17	Peter	WAS 115		PRI 224
Elizabeth	BAL 9	Philip	WAS 84	ATHEY, John	ALL 31
Ephraim	HAR 27			Margaret	ALL 22
Esther	BAL 52			Walter F.	BCI 518

8

ATHEY (continued),		ATWOOD (continued),		AUSTON, ---	
William	ALL 5A	William	FRE 84	(See HISS & AUSTON)	
ATHOE, Dorathy	BCI 10	AUBURT, Catherine	WAS 118	John	QUE 12
ATKINS, Benjamin	FRE 115	AUCHINBACK, Croft	BCI 486	John; J.	WOR 203
James	FRE 115	AUCKUS, Fred.	BCI 526	AUTHER, Hu.	BCI 229
Ryly	TAL 49	AUD, Asa (?)	FRE 85	Michal	BAL 8
Samuel	FRE 163	Ignatious	SAI 75	AUTTHOUSE, George (?)	
Thomas	CEC 153A	William	SAI 66		FRE 204
William	FRE 118	AUDDLESPERGER,		AVARD, Ann	D.C. 29
Wm.	BCI 169	Jacob	FRE 145	AVELIN ROLING & SLIT-	
ATKINSON, Alexander		John	FRE 141	ING MILL & NAIL	
	CEC 131A	Michael C.	FRE 141	FACTORY-Nathaniel	
Angleo	WOR 213	Sebastion (?)	FRE 140	ELLICOTT & Co.-	
Ann M.	BCI 220	AUGBORN, John	FRE 200	John DYKE-manager	
Asaac	SOM 115	AUGUSTINE, Elizabeth			BAL 192
Edwd.	BCI 325		BCI 436	AVERARY, Philip	D.C. 192
George D.	SOM 116	AUGUSTING, Sizar	BCI 339	AVERY, Ann	D.C. 191
Guy	D.C. 165	AUGUSTIS, S.	BCI 398	James	D.C. 174
Isaac	BCI 9	AUGUSTUS, Abraham		John	D.C. 190
Isaac	BCI 253		BCI 90	Samuel	BCI 5
Isaac	HAR 45	Ceesar	ANN 302	AVEY, Andrew	WAS 87
Isaac	TAL 9	AUHELBERGER,		Chrislly	WAS 88
James	ANN 321	George (?)	FRE 117	Christian	BAL 138
James	ANN 375	Philip (?)	FRE 115	Christian	WAS 87
James	D.C. 210	AUKERMAN, James	BCI 27	Henry	WAS 88-
James	WOR 214	AUL, Benjamin	BCI 14		89
John	BCI 7	AULD, Daniel	TAL 27	Jacob	WAS 82
John	FRE 95	Dawson, Ovsr.	TAL 6	Jacob	WAS 95
John	KEN 89	Edward	TAL 14A	Michael	WAS 82
John	QUE 29	Elizth.	BCI 247	Samuel	WAS 82
John of Ho.	WOR 214	Frances	TAL 22	Samuel	WAS 87
John of J.	WOR 212	Francis?	TAL 22	AVIS, David	CAL 41A
John, of Wm.	WOR 213	Hugh	TAL 23	David, Junr.	CAL 41A
Joseph	ANN 349	John	TAL 24	James	CAL 41A
Joseph	BCI 16	William	TAL 22	AVRY, David	WAS 74
Josh.	D.C. 212	AULL, James	BCI 121	AWKWARD, Ann	D.C. 121
Lidge	WOR 212	AULT, ---		Francis	D.C. 120
Mary	BCI 314	(See AULT & GEATY)		Heny.	D.C. 125
Milby	WOR 189	Henry	D.C. 89	AYDELOTT, Peter	BCI 317
Sarah	QUE 46	Samuel	BAL 106	AYDOLET, Benja.	
Solomon	CLN 90	William	WAS 63	(Captn.)	WOR 160
Thomas	ANN 309	AULT & GEATY	FRE 186	Margaret	WOR 160
Thomas	DOR 56	AULTHOUSE, George	FRE 204	AYDOLETT, Joseph	SOM 118
Thomas	TAL 8A	AUODOUN, Louis	BCI 21	AYDOLIT, Benja. (of	
Thomas	WOR 213	AUSBOURN (See also		Wm.)	WOR 162
ATKINSONS, Angello		OSBORN)		Jno.	WOR 163
	BCI 285	Saml.	QUE 7	Thos.	WOR 161
ATKISSON, John	BCI 139	AUSHINS, Ann	WAS 80	Wm.	WOR 162
ATLEE, Isaac	FRE 200	AUSTEN, Richard,		AYEARS, James	WAS 146
ATMAN, Peter	BAL 105	Ovsr.	TAL 7	AYERS, Abraham A.	CLN 76
ATTEE, Isaac (?)	FRE 200	William	TAL 13	Anthony	QUE 25
ATTIX, Thos.	QUE 19	William K.	TAL 14	Henny	QUE 39
ATTLEY, Samuel J.	BAL 139	AUSTERDIGH, Michael		AYES, George	WAS 63
ATWELL, Austin	ANN 315		WAS 72	AYLER, Henry	CLN 91
Benjamin	CLN 82	AUSTIN (See also OSTIN,		AYMANT, Henry	BCI 46
Benjamin	CEC 119	OSTON),		AYRES, Benjamin	TAL 37
Daniel	ANN 285	Amos	MON 132	Benjamin, Senr.	ALL 5A
John	BCI 9	Archibald	HAR 20	Benjamin, Jr.	ALL 5A
John	D.C. 185	David	CEC 131A	Catherine	WOR 176
Nathaniel	BCI 30	Edward	SOM 108	Comfert	WOR 188
Saml.	D.C. 157	Elenor	CAL 60	Elizabeth	WOR 188
Samuel	D.C. 185	Francis	BAL 233	Isaac	WOR 188
Samuel	PRI 229	Jas.	MON 177	John	HAR 59
ATWILE, Rachel (?)	ANN 258	John	D.C. 185	John	WOR 164
ATWILL, John (?)	TAL 51	John	SOM 105	John, Ovsr.	TAL 8A
John	ANN 280	John	SOM 135	John K.	KEN 86
Joseph	ANN 271	John	TAL 48	Lambert	WOR 171
Rachel	ANN 258	John, Senr.	MON 129	Moses	ALL 12
Robert	ANN 256	Jonas	MON 142	Samuel	ALL 12
Rodger	ANN 278	Richd. L.	TAL 46	Samuel	BCI 23
Thomas	ANN 259	Sally	SOM 152	Thomas	BCI 426
ATWOOD, Catharine	TAL 23	Tamar	BAL 233	Thomas, Senr.	HAR 63
George P.	D.C. 53	Thomas	WAS 57	Thomas W.	HAR 62
James	FRE 81	Will	D.C. 108	AYRS, Mycagy	WOR 156
John	D.C. 29	William	SOM 129	AYSTERDAUGH, Michael	
John L.	FRE 81				WAS 73

BAKER (continued),					
Barbary	BAL 83	Maria	BCI 443	BALDWIN, --- (Mrs.)	PRI 186
Bazil	FRE 226	Mary	D.C.21	Abraham	BCI 7
Benj.	BCI 215	Michael	FRE 191	Charles E.	ANN 349
Benjamin (?)	TAL 51	Michey?	BAL 40	Edward (Overseer)	ANN 283
Benjamin	ANN 336	Mickey	BAL 40	Francis	ANN 293
Benjamin	BCI 45	Morris	BAL 37	Geo.	D.C.117
Bridget	ANN 347	Morris	WAS 102	James	HAR 56
Brook	FRE 226	Moses	D.C.130	John	BAL 239
Charles	BCI 58	Nathan	CEC 154	John	PRI 184
Christian	BAL 83	Nathan	CEC 154	John	PRI 195
Christian	FRE 162	Nathan	FRE 227	Marshal	HAR 40
Danl.	D.C.215	Nathaniel	BAL 239	Nace	ANN 328
David	WAS 71	Nathaniel	CAL 44	Nancy	PRI 203
Dorsey	FRE 71	Nicholas	HAR 26	Nicholas	BAL 208
E.	BCI 380	Peter	BAL 82	Rezin D.	ANN 393
Elias	WAS 60	Peter	BCI 225	Rignale?	ANN 351
Elick	WAS 102	Peter	WAS 59	Rignall	ANN 351
Elihu	WOR 201	Peter	WAS 71	Sarah	PRI 196
Elijah	WOR 193	Peter	WAS 84	Theophs.	D.C.135
Elizabeth	BAL 206	Pheby	BAL 186	Thomas	PRI 195
Elizabith?	BAL 206	Philip	FRE 131	Thomas	PRI 196
Enoch	BAL 57	Phillip	BAL 81	Thos.	D.C.122
Frances	DOR 56	Polly	D.C.216	Tiler	BAL 209
Francis	TAL 39	Prevose	BCI 185	Tyler	HAR 26
Frederick	FRE 230	Reuben	MON 148	William	ANN 347
Frederick	FRE 234	Richd.	QUE 12	William	HAR 64
Frederick	WAS 71	Richd.	TAL 48	William H.	ANN 293
Geo. S.	BCI 376	Robert M.	WOR 196	Wilim.	D.C.131
Gideon	HAR 8	Salathel	WOR 193	BALDWING, Piercin	BCI 20
Grafton	HAR 73	Saml. (Dr.)	BCI 294	BALE, Lissa Ann	PRI 236
Henry	ALL 28	Samuel	CEC 132	BALEMAN, Nicholas (?)	
Henry	CEC 171A	Samuel	KEN 94		BCI 522
Henry	FRE 219	Sarah	BAL 40	BALES, Joseph	BCI 479
Henry	WOR 178	Sarah	BCI 58	BALEY (See also RALEY),	
Isaac	ANN 354	Sarah	WAS 78	Dareathy	BCI 225
Isaac	CAL 42	Shdrick	WOR 206	Elenor	SAI 87
Isaac	D.C.35	Silvester	FRE 72	Jacob	BCI 304
Isaac	WOR 188	Tacy	BAL 202	John	BCI 158
Ishmeal	WOR 197	Thomas	CLN 74	William	ALL 22
Jacob (?)	WAS 139	Thomas	CLN 110	BALINGER, Valentine	D.C.173
Jacob	BCI 494	Thomas	FRE 71	BALL, Amelia (?)	SOM 151
Jacob	FRE 150	Thomas	KEN 91	Aquila	D.C.83
Jacob	WAS 61	Thomas	TAL 37	Basil	D.C.217
James	BCI 31	Thomas, Senr.	CLN 79	Bennett	PRI 237
James	BCI 181	William	BAL 58	Christopher P.	WOR 162
James	D.C.19	William	BCI 143	Daniel	FRE 72
James	D.C.131	William	CHA 196	Eleanor	BCI 55
James	WOR 192	William	FRE 211	Elleanor	MON 164
Jesse	D.C.96	William	WOR 193	Fanny	CLN 95
Jesse	SAI 69	William Werten	FRE 68	Henry	BCI 84
Jesse	WOR 193	Wm.	BCI 537	Henry	PRI 236
Jesse D.	WOR 187	Wm. (Doct.)	PRI 195	Henry U.	D.C.100
Jno. M.	D.C.91	Zacheriah	D.C.25	Henry W.?	D.C.100
Job	TAL 37	BALCH, Stephen B.	D.C.22	Horatio	D.C.213
John (?)	TAL 51	BALD, Richard	BCI 38	Horatio	FRE 123
John	ANN 316	BALDEN, Joseph (negro)		Isaac	CEC 132
John	BAL 109		TAL 49	Isaac	PRI [200]
John	BAL 125	BALDERSON, Isaiah (?)		James	BCI 110
John	BAL 194		BAL 185	James	TAL 24
John	BAL 238	Isaiah, Junr.	BAL 203	John	D.C.195
John	BCI 193	Jacob	HAR 78	John	D.C.197
John	BCI 339	John	FRE 102	John	TAL 25
John	CEC 154	Jonathon	BAL 203	Jos.	MON 176
John	D.C.58	BALDERSTON, Ely	BCI 178	Lissa Ann (?)	PRI 236
John	D.C.103	Isaiah	BAL 185	Mary	TAL 25
John	D.C.130	BALDING, Daniel	FRE 175	Miram	D.C.88
John	FRE 73	Daniel, Senr.	FRE 172	Robt.	D.C.212
John	MON 148	Geo.	BCI 395	Stephen	MON 132
John	WAS 63	Isaac	FRE 172	Thomas	DOR 39
John	WAS 78	Mary	FRE 79	Thomas	TAL 24
John	WAS 95	Thomas	FRE 79	Thomas	TAL 25
John W.	D.C.20	BALDLESTON, Richard		Thos.	CAL 42
Leakin	MON 174		BCI 356	Thos.	WOR 162
Levi	MON 166			Timothy	QUE 27

11

BALL (continued),		BANDALL, Michael	BCI 146	BANTOM (continued),	
Walter	BCI 385	William	BCI 149	Milly	DOR 45
William	WOR 159	BANDEL, Frederick	BCI 98	Rhody	TAL 40
Wm.	BCI 502	George	BCI 81	Susan	DOR 52
Wm.	BCI 507	BANDLE, John	BCI 79	BANTUM, Charles	BCI 457
Wm. O.	MON 162	BANE, John	BAL 225	BANTZ, Elizabeth	FRE 104
BALLARD, Benj.	WOR 157	John	BCI 4	Gideon	FRE 95
Betsey	WOR 157	BANEKE, --- (Mrs.)	BCI 347	Henry	FRE 103
Daniel	SOM 153	BANER, Henry	BCI 399	BANZETT, Christian	BCI 102
Eleanor	WOR 153	BANES, Francis	FRE 117	BAOLEY, Thomas	QUE 16
Hetty	SOM 132	Isaac	HAR 56	BAPTISTE, G.	D.C. 96
Hetty	WOR 157	Thomas	CAL 66A	BARACK, Christian	HAR 19
Hetty	WOR 160	BANETT, John (?)	PRI 229	BARACKMAN, Catherine	
Jarvis	SOM 123	John H. (?)	PRI 230		BCI 161
Jeffry	WOR 213	Joseph L. (?)	PRI 230	BARBER, Acquillo	ANN 316
John	WOR 213	BANEY, Anthony	FRE 162	Allen	WAS 125
Jonathan	FRE 94	BANGS, David	D.C. 167	Barney	D.C. 62
Levin, Sen.	SOM 139	John	BCI 122	George	ANN 388
Levin, Senr.	SOM 122	BANISTER, Aron	BCI 286	George	SAI 86A
Levin (Taylor)	SOM 140	Joseph	BAL 20	George	WAS 80
Levin W.	CAL 62	Richard	D.C. 10	Ignatius	WAS 87
Littleton	SOM 131	BANKARD, Abraham	FRE 194	James	BCI 369
Lucey	SOM 139	Christiana	FRE 190	John	ANN 393
Richd.	D.C. 90	Jacob	FRE 194	John	BAL 21
Robert	SOM 126	John	FRE 194	John	BCI 211
Sarah	SOM 133	Peter	FRE 195	Jose	FRE 214
Severn	SOM 125	Peter	FRE 196	Luke L.	SAI 92
Tabbitha	SOM 128	BANKERD, Jacob	BCI 34	Luke W.	SAI 92
William	SOM 140	BANKHEAD, Bash-Negro		Rebecca	BCI 530
BALLENGER, Mary	FRE 68		HAR 65	Rezin	MON 176
Saml.	BCI 505	Bast?-Negro	HAR 65	Rezson	WAS 83
BALLIER, Willm.	BCI 175	Hugh	HAR 55	Thomas	BCI 232
BALLINGER, Letty (?)		BANKS, Aaron	DOR 9	Walter	SAI 92
	D.C. 155	Allin	ANN 360	Wm.	MON 173
BALONY, John	SOM 140	Basil	ANN 360	BARBERRY, Ann	BCI 283
BALTIMORE, Archd.	D.C. 114	Betsy	FRE 184	BARBI, Lewis	BCI 265
Henry	DOR 7	David	BAL 122	BARBINE, Charles	BCI 322
Leah	DOR 45	Gabriel	SOM 136	Mary	BCI 303
Will.	D.C. 87	Gamelia M.	DOR 40	BARBOUR, Clement	D.C. 88
BALTIMORE ALMS		George	FRE 80	BARCLAY, John	ALL 6
HOUSE	BCI 464	Henry, Senr.	SOM 136	John	HAR 71
BALTIMORE, ARBISHOB		Henry, Jun.	SOM 136	John D.	D.C. 18
of	BCI 391	Hugh	D.C. 200	Samuel	CHA 212
BALTIMORE, ARBISHOP		James	DOR 6	Thomas	D.C. 4
of (?)	BCI 391	Jesse	BAL 174	Travers	D.C. 134
BALTIMORE CITY &		Jinny	DOR 50	BARCROFT, Titus	D.C. 127
MARINE HOSPITAL		John	FRE 186	BARCUS, John	CLN 80
	BCI 40	Levi	CLN 77	Sewel	CLN 79
BALTINGER, Letty	D.C. 155	Margaret	BCI 142	BARD, Anthony	BCI 535
BALTR. COUNTY JAIL		Nancy	D.C. 154	Jacob	FRE 179
	BCI 203	Samuel	ANN 366	BARDETEY, Margerata	
BALTZAL, Thomas	BCI 375	Samuel	BAL 186		BCI 338
BALTZEL, Anna	FRE 156	BANKSON, Mary	BCI 299	BARDLE, Charles	BAL 6
BALTZELL, Charles	FRE 225	Sarah	BCI 178	BARE, Jacob	BAL 217
Chars.	BCI 358	BANNING, Andrew	DOR 49	Susannah	BCI 30
George	BCI 479	Anthony	TAL 21	BAREFORD, Wm.	CAL 42
Jacob	FRE 96	Anthony	TAL 32	Wm.	CAL 45
Leuis	BCI 352	Edward	TAL 35	BARENS, Patrick	CEC 133
Michael	FRE 101	Freburn	TAL 39	BARGER, Benjamin	KEN 106
Michael	FRE 103	James	CLN 113	Fredk., Senr.	FRE 122
Wm.	BCI 357	Robert	TAL 19	Henry	FRE 126
BALTZER, --- (Mrs.)		Thomas	TAL 19	John	BCI 441
	D.C. 50	BANNISTER, Moses	BCI 323	Joseph	BCI 533
Jacob	D.C. 54	Richd.	D.C. 97	BARGHOUSE, Henny C.?	
Margaret	D.C. 48	BANNS, Sippio (?)	DOR 35		BAL 139
Susan	D.C. 81	BANON, Leah	DOR 44	Henry C.	BAL 139
BAMFORD, Hugh	CEC 172	BANTER, Caleb (?)	PRI 226	BARHAN, George	FRE 219
BAMGARDNER, Jacob,		BANTERM, Charles (?)		BARKDALL, George	WAS 98
Senr.	FRE 180		BCI 457	Jacob	WAS 98
Jacob, Jr.	FRE 180	BANTOM, Abraham	TAL 8	John	WAS 98
John	FRE 180	Henry	TAL 35	Joseph	WAS 98
BAMSBURRY, Jacob	BCI 304	James	TAL 2	Peter	WAS 98
BANBURY, Jacob	KEN 108	John	BCI 296	Susan	WAS 99
BANCK, C.	BCI 380	John	TAL 33	BARKDOLL, Jacob	FRE 142
BAND, --- (Mrs.) (?)		Joseph	CLN 109	BARKER, --- (Mrs.)	BCI 414
	BCI 437	Martin	TAL 31	Alexander	BAL 185

12

BARKER (continued),		BARNARD (continued),		BARNES (continued),	
Basil	FRE 93	Notley	ALL 15	Mathew (Overs.)	PRI 224
Ephraim	BCI 253	BARNES, --- (Mrs.)	PRI 195	Mordecai	HAR 25
Gilbert (?)	CHA 193	Abraham	SAI 57	Moses	BAL 49
Isaac	CHA 195	Abraham	SAI 63	Moses	SAI 69
James	BCI 248	Adam	ANN 367	Nancy	SAI 69
John	ALL 7	Adam	BAL 44	Ned-f.c.p.	HAR 11
John	BCI 258	Adam	BAL 58	Osias	WAS 147
John	CHA 193	Alexander	D.C. 66	Parker	SOM 146
John	FRE 83	Amos	HAR 25	Patience	BCI 33
John W.	DOR 30	Andrew	FRE 209	Peter	SAI 76
Joseph	CHA 224	Ann	ALL 37	Philip	MON 148
Lewis	BCI 196	Ann	SAI 56	Philip	SAI 67
Murray	D.C. 52	Ann	SAI 67	Priscilla	SAI 67
Prissilla (Mrs.)	CAL 53A	Archibald	FRE 210	Pristen	KEN 114
Resin	D.C. 200	Basil	PRI 230	Richard	HAR 20
Sarah	BCI 71	Bennett	HAR 20	Richard	HAR 25
Thomas	D.C. 11	Brice	ANN 356	Robert	BAL 55
William	ALL 23	Bristo	BCI 75	Robert	SAI 79
William	BCI 31	Cecelia	D.C. 114	Robt.	D.C. 13
William	BCI 277	Charles	SAI 74	Rosey	SAI 75
BARKES, Gilbert	CHA 193	Daniel	DOR 8	Saml.	D.C. 86
BARKLEY, Abraham		Dennis	BAL 68	Saml.	D.C. 113
(Jur.)	SOM 114	Dorsey	BAL 49	Samuel	BCI 195
Betsy	SOM 132	Drady	SAI 73A	Samuel	FRE 101
Catherine (f.n.)	SOM 119	Edward	CHA 203	Sarah	BAL 187
George	BCI 258	Edward	D.C. 23	Sarah	SAI 64
George	DOR 31	Elisha	ANN 369	Simon	BCI 305
Henry	SOM 115	Elizabeth	CEC 173	Thomas	HAR 70
Hugh	BCI 195	Elizabeth	SAI 67	Thomas	MON 148
James	DOR 41	Ely	FRE 75	Thomas	PRI 193
John	BCI 495	Enock	BAL 50	Thomas	SAI 67
John M.	BCI 294	Ford	BCI 312	Thomas W.	QUE 46
Johnathan	SOM 115	Gabe	SAI 67	Titus	SAI 67
Joseph	SOM 134	George N.	PRI 185	William	ANN 367
Littleton	SOM 132	Gerrard	SAI 67	William	PRI 180A
Obidiah	DOR 35	Godshall	CHA 191	William	TAL 5
Thos.	BCI 531	Gregory	HAR 27	William	WAS 147
BARKLY, Francis	BCI 404	Gregory	SAI 67	William P.	BCI 45
Saml.	BCI 378	Henry	BAL 55	Willm.	D.C. 111
BARKMAN, C.	BCI 435	Henry	BAL 64	Winny	SAI 56
Cath.	BCI 354	Henry	BCI 79	Wm.	KEN 121
Danl.	FRE 129	Henry	D.C. 8	Zachariah	FRE 211
Darky	WAS 140	Henry N.	PRI 182	BARNET, Benjamin	BCI 28
Eve	WAS 139	Hester	ALL 21	David	WAS 145
Henry	WAS 60	Hosier	HAR 22	Frank	ANN 266
Jacob	WAS 139	Humphrey	CHA 192	Isaac	BCI 60
John	BCI 4	Jacob	SAI 67	John	BCI 431
John	BCI 479	James	BCI 5	BARNETT, Elizabeth	WAS 138
Peter	QUE 25	James	BCI 295	Ezekiel	HAR 71
BARKMON, Peter	WAS 88	James-Negro	HAR 80	Henry	WAS 134
BARKS, Jacob	WAS 65	Jas.	D.C. 105	Isaac	ANN 267
John; S.	WAS 65	Jesse	D.C. 133	Jacob	TAL 40
Joseph	WAS 72	Jesse	SAI 67	Jacob	WAS 134[A]
BARKUS, John	ALL 15	Jessee	DOR 57	James	HAR 78
Nathan (?)	QUE 11	John	ALL 12	John	CEC 132
BARLEY, Thomas	ANN 284	John	CHA 192	John	CEC 155
BARLING, Joseph	BCI 115	John	CLN 74	John	DOR 56
Sarah	BCI 115	John	D.C. 28	John	TAL 20
BARLONE, Elizabeth (?)		John	FRE 68	John	WAS 134[A]
	BCI 8	John	FRE 128	John	WAS 146
BARLOW, Elizabeth	BCI 8	John	HAR 27	Manassah	HAR 78
Israel (f.n.)	SOM 120	John	MON 149	Perry (negro)	TAL 21
James	BAL 60	John	SAI 74	Richd.	TAL 48
John	BCI 54	John	SAI 93	Robert	HAR 76
Joshua	BAL 61	John B.	DOR 25	Sarah	BCI 64
BARNABY, John	CEC 120	John H.	CHA 189	Thomas	CLN 106
Richard	CEC 120	Joseph	DOR 56	Thomas	DOR 51
Sophia	BCI 52	Joseph	HAR 39	Thomas	HAR 78
BARNACE, Andrew	MON 164	Joshua	BAL 50	Thomas	TAL 41
BARNACLOE, Risden,		Josiah	FRE 176	Thos.	BCI 335
Ovsr.	TAL 5	Julia	BCI 487	William	TAL 10
BARNARD, Edward	ALL 3	Levin	FRE 178	BARNEY, --- (Mrs.)	BCI 383
James	ALL 3	Levin P.	BCI 252	Jno. H.	BCI 178
James	BCI 145	Lucy-Negro	HAR 80	John	BCI 440
Mary	BCI 168	Mary	ALL 24	Louis	BCI 250

13

BARTON (continued),	BAST, John	FRE 86	BAUGHER, Isaac	FRE 141

BARTON (continued),
Aquilla	PRI 229
Ashael	BAL 123
Edward	CLN 116
Geo.	BCI 209
Jacob	BCI 427
James	BAL 200
James	BCI 37
James	BCI 510
James	CEC 172
Jas. of Wm.	HAR 44
Levin	CLN 115
Lloyd H.	WAS 146
Mary	D.C.169
Nancy	PRI 226
Nicholas	BCI 33
Peter	BCI 184
Sarah	FRE 107
Stephen	WAS 139
Thomas	BCI 92
Thomas	PRI 226
Thomas	PRI 232
William	CLN 95
William	WAS 139
William, Jr.	HAR 58
William H.	HAR 58
BARWICK, Edward F.	CLN 93
Elijah	CLN 95
James	CLN 78
Nathan	CLN 92
Nimrod	CLN 92
Peter	TAL 14A
Sarah	CLN 97
BARZE, Benja.	CAL 42
John	CAL 51
John L.	CAL 45
BASCO, John	BCI 76
BASE, Levin	BCI 74
BASEMAN, Geo.	FRE 191
Joshua	BCI 503
BASFORD, Alphred	MON 174
Anne	ANN 263
Cassandra	MON 172
Elijah	CAL 52
Henry	ANN 273
Jacob	PRI 206
John	D.C.78
John	PRI 182
BASH, Catharine	FRE 73
BASIL, Henry	BCI 101
John	ANN 402
Ralph	ANN 393
BASK, Adam	BCI 61
BASLEY, Peter (?)	BAL 249
BASLIN, Spencer	TAL 50
BASS, Adam	BCI 79
Griffin	CEC 132
Philimon	TAL 8
Thomas A.	BCI 89
BASSET, John	WOR 172
Wm., Senr. ?	WOR 172
Wm., Senr.	WOR 172
BASSETT, A.	D.C.118
Ann	BCI 278
John	DOR 46
John	DOR 59
Rabacca	BCI 333
Saml., Senr.	SOM 136
Samuel, Junr.	SOM 136
Simeon	D.C.77
Thomas	DOR 8
William	WOR 200
William of J.	WOR 199A
BASSFORD, Stephen	FRE 72

BAST, John	FRE 86
Leonard	FRE 198
Saml.	FRE 122
Sydney	FRE 204
BASTINE, John B.	BCI 495
BASTON, Duke (?)	BAL 79
BASTPITCH, William	DOR 43
BASWELL, Benjamin (?)	D.C.63
Martha	D.C.210
BATCHELDER, John A.	CLN 87
BATCHELDOR, Smith	BCI 68
BATCHELOR, --- (Mr.)	BCI 119
Joshua	BCI 312
Mary	BCI 258
Nathaniel	BCI 116
BATE, James	BCI 203
BATEMAN, Artemas	BCI 282
Benjamin	BCI 124
Brice	ANN 333
Catherine	BCI 84
George	CHA 200A
Gustavus	CHA 200A
Hezekiah	CHA 201
James	CHA 200A
James	QUE 7
Mary	D.C.57
Melinda	CHA 212
Michael	CLN 92
Nicholas	BCI 522
Richard	CEC 120
Richard	CHA 200A
William	D.C.36
William	HAR 77
William, Senr.	CHA 201
William, Jun.	CHA 201
Wm.	BCI 219
BATES, David	D.C.94
Jacob	SOM 124
John	ANN 369
John	BCI 92
Nehemiah	ALL 21
Thomas	D.C.79
Wm. H.	BCI 255
BATLER, John	BAL 24
BATSON, George	BAL 45
Thomas	ANN 272
Thomas	ANN 372
BATTE, Eleanor	BAL 126
BATTEE, John W.	TAL 20
Richard H.	ANN 264
Sarah	ANN 271
BATTEIS, Richard	BCI 268
BATTEN, --- (See Solomon OSBORN & BATTEN)	
James	KEN 91
Robert	BAL 219
BATTERS, Nancy	D.C.155
BATTERSON (See also PATTERSON),	
Archibold	WAS 66
BATTINGER, Letty (?)	D.C.155
BATTIS, Ann	TAL 50
BATTNER, Michael	FRE 196
BATTON, Zacheriah	BAL 4
BATTS, Henry	WOR 211
Lemuel	WOR 210
BAUCKMAN, Jacob	ALL 17
BAUDSON, Peter	BCI 276

BAUGHER, Isaac	FRE 141
John	FRE 192
Saml.	FRE 230
Saml.	FRE 234
BAUGHMAN, Adam	FRE 124
Andrew	WAS 96
Charlotte	FRE 109
Frederick	BCI 464
Henry	BAL 142
Jacob	BAL 163
Jacob	FRE 153
Wm.	D.C.10
BAUGHN (See also VAUGHN),	
Augustin	BCI 485
Robt.	D.C.208
BAUGN, Charles	BCI 118
BAUKMAN, Henry	BAL 5
John	BAL 5
BAULDING, Andrew	QUE 23
BAUM, John C.	D.C.33
Mary	BCI 503
Saml.	BCI 503
BAUMAN, William	ANN 324
BAUMBAUGH, Henry	FRE 93
BAUMGARDNER, Daniel	FRE 188
Henry	FRE 189
Jacob	FRE 190
BAUMWARD, Peter	ALL 26
BAUSER, Robert	BCI 336
BAUSMAN, John	BCI 375
BAUST, Cornelius	FRE 181
BAUYEA, Fanny	BCI 429
BAVAN, Francis	CHA 216
Waller	CHA 207
Walter?	CHA 207
BAVEN, Basil W.	CHA 225
Elizabeth M.	CHA 225
Francis	CHA 225
John	CHA 225
John, Junr.	CHA 225
Richard	CHA 225
BAWDEN, William	BCI 91
BAWIE, Washington (?)	D.C.45
BAWLDING, Samuel	ANN 333
BAWLEY, Thomas (?)	QUE 16
BAWLIN, John	D.C.17
BAWLINGER, Conrad	D.C.17
BAWMAN, Charles	D.C.58
Luke	D.C.51
Nathaniel	D.C.58
BAXLEY, Jas.	BCI 189
John	BCI 249
Peter	BAL 249
BAXLY, Geo.	BCI 412
BAXTER, Anthony	BCI 458
Caleb	PRI 226
Catharine	CHA 192
Greenberry	QUE 49
Jacob	HAR 45
James	BCI 255
John	QUE 16
John	SAI 69
Joseph	QUE 49
Sarah	BCI 16
Sarah	BCI 21
Thomas	HAR 45
Vinsent	QUE 36
William	HAR 42
William	QUE 49
Wolsey	BCI 315

BAY, John	HAR	60	BAYNUM, Elisha	WOR	192	BEALHARD, Richard M.		
Sarah	HAR	74	Wm.	WOR	197		WOR	204
Sary	BCI	344	BAYOR, Bennidicial	WAS	123	BEALL, Alexander	FRE	81
BAYARD, Arrabella	CLN	88	BAYS, Andrew	CEC	155	Alpheus	ALL	23
John H.	ALL	23	BAYSE, --- (Mrs.)	BCI	402	Ann	D.C.	33
Pere	CLN	75	H.	BCI	406	Ann	D.C.	45
BAYER, Charles	BCI	404	BAYWARD, John (?)	TAL	51	Aquila	PRI	219
David	BCI	276	BAZLER, Godlep	WAS	118	Archibald	PRI	194
Frederick A.	BAL	156	BAZONRIFF, Valentine			Aza	ALL	27
Jacob	FRE	97		D.C.	34	Azel (?)	PRI	194
Saml.	MON	175	BCRAFT (See also BE-			Basil	D.C.	56
Victor	ANN	287	CRAFT),			Basil M.	MON	168
BAYLE, Hambleton	WOR	210	Abram	MON	138	Benj. L.	D.C.	40
John	D.C.	10	BEAALE, Oston	PRI	186	Benjamin	FRE	80
Moses	WOR	201	BEABAN, Thos.	BCI	201	Benjamin	PRI	184
Purnell	WOR	216	BEACCO, Nathan D.	QUE	5	Benney	CHA	214
BAYLES, --- (Widaw)			BEACH, Anthony	BAL	110	Charles	D.C.	87
	BCI	387	John	BAL	4	Charles	MON	149
John, Jun.	WAS	65	Willm.	D.C.	132	Charles	PRI	237
BAYLESS, Asael	HAR	21	BEACHAM, Andrew	QUE	39	Daniel	MON	148
Asel	HAR	20	James	BCI	20	Danl.	MON	175
Zephaniah	HAR	19	Mary	CLN	100	David	ALL	23
BAYLEY, Betsy	SOM	155	BEACHAMP, Andrew	CLN	89	Dennis	ALL	15
Daniel	FRE	142	Jeremiah	CLN	110	Easther	MON	134
Esme	SOM	106	John	CLN	111	Eden	MON	148
Frank (f.n.)	SOM	120	BEACHBOARD, Wiltha	WOR	164	Edwd.	MON	143
George W.; of ---	BCI	347	BEACHEM, William	BCI	296	Elemma (?)	PRI	180A
Isaac	CLN	90	BEACHER, Samuel	WAS	117	Elenor	PRI	225
John	WAS	116	William	WAS	117	Elijah	PRI	183
Josiah	DOR	3	BEACHEY, Joseph	FRE	141	Elisha	FRE	73
Margaret	CHA	208	BEACHGOOD, James	ANN	361	Eliza	MON	160
Robert (f.n.)	SOM	120	BEACHTEL, Isaac	WAS	150	Elizabeth	MON	167
Samuel	WAS	120	BEACHUMP, Betsy	SOM	156	Enoch	MON	148
Sarah (f.n.)	SOM	120	Easter	SOM	155	Geo.	D.C.	108
Thomas	CLN	81	Elisha	SOM	148	George (?)	PRI	180A
William	FRE	150	Henry	SOM	156	George	BCI	515
William	FRE	162	Isaac	SOM	145	George	PRI	192
BAYLIS, Jacob	DOR	18	James	SOM	153	George	PRI	237
BAYLOR, John	BCI	438	Josiah	SOM	145	Harriet	D.C.	18
Martha	BCI	437	Nathan	SOM	146	Henry	PRI	193
BAYLY, Benjamin	SOM	125	Nathan H.	SOM	156	Hezikiah	MON	173
Even	BCI	337	Samuel	SOM	145	Horatio	MON	147A
Isaiah	SOM	122	Stephen	SOM	154	Horatio	MON	166
Jacob (?)	DOR	18	Thomas	SOM	145	Horatio	PRI	196
James	SOM	133	Zarah	SOM	156	Isaac	PRI	225
John	BCI	351	BEACK, James	PRI	182	James (?)	PRI	183
Lizzy	SOM	140	BEACKER, William (?)	WAS	117	James	ALL	23
Sinah	CLN	80	BEACLAY, Peter	FRE	132	James (Ovrs.)	PRI	236
Thomas	WAS	106	BEACON, James	BAL	187	James, of Jas.	MON	129
Thomas, Esqr.	SOM	111	Moses	BAL	201	Jami?	BCI	336
Thomas D. (B.smith?)			BEADLEY, Henry (?)	DOR	55	Jann?	BCI	336
	SOM	101A	BEADS, Elizabeth	BAL	43	Jeremiah	MON	136
BAYNARD, Aaron	CLN	93	BEAGLE, Henry	FRE	130	Jno. of Leven	MON	130
Abraham	CLN	97	BEAHAN, Samuel (?)	D.C.	17	John	FRE	93
Ann	CLN	73	BEAKAN, Samuel (?)	D.C.	17	John	PRI	237
George	CLN	75	BEAL, David	FRE	195	John W.	BCI	241
James	QUE	11	Evan	BCI	175	Jonathan (?)	PRI	193
James	QUE	38	Thomas	SAI	65	Josiah	MON	147A
John	CLN	74	BEALE, Azel	PRI	194	Josiah	MON	148
John	TAL	24	Basil	MON	141	Kinsey	MON	162
John	TAL	51	Elemma	PRI	180A	Levin	ANN	333
Letitia	CLN	76	Geo., Jun.	D.C.	102	Margaret	D.C.	45
Nathan	CLN	72A	George	D.C.	100	Margaret B.	CHA	210A
Nathan	QUE	27	George	PRI	180A	Mary	PRI	196
Robert C.	CLN	89	James	PRI	183	Mary Ann	FRE	113
Saml.	TAL	48	Jonathan	PRI	193	Ninian	D.C.	31
Sarah	TAL	39	Obed	PRI	183	Obed.(?)	PRI	183
BAYNE, Ebsworth	PRI	235	Offa	PRI	180A	Offa (?)	PRI	180A
Henry	D.C.	206	Samuel	PRI	185	Otho. B.	PRI	198
John E.	SAI	54	Thomas	PRI	193	Ralph	PRI	182
Nancy	SOM	135	Trylas	BCI	529	Rebecca (?)	D.C.	23
Thomas	TAL	36	William	ALL	5A	Rezin	ALL	23
William	FRE	69	BEALER, Christiana	WAS	58	Richard	MON	129
William	PRI	236	George	WAS	68	Richd. D.	BCI	175
William, Junr.	PRI	236				Robt. L.	MON	164

16

BEALL (continued),		BEANS, Colmore	PRI 182	BEATTY (continued),	
Samuel (?)	PRI 185	Colmore	PRI 222	James	BCI 259
Samuel	MON 148	John H.	PRI 225	John	D.C.160
Samuel	PRI 240	Stephen	CEC 133	John M.	FRE 101
Shadrach, Senr.	PRI 183	BEAR, Jacob	FRE 212	Levy A.	FRE 73
Shadrach, Junr.	PRI 183	John	BCI 336	Samuel	WAS 113A
Theodore	PRI 186	John	FRE 221	Sarah	FRE 93
Theophilus	ALL 21	William	FRE 128	William	D.C.58
Thomas (?)	PRI 193	Wm.	BCI 353	BEATY, James	BCI 5
Thomas	ALL 31	BEARCROFT, Domini		James	HAR 29
Thomas	FRE 79		D.C.168	James	HAR 60
Thomas	MON 148	BEARD, --- (See		John	HAR 59
Thomas of L.	ALL 29	BEARD & TYLER)		Mary	BCI 6
Thomas D.	ALL 21	Alexander	BCI 98	Samuel	CEC 171A
Thomas H.	D.C.49	Andrew	WAS 104	Samuel	HAR 60
Thos.	FRE 125	Charles	DOR 41	Sarah	BCI 27
Tyson	MON 148	David	WAS 150	Sarah	HAR 70
Upton	MON 158A	Elizabeth	WAS 59	BEAUCHAMP, Benjamin	
Waltee	PRI 237	George	PRI 229		SOM 131
Walter?	PRI 237	George	WAS 103	Edward	SOM 124
Walter B.	D.C.4	George	WAS 104	Fountain	SOM 136
Warren B.	D.C.18	George	WAS 150	Handy	SOM 131
Washn. B.	D.C.77	Hugh	BCI 148	Jesse	SOM 123
William	ALL 24	Hugh	CEC 172	John	SOM 125
William	PRI 211	Jacob	FRE 228	Leah	SOM 127
William B.	D.C.59	Jacob	WAS 102	Planner	SOM 131
William M.	FRE 99	James	CEC 172	Selby	SOM 124
William M., Junr.	FRE 101	John	ANN 275	Wm.	WOR 154
Wm. L.	MON 141	John	BAL 206	BEAUMONT, Pascal	FRE 216
Zadock	PRI 183	John	BCI 303	BEAVER, Adam	BAL 52
Zephaniah	PRI 183	John	DOR 43	BEAVERS, Francis	FRE 156
BEALLE, Allison F.	PRI 223	John	MON 133	Susanna	BAL 53
BEALLER, Peter	WAS 57	John	QUE 35	BEAVIN, Benjamin	PRI 214
BEALMEAR, Absalom	ANN 343	John	WAS 57	Henry	PRI 215
Francis	ANN 343	John	WAS 150	BEAZIL, Robt. Wm.	D.C.41
BEAM, George	BAL 195	John W.	ANN 390	BEBY, James	WOR 164
Jacob	FRE 181	Lambert	CEC 120	BECHIM, John	BCI 6
John	FRE 193	Mary	D.C.60	BECHLEY (See also BECKLEY),	
William	BAL 183	Michael	WAS 150	Henry (?)	WAS 57
BEAMER, Henry	FRE 181	Nathan	KEN 125	Jacob (?)	WAS 55A
Philip	BAL 122	Philip	WAS 101	Mary (?)	WAS 58
BEAN, A.	D.C.111	Rebecca	ALL 29	Philip (?)	WAS 57
Barton	WAS 95	Rebecca	QUE 45	BECK, --- (?)	BCI 395
Benjamin	WAS 146	Richard	ANN 253	Andrew	WAS 121
Elizabeth	SAI 67	Robert	BAL 84	Caezar	QUE 5
Geo.	D.C.132	Saml.	FRE 131	Ceasor	QUE 35
George	WAS 113A	Stephen	ANN 284	David	CEC 132
James	ALL 27	Susannah	ANN 268	Dorcas	D.C.30
Jane	SAI 54	Thomas	DOR 40	Edward	KEN 89
Jno.	D.C.134	Will. H.	D.C.80	Elijah	KEN 89
John	D.C.122	William	WAS 134	George	BAL 155
John (Pilot)	SAI 69	Zebulon	DOR 43	George	KEN 106A
John, Senr.	SAI 68	BEARD & TYLER	D.C.172	Godfrid	BCI 444
Josias	BCI 437	BEARDS, Barnhard	FRE 110	Henry	HAR 61
Launcelot	D.C.104	John	FRE 110	Jacob	WAS 105
Leonard	MON 137	BEARDSLEY, Joseph	D.C.8	John	BCI 120
Noble	MON 167	BEARHOPE, Robt.	BCI 184	John	KEN 87
Ricd.	D.C.134	BEARNS, Henry	DOR 22	John	KEN 114
Richd.	MON 165	Mary?	DOR 22	Joseph	D.C.107
Robert (of Robt.)	SAI 67	Mayg	DOR 22	Martha	PRI 186
Robert, Junr.	SAI 63	Steuart	DOR 24	Peggy	D.C.209
Samuel	SAI 55	William	DOR 24	Pue	KEN 105
Susan	SAI 67	BEARSHING, Henry	WAS 117	Simon	KEN 93
Susanna	PRI 236	William	WAS 117	Trueman	D.C.32
Thomas (Capt.)	SAI 69	BEASH, David	WAS 114	William	CEC 120
Timothy	D.C.97	BEASLEY, Temperance		Wm.	QUE 17
William	PRI 194		WAS 83	BECKE, Adam	FRE 226
William (of Jno.)	SAI 64	BEASTEN, George	CEC 120	Michael	FRE 227
Wm. (Capt.)	SAI 66	Sarrah	CEC 133	BECKENBAUGH, Cath-	
BEANE, Edward	CHA 197	BEASTON, Zebulon	CEC 132	arine	FRE 156
Henry H.	CHA 225	BEATHERDS, Amey	WOR 188	Geo.	FRE 134
John H.	CHA 222	BEATTY, C. A. (Doc)		Michael	FRE 134
BEANES, Eleanor	PRI 201		D.C.24	Sus.	FRE 133
William	PRI 201	Elie	WAS 112	BECKET, Sarah	BCI 97
		Guy	BCI 239	BECKETH, John	TAL 14A

17

BECKETT, Ann	ANN 343	BEGOING, Mary	BCI 122	BELL (continued),		
Ann	PRI 204	BELFAST, John	KEN 120	Robert	WOR 160	
Benjamin H.	PRI 182	BELL (See also RELL),		Robt.	D.C.167	
Betty H. (Mrs.)	CAL 51	--- (Mrs.)	D.C.134	Sally	FRE 228	
Elleanor	MON 148	Abraham	CLN 85A	Samuel	CHA 194	
John	PRI 191A	Alexander	BAL 48	Samuel	D.C.181	
John	WOR 154	Amelia (?)	SOM 151	Sarah	BAL 80	
BECKLE, Henry	FRE 196	Andrew	D.C.185	Thomas	BCI 416	
Nicholas	FRE 196	Andrew	WAS 97	Thomas	CEC 154	
BECKLEY (See also		Ann	TAL 12	Thomas	DOR 18	
BECHLEY),		Arthur	DOR 5	Thomas	DOR 36	
--- (Mrs.)	BCI 435	Benjamin	WAS 69	Thomas	DOR 55	
Henry	WAS 57	Catharine	FRE 126	Thomas	DOR 60	
Henry	WAS 114	Chs.	QUE 13	Thomas, Junur	DOR 18	
Henry, Jun.	WAS 125	Cloye	WAS 61	William	BAL 185	
Jacob	WAS 55A	Daniel	DOR 37	William	BAL 203	
Jesse (?)	D.C.159	Daniel	WAS 74	William	CLN 114	
John	BAL 19	Daniel, Sr.	CLN 94	William	HAR 26	
John	WAS 108	Daniel, Jr.	CLN 96	William	SOM 122	
Mary	WAS 58	Doll	D.C.188	William B.	SOM 118	
Philip	WAS 57	Elizabeth	HAR 60	William D.	WAS 117	
BECKS, Jonathan	DOR 52	Ezekiel	BCI 297	BELLICA, Joseph	CEC 133	
BECKWARD, E.	BCI 377	Francis	CHA 194	BELLINGER, John (?)		
BECKWITH, Alley	MON 167	Frederick	WAS 96		BAL 159	
Charles	MON 147A	George	WOR 162	BELLMIN, Grabriel	WAS 105	
Clement	TAL 11	Godfrey	CHA 194	BELLON, Pere	QUE 25	
George	MON 159	Hannah	FRE 147	BELLONA POWDER MILL-		
Henry	DOR 14	Henry (?)	WAS 57	John YOUNG, manager		
Jeremiah	DOR 14	Hugh	BCI 256		BAL 182	
Nehemiah	DOR 14	Hugh	BCI 389	BELLOTE, William	BCI 68	
Rezen	SAI 54	Isiah	BAL 181	BELLOWS, Isaac	ANN 375	
Sykes	MON 167	Jacob	DOR 36	BELMEAR, Elizabeth	MON 162	
William	DOR 13	Jacob	FRE 228	BELONE, Pasco	BCI 99	
BECKWORTH, Lenox	FRE 133	Jacob	SOM 127	BELSAN, Joseph	BCI 457	
BECRAFT (See also		Jacob	WAS 96	BELSCHER, William	BCI 88	
BCRAFT),		Jahue	BAL 183	BELSHOVER, Henrey	BCI 405	
Abraham	ANN 361	Jas.	BCI 296	BELSON, William	BAL 59	
Aquilla	MON 148	Jerry	ANN 365	William	BAL 62	
John	ANN 361	Jno. H.	D.C.113	BELT, --- (Mrs.)	PRI 186	
Peter	ANN 361	Jno. H.	D.C.135	Adison	D.C.49	
Peter	FRE 209	John	ANN 378	Anthony	D.C.66	
Peter	FRE 214	John	BAL 175	Benjamin	PRI 203	
BEDDERS, Allen	CAL 49	John	BAL 182	Benjn. M.	D.C.85	
John	CAL 49	John	D.C.112	Charles R.	D.C.66	
BEDDO, Edward	CHA 221	John	D.C.114	Enos	MON 133	
BEDDOW, Richard	PRI 212	John	DOR 23	Evan	MON 161	
BEDFORD, Benjamin	BAL 110	John	DOR 62	Hanah	BAL 28	
Charles	PRI [200]	John	FRE 228	Henry	D.C.59	
BEDINGER, Henry	ALL 9	John	HAR 61	Humphrey	PRI 204	
BEDLEY, William (?)	WOR 194	John	WAS 71	James	ANN 335	
BEDSWORTH, Amelia	SOM 129	John	WAS 96	James	PRI 204	
Isaiah	SOM 124	John	WOR 169	James, Junr.	BCI 2	
Tubman	SOM 105	John, Senor	DOR 23	Jane	ANN 373	
Whittington	SOM 122	John, Junr.	HAR 58	Jerry	BAL 51	
BEEDING, Craven	D.C.45	John B.	D.C.175	John	PRI 180A	
BEEDLE, John W.	D.C.187	John H.	SOM 129	John L.?	MON 174	
BEEHO, Limas	BCI 427	John P.	BCI 101	John S.	ANN 318	
Moses	BCI 427	Joseph	HAR 43	John S.	MON 174	
BEEKLEY, Jesse	D.C.159	Joshua	BAL 183	Joshua	BCI 322	
Wm. A.	D.C.205	Kate	ANN 346	Leonard	BAL 165	
BEELER, Lewis (?)	D.C.163	Lawson	D.C.138	Levi	D.C.137	
BEELMAN, Mary (?)	WAS 149	Lucy	D.C.114	Mordica	BAL 29	
BEEMAN, Moses	ALL 17	Manassa	PRI 207	Osborn	PRI 181	
William	ALL 12	Mary	BAL 183	Rebecca	PRI 183	
BEEN, John	MON 147A	Michael	BAL 189	Richard	BAL 51	
Josiah	MON 147A	Monica	D.C.157	Thomas	D.C.137	
BEER, John	MON 142	Nathaniel	ANN 373	Thomas	WAS 114	
Michael	FRE 71	Peter	WAS 96	Thomas H.	BAL 178	
BEERBROUGHER,		Peter	SOM 111	Thomas J. (I.?)	D.C.67	
Casper	WAS 147	Peter	WAS 118	Tobias	FRE 125	
BEESTON, Jno. S.	QUE 13	Prisciller	ANN 391	Tobias J.	BCI 30	
BEETLEY, Mary	CLN 96	Rachel	CEC 171A	William D.	FRE 79A	
BEEVER, Martain	BAL 164	Richard	BCI 16	BELTON, John	BCI 50	
BEFELT, Margarett	BCI 439	Robert	CLN 95	BELTZ, Henry (?)	BAL 138	
BEGERSTAFF, Andrew		Robert	HAR 26	BELTZER, Margaretta		
	WAS 55A	Robert	SOM 145		WAS 59	

BELTZHOOVER, George	BENNETT (continued),	BENSON (continued),
WAS 115	Ely BAL 69	Benjamin HAR 43
Henry WAS 138	Ely HAR 9	Cephas W. (?) PRI 206
BELWOOD, Susanah SAI 53A	Equillar WAS 72	Charles TAL 20
BEMIS, Nathan S. HAR 76	Fielding BCI 60	Edward CLN 90
BEN, Thomas WAS 65	George BCI 500	Elijah WOR 158
BENCE, Catherine WAS 58A	George SOM 118	George SOM 109
Henry WAS 94	Henry CEC 133	Henry SOM 125
Jacob, Senr. WAS 126	Henry SOM 112	Isaac QUE 38
Jacob, Junr. WAS 126	Henry, Senr. CEC 132	Isaac TAL 12
John WAS 108	James HAR 7	Isaac WOR 158
BENCKERT, John D. D.C.172	Jane SOM 136	James BAL 25
BEND, James BAL 21	Jessey BAL 44	James BCI 221
BENDEN, William TAL 46	John ANN 373	James DOR 55
BENDER, --- (Mrs.) BCI 456	John BAL 123	James TAL 20
Christian WAS 55A	John CEC 154	James WOR 196
Daniel WAS 67	John D.C.128	James H. SOM 132
Elizabeth WAS 67	John HAR 27	Jeremiah TAL 20
George WAS 114	John MON 176	Jno. MON 132
Henny BCI 477	John TAL 12	John ANN 330
Jacob D.C.93	Joshua CEC 155	John BCI 11
John FRE 190	Joshua SOM 111	John BCI 146
Yost FRE 178	Larkin BAL 47	Joseph BCI 243
BENDING, Thomas, Sr.	Margt. BCI 223	Joseph DOR 64
CLN 106	Matthew BCI 48	Levi HAR 43
William CLN 100	Mordecai D.C.181	Levin M. SOM 137
BENDY, Anthony D.C.72	Pat BCI 513	Loyde BAL 10
BENEDICT, Charles M.	Peter BCI 140	Milly SOM 140
BCI 123	Resin BAL 45	Moses WOR 157
BENJAMIN, George CEC 154	Richard BCI 72	Nicholas TAL 20
Isaac CEC 155	Richard BCI 160	Nicholas TAL 46
Levi BCI 74	Richard SAI 55	Ninian MON 144
William CEC 154	Richd. QUE 12	Niniar? MON 144
BENNER, Daniel WAS 66	Robert BAL 47	Pere QUE 11
Geo. BCI 168	Spencer D.C.202	Pere QUE 13
Henry WAS 56	T. George CEC 132	Perry TAL 6
Henry WAS 83	Thomas BAL 44	Peter BCI 399
Jacob WAS 56	Thomas I. (J.?) SAI 57	Peter DOR 8
John BCI 297	Thomas P. TAL 8A	Richard ANN 330
John WAS 56	Thomas W. SOM 104	Robert BCI 273
Mary BCI 153	Thos. MON 140	Ruben BAL 25
BENNET, Burtes FRE 163	Westley BAL 44	Samuel ANN 330
Elijah WOR 157	William SAI 75	Samuel BCI 249
George WOR 155	William SAI 82	Samuel WOR 158
Gerard SAI 89	William SOM 103	Solomon TAL 39
Henry WOR 174	William B. SAI 56	Stephen DOR 15
J. BCI 410	William R. KEN 90	Susan SOM 117
Jane BCI 11	Willm. D.C.208	Thomas ANN 330
John, Sen. SAI 89	Willm. MON 130	Thomas PRI 184
John, Jun. SAI 89	Wm. MON 177	Thos. MON 135
Jos. BCI 220	Wm., Senr. WOR 174	Wm. BCI 506
Lloyd FRE 198	Wm., Captn. WOR 170	Wm. MON 141
Rebecca FRE 198	BENNEY, John, Ovsr.	BENSOR, Ninian (?) MON 144
Robert FRE 192	TAL 7	Niniar? (?) MON 144
Thomas BCI 8	Jonathan N. TAL 10	BENSTON, Daniel SOM 145
Thomas BCI 153	Mingo TAL 7	Daniel WOR 162
Uphama WOR 169	William (?) DOR 25	Gideon WOR 158
Warner WOR 155	BENNINGTON, Jeremiah	Hector SOM 142A
William FRE 176	HAR 73	Jesse SOM 144
Wm. (of Jas.) WOR 154	John WAS 150	Polly SOM 148
Wm. (of Jesse) WOR 171	Moses WAS 150	Wm. WOR 158
BENNETT, Abraham CEC 132	BENNITT, Emanuel DOR 59	BENTALOU, Paul BCI 425
Ann WOR 172	BENNY, Benjn. TAL 46	BENTER, Willm. D.C.192
Anthony SOM 134	Charles TAL 46	BENTLER, Susanah WAS 125
Arromenta SAI 53A	James TAL 48	BENTLEY, Caleb MON 148
Benjamin BAL 44	Ryley TAL 52	Eli FRE 170
Benjamin BAL 55	William, Senior TAL 45	Eliza BCI 488
Benjn. WOR 174	William, Junior TAL 45	Israel FRE 202
Charles WOR 209	Williand?, Junior TAL 45	Joseph E. MON 148
Chas. D.C.183	BENSAN, Cephas W. PRI 206	Jude BAL 123
Danl. MON 172	BENSELEY, Henry WOR 153	BENTLY, Jno. H. BCI 194
David FRE 98	BENSIN, John CEC 120	BENTNEY, Samuel HAR 18
Eliakim WOR 161	BENSKIN, Zack FRE 123	BENTON, Anne MON 133
Elijah BAL 55	BENSON, --- (?) BCI 404	Benjamin KEN 86
Elisha BAL 47	A. BCI 368	Benjamin KEN 100
Elizabeth SOM 113	Amos HAR 42	Benjamin, Senr. KEN 89

19

BENTON (continued)		BERRY (continued),		BETT, Henry	WAS 119
Benjn.	MON 142	James S.	PRI 227	Thomas H. (?)	BAL 178
E. (Widaw)	BCI 393	Jeremiah	DOR 5	BETTERTON, Benj.	ALL 28
Edward	FRE 79A	Jeremiah, 3d	ALL 30	BETTON, John	BCI 132
Elijah	QUE 4	John	BCI 64	Joseph E.	QUE 46
Francis	KEN 86	John	BCI 153	Nathan	QUE 24
Nathl.	MON 166	John	BCI 241	Pere (?)	QUE 25
Samuel	D.C. 194	John	BCI 367	Turbott	QUE 31
Thomas	FRE 79A	John	CLN 93	BETTS, Alfred	BCI 315
Vincent	QUE 11	John	CEC 154	Catherine	KEN 123
Wm.	MON 160	John	CEC 154	Enoch	BCI 169
BENTZ, Catharine	FRE 112	John	CEC 172	Enoch	SAI 80
George	FRE 98	John	CHA 216	John	BAL 196
BENWARE, Lewis	BCI 8	John	PRI 208	John	SAI 80
BEO, Robert	ANN 364	John N.	CHA 216	Mary K.	BCI 23
BEOARD, George	BCI 491	John O.	CHA 228	Solmon	BCI 267
BEOUCHET, Anthy	BCI 216	John W.	BCI 477	BETTY, George	BCI 94
BERD, John	FRE 126	Lucey	WAS 84	BETTZ, Henry	BAL 138
BERDSLEY, Davd. H.	BCI 348	Mary	BCI 275	BETTZER, Anthoney	WAS 90
BERGER, Geo.	BCI 414	Mary	CHA 214	BETZ, Catherine	WAS 123
Henry	FRE 104	Mary	PRI 239	David	WAS 89
Jacob	FRE 96	Merrick	TAL 11	Frederick	WAS 58A
BERGES, And.	BCI 354	Michael-negro	CEC 120	Jacob	WAS 108
BERKLEY, Mary	D.C. 124	Richard	BAL 214	John	WAS 105
BERKS, James	HAR 30	Robert	BCI 31	BEUCH, Anthony (?)	BAL 110
BERLY, Jacob	FRE 221	Rosanna	FRE 140	BEULL, Rebecca	D.C. 23
BERNARD, Chs.	BCI 498	Sanda-ngro.	CEC 120	BEVAN, Charles	CAL 64
Grafton	FRE 226	Sarah	KEN 91	Horatia	BCI 464
Jesse	BCI 322	Staten	CLN 87	Richard	BCI 340
Joseph	BAL 108	Staten	CLN 98	Thomas	BCI 80
Malachi	FRE 226	Thomas	CLN 76	Thos.	D.C. 117
William	FRE 202	Thomas	PRI 236	William	CAL 63.
BERNECE, William	BCI 17	Thomas L.	BCI 367	BEVANS, James	WOR 155
BERNEY, William (?)	DOR 25	Walter	D.C. 205	John	WOR 212
BERNHARD, Henry	BCI 244	Washington	PRI 219	Joshua	WOR 217
BERR (See also KERR),		William	BCI 132	Roland	WOR 212
Meriah (?)	TAL 9	William	BCI 320	Wm. (of Rowland)	WOR 163
BERRANG, Jerome	D.C. 34	William	CHA 202	BEVARD, James	HAR 72
BERREO, Noel	D.C. 98	William	CHA 221	Samuel	HAR 72
BERRES, Noel (?)	D.C. 98	William	TAL 37	BEVERAGE, Francis	MON 135
BERREY, William	DOR 25	Willm.	D.C. 182	BEVERLY, Charles	CAL 50
BERRIDGE, John	TAL 23	Zachariah	PRI 194	James B.	D.C. 65
Mary	TAL 35	Zachariah	PRI 198	Jeremiah	CAL 45
BERRY, Abarilla	BCI 90	BERRYCOLLEAU, Jacen		P. R.	D.C. 173
Abraham	KEN 115		BCI 347	BEVERS, Andrew	D.C. 129
Ann	CHA 214	BERRYMAN, Charles	KEN 90	BEVINS, Brittingham	WOR 155
Ann	PRI 208	Elijah	KEN 89	James	BAL 129
Ann	PRI 224	Mary	KEN 89	James	KEN 108
Anne (Mrs.)	PRI 203	Sarah	BCI 75	Joshua	BAL 118
Bayne	D.C. 173	BERSCH, Henry	BCI 174	Thomas	KEN 108
Benjamin	BAL 222	BERTEAU, Nicholas	BCI 143	BEVIRIDGE, John	BCI 306
Benjamin	CHA 212	BERTHEUR, John	BAL 106	BEWARD, James	ANN 361
Benjamin	PRI 197	BERTHIER, Joseph	BCI 73	BEWLEY, Lemuel	QUE 2A
Benjamin	PRI 202	BERTON, Joshua	ANN 354	BEWSICK, Thomas	DOR 4
Brooke M.	D.C. 106	BERYMAN, William	BAL 14	BEYER, Henry	FRE 77
Chas.	D.C. 109	BESFORD, Thomas	BCI 278	BEYERLY, Catharine	BAL 165
Christopher	BCI 7	BESHEARS, Otha	FRE 214	BEYERS, David	FRE 186
Elisha (?)	PRI 197	BESHIN, Charles G.	BCI 280	BIACH, Danl. (of North	
Elisha D.	MON 147A	BESITER, I. W.	BCI 403	beach)	WOR 175
Eliza	BCI 476	BESS, Sarah	BCI 15	BIARD, David	CEC 133
Esther	WOR 197	BESSE, Margaret	BCI 80	BIAS, James	QUE 39
Fielder	CHA 214	BESSEX, Brdford	QUE 39	John	DOR 26
George	CHA 213	Jacob	KEN 91	Mary	BCI 530
George	CHA 214	BESSY, Dinah (?)	BCI 148	Perry	BCI 426
George	D.C. 194	BEST, Elizabeth	WAS 65	Thomas	DOR 19
Hanta	BCI 343	George	FRE 226	BIASS, Mathew (free)	CAL 64
Heburn S.	PRI 224	BESTOR, Harvey	D.C. 82	BIAYS, James, Jr.	BCI 64
Henry	CHA 211	BESWICK, Sarah	KEN 101	BIBBY, Jahn	DOR 36
Hezekiah	CHA 212	BETHARDS, Benjn.,		John?	DOR 36
Hezekiah	CHA 215	Senr.	WOR 178	John	BAL 115
Hezekiah	D.C. 58	Danl.	WOR 175	John	WOR 195
Horatio	BCI 477	Isaac, Senr.	WOR 178	BICHEL, Philip	BAL 15
J.	BCI 401	James	WOR 172	BICKET, James	FRE 145
James	D.C. 127	BETHRY, Susan	BCI 227	BICKFORD, James	BCI 124
James	TAL 48	BETSWORTH, Benjn.	SOM 148	BICKHAM, James	BCI 354
James	WAS 111			BICKLAND, John	QUE 32

BICKLEY, John	ANN 356	
BICKNELL, Thomas	ANN 288	
BIDDE, Jacob	CEC 132	
BIDDINGER, Philip	FRE 222	
Wm. (?)	FRE 217	
BIDDISON, Abednigo		
	BAL 122	
Abraham	BCI 154	
Jeremiah	BAL 123	
Mary	BAL 130	
Salem	BAL 249	
Zachariah	BAL 117	
BIDDLE, Abraham	BCI 320	
Andrew	CEC 132	
Augustine	CEC 120	
B. Thomas	CEC 133	
Elizabeth	CEC 120	
Eve	FRE 123	
Frisby	CEC 133	
Jacob	CEC 133	
Jesse	BCI 530	
John	BCI 243	
John	CEC 120	
John	CEC 132	
John B.	HAR 63	
John S.	CEC 120	
Mathew	CEC 133	
Pat-ngro.	CEC 120	
Peregrin	CEC 120	
Raymon	CEC 133	
Saml. R.	BAL 113	
(See Elias LEE &		
Saml. R. BIDDLE)		
Spencer	CEC 133	
Stephen	DOR 9	
Thomas	BCI 305	
Thomas	CEC 133	
Thomas, Senr.	CEC 132	
Thomas, Jr.	CEC 133	
Tobias	CEC 120	
BIDEMAN, Jacob	WAS 63	
BIDEN, John	ANN 316	
William	ANN 316	
BIDINGER, Wm.	FRE 217	
BIDISON, Danl.	BCI 243	
BIDMAN, Jacob	D.C.24	
BIER, George	FRE 128	
Jacob	BCI 64	
BIERLY, Philip	BAL 22	
BIERS, Isaac	PRI 230	
BIGERS, Henry	FRE 75	
BIGGART, Samuel	BCI 130	
BIGGERS, Henry	FRE 213	
BIGGERTON, Alexr.	D.C.152	
BIGGS, Ann	D.C.212	
Benjamin	FRE 162	
Darky	PRI 237	
Elizabeth	FRE 145	
Frederick	FRE 174	
Green	MON 136	
Jacob	FRE 174	
James	MON 161	
John	ANN 344	
John	CEC 133	
John	FRE 149	
Joseph	ALL 4	
Joseph	FRE 173	
Joseph (of Jno.)	FRE 157	
Saml.	MON 161	
Susanna	PRI 237	
William	FRE 94	
William	FRE 174	
William	KEN 108	
William (of Ben)	FRE 145	
William (of Jacob)		
	FRE 145	
BIGGUM, Joseph	WAS 103	
BIGHAM, Bryan	FRE 144	
Charles W.	FRE 141	
Robert	BAL 193	
Thomas	ANN 380	
BIGLEY, James	CEC 173	
BIGNAL, John	CHA 226	
Thos. W. T.	BCI 514	
BIGS, Joseph	CEC 120	
BIJAS, Joseph (?)	DOR 10	
BILAFELT, William	BAL 12	
BILES, John	TAL 45	
William	QUE 33	
BILFERE, ---		
(See FINN & BILFERE)		
BILL, Levin	DOR 36	
BILLETTER, Clark	TAL 51	
BILLINGSLEA, Abraham-		
Negro	HAR 80	
Jack-Negro	HAR 50	
James	HAR 8	
Walter	HAR 40	
William	HAR 4	
BILLINGSLEY, Thomas		
	CAL 67	
BILLINGSLY, Bazil	BAL 239	
BILLINGTON, James		
	BCI 127	
Mary Ann	BAL 224	
BILLITER, John	CLN 105	
Joseph	CLN 106	
BILLMEIR, John	WAS 115	
BILLMYER, Jacob	BCI 300	
Martin	FRE 202	
BILSON, John	BCI 501	
William	BAL 122	
BINDER, Jared	D.C.65	
William	WAS 107	
BING, Mary	PRI 195	
BINGEY, Thomas	D.C.6	
BINGHAM, Elizth.	D.C.158	
J.A.	MON 159	
Thomas	BCI 25	
BINILLANH, Stephen		
	BCI 69	
BINKLEY, Eve	WAS 117	
Philip	WAS 102	
BINNIX, Barnet	BAL 231	
Ellen	BAL 231	
Samuel	BAL 232	
BINNY, Archibald	SAI 70	
BINS, Thomas	BCI 20	
BINT, Francis	BCI 240	
BINTER, Willm. (?)	D.C.192	
BINTZER, Frederick		
	BCI 286	
BINYON, Elizabeth		
(Miss)	CAL 46	
John	CAL 45	
Parslow	CAL 46	
BIONS, Ann (?)	DOR 42	
BIOUS, Ann	DOR 42	
BIRCH, Caleb	D.C.215	
Isaac	D.C.214	
James	D.C.211	
John	D.C.211	
Joseph	D.C.214	
Molly	SOM 127	
Rachel	KEN 116	
Saml.	D.C.212	
Thos.	D.C.211	
William	BCI 446	
Willm.	D.C.211	
BIRCKHEAD, Elizabeth		
	HAR 8	
John	CAL 48	
BIRCKHEAD (continued)		
Mathew	HAR 7	
Samuel	CAL 51	
Samuel, Junr.	CAL 51	
BIRD, --- (Major?)		
	WOR 213	
Alice	D.C.75	
Anne	ANN 365	
Francis	ANN 269	
Jacob	ANN 271	
Jacob	BCI 166	
Jacob	SOM 147	
John	ANN 261	
John	FRE 157	
John	PRI 202	
Joseph	WAS 140	
Major	WOR 213	
Mary	D.C.57	
Saml.	WOR 178	
Thomas	ANN 272	
Thos.	D.C.171	
William	ANN 287	
William C.	BAL 220	
Wm.	BCI 414	
BIRDIN, Phenix	QUE 18	
BIRDSLY, --- (Widaw)		
	BCI 384	
BIRELY, Elizabeth	FRE 96	
George	FRE 159	
George	FRE 162	
John	FRE 132	
Lewis	FRE 98	
Lewis	FRE 132	
Philip	FRE 132	
Valentine	FRE 118	
William	FRE 104	
BIRKHEAD, Edwd.	D.C.92	
Hugh	BCI 382	
Robert	CAL 62	
Soln. (Doctr.)	BCI 278	
William	SOM 134	
BIRMINGHAM, Rebecca		
	HAR 61	
BIRNIE, C.	FRE 181	
BIRTH, Eliza. B.	BCI 341	
James	D.C.9	
BIRTIN, John	WOR 158	
BISBID, Rosetta	BCI 256	
BISCOE, Benidict	SAI 86A	
George	QUE 42	
George W.	PRI 219	
James	BCI 253	
James	SAI 57	
Josiah	SAI 55	
Langley	SAI 55	
Margaret	SAI 55	
Mary	QUE 34	
McKay	SAI 55	
Philip	CAL 44	
Richard	SAI 64	
Samuel C.	SAI 54	
Susan	QUE 34	
Thomas	QUE 27	
William	BCI 79	
BISER, Danl.	FRE 130	
Fredk.	FRE 130	
Jacob	FRE 130	
John	FRE 124	
BISFAM, Benjamin	HAR 60	
BISH, Adam	FRE 189	
Daniel	FRE 189	
Elizabeth	FRE 194	
BISHIERS, Richard		
	BAL 67	
BISHOP, Abram	DOR 28	
Airy	BCI 159	

21

BISHOP (continued),		BLACK (continued),		BLACKISTON (continued)	
Ann	D.C. 179	David	BCI 516	Martha	KEN 124
Cealey (f.n.)	SOM 120	David	D.C. 207	Saml.	KEN 123
Deter	FRE 168	Elizabeth	ANN 352	Thomas	SAI 96
Elizabeth	BCI 10	Eveline	D.C. 16	BLACKLEY, Thomas	BAL 246
George	BAL 181	FAMILY	BCI 88	BLACKLOCK, Davis	BAL 216
George	WOR 179	Frederick	FRE 179	Robt. S.	D.C. 167
Jacob	FRE 181	Frederick, Junr.	FRE 171	BLACKMORE, Wm.	WAS 144
Jacob	WOR 205	George	FRE 190	BLACKNEY, Abel	BAL 215
John	BAL 112	Henry	FRE 182	Richard	BAL 249
John	FRE 188	Henry	FRE 182	BLACKSTOCK, Robert	
John	WOR 170	Jacob	FRE 145		CHA 204
John, Senr., Esqr.		Jacob	FRE 203	BLACKSTON, Charles	
	WOR 175	James	ALL 36		BCI 449
John, Captn., (of		James	BCI 181	John	FRE 214
Wm.)	WOR 174	James	CEC 172	Ross	ANN 400
Joshua	WOR 195	James	D.C. 79	Sally	BCI 535
Levi	SOM 155	James	WOR 162	BLACKSTONE, Dent	
Levin	WOR 161	Jenny	D.C. 14		SAI 96
Mark	FRE 228	Jenny	D.C. 18	George	SAI 96
Minta	KEN 123	John	BAL 220	Kenelm	SAI 96
Pere	QUE 12	John	BCI 13	BLADEN, Joseph	D.C. 213
Richard R.	BCI 12	John	BCI 528	Peggy	SOM 138
Robert	QUE 24	John	FRE 142	Thos.	D.C. 186
Sarah	QUE 3	John	FRE 143	BLADES, Ben	QUE 3
Smith	QUE 7	John N.	CEC 155	Benj.	WOR 159
Thomas	DOR 30	Joseph	BAL 46	Benjamin	TAL 22
William	ANN 397	Joseph	PRI 187	Bowdle	CLN 100
William	BAL 242	Joshua	ANN 354	Bowdle	CLN 108
Wm.	QUE 11	Junor	FRE 204	Edmund	TAL 22
Wm.	WOR 169	Lucretia	CLN 98	Eli	DOR 8
Wm. (of Benj.)	WOR 171	Lucy	BCI 230	George	BCI 90
Wm. (of Wm.)	WOR 173	Mary	CLN 86	Gouldsborough	WOR 195
BISSAM, Benjamin (?)		Mary	FRE 190	Handy	WOR 157
	HAR 60	Mary-Negro	HAR 65	Hulda	WOR 194
BISSANT, John	MON 130	Nancy	D.C. 170	Isaiah	CLN 115
BISSELL, Phebe	BCI 34	Noah	CLN 90	James	CLN 75
BISSETT, Thomas	BAL 98	Peter	FRE 172	James	TAL 27
BITLAR, Jacob	FRE 115	Philip	CEC 120	James	WOR 161
BITTINGER, Adam	FRE 228A	Polly	FRE 172	James (of Saml.)	WOR 158
BITTLE, Marey	BCI 413	Richard	BAL 194	Jessee	CLN 109
BITTO, Mary Ann	BCI 18	Rosetta	D.C. 17	John	TAL 24
BITTS, Sol.	BCI 537	Sahel	BCI 345	John, Senr.	WOR 157
Thos.	D.C. 157	Sam.	BCI 358	Joseph	CLN 106
BIVAN, Charles	CHA 211	Sam-Negro	HAR 65	Levin	TAL 22
BIVANS, Henry	ALL 38	Saml.	D.C. 117	Mary	CLN 116
Mary A.	ALL 37	Samuel-f.n.	SOM 120	Periguin	BCI 29
Walter	ALL 37	Thomas	WAS 62	Rachel	CLN 116
BIVENS, Lennard	WAS 149	Vachel	BCI 188	Samuel	SOM 154
Richard	D.C. 20	Violet	D.C. 13	Thomas	CLN 105
Thomas	WAS 145	William	ANN 352	Thomas	TAL 4
BIXBY, Nathl. P.	BCI 272	William	KEN 116	Thomas, Jr.	CLN 109
BIXLER, Abraham	BAL 147	William	SOM 134	BLAGDEN, George	D.C. 113
Benjamin	FRE 188	William, Sen.	ANN 353	BLAGROVE, Ann	D.C. 101
Christopher	BAL 152	William, Jur.	ANN 352	Will.	D.C. 92
David	BCI 447	BLACKBURN, Jehu	CEC 173	BLAIN, James	SOM 124
Elizabeth	BAL 139	John	CAL 46	BLAIR, Andrew, Sen.	
Elizabeth	FRE 188	Robert	MON 148		WAS 135
Emanuel	FRE 189	Uriah	CEC 171A	Andrew, Jun.	WAS 135
Frederick	BAL 141	William	ANN 363	Elizabeth	WOR 177
Jacob	BAL 141	Wm.	CAL 44	Elizh.	BCI 178
John	BAL 164	BLACKBURNE, George		James	BAL 40
John, of J. (I.?)			BCI 273	James	WAS 135
	BAL 147	BLACKEWELL, John	WAS 62	Lewis	FRE 159
Peter	FRE 188	BLACKFORD, John	WAS 62	Thomas	ALL 17
Samuel	FRE 180	BLACKHEAD, Jacob	FRE 131	William (Overs.)	PRI 225
BLACK, Anna	D.C. 3	BLACKISTON, Ebenezer		BLAK, Isaac	BCI 38
Archer	BCI 13		KEN 93	BLAKE, Alfonsa	KEN 92
Arthur	BCI 425	Jabus	QUE 11	Ann	TAL 11
Betsy	BCI 231	Jacob-ngro.	CEC 120	Archibold	KEN 92
Charles	BAL 23	James	QUE 38	Betty H.	D.C. 79
Charles G.	CEC 155	Jamima	KEN 123	Charles	QUE 35
Cornelius-Negro	HAR 49	Joseph	KEN 87	Charles	TAL 3
Daniel	CEC 154	Joseph	KEN 114	Charles P.	QUE 31
Daphne	D.C. 27	Joseph	KEN 120	Cleary	BCI 158

22

BLAKE (continued),		BLISSARD, John	BAL 51	BOARSHLER, George W.	
Conl. Jo.	CAL 61	William	BCI 457		WAS 126
Daphne	QUE 36	BLISZARD, Isack	BAL 21	BOAZ, George	DOR 36
Edward	DOR 13	BLIZARD, Isack	BAL 21	Lenard	DOR 21
Edward U.	SOM 118	Margaret	BAL 22	Thomas	DOR 29
Edwd.	WOR 162	Sarah	BAL 22	Zebulan	DOR 35
George	QUE 26	Stephen	BAL 165	BOBERY, Jacob	WAS 119
Jacob	WOR 162	William A.	BAL 156	BOBEY (See also ROBEY),	
James	BCI 109	BLIZZARD, William	WOR 193	Adam	WAS 105
James	DOR 13	BLOCHER, Andrew	ALL 8A	Christian	WAS 127A
Janus?	DOR 13	John	ALL 9	Christian	WAS 140
John	BCI 499	BLOCK, Elizh.	BCI 191	Daniel	WAS 117
John	KEN 86	BLOCKBANK, Sharper		Daniel	WAS 133
John	KEN 92		SAI 96	Elizabeth	WAS 114
John	TAL 7	BLONDALE, Nichl.	BCI 525	Jacob	WAS 134
John	TAL 8	BLONDEL, John M.	BCI 70	John	WAS 86
John S.	QUE 42	BLOODSWORTH, Risdon		BOBST, Daniel	FRE 111
Leven	WOR 184		SOM 141	John	FRE 111
Levin	WOR 214	Robert	SOM 141	BOBY, Michael	WAS 140
Levin, Jun.	WOR 161	BLOODWITH, John	DOR 33	BOCKMAN, Ferdinand	FRE 97
Levin F., Senr.	WOR 161	Robert?	DOR 33	BOCKMILLER, Eliza	BCI 492
Nathan	CEC 155	Robrt	DOR 33	BODEN, Francis	BCI 139
Polly	DOR 13	BLOOM, Enoch	WAS 82	James	BAL 113
Rachell	BCI 75	John	FRE 79	John	BAL 111
Samuel	CAL 42	Maria	D.C. 155	Samuel	MON 147A
Sarah	CLN 91	Peter	FRE 178	BODFIELD, Obednigo	TAL 5
Sarah	KEN 102	BLOSS, John	SOM 109	BODLEY, Joseph	BCI 58
Sarah	QUE 25	BLOWER, James	FRE 75	William (?)	WOR 194
Solomon	CEC 120	BLOWERS, Anne	ANN 373	BODY, George	CEC 172
Thomas	BAL 96	BLOWES, Benjamin	ANN 372	BOENICKS, Henry	BCI 354
Thomas, Jun.	CAL 62	BLOXHAM, Edmond	WOR 159	BOGAN, Caroline	FRE 96
Thomas (Capt.)	CAL 61	James	D.C. 182	Jas.	D.C. 86
William	BAL 227	BLUBOUGH, Benjamin	ALL 23	BOGGS, A.L.	BCI 244
William H.	QUE 24	Raphael	ALL 16	Harmanious	BCI 265
BLAKELY, Matthew	BCI 220	BLUE, John	D.C. 203	John	BCI 500
Sally	FRE 209	John H.	ANN 316	Levin	SOM 155
BLAKEMAN, Joab	D.C. 92	BLUFFORD, Sarah	BAL 180	William	SOM 146
BLAKER, Ann	CEC 133	BLUIT, Levin	SOM 135	BOGGUS, Robert S.	BCI 444
BLAKEWAY, John	KEN 118	BLUME, Adam	FRE 223	BOGS, James	BAL 115
BLAMER, Perry	TAL 35	BLUNKALL, Joseph	CEC 155	BOHAM, Mary	FRE 200
Richard	TAL 36	Margaret E.	CEC 155	BOHANNAN, James	SAI 54
BLAN, Jenny	D.C. 208	BLUNNT, Benjamin	QUE 37	Jonathon	SAI 65
BLANCH, Jeremiah	KEN 86	BLUNT, Henriette M.	QUE 27	BOHART, Phillip	FRE 124
William	TAL 50	Josh.	D.C. 151	BOHEN, James	CAL 63
BLANCHARD, ---		Nathan	CLN 76	Jas.	BCI 306
(Mrs.)	D.C. 102	Samuel	D.C. 60	Mary	ANN 363
Will.	D.C. 73	Wm.	QUE 13	BOHN, Anthony	FRE 140
BLAND, Edwd.	D.C. 131	BLUNTS, --- (Miss)	D.C. 175	Charles	BAL 180
George, Sen.	CLN 106	BLUNTT, Edward	CAL 63	Jacob	FRE 142
George, Jr.	CLN 107	BLYDEN, John	SOM 138	John	FRE 222
James	D.C. 204	BOADEN, James	BCI 73	Nicholas	FRE 217
Levina	CLN 111	BOADLEY, John	BAL 248	Solomon	FRE 228A
Theoderick	BCI 443	BOALT, John	WAS 102	Susan	FRE 216
BLANDFORD, Jos.	D.C. 124	William	WAS 108	BOHOFFEN, Thomas (?)	
BLANDY, Thomas	BAL 7	BOALTON, John	WAS 82		CEC 119
BLANEY, John	HAR 47	BOARDING SCHOOL-		BOHOTTEN, Thomas (?)	
BLANFORD, Joseph	PRI 218	FAIRHILL BOARDING			CEC 119
Walter	CHA 211	SCHOOL	MON 154	BOHRER, Mary	D.C. 49
BLANSET, Joseph	SAI 89	BOARDLEY, Catherine		BOICE, John	BCI 210
BLANTZ, Charles	FRE 227		KEN 106	BOIE, Denis	FRE 143
BLARE, Jane	SAI 77	BOARDLY, Stephen	BCI 303	BOING, Lydia	FRE 216
BLASDELL, Nics.	D.C. 152	William	KEN 119	BOIS, Sutton	BCI 306
BLASS, Christ.	BCI 481	BOARMAN, A.J.P.	PRI 218	BOLD, Martha	CEC 132
BLAWER, James (?)	FRE 75	Alecius	CHA 223	BOLDEN, John	BAL 231
BLAYCE, Jonathan	D.C. 42	Benedict L.	CHA 206	BOLDING, Geo. (?)	BCI 395
BLECKER, John	WAS 71	Edward	HAR 43	Jehu	BCI 36
BLESSEN, Michael	FRE 145	George W.	CHA 207	BOLENEA, John	BAL 19
BLESSING, Geo.	FRE 123	Horace	CHA 207	BOLENED, John (?)	BAL 19
Henry	WAS 58A	John C.	CHA 222	BOLEY, Simon	DOR 11
Phil.	FRE 123	Joseph	CHA 207A	BOLGIANO, Fras. M.	BCI 215
BLEW, Patrick	BAL 223	Joseph G.	CHA 214	BOLIN, Stephen	TAL 4
BLICKENSTAFF, Yost		Monica	CHA 228	BOLING, Elijah	BCI 27
	FRE 133	Raphael	CHA 207	BOLLARD, William	FRE 163
BLISS, Calvin	BCI 54	Rapheal	CHA 222	BOLLES, Jacob	MON 173
William	BCI 56	Robert	HAR 41	BOLLINGER, John	BAL 159
		Thomas C.	CHA 205	Joseph	BAL 159

BOULDEN (continued),
John CEC 132
R. Richard CEC 133
Richard CEC 133
William BAL 105
William CEC 133
BOULEN, Mary CEC 173
Samuel CEC 173
BOULS, Nancy WOR 194
Thos. WOR 186
BOULTEN, William CEC 132
BOULTON, Joseph SAI 92
BOUND, Barbary ANN 355
BOUNDS, Ann Maria
BCI 57
Collins (f.n.) SOM 119
Doubty SOM 109
James SOM 104
John SOM 105
Richard ANN 336
William SOM 138
William, of Jas. SOM 110
BOURDLEY, Lisban KEN 89
Thomas KEN 86
BOURKE, James QUE 36
Thomas C. QUE 40
Thomas F. CLN 86
Tobias QUE 37
William Y. QUE 40
BOURNE, George CAL 44
James I. CAL 42
John CAL 42
BOURY, Sophia BCI 225
BOUSER, Stephen CEC 120
BOUSHELL, John CEC 120
Peter CEC 119
BOUSMAN, John BAL 20
BOUTCHER, Alfred D.C. 26
BOUTMAN, John (?)
BAL 20
BOUZER, Harry CEC 154
BOVEINGER, George
BAL 138
BOWAN, Thomas BCI 309
BOWARD, George WAS 122
Henry WAS 105
Jacob WAS 99
Jacob WAS 99
Jacob WAS 106
Jacob WAS 122
John WAS 101
Margaretta WAS 122
Michael WAS 122
William WAS 105
BOWARS, Jacob WAS 108
BOWCOCK, Elizabeth
BAL 61
BOWDEN, Isaac (?) WOR 192
James CEC 133
James FRE 140
Littleton WOR 177
Littleton R. WOR 174
BOWDLE, Carson TAL 41
Edward TAL 40
Jacob TAL 33
John CLN 105
John, Jr. CLN 113
Loftis TAL 39
Tristram TAL 33
William CLN 108
BOWEN, Absolem BAL 113
Aquilla G. CAL 43
Artimas D.C. 80
Asa WOR 178
Basil CAL 50
Benjamin (?) CEC 133

BOWEN (continued),
Benjamin BAL 174
Benjamin BAL 226
Benjamin BAL 247
Benjn. D.C. 80
Benjn. WOR 173
Catharine BCI 155
Chas.? MON 144
Chos. MON 144
Cyrus MON 176
Edward J. (I.?) BAL 125
Edwd. WOR 173
Elenor CAL 67
Elisha BAL 226
Elisha WOR 181
Elizabeth BAL 226
Elizabeth MON 152
Elizh. BCI 176
Gambrul CAL 48
Gedun CAL 44
George WOR 177
George WOR 178
Hannah WOR 178
Henry HAR 28
Isaac, of James CAL 48
Isaac, of Jesse CAL 47
Isaac (of Jethro) WOR 174
James D.C. 92
James (Capt.) WOR 172
James C. WOR 173
Jasper CAL 46
Jenkins WOR 177
Jeptha WOR 177
Jesse CAL 47
John BCI 20
John BCI 132
John CAL 44
John D.C. 95
Joshua BCI 411
Josiah WOR 173
Josiah WOR 177
Kendal WOR 179
Kendal T. WOR 181
Littleton WOR 174
Lydia CHA 223
Maryland CAL 50
Miles Y. CAL 43
Nathl. D.C. 113
Nathl. M. CAL 48
Parker WOR 175
Peregrine CAL 47
Peregrine CAL 58A
Peter FRE 177
Philip BAL 126
Pitt E. BAL 231
Ralph W. MON 160
Richard BCI 117
Richd. CAL 47
Robert HAR 6
Samuel MON 148
Sarah (Mrs.) CAL 45
Solomon BAL 226
Somercett CAL 47
Thomas D.C. 82
Thomas MON 148
Thos. CAL 48
William BAL 224
William CAL 66A
Willm. D.C. 213
Wm. CAL 47
Wm., Senr. WOR 178
BOWENS, Jacob CEC 155
BOWER, Barbara FRE 170
Chas.? (?) MON 144
Chos. (?) MON 144
Daniel FRE 177

BOWER (continued),
Frederick FRE 161
George WAS 102
Henry WAS 126
Hester FRE 177
J. BCI 398
Jacob FRE 177
Lawrence FRE 148
Mary (?) BCI 239
Michael CEC 133
Stephen FRE 177
Susan FRE 156
BOWERD, Jacob WAS 58A
BOWERICE, Christian
FRE 87
BOWERS, Adam FRE 194
Benjamin QUE 35
Christian FRE 194
Conrad WAS 62
Daniel FRE 225
Everhart BCI 496
Frederick ALL 27
George WAS 56
Henry BCI 200
Howell TAL 39
Jacob BCI 505
Jacob WAS 56
James BCI 142
James KEN 101
John FRE 195
John KEN 106
John TAL 40
John WAS 62
John WAS 108
Martin BCI 191
Nathan BCI 428
Sarah KEN 93
William KEN 92
William KEN 116
Willm. BCI 199
BOWERSOCK, Valentine
FRE 159
BOWERSOX, Christian
FRE 186
Geo. A. BCI 517
Jacob FRE 179
Maria FRE 179
BOWES, Christopher SAI 74
Elisha CAL 62
BOWIE, Abraham CHA 197
Allen TAL 4
Alley MON 176
Ann Elizabeth PRI 226
Charles PRI 203
Daniel PRI 182
David BCI 88
Davis D.C. 152
Elizabeth A. PRI 219
Elizh. BCI 186
Elizth. D.C. 191
Fielder PRI 219
Isaac CHA 191
James D.C. 47
John PRI 204
John (Dr.) MON 148
Joseph CHA 196A
Mary PRI 208
P. (Mrs.) PRI 219
Reuben S. D.C. 176
Robert W. PRI 211
Sarah CHA 197
Thomas PRI 195
Thomas, Junr. PRI 203
Thomas H. ANN 389
Walter PRI 184
Washingtin MON 136

BOWIE (continued),		BOWMON, George	PRI 196	BOYD (continued),	
Washington	D.C.45	BOWSER, Bill	HAR 30	Saml.	D.C.138
William	PRI 205	Charlottee	KEN 103	Samuel	BCI 102
William	PRI 207	D.	BCI 239	Samuel	BCI 296
BOWIN, Lewis	CEC 120	Easter	KEN 118	Samuel	PRI 214
Oswell	BAL 179	Frederick	WAS 133	Thomas	HAR 70
Whittington	WOR 179	Frederick	WAS 134	Walter	WAS 105
BOWINE, James E.	CAL 42	Isaac	BAL 163	Washington	D.C.137
BOWIR, Ann	BCI 286	John	WAS 109	Washington S.	MON 148
BOWLAND, John N.	SOM 112	John	WAS 140	William	BCI 318
John N.	SOM 125	Joseph	BAL 164	William	WAS 135
BOWLEN, Martin	BCI 500	Moses	BCI 295	BOYE, Lucue	BCI 346
BOWLES, Betsey	D.C.189	Sam	QUE 20	BOYED, David	FRE 100
Christiana	WAS 121	Shaderick	KEN 102	Robert	WOR 197
Elizabeth	SAI 89	Thomas	KEN 92	BOYEN, --- (Mr.)	ANN 291
Isaac	WAS 135	BOWSIER, Perry	DOR 65	BOYER (See also VOYER),	
James H.	WAS 146	BOWSON, Benjamin	CEC 133	Augustin	KEN 123
John	WAS 120	BOWUS, James (?)	KEN 101	Danl.	FRE 129
John	WAS 134[A]			Detrick	FRE 228A
Thomas C.	WAS 133	BOWYER, John	MON 142	Eve	D.C.164
BOWLEY, Elizabeth	BCI 62	Mary	MON 142	F.A. (Doctr.)	WOR 180
George	CLN 98	BOXE, Martin (?)	ALL 25	Frederick	KEN 122
Sam. H.	BCI 473	BOXEL, Robert	ALL 37	Gabriel	KEN 125
William D.	BAL 108	BOYCE, David	MON 134	Isaac-ngro.	CEC 120
BOWLIN, Charles	BCI 279	Jas.	D.C.156	Jacob	BCI 170
Eleonor	SAI 56	Sarah	D.C.121	Jacob	MON 165
Hester	DOR 4	Silas	CLN 112	James	QUE 4
Roger	DOR 12	Theodore R.S.	ANN 349	John	D.C.151
BOWLING, Austin	PRI 225	BOYD, Alex H.	BCI 494	John	FRE 109
Basil	PRI 201	Alexander	CEC 154	John	KEN 104
Dick	DOR 12	Alexander	HAR 58	Johnathan (?)	FRE 129
Edward	PRI 225	Alexr.	BCI 198	Johnathan	FRE 131
Emily (See Peter		Cooper	HAR 73	Lucy	KEN 102
DRURY, agent to		Dennis	ANN 291	Michael	CEC 133
Emily BOWLING)		E. (Miss) & Mary	BCI 266	Michiel	KEN 125
Francis	D.C.185	Francis	CAL 59	Nathaniel	KEN 110
John F. R.	CHA 215	Hanah	WAS 56	Nicholas	ANN 336
Kesiah	D.C.200	Hugh	BCI 156	Nicholas	FRE 213
Marsham	CHA 227	Hugh	CEC 172	Peter	FRE 213
BOWLUS, David	FRE 133	Hugh, of J.	CEC 154	Phillip	KEN 102
George	FRE 132	Jacob	KEN 115	Reason	ANN 337
Henry	FRE 127	James	BAL 230	Saml.	BCI 167
Jacob	FRE 131	James	BCI 4	Stephen	KEN 120
John	FRE 131	James	CEC 154	Thomas	FRE 201
Nicholas	FRE 127	James	CEC 154	Terissa	KEN 123
BOWMAN, Aden	MON 139	James (Farm)	BAL 246	William	KEN 116
Allen	MON 139	James P.	BCI 519	BOYERS, Elizabeth	WAS 63
Alley	BCI 150	Jane	CEC 154	Gabriel	FRE 204
Baltzer	WAS 122	Jas.	D.C.168	George	WAS 100
Carlton	ALL 35	Jeremiah L.	PRI 206	Jacob	WAS 108
Cornelius	PRI 224	John	BAL 215	Jacob	WAS 123
Daniel	BAL 144	John	BCI 28	John	WAS 126
Danl.	BCI 529	John	BCI 171	Peter	WAS 108
Fredk.	MON 178	John	BCI 213	William	WAS 81
George	FRE 149	John	CEC 154	BOYES, Andrew	CEC 133
George	WAS 78	John	D.C.175	Hugh	BCI 71
George	WAS 93	John	HAR 21	BOYLE, Danel	FRE 170
Henry	HAR 26	John	HAR 70	Edward	BCI 125
Henry; S.	WAS 88	Joseph	BCI 397	Francis	BCI 382
Henry; J.	WAS 88	Joseph	WAS 116	George S.	BCI 425
Ignatius	BCI 456	Margarel?	BCI 499	James	ANN 392
Isaac	WAS 87	Margaret	BCI 499	Jna.	BCI 226
Jacob	MON 178	Mary (See Miss E.		Mary	FRE 141
Jacob	WAS 88	& Mary BOYD)	BCI 266	Patrick	CEC 173
Jacob	WAS 98	Mary	CEC 154	Peter	FRE 143
Jacob	WAS 125	Mathew	KEN 118	Thomas	BCI 114
John	WAS 78	Matthew	BCI 58	Wm.	BCI 509
John	WAS 88	Nicholas	HAR 78	BOYLES, William B.	CEC 172
Joseph	BCI 3	Patrick	BCI 72	BOYLEY, Philip	BAL 200
Joseph	WAS 125	Patrick	BCI 181	BOYS, Andrew (?)	CEC 155
Margaret	WAS 144	Peter	BCI 172	John (?)	HAR 21
Mary	ALL 35	Reuben T.	BCI 446	BOYSE, Samuel	BAL 14
Mary	PRI 225	Richard	PRI 206	BOZMAN, David	SOM 125
Peter	WAS 103	Robt.	D.C.78	George	CLN 107
Samuel	FRE 221	Robt.	D.C.145	Levin	SOM 126
Sarah	BCI 51				

BOZMAN (continued),			BRADLEY (continued),			BRAMBLE (continued),	
William	SOM 129		Harisson	D.C. 191		Edmonson	DOR 36
BOZMON, John L.	TAL 38		Henry	DOR 55		Geo.	QUE 11
BRABSON, Calep	CEC 173		Henry	MON 147A		James	KEN 121
BRACCO, Bennett	TAL 6		Isabel	ALL 27		Jeremiah	DOR 53
Jas. D.	QUE 5		John	D.C. 54		John	KEN 86
Philip	CLN 109		John, Sr.	CLN 92		John	QUE 17
William	QUE 33		John, Jr.	CLN 90		Jonas	DOR 3
BRACES, Bennett (?)			Mary	ALL 24		Levin	DOR 34
	TAL 6		Mary	MON 160		Lydia	TAL 8
BRACKEN, Bennett	CLN 81		Patrick	FRE 141		Mary	DOR 36
John	BCI 460		Patrick	FRE 159		Masheck?	DOR 22
BRACKENRIDGE, ---			Phineas	D.C. 102		Mashuk	DOR 22
(Widow)	FRE 171		Rob.	BCI 225		Mathew	DOR 34
BRADA, Owen	PRI 194		Samuel	BAL 189		Rachel	DOR 40
BRADAHOUSE, Ann	BCI 51		William, Sr.	DOR 52		Robert	WAS 126
BRADAY, Charles	SAI 95		William, Jr.	DOR 52		Samuel	KEN 92
BRADBURN, Chas.	D.C. 131		BRADLY, Francis	CEC 132		Stephen	DOR 40
Edward R.	SAI 77		Isaac	BCI 384		Thomas	BAL 233
Peter	D.C. 158		John	DOR 19		Thomas	DOR 34
Samuel	BAL 215		BRADSHAW, Edward	DOR 4		Thomas	DOR 61
BRADBURY, Stephen	BCI 10		Elizabeth	CHA 196		William	BAL 249
BRADDOCK, John	MON 158A		Hambleton	SOM 148		William	DOR 36
Thos.	D.C. 186		Jacob	SOM 148		William	SOM 108
Wm.	MON 159		James	KEN 114		William	TAL 47
BRADEBAUGH, John	BCI 254		John	KEN 85		Wm.	QUE 12
BRADEN, Elizabeth	D.C. 30		John	WAS 118		Zechariah	DOR 36
Rebecca	CEC 133		Joseph	FRE 99		BRAMLLE, Thomas	BAL 219
William	BCI 450		Lewis	BCI 156		BRAMSER, Adam (?)	BAL 14
BRADENBAUGH, Jacob			Littleton	SOM 148		BRAMWELL, Henry	BAL 10
	BCI 83		Nathan	SOM 142A		BRANAN, ---- (Widow)	
Jacob	HAR 61		Rachel	KEN 85			FRE 170
BRADENBEAU, John	BCI 151		Richard	SOM 147		Hugh	BCI 255
BRADEY, Caleb, Senr.			Richd.	BCI 253		Martha	BAL 118
	D.C. 213		Sarah	CHA 195		Sara	WAS 149
Caleb, Junr.	D.C. 213		Sarah	DOR 3		BRANCH, Alexander R.	
John M.	BCI 160		Thomas	TAL 11			BCI 449
BRADFIELD, Enos	HAR 23		Wm.	BCI 494		BRANCOM, John (?)	SAI 97
BRADFORD, ---			BRADY, Andrew	D.C. 98		BRAND, David	BCI 254
(Widaw)	BCI 383		Benjamin	ALL 11		BRANDENBURG, Jacob	
Ben-Negro	HAR 49		Caleb	CEC 132			FRE 70
Betsy	WOR 193		Edward	BCI 378		Jacob	FRE 163
Chas.	D.C. 207		Edward	QUE 33		Jacob, Jr.	FRE 79
George	ANN 335		Felix	D.C. 82		BRANDT, --- (See	
George	HAR 6		George	FRE 86		SMOOT & BRANDT)	
George W.	HAR 29		Israel	BCI 46		Charles	CHA 224
Henry	WOR 172		James	HAR 21		Jacob	BCI 515
Jeffrey	PRI 197		John	CHA 207		John	ALL 3
John	BCI 37		John	D.C. 63		Sarah	ALL 36
John	BCI 268		John	WAS 146		William	BCI 84
John	WOR 163		John, Revd.	SAI 68		BRANGLE, Nicholas	FRE 77
Kendal	WOR 179		Joshua	WAS 150		BRANHAM, Rachael	D.C. 196
London-f.c.p.	HAR 10		Mary	SAI 66		BRANHAN, Wilson	D.C. 182
Mary	BAL 241		Michael	D.C. 66		BRANICK, Edmond	DOR 5
Moses	CEC 120		Nathl.	D.C. 121		Henry	DOR 11
Petee?	PRI 229		Phillip	CEC 132		Henry	DOR 26
Peter	PRI 229		Thomas	BAL 192		BRANING, Juliann	BAL 207
Robert	HAR 8		William	ALL 12		BRANISER, Adam	BAL 14
Saml.-Negro	HAR 79		BRAFFEN, Henry	CEC 133		BRANNAM, Julia	BCI 38
Samuel	ANN 335		BRAGGOONIER, Daniel			BRANNAMAN, Geo.	BCI 186
Samuel	HAR 48			WAS 111		BRANNAN, Jane	BAL 130
Sarah	WOR 180		Jacob	WAS 101		John	BCI 87
Sophia	WOR 172		Samuel	WAS 109		John	D.C. 93
William	ANN 318		BRAGONYER, Henry	WAS 149		John	D.C. 131
William	D.C. 49		BRAHAN, Samuel (?)	D.C. 17		John	D.C. 138
William	FRE 96		BRAHAWN, John	DOR 21		Thomas	BAL 113
William	HAR 8		BRAIKLEY, Joakim	CEC 173		Thomas	BAL 118
William-Negro	HAR 65		John	CEC 173		William	BCI 301
Wm. ? (of Avra)	WOR 171		BRAIN, Benjamin	FRE 112		BRANNER, Patrick	BCI 416
Wn. (of Avra)	WOR 171		John	FRE 112		William (?)	FRE 201
Zelitha	WOR 172		Mary	D.C. 86		William (of Edwd.) (?)	
BRADGES, Robert	WAS 146		BRAISER, William	WAS 115			CHA 190
BRADLEY, Abram	MON 164		BRAKAN, Samuel	D.C. 17		BRANNOCK, James	CLN 104A
Ann	CHA 195		BRAMBLE, Banzilla?	DOR 34		Thomas	CLN 104A
Ezekiel	DOR 10		Barzilla	DOR 34			

BRANNON, John	HAR 79	BRAWN, --- (?)	BCI 388	BRENT (continued),	
Philip-Negro	HAR 65	Able	BCI 372	R.Y.	D.C.138
BRANSBY, William	FRE 99	Charles	BCI 368	Robert	BCI 377
BRANSON, Batty	BCI 337	John (?)	BCI 395	Sally	D.C.204
Ben.	D.C.150	John	BCI 374	Thos. C.	WAS 146
James	SAI 81	Michael (?)	BCI 370	Willm.	D.C.100
John B.	SAI 78	Sarah (?)	BCI 368	BRERESINGER, George (?)	
Wm.	BCI 476	Thomas	BCI 396		BCI 461
BRANSTETTER, Daniel		BRAWNER, Catharine	CHA 191	BRERETON, Henry	SOM 136
	WAS 100	Habk.	D.C.124	Joseph	SOM 103
BRANTNER, George	WAS 59	Henry	CHA 212	Patty	SOM 133
Jacob	WAS 85	Henry	FRE 143	Patty	SOM 134
Michael	WAS 88	Henry, Senr.	CHA 193	Scott	SOM 134
Nelly	WAS 72	Henry, Junr.	CHA 208	Stephen (f.n.)	SOM 119
Susanah	WAS 59	Hezekiah	CHA 211	BREVARD, Adam	WOR 197
BRANZIL, John	SAI 68	Ignatius	FRE 145	James	WOR 192
BRASH, David	FRE 71	James	CHA 191	BREVETT, Benje.	BCI 507
BRASHEAR, Ausburn		Robert	CHA 194	John	BCI 507
	FRE 75	Thomas S.	CHA 194	Joseph	BCI 155
Belt	FRE 69	William	FRE 143	BREWEN, Cornelius	BAL 235
Dora	FRE 85	William (of Edwd.)	CHA 190	BREWENTON, Stephen	CLN 112
Ely	FRE 70	William (of Wm.)	CHA 190	BREWER, Barbary	D.C.143
Otho	FRE 76	BRAWNING, --- (Widaw)		Betsey	FRE 229
BRASHEARS, Bennedik			BCI 370	Brice	ANN 394
	PRI 180A	BRAY, Philip H.	ALL 2	Catharine	SAI 82
Dowell	ANN 274	BRAYDAY, Isaac (?)	TAL 5	Daniel	WAS 132
Eliza.	MON 135	BRAYFIED, John	SAI 94	David	WAS 136
Elizh.	D.C.124	BRAYGOONIER, Jacob	WAS 94	Edward	SAI 79
Francis	PRI 204	BRAZIER, Levin	WOR 192	Elizabeth	ANN 403
Green	PRI 182	William	HAR 8	Elizabeth	SAI 80
Ignatius	PRI 205	BREADY, Frances	SOM 106	George	WAS 132
Jeremiah	PRI 204	BREARETON, John A.		Hannah	ANN 300
Jno. U.?	D.C.105		D.C.4	Henry	ALL 8A
Jno. W.	D.C.105	BREATHOD, James	WAS 89	Henry	WAS 136
John	ANN 254	BRECHT, Danl.	BCI 285	Isaac	HAR 25
John	PRI 195	BRECKENRIDGE, James		Jacob	WAS 80
Noah	D.C.129		PRI 191A	Jacob	WAS 140
Rebecca	PRI 182	BREDEN, Jacob	CAL 42	Jacob	WAS 134
Robert	D.C.95	Richard	CAL 41A	James	HAR 25
William	ANN 272	BREEDING, Anderton O.		John	ANN 388
William	PRI 183		CLN 98	John	BCI 453
Wm.	MON 165	Ennalls	CLN 94	John	WAS 137
Zedock	ANN 263	BREESE, Betey	TAL 8	John A.	WAS 132
BRASHERE, John	ANN 336	Joanna	CAL 63	Joseph	ANN 255
BRASHERS, William	ANN 262	BREMER, Caleb T.	WOR 156	Joseph	D.C.60
BRASS, Joseph	BCI 239	Leu	WOR 189	Joseph	SAI 75
BRATSHAW, Martha	WAS 115	Levi (?)	WOR 189	Lloyd	ANN 306
BRATT, John	BCI 325	BREMERMAN, Herman	BCI 301	Nicholas	ANN 397
BRATTAN, Joshua	SOM 105	BRENDAN, R.	BCI 379	Nicholas	BCI 45
BRATTEN, Bruff	WOR 219	BRENDLE, George	WAS 114	Nicholas (Covington)	
Ebenezer	WOR 188	BRENESER, George	BCI 475		ANN 291
Ebenezer	WOR 191	BRENGLE, Christian	FRE 117	Peter	WAS 137
Eli	WOR 206	Elizabeth	D.C.34	Richard	SAI 79
Jesse	WOR 202	Jacob	FRE 109	Thomas S.	ANN 388
Jesse	WOR 205	Jacob	FRE 163	William	ANN 392
John	WOR 192	John	FRE 105	William	BCI 453
John	WOR 215	John	FRE 117	Wm.	MON 132
Josiah, Sen.	WOR 171	Lawrence	D.C.14	BREWN, Jos.	MON 162
Nathl.	WOR 191	Lawrence	FRE 104	BREWNER, Elias	BCI 191
Sally	WOR 205	Peter	FRE 97	Jacob	FRE 83
William	WOR 191	BRENLLINGER, Conrad		John, Sr.	FRE 83A
BRAU, Anthoney L.	BCI 283		WAS 121	John, Jr.	FRE 83A
BRAUGHTON, Henry	SOM 146	BRENNER, Anthony	FRE 104	BRIAN (See also O'BRIAN),	
James	SOM 156	Margaret	BCI 19	Abraham	BCI 466
John H.	SOM 155	BRENNING, Christian	WAS 123	Charles	BCI 324
Killiam	SOM 145	BRENSINGER, George	BCI 461	Daniel	KEN 117
William	SOM 156	BRENT, Ann	PRI 214	Elizabeth	CEC 132
BRAUGTON, Isaac M.		Charles	SAI 80	Isaac	BCI 242
	SOM 148	Danl.	D.C.100	Joseph	BAL 77
BRAUHAN, Sarah	DOR 60	George	CHA 203	William	SAI 63
BRAVO, John	CEC 172	George	D.C.194	William O. (?)	PRI 193
BRAWHAN, John	DOR 54	George	PRI 229	BRIANT, David	BAL 161
Keziah	DOR 19	Henry	D.C.203	BRICE, Ann	KEN 88
BRAWHAW, William	DOR 49	Jane	CHA 204	Cloudsberry	QUE 3
		Moses	D.C.209	Edmund	ANN 296

BRICE (continued),		
George-Negro	HAR 79	
Hannah	D.C.144	
Henry	BCI 433	
Hewlet	DOR 7	
James	KEN 124	
John	BCI 251	
John P.	ANN 288	
Joseph W.	QUE 2A	
Julianna	ANN 402	
Nichs.-Judge	BCI 278	
Richard	BCI 60	
Richard	KEN 110	
Sarah	KEN 88	
Stephen-Negro	HAR 79	
Susan?	KEN 89	
Theadore	KEN 102	
William	TAL 33	
BRICKENHAM, Jas.	D.C.94	
BRICKER, Christiana	ALL 37	
Elizabeth	ALL 37	
John	ALL 37	
BRICKLE, Isaiah	DOR 12	
Maycall	DOR 12	
Washington	DOR 12	
BRIDDENDON, Phillip		
	BCI 92	
BRIDDLE, David	WOR 200	
John	WOR 218	
BRIDE, John -ngro.	CEC 120	
M.	BCI 407	
BRIDELL, Isaac	WOR 184	
Mary	WOR 189	
BRIDEN, William	BCI 36	
BRIDENALL, Anthonay		
	WAS 149	
Anthonay, Jr.	WAS 149	
BRIDENER, Martin	BCI 56	
BRIDES, Lydia	D.C.35	
BRIDGATT, Charles	D.C.33	
BRIDGE, Isabelea?	BCI 254	
Isabella	BCI 254	
BRIDGEMENT, Heziciah		
	WAS 64	
BRIDGES, Daniel	TAL 25	
J.S.	BCI 251	
John	TAL 26	
Rebecca	BCI 230	
Thomas	TAL 25	
Thomas	TAL 27	
BRIDGET, William	CHA 201	
BRIDLE, Elihu	WOR 217	
BRIDLES, Wm.	QUE 10	
BRIDLEY, Elizabeth	CLN 81	
BRIDGMAN, Ann	CLN 75	
BRIEN, John	FRE 102	
BRIERLY, William	HAR 60	
BRIERWOOD, Jobe	DOR 8	
Jonathan	DOR 6	
Joshua	DOR 4	
Thomas	DOR 59	
BRIGGS, Isaac	MON 148	
John	MON 140	
Mary	BCI 100	
Robert	MON 163	
BRIGHT, Dominic?	DOR 22	
Dominie	DOR 22	
Horace	BCI 320	
Ignatius	ANN 312	
James	QUE 45	
Mary Ann	ANN 402	
Mosses	DOR 18	
Nancy	QUE 11	
Rosanna	CLN 80	
Susana	SAI 82	
William	CLN 82	

BRIGHT (continued),		
Wm.	MON 165	
BRICHTMAN, Israel	CHA 194	
BRIGHTNAN, Rebecca		
	BCI 526	
BRIGHTWELL, Cathirine		
	PRI 213	
Cathirine	PRI 214	
John	D.C.106	
Levin	PRI 213	
Peter	PRI 214	
Richard	FRE 213	
Sibby	MON 149	
BRIGHTWON, Toby	BCI 334	
BRIGS, James	BCI 38	
BRILEY, James	DOR 61	
John	QUE 28	
Samuel	DOR 57	
Thomas	DOR 61	
Thos., Jr.	DOR 57	
BRIMMER, --- (Mr.)		
	BAL 127	
BRINCEFIELD, Elijah		
	DOR 57	
James	DOR 58	
BRINCKLY, James	CAL 48	
William	CAL 49	
Wm.	CAL 48	
BRINDLE, Mary	BCI 513	
BRINDLEY, Benjn.	HAR 57	
BRINER, Robert	MON 148	
BRINKIT, --- (See		
WELLS CHASE, BRINKIT		
& CO. WOOLEN MANU-		
FACTORY)		
William	BAL 179	
BRINKLEY, Dick	QUE 19	
James	SOM 116	
Joseph B.	SOM 142A	
BRINKMAN, Henry	BAL 140	
BRINN, Henny	SAI 63	
BRINNER, John	WAS 107	
BRINSFIELD, Elijah	DOR 39	
Peter	TAL 34	
Sarah	TAL 33	
William	TAL 39	
BRINTON, Edward	HAR 43	
BRION, William	ANN 254	
BRIOOS, James (?)	BCI 345	
BRISCO, Isaac	FRE 161	
John	FRE 151	
Joseph	MON 148	
BRISCOE, Betsey	BCI 115	
Caleb	KEN 120	
Charles	WAS 140	
Edward	SAI 92	
Eleanor B.	CHA 204	
James	FRE 96	
James	KEN 108	
James	KEN 121	
Jane	KEN 108	
John	CEC 172	
John	FRE 116	
John	SAI 87	
John H.	SAI 92	
John Ll.	SAI 88	
Leonard	SAI 88	
Margaret	KEN 107	
Martha	KEN 123	
Mary Ann	ALL 27	
Nathan	BCI 142	
Philip	SAI 93	
Polly	D.C.150	
R.S.	D.C.7	
Saml. J. (I.?)	CHA 204	
Sarah M.	CHA 211	

BRISCOE (continued),		
Thomas	KEN 106	
Thomas B.	SAI 86A	
William	SAI 94	
William H.	SAI 91	
BRISH, Barbara	FRE 94	
Harriot	FRE 103	
BRISLAND, Nancy	BAL 158	
BRISON, Charles	WAS 115	
Thomas	CEC 133	
William	CEC 173	
BRISTER, Big	SOM 130	
David	BCI 141	
Nat-Negro	HAR 50	
Rachael	WAS 94	
BRISTO, Mary	BCI 71	
Richard	CEC 133	
William	CEC 132	
BRISTON, --- (?)	BCI 404	
Jane	BCI 91	
BRISTOR, George	BCI 100	
BRITHARD, Isaac	MON 176	
BRITT, Joshua	WOR 212	
S.	BCI 389	
BRITTINGHAM, Elijah	WOR 187	
George	WOR 199A	
Isaac	WOR 177	
James	WOR 160	
Jas. (of Purnell)	WOR 159	
John of J.	WOR 199A	
John, S. (of J. (I.?) ?)		
	WOR 199A	
Joshua	WOR 170	
Josiah	WOR 211	
Leah	WOR 184	
Leah	WOR 191	
Levi (of Purnell)	WOR 159	
Margaret	WOR 159	
Nathan	WOR 157	
Nathan M. (?)	WOR 199A	
Nathanell	WOR 199A	
Sally	WOR 192	
Sam	WOR 160	
Stephen	WOR 215	
Tab	WOR 218	
Thos.	SOM 137	
Thos.	WOR 173	
Thos. E.	WOR 176	
William	WOR 217	
William, J.	WOR 199A	
William (of J. (I.?) ?)		
	WOR 199A	
Wm.	WOR 179	
Wm. E.	WOR 169	
BRITTON, Edward	BAL 230	
Jas.	QUE 8	
John	BCI 125	
William	QUE 8	
BRIZARD, Charles	BCI 296	
BROADAWAY, James	QUE 33	
BROADBECK, Jacob	D.C.17	
BROADBEEK, Jacob (?)		
	D.C.17	
BROADWATER, Charles		
	ALL 2	
Elias	WOR 179	
Henry	WOR 160	
James	WOR 156	
BROADWATERS, Guy	ALL 2	
Mary	ALL 12	
William	ALL 13	
BROADWELL, James	D.C.28	
BROCHUS, Milly	D.C.189	
Thos.	D.C.163	
BROCK, Fradinan	BAL 208	

BROCKETT, Robt.,	BROOKES (continued),	BROOMBAUGH (continued),
Senr. D.C.202	George W. PRI 205	David WAS 111
Robt., Jr. D.C.184	Ignatias D.C.33	George WAS 122
BROCKINS, Peter (?)	Ignatius? D.C.33	Henry WAS 112
BCI 49	BROOKHART, Henry BAL 215	Joseph WAS 111
BROCKIUS, Peter BCI 49	BROOKINGS, Margaret	BROOMCORD, John WAS 62
BRODERICK, Thos. D.C.107	CEC 154	BROOME, Benjamin SAI 57
BRODRUP, George FRE 115	BROOKLIN, Cassin D.C.58	James M. SAI 57
William FRE 115	BROOKOVER, Thomas FRE 77	BROOMETT, Michael WAS 96
BROGDEN, Abraham ANN 343	William FRE 77	BROOMFIELD, Edwd. BCI 169
Sollomon ANN 343	Wm. MON 172	BROOMHALL, John WAS 69
William ANN 275	BROOKS, Amia TAL 37	BROOMWELL, Henry WAS 78
BROKIUS, Peter BCI 95	Ann D.C.100	BROON, Cath. BCI 496
BROME, Alexander CAL 46	Benjamin CAL 65	BROOSE, Isaac BCI 181
Benja. CAL 46	Benjmn. BCI 306	BROPHY, William FRE 81
James CAL 43	D. BCI 435	BROSE, Mary FRE 179
John CAL 45	David TAL 39	BROSEAUS, Jacob WAS 145
BROMLEY, Archibald D.C.59	Dennis DOR 57	John WAS 146
Joseph D.C.8	Denniss DOR 45	BROSEOUS, Jacob WAS 149
BROMWELL, Edward TAL 39	Elizabeth HAR 23	Samual WAS 149
Harrieta BCI 274	Elizh. D.C.112	BROSSER, Isaac (?) BAL 83
Jacob S. TAL 38	Fanny TAL 37	BROTHERS, --- (?)
John K.? TAL 37	George BAL 184	(See POPPLEIN &
John R. TAL 37	George BCI 82	BROTHERS)
Robert TAL 14	George DOR 43	Joshua BAL 52
Sarah CLN 91	George TAL 33	BROTTON, George WOR 175
Thomas S. TAL 38	George TAL 38	Mary CEC 171A
William TAL 20	Hannah KEN 102	BROUDAWAY, Wm. QUE 16
William H. BCI 248	Henry DOR 25	BROUDMARKLE, Chris-
Wm. BCI 169	Isaac D.C.114	topher ALL 25
BRONAUGH, Jer. W. D.C.47	Isaac SOM 127	BROUGDEN, George D.C.203
John W. D.C.59	James D.C.87	BROUGHTAN, Noah BCI 460
BRONNICK, Jahn DOR 26	James D.C.202	BROUGHTON, Alcy SOM 131
John? DOR 26	James B. D.C.59	Benjamin SOM 128
BRONWELL, Edward BCI 65	John BAL 207	Isaac BCI 256
BROOGONIER, David WAS 93	John CEC 172	Jonah SOM 123
BROOK, Ann ANN 345	John DOR 20	William BCI 434
George PRI 187	Jonathan BAL 193	BROUNE, James KEN 104
Henry TAL 10	Jos. BCI 228	BROW, Mary BCI 295
Jesse CAL 44	Joseph BAL 193	BROWER, Emanuel FRE 182
Joliet BCI 459	Joseph D.C.60	Emanuel FRE 191
Joseph D.C.58	Joseph DOR 20	Frederick D.C.6
Mary PRI 187	Joseph DOR 25	John FRE 182
Samuel D.C.7	Joseph R. BCI 276	John FRE 200
Thos. D.C.175	Joshua BAL 208	John D. SOM 153
BROOKBANK, John SAI 92	Nancy BCI 431	BROWERS, John D.C.162
BROOKE, Basil MON 149	Nancy DOR 27	BROWIN, Oswell (?) BAL 179
Bassil FRE 174	Nathan BAL 227	BROWM, John? FRE 218
Clement PRI 204	Nelly CAL 67	BROWN, --- (?) BCI 388
Clement H. PRI 205	Nelly WAS 87	--- (?) BCI 395
Francis D.C.75	Phillip KEN 110	--- (Mrs.) BCI 449
Harriott PRI 219	Robert BCI 435	--- (Negro) (?) BAL 129
Ignatius R. CHA 222	Sarah D.C.104	--- (Widow) BCI 372
James KEN 109	Sarah DOR 20	A.C. PRI 194
John ANN 345	Sibert WAS 136	Abel BAL 60
John J. (I.?) CAL 43	Thomas HAR 72	Abel BAL 61
Jos. MON 164	Thomas KEN 110	Able (?) BCI 372
Oswald B. SAI 79	Tower D.C.120	Able BCI 284
Rachel PRI 216	William ANN 286	Abraham BAL 234
Rebecca PRI 224	William BAL 3	Addison D.C.131
Richard CHA 189	William BAL 189	Alee CEC 155
Richard MON 148	William BCI 321	Alexander D.C.65
Robert (See Rich-	William BCI 450	Alexr. BCI 280
ard. SPALDING-	William D.C.57	Allen CEC 172
oveser. Robert BROOKE)	William SOM 126	Amos BCI 438
Roger FRE 143	Willm. D.C.192	Andrew BAL 45
Roger MON 148	BROOM, Delila DOR 24	Andrew D.C.131
Thomas PRI 204	George D.C.53	Ann BCI 228
Thomas F. ALL 2	Henry BCI 23	Ann D.C.27
Thos. A. MON 164	Hooper CHA 223	Ann D.C.109
Walter B. PRI 216	Thomas BCI 19	Ann D.C.184
William J. (I.?) SAI 74	Thos. MON 168	Ann DOR 5
William R. HAR 21	BROOMBAUGH, Catherine	Archabold BAL 60
BROOKES, Eleanor MON 131	WAS 112	Barthoshaba WOR 171
Fanny D.C.143	Daniel WAS 112	Basil D. PRI 182

BROWN (continued),			BROWN (continued),			BROWN (continued),		
Benj.	FRE	123	Elsa	ANN	346	James (free negro)		
Benjamin	ALL	20A	Emanuel (?)	FRE	182		SOM	118
Benjamin	ANN	286	Emma	BCI	128	James (Thr.)	MON	140
Benjamin	CEC	155	Ephm.	MON	142	James (Ths.?)	MON	140
Benjn.	D.C.	146	Ephraim	FRE	203	James F.	KEN	88
Benjn.	D.C.	192	Fanny	BCI	161	Jas.	WOR	170
Betty	DOR	6	Francis	BCI	317	Jane	ANN	403
Brice	BAL	62	Francis	PRI	195	Jane	BCI	81
Bristol	BCI	506	Francis	PRI	202	Jane	BCI	493
Caleb	BCI	520	Frederick	FRE	74	Jas.	D.C.	101
Caleb	TAL	32	Fredk.	MON	141	Jas.	D.C.	106
Calep of J.	CEC	172	Freeborn	HAR	46	Jehu	CEC	172
Calep of R.	CEC	172	G.	D.C.	198	Jehu of J.	CEC	172
Cassa	MON	139	Gabaral	BAL	11	Jemima	PRI	237
Cathe.	D.C.	88	Garrett	BCI	50	Jenny	TAL	48
Catherine	ANN	352	George	BCI	198	Jess-Negro	HAR	49
Catherine	D.C.	40	George	BCI	252	Jess-Negro	HAR	50
Cathn.	BCI	180	George	CEC	172	Jesse	CEC	172
Cato	SOM	138	George	CHA	221	Jesse	D.C.	167
Charles (?)	BCI	368	George	D.C.	21	Job	QUE	19
Charles (?)	BCI	368	George	HAR	24	Joel	BCI	315
Charles	BCI	63	George	PRI	238	John (?)	BCI	374
Charles	BCI	308	George	WAS	137	John (?)	WAS	70
Charles	CAL	50	George T.	PRI	222	John	ANN	264
Charles	CEC	173	George T.	WOR	217	John	ANN	322
Charles	HAR	21	Gustavus A.	BCI	60	John	ANN	371
Charles	MON	148	Gustavus R.	CHA	207B	John	BAL	17
Charlotte	BCI	24	Gustavus R.	PRI	226	John	BAL	148
Charlotte	BCI	308	Gusty	SAI	89	John	BAL	192
Christopher	BAL	181	Hager	ANN	277	John	BAL	216
Clara	D.C.	108	Hannah	ANN	376	John	BCI	29
Clement	SAI	96	Hannah	BAL	242	John	BCI	55
Clement T.	FRE	109	Hannah-Negro	HAR	49	John	BCI	57
Cornelius P.	BCI	174	Harry	KEN	93	John	BCI	86
Daniel	CLN	114	Henrietta	ANN	286	John	BCI	93
Daniel	CEC	154	Henrietta	CLN	97	John	BCI	196
Daniel	CEC	155	Henry	BAL	151	John	BCI	224
Daniel	D.C.	15	Henry	BAL	201	John	BCI	395
Daniel	WAS	68	Henry	D.C.	190	John	BCI	454
Daniel	WAS	88	Henry	FRE	196	John	BCI	529
Danzey	ANN	278	Henry	FRE	203	John	CEC	154
Daphney	ANN	308	Henry	KEN	91	John	CEC	171A
David	ANN	334	Henry	SAI	75	John	D.C.	13
David	BCI	128	Henry H.	ANN	342	John	D.C.	33
David	BCI	507	Hiram	KEN	90	John	D.C.	52
David	CEC	172	Horatio	ANN	277	John	D.C.	90
David	D.C.	156	Hugh	CEC	155	John	D.C.	159
David	FRE	154	Ignatius	FRE	149	John	FRE	145
David	SOM	126	Isaac	PRI	217	John	FRE	187
David	WAS	110	Isaiah	CEC	172	John	WAS	63
David; S.	WOR	211	Jacob	BAL	22	John	WAS	85
Debby	BCI	431	Jacob	BCI	100	John	WOR	202
Delia	BCI	496	Jacob	BCI	198	John, Esqr.	CLN	99
Dickson	BCI	59	Jacob	BCI	298	John (of Thos.)	FRE	149
Dixon	BAL	78	Jacob	BCI	516	John B.	BAL	3
Dorethy	BCI	126	Jacob	FRE	195	John E.	BCI	139
E. & William	BAL	60	Jacob	HAR	24	John G.	BCI	315
Eccleston	DOR	56	Jacob	MON	144	John H.	ANN	285
Edmund	CEC	132	Jacob	PRI	195	John H.	D.C.	169
Edward	BAL	61	James	ANN	281	John H.	PRI	202
Edward	BCI	101	James	ANN	299	John M.	BCI	48
Edward	BCI	462	James	BAL	121	Joseph	ANN	377
Edward	DOR	40	James	BAL	245	Joseph	DOR	4
Edward	KEN	91	James	BCI	33	Joseph	BCI	40
Eleanor	CHA	202	James	BCI	61	Joseph	CEC	172
Elihu	HAR	62	James	BCI	214	Joseph	CEC	173
Elisha	ANN	324	James	BCI	490	Joseph	FRE	168
Elisha	ANN	374	James	BCI	510	Joseph	HAR	45
Elisha	CEC	172	James	D.C.	64	Joseph	MON	148
Elizabeth	ANN	266	James	D.C.	66	Joseph	SAI	81
Elizabeth	ANN	318	James	D.C.	83	Joseph, Senr.	KEN	90
Elizabeth	BCI	68	James	DOR	50	Joseph, 3d.	KEN	94
Elizabeth	BCI	75	James	KEN	91	Joseph, 4th	KEN	86
Elizh.	BCI	176	James	MON	148	Joseph G.	WAS	83
Elizh.	D.C.	122	James	TAL	33			

32

BROWN (continued),			BROWN (continued),			BROWN (continued),		
Joshua	BAL	53	Robert	D.C.	35	Tobias	WAS	70
Joshua	BAL	56	Robert	D.C.	68	Tubman	SOM	126
Joshua	BAL	155	Robert	HAR	30	Uriah	BCI	153
Joshua	BCI	536	Robert	SOM	105	Uriah	D.C.	16
Joshua	CEC	172	Robert, J.	CEC	172	Vachel	BAL	67
Joshua	FRE	203	Robt.?	MON	143	Violet	ANN	324
Joshua	MON	149	Robt.	D.C.	106	Virlinda	D.C.	190
Josiah	BCI	170	Robt.	D.C.	131	Walter	ANN	378
Juliana	D.C.	71	Robt.	HAR	30	Will.	D.C.	121
Kinzir	ANN	266	Rudolp	WAS	70	Will	PRI	238
Lanty	HAR	30	Rush?	CEC	172	William	ANN	290
Levi	DOR	4	Ruth	CEC	172	William	ANN	374
Levi	WOR	202	Sam.	QUE	19	William	BAL	60
Levin	TAL	9	Saml.	D.C.	83	William	BAL	150
Limas	ANN	315	Saml.	D.C.	158	William	BAL	215
Loring	BCI	282	Saml.	KEN	116	William	BCI	36
Lucretia	DOR	12	Saml.	SOM	140	William	CLN	81
Luke	BCI	257	Samuel	ALL	8A	William	CEC	172
Magdalene	FRE	113	Samuel	ANN	323	William	D.C.	5
Margaret	HAR	8	Samuel	BAL	198	William	D.C.	20
Margt.	D.C.	80	Samuel	BAL	202	William	D.C.	83
Martha	KEN	94	Samuel	CEC	171A	William	DOR	9
Marton	SAI	79	Samuel	D.C.	41	William	DOR	35
Mary	BAL	60	Samuel	D.C.	208	William	FRE	82
Mary	BCI	520	Samuel	FRE	78	William	FRE	164
Mary	CEC	172	Samuel	HAR	76	William	HAR	24
Mary	D.C.	66	Sarah	ANN	352	William	HAR	31
Mary	D.C.	112	Sarah	BAL	46	William	HAR	46
Mary	FRE	87	Sarah	BAL	119	William	SAI	93
Mary	KEN	94	Sarah	BAL	210	William	TAL	32
Mary	MON	144	Sarah	BCI	368	William	WAS	85
Mary	MON	147A	Sarah	PRI	196	William	WOR	214
Mary	WAS	57	Siderwil	ANN	272	William W.	KEN	86
Matilda	D.C.	62	Simon	DOR	4	Willm.	D.C.	122
Matthew	FRE	82	Simon	HAR	74	Willm.	D.C.	123
Michael	ANN	358	Stephen	BCI	142	Wm.	BCI	180
Michael	BCI	370	Stephen	CEC	133	Wm.	BCI	228
Miller	CHA	211	Stephen	CEC	172	Wm.	BCI	499
Milly	BCI	310	Stephen-free	CAL	59	Wm.	BCI	513
Montelion	CEC	172	Stewart	BCI	273	Wm. H.	D.C.	178
Morgan	BCI	306	Suck	PRI	197	Zachariah	ANN	334
Moses	BAL	205	Sucky	PRI	236	Zephh.	D.C.	138
Nancy	FRE	203	Susan	ANN	393	BROWNE, Andrew	QUE	48
Ned	SOM	133	Susan	D.C.	27	Benjamin	QUE	45
Nelly	CEC	154	Susan	D.C.	147	Bill	QUE	6
Nelly	D.C.	59	Susana	SAI	81	Charles C.	QUE	38
Nelly	D.C.	63	Susanah	WAS	116	Darcus	KEN	124
Nicholas	BAL	148	Sylvester	BCI	55	Henry	QUE	16
Nicholas H.	FRE	193	T.	BCI	411	Jacob	QUE	31
Ob. B.	D.C.	87	Tabitha	CHA	202	James (?)	KEN	104
Oswell (?)	BAL	179	Tamar	BAL	233	James	KEN	103
Paul	D.C.	171	Tamsey	CLN	114	James	KEN	104
Perry	KEN	90	Thomas (?) (See			James	KEN	116
Perry	TAL	50	Brown THOMAS)			James	QUE	5
Peter	BCI	433	Thomas (?)	BCI	396	James	QUE	12
Peter	FRE	195	Thomas	ANN	297	James	QUE	25
Peter, Jr.	FRE	195	Thomas	ANN	303	James (Col.)	QUE	6
Phebe	BCI	427	Thomas	BAL	14	James W.	QUE	5
Rachel	SAI	64	Thomas	BAL	196	Jinny	QUE	48
Rebecca	BAL	228	Thomas	BCI	82	Manuel	KEN	123
Rebecca	BCI	66	Thomas	BCI	304	Marla	KEN	107
Rebecca	CEC	132	Thomas	CEC	172	Mary Ann	KEN	124
Rebecca	CEC	133	Thomas	CEC	172	Morgan	KEN	100
Rebecca	CEC	173	Thomas	D.C.	48	Pere	QUE	7
Rebt.	MON	143	Thomas	D.C.	50	Pheby	QUE	46
Reese	BAL	48	Thomas	D.C.	53	Philip	KEN	120
Remus	QUE	17	Thomas	D.C.	59	Richd.	QUE	12
Richard	BAL	22	Thomas	D.C.	105	Robert	QUE	24
Richard	BAL	158	Thomas	FRE	164	Thos.	KEN	122
Richard	BCI	445	Thomas	HAR	18	William	QUE	47
Richard	SAI	55	Thomas	PRI	183	BROWNHILL, James	D.C.	89
Richard	SAI	91	Thomas	SOM	125	BROWNING, --- (Wid-		
Richd.	BCI	229	Thomas	WAS	95	aw) (?)	BCI	370
Robert	CEC	172	Thomas, Jr.	FRE	149	Archd.	MON	140
Robert	CEC	173	Thomas C.	BAL	46	Benjn.	MON	175

BROWNING (continued),		BRUNER, John	FRE 205	BRYON, Jeremiah	SAI 81

BROWNING (continued),
Edward MON 148
Ish.? MON 176
Jah. MON 176
Jno. KEN 125
Jonathan FRE 78A
Jono. MON 141
Jono. MON 141
Jos. MON 175
Josiah D.C. 211
Levi BCI 216
Lewis MON 175
Meshac ALL 4
Meshick MON 175
Retson BCI 349
Saml. of Jno. MON 177
Saml. B. MON 171
Wm. BCI 192
BROWNLEY, James HAR 23
Joseph HAR 29
BROWNS, John BCI 335
BROWNSBERRY, Peter
FRE 103
BROWNSON, Hector D.C. 78
BROZIER, Michael BCI 25
BRUBAKER, John FRE 113
BRUCE, Andrew ALL 27
Charles PRI 184
David D.C. 181
Edward FRE 218
Francis ALL 15
George ALL 27
Hanah D.C. 191
Hariet D.C. 59
Henrietta CHA 203
John HAR 77
Rachael FRE 201
Upton FRE 183
William CHA 196
BRUCHEE, Catharine
FRE 210
BRUFF, Elizabeth SOM 155
Jack QUE 26
James WOR 187
John TAL 26
Joseph TAL 26
Margarett QUE 29
Mary D.C. 10
Thomas TAL 22
Wm. BCI 492
BRUICE, William SAI 91
BRUINGTON, George
WOR 204
Harah WOR 205
John WOR 204
Smith WOR 204
Thomas WOR 203
William WOR 204
BRUMBLY, Benjamin
WOR 200
David SOM 136
Elisha WOR 212
Isaac WOR 200
Jabez WOR 164
Jesse SOM 136
BRUMELL, John DOR 20
BRUMFIELD, Daniel CEC 171A
BRUMINET, Josephus
CHA 190
BRUMLY, Lewis BCI 405
BRUMMELL, Henry BCI 503
BRUMMER, Cuffey ANN 394
BRUMWELL, Joseph BAL 149
BRUNDIGE, James BCI 353
BRUNE, F.W. BCI 258

BRUNER, John FRE 205
John WAS 100
Michl. MON 131
Peter WAS 100
BRUNETT, James ANN 334
John ANN 334
William ANN 334
BRUNIP, Thos. BCI 181
BRUNNEL, Jacob BCI 109
BRUNNER, Andrew BCI 433
Daniel FRE 113
Elias FRE 113
Jacob D.C. 24
Jacob FRE 93
Jacob FRE 101
John FRE 102
John FRE 113
John, of Jacob FRE 105
Stephen FRE 113
Valentine FRE 102
BRUNT, George ALL 25
John ALL 25
BRUSCOP, Harriott QUE 25
BRUSH, John D.C. 88
BRUSHWELLER, Ferdd.
BCI 200
BRYAN, A. BCI 368
Albert CEC 120
Arthur BAL 126
Benjn. D.C. 119
Benjn. D.C. 130
Bernard D.C. 165
Charles BAL 227
Charles K. DOR 3
Enoch D.C. 127
Frederick BAL 111
Guy CEC 120
Hager BCI 521
Henrietta QUE 37
Henry PRI 237
Isaac CEC 133
James FRE 143
James, Sen. ALL 22
Jesse CEC 120
John BCI 85
John, Esqr. CEC 133
John B. PRI 228
Joseph CEC 120
Joseph PRI 231
Levin TAL 13
Milly ANN 319
Nathaniel ALL 27
Nicholas BAL 131
Robert QUE 45
Ruth BAL 14
Samuel ANN 337
Samuel CEC 120
Samuel QUE 41
Silve K., C.W. BCI 281
Susan BAL 14
Thomas CHA 226
Thomas PRI 231
Valentine QUE 40
William PRI 226
William PRI 231
William QUE 40
BRYANS, Dorathy BCI 283
BRYANT, John BCI 233
Rachel BCI 127
BRYARLY, Wakeman HAR 47
BRYDENHART, Mary ALL 26
BRYLEY, Collerson FRE 150
John WAS 108
BRYNE, Edward PRI 225
Osburn PRI 225
T. BCI 394

BRYON, Jeremiah SAI 81
Stephen SAI 81
Thomas KEN 86
BRYSON, James BAL 184
John BCI 152
Nath. G. BCI 188
BUCEY, Benjamin ANN 258
Joseph ANN 257
BUCHAM, Samuel CEC 119
BUCHANAN, Edward BAL 227
Elizabith BCI 273
James BCI 335
James A. BCI 279
John M. WOR 158
Lloid BCI 411
Peter-Negro HAR 65
Rebecca ANN 273
Solomon BAL 234
Sydney BCI 252
Wm. BCI 418
BUCHANNAN, Chas. D.C. 81
BUCHEN, --- BCI 442
Charles BCI 417
BUCHER, Christopher
BAL 149
David BAL 149
Thomas KEN 115
Ulerick Z. BAL 148
BUCK, --- (Mrs.) BCI 397
Benjamin BAL 120
Benjamin BCI 114
Casire BCI 113
Dorcas BAL 114
Henry WAS 65
Jacob BCI 117
James BAL 128
John BAL 113
John BCI 80
John BCI 97
John BCI 117
John CLN 95
John WAS 66
Ned PRI 185
Robert BCI 302
Samuel BCI 80
Selvester BAL 58
Wm. BCI 257
BUCKANAN, Joshua BCI 140
BUCKER, Catherine WAS 117
Daniel FRE 189
BUCKET, Maria KEN 122
BUCKEY, Daniel FRE 81
David FRE 117
George FRE 77
George FRE 81
John FRE 94
Michael FRE 97
Peter FRE 110
Valentine FRE 113
BUCKHANAM, John CEC 133
Margaret CEC 132
BUCKHANNAN, James
KEN 105
John WAS 83
Thomas WAS 82
William CHA 193
BUCKINGHAM, Archabold
BAL 68
Beal BAL 68
Benjamin BAL 58
Benjamin BAL 161
Caleb D.C. 126
Elizabeth BAL 49
Ephream BAL 66
Ezekiel FRE 211
George BAL 68

BUCKINGHAM (continued),
Isaiah BCI 456
James HAR 46
John BAL 57
Larkin BAL 65
Leven BAL 56
Margarett FRE 123
Mary BAL 68
Nathan, Senr. BAL 58
Nathan, Junr. BAL 59
Nicholas BAL 58
Obadiah BAL 7
Obediah BAL 58
Obediah, Senr. BAL 58
Saml. BCI 302
Thomas BAL 175
Thomas PRI 216
Thos. BCI 314
Will. D.C. 86
William BAL 59
Wm. HAR 42
BUCKINHAM, Levy BCI 393
BUCKLEAR, Georg SAI 89
BUCKLER, John CAL 48
William BAL 180
William DOR 20
BUCKLEY, Arnold TAL 52
Bennett TAL 46
C. D.C. 85
Henry BCI 139
James BCI 256
Jas. D.C. 123
John QUE 32
Joseph D.C. 117
Samuel TAL 36
BUCKLY, Charles TAL 49
BUCKMAN, Abner ANN 378
Elijah BAL 21
Jesse BAL 11
Loyde BAL 9
Loyde BAL 24
Samuel BAL 9
Thomas ANN 351
William ANN 382
BUCKMASTER, Alxd.
CAL 47
Benja. CAL 53A
Elisha CAL 51
Gidion CAL 66A
Henry CAL 53A
Jesse CAL 50
Thomas CAL 66A
BUCKSKIN, Rachel KEN 110
BUCKSTON, John FRE 213
BUCKWALLER, Ghear-
heart WAS 94
BUCRY, Benjamin (?)
ANN 258
Joseph (?) ANN 257
BUDD, George HAR 24
John CHA 204
Julius BCI 155
Wm. QUE 15
BUEFFETT, John (?)
KEN 105
BUERY, Benjamin (?)
ANN 258
Joseph (?) ANN 257
BUFFENDON, Abraham
FRE 175
Jacob FRE 177
BUFFINGTON, Jonah
FRE 124
BUFFORD, Benjamin CAL 61
BUFNENS, John BCI 334

BUGH, John MON 164
Richd. J. MON 174
BUGLE, James D.C. 26
BUIFFETT, John KEN 105
BUILY, William L. BAL 198
BUINS, Walter FRE 213
BUKLEY, Wm. A. (?)
D.C. 205
BULER, Lewis D.C. 163
BULEY, Philip BCI 61
Titus (f.n.) SOM 120
BULFINCH, Chas. D.C. 104
BULGEAN, James BCI 9
BULGER, --- (Mr.) BCI 463
James D.C. 56
BULL, Ambress BAL 97
Aquila BCI 20
Betsy WOR 194
Christopher BAL 98
Cordelia BCI 212
Elisha BCI 154
George S. SAI 88
Jacob BAL 85
Jamima BAL 94
Jarrett BCI 460
John D.C. 90
Maria BCI 305
Mary (?) TAL 25
Mary BAL 97
Nicholas BAL 100
Robert BAL 82
Sarah HAR 37
Susan SAI 93
Walter HAR 38
William FRE 200
William HAR 47
Wm. BAL 91
Wm. BAL 95
Wm. BCI 490
BULLAR, Charlotte SAI 96
Susan SAI 90
BULLEN, Moses ANN 392
Thomas TAL 5
Thomas TAL 36
William TAL 12
BULLER (See also
BUTLER),
Henry (?) D.C. 63
Jacob D.C. 53
Samuel PRI 207
BULLETT, Thomas J.
TAL 10
BULLEY, Michl. D.C. 128
BULLHIME, William BCI 324
BULLIN, Henry QUE 47
BULMAN, Mary (?) WAS 149
BULTAR, Leonard SAI 93
BULTER (See also
BUTLER),
Letitia (?) D.C. 129
Walter (?) D.C. 132
BULY, Levin (f.n.) SOM 119
BUMBARGER, Christian
WAS 126
Jacob WAS 88
John WAS 88
John; S. WAS 88
Moses WAS 88
BUMBERRY, Ann BCI 170
BUMS, Philadelphia (?)
ALL 14
BUNCH, Jesse BCI 322
BUNDY, James BCI 13
BUNE, --- (?) BCI 387
BUNNELL, Eliab D.C. 56
John CAL 64

BUNNIER, Gottfrid BCI 306
BUNSTEAD, Frances BCI 512
BUNTING, Esme WOR 156
John BCI 195
William J. BCI 459
BUNTON, Charles MON 148
Isaac SOM 127
William (?) DOR 32
BUNTRAM, Jno. D.C. 96
BUNTS, Robert S. WOR 213
BUNYIE, Robert BCI 241
William BCI 79
BURALL, George FRE 75
John FRE 78A
BURBAGE, Ann WOR 171
John (of Nehal.) WOR 178
Sampson WOR 217
Samson WOR 171
Thos. WOR 172
BURBANK, Isaac FRE 142
BURBAYGE, Henry WOR 189
BURBECK, Henry D.C. 26
BURBER, Daniel BAL 233
BURBRIDGE, John ALL 21
BURBROUGHER, Casper (?)
WAS 147
BURCH, Alexr. D.C. 91
Ann CHA 222
Augustin C. CHA 220A
Ben D.C. 105
Edward CHA 222
Edwd. D.C. 94
Fredeick? D.C. 36
Frederck D.C. 36
George BCI 39
Gustavus CHA 224
James CHA 223
Jarrad D.C. 108
Jesse CHA 226
John TAL 4
Jonathan T. PRI 217
Joseph N. PRI 221A
Lucinda CHA 225
Reznijah? D.C. 92
Richd. D.C. 87
Saml. D.C. 109
Thomas BCI 265
Thomas FRE 156
Thomas PRI 204
Thomas N. PRI 221A
Thos. D.C. 95
William QUE 37
Wm. BCI 489
BURCHAL, Rebert BCI 40
BURCHENAL, Thomas CLN 74
BURCHET, Benjamin MON 147A
BURCHHART, Catherine
WAS 101
George WAS 96
BURCHHOLDER, Ulrich?
WAS 59
Ulrick WAS 59
BURCHINAL, Wm. QUE 10
BURCHINALL, James QUE 28
BURCHIS, --- (Mr.) BCI 368
BURCHNELL, Martha KEN 92
BURCKHART, Christopher
WAS 97
Jacob WAS 122
Jacob WAS 132
John WAS 98
BURD, --- (Major?) WOR 179
Major WOR 179
BURDEN, James KEN 89
James (Doctr. James STE-
WART's farm) BAL 129

35

BURDEN (continued),			BURGESS (continued),			BURKETT, William	D.C.13
James D.	HAR 63		Thomas	ALL 33		BURKHARTT, John	FRE 125
John	KEN 86		Thomas	ANN 354		BURKHEAD, Thomas	BAL 142
Willm.	BCI 202		Thomas	CHA 192		BURKINS, Charles	HAR 77
BURDET, Wilton	FRE 74		Thomas	D.C.51		Isaac	HAR 71
BURDETT, Benjn.	MON 137		William	ANN 349		BURKITT, Fredk.	D.C.89
Benjn., Junr.	MON 141		William	PRI 218		Henry	FRE 128
Jas.	MON 176		William P.	FRE 74		BURKMAN, John	BCI 456
Saml.	MON 142		BURGIS, Willm.	D.C.149		BURLAND, James	BCI 90
Thos.	MON 174		BURGOINE, Augustine			Mary	BCI 172
BURDINE, William	D.C.132			BCI 78		BURLINE, John	ANN 328
BURDITT, Basil	MON 129		BURGOON, Francis	FRE 181		BURLINGTON, James	D.C.20
BURDON, Benjamin	WAS 135		Jacob	FRE 181		BURLY, Richd.	TAL 49
BURDSALL, Andrew	MON 148		BURGOONE, William	FRE 194		BURN, --- (Widaw)	BCI 407
BURDWELL, James	PRI 229		BURGOYNE, Elizabeth			Adam	BAL 147
BURDY, --- (Widaw)	BCI 384			BCI 11		Henry	DOR 4
BURFORD, Robert	SAI 66		Keron	CEC 133		Jacob	BAL 147
Rosetta	D.C.122		BURGUINE, --- (Widaw)			James	BAL 62
Thomas	BAL 210			BCI 393		James	BCI 15
BURG, Richard	BCI 392		BURGUS, John	BCI 121		John	BAL 147
BURGAN, Nicholas	WAS 85		BURIER, Adam	FRE 79		John, of Jno.	BAL 140
Philip	BAL 225		BURJESS, James	TAL 10		BURNABUE, Chars. D.	
Thomas	BAL 225		Saml.	FRE 222			BCI 374
Thomas, Senr.	BAL 110		BURJISS, West	FRE 222		BURNES, Andrew	HAR 45
BURGEE, Mial	FRE 70		BURK, Andrew	BAL 143		Edward H.	ALL 33
Nathan	FRE 228A		Edward	CEC 133		Fanny	BCI 277
Singleton	FRE 70		Ezekiel	BCI 197		James	BAL 183
Thomas	PRI 180A		George	BAL 156		Jas.	QUE 7
Thomas, Sr.	FRE 70		Jacob	BAL 178		Theodore	BCI 11
Thomas, Jr.	FRE 70		Jacob	BCI 532		Thomas	CEC 155
BURGER, Daniel	WAS 102		Jane	HAR 31		Thomas	CEC 173
Daniel	WAS 127A		Jessee	BCI 144		Thos.	D.C.106
John	BCI 159		John	CEC 155		BURNESTON, Isaac	BCI 466
BURGES, John	BCI 40		John	FRE 146		Joseph	BAL 187
BURGESS, Alfred	ALL 34		John	WOR 204		BURNET, James	WOR 158
Barney	BCI 33		Joseph	HAR 20		BURNETT, --- (Mr.)	BCI 138
Basil	ANN 371		Margaret	BCI 513		Ann	D.C.57
Basil	BCI 512		Marshall (f.n.)	SOM 120		Asa	HAR 45
Ben.	D.C.133		Micajah	BAL 41		Charles A.	D.C.39
Benjamin	CHA 191		Nathl.	HAR 21		James	ANN 310
Charles	PRI 206		Stephen	MON 132		John	BCI 84
Charles	PRI 226		Susan	HAR 21		Mary	BCI 93
Dawson P.	D.C.46		Thomas	BAL 210		Richard	BCI 100
Dennis	PRI 201		Thomas	BCI 212		Thomas	D.C.30
Edwd.	MON 139		Thomas	BCI 508		BURNEY, Benjamin	QUE 36
Elijah	ANN 332		William	BAL 194		BURNHAM, Benjamin	BCI 86
Elizabeth	BCI 93		William	CEC 133		Edward	BAL 11
Elizabeth	PRI 184		William	CEC 133		Harvey	ALL 30
Geo. B. (Dr.)	QUE 11		BURKART, Daniel	FRE 160		John	BAL 11
George	ANN 380		BURKE, David	BCI 20		Saml.	BCI 244
Hellen	MON 147A		Edmond, Sen.	CEC 155		BURNIBUE, J. J.	BCI 374
Henery	BAL 78		Edward	D.C.48		BURNITE, Samuel	CEC 155
James	PRI 239		Edward	FRE 109		BURNS, Adam	BAL 91
John	CLN 85A		Francis	D.C.91		C.	BCI 369
John	CHA 196		Henry	BCI 92		Cavin	BCI 73
John	MON 148		James	ANN 266		Chars.	BCI 198
John	PRI 204		James	BCI 144		Dennis	WAS 63
John	PRI 226		James	BCI 240		Elizabeth	KEN 86
John	QUE 30		James	FRE 71		Frances	BCI 480
John, Jr.	FRE 69		James, 1st	D.C.11		Geo.	D.C.104
John H.	FRE 69		James, 2d.	D.C.11		Jacob	WAS 139
Joseph	BAL 243		John	CHA 205		James	BCI 317
Josiah	D.C.49		John	D.C.66		James	TAL 21
Micheal	ANN 354		John	D.C.73		John	BAL 91
Nancy	MON 139		John	QUE 8		John	BCI 395
Nathaniel	PRI [200]		Michael	FRE 170		John	WAS 78
Perrygreen	ANN 382		Nathl.	BCI 519		Margt.	D.C.213
Peter, Ovsr.	TAL 3		Nicholas	BCI 146		Martha	MON 135
Richard	D.C.44		Patrick	FRE 171		Mary	KEN 103
Richard, Sen.	ALL 31		Thomas	BCI 11		Patrick	WAS 63
Roderick	ANN 322		William	BCI 301		Philadelphia	ALL 14
Ruthy	ANN 338		William	CEC 155		Saml.	BCI 227
Saml.	QUE 10		William B.	FRE 95		W.	BCI 406
Samuel	KEN 104		BURKENS, Jacob	CEC 154		Wm.	MON 139
Sarah	ANN 292		BURKET, Eleanor	ANN 277		BURNSIDES, --- (Mrs.)	
Sary	PRI 226		Nehemiah	ANN 277			BCI 383

BURNSIDES (continued),		BURTS, Thomas	CEC 172	BUTCHER (continued),	
Anne	MON 175	BURTSELL, John	MON 148	John	FRE 84
Henry	MON 175	William	MON 148	Jonatn.	D.C.177
John N.	MON 173	BURTTON, James	DOR 19	Moses	FRE 161
BURNUM, Wm.	BCI 500	BURWELL, Francis	ALL 33	Robert	KEN 124
BURR, Abraham	D.C.51	BURY, William	PRI 197	William	FRE 211
BURRAGE, Martain	SAI 89	BUSCH, Abraham	BCI 312	BUTLAR, Charles (?)	
BURRAT, William	BCI 323	BUSEY, Charles	ALL 25		SAI 97
BURRAWS, Moses	D.C.6	Edward	ALL 24	Charlotte (?)	SAI 96
BURRELL, Charles	BCI 433	John	D.C.64	John	SAI 98
Nat	D.C.187	Saml.	MON 164	Leonard (?)	SAI 93
BURRENGER, John	BCI 36	Thomas	ALL 24	Mary	SAI 90
BURRESS, Asher	WOR 202	BUSH, Aaron	CLN 79	Prichard?	SAI 87
Edward	BCI 14	Catharine	BCI 158	Richard	SAI 87
Elisha	CHA 202	Elizabeth	BAL 227	Susan (?)	SAI 90
William	ALL 37	Elizabeth	CHA 192	BUTLEE, James (?)	PRI 226
BURREST, Mary	BAL 187	Francis	DOR 63	James	PRI 224
BURRIER, Jacob	FRE 228A	George	BCI 500	Patrick	PRI 228
John	BCI 89	George	FRE 157	BUTLER (See also BUL-	
BURRIS, John	CEC 154	Henny?	CHA 223	LER, BULTER,	
John	CEC 172	Henry	CHA 223	BUTTER),	
Leah	CEC 154	James	BCI 218	--- (Widaw)	BCI 377
Peter E.	ANN 262	John	BAL 188	Abitha	D.C.78
BURRISS, Anne	MON 160	John	FRE 162	Abraham	D.C.29
Basil	MON 147A	John K.	BCI 438	Absolum	BCI 449
Benjamin	CLN 115	Joshua	BCI 146	Adam	WAS 150
John	MON 148	Precella	BCI 431	Ann	CHA 208
Proverb	MON 161	Sadrick	BAL 165	Ann	D.C.49
Thomas	MON 167	Samuel	TAL 9	Ann	D.C.96
Tyson	MON 159	Silas C.	SOM 101A	Benjamin	WAS 145
William	MON 148	Spencer	DOR 49	Benjn.	D.C.78
Zadoc	MON 160	William	BCI 56	Betsey	D.C.211
BURROUGHS, Elizabeth		BUSHEY, Henry	BAL 17	Betsey	D.C.212
	SAI 89	John	BAL 23	Catharine	ALL 29
Esther	SAI 87	BUSHOFF, John R.	SAI 92	Charles (?)	BCI 150
Hanson	SAI 91	BUSHOP, Joseph	ANN 379	Charles	CHA 211
Henry	SAI 90	BUSICK, Henry	QUE 14	Charles	D.C.37
Hezikiah	SAI 91	Jno.	QUE 14	Chas. U.?	D.C.90
James	SAI 87	Sarah (?)	QUE 10	Chas. W.	D.C.90
Jesse	WOR 192	Senah	QUE 10	Clem	BCI 344
Jesse C.	SAI 86A	Solomon	QUE 19	Clement	SAI 82
Joseph	SAI 81	BUSSARD, Daniel	D.C.50	David	D.C.162
Joshua	WOR 185	Daniel	BAL 67	Edward	CHA 212
Mary	WOR 190	David	FRE 133	Edward	PRI 183
Philip	SAI 87	Elenor	BAL 67	Edward	WAS 69
Samuel	WOR 187	Henry	BAL 67	Elias	WAS 73
Samuel (of Z.?)	SAI 90	John	FRE 164	Ezekel	WOR 216
William	DOR 5	Margaret	FRE 164	George	CHA 191
William	SAI 90	Solomon	CHA 223	George	CHA 203
BURROWS, Alexander		BUSSEL (See also RUS-		George	CHA 208
	D.C.62	SEL),		George	D.C.50
Alexander	D.C.64	William (?)	CHA 207	George-Negro	HAR 80
Ed	QUE 10	BUSSELLS, James	WOR 215	Harry-f.c.p.	HAR 10
Henry	TAL 27	Pracilla, Wd.	WOR 215	Henny	SAI 80
Hugh	BCI 117	BUSSERD, E.	BCI 375	Henry	CHA 200A
John	D.C.42	BUSSEY, Bennet	HAR 46	Henry	CHA 211
John	D.C.64	Edward F.	HAR 43	Henry	D.C.47
Joseph	D.C.87	Elizabeth S.	HAR 46	Henry	D.C.63
Moses (?)	D.C.6	BUSSICK, James	DOR 18	Henry	D.C.74
Samuel	D.C.64	BUSSLER, Francis	QUE 2A	Henry	D.C.133
Thomas	FRE 106	BUSSURD, Samuel	FRE 130	Henry	FRE 146
BURSER, John	KEN 117	BUSTEED, Warner	CLN 78	Hezhiak	WAS 69
BURTAIN, Isaac	PRI 183	BUSTPITCH, Jessee	DOR 41	Ignatius	CHA 207B
William	PRI 185	BUSY, Jane	CAL 63	Jacob	CHA 208
BURTGESS, Elizabeth		John	ALL 24	Jacob	D.C.17
	FRE 122	Paul, Sen.	ALL 24	Jacob	PRI 217
BURTON, Basil	MON 148	Saml. P.	BCI 316	James (?)	PRI 224
Elijah	BAL 219	Samuel	ALL 23	James	BAL 192
James	FRE 77	Samuel, Jr.	ALL 24	James	BCI 173
James	QUE 46	BUTCHER, Ann	D.C.161	James	BCI 432
John	BAL 249	Henry	FRE 221	James	CLN 87
Joseph, Senr.	BAL 248	Jacob	FRE 215	James	CEC 120
Joseph, Junr.	BAL 248	James	BCI 475	James	CHA 207B
William	BAL 242	Jas.	QUE 3	James	D.C.12
William	DOR 32	John	BAL 64	James	KEN 106
Wm.	BCI 476	John	D.C.216	James	PRI 226

37

BUTLER (continued),		BUTLER (continued),		BYARD (continued),	
James	QUE 48	William	HAR 28	Henry-negro	CEC 120
James	WOR 212	William	PRI 214	Lewis	HAR 20
James (of M.)	CLN 98	William	WAS 65	Richd.	BCI 199
Jane	D.C.31	William	WOR 212	Ruth-negro	CEC 120
Jane	FRE 107	Wm.	BCI 381	Stephen	CEC 120
Jane	PRI 212	BUTSAUR, --- (Widaw)		Thomas-negro	CEC 120
Jas.	D.C.112		BCI 390	BYAS, James	BAL 109
Johannah	PRI 216	BUTT, Basil	MON 148	James	BCI 535
John	BAL 17	Benjamin	WAS 95	Joseph	DOR 10
John	BAL 66	Hazael	MON 147A	BYASS, Henry	CLN 87
John	BAL 190	Hazael S.	MON 159	Philip	CLN 97
John	BCI 372	John	PRI 186	BYENS, John	QUE 28
John	CLN 93	Proverb	MON 160	BYERS, Jacob	WAS 138
John	CHA 207B	Richard	MON 148	John	WAS 99
John	CHA 224	Rignal	MON 147A	John	WAS 140
John	D.C.72	BUTTAN, James	DOR 26	Louisa	BAL 187
John	D.C.198	BUTTAR, Charles	SAI 97	BYHEW, John	BCI 141
John	FRE 161	John (?)	SAI 98	BYLAND, Andrew	CLN 113
John	FRE 211	Leonard (?)	SAI 93	BYMOND, James (?)	WAS 119
John	HAR 23	Mary (?)	SAI 90	BYONHEIDT, Alexandria (?)	
John	HAR 71	Prichard (?)	SAI 87		FRE 187
Jonathan	CLN 86	Richard (?)	SAI 87	BYRAM, Thomas	BAL 88
Joseph	BAL 17	BUTTER (See also		William	KEN 108
Joseph	BCI 52	BUTLER),		BYRD, Thomas	SOM 111
Joseph	D.C.31	Ann (?)	D.C.96	Thomas (Jur.)	SOM 118
Josias	BCI 428	Charles	BCI 150	BYRN, Henrietta	CLN 99
Julianna	WAS 151	Clem (?)	BCI 344	BYRNE, Bernard	BCI 532
Leonard	D.C.14	Henry (?)	D.C.133	Christr.	D.C.85
Letitia	D.C.79	Henry S.	BCI 210	Patrick	BCI 416
Letitia	D.C.129	Letitia (?)	D.C. 129	BYRNES, Saml.	BCI 486
Letty	CHA 208	Malan (?)	D.C.93	William	HAR 47
Letty	D.C.22	Margaretta (?)	WAS 73	BYRON, Michael	KEN 92
Letty	WAS 120	Richard	ANN 261	BYRUM, Martin	BAL 54
M.	BCI 397	Walter (?)	D.C.132	BYSHER, Francess	BCI 152
Malan	D.C.93	BUTTERWITH, William			
Margaret	D.C.54		PRI 228		
Margaretta	WAS 73	BUTTERWORTH, John			
Mary	BAL 184		BCI 324		
Mary	BCI 380	Thomas	BAL 233	--- C ---	
Milly	SAI 78	BUTTLER, Abby	SAI 96		
Minty P.	D.C.20	George	CEC 154	CABLE, George	WAS 97
Monicka	SAI 73A	James	KEN 119	John	D.C.117
Moses, Sr.	CLN 89	Jno.	KEN 121	Martha	WAS 59
Moses, Jr.	CLN 92	Julia	BCI 497	CABLES, Samuel	BAL 8
Nancy	D.C.20	Mary	BCI 503	CACH, Benjamin (?)	BAL 80
Nelly	D.C.19	Mintey	BCI 536	CACHRANE, John (?)	
Noble	ANN 392	Ralph	BCI 490		D.C.51
Ormond	FRE 102	Sally	BCI 535	CADDEN, Catharine	SAI 74
Patrick (?)	PRI 228	Saml.	BCI 512	Frances	SAI 76
Paul	ALL 15	Thos.	BCI 353	CADE, Charles	BCI 34
Philis	PRI 213	Zachriah	WAS 69	Elijah	CLN 95
Rezin	PRI 215	BUTTON, Elias	BCI 7	Robert J. (I.?)	CLN 105
Richd.	BCI 217	George	ANN 395	CADEL (See also CADLE,	
Richd.	QUE 11	James (?)	DOR 26	KADEL, KEADLE)	
Robt.	D.C.190	Nany	DOR 30	Agnes	ANN 347
Samuel (?)	PRI 207	Robert	BAL 108	CADEN, Jas.	D.C.154
Samuel	DOR 62	BUTTRUM, John	WOR 203	CADIS, David	D.C.177
Samuel	WOR 214	BUTTS, Augustus	D.C.166	CADLE (See also CADEL,	
Sarah	D.C.78	Mark	D.C.180	KADEL, KEADLE),	
Sarah	PRI 213	Noah	BCI 143	Horatio	ANN 305
Sarah	SAI 63	BUVY, Dennis	D.C.39	Thomas	ANN 288
Sarah	WAS 79	BUXTON, John, of		William	PRI 227
Sollimon	WOR 212	Thos.	MON 137	CADUC, John	BCI 168
Sukey	D.C.143	Thos.	MON 178	CAETZER (See also CRETZER),	
Thomas	ANN 283	Wm.	MON 166	George	WAS 66
Thomas	BAL 194	BUZINES, Samuel	QUE 30	John	WAS 57
Thomas	DOR 13	BUZZARD, Catharine		CAFFEL, Simon	WAS 148
Thomas	HAR 64		FRE 131	CAFFERTY, Thomas	BCI 258
Thomas	SAI 66	George	WAS 133	CAFFERY, John	BCI 76
Thomas	WAS 68	Samuel	FRE 132	CAGE, Thomas S.	PRI 212
Thos.	D.C.132	BYAN, James	QUE 47	William W.	PRI 212
Tom-f.c.p.	HAR 10	James L.	QUE 46	CAGER, John	ANN 287
Walter	D.C.132	BYARD, Benjamin	CEC 120	William	BCI 121
William	ANN 267	Elizabeth	HAR 24		
William	D.C.19	Gabrial-negro	CEC 120		

CAHAGAN, B.	D.C. 97	
CAHALL, Francis	CLN 93	
Gove	CLN 94	
James	CLN 80	
John	CLN 75	
John (of Solo.)	CLN 94	
Solomon	CLN 92	
William	TAL 49	
CAHEY, Michael	BCI 91	
CAHILL, Edmond	BCI 319	
CAHO, Rebecca	CHA 226	
CAHOON, Sarah	CLN 111	
CAIN (See also KAIN,		
KAINE, KANE),		
Aron	BCI 132	
Cumberland-Negro	HAR 80	
Elizabeth	HAR 47	
Ephraim	FRE 76	
James	BCI 148	
James	BCI 429	
James	TAL 36	
Jane	BCI 109	
Jas.	D.C. 212	
John	HAR 41	
John M.	BCI 136	
Levin	TAL 37	
Mathew	HAR 46	
Samuel	HAR 50	
Sarah	FRE 76	
Thomas	ALL 22	
Thos.	BCI 201	
William	ANN 403	
William	FRE 72	
CAINE, Benjamin	FRE 212	
CALAHAN, Nancy	WOR 155	
Turbutt	TAL 36	
CALAMAN, Aaron	FRE 83A	
CALAWAY, Job	SOM 117	
John	SOM 103	
Matthew	SOM 117	
Nathan	SOM 113	
Phillip	DOR 64	
CALDER, Becky	QUE 15	
James	D.C. 23	
Joseph	QUE 9	
Simon	QUE 17	
William	ANN 398	
William	D.C. 23	
CALDWELL, Charles	ALL 35	
David	ANN 291	
E.B.	D.C. 107	
Elijah	BCI 474	
Jabez	TAL 49	
Jeremiah	BCI 310	
Joe (negro)	TAL 26	
John	HAR 72	
John	QUE 13	
John M.	MON 166	
Joseph	BCI 211	
Josiah T.	D.C. 102	
Rachel	BCI 122	
Silas	CLN 93	
Susanna	BAL 233	
Thomas	CEC 174	
CALEB, James	KEN 122	
Samuel	KEN 88	
Samuel, Jun.	KEN 93	
CALEF, Achsah	BCI 94	
CALENDER, William	CEC 156	
CALFLESH, Eve	ALL 21	
CALHAUN, William (?)		
	D.C. 57	
CALHOON, Benja.	BCI 476	
CALHOUN, J. C.	D.C. 93	
John	BAL 121	
Thomas	CEC 156	

CALHOUN (continued)		
William	D.C. 57	
Wm.	BCI 527	
CALINDER, John	DOR 10	
CALL, Sally	FRE 195	
CALLAHAN, George	CLN 99	
Joseph	TAL 49	
Mary	ANN 398	
Sarah	ANN 392	
William	HAR 44	
CALLAN, James	D.C. 122	
John	D.C. 103	
Nichs.	D.C. 76	
CALLENDAR, John	BCI 132	
CALLENDER, Bartw.		
	D.C. 145	
James	BCI 267	
Robert	SOM 126	
CALLIGHAN, John	BCI 242	
Peter	BCI 74	
CALLIMER, Betsy	WAS 66	
Thomas	WAS 66	
CALLIN, --- (Mrs.)	BCI 408	
CALLIS, Daniel	ANN 305	
Henry A.	PRI 238	
CALTON, George	PRI 198	
CALVERT, Alee	CEC 156	
Charles	ANN 273	
Dinah	ANN 272	
Edward H.	PRI 204	
George	PRI 196	
Hannah	D.C. 205	
Jas.	D.C. 115	
Leonard	MON 149	
Rodeham	BCI 135	
Saml.	D.C. 157	
Thomas	ANN 278	
CALVIN, Charles	D.C. 218	
Harriot	BCI 109	
CALWELL, David	HAR 56	
Thomas	HAR 9	
Thomas	HAR 43	
CAMARUN, John	WOR 176	
CAMBELL, Anthoney		
	WAS 115	
Jane	D.C. 55	
John	SOM 154	
John, Jr.	FRE 212	
Patrick	WAS 64	
CAMBRIDGE, Francis M.		
	ALL 7	
CAMDEN, John	ANN 281	
John S.	ANN 285	
CAME, Susanah	CEC 134	
CAMEL, Aaron	BAL 83	
Elizabeth	CEC 156	
Michael	CEC 173	
CAMERON, Hugh	BCI 510	
James	CEC 174	
John	CEC 156	
John C.	CEC 174	
Matthew	CEC 156	
Robert	CEC 156	
William	CEC 156	
CAMLIN, Charles	PRI 197	
Richard	PRI 193	
William	PRI 193	
CAMMACK, Edward	D.C. 67	
CAMMELL, Enoch	ANN 288	
James	CEC 155	
CAMP, Joseph	BCI 176	
Thos.	D.C. 87	
William	BCI 230	
CAMPBELL, Abram	DOR 42	
Alexander	MON 163	
Ann	CEC 156	

CAMPBELL (continued),		
Anne	MON 142	
Archibald	BAL 191	
Benjamin	FRE 186	
Daniel	D.C. 89	
Daniel W.	SAI 57	
Edward	ALL 27	
Eli	WOR 154	
Elisabeth	KEN 101	
Emmy	D.C. 9	
Fanny	ANN 404	
George	BCI 485	
Iver	MON 158A	
James	BAL 191	
James	BCI 141	
James	BCI 144	
James	BCI 275	
James	BCI 293	
James	CEC 156	
James	MON 132	
Jas.	D.C. 168	
John	BCI 75	
John	CLN 79	
John	CEC 134	
John	CEC 135	
John	CEC 174	
John	D.C. 15	
John	FRE 104	
John	FRE 155	
John	FRE 212	
John	MON 161	
John	QUE 7	
John	SAI 64	
Loudon	D.C. 182	
Mariah	DOR 5	
Marlboro	D.C. 11	
Matthew	BAL 84	
Meshack	D.C. 25	
Nancy	BCI 50	
Nicholas	D.C. 210	
Rob.	BCI 229	
Robert	FRE 80	
Samuel	CEC 135	
Sophia	BCI 9	
Thomas	BAL 111	
Thomas L.	BAL 199	
Will.	D.C. 118	
William	BCI 247	
William	BCI 274	
William	CEC 156	
William	FRE 78	
William	FRE 187	
Willm.	D.C. 198	
Wm.	MON 165	
CAMPBLIN, William	CEC 134	
CAMPDEN, William (Overs.)		
	PRI 228	
CAMPELL, Ben	FRE 210	
John	FRE 226	
CAMPER, Denny	DOR 22	
Isaac	DOR 43	
Jacob	DOR 7	
James	MON 175	
John	CLN 75	
John	CLN 112	
John	TAL 24	
Leah	DOR 45	
Lilly	DOR 45	
Lotty	DOR 4	
Mary	DOR 6	
Rhoda	DOR 11	
Richard	DOR 40	
Richard	DOR 43	
Stephen	DOR 49	
Susan	BAL 11	
Thomas	TAL 25	

CAMPHER, Catharine		CANNON (continued),		CAREY (continued),	
	BCI 520	Thomas	SOM 103	Levin	WOR 194
Joseph	BCI 519	William	CLN 80	Louis	D.C.202
Wrightson	TAL 5	William, Senr.	ANN 351	Moses	SOM 118
CAMPLER, Levin	DOR 4	William, Junr.	ANN 351	Obediah	WOR 155
CAMREN, John	WOR 179	William E.	CLN 79	Richard	HAR 44
CAMRON, William	BCI 137	William E.	TAL 34	Solomon	WOR 191
CAMSELL, Wm.	BCI 382	CANOLES, Charles	BAL 214	Thomas	BAL 225
CAN, Thomas	FRE 215	CANRPER, Denny (?)		CARGIN, John	BAL 206
CANA, Frederick	D.C.94		DOR 22	CARICO, Elizabeth	PRI 214
John	D.C.72	CANT, Jauris	QUE 31	CARK, John	WAS 74
CANAAR, William	BCI 96	CANTER, Eleanor	CHA 223	CARLAN, Mary	FRE 100
CANAHAN, Wm. (overeer)		Erasmus	D.C.128	Thomas	FRE 104
	ANN 293	Henry	SAI 90	CARLAND, Philip	MON 163
CANAWK, Micl.	FRE 126	James	CHA 223	CARLEN, George	BAL 126
CANBY, Benje.	BCI 496	Margaret	CHA 225	CARLETON, James P.	
Lewis (?)	D.C.52	William L.	CHA 225		ALL 30
Samuel	BAL 205	CANTERBURY, Bishop		CARLILE, David	BAL 11
Thomas	BCI 461		CLN 105	Lancelot	HAR 56
Whitson	MON 149	CANTLER, David	CEC 174	CARLIN, Elizth.	D.C.217
CANDERS, Aunt (?)		CANTLIN, Robert	HAR 77	George H.	D.C.214
	D.C.54	CANTWELL, Dinali	BCI 453	Westley	D.C.217
CANDLER, John	MON 162	John	SOM 138	CARLISLE, Amos	BAL 204
CANDOLLE, Rachel	BCI 316	Mathew	CEC 134	David	FRE 192
CANE (See also KAIN,		Nancy	SOM 135	David	MON 130
KAINE, KANE),		Thomas	DOR 14	David J. (1.?)	MON 133
Arom	WAS 12	CANVENTER, Robert (?)		Ebenezer	FRE 200
Charles	ANN 285		BCI 343	Elizh.	BCI 184
Hewie	ANN 357	CAPALINO, Anthony		John M.	FRE 227
J.	BCI 398		BCI 442	Purnell	CLN 81
Joshua	FRE 75	CAPEL, Samuel	BAL 50	Tapey	CLN 81
Margarett	QUE 41	CAPITO, Chris	BCI 485	CARLLON, Margl. (?)	BCI 228
Thomas	QUE 30	Frances	BCI 481	Margt. (?)	BCI 228
William	QUE 36	Peter	BCI 334	CARLON, James	HAR 60
CANEL, Elizabeth (?)		CAPLES, Hannah	ANN 329	Jas.	D.C.105
	PRI 227	Jacob	ANN 329	Robert	BCI 132
CANIER, William	BCI 37	Liby	ANN 316	Robert	D.C.4
CANLEY, Lewis	D.C.52	Lily?	ANN 316	CARLSE, Geo.	FRE 125
CANN, Charles, Senr.		Robert	ANN 329	CARLTON, Margl.? (?)	
	ANN 297	CAPOT, Jeremiah	BCI 445		BCI 228
Nancy	BCI 321	CAPPAU, Joseph	BCI 446	Margt.	BCI 228
CANNADY, David	CLN 90	CAPPER, Leah	DOR 26	Thomas	FRE 103
Ezekiel	BAL 191	CAR, Catharine	FRE 220	CARMACH, Samuel	FRE 95
Thomas	DOR 18	CARAGAN, Daniel	D.C.73	CARMACK, Evin	FRE 226
CANNALL, Isaac	KEN 104	CARBACK, Ephraim	BAL 115	John	FRE 223
CANNAN, Luke	DOR 33	Ephraim	BAL 130	Lydia	FRE 223
CANNE, Anthony	BCI 65	Hezekiah	BAL 114	Paul	FRE 222
Brogit	BCI 351	Hezekiah	BAL 123	William	FRE 223
CANNER, Robert (?)		John	BAL 115	Wm.	FRE 222
	D.C.55	John	BAL 128	CARMAN (See also EAR-	
CANNOLLS, William	BCI 222	Thomas	BAL 124	MAN),	
CANNON (See also PAN-		CARBERRY, Henry	D.C.63	Andrew	HAR 62
NON),		Joseph (Revd.)	SAI 57	Greenberry	QUE 8
Abel	D.C.111	Lewis	D.C.63	Mary	D.C.20
Belus	DOR 10	Thomas	D.C.3	Pere (?)	QUE 19
Bevas	DOR 61	CARBERY, Jas.	D.C.108	William	BCI 86
Clement	CLN 99	CARBRICK, John	BAL 81	William	BCI 124
Comphart	DOR 34	CARDIFF, William	CLN 86	CARMEAN, Anderton	CLN 108
Daniel	DOR 63	CARDON, John	BCI ?75	Elijah	CLN 112
Dominick	BCI 57	CAREINS, George	HAR 59	Seth	CLN 109
Edward	KEN 88	Mary	HAR 59	CARMICHAEL, Alex.	D.C.32
Henry	CLN 79	William	HAR 60	Mary	BCI 75
Hetty (f.n.)	SOM 118	CARERE, John	BCI 249	Mary	BCI 195
Jahn	DOR 32	CAREW, Richard	SOM 114	Robt.	BCI 252
James	DOR 34	CAREWELL, Mecine	WOR 175	Sarah	D.C.118
Jane	DOR 61	CAREY, ---	BCI 453	William	BCI 449
John?	DOR 32	Collins, Esqr.	CLN 97	CARMICHEAL, Richard	
John	DOR 34	David	BCI 76		QUE 41
John	HAR 22	Elijah	WOR 194	William	QUE 42
Lovey	DOR 63	Elizabeth	CLN 97	CARMICHIEL, William	
Mary	BCI 248	Henry	TAL 46		KEN 119
Mary	BCI 457	James	BCI 393	CARMIN, Samuel	DOR 23
Moses N.	CEC 121	John	BCI 136	Thomas	DOR 23
Rebecca	CLN 79	John	D.C.115	CARMINE, Elizabeth	SOM 107
Sally	SOM 127	John	HAR 63	Isaac (?)	SOM 116
Susanna	D.C.155	Josiah	WOR 194	Nathan	SOM 117

CARMION, Jos.	QUE 9	CARR (continued),		CARROLL (continued),		
CARMON, Joseph	ANN 344	John	BCI 447	Henry	SAI 66	
Wm.	QUE 15	John	CAL 61	Horatio	PRI 204	
CARMONEY, Joseph	WAS 95	John	CAL 64	Ignatious	SAI 89	
CARN, Jacob	FRE 159	John	DOR 59	Jacob	ALL 37	
CARNAHAN, James	D.C. 45	John	FRE 159	Jacob	BCI 297	
CARNAN, Bridget	BCI 508	John	WAS 148	James	BCI 101	
Chistorphor	BAL 2	Levi (f.n.)	SOM 120	James	BCI 538	
Robert	BAL 2	Marry	BCI 342	James	CLN 108	
CARNEIGHAN, Jas.	BCI 212	Matilda	FRE 110	James	DOR 50	
CARNES, Adam	FRE 124	Middleton	BCI 147	James	DOR 55	
Daniel	FRE 129	Overton	D.C. 85	John	BCI 99	
Jacob	FRE 102	Richard	MON 149	John	CLN 111	
John	BCI 22	Robert	ANN 272	John	CLN 113	
Maria	D.C. 102	Robert	CEC 135	John	D.C. 44	
Peter A.	BCI 493	Rowley	BCI 71	John	HAR 26	
Phil.	FRE 124	Sarah	ANN 292	John	HAR 72	
Sus.	FRE 123	Teage	BCI 458	John	TAL 27	
CARNEY, Elizh.	D.C. 123	Thomas	BCI 250	John B.	HAR 63	
Esther	CLN 74	Walter	ANN 281	John S.	BCI 461	
Hewe	BAL 24	Walter	ANN 371	Joseph	CEC 174	
John	WAS 81	William	ANN 268	Keely	DOR 53	
Joseph	D.C. 167	William	ANN 351	Mary	BCI 453	
Levi	CLN 74	William	HAR 44	Mary	DOR 50	
Maranda	FRE 106	CARRALL, Henry	D.C. 63	Mary	FRE 88	
Montgomery	CLN 94	CARRAN, Mary	ANN 397	Mary Ann	BAL 182	
Thomas	CLN 89	CARREL, Elizabeth	PRI 227	Michael B.	SAI 66	
CARNEYHAM, Geo.	BCI 200	James	PRI 236	Patrick	BCI 114	
CARNIAN, Greenberry (?)		CARRELL, Henry	CEC 135	Peter	DOR 57	
	QUE 5	CARREY, Hester	BCI 337	Rachel	PRI 213	
CARNS, John	BCI 100	CARRGAN, William	ANN 350	Richard	BAL 238	
CAROL, Sara	BCI 346	CARRICK, Benjamin	ANN 253	Richard	BCI 270	
CAROLE, John	BCI 47	CARRICO, James	D.C. 16	Samuel	DOR 57	
CAROLIN, Hugh	D.C. 170	Jane	D.C. 118	Samuel	MON 149	
CAROLL, Terre	KEN 118	Milly	PRI 214	Thomas	BCI 323	
CARPENTER, Charles		Peter	D.C. 125	Thomas	CEC 121	
(negro?)	CEC 121	Thomas	CHA 223	Thomas	DOR 19	
Danl.	FRE 128	William H.	CHA 224	Thomas K.	SOM 146	
Edward	CLN 89	CARRICOE, Alexander		Thos.	BCI 214	
Edward T.	SAI 77		D.C. 38	Tilghman	DOR 52	
Frances	CHA 194	CARRINGTON, Daniel		William	BCI 315	
Francis	CHA 196A		CHA 217	William	CEC 121	
Isaac	BCI 534	CARROL, Gracy	BCI 112	William	HAR 74	
John	BCI 428	Michal (?)	BCI 412	William	PRI 195	
John	CHA 196	Micheal	ANN 358	William	WAS 59	
John	WAS 97	Mima	PRI 196	William	WAS 108	
Richard	CEC 134	Ruthy	BCI 293	CARROW, William	DOR 7	
Sally	D.C. 151	Thomas	KEN 122	CARRVENTER, Robert (?)		
Saml.	BCI 527	Thomas	PRI 181		BCI 343	
Samuel	SAI 95	William	TAL 25	CARSELL, Sary Ann	PRI 221A	
Sarah	BCI 484	CARROLL, Amla	TAL 6	CARSLILE, Amos	ANN 283	
Susanna	D.C. 159	Ann	ANN 395	Amos	BCI 481	
Thomas, Ovsr.	TAL 6	Ann	BCI 308	CARSON, D.	BCI 259	
Urih	BCI 345	Ann	MON 149	David	BCI 509	
Whittington	D.C. 192	Aquila	HAR 25	Ephram (negro?)	CEC 121	
William	ANN 369	Aquilla	BCI 120	Frederick	ALL 4	
William	CHA 193	Benjamin	HAR 5	George	BCI 486	
CARR, Abraham	BCI 296	Charles	ALL 37	James	D.C. 182	
Ann	BCI 413	Charles	ANN 324	John	HAR 27	
Benjamin	ANN 263	Charles	DOR 52	John	WAS 99	
Benjamin	ANN 374	Charles of Carlt	ANN 388	Joseph	BCI 464	
Benjamin	CAL 63	Charles of Carroln		Joseph	BCI 511	
Benjamin	PRI 185	family	ANN 383	Nehemiah	D.C. 162	
Benjamin P.	ANN 372	Chris	BCI 475	Saml.	D.C. 161	
Daniel	BAL 63	Daniel	BAL 197	William	BCI 123	
Edward	ANN 355	Daniel	D.C. 113	CARSONS, Araminta	KEN 125	
Elizabeth	WAS 114	David	ALL 37	Pere	QUE 17	
Emanuel	BCI 2	David	D.C. 75	Robert	QUE 34	
George	BAL 127	Dickinson	CLN 112	CARSSON, Richard	WAS 106	
Henry	ANN 261	Dinah	BCI 482	CARTEE, John	FRE 127	
Isaac	FRE 102	Edward	DOR 57	William P.	FRE 98	
James	ANN 325	Eliza	BCI 258	CARTEN, S. (?)	BCI 408	
James	BCI 416	Elizabeth	MON 149	CARTER, --- (Mr.)	BCI 127	
Jane	D.C. 23	Henry (?)	D.C. 63	--- (Widaw)	BCI 393	
John	BAL 206	Henry	BAL 123	Arthur	QUE 37	
John	BCI 8	Henry	BAL 241	Charles	BAL 197	

43

CHAMPAYNE, Mary Ann		CHANNING, Burton	CHA 190	CHARRIER, John	BCI 172
	BAL 201	James	CHA 189	CHARS, Mary (?)	QUE 39
William R.	BAL 201	Zachh.	CHA 195	CHARSHA, James	HAR 27
CHAMPLAIN, Ann	BCI 59	CHANS, Titus (?)	DOR 19	CHASE, --- (Mrs.)	BCI 442
CHAMPLIN, Frances	BCI 9	CHANY, Elijah	FRE 72	Abraham	DOR 65
CHANBERS, John	MON 178A	Thomas	KEN 106A	Abraham	FRE 100
CHANCE, Atwell	CLN 87	CHAPELEAR, Marg.	SAI 90	Abraham	WAS 74
Batchelder	CLN 72A	Mary?	SAI 90	Anthony	FRE 111
Boon	CLN 74	CHAPLAIN, Henry	TAL 40	Ennels	BCI 133
Elijah	CLN 111	James	DOR 3	James	CLN 109
Jona	QUE 11	James	TAL 35	James-Slave	CAL 61
Levi	CLN 73	James, Jr.	TAL 35	Jeremiah T.	ANN 403
Noah	CLN 116	Mary	TAL 40	Jerimiah	ANN 255
Peter	CLN 90	Nancy	TAL 41	John	BCI 64
Richard	CLN 76	Philemon	TAL 35	John	BCI 145
Samuel	CLN 90	CHAPLAN, Mary	BCI 344	Letty	WAS 116
Skinner	CLN 85A	CHAPLIN, James N.	WAS 61	Nelly	PRI 187
Warner	KEN 88	Joseph	WAS 61	Richard M.	ANN 400
William	CLN 91	Samuel	QUE 24	Robert	SOM 137
CHANCEY, Susan	BCI 520	CHAPMAN, Amos	BCI 174	Saml.	KEN 117
CHANCY, Elijah (?)	WOR 176	Ann	BAL 43	Samuel	ANN 381
Javiss	WAS 107	Chas. T.	D.C. 164	Samuel	ANN 388
CHANDLE, Ann	CEC 121	Christopher	BCI 95	Samuel	CLN 109
CHANDLEE, Elizabeth G.		Collimore	ALL 23	Thomas	ANN 283
	CEC 173	Harriett	KEN 91	Thorndike	BCI 58
Evan	CEC 173	Harry	CEC 155	Wells	BAL 179
Mahlon	MON 149	Henry H.	D.C. 40	(See WELLS CHASE
CHANDLER, Daniel	CEC 156	Isaac	BCI 305	BRINKIT & CO. WOOLEN
Jehu	ANN 389	James	BAL 51	MANUFACTORY)
Rosanna	CEC 157	James	TAL 5	William	FRE 99
Samuel V.	BCI 16	John	BCI 449	CHASELY, Hulda	WOR 194
Thomas	BCI 99	John	BCI 509	CHASER, Daniel	D.C. 85
Walter	D.C. 47	John	DOR 56	CHASES, Titus (?)	DOR 19
CHANDLEY, Benjamin		John	QUE 31	CHATHAM, Henry	D.C. 181
	HAR 20	John	SOM 156	CHATTEN, Thomas	KEN 121
Cornelius	HAR 21	Joseph	BCI 219	CHATTON, Elizabeth	CAL 42
Thomas	HAR 20	Joshua	WOR 160	Wm.	QUE 4
William	HAR 20	Mary	BCI 275	CHAUNCEY, John	D.C. 154
CHANDLY, Benjamin	BCI 155	Nathan	BAL 6	John	HAR 19
CHANES, Jona (?)	QUE 11	Robert	ALL 20A	CHAUX, John B.	BCI 173
CHANEY, Absolum	BAL 174	Samuel	CHA 207A	CHAYTOR, Daniel	BCI 22
Benjamin	ANN 254	Uriah	TAL 5	James	BCI 131
Benjamin	ANN 304	William	ALL 32	CHEANEY, Zachariah	BAL 234
Cornelius	BCI 142	CHAPPEL, Robert	CEC 134	CHEARS, Robert	QUE 35
Dennis	ANN 344	CHAPPELL, John	BCI 357	CHEARSE, John	QUE 34
Elija	ANN 270	John	D.C. 66	CHEATLE, George	FRE 105
Elijah	WOR 176	Richard	BAL 116	CHEATUM, Josiah	WOR 217
Elizabeth	WAS 86	Wm. L.	BCI 172	CHEDAL, Mary	BCI 68
Henry	PRI 183	CHARE, Elizabeth (Mrs.) (?)		CHEEKE, Jesse	CEC 134
Javiss (?)	WAS 107		CAL 44	Joseph	CEC 134
Jeremiah	WAS 89	CHARICK, Henry	PRI 184	CHEESE, Richard (?)	TAL 50
Jesse	MON 149	William	PRI 187	CHEISBOROUGH, Isaac M.
John	PRI 204	CHARITY, SISTERS OF			BCI 441
John	WAS 86		FRE 153	CHELCOAT, Mary	BCI 517
Joseph	ANN 265	CHARLES, --- (?)	BCI 458	CHELL, Charles	D.C. 75
Joseph	ANN 267	Andrew	WAS 113A	Seth	D.C. 24
Joseph	ANN 339	Cannon	CLN 112	CHENAULT, Elija	D.C. 186
Richard	ANN 302	Christopher	BCI 39	CHENEY, David	ALL 34
Richard	ANN 332	Elizh.	D.C. 121	David	WAS 86
Richard	HAR 77	Jacob	CLN 112	Ezekiel	ALL 32
Richard	PRI 204	John	DOR 52	Isaac	ALL 34
Robert	WAS 87	Joseph, Senr.	WAS 138	Jeremiah	ALL 35
Saml.	D.C. 106	Joseph, Jun.	WAS 138	Jesse	ALL 33
Samuel	ANN 305	Levin	CLN 96	John	ALL 33
Samuel	ANN 344	Moses	WAS 125	John of N.	ALL 11
Shadrach	MON 176	Solomon	CLN 86	Thomas	ALL 32
Thomas	ANN 267	Willis	CLN 89	Thomas of N.	ALL 34
Thomas	ANN 299	CHARLETON, Elizabeth		William	WAS 81
William	WAS 78		FRE 228A	CHENOWETH, George	BAL 243
Zachariah	ANN 341	CHARLEY, George	FRE 70	William	BAL 230
Zeph	BCI 534	CHARLSTON, Joshua	BCI 71	CHENOWITH, Richd.	BCI 179
CHANLER, Jacob	BAL 186	CHARLTON, James	CAL 45	CHENY, Ruthy	BCI 310
CHANLEY, James	BCI 356	John	HAR 63	CHERRIX, Arthur	WOR 162
James	HAR 24	Jonathan	WAS 140	Francis	WOR 163
CHANNELL, --- (Mrs.)		Ralph	D.C. 85	James	WOR 155
	BCI 349	Thomas	WAS 100		

CHERRIX (continued),		CHILDS (continued),		CHRIST, Henry	WAS 120	
James	WOR 162	Nathaniel	BAL 245	Jacob	FRE 154	
John (of Jas.)	WOR 164	Peter	ANN 277	John	BAL 22	
CHERRY, Charles	BCI 536	Saml .	D.C.111	CHRISTE, Robert	BAL 163	
Edwd.	BCI 530	Samuel	D.C.28	CHRISTFIELD, William		
CHERRYTREE, Peter	QUE 25	CHILISON, Levin W.			WAS 65	
CHESHOLM, Sarah	BCI 316		DOR 10	CHRISTIE, Gabriel	HAR 30	
CHESLEY, Edwd.	BCI 524	CHILLCOAT, Elijah	BAL 245	George	BAL 124	
John (overseer)	BAL 61	CHILLISON, John	DOR 14	George	HAR 26	
Lidly	WAS 79	William	DOR 14	Henry	BCI 452	
Richard	D.C.18	CHILLMAN, Thomas	BCI 85	James	CEC 174	
Zadock C.	D.C.47	CHILTON, Andrew	CLN 81	John	HAR 22	
CHESLON, Anne	ANN 271	Charles	SAI 64	Michael	HAR 29	
CHESNER, Jacob	DOR 15	William	CLN 96	CHRISTMAN, Daniel; S.		
CHESNEY, James	HAR 22	CHINA, Sarah	D.C.16		WAS 74	
William	HAR 18	CHINAWITH, Elizabeth		Daniel; J.	WAS 74	
CHESSHIRE, Richd.	D.C.83		FRE 226	George	WAS 78	
CHESTER, George	QUE 30	CHING, Thomas	CHA 204	Jacob	WAS 74	
Hannibal	BCI 88	CHINN, Charles	CHA 203	Michael	WAS 82	
James	WOR 201	Manavill	D.C.150	CHRISTOPHER, Belitha?		
John	WAS 97	Willm.	D.C.206		SOM 107	
Rachel	QUE 28	CHINOETH, John	BAL 219	Betitha	SOM 107	
Saml .	D.C.90	CHINOWETH, William		Charles	DOR 31	
Samuel	WAS 87		BAL 24	Eli	WOR 204	
Stephen	BCI 85	CHINOWTH, John B.		Elijah	SOM 105	
CHESTON, Anne (?)	ANN 271		BAL 17	Elizabeth	BAL 130	
Daniel	BCI 126	CHINWORTH, Thomas		Harriet	SOM 134	
James	BCI 347		HAR 42	Heny	DOR 7	
CHEW, Anne	ANN 266	CHIPMAN, Daniel	HAR 73	John	BAL 225	
Benjamin	CEC 121	CHIPPEY, Joshua	CLN 90	Levin	DOR 56	
Charles-negro	CEC 121	CHIRACK, Joh. F.	BCI 350	Mary	WOR 215	
Dinah	ANN 393	CHISELDINE, Canelm,		Sophia	WOR 188	
Henry	ANN 276	Sen.	SAI 97	Thomas	BAL 131	
James	BAL 106	Canelm G.	SAI 96	Tubmon	WOR 211	
John	CAL 41A	Cyreanus	SAI 97	William	CLN 109	
John H.	CAL 67	CHISELTINE, Charles		CHRISTY, Francis	BAL 173	
John L.	ANN 279		SAI 96	John	ALL 22	
Lindy	BAL 174	Kanelm	SAI 96	Robert	CEC 135	
Nancy	BCI 147	CHISHOLM, John	HAR 9	CHRUCHES, Danl.		
Nathaniel	CEC 155	CHISLEY, Elizabeth	SAI 54	(Negro)	BAL 235	
Nathaniel, Jnr.	ANN 267	Sarah	PRI 184	CHUB, Priscilla	D.C.105	
Phil., J.	PRI 219	CHISLY, Fany	PRI 237	Robert	FRE 87	
Philip	PRI 195	CHISM, Alexander	ALL 3	CHUBB, Henry	D.C.129	
Richard	ANN 390	Archibald	ALL 3	CHUCHES, Danl.		
Robert	PRI 195	Lewis	D.C.137	(Negro) (?)	BAL 235	
Roger-Negro	HAR 80	CHISSELLINE, Thomas (?)		CHUCKLIN, John	CEC 134	
Samuel A.	WAS 79		BAL 225	CHULE, Robert (?)	FRE 87	
Solomon	KEN 120	CHISSELTINE, Thomas		CHUNER, Elijah	DOR 21	
Thomas	HAR 76		BAL 225	CHUNES, Elijah (?)	DOR 21	
CHEZUM, Daniel, Sr.		CHISTOPHER, John	DOR 25	CHURB, Easter	PRI 211	
	CLN 104A	CHISWELL, Jos. N.	MON 134	CHURCH, Abram	DOR 19	
Daniel, Jr.	CLN 104A	Wm.	MON 135	John	BCI 151	
Mary	CLN 96	CHISWINE, Wm.	BCI 380	Jonathan	WOR 161	
Richard	CLN 104A	CHITTAM, John	SOM 138	Lewis	D.C.120	
Thomas	CLN 106	CHITTENDEN, Nathanil		Nathaniel	BCI 10	
William	CLN 86		BCI 62	Sephard S.	FRE 125	
CHICKES, Barick	QUE 40	CHITTON, Richard	CAL 66A	CHURCHES, Danl.		
CHILCOAT, --- (Mrs.)		CHIVALIER, Charles		(Negro) (?)	BAL 235	
	BCI 389		CAL 63	CHURCHMAN, David	CEC 173	
George	BCI 507	CHIVREL, James	SAI 67	Enoch	BCI 248	
CHILCOTH, George	BAL 29	CHOATE, Austin	BAL 13	George	CEC 174	
CHILCUTT, Elizabeth		Edward	BAL 5	John	D.C.144	
	CLN 115	CHOCKE, Benjamin	HAR 57	Mary	BCI 182	
John	CLN 72A	Esrom	HAR 57	Michajah	BAL 207	
Joshua	CLN 92	George	HAR 57	CHURE, Elizabeth (Mrs.) (?)		
CHILD, Thos.	BCI 335	Naason	HAR 57		CAL 44	
Thos.	BCI 488	Zenas	HAR 57	CHUSE, Richard	TAL 50	
CHILDS, Ann	ANN 285	CHOICE, Henry	BCI 316	CHYNOWETH, William	FRE 103	
Ben.	D.C.122	CHOIN, Willm.	D.C.203	CIECILL (See also CECIL,		
Benjamin	BAL 227	CHOWMING, William	BCI 85	CISSALL, CISSELL,		
Cephas	MON 162	CHRISFIELD, Arthur		SISSEL),		
Eleanor	ANN 278		KEN 122	Mortin	QUE 38	
Enos	MON 165	Gilbert	KEN 125	CILER, Jacob	FRE 213	
Henry	ANN 279	CHRISINGER, Catherine		CIRCLE, Jacob	FRE 204	
James	BCI 8		WAS 116	Mary	FRE 197	
John	D.C.179					

CIRKBY, Mass	BCI 136	CLAPPER, F. C.	MON 161	CLARK (continued),			
CISE, George	FRE 223	John	WAS 70	James H.	KEN 109		
CISS, Sarah (negro)	TAL 21	Nicholas	FRE 84	Jamima	BAL 204		
CISSALL (See also CECIL,		Nicholas	MON 167	Jas.	BCI 191		
CIECILL, SISSEL),		CLAPSADDLE, Paul	FRE 73	Jesse	KEN 121		
Archd.	MON 174	Paul	FRE 216	John	ANN 376		
Saml.	MON 174	CLAPSADLE, Jacob	WAS 94	John	ANN 381		
Samuel	MON 149	Jacob	WAS 137	John	ANN 397		
Thomas	MON 149	Michael	FRE 175	John	BAL 125		
CISSEL, Thomas, Junr.		CLAR, J.	BCI 351	John	BAL 243		
	SAI 70	CLARAGE, Solomon	ANN 309	John	BCI 149		
CISSELL, Ethelbert	SAI 77	CLARCK, John	BCI 352	John	CEC 156		
George	SAI 62A	Mathew	WAS 125	John	CEC 157		
Jeremiah	SAI 56	Thomas	WAS 128A	John	D.C.28		
John	SAI 62A	CLARE, Jas.	D.C.151	John	D.C.36		
Margery	ANN 331	John	CAL 45	John	D.C.116		
Thomas, Senr.	SAI 68	John	D.C.112	John	FRE 202		
CISSIL, Samuel	ANN 373	Wm.	CAL 45	John	HAR 55		
Samuel	PRI 181	CLARTAGE, Edward	DOR 24	John	KEN 89		
CISSON, Ellen	D.C.147	CLARIDGE, Acha	BCI 180	John	KEN 90		
CITHCART, Joseph	HAR 57	Catherine	BCI 74	John	MON 135		
Thomas M.	HAR 57	CLARK, A.	D.C.72	John	SAI 56		
William	HAR 58	Abraham	PRI 192	John	WAS 57		
CLABBAUGH, Martin	ALL 35	Alexander	BCI 13	John	WAS 150		
CLACKEN, Rebecca	BCI 118	Alfred	ANN 316	John	WOR 170		
CLACKNER, Adam	BCI 118	Ann	ANN 343	Johnson	BAL 40		
Joseph	BCI 118	Augustavious	BAL 243	Johnson	BAL 201		
CLACKSON, Sarah (?)		Barnett	HAR 75	Johnson	MON 149		
	KEN 102	Basil	D.C.10	Joseph	BCI 219		
CLADEN, Saml.	BCI 372	Benj.	BCI 400	Joseph	BCI 368		
CLADON, Saml.	BCI 374	Benjamin	WOR 189	Joseph I. (J.?)	BCI 188		
CLAGETT, Alexander		Benjamin	WOR 194	Joseph N.	BCI 188		
	BCI 123	Caleb	PRI 184	Joshua	TAL 45		
Amelia-Slaves	ANN 261	Catharine	BCI 151	Joshua T.	PRI 181		
Asa	MON 161	Catherine	WAS 126	Keziah	HAR 62		
Charles	PRI 202	Chancery	BCI 312	Lawson	MON 149		
Charles N.	FRE 109	Charles	ANN 382	Margaret	BCI 37		
David	MON 163	Charles	KEN 114	Martha	KEN 90		
Elie	ANN 350	Chs.	QUE 10	Mary	FRE 162		
Elie	BCI 171	Cloe	PRI 187	Mathew	BAL 176		
Elizabeth	ANN 290	Cornelius	D.C.126	Matilda	BCI 478		
Hezekiah	BCI 437	Daniel	D.C.11	Nathin	BCI 403		
James	MON 149	David	ANN 381	Ned	QUE 20		
Jno.	MON 176	Ebenezer	ALL 11	Nelson	BAL 177		
John H.	MON 161	Edward	TAL 51	Patrick	BAL 227		
Joseph	MON 160	Edwd. W.	D.C.123	Patrick	BCI 194		
Joseph W.	PRI 208	Eleanor	ALL 29	Patty	BCI 429		
Nathan	MON 174	Eleanor (Mrs.)	CAL 42	Peter	KEN 118		
Nathan W.	MON 173	Elias	WAS 80	Ralph	HAR 39		
Ninian	MON 142	Eliza	D.C.77	Richard	ALL 14		
Niniar?	MON 142	Elizabeth	BAL 5	Richard	BAL 6		
Posthmas	WAS 70	Elizabeth	BCI 19	Richard	BAL 131		
Robert	WAS 68	Elizabeth	D.C.25	Robert	CEC 134		
Saml. M.	MON 142	Elizabeth	KEN 87	Robert	D.C.50		
Samuel	PRI 207	Elizh.	D.C.122	Samuel	BCI 425		
Samuel	WAS 68	Francis	ANN 355	Samuel	D.C.26		
Samuel	WAS 108	George	CEC 157	Samuel	D.C.43		
Samuel B.	WAS 108	George (Doc)	D.C.38	Satterlee	D.C.9		
Thomas	PRI 204	Hannah	BCI 156	Shadrach	PRI 196		
Thomas D.	CHA 211	Henry	BAL 20	Solsbury	BCI 311		
Thos.	MON 167	Henry	CEC 157	Spencer	DOR 29		
Thos. M.	MON 166	Henry	CEC 157	Stephen	BCI 218		
Zachriah	WAS 68	Henry	MON 149	Stephen	CEC 157		
CLAGGETT, Horatio	D.C.174	Henson	MON 149	Susan	D.C.128		
CLAIBORNE, Jane	D.C.6	Horatio D.	D.C.82	Thomas	HAR 40		
CLAINS, Fargue	CEC 134	Hyram	WAS 146	Walter	D.C.94		
CLAIRBERN, Ann C.	BCI 150	Isaac	D.C.68	Walter S.	PRI 181		
CLAMPET, Willm.	D.C.127	Isaac	D.C.94	William	BAL 117		
CLANAHAN, Joshua	QUE 24	Isaac	PRI 183	William	BAL 187		
CLANTON, Jane (?)	PRI 236	Jacob	CEC 135	William	BAL 206		
Thomas	PRI 236	James	BCI 113	William	D.C.36		
CLANTS, Sarah	FRE 229	James	BCI 192	William	HAR 37		
CLAP, Aron	BCI 277	James	BCI 454	William	HAR 74		
Eanoch	BAL 176	James	HAR 31	William	KEN 86		
CLAPHAM, Jonas	BCI 441	James	WAS 70	William	PRI 181		
		James H.	BCI 2	William	TAL 51		

46

CLARK (continued),		CLARKSON (continued),		CLAZE, Vindle	WAS 72
William	WOR 196	Vincent	DOR 58	CLEARY, James	ANN 401
William, Senr.	BAL 122	CLARON, Lydia	PRI 197	Jessey	BAL 67
William, Junr.	HAR 37	CLAROU, --- (Madam)		Jno.	BCI 168
William H.	KEN 108		BCI 456	Samuel	BAL 67
Willm.	D.C.116	CLARRIDGE, James	DOR 16	William	WAS 72
Willm.	D.C.127	CLARVEAUX, Jane	WOR 154	CLEAVELAND, Elizabeth	
Wm.	BCI 225	John	WOR 153		BCI 27
Wm. H.	KEN 117	CLARY, Gerrard	ALL 16	CLEAVER, Joseph	BAL 236
Zadok	ALL 28	John	FRE 213	Richard	KEN 90
CLARKE, Aaron	CLN 106	Reubin	FRE 75	CLEAVES, Nathan	KEN 86
Abraham	PRI 231	CLASBY, William A.	BCI 16	CLEFLOWER, Michael	FRE 162
Alexr.	D.C.190	CLASH, Anthony	DOR 7	CLEGETT, John	PRI 225
Ann	CLN 97	Anthony	DOR 58	Thomas H.	PRI 225
Barney	WAS 137	Cloudsbury	TAL 36	CLEGGETT, Darias	D.C.35
Benjamin	ANN 340	Greenbury	TAL 36	Jane	D.C.38
Benjamin	PRI 204	James	DOR 44	Thos. J. (I.?)	FRE 124
Christiana	CLN 106	John	TAL 35	William	D.C.41
Cuthbert	SAI 53A	Jonathan	TAL 41	CLEM, Adam	FRE 160
Edward	SAI 76	Leucretia	TAL 37	George	FRE 130
Elizabeth	BCI 95	CLATEN, --- (?)	BCI 408	Henry	FRE 160
Elizabeth	SAI 64	CLAUBAUGH, Elizabeth		Jacob	FRE 163
Elizth.	D.C.204		FRE 182	John	FRE 160
George	FRE 69	Frederik	FRE 182	CLEMAN, Thomas	CEC 134
George	SAI 64	Jacob	FRE 169	CLEMANTS, Sarah	BCI 524
George	SAI 79	James	FRE 169	CLEMENS, Abraham	FRE 202
Hester	QUE 39	John	FRE 169	Henry	D.C.206
Hezekiah	ANN 341	John	FRE 175	CLEMENT, Ann	D.C.81
Israel	BCI 80	John	FRE 182	Edward	FRE 156
James	SAI 79	Thomas	FRE 181	CLEMENTS, Abednigo	CHA 216
Jane	SAI 82	CLAUDE, Dennis	ANN 393	Albin	D.C.124
Jessee	QUE 48	CLAUTICE, Peter	BCI 526	B.	D.C.16
John	BAL 225	CLAUTUS, Joseph	BCI 183	Benjamin	QUE 27
John	BCI 78	CLAVER, Joseph	BAL 3	Charlotte	BCI 465
John, Junr.	SAI 55	Samuel	PRI [200]	Cleon	CHA 207
John M.	D.C.185	CLAVILLE, Peter	WOR 176	Edward	BAL 192
Joseph	MON 149	CLAWILL, Moses	WOR 179	Edward, Junr.	BAL 193
Joseph S.	D.C.94	CLAXTON, Jane	PRI 236	Eleanor	CHA 196
Josiah	FRE 77	John	D.C.48	Elizabeth (Mrs.)	BCI 282
Lawson A.	PRI 217	Thos.	D.C.101	Francis	D.C.134
Levy	FRE 81	CLAY, Adam	FRE 72	Francis A.	CHA 191
Mary	SAI 54	Adam, Jr.	FRE 72	George	CHA 191
Matthias, Col.	SAI 55	George	FRE 69	George	D.C.28
Nancy	CLN 107	George	FRE 72	Henry	CHA 217
Nancy	PRI 228	John	FRE 74	Henry	PRI 224
Patrick	BCI 504	John	WAS 121	Henry H.	SAI 96
Philip	WAS 124A	Samuel	FRE 72	Jacob	CHA 196A
Rachel	BCI 489	CLAYLAND, Lambert		Jacob	CHA 200A
Robert	TAL 31		TAL 12	James	CHA 196
Robt.	D.C.125	Sarah	TAL 40	John	BAL 192
Robt.	D.C.129	CLAYLEY, Jerry	BAL 180	John	CLN 77
Saml.	BCI 501	CLAYPOLE, James	KEN 102	Martha	CHA 222
Samuel	PRI 205	CLAYTON, Ann	WAS 55A	Mary	CHA 196
Sarah	BCI 77	Anna	QUE 37	Nathan E.	QUE 34
Susanna	PRI 228	Charles	CLN 77	Nicholas	BCI 282
Thomas	PRI 206	Daniel	WAS 66	Robert	D.C.53
Thomas	SAI 54	Jacob	KEN 123	Robt. H.	D.C.143
Thomas	SAI 56	James	BCI 81	Sarah	ANN 293
Violet	BCI 72	John	ANN 377	Sarah	ANN 389
William	ANN 340	John	BAL 119	Sarah	D.C.114
William	CLN 91	John	BAL 249	Seth	QUE 34
William	PRI 212	John	CLN 77	Teresa	CHA 213
William	QUE 34	Joseph	BAL 238	Thomas	BCI 464
William	SAI 68	Perry	BCI 81	Thomas C.	CHA 212
William	TAL 11	Philip	ANN 388	Thos.	D.C.137
William	TAL 32	Philip	BCI 463	CLEMM, Wm.	BCI 480
William, Junr.	BAL 122	Richard E.	QUE 27	CLEMMENT, Hezicish	WAS 77
William T.	CLN 73	Thomas D.	CEC 173	CLEMMON, Louisa	BCI 8
Willm.	D.C.218	Thos. (?)	D.C.101	CLEMMONS, Bennet	MON 165
CLARKSON, Alex	BCI 514	Walter J. (I.?)	KEN 100	Edward	MON 149
Charles	PRI 236	William	CLN 77	Thos.	MON 160
Jacob	CLN 98	William C.	QUE 27	CLEMONCY, Zachariah	
Jeremiah	BCI 88	CLAYTOR, John	ANN 272		TAL 32
Joseph	CEC 134	CLAYVELL, Selby	WOR 210	CLEMONS, Oswald	MON 137
Richard	BCI 283	Wm.	WOR 175	Samuel	CEC 174
Sarah	KEN 102	CLAYVILL, Eli	WOR 210	CLEMONSAN, John	D.C.29

47

CLEMPSON, James	FRE 214	CLOUD, Enoch	CEC 134	COATS (continued),	
John	FRE 214	James	D.C.193	Francis	BCI 285
Sarah	FRE 220	Jesse	FRE 174	Francis	CAL 50
CLENDENIN, James	CEC 173	William	D.C.68	Jeremiah	BCI 140
CLENDENING, Thomas		CLOUDSLEY, Jane	BCI 433	Lucinda	D.C.148
	CLN 78	CLOUGH, John	CLN 80	Mathew-free	CAL 61
CLENDENNIN, Wm. H.		CLOVER, --- (?)	BCI 406	Nelson	CAL 49
(Doctr.)	BAL 210	CLOVES, Conrad	WAS 133	Saml.	D.C.217
CLENDINEN, A.	BCI 10	CLOW, Chany	KEN 102	Stephen	FRE 145
John	HAR 60	China	QUE 10	Wm.	CAL 49
William H.	BCI 10	Isaia	QUE 17	COBB, ---	BCI 433
CLEPHAN, Lewis	D.C.84	Jas.	QUE 9	Elizh.	D.C.81
CLERAGE, Leven	FRE 155	Nathl.	QUE 9	Jas. D.	D.C.136
CLERK, Levi	DOR 14	CLOWARD, George	QUE 39	COBBETT, Daniel	D.C.32
William	TAL 51	CLUB, Elizh.	D.C.115	Peter	ANN 316
CLERMONT, George F.		Horatio	PRI 217	COBER, Catherine	D.C.43
	FRE 151	John	PRI 218	COBERTH, Catherine	
CLETTON, Richad.	BCI 338	Levin	PRI 227	(Mrs.)	CAL 48
CLEVENSON, George	WAS 106	Thomas	PRI 219	Hezekiah	CAL 44
CLEVER, Barbara	BCI 296	William	PRI 217	COBEY, Elizabeth W.	CHA 193
CLEYLER, Thomas	BCI 89	CLUBB, Benjamin	PRI 204	John	CHA 215
CLEZZY, George	BCI 115	Sarah	PRI 203	COBLENTZ, Danl.	FRE 130
CLICE, Elizabeth	ALL 29	CLUFF, Jonathan	WOR 162	Elizabeth	FRE 178
CLIFF, Henry	BCI 369	Micheal	SOM 153	Jacob	FRE 134
CLIFFIN, Betsey	MON 149	Robert	SOM 149	Jno.	FRE 126
CLIFFORD, Joseph	BCI 506	Sarah	SOM 128	Phil.	FRE 126
Sylvester	BCI 489	CLUFFER, Chris	BCI 182	Philip	FRE 132
CLIFT, George	BAL 46	CLUNK, Peter	BCI 522	COBOURN, James	TAL 32
Henry	DOR 3	CLYMER, Isaac	WAS 97	COBOURNE, Daniel	KEN 106A
Henry	TAL 47	CO, Mark	BAL 100	William	KEN 106
CLIFTON, Frances	D.C.120	COACH, George	QUE 18	COBURN, Primus	BCI 47
William	CEC 122	COAD, Joseph	SAI 66	Vinton	TAL 21
CLINE, Adam	FRE 214	COAFFER, Sarah	D.C.103	COBY, Danuel	BAL 21
Casper	FRE 68	COAKE, George	WAS 118	William	PRI 225
Catherine	BCI 18	COAKEY, Saml.	D.C.78	COCHARAN, Debby	BCI 537
Jacob (?)	HAR 20	COAL, Christophor	BAL 25	COCHE, Eleanor (?)	D.C.25
John	BCI 194	Edward	ANN 373	COCHRAN, --- (Mrs.)	
CLINEDINTS, Andrew		Henry	ANN 373		BCI 449
	BAL 141	James	HAR 24	David	D.C.77
CLINEFELTER, Peter		John S.	ANN 253	Hiram	BAL 220
	BAL 144	Joseph	BAL 27	James	HAR 4
CLINGAN, Mary	MON 160	Rebeca	BAL 25	John	HAR 19
William	FRE 172	Saml.	BCI 526	Nathan (?)	CLN 112
Wm.	MON 131	Samuel	ANN 256	Ninian	ALL 29
CLINGEN, Archibald	FRE 181	Sarah	BAL 27	Rebecca	BCI 59
CLINKSCTALE, Jane (?)		Thomas	ANN 325	Saml.	BCI 173
	CHA 217	Vachel	BAL 25	Susan G. (Mrs.)	BCI 267
CLINKSETALE, Jane	CHA 217	William	ANN 256	Thomas	CEC 134
CLINTON, Peter	CEC 156	William	ANN 259	Walter	D.C.129
Thomas	ALL 29	COALE, Benjamin	HAR 27	Wm.	BCI 348
William	ALL 29	Dan-Negro	HAR 50	COCHRANE, John	D.C.51
CLIPHAN, James	D.C.91	Debby	BCI 506	COCHREN, Alexander	
CLITON, Sam.	BCI 337	Edward J.	BCI 251		WAS 100
CLOAK, Samuel M.	KEN 103	Isaac	HAR 29	COCK (See also CORK),	
CLOCKER, Benjamin	SAI 53A	Jesse	HAR 27	George (?)	KEN 109
Daniel	SAI 65	Samuel	HAR 41	Isaac (?)	KEN 109
William	SAI 56	Sarah	HAR 27	Jacob (?)	KEN 109
CLOCKS, Conrad D.	BCI 91	Skipwith	CEC 173	Saml.	FRE 230
CLODEN, Saml. (?)	BCI 372	Skipwith	HAR 46	COCKANE, James	TAL 9
CLODMAN, Thomas	BCI 465	Thomas	HAR 27	COCKAYNE, Jane	TAL 9
CLOGG, Henry	WOR 214	William	HAR 20	John	CLN 88
William	WOR 213	COALGATE, Richard		COCKBURN, James	CEC 173
CLONEY, James	BCI 49		FRE 87	COCKE, Eleanor	D.C.25
CLOPPER, Abm. D.	MON 130	COALKAS, Henry	FRE 81	Elizth.	D.C.187
Andrew	BCI 259	COALL, Richard	FRE 219	Samuel	FRE 234
Cherine	WAS 70	COALMAN, Patrick	ANN 364	COCKEY, Andrew	BAL 6
Edwd. N.	BCI 538	Robert	CEC 174	Ann	BAL 247
Peter	BCI 169	COALSON, John	ANN 365	Charles	BAL 6
CLOSE, Christian	FRE 145	COARSEY, Jacob	TAL 34A	Charles	BAL 21
David	ALL 25	COATES, James?	FRE 183	John	BAL 246
George	FRE 80	Janus	FRE 183	John	QUE 45
Peter	ALL 25	John	BAL 202	John C.	FRE 187
Samuel	ANN 370	COATH, Wm.	BCI 247	Joseph C.	BAL 5
CLOTHIER, Saml.	KEN 118	COATS, Benja.-free	CAL 61	Joshua	FRE 188
CLOTHYER, James	KEN 120	Chas.	MON 177	Joshua F.	BAL 243
CLOTTIS, Peter	FRE 183	Elijah-free	CAL 61	Patrick	BCI 298

COCKEY (continued),			COKE, Baltzer	FRE 192	COLE (continued),	
Thomas	BCI 6		COKELEY, Daniel	ALL 20A	Margaret	BCI 12
Thomas	BCI 187		COKENDORFER, Leond.		Margt.	D.C. 192
Thomas B.	BAL 2			D.C. 39	Mark	BCI 160
William	FRE 75		COKER, Abner	BCI 139	Mary	BAL 218
COCKING, James	D.C. 49		Moses	CLN 86	Mary	D.C. 199
Will	D.C. 88		Patty	CLN 87	Mary	SAI 97
COCKLEN, William	FRE 196		Philip	CLN 91	Mary Ann	D.C. 201
COCKLIN, William	CLN 97		Walter	FRE 188	Minty	SAI 54
COCKRAN, George	CEC 156		COLAMAN, John	FRE 87	Nancy	DOR 57
James	CEC 122		COLBERT, Isaac	SOM 156	Nathan	D.C. 21
Jas.	FRE 131		James	WAS 63	Nelly	D.C. 150
John (?)	CLN 112		Joseph	D.C. 65	Philemon	BAL 226
Letitia (?)	CLN 112		Joseph	WAS 63	Prince	BCI 443
Nathan (?)	CLN 112		Levi	D.C. 13	Richard	BAL 197
COCKS, Isaac	BCI 39		Neal	SOM 156	Richard	HAR 75
John	ANN 319		Nicholas	D.C. 11	Robert	DOR 13
Thomas	ANN 319		R.	BCI 404	Robert	SAI 57
William	WAS 61		William	D.C. 9	Sabathiel?	BAL 96
COCKY, John	FRE 226		COLBOURN, Elijah	WOR 210	Salathiel	BAL 96
COCLAZIER, Jacob	D.C. 66		William	WOR 219	Samuel	BCI 171
COCOO, Levin	TAL 4		COLCLAZIER, Thos.		Sarah	MON 132
CODD, John	BAL 47			D.C. 90	Thomas	ANN 329
William	BCI 34		COLCLEASER, Abraham (?)		Thomas	CEC 157
CODDINGTON, Benj.	ALL 7			FRE 76A	Thomas	SAI 67
Samuel	ALL 6		COLDEN, Joseph	TAL 3	Vincent	BAL 153
William	ALL 6		COLDER, Charles	BCI 310	Walter	SAI 87
CODE, John	D.C. 82		COLE, --- (Mrs.)	BCI 426	William	BCI 37
COE, Basil	FRE 204		--- (Widaw)	BCI 396	William	BCI 101
Charles	BCI 92		Abham	BAL 95	William	BCI 146
Greenbury	BAL 234		Abraham	BAL 245	William	BCI 246
Isaac (?)	BAL 243		Abraham	KEN 125	William	CLN 78
James	BAL 107		Abraham, Junr.	BAL 95	William	FRE 68
Jasse	FRE 228A		Allen	ANN 319	William	HAR 47
John	FRE 204		Allen	D.C. 22	William	HAR 76
Joshua	FRE 204		Ann	BCI 214	William S.	CEC 156
Richard	PRI 224		Charles	DOR 8	Wm.	BCI 225
Samuel	PRI 222		Cornelius	HAR 19	COLEBY, John	KEN 88
Samuel, Junr.	PRI 222		Daniel	BCI 128	COLEGATE, George	FRE 186
William	BAL 248		David	QUE 18	COLEHOUR, Henry	BAL 244
COEN, John	HAR 25		Eliza	BCI 194	COLELEASER, Abraham	
COES, Peter (?)	FRE 220		Elizabeth	BAL 226		FRE 76A
COFER, Godshall	CHA 193		Elizabeth	BAL 244	COLEMAN, Adam	FRE 179
John	CHA 201		Francis	BCI 66	Allice	D.C. 156
Martha	CHA 207A		Francis	SAI 56	Alten	ALL 13
COFFIELD, Hugh	BCI 459		Frederick	BCI 52	Arthur-Negro	HAR 79
William	CEC 155		George	BAL 110	Catharine	QUE 12
COFFIN, Abner	WOR 187		George	BCI 144	Chs.	BCI 529
Hetty	WOR 195		George	PRI 222	Daniel	DOR 51
Jacob	WOR 197		Giles	BAL 219	David-Negro	HAR 50
John	WOR 196		Hannah	BAL 218	Ezekiel	KEN 89
Joseph	WOR 197		Hynson	QUE 16	Frances	BCI 26
Nancy	D.C. 50		Jack	D.C. 155	George	BCI 509
COGGIN, John	BAL 84		James	BCI 426	George	D.C. 59
COGGINS, Joseph	HAR 47		James	HAR 75	George	D.C. 175
COGHER, Hanson	D.C. 38		James-Negro	HAR 79	Henry E.	CEC 121
COHAGAN, Joshua	BCI 448		James A.	BCI 79	Hesekiah	KEN 87
COHAGEN, John	D.C. 202		Jane	SAI 67	Isaah	KEN 102
John	PRI 229		Jesse	SAI 63	Israel	DOR 56
COHEE, Benjn.	KEN 124		John	BCI 270	James	KEN 101
James	TAL 33		John	D.C. 153	Jesse	ALL 10A
William	DOR 53		John	FRE 160	John	BAL 52
COHEN, A. H.	BCI 240		John	KEN 117	John	BCI 60
Benjanin J.	BCI 428		John	PRI 185	John	BCI 258
Judith J.	BCI 251		John	QUE 8	John	BCI 381
COHILL, Peregrine	CHA 207A		John	WOR 202	John	HAR 55
William	CHA 201		John (of Geo.)	SAI 66	Joseph	BCI 60
COHLSON, Thomas	BCI 465		John (of Jno.)	SAI 69	Joseph	KEN 94
COHOON, John H.	SOM 147		Joseph	D.C. 51	Phineas	ALL 12
Nathan	SOM 157		Joseph	SAI 78	Richard	BCI 27
Samuel A.	SOM 148		Joshua	BCI 463	Richd.	QUE 11
COIL, Edward	BCI 255		Judah	BCI 144	Risdon	DOR 50
COILER, John	CAL 62		Levi	D.C. 96	Ruth	QUE 15
COIN, Elizabeth	BCI 6		Lewis	D.C. 64	Samuel	KEN 93
James	HAR 76		Luther	BAL 3	Thomas	ANN 359
COINS, John (?)	BAL 120		Lydia	D.C. 118	Thomas	QUE 6

COLEMAN (continued),		COLLINS (continued),		COLLINS (continued),	
William	D.C.72	Elsey	D.C.80	Zacheriah	D.C.67
Wm.	MON 161	Ennalls	CLN 107	COLLISON, Andrew	CLN 85A
Wm.	QUE 7	George	BCI 443	Edward	TAL 22
Wm.	QUE 12	George	CLN 107	Edward, Ovsr.	TAL 2
COLENTZ, Peter	FRE 126	George	KEN 94	Fountain	CLN 89
COLES, Charles	MON 149	George	PRI 239	George W.	CLN 86
Conels.	BCI 192	George C.	BAL 130	Job	TAL 26
William	BAL 59	Henry	CHA 214	John	CLN 94
COLESCOTT, William	CLN 99	Henry	D.C.42	Joseph	WAS 146
COLESTON, William	DOR 64	Henry	D.C.105	Reuben	TAL 23
COLEY, Stephen	CLN 73	Henry	FRE 215	Sarah	CLN 94
COLGIN, Esau	KEN 124	Hezekiah	D.C.66	William	TAL 27
COLL, Richard	FRE 212	Isaac	BAL 191	COLLISSON, Edward	ANN 261
COLLAGE, ST. MARY'S		Isaac	WOR 210	John	ANN 257
	BCI 517	Isabella	BCI 320	William	ANN 261
COLLARD, Elizh.	D.C.115	Jacob	BAL 159	COLLUM, Nancy	BCI 160
Joseph	CEC 174	James	BCI 143	Temperance W.	BCI 172
COLLEER, Peter	WOR 190	James	CLN 114	COLMAN, Catharine	(?)
COLLEFLOWER, George		James	D.C.64		BCI 521
	FRE 158	James	KEN 87	Goldsbury	BCI 118
John	WAS 106	James	SOM 127	Jacob	FRE 128
Michael	FRE 156	James	TAL 34A	John	KEN 114
COLLEGE OF GEORGETOWN		James	WOR 157	Samuel	BCI 137
	D.C.61	James A.	WOR 186	William	D.C.73
COLLEGE, ST. MARY'S (?)		James H.	SOM 139	COLMARY, James H.	CEC 121
	BCI 517	James W.	BAL 41	COLMERS, Levy	BCI 415
COLLENBERGER, John		Jeremiah	CLN 107	Lucy?	BCI 415
	FRE 218	Jessee	CLN 107	COLON, Catherine	BAL 5
COLLENS, George	ANN 307	John	BAL 119	COLSON, George	D.C.72
Mary	SAI 82	John	BCI 482	John	D.C.115
Stephen	BCI 30	John	MON 149	COLSTON, Andrew S.	
COLLET, Aaron	BAL 83	John	WOR 195		CLN 72A
J.	BCI 367	Johnson	ALL 38	Deborah	CLN 72A
Mary	BAL 80	Joseph	BCI 138	Dzire	DOR 21
Moses	BAL 91	Joseph	BCI 482	Henry	DOR 49
Stepen	BAL 91	Joseph	FRE 220	Henry	TAL 20
COLLEY, George	BCI 537	Joseph S.	D.C.29	Humpy.	D.C.209
Isabella	HAR 55	Joshua	D.C.66	Jacob	TAL 35
COLLIAR, Robert	SOM 133	Josiah	WOR 173	James	DOR 7
COLLICK, Wm.	WOR 176	Lamuel	CEC 122	James	TAL 20
COLLIER, Cheney	SOM 116	Levin	CLN 114	Jeremiah	DOR 59
Elizabeth	SOM 108	Mark	ANN 397	Jessee	DOR 9
Esme	SOM 108	Martha	ANN 311	Lucy	D.C.169
George W.	SOM 103	Mary	KEN 87	Samuel	TAL 4
James	ANN 300	Michael	ANN 262	Wm.	BAL 79
Kendal	WOR 190	Milly	SOM 127	COLTER, Daniel	FRE 111
Levin D.	SOM 103	Nathan	D.C.43	COLTON, Isaac (?)	KEN 125
Martha	SOM 103	Parker	WOR 175	John (?)	KEN 107
Sassa	MON 149	Peter	SOM 118	John	SAI 73A
Thomas	FRE 103	Rebecca	TAL 8A	COLTRIDER, Frederick	
William	WAS 114	Richard	BAL 249		FRE 194
William	WOR 190	Robert	D.C.67	George	BAL 81
COLLINEE, C.	BCI 368	Salisburry	DOR 54	George	BAL 154
COLLINGS, Abraham	WAS 112	Samuel?	CEC 122	Jacob	BAL 154
Elam	WAS 60	Samuel	CHA 207A	John	BAL 144
Mary Ann	PRI 218	Sarah	ANN 304	John, Junr.	BAL 154
Mathew	WAS 60	Sarah	QUE 31	COLVELL, Clarinda	BCI 282
COLLINGWOOD, John		Sophia	WOR 174	COLVIN, Ann	BCI 174
	D.C.33	Stephen	SOM 154	John	BCI 390
Saml.	D.C.24	Stephen	WOR 154	John B.	D.C.95
COLLINS, Abraham	CLN 114	Sterling	WOR 154	COLWELL, Ally	KEN 104
Alice	TAL 31	Tabitha	WOR 184	Charles	BAL 92
Allen	D.C.59	Thos.	WOR 163	COLYER, James	QUE 37
Andrew	CLN 112	Timothy	BAL 63	James	QUE 39
Ann	D.C.66	Timothy	WOR 206	COMBS, Adam	FRE 106
Benjamin	BCI 111	W.	BCI 349	Cornelius	SAI 68
Branson	WOR 218	William	BCI 134	Cuthbert	ALL 15
Danl.	MON 175	William	D.C.21	Elijah	ALL 17
Deborah	DOR 49	William	SOM 137	Enoch	SAI 94
Ebenezer	DOR 28	William	TAL 34A	Henry	FRE 124
Edward	BCI 453	William, Jr.	TAL 33	John	ALL 15
Eleanor	MON 136	William A.	D.C.27	John of C.	ALL 14A
Ell	WOR 185	Williams	BAL 20	Joseph	SAI 76
Elizabeth	ANN 300	Wm.	MON 164	Mary	SAI 69
Elizabeth	FRE 156	Zachariah	ANN 307	Nathaniel	SAI 67

CONWAY (continued),		COOK (continued),		COOLEY (continued),	
Margret	BAL 46	Robert	BCI 113	Carvell	CEC 155
Robt.	D.C.168	Rosetta	BCI 505	Charles	CEC 173
Thomas	CEC 174	Samuel	ANN 332	Eleanor	ANN 254
Thos.	BCI 194	Samuel	DOR 64	Henry	MON 129
Zachariah	BAL 46	Stephen	ANN 299	Isaac	ANN 270
CONYNGHAM, Geo.	BCI 317	Susan	QUE 40	James	MON 130
COOCH, Collen	WAS 81	Theodore	PRI 239	John	CEC 174
Zebulon	BCI 258	Thomas	ANN 368	Joseph	QUE 32
COOCK, David	WAS 118	Thomas	BCI 131	R. R.	BCI 410
John	WAS 115	Thomas	FRE 202	Sarah	HAR 24
John	WAS 121	Thos., Senr.	DOR 16	Thos. A.	MON 133
Mary Ann	WAS 106	Thos., Jr.	DOR 16	William	HAR 72
Susan	WAS 94	William	BAL 5	COOLIDGE, --- (Mrs.)	
COOGLE, Christian	FRE 132	William	BAL 125		D.C.15
COOK, --- (Mrs.)	BCI 455	William	D.C.36	William	BCI 269
Aaron	DOR 46	William	FRE 171	COOMBE, Griffith	D.C.102
Aaron	DOR 49	William	HAR 22	COOMBS, Elizabeth	BCI 62
Acco	QUE 30	William	PRI 217	Mary M.	PRI 230
Amos	MON 176	Wm.	BCI 225	COOMES, Aloesius	CHA 217
Andrew	DOR 14	Zadock	MON 137	James	BCI 47
Ann	D.C.113	Zedock	PRI 239	Jane	CHA 213
Anne	MON 133	COOKE, --- (?)	BCI 407	Leonard	CHA 214
Anthy. L.	BCI 195	Amus	BCI 389	Sarah	CHA 214
Archd.	BCI 193	Archibald	BCI 414	Stans.	CHA 213
Benjamin	PRI 239	Barnet H.?	BAL 121	William	CHA 213
Catharine	BAL 16	Basil	D.C.37	COOMS, James	MON 136
Charles	BCI 447	Benjamin	ANN 344	Richard	WAS 78
Charles	QUE 30	Burnet H.	BAL 121	COON, Gabiel	FRE 123
David	D.C.113	Christiana	D.C.209	John	WAS 67
David	D.C.193	Christopher	BAL 58	Michael	WAS 67
Dinah	BCI 426	Donaldson	CHA 203	Samuel	WAS 70
Edward	PRI 184	Fanny	D.C.169	Thomas	WAS 64
Elisha	BCI 460	Gasper	BAL 46	COONEER, John	BCI 47
Elisha	HAR 41	George	ANN 323	COONES, Cathe.	D.C.92
Elizabeth	BCI 440	George	D.C.204	Fredk.	D.C.86
Ellender	D.C.183	George; J.	ALL 25	COONEY, Patrick	BCI 10
Fredk.	BCI 334	Jacob	BCI 408	COONS, Abraham	FRE 174
George	BCI 155	Jesse C.	CHA 227	Andrew	FRE 171
George	BCI 286	Jo.	QUE 16	Anna	FRE 175
George	FRE 79	John	BAL 54	Benjamin	FRE 150
H.	BCI 389	John	SAI 93	Henry	FRE 172
James	BAL 43	Joseph	FRE 199	Henry	FRE 173
Jannett	PRI 227	Leonard	D.C.209	Henry	FRE 174
Jeremiah	BAL 5	Lyda	SAI 98	Jacob	FRE 173
Joel	HAR 22	Manuel	BAL 44	Mary (Widow)	FRE 172
John	ANN 349	Nancy	BAL 50	Peter	FRE 172
John	ANN 359	Peter	ALL 10A	William	FRE 178
John	ANN 359	Peter	BAL 5	COOPER, --- (Mrs.)	BCI 388
John	BCI 202	Richard	CHA 216	Aaron	BCI 310
John	BCI 322	Thomas	BAL 54	Ambrose	BCI 514
John	BCI 515	Thomas	D.C.9	Ann	BCI 258
John	CEC 173	Thomas	PRI 236	Ann	KEN 120
John	D.C.129	Thomas B.	QUE 23	Ann	QUE 14
John	D.C.212	COOKENDOFFER, Thomas		Ann B.	BCI 231
John	FRE 204		PRI 180A	Benjamin	ANN 312
John	FRE 219	COOKERLEY, John	FRE 156	Betcy?	TAL 6
John	MON 167	COOKERLY, Jacob	FRE 97	Betey	TAL 6
John	PRI 181	John, of Jac.	FRE 162	Bob	QUE 6
John B.	D.C.35	Peter	ANN 380	C.	BCI 229
John F.	BCI 134	Rosanna	FRE 224	Cezar	KEN 107
John L.	BCI 127	William	FRE 216	Clenus	KEN 94
Joseph	BCI 484	COOKSEY, Charlotte G.		Daniel	ANN 319
Joseph	D.C.201		CHA 207A	Dolly	DOR 4
Kinsey	CLN 99	Isaac	PRI 215	Edward	D.C.23
Lenard	DOR 14	James	PRI 212	Elisha	HAR 62
Levin	BCI 101	Jonathan	PRI 214	Elizabeth	SAI 92
Mark	DOR 12	Samuel	PRI 214	Esther	QUE 14
Mary	D.C.96	Townley	SAI 91	Geo.	D.C.108
Mattw.	D.C.96	COOKSON, Samuel	FRE 203	Gideon	CLN 75
Moses	CEC 155	COOL, John	CEC 155	Henry	BCI 307
Nancy	BCI 35	COOLEN, Lydia	CEC 157	Henry	KEN 117
Nathan	CLN 99	COOLER, Esther	MON 144	Henry	TAL 7
Orlando	D.C.94	Jas.	MON 137	Isaac	BCI 128
Perry	BCI 427	COOLEY, Anne	MON 134	Isaac	D.C.71
Rezin	FRE 198	Benjamin	ANN 279	Isaiah	CEC 173

COOPER (continued),		COOTS, William	D.C. 52	CORCORAN (continued),	
Jacob	CEC 134	COOXEY, Robert	SOM 135	Thomas	D.C. 39
James	BAL 83	COPE, Thomas	HAR 47	CORD, Amos	HAR 24
James	FRE 144	COPELAN, Josiah S.		Elizabeth	CEC 156
James	PRI 223		BAL 201	Elizabeth (Mrs.)	CAL 50
Jane	TAL 34	COPELAND, Rachel-		Geo.	BCI 389
Jery	SAI 93	Negro	HAR 50	Henry	ANN 352
Jo.	QUE 14	COPELIN, Samuel	FRE 84	John	CEC 156
John	ANN 316	COPENHAFER, Barbara		John	HAR 42
John	BCI 83		FRE 105	John R.	WOR 186
John	BCI 405	COPENHAVER, Jacob		Thomas M.	QUE 48
John	CLN 94		FRE 204	William	CEC 156
John	CEC 155	William	FRE 197	CORDELL, John J. (I.?)	
John	FRE 147	COPES, Augustus	WAS 99		CHA 228
John	PRI 197	Beverly	WOR 159	CORDEN (See also COS-	
John	PRI 197	Giles	BCI 311	DEN),	
John	TAL 50	John	CLN 77	Ben (?)	QUE 13
John	WOR 192	Robert	CEC 121	Eliza G. (?)	QUE 16
John W.	TAL 22	COPP, Joseph	BAL 146	Wm. (?)	QUE 11
Joseph	BAL 80	COPPAGE, Edwd.	QUE 8	Wm. (?)	QUE 13
Joseph	BAL 222	Jo	QUE 20	CORDERY, Doughty	SOM 115
Joseph	D.C. 165	John	QUE 8	Maria	BCI 59
Joseph	DOR 40	John	QUE 21	CORDEY, Phill-Negro	
Joseph	SAI 77	COPPAU, Joseph(?)	BCI 446		HAR 65
Joseph	TAL 9	COPPER, Charles	QUE 31	CORDIMAN, Samuel	WAS 112
Joseph (negro)	TAL 27	Danniel N.	QUE 24	CORDRAY, David	SOM 105
Joshua	CLN 94	Hagar, Col'd.	BAL 216	Henry	BCI 23
Lewis	SAI 74	Jane	KEN 85	CORDREY, Covington	
Liydea	SAI 97	Leah (?)	DOR 26		SOM 116
Margaret	BCI 50	Mary	KEN 91	CORDRICK, Henry	CHA 226
Maria	ANN 382	Nathaniel	KEN 105	CORE, Danl.	D.C. 209
Mark G.	CLN 75	Perre	QUE 6	John	BAL 245
Mary	BCI 93	Robert N.	BCI 150	John	CAL 59
Merchant	CLN 97	Thomas	KEN 110	CORGAN, John	QUE 9
Mike	QUE 3	William	DOR 25	CORHRAN, Nathan	CLN 112
Nancy	TAL 27	William	KEN 87	CORK (See also COCK),	
Nelly	PRI 197	COPPERAL, Abraham		George	KEN 109
Nelly	SOM 111		KEN 105	Isaac	KEN 109
Nicholas	HAR 71	Isaac	KEN 106A	Jacob	KEN 109
Peregrine	KEN 109	COPPERAS COMPANY,		James	TAL 35
Peter (negro)	TAL 27	ALLUM &	ANN 311	Lewis	CEC 121
Philemon	TAL 3	COPPERSMITH, Jacob		Thomas	TAL 7
Philis	SAI 77		FRE 196	CORKIN, Thomas	CLN 108
Phineas	CEC 174	Peter	BAL 157	CORKRAN, Algernon	DOR 57
Richard	CLN 90	COPPICK, William	TAL 11	Charles	DOR 60
Robert	BCI 30	COPPIN, John	CEC 121	Elisha	CLN 112
Robert	BCI 166	COPPLE, Rachel	BCI 304	Ezekiel	DOR 62
Robert	CLN 72A	COPS, John	WAS 77	Henry	DOR 62
Robt.	QUE 18	COPSEY, Elenor	SAI 91	James	CEC 134
S. P.	BCI 340	John	SAI 90	James	DOR 64
Sally	SOM 138	CORBALEY, John	FRE 125	James (H.C.)	DOR 64
Sam.	BCI 343	CORBAN, Nathan	BAL 249	John	CLN 112
Samuel	BCI 103	William	BAL 222	John	DOR 55
Samuel	SOM 111	CORBAR, Henry	BCI 102	John	DOR 58
Solomon	CLN 90	CORBEN, Edward	BAL 16	Letitia	CLN 112
Spindler	CLN 113	CORBET, Lucas?	WAS 149	Nancy	DOR 52
Susanna	HAR 41	Lucay?	WAS 149	Nathan (?)	CLN 112
Thomas	ALL 23	Samuel	BAL 41	Peter	DOR 56
Thomas	BCI 446	CORBETT, Agness	CEC 156	Samuel	DOR 4
Thomas	CEC 134	Sarah	D.C. 5	Timothy	DOR 50
Thomas	SOM 111	CORBEY, Elizabeth	WAS 64	William	DOR 52
Thomas	TAL 6	William	WAS 78	CORKRELL, James?	TAL 50
Thomas (negro)	TAL 21	CORBIN, Henry (?)	BCI 102	Jumes	TAL 50
Wels	BCI 392	James	WOR 178	John	TAL 50
William	BAL 155	John	WOR 213	Mary	TAL 50
William	TAL 13	Joseph	BAL 21	CORLS, John	BCI 405
William A.	CLN 91	Micajah	ANN 378	CORMACKLE, William	BCI 40
Willm.	D.C. 85	William	FRE 178	CORNAL, Jesse	FRE 168
COOPERLEY, Rebecca		Wm., Senr.	WOR 161	Smith	FRE 183
	D.C. 5	Wm. S.	WOR 162	William	FRE 168
COOPPER, Charlotte	QUE 40	CORBLEY, Elizabeth		CORNDEL, Wester	CEC 134
Henry	QUE 40		BCI 34	CORNELIAS, Sally	WAS 107
William	WAS 123	CORBLY, Richard	CEC 121	CORNELIOUS, Peter	CAL 46
COOSER, Saml.	FRE 226	CORBUS, Conrad	ALL 11	CORNELIUS, Campbell J.	
COOTE, Clement	D.C. 89	CORCORAN, James	D.C. 39		QUE 6
Thos.	D.C. 111	Jesse	D.C. 215	Evert	BAL 233

COUNTY, Edward	BCI 78	COVINGTON, Ben	QUE 10	COX (continued),			
COUPLE, Joseph	BCI 463	Ebenezer	QUE 25	James	HAR 38		
COUR, Alexr. de Val	BCI 247	Ebenezer M.	QUE 28	James	SAI 75		
COURAGE, Anthany	BCI 386	Elijah	QUE 28	James	SAI 97		
COURSANTT, --- (Mrs.)		Henry	QUE 31	James	SOM 109		
	BCI 342	Isaac	SOM 123	James-Cashr.	BCI 279		
COURSE, George	FRE 201	James	SOM 103	Jeremiah	CAL 59		
Jessee	KEN 101	Jenny	SOM 125	Jesse	CHA 210A		
COURSEY, Edward D.	QUE 33	Leonard	PRI 214	Jessee	CLN 88		
Edward H.	QUE 23	Luther J. (I.?)	QUE 26	John	BAL 100		
Gerald	QUE 27	Nathaniel	QUE 45	John	BAL 157		
James	CLN 74	Nehemiah	SOM 125	John	BCI 194		
Jane	BCI 320	Phillip	SOM 113	John	CHA 211		
Jeremiah	QUE 29	Samuel	KEN 92	John	D.C.60		
Louisa	BCI 297	Samuel	SOM 111	John	SOM 108		
Saml.	QUE 8	Thomas	BCI 314	John	SOM 142A		
Thomas	QUE 25	Thomas	SOM 110	John	WAS 89		
Tom	QUE 15	Wealthy Ann	BCI 147	John J.	CEC 121		
William	CLN 74	Zache.	QUE 13	Johnston	SOM 137		
William	QUE 25	COVY, Archd.	QUE 6	Jonathan	ALL 23		
William	QUE 49	COW, Asel (?)	BAL 81	Joseph	BCI 282		
William T.	CLN 74	Christly	WAS 122	Joseph	KEN 90		
COURSLL, Peter	BCI 114	John	WAS 123	Josias	CHA 200A		
COURTESS, Elenor	PRI 226	COWAN, Samuel-Negro		Kesiah	BCI 455		
COURTLAN, James	BCI 134		HAR 49	Keziah	DOR 35		
COURTLEY, Aaron	D.C.44	COWARD, Slyder?	DOR 37	Kitty	BCI 484		
COURTNAY, Mary	BAL 242	Sophia	BAL 2	Levi	WAS 136		
COURTNEY, Cyrus	HAR 27	Thomas	TAL 38	Levin	TAL 38		
Edward	HAR 24	COWEN, Thomas	BCI 169	Luther J.	QUE 23		
George W.	HAR 18	William	CEC 134	Mackall S.	PRI 211		
Hannah	BCI 534	COWIN, John	KEN 93	Mary	BCI 350		
Hanson	HAR 27	COWING, Joseph	D.C.179	Meriah	TAL 8A		
Henry	BAL 242	COWLER, Catherine	WAS 100	Michiel	KEN 124		
Hollis	HAR 21	George	WAS 100	Molley	SOM 155		
John	D.C.127	COWLEY, Samuel	WOR 156	Peggy	SOM 144		
Matthew B.	CHA 202	Thomas	BAL 115	Peregrin	CEC 121		
Thomas	HAR 18	COWMAN, Gared	FRE 68	Peter	BCI 227		
Thomas	HAR 26	John	ANN 289	Samuel	TAL 19		
Thomas, Sr.	HAR 27	John	D.C.186	Sarah (Mrs.)	CAL 52		
William	BCI 271	Philip	ANN 256	Thomas	CEC 121		
COURTS, Elenor C.	PRI 236	COX (See also VOX),		Thomas	QUE 31		
Henry	PRI 218	Aaron	WOR 204	Thomas	SOM 134		
Sauyson	BCI 515	Abraham	D.C.132	Thomas	SOM 154		
William	ANN 263	Alexander	CHA 200A	Walter	D.C.112		
William	CHA 201	Ann	DOR 23	Wheeler	BAL 18		
COURTWRIGHT, Margt.		Banjamin	BCI 87	William	ANN 394		
	D.C.8	Benjamin	HAR 62	William	CAL 51		
COVELL, Jonathan	FRE 73	Cathn.	BCI 176	William	CLN 86		
COVENHOVER, Jacob	BCI 149	Charles	CAL 61	William	D.C.76		
COVER, Daniel	FRE 202	Charles	PRI 238	William	HAR 46		
Daniel, of Jno.	FRE 193	Christopher	QUE 41	William	PRI 236		
Danl.	MON 143	Daniel	TAL 34A	William	SOM 148		
David	FRE 154	Darbey	QUE 28	William	TAL 12		
George	D.C.50	Elisha	BAL 149	William W.	CHA 211		
Henry	BAL 56	Elizabeth	HAR 73	Williamson	CHA 204		
Joseph	FRE 154	Elizabeth	TAL 13	Willm.	D.C.125		
Elizabeth	FRE 170	Elizabeth	WAS 90	Wm. (?)	BCI 524		
Jacob	FRE 174	Ellen	D.C.156	COXE, George	FRE 96		
Jacob	FRE 178	Emory	CEC 121	John (?)	BAL 245		
John	FRE 191	Francis	CHA 214	William	FRE 177		
John	FRE 224	Francis	PRI 238	COXEN, Washington	D.C.37		
Mary	FRE 202	Geo.	D.C.122	William	FRE 73		
Tobias	FRE 174	George	FRE 176	COY, Peter L.	BCI 5		
Yost	FRE 174	Harman	BCI 317	COYLE, Andw.	D.C.94		
COVERNTON, James	WAS 107	Henry	QUE 12	Francis	D.C.79		
COVEY, Andrew	CLN 114	Herculees	TAL 32	John	D.C.101		
Francis G.	CLN 112	Herculus?	TAL 32	John	D.C.118		
Hutton	CLN 100	Hester	BCI 116	COZEN, Elizabeth	HAR 28		
Jacob	CLN 112	Hester	CHA 217	COZENS, Wm. R.	D.C.9		
Peter	DOR 52	Hugh	CHA 206	COZIER, Thomas	CEC 157		
Thomas	DOR 10	Isaac	TAL 19	CRABB, Elizabeth	MON 163		
William	CLN 112	Isaac P.	TAL 34A	John	D.C.120		
COVIN (See also COUIN),		Jacob	BAL 148	Richard J.	ANN 291		
James (?)	KEN 107	James	BAL 209	Thomas	ANN 368		
Maria (?)	KEN 103	James	CAL 59	CRABBIN, Wm.	BCI 501		
		James	FRE 83				

CRABBS, Eve	FRE 146
Frederick	FRE 146
Joseph	FRE 143
CRABLE, Elizabeth	FRE 101
Jane	FRE 93
CRABS, George	FRE 183
John	FRE 173
CRABSON, Moses	HAR 22
CRABSTER, Basil	ANN 363
CRABTREE, Baltzer	ALL 31
James	ALL 35
Jonas	ALL 31
Lewis	ALL 36
Thomas of J.	ALL 34
Willm.	D.C. 200
CRACRAFT, Benjamin	
	MON 149
CRACROFT, Jerrard	ANN 323
CRADDOCK, Benedict	
	CEC 121
Daniel	CEC 121
Eliza	D.C. 159
James	CEC 121
Joseph	BCI 89
Malacca	D.C. 18
Malacea?	D.C. 18
Richard	CEC 121
William	CEC 121
CRAFT, Elizabeth	BAL 140
George	BCI 277
John	D.C. 80
John	DOR 45
John B.	BAL 69
Thomas	DOR 58
William	DOR 43
CRAGE, Isaac	WAS 146
Isaac	WAS 148
CRAGG, Jonan. W.	BCI 198
CRAGGS, George	ANN 315
Robert	BCI 56
CRAGH, John	BAL 149
CRAIE, Phebe (?)-	
Negro	HAR 50
CRAIG, Alexander	CEC 156
Alexandra J.	CEC 122
Alexandra S.	CEC 121
Ann	BCI 284
Augts.	D.C. 100
Benjamin	CEC 121
Henry	BCI 113
Jas.	BCI 211
John	ALL 31
John	BCI 4
John	DOR 31
John, Esqr.	DOR 45
John D.	BCI 378
Kitty	D.C. 215
Levi	CEC 121
Nany	DOR 22
Nehemiah	DOR 19
Polly	DOR 20
Richard-negro	CEC 121
Sally	DOR 20
Samuel	DOR 19
Thomas	BAL 87
William	ANN 256
William, Sen.	CEC 121
William, Jr.	CEC 121
CRAIGE, Benjamin	CEC 134
Benjamin	CEC 156
CRAIL, Joseph (?)	BCI 409
Phebe-Negro	HAR 50
CRAIN, Alexander	CHA 204
Robert	CHA 201
CRAINE, Joseph	BCI 498
CRAIRO, --- (?)	BCI 388

CRAIT, Joseph	BCI 409
CRALEY, John	WAS 94
Michael	FRE 99
CRALL, Isaac	FRE 162
CRAM, Saml.	D.C. 179
CRAMER, A. M. C.	WAS 80
Christopher	BAL 149
David	FRE 234
Ezra	FRE 234
Fred.	BCI 380
Henry	FRE 179
Jacob	FRE 160
Jacob	FRE 220
Jacob	FRE 229
Jacob	WAS 137
John	BAL 69
John	D.C. 83
John	FRE 160
John	WAS 120
Mary	D.C. 118
Peter	D.C. 52
Philip Henry	FRE 163
CRAMFIELD, Isaah	WOR 201
CRAMLET, Stephen	BAL 207
CRAMPFORD, Robert	
	CAL 51
Samuel	CAL 49
CRAMPHIN, Thomas	MON 149
CRAMPTON, Elias	WAS 68
Elisha	FRE 131
John	WAS 70
Joseph	WAS 68
Josiah	WAS 69
Moses	WAS 66
Nancey	WAS 70
CRAMSHIRE, Chas.	FRE 127
CRAMWER, Hepher	FRE 223
CRANCH, Wm.	D.C. 199
CRANDALL, Allison	CEC 155
CRANDELE, Thomas (?)	
	ANN 276
CRANDELL, Abel	ANN 253
Amelia	ANN 257
Francis	ANN 266
Henry	ANN 257
Jane	D.C. 161
Thomas	ANN 276
CRANDLE, Abel	CAL 63
Geo.	D.C. 81
Willm.	D.C. 92
CRANE, David	D.C. 109
George	SAI 73A
George W.	CAL 51
James	D.C. 73
James A.	SAI 65
John	CAL 52
John	QUE 42
Jonathan	QUE 5
Margaret	ANN 309
Thos.	QUE 5
William	KEN 85
Wm.	CAL 52
CRANEFARD, John	DOR 18
CRANFORD, George R.	
	CAL 68
James	CAL 61
Robert	CAL 67
CRANFURD, David (?)	
	PRI 201
CRANGLE, Mary	BCI 348
CRANON, Celia (?)	CLN 95
CRANOR, Benedict	CLN 97
Celia	CLN 95
Joshua	CLN 89
Solomon D.	CLN 94
CRANSTON, John	D.C. 167

CRANTZ, John D.	FRE 78A
CRAPSTER, John	FRE 169
John, Junr.	FRE 170
CRASH, Sally	D.C. 188
CRATHERS, John	D.C. 82
CRATIN, John	FRE 210
CRAUFORD, James (?)	
	CAL 61
CRAUFURD, David	PRI 201
CRAUGH, Mary (?)	BCI 348
CRAUS, Loranie	BCI 374
CRAUSIN, Saml.	D.C. 114
CRAUT, --- (Mr.)	BAL 250
CRAVEN, John	D.C. 15
Thomas	FRE 95
CRAVER, Henry	WAS 111
Jacob	FRE 161
John	ANN 364
Peter	FRE 116
Philip	D.C. 123
CRAW, John	TAL 4
CRAWFARD, John (?)	
	DOR 18
CRAWFERD, Jas. L.	BCI 209
Priscilla	PRI 193
Thomas	PRI 193
CRAWFORD, --- (Mrs.)	
	PRI 198
Aaron	FRE 71
Adam	PRI 194
Ann	CLN 74
Diana	WAS 120
Henry	SOM 109
Isaac	D.C. 158
James	CEC 174
James	FRE 191
James	PRI 196
Jas.	BCI 193
John	ANN 365
John	ANN 377
John	D.C. 149
John	HAR 77
John	WAS 99
John	WAS 106
Jonathan	FRE 158
Joseph	FRE 227
Leven L.	BAL 62
Mattw.	D.C. 102
Priscilla (?)	PRI 193
Robert	FRE 194
Samuel	FRE 80
Samuel	FRE 190
Sarah	D.C. 41
Sarah	HAR 75
Stacy	MON 173
Thomas (?)	PRI 193
Thomas	D.C. 59
Thomas B.	ALL 14
Tilghman	ANN 377
W. H.	D.C. 83
William	CEC 134
William	FRE 125
Wm.	FRE 209
CRAWLEY, Benjamin	SAI 70
Mema	D.C. 149
William	SAI 76
CRAWLY, Sary	SAI 96
CRAWMER, Apalonia	FRE 228
Daniel	FRE 155
David	FRE 230
Ezra	FRE 230
Henry	FRE 225
John	FRE 211
John	FRE 230
Philip	FRE 209

CRAWS, George	BAL 151	CRESE, Leuis	BCI 349	CROCKETT (continued),			
CRAY, --- (Mrs.)	BCI 373	CRESFIELD, Peregine		George	SOM 115		
John	QUE 48		BCI 405	Henry	MON 144		
CRAYCROFT, Ann	BCI 474	CRESIMER, Nicholas	FRE 179	John	SOM 140		
William C.	PRI 214	CRESS, Jacob	FRE 143	Levin	SOM 103		
CRAYTAN, Thomas	DOR 28	John	ALL 26	Nehemiah	SOM 103		
CRAYTON, Draiper	DOR 25	CRESSWELL, Elijah	BAL 51	Nicholas	SOM 106		
Elias	DOR 29	Hannah	BAL 58	Shiles	SOM 103		
Henry	DOR 30	James	BAL 57	William	SOM 129		
Iasc?	DOR 32	James	BAL 57	CROFFERD, --- (Widaw)			
Iasl	DOR 32	CRESWELD, Elizabeth			BCI 389		
Jeremiah	DOR 29		CEC 173	CROFT, John (?)	DOR 45		
John	DOR 28	CRESWELL, John	CEC 156	John	FRE 147		
Robert	HAR 59	John-negro	CEC 121	CROGGAN, John	D.C.208		
Samuel	DOR 29	CRETZER (See also		Wm. N.	D.C.208		
Thomas (?)	DOR 28	CAETZER),		CROGCON, Thos.	D.C.208		
Thomas, Senr.	DOR 28	George (?)	WAS 66	CROKER, Abraham	BCI 123		
Vernon	DOR 13	John (?)	WAS 57	Mary	BCI 88		
CRAZER, Saml.	BCI 523	Leonard	WAS 62	CROMER, Daniel	BCI 439		
CREAGBAUM, Conrad		CRETZLEY, Thomas	WAS 69	George	BAL 145		
	ALL 17	CREVISTON, George		George W.	BCI 439		
CREAGER, Daniel	FRE 223		HAR 18	John (?)	WAS 120		
George	FRE 77	CREW, Charles	HAR 75	John	DOR 12		
Lewis	FRE 135	John	KEN 107	Jonas	WAS 123		
Michael	D.C.6	Jonathan	KEN 107	CROMMILLER, Thos.	BCI 352		
Michael	FRE 223	Richd.	BCI 512	CROMWELL, Charles	ANN 309		
Solomon	FRE 228A	Willm.	BCI 184	Elizh.	BCI 179		
CREAGH, John	BCI 180	CREWS, Clinton	QUE 40	George	ANN 331		
John	BCI 375	CREY, Fredk.	BCI 194	Isaac	TAL 31		
CREAKBAUM, Peter	ALL 15	CRICK, Peter	WAS 94	Jacob	BAL 189		
CREAKBAURN, Peter		CRIDDLE, Jonathan	D.C.122	Jacob J.	BCI 462		
	ALL 15	CRIEGER, Lucy	PRI 197	James	BAL 7		
CREAMER, Christian	FRE 203	CRIER, Benjn.	D.C.201	James, Jur.	BAL 7		
Daniel	WAS 58A	CRIGLOW, William	FRE 105	John	ANN 308		
Emanuel	BAL 127	CRILL, Martin	FRE 110	John	BAL 189		
Frederick	FRE 128	CRIPPIN, George	WOR 189	John	FRE 98		
Joshua	BCI 200	CRIPPLEAVER, John		John (Doct.)	BCI 268		
Mary	BAL 202		ALL 7	John G.	ANN 331		
CREASE, Anty.	D.C.189	CRISDON, Ben	QUE 20	Joseph	WAS 133		
John H.	D.C.160	CRISE, George	FRE 180	Joseph M.	FRE 103		
CREDDICK, Chas.	MON 131	Henry	FRE 224	Nathaniel	WAS 111		
Chos.?	MON 131	Jacob	FRE 159	Nimrod	BAL 17		
Samuel	CLN 75	Margaret	FRE 224	Oliver	ALL 31		
CREDIT, Henry	D.C.208	Volentine	FRE 179	ONeal	ANN 309		
CREE, Samuel	BAL 89	CRISHER, Conrod	FRE 189	Philerman	FRE 225		
CREEGER, Daniel	FRE 157	CRISMAN, John M.	BCI 93	Richard	BAL 17		
Henry of Jno.	FRE 154	CRISMAND, John	CHA 200A	Richard	FRE 86		
Henry (of L.)	FRE 157	CRISMER, Henry	SAI 93	Richard	WAS 133		
Jacob	FRE 159	CRISMOND, Viotte	CHA 206	Richard, of Osln.			
John	FRE 157	CRISP, Elijah	QUE 34		ANN 315		
John, of L.	FRE 154	John	QUE 47	Richard, of Ricd.			
Joseph	FRE 155	John-Negro	HAR 65		ANN 315		
Lawrence	FRE 157	Mary	TAL 48	Rosanna	DOR 11		
Samuel	FRE 158	CRISSAL, Richd.	BCI 223	Stephen	ANN 298		
William	FRE 154	CRISSEE, James	HAR 39	Thomas	BCI 137		
CREEK, James	BCI 96	CRISSEL, George	HAR 44	William	BAL 217		
Pompi	ANN 263	CRISSMAN, George	BAL 49	Wm.	BCI 508		
William	ANN 266	CRIST, Jacob	FRE 160	CRON MILLER, Philip (?)			
CREERY, --- (Mrs.)	BCI 357	Jacob	FRE 202		BCI 3		
John	BCI 436	John	FRE 161	CRONAM, John	BCI 255		
CREGLOW, John	FRE 76A	Valentine	FRE 161	CRONDY, Polly (?)	D.C.171		
CREICH, Fredirck	BCI 443	William	BCI 161	CRONE, Conrod	FRE 130		
CREIGER, Ann	D.C.52	CRISTIE, David	SAI 79	John	BCI 14		
Lewis	D.C.46	Pricilla	BCI 144	Sarah (?)	BCI 10		
CREIGHTON, James	D.C.3	CRISTY, Robert	BCI 9	CRONEMILLER, John	BCI 490		
John	D.C.143	CRISWELL, Jehu	FRE 192	CRONEY, Elizabeth	BCI 37		
CREMAR, Cornelius	FRE 225	Richard	BAL 203	Gillis	TAL 45		
CREMER, Elizab.	BCI 346	Thomas	BAL 28	Philemon	TAL 50		
Margaret	FRE 225	CRITZER, Jacob	FRE 133	CRONIA, Henry (?)	WAS 113A		
Mary	FRE 225	CROCK, John	ALL 34	Mary	WAS 114		
CRESAP, James D.	ALL 22	CROCKER, Assa	BCI 125	CRONIAN, Philip	D.C.118		
James M.	ALL 31	Barney	BCI 59	CRONIN, George	WAS 55A		
John M.	ALL 22	CROCKET, James	FRE 161	William	HAR 19		
Joseph	ALL 20A	Sarah	KEN 117	CRONISE, Jacob	FRE 160		
Robert	ALL 23	CROCKETT, ---		John	FRE 114		
Thomas	ALL 22	(Widaw)	BCI 372	Simon	FRE 117		

CRUMPTON, Susannah		
	ANN	276
CRUMRINE, Henry	FRE	189
John	FRE	159
John	FRE	189
Philip	BAL	138
Philip	BAL	141
CRUMWELL, Gabriel	CAL	50
George	BCI	432
Michail	BCI	39
CRUPPER, Stephen	BCI	487
CRUSE, George	ANN	283
Thos.	D.C.	170
CRUSER, Mary	BCI	504
CRUSEY, Frederick	FRE	211
CRUSHONG, John	FRE	228
CRUSSETT, Thos.	BCI	184
CRUTCHER, Vincent	FRE	161
CRUTCHLEY, Eli	FRE	118
CRUTHERS, Francis	CEC	134
Samuel	CEC	134
Weather	CEC	134
CRUTT, John (?)	DOR	26
CRUTTENDEN, George		
	D.C.	38
Harvey	D.C.	101
CRUTZER, Catherine	WAS	56
Lenorad	WAS	66
CRYEN, Jacob	DOR	21
CRYER, John	DOR	21
CUDDY, Lawson	BAL	77
CUDGER, James	KEN	120
CUDLIPP, Luisa	SAI	55
CUE, Ann W. (?)	BAL	53
CUFF, Nelly (negro)	TAL	20
Perre	CLN	96
CUFFEY, Charles	BCI	525
CUFSHAW, Abraham (?)		
	FRE	111
CUGLE, Christopher	ANN	362
George	ANN	361
John	BCI	491
CUIKSHANK, Charls	D.C.	47
CUISON, Elizabeth (Mrs.)		
	BCI	270
CULBERT, Thomas	BCI	464
Wm.	BCI	189
CULBRETH, Samuel	CLN	76
Thomas	CLN	88
CULL, John	D.C.	114
CULLEN, Edward	SOM	134
CULLER, Henry	FRE	126
Jacob	FRE	126
John	FRE	125
Phillip	FRE	128
CULLERSON, Silvey	SAI	98
Wheeler	BAL	28
CULLEY, Ann	CEC	173
Robert	BCI	321
CULLIMORE, William	BCI	313
CULLING, Jacob	SOM	144
Jacob (of E.)	SOM	150
John	SOM	151
Laurence	BCI	84
CULLINGS, James	BAL	162
CULLINS, Thomas	BAL	84
Thomas	BAL	165
CULLISON, Cornelius		
	SAI	65
Elizabeth	SAI	54
Elizabeth	SAI	55
George	SAI	68
Helen	SAI	64
Jessee	BAL	166
Joseph	SAI	54
Joshua	BAL	164

CULLISON (continued),		
Noah	BAL	175
Shadrick	BAL	164
Wesley	BAL	188
Wesley	BAL	193
William	BAL	164
CULLUM, Jesse	HAR	6
John	BAL	221
Richard	HAR	56
CULLUMBER, ELeanor		
(Miss)	CAL	47
Hezekiah	CAL	42
Joshua	SAI	69
Sarah (Mrs.)	CAL	45
Sofia (Mrs.)	CAL	48
CULLY, Sina	CEC	134
Thomas	CEC	121
CULPEPPER, Thos.	CAL	45
CULVEE, Henry	PRI	180A
CULVER, Benjamin	HAR	79
Burgess	MON	149
Elijah	SOM	106
Henry (?)	PRI	180A
John	SOM	105
Richard	SOM	115
Tabitha	SOM	113
William	MON	149
William	SOM	118
CULVERSON, Elizabeth		
	BCI	34
Thomas	CEC	156
CULVERVELL, Richard		
	BCI	384
CULVERWELL, Richard		
	BCI	435
CUMBERLAND, John		
	BCI	448
CUMLER, William	D.C.	10
CUMMIN, Samuel	BCI	116
William	BCI	116
CUMMING, Jno.-his		
Quarter	QUE	19
Robert	FRE	219
CUMMINGS, Alexander		
	BCI	48
Ann	BCI	87
Aquilla	TAL	26
E. H. (?)	BCI	501
Francis D.	BCI	523
James	CEC	174
John	ALL	7
John	BCI	94
Michael	TAL	26
Sarah	TAL	26
Solomon	TAL	26
Thomas	TAL	26
CUMMINS, Christr.	D.C.	73
James	BAL	124
James	CEC	135
John	BCI	308
Richard	BCI	395
William	QUE	29
CUMMONS, David	TAL	48
CUMPTON, Henry	PRI	212
CUNINGHAM, Absolon		
	WAS	146
Bassel	CEC	134
Catharine	CEC	157
Daniel	BCI	129
David	CEC	156
Isabella	CEC	156
James	BAL	191
James	CEC	173
John	BAL	180
Thomas	CEC	134

CUNINGHAM (continued),		
Thomas	CEC	173
CUNNIGHAM, James	BAL	216
CUNNING, Barney	WAS	63
Catharine	BCI	303
CUNNINGHAM, Aquilla		
	BAL	249
Arthur	BAL	108
Barthia	HAR	43
Charly	CEC	122
Crispin	HAR	8
Daniel	HAR	6
George	HAR	8
James	ALL	2
James	BCI	405
John	BAL	105
John	BCI	61
John C.	PRI	226
Joseph	HAR	78
Lloyd	HAR	4
Robert	WAS	66
Stephen	BAL	109
Susannah	BCI	71
Thomas	HAR	79
Thornton	D.C.	79
Walter	HAR	41
Walter	WAS	56
William	BCI	456
Wm.	BCI	512
CUPPOLD, Betsey	BCI	480
CURBY (See also KERBY, KIRBY),		
John	BCI	149
CURE, Rachel	BCI	538
CURFMAN, Adam	FRE	124
CURLET, Thos.	BCI	197
CURLETT, Jno.	QUE	20
John	BCI	183
CURLEY, James	BCI	285
James	BCI	384
Patrick	HAR	75
William	BCI	39
CURLY, Thomas	FRE	225
CURPMAN, Barbara	FRE	113
Peter	FRE	116
CURRAN, Joshua	CHA	204
Micha	BCI	214
Moses	BCI	298
Philip	ANN	394
William	D.C.	23
CURRANS, Elijah	FRE	169
CURRE, James	SOM	134
CURRELL, James	D.C.	12
CURREN, Benjn.	MON	158A
William	FRE	144
CURRENCE, William	FRE	143
William, of Tho.	FRE	146
CURRER, Samuel	BCI	444
CURRIE, James	BCI	343
CURRIER, Jonathan	CEC	155
CURRIOUS, Harry	WAS	138
CURRIR, Victor	CEC	155
CURRURTHURS, Hanah		
	WAS	84
CURRY, Abraham	HAR	7
Arthur	HAR	41
Benjn.	D.C.	79
Edward	KEN	90
Henry	KEN	88
Israel	HAR	63
James	D.C.	173
James	FRE	200
James	HAR	63
Jane	D.C.	185
John	HAR	44

DANIKER, John	BCI 303	DARNALL (continued),		DAST, Dorcas	BCI 94
DANISON, Mary	ANN 345	Mary	BCI 503	DATER, Jacob (?)	WAS 108
Moses	ANN 339	Nicholas (See Henry		DATON, Isaac	D.C.33
Reason	ANN 339	& Nicholas DARNALL-		DAUB, Jacob	FRE 113
Thomas	ANN 345	their Slaves)		DAUGHADAY, Joseph	
DANNA, Zachariah	FRE 220	Philip	ANN 272		BAL 219
DANNENMANE, C. H.		Ralph	FRE 80	Samul?	BAL 216
	BCI 348	Thos.	MON 133	DAUGHADY, John	BAL 230
DANNER, Jacob	FRE 141	DARNE, Wm.	MON 133	John	BAL 243
DANNIALS, Nathan	BAL 78	DARNEL, Maria	QUE 15	Richard	BAL 244
DANNISON, Elijah	ANN 343	DARNELD, Henry	D.C.192	DAUGHARTY, Conn	WAS 68
Samuel	ALL 31	DARNELL, Philip	ANN 280	DAUGHERDY, Caleb	
DANOM, Benjamin	ANN 329	DARNER, Fredk.	FRE 135	J. (1.?)	BAL 191
DANOON, Bartley	ANN 370	Henry	FRE 130	DAUGHERTY, Charles	
DANSKIN, --- (Mrs.)		John	FRE 130		WAS 62
	BCI 357	DARNES, Belinda	D.C.214	Dickerson	SOM 147
DANZELL, James	BCI 525	DARNEY, Bartholomew		Elijah	SOM 149
DAPLE, Jacob	WAS 88		BCI 49	Elizabeth	SOM 114
DAPU, John	CLN 76	DARNON, Jusan? (?)		Hugh	D.C.98
DAR, Chars.	BCI 336		DOR 58	Isaac	SOM 107
DARBY, Aden	MON 137	Susan (?)	DOR 58	Isaac	SOM 150
Asa	MON 150	DARON, Amos	KEN 102	James	CEC 157
Basil	MON 131	DARR, Jacob	FRE 132	James	HAR 39
Dathan	MON 136	John, of Martin	FRE 162	Jesse	SOM 146
Geo. W.	MON 172	DARRAUGH, Sarah	HAR 73	John	BCI 269
James	D.C.203	DARRINGTON, Wm.	BCI 256	John	HAR 22
John	DOR 61	DARSEY, Ann	PRI 240	John	SOM 115
John	DOR 64	Llayd (?)	MON 177	John (of Jesse)	SOM 144
John	FRE 170	DARST, John	FRE 111	John (of Obed)	SOM 149
John	WAS 103	DART, John	ALL 24	Johnathan	SOM 112
John W.	D.C.51	Joseph	SAI 77	Joseph	D.C.87
Magor	DOR 64	Mary	BCI 4	Joshua	SOM 147
Mary	SOM 112	DASHIEL, Warren	D.C.74	Josiah	SOM 148
Rezen	MON 177	DASHIELD, Alfred H.		Nathaniel	SOM 144
Ruth	MON 139		ANN 377	Nathaniel	SOM 149
Saml.	MON 139	Henry	BCI 49	Noah	SOM 150
Samuel	SOM 155	DASHIELDS, G.	BCI 352	Peter	SOM 149
Thomas	SOM 105	DASHIELL, Benjamin		Severn	SOM 144
Thos.	MON 138		SOM 116	T. F.	BCI 367
Walter	FRE 69	Chapman	SOM 101A	Thos.	D.C.117
DARCAS, Henry	FRE 227	Charles	SOM 117	DAUGHITY, Partrick	SAI 94
DARCEY, Edward	PRI [200]	David (f.n.)	SOM 119	DAUGHTERS, Samuel	SOM 117
Francis	PRI 202	Della	SOM 116	DAUGLASS, Edward	D.C.13
DARCUS, Frederick	FRE 226	Eleanor	SOM 111	John (?)	D.C.58
DARCY, J. N.	BCI 40	Elizabeth	SOM 110	DAUHERTY, Jno.	BCI 182
DARDEN, Richd.	TAL 46	Esther	SOM 113	DAUHTY, Peter	D.C.52
Stephen	TAL 6	George (of Jno.)		DAUNT, James	D.C.77
DARE, Elizabeth (Mrs.)			SOM 107	DAUNY, John E. (?)	QUE 33
	CAL 49	George (of Wm.)	SOM 109	DAVENPORT, Lewis	BCI 123
Gidun	CAL 49	George A.	SOM 128	DAVID, Joseph, Senr.	
Henry	CAL 49	Haste W.	SOM 105		CAL 60
John	FRE 128	Hetty (Junr.)	SOM 110	Joshua	QUE 29
John (Doctr.)	CAL 49	Ichabud	DOR 43	DAVIDGE, --- (Doct.)	
John, Junr.	CAL 42	James	SOM 109		BCI 386
Mary	BCI 333	James F.	SOM 134	DAVIDSEN, B. A.	BCI 400
Thos. C.	CAL 53A	James W.	SOM 109	John	BCI 387
DARIS, Thomas	MON 150	John	SOM 104	DAVIDSON, Cordelia	FRE 75
DARLES, Joseph	D.C.36	Leah (free negro)		Daniel	BCI 131
DARLEY, James	BCI 411		SOM 118	George	CEC 157
John (?)	FRE 170	Levina (f.n.)	SOM 119	Henry	CHA 216
Thos.	D.C.162	Matthias	SOM 106	Henry	WAS 119
DARLINGTON, Thomas		Mattilda (f.n.)	SOM 120	James	ANN 261
	ANN 378	Messer (free negro)		James	BCI 299
DARMERTEY, Richard			SOM 118	James	CEC 135
	BCI 286	Mitchel	SOM 116	Jane	BCI 169
DARMON, John	BAL 88	Pitt	SOM 108	Jas.	BCI 166
DARNAL, Ann	SAI 95	Priscilla	SOM 135	Jas.	D.C.74
Francis L.	PRI 197	Prisella (f.n.)	SOM 120	John	ALL 23
Lucy	MON 137	Robert	SOM 106	John	CEC 135
DARNALE, Henry (?)		Robert	SOM 125	John	CEC 135
	ANN 269	Samuel	SOM 131	John	D.C.10
Philip (?)	ANN 272	Samuel	SOM 141	John	PRI 227
DARNALL, Fielder	MON 174	Thomas	D.C.14	John	WOR 189
Henry	ANN 269	William	SOM 109	John M.	ALL 31
Henry & Nicholas-		DASHILL, Charles	WOR 205	Lanclote?	PRI 227
their Slaves	ANN 264	Robert	WOR 207	Lanclott	PRI 227

DAVIDSON (continued),			**DAVIS (continued),**			**DAVIS (continued),**		
Lewis	ALL	20A	Eleanor	HAR	70	James	PRI	208
Lewis G.	D.C.	44	Elender	SAI	78	James	SAI	69
Margt.	BCI	232	Elias	BCI	229	James	SOM	154
Martha	HAR	77	Elija	D.C.	182	James, Ovsr.	TAL	40
Nelson	D.C.	36	Elijah	HAR	21	James of J.	WOR	206
Patrick	FRE	100	Elijah	FRE	83A	James (of Jon.)	WOR	159
Robert	CEC	135	Elijah	SAI	92	Jane	SAI	92
Robt.	BCI	174	Elisha	ANN	372	Jas. G.	HAR	19
Thomas	BCI	65	Elisha	DOR	53	Jenifer	CHA	190
Thos.	D.C.	94	Elisha	WOR	193	Jeremiah	BCI	493
W. John	CEC	135	Elizabeth	ANN	268	Jeremiah	TAL	51
William	ALL	24	Elizabeth	ANN	399	Jess	BCI	346
William	CEC	135	Elizabeth	BAL	59	Jesse	BCI	297
DAVIN, Esabella	BCI	161	Elizabeth	CEC	135	Jesse	BCI	417
DAVIS, Abel	MON	150	Elizabeth	FRE	104	Jesse	CHA	217
Abraham	D.C.	21	Elizabeth	SAI	90	Jo-f.c.p.	HAR	11
Abraham	TAL	38	Elizabeth S.	SAI	87	John	ALL	3
Ahasuarus	CHA	223	Elizabith	WOR	169	John	ALL	21
Albain	BAL	54	Elizth.	D.C.	171	John	ALL	32
Ambrose	ANN	372	Ely	FRE	215	John	ANN	289
Amelia	BCI	15	Elzy	SOM	137	John	BAL	112
Amos	ALL	24	Ephram	WAS	59	John	BAL	216
Amos	BAL	229	Essex Y.	CHA	227	John	BAL	239
Amos	BCI	313	Esther	BCI	126	John	BCI	84
Amos	D.C.	34	Evan	BCI	130	John	BCI	153
Andrew	WOR	216	Ezekiel	BAL	129	John	BCI	187
Ann	ANN	287	Ezekiel S.	CLN	106	John	BCI	222
Ann	ANN	390	Fanny	D.C.	146	John	BCI	432
Ann	BAL	84	Francis	D.C.	37	John	CLN	108
Ann	CEC	122	Franes	WAS	61	John	CEC	122
Ann	CHA	228	Gearge?	DOR	23	John	CEC	135
Ann	D.C.	134	Gelbert	WAS	135	John	CEC	135
Ann	D.C.	186	George	CHA	205	John	D.C.	49
Anna	WOR	178	George	D.C.	26	John	D.C.	94
Anne	MON	167	George	DOR	23	John	D.C.	113
Annonias	WOR	206	George	FRE	75	John	D.C.	174
Anthony	SAI	88	George	KEN	106A	John	FRE	213
Archibald	BAL	124	George	WOR	188	John	KEN	118
Arthur	SOM	130	George (of James)	CHA	193	John	QUE	6
Asa	CHA	193	George (of Richd.)			John	QUE	24
Benjamin	CHA	196		CHA	193	John	SOM	122
Benjamin	MON	150	Gerard	SAI	94	John	WAS	116
Benjamin U.	CEC	175	Gideon	D.C.	28	John	WAS	136
Betsy	BCI	431	Gideon	D.C.	40	John	WOR	177
Blany, Ovsr.	TAL	8	Gilbert	FRE	71	John	WOR	189
Briscoe	SAI	93	Handy	WOR	178	John	WOR	193
Caleb	BCI	485	Harry	D.C.	156	John, Jnr.	QUE	32
Caleb P.	CLN	112	Henny	BAL	204	John (of Abel)	D.C.	129
Calib	FRE	74	Henry?	BAL	204	John (of Charles)	WOR	171
Canelm	SAI	94	Henry	BCI	417	John (of Jas.)	WOR	159
Canelon?	SAI	94	Henry	D.C.	42	John B.	WAS	123
Carlos	BCI	426	Henry	D.C.	153	John B.	BCI	442
Cath.	D.C.	96	Henry	WAS	148	John P.	D.C.	71
Catharine	D.C.	174	Henry	WOR	157	John R.	TAL	5
Catherine	CEC	122	Henry, Junr.	WOR	160	John S.	PRI	222
Charles	CLN	88	Henry L.	ANN	403	Jonas	D.C.	34
Charles	SAI	67	Hezekiah	CHA	193	Jonathan	FRE	71
Charles (of Benj.)	WOR	172	Hugh	CEC	174	Jonathan	FRE	201
Charles S.	BAL	107	Iagnatius	FRE	87	Jos.	QUE	10
Chars.	BCI	352	Isaac	ALL	8A	Joseph	ALL	3
Chas.	MON	177	Isaac	ANN	257	Joseph	BAL	29
Chas. B.	D.C.	87	Isaac	HAR	60	Joseph	BCI	19
Christopher	BCI	304	Isaac	WOR	216	Joseph	BCI	60
Cornelious	SAI	77	Isaiah	BCI	464	Joseph	BCI	128
David	ALL	24	Israel	ANN	287	Joseph	CEC	122
David	BAL	111	Jacob	TAL	33	Joseph	CHA	194
David	BCI	392	Jacob	WAS	132	Joseph	FRE	126
Debora Ann	PRI	231	James	BAL	99	Joseph	HAR	28
Dennis	BAL	138	James	BCI	17	Joseph	HAR	76
Edward	CHA	223	James	BCI	28	Joseph	TAL	13
Edward	D.C.	39	James	BCI	395	Joseph	WAS	134
Edward	QUE	30	James	BCI	529	Joseph H.	BCI	136
Edward	TAL	35	James	FRE	159	Joseph W.	MON	150
Edwd.	D.C.	209	James	KEN	94	Joshua	ALL	35
Edwrd.	WOR	173	James	MON	150			

DAWSON (continued),		DAY (continued),		DEAN (continued),	
James of E.	ALL 10A	William	ANN 380	James	ANN 360
James of Jas.	ALL 11	William	BAL 121	James	DOR 32
Jas. M.	MON 131	William	D.C.108	James	DOR 54
John	BCI 496	William	HAR 72	James	FRE 94
John	CLN 110	Willm.	D.C.97	James	SAI 82
John	CEC 135	DAYHOFF, Andrew	FRE 223	James	WAS 63
John	CEC 175	Jacob	FRE 175	James, Sen.	SAI 88
John	TAL 13	John	BAL 144	John	DOR 3
John	TAL 21	Peter	BAL 142	John B.	SAI 91
John of Jas.	ALL 11	DAYHOOF, Jacob	WAS 100	Joseph	ALL 32
John P.	ALL 10A	Samuel	WAS 100	Joseph	DOR 39
Jonas	ANN 308	DAYLE, Isaac	WOR 203	Joseph	SAI 87
Joseph	TAL 14	Isaac	WOR 204	Josiah	DOR 55
Joseph	BCI 16	James	WOR 204	Mary	CLN 96
Joseph H.	TAL 27	John	WOR 204	Matthew	DOR 43
Levi	ALL 24	William	WOR 204	Michael	CLN 105
Levin	QUE 27	DAYLONG, David	ALL 29	Nathan	HAR 39
Mary	CHA 193	DAYLY, Elizabeth	SOM 118	Nelly	WAS 66
Nancy	ALL 11	DAYMAN, John	FRE 132	Richard	DOR 36
Nichls.	MON 131	DAYMOUTH, John	FRE 192	Robert	ALL 37
Nicholas	TAL 27	DAYNE, Jane	D.C.33	Saml.	D.C.207
Noah	ALL 10A	DAYTON, John	ALL 14	Solomon	CLN 86
Obediah	DOR 9	Thomas	DOR 42	Thos.	MON 163
Otho	ALL 11	DEAGEN, Henry B.	D.C.180	Whitington	DOR 32
Peter	CLN 110	DEAKENS, Edward	CHA 221	Will.	D.C.88
Richard	TAL 7	DEAKINS, --- (Mrs.)		William	DOR 39
Richd.	MON 140		PRI 195	William	DOR 55
Robert	TAL 20	James	PRI 193	Wm.	BCI 474
Robt. D.	MON 130	John	ALL 11	DEANE, Charles	CHA 193
Sovern	DOR 64	Leonard M.	PRI 197	Felix	D.C.43
Sovren	CLN 113	Walter	PRI 194	Williaim	DOR 32
Theodorus	ALL 11	DEAL, Christian	BCI 158	William	DOR 31
Thomas	ALL 14A	Christian	WAS 132	DEAR, Jesse	WOR 185
Thomas	BCI 314	Fled?	BCI 526	Jno.	BCI 225
Thomas C.	QUE 24	George	BCI 162	DEARBORN, Simon	D.C.152
Thomas H.	TAL 11	George	BCI 538	DEARHOLT, Henry	HAR 78
Thomas M.	ALL 11	Hannah	BCI 5	DEATH, Joseph	CEC 174
Thomas R.	BCI 281	Jacob	BAL 208	Randall	CEC 174
Thos. of Robt.	MON 129	Jacob	WAS 140	DEATLY, Thomas	CHA 192
W.	BCI 340	James	BCI 36	DEATS, John	BAL 240
Warner	CLN 110	James	CAL 47	DEAVER, Abraham	FRE 125
William	ANN 308	James	CAL 64	Aquila	HAR 19
William	BCI 12	James	DOR 18	Aquila	HAR 23
William	CEC 135	John	BCI 194	Benj.	FRE 135
William	DOR 51	John	FRE 217	George	HAR 23
William (negro)	TAL 23	John, Jr.	FRE 216	James	BCI 142
William, Senr.	ALL 11	Martin	FRE 221	James	HAR 57
William, Jr.	ALL 11	Michael	BAL 129	James	HAR 75
William R.	ALL 10A	Moses	DOR 57	John	HAR 55
Wm.	BCI 514	Reachel	BAL 148	Joshua	BAL 26
DAY, Aquilla	ANN 356	Richard	CAL 61	Joshua	HAR 22
Betsey	CHA 194	Richard	CAL 64	Richard	HAR 73
David	CEC 122	Sally-(Quarter in		Richard, of Jas.	HAR 57
Edward	BAL 238	S.H.)	WOR 170	Sarah	BCI 504
Eleanor	CHA 193	Stephen	KEN 93	DEAVIN, John	BAL 210
Francis	ANN 354	Thomas	DOR 9	DEAVOUR, Aron	BAL 173
George	CLN 77	Thomas	KEN 94	DEBB, James (?)	BAL 109
Goldsmith	HAR 7	DEALE, Danniel (?)	WOR 206	DEBEET, Corns.	BCI 256
Henry	BCI 498	Elijah	WOR 206	DEBERRY, John	FRE 162
Horatio	D.C.196	DEALES, Sally, wd.	WOR 210	DEBIL, Edward	D.C.41
Jacob	MON 149	DEAMS, Chris	BCI 474	DEBOROUGH, Peter L.	
James	MON 139	DEAN, Ann	DOR 49		TAL 14
John	ANN 312	Charles	CLN 87	DEBOW, John	BAL 210
John	HAR 73	Charles	CLN 108	Mehlon	BAL 61
Juda	D.C.218	Charles	D.C.44	DEBRULER, Micajah	HAR 7
Lavina	CHA 196A	David (of Elijah)	CLN 111	DEBUTTS, --- (Doctr.)	
Luke	PRI 236	Deborah	CLN 115		BCI 391
Nathan	PRI 207	Elisha	D.C.88	John H.	PRI 237
Rebecca	ANN 302	Ephraim	DOR 54	DECKER, Cornelius	BCI 35
Robert I. (J.?)	CAL 41A	George	DOR 37	George	BAL 12
Sarah	HAR 9	George	DOR 57	Jacob	BAL 2
Thomas	ANN 383	Godfry	DOR 21	James	D.C.30
Thomas	FRE 228A	Hannah	D.C.176	Mary	BCI 381
Tom	FRE 222	Henry	QUE 33	DECKESS, David	WAS 107
Urbin	ANN 358	Isabella	BCI 67	DE CORSE, Barney	KEN 90

DECOURSEY, Edward	QUE 37	DELANY (continued),		DEMENT (continued),	
Mary	BCI 85	Mary	D.C. 167	Mary S.	CHA 213
DECROW, William	ANN 279	Robert	PRI 197	Richard	CHA 213
DEEL, Elizabeth	ANN 256	William	BCI 459	William	CHA 211
Henry	ANN 254	DELAPLAINE, John	FRE 224	DEMET, John	ALL 31
Rachel	ANN 260	Joseph	FRE 224	DEMIT, Elizabeth	FRE 210
Samuel	ANN 269	Wm.	FRE 224	DEMMENICK, Michael	
Samuel L.	ANN 260	DELAPLANE, Daniel	FRE 173		BAL 190
DEELON, Christr.	D.C. 167	John	FRE 174	DEMMET, William	BAL 5
DEEMS, --- (Widaw)	BCI 396	Joseph	MON 150	DEMMETT, Andrew	ALL 35
Augustus	BAL 231	Joshua	FRE 175	DEMMIT, Stansbury	BAL 4
Frederick	ALL 29	Joshua	FRE 224	Thos.	BAL 4
Jacob	BCI 489	DELAPORTE, Francis		DEMMITT, Stansbury	
DEEN, George (?)	WAS 149		HAR 46		BAL 41
Jacob (?)	WAS 149	DELAROY, Ann	BCI 518	DEMOSS, John	HAR 60
Joshua	SOM 113	DELASHMET, Basil	FRE 84	Thomas	HAR 78
Steward	FRE 159	DELAUDER, Adam?	ANN 359	DEMOTH, Peter	BCI 477
DEENER, Conrad	WAS 72	Adames	ANN 359	DEMPSEY, --- (Mrs.)	
Henry	WAS 64	David	ANN 359		BCI 458
Joseph	WAS 67	George	ANN 359	John, Senr.	ANN 360
William	WAS 69	DELAUGHTER, George		Robert	CEC 175
William, Junr.	WAS 64		FRE 161	Thomas	ANN 360
DEER, William	FRE 193	John	FRE 158	Thomas	HAR 21
DEETER, Philip	WAS 72	DELAWARE, John	D.C. 159	DEMPSTER, Thomas	BCI 322
DEETON, Christr.	(?)D.C. 167	DELAWDER, Jacob	FRE 130	DEMUST, William	D.C. 11
DEETZ, George	ALL 26	DELCHER, Jemima	BCI 197	DENBOW, Basil	HAR 56
DEEVER, --- (?)	BCI 387	John	BCI 196	John	HAR 37
--- (Widaw)	BCI 416	DELEHUND, Charles	BCI 395	John, Junr.	HAR 63
DEEVES, Garrett	BAL 221	DELIAN, --- (Widow)		John, of Thos.	HAR 62
DEFERD, John	QUE 34		BCI 399	Juliann	BAL 199
DEFORD, Edward	CLN 79	DELIGNEY, Peter	CEC 175	Thomas	HAR 60
Henry	QUE 6	DELL, Adam	FRE 203	DENEALE, Mary	D.C. 183
James	QUE 36	David	BAL 55	DENEHOE, Patrick	FRE 177
Jos. M.	QUE 8	John	FRE 186	DENELBARGH, Eliz.	BCI 528
Nancy	QUE 17	John	FRE 188	DENFAR, Edward	ANN 400
Nathan	QUE 16	Nicholas	FRE 191	DENHAM, Lewis	D.C. 76
Price M.	QUE 23	Peter	FRE 186	DENIER, S. (J.?) H. (?)	
Thomas	KEN 104	William	BCI 279		BCI 334
DEGAN, Thomas	BAL 12	DELLA, Jarett	BCI 302	DENING, Stephen	KEN 106
DEGARE, Bathw.	BCI 218	DELLAM, F. J.	BCI 412	DENIOUS, Samuel	BAL 165
DEGARIS, John	BCI 69	DELLASHMUTT, Basl., Jn.?		DENISON, Edwd.	BCI 179
DEGILOIN, John	BCI 11		FRE 123	Jerusha	HAR 27
DEGINS, Ann	BCI 190	DELLON, R. (?)	BCI 413	Joseph	CEC 157
DEGRAFT, Abraham	WAS 124A	DELLOW, R. (?)	BCI 413	DENMEAD, Adam	BCI 153
Lewis	BAL 200	DELMAN, Peter	BCI 497	DENNER, Jacob	FRE 113
DEGRANGE, Peter	FRE 93	DELMAS, Francis	HAR 6	DENNEY, David	BCI 484
DEHEALME, Anna E.	FRE 101	DELOSTE, Francis	BCI 175	James	TAL 4
DEHEREGUSS, Charles		DELOUGHERY, John	BCI 128	James, of Joseph	TAL 8
	BCI 80	DELOZEIR, Richard	CHA 215	Jere	TAL 37
DEIGO, Edward	BAL 23	DELOZIER, --- (Madam)		John	DOR 37
DEIL, Henry	WAS 117		BCI 456	John	QUE 45
Thomas	WAS 63	--- (Mrs.)	BCI 442	Patrick	DOR 37
DEINNCK, Jeseph (?)	BAL 79	Alexander	BCI 537	Peter	TAL 12
DEINNEK, Jeseph (?)	BAL 79	Daniel	CHA 194	Theodore	TAL 12
DEITER, Jacob	WAS 108	Ignatius	FRE 149	Thomas	TAL 5
DEJEAN, Peter	PRI 224	John	CHA 196A	DENNING, Daniel	KEN 88
DE KRAFFT, Corns.	D.C. 82	DELPHY, Michl.	D.C. 101	James	BAL 54
Edwd.	D.C. 85	Richd.	D.C. 152	DENNIS, Abram	MON 150
DELACOUR, David	BCI 515	DELSHER, James	ANN 398	Ann	BCI 293
James	BCI 516	DELVILBISS, Susannah		Annias	WOR 205
DELAHAY, Edward	TAL 40		FRE 225	Benjamin	CEC 157
Henry	BCI 24	DEMAINE, Job	D.C. 156	Cata	SOM 124
Henry	TAL 31	DEMASTEE, Philip	PRI 228	Cata	SOM 124
Marke	TAL 32	DEMASTER, Philip (?)		Comfort	WOR 217
Mary	TAL 39		PRI 228	Durham	SOM 138
DELAHUTT, George	BCI 497	DEMBAR, Mary	BCI 308	Eleanor	SOM 139
DELAKUTT, George (?)		DEMBEY, Lydia	QUE 48	Frederick	BCI 60
	BCI 497	Robert	QUE 48	Geo.	WOR 192
DELAMAR, Robt.	D.C. 160	Thomas	QUE 26	Henry	ALL 24
DELANY, Andrew	FRE 68	Thomas	QUE 48	Henry	WOR 205
Easter	KEN 121	DEMBY, Henry	TAL 36	Henry; S.	WOR 200
Elizabeth	CEC 174	Richard	BCI 85	Henry; J.	WOR 200
James	D.C. 86	Samuel	TAL 34	James	BCI 445
John	BCI 45	DEMENT, Edward	CHA 205	Jas., Captn.	WOR 180
John	D.C. 91	Eleonor	SAI 65	Jesse	WOR 217
		George	CHA 189	John, Esqr.	WOR 158

65

DENNIS (continued),		DENT (continued),		DEVAN, Wm.	FRE 229
John; S.	WOR 200	Richd.	BCI 515	DEVANEY, Wm.	BCI 406
Johnson	WOR 200	Theophilus	CHA 220A	DEVANN, William	CAL 60
Lane	ANN 258	Thomas	DOR 51	DEVAUGHN, John	D.C. 201
Littleton	WOR 199A	William	SAI 69	Saml.	D.C. 183
Littleton, Esq.	WOR 156	William, senr.	CHA 190	Thos.	D.C. 111
Littleton P.	SOM 139	Zachariah, Senr.	CHA 221	DEVEDER, R.	BCI 398
Nathan	D.C. 113	Zachariah, Junr.	CHA 221	DEVENNEY, James	BCI 198
Neoma (of Geo.)	WOR 178	DENTON, James D.	CAL 43	DEVENPORT, Thomas	MON 150
Nias	WOR 200	John A.	CAL 49	DEVER, Moses	ANN 317
Philip	MON 150	Rezin	BCI 508	Hugh	HAR 78
Rebecca	CEC 122	Susanna-free	CAL 62	James	ANN 336
Robert, Esqr.	DOR 44	DENTTEN, Levin	WOR 211	Margaret	HAR 44
Sabour	TAL 10	DENTY, William	ANN 317	Michael	PRI 235
Sally	WOR 170	DEPISS, Ann	BCI 342	Robert	HAR 28
Sophia	BCI 121	DEPMAN, Elizh.	BCI 197	Samuel	HAR 39
Thomas	WOR 202	DEPUTY, Silvester	BAL 24	Thomas	HAR 19
Valentine	WOR 181	DEREW, Amri	CEC 175	DEVERBAUGH, Benjamin
Vallentine	WOR 217	DERGEN, John	BCI 19		ALL 35
Zadoc	SOM 136	DERHAM, Eliza	BCI 491	John	ALL 36
DENNISON, Elijah	ALL 33	Lloyd	BCI 479	Peter	ALL 32
Heziciah	WAS 89	Mary	BCI 473	DEVEREU, Patk.	D.C. 147
John	D.C. 54	DERINE, Valentine	BCI 519	DEVERIES, Christian	BAL 60
John	D.C. 85	DERK, Ann	BCI 311	DEVERING, Edward	BAL 210
Richard	BCI 87	DERKEY, Pearl	BCI 117	DEVERIX, Delia	QUE 18
Thomas	ALL 34	DERN, Fred. W.	BCI 370	Elizah	QUE 3
Thomas	D.C. 58	Frederick	ALL 35	Geo.	QUE 3
Thomas	WAS 89	Frederick	FRE 173	DEVERO, Francis	BCI 216
Thos.	BCI 481	Isaac	FRE 116	DEVICE, John	KEN 107
Thos.	D.C. 214	William	FRE 145	Mary	KEN 107
William	CEC 157	DERNING, James	BCI 125	DEVILBISS (See also DEL-
DENNISS, Ann	BCI 473	DEROCHBRUNE, Philip S.		VILBISS),
James	BCI 523		CLN 90	Adam	FRE 212
Littleton	SOM 155	Thomas	CLN 115	Becky	FRE 159
DENNY, Adam (negro)		DERONSEY, Charles	BCI 127	Casper	FRE 209
	TAL 24	DERR, Abraham	FRE 204	Casper	FRE 209
Benjamin	TAL 20	Abraham, Jr.	FRE 204	Catharine	FRE 161
Benjamin, Jr.	TAL 20	Elizabeth	D.C. 29	Charles	FRE 205
Benjamin, of Rd.	TAL 21	Jacob	FRE 102	David	FRE 212
Joseph	KEN 94	John	BAL 161	David	FRE 225
Joseph	TAL 20	John	FRE 117	George	FRE 215
Richard	TAL 20	John (Fuller)	FRE 163	John	ALL 37
Rudy	BCI 430	Thomas	FRE 117	John	FRE 225
Samuel	QUE 39	DERRICK, Susan	BCI 49	John (of Cas.)	FRE 162
William	ANN 321	DERROW, Samuel	BCI 303	Levi	FRE 209
William	BCI 2	DERRY, James	KEN 90	Samuel	FRE 160
DENOON, Elie	WAS 79	Joseph	KEN 90	William	FRE 180
Eliz.	D.C. 116	DERSCHBRUNE, Pere		DEVIRE, James	MON 143
James	WAS 109		CLN 94	DEVIT, Mary	FRE 214
DENSAR, Edward (?)		DERUMPLE, James	CEC 135	DEVITT, William	BCI 216
	ANN 400	DESANT, Lemo	BCI 504	DEVLING, Patrick	FRE 194
DENSLEY, Hugh	D.C. 117	Nicholas	BCI 488	DEVOE, John	HAR 38
DENSON, Ephraim	SOM 128	DESARE, Janet	BCI 216	DEVONISH, William	QUE 35
Isaac	SOM 111	DESHA, R. M.	D.C. 127	DE VOS, Peter Jno.	MON 159
James	SOM 111	DESHAM, Valentine	BCI 514	DEVOSS, William	BCI 325
John	BCI 71	DESHIELDS, Mary	BCI 20	DEW, Ann	BCI 174
Milby	SOM 125	DESHON, Christopher		James C.	BCI 155
Parker	SOM 134		BCI 119	William	BCI 118
William	WOR 188	Mary	BCI 293	DEWEES, Samuel	BAL 138
DENSTON, Nancy	WOR 218	DESNER, George	FRE 84	Willm.	D.C. 74
DENT, Alexander	CHA 205	DESPAUX, Alexander		DEWES, And	BCI 335
Ann Brooke	PRI 225		BCI 61	Simon	BAL 47
Benjamin	CHA 222	John	BCI 60	DEWEY, Eliza	BCI 71
Catharine	CHA 192	Joseph	BCI 59	DEWLAND, John	KEN 115
Eleanor	CHA 212	Thomas	BCI 63	DEWORD, Elizabeth	QUE 28
George	CHA 203	DETCHER, Hannah	D.C. 201	DEYMOND, Catharine	FRE 189
George	SAI 68	DETERICK, George	WAS 88	DEYOUNG, Michl.	BCI 250
Jane	CHA 203	Jacob	WAS 88	DEYSOT, Ruth	BCI 249
John B.	CHA 223	DETMAR, Elizabeth	BCI 456	DEZELLUM, James	MON 160
John B.	CHA 223	DETRADY, James	CEC 135	DIAL, David	CHA 195
John B. E.	CHA 220A	DETRICK, Philip	FRE 215	DIALE, Danniel	WOR 206
John C.	ANN 335	DETTROW, John	WAS 73	Elijah (?)	WOR 206
Leonard	CHA 228	DEUON, Henry	BCI 220	DIBB, James	BAL 109
Margaritta	CHA 206	DEUVALE, Aquilla	ANN 365	DIBERT, Christian	WAS 56
Mary	CHA 207	Edward	ANN 381	DIC, James (?)	WAS 63
Nathan S.	CHA 206	DE VAL COUR, Alexr.		John	WAS 69
Peter	CHA 221		BCI 247		

Name	Loc
DISHEROON, James?	WOR 217
DISNEY, --- (Mrs.)	BCI 392
Harry	CEC 157
James	ANN 287
James	ANN 334
James	BCI 369
James	BCI 487
James, Junr.	ANN 340
John	ANN 335
John	BCI 501
Margaret	ANN 392
Richard	ANN 339
Richard	ANN 350
Richard of Edwd.	ANN 339
Richard, of Jas.	ANN 340
Richard, of Thos.	ANN 339
Samuel	BCI 395
Snowden	BAL 181
Thomas	DOR 3
Thomas of Wm.	ANN 340
Westley	BCI 492
William	ANN 335
William	ANN 347
William	BCI 432
William of Ths.	ANN 340
William J. (I.?)	ANN 332
DISSELL, James	MON 150
DISSNEY, Peter	BCI 401
DITMAN, John	BCI 156
DITMORE, Henry	BCI 249
DITTO, Abraham	WAS 136
David	BCI 13
DITTON, Allexd.	BCI 337
DIVENPORT, David	BCI 379
DIVERS, Christopher	BAL 240
Henry	BAL 236
William	HAR 45
DIVILL, Whelhelm	WAS 96
DIVINNY, George	CEC 135
DIVINPORT, Joseph	BCI 417
DIX, George	SAI 76
John	D.C. 79
John	D.C. 192
Jonas	D.C. 34
Mary	WOR 177
Patty	SOM 147
DIXEN, Elisha	TAL 31
Joshua	TAL 46
DIXERSON, Gidion	BAL 184
DIXON, --- (?)	BCI 386
--- (?)	BCI 411
Ben	QUE 20
Betty (of J. (I.?)	SOM 151
Catharine	CHA 207
David	CEC 175
Edward	PRI 225
Elizabeth (of Wm.)	SOM 142A
Frances	MON 162
George	BCI 409
George	CHA 214
George L.	CHA 213
Hanes	FRE 117
Hezakia	WAS 145
Isaac	SOM 147
Isack	BAL 23
James	BAL 130
James	CAL 45
James	D.C. 41
James	FRE 107
James	TAL 51
Jessy (Cold.)	SOM 147
Joe (Negro)	HAR 29
John	ANN 384
John	CLN 73
John	CEC 175
John	CHA 212

Name	Loc
DIXON (continued),	
John	HAR 7
John, Jur.	CEC 175
Joseph	CAL 66A
Joseph	CHA 218
Moses	D.C. 161
Nathaniel	WOR 173
Patrick	CHA 222
Rachel	BAL 247
Rachel	KEN 119
Rachel	WAS 151
Robert	TAL 24
Sally	SOM 151
Sally S. (Mrs.)	CAL 43
Sally T.? (Mrs.)	CAL 43
Samuel	BAL 118
Susan	SAI 91
Thomas	CEC 122
Thomas	CEC 157
Thomas	D.C. 36
Thomas	DOR 20
Thomas	SAI 80
Thos.	CAL 50
Walter G.	CHA 196A
William	BAL 192
William	BCI 112
William	CHA 214
William	SAI 57
Wm.	WAS 145
DIXSON, Ambey?	WOR 218
Harrison	BCI 337
James	WOR 173
Jonas	KEN 107
Leah-Wd.	WOR 220
Naah	DOR 26
Noah?	DOR 26
Nutter	WOR 204
Peter	WOR 204
Sampson	WOR 220
Samuel	WOR 220
Susan, wd.	WOR 213
Wm.	BCI 339
DIZE, Feilde	SOM 146
John, Senr.	SOM 149
John, Junr.	SOM 149
Richard	SOM 152
William	SOM 131
DOBBIN, Archibald	BCI 91
Catharine	BCI 130
John	BCI 305
John	MON 164
DOBBINS, John	HAR 9
William	BCI 302
DOBLER, John	BCI 196
DOBSON, Abraham	TAL 36
Cassy	TAL 48
Delia	DOR 8
Dolly	DOR 9
Isaac	TAL 48
James	QUE 38
Jessee	TAL 14A
Matthew	BCI 229
Pompy	TAL 48
William	TAL 14A
DOCKER, Jane	D.C. 102
DOCKIN, Richd.	BCI 345
DODA, Julian	BCI 178
DODD, Charles	BCI 15
Eben	QUE 11
Henry	TAL 47
James	CLN 87
James	D.C. 39
Mark	QUE 30
Thos.	QUE 7
William	D.C. 18

Name	Loc
DODDRELL, James C.	BCI 418
DODDS, Andrew	FRE 176
John	FRE 180
Joseph	D.C. 144
Robert	FRE 201
DODGE, Francis	D.C. 45
DODGING, Francis	D.C. 16
DODLEY, Anna	BCI 350
DODSAN, Henry	PRI 207
DODSON, Barton	CHA 217
Betsey	CHA 195
James	TAL 23
John S.	PRI 235
Luckey	ANN 400
Midleton	PRI 235
Priscilla	FRE 187
Robert	TAL 23
Samuel	PRI 235
Thomas	KEN 95
William	KEN 114
William	TAL 23
Wm.	KEN 124
DODY, Marey	BCI 391
DOFFMAN, Thomas	BCI 59
DOFLER, George	FRE 117
DOGEN, John	D.C. 207
DOHERTY, --- (Mrs.)	FRE 143
Henry	HAR 70
Moses-Negro	HAR 49
Rachel	HAR 70
Samuel	HAR 46
DOLAN, Lawrence	BCI 255
Peter	BCI 409
DOLIN, Edward	BCI 67
DOLL, Catharine	FRE 101
George	FRE 97
Jacob	FRE 101
John	FRE 106
Michael	FRE 101
DOLLEY, Stephen	DOR 8
DOLLIHIDE, James	FRE 158
DOLLIS, Thos.	KEN 120
DOLPHIN, Jacob	TAL 8
DOLSON, James	CAL 43
DOLVICHIO, Petr. (?)	BCI 376
DOMAIN, Julious	BCI 524
DOMAN, Ann	KEN 115
Daniel	KEN 116
Joe	KEN 122
DOMER, Daniel	FRE 163
Dorathy	FRE 163
Hugh	WAS 62
DOMINICK, Rachel	CLN 80
DOMONICK, --- (?)	BCI 465
DONAHOE, Teague	WOR 212
DONAHOO, Daniel	HAR 27
John	HAR 18
DONALD, Thomas	D.C. 50
DONALDSON, --- (Doct.)	BCI 386
--- (Mrs.)	BCI 461
--- (Widaw)	BCI 384
Aaron	BCI 53
Benjn.	D.C. 217
Daniel	BCI 150
John	WAS 115
John J.	BCI 272
Joseph	BCI 438
Lewis	D.C. 191
Richard	ANN 324
Richard	BCI 384
Robert	CEC 135
Robt.	D.C. 211

DORSEY (continued),	
Michl.	D.C. 98
Milly	D.C. 150
Mortimer	ANN 365
Nace	BCI 308
Nerse	DOR 14
Nichl. W. (?)	MON 141
Nicholas	ANN 321
Nicholas	ANN 327
Nicholas	BAL 47
Nicholas	BAL 61
Nicholas	BAL 77
Noah	ANN 327
Owen	BCI 513
Peter	ANN 367
Peter	FRE 147
Rachl.	PRI [200]
Reescaw	BAL 64
Richard	ANN 323
Richard	ANN 365
Richard B.	MON 150
Roderick	ANN 359
Ruscaw?	BAL 64
Ruth H.	ANN 366
Samuel	FRE 71
Samuel F.	FRE 215
Sarah	CEC 174
Simon-Negro	HAR 79
Sophia	BAL 47
Stephen H.	CEC 174
Thomas	ANN 381
Thomas	BAL 108
Thomas	SOM 146
Thomas B.	ANN 350
Thomas Beal, of Thos.	ANN 376
Thomas H.	ANN 292
Umphrey	ANN 366
Upton	FRE 215
Vachiel	FRE 212
Walter	BAL 192
William	ANN 376
William C.	CEC 157
William E.	CEC 174
William E.	CEC 175
Wm.	BAL 83
DORSON, Isaac	WAS 147
DORUS, Francis	BCI 7
DORY, Betty	SOM 133
DOSEN, --- (?)	BCI 409
DOSEY, John B.	BCI 523
Louisa	BCI 517
DOSH, Rebecca	BCI 299
DOSSEY, Benja. of James	CAL 46
Benja. S.	CAL 47
David	CAL 45
Francis	CAL 53A
James	CAL 50
James, of John	CAL 44
John S.	CAL 49
Mary	CAL 68
Michael	PRI 185
Prindowell M.	CAL 67
Samuel of John	CAL 52
Samuel Y.	CAL 49
Somersett	CAL 53A
Thomas	CAL 47
Walter?	CAL 59
Watter	CAL 59
William C. (?)	CEC 157
Young	CAL 67
DOSSY, Samuel	CAL 67
DOTSON, Elijah	FRE 209
James (?)	CAL 43
James	CAL 47

DOTSON (continued),	
James, Jun.	CAL 51
DOTTON, John	BAL 197
DOUB, Jacob	FRE 87
DOUBLEDAY, Joshua	ANN 293
DOUD, John	MON 162
DOUDS, George	FRE 148
DOUGHERTY, Danl.	D.C. 179
Dennis	CEC 135
James	BCI 315
James	D.C. 73
John	BCI 460
John	FRE 160
John	FRE 193
Joseph	BCI 275
Nancy	SOM 140
Neal	BCI 454
Patrick	CEC 135
Patrick	FRE 151
DOUGHTY, James	FRE 211
Willm.	D.C. 137
DOUGLAS, Jacob	D.C. 183
James	D.C. 183
John	D.C. 153
John	D.C. 203
Richard L.	PRI 224
Samuel	FRE 180
Susanna	D.C. 207
DOUGLASS, Benjamin	CHA 216
Casandra	BCI 457
Daniel	D.C. 18
David	CEC 175
Edward (?)	D.C. 13
Eliz.	D.C. 102
Geo.	BCI 293
Godshall	MON 131
Hannah	DOR 59
Henry	D.C. 112
Hugh	MON 136
Jane	D.C. 7
Jno.	MON 130
John	CLN 87
John	D.C. 58
John	D.C. 92
John	SOM 107
John L.	BCI 438
Joseph	CLN 107
Levi	ANN 327
Robert	WAS 113A
Saml.	MON 132
Thomas	ANN 320
William	CEC 175
William	SOM 114
York	DOR 9
DOUGLES, Peter	BCI 200
DOULAN, Nicholas (C. Man)	BCI 269
DOULY, James	BAL 120
DOUNEY, Valentine	QUE 24
DOUNY, John E.	QUE 33
DOUP, Henry	FRE 127
John	FRE 132
DOUTY, James (?)	BAL 120
DOVE, Adam	BCI 39
James	TAL 9
Jeremh.	D.C. 158
Jilson	D.C. 166
John	CAL 51
John	D.C. 92
John	MON 150
Joseph	D.C. 80
Marmdke.	D.C. 127
Saml.	D.C. 91
Samuel	ANN 279

DOVE (continued),	
Thomas	D.C. 16
William	ANN 279
William G.	HAR 7
Zachh.	D.C. 163
DOVEE, Punch	PRI 237
DOVER, Alexander	D.C. 24
Geo.	D.C. 106
Jas.	D.C. 106
Julian	BCI 315
Moses (?)	ANN 317
Punch (?)	PRI 237
DOWALLY, James	BCI 151
DOWBOKER, Adam	BCI 482
DOWD, Ann	BCI 53
DOWDEN, Adam, col'd.	BAL 216
Isaac	BCI 144
James H.	MON 159
Michael	BCI 304
Nicholas	BAL 181
Solomon, col'd.	BAL 216
Thomas	ALL 26
Zachr.	MON 141
DOWDLE, William	FRE 102
DOWEL, Harrison	CAL 43
John	CAL 42
DOWELL, Francis S.	CAL 60
Harrison	CAL 60
Henry	CAL 65
Hillery	CAL 60
John	CAL 61
Sarah	CAL 65
William	CAL 61
DOWLASS, Robert	BCI 522
DOWLER, James C.	WAS 145
DOWLIN, Hezekiah	CEC 122
DOWLING, Anthy.	D.C. 207
Eliphalet	KEN 86
John	BCI 48
Michl.	D.C. 75
Patk.	D.C. 86
Patrick	BCI 168
William	BCI 73
William	D.C. 73
DOWNES, Benjamin	CLN 78
Charles	CLN 82
Charles	CLN 111
Edwd. P.	D.C. 145
George	CHA 212
Hawkins	CLN 95
Isaac	CLN 90
Jacob-free	CAL 61
Joseph (?)	D.C. 60
Lott	CLN 91
William	CLN 81
Wm.	QUE 18
DOWNEY, Edmund	BCI 442
George (?)	BAL 157
Howell	BCI 527
James	BAL 116
James	KEN 86
Robert	BAL 130
Walter	BAL 162
William	BCI 432
William	FRE 69
William	FRE 75
William	KEN 93
Wm.	BCI 528
DOWNING, John	BCI 325
John	KEN 88
John	WAS 110
John	WAS 136
John	WOR 202
Joseph	D.C. 92
Margaret	BCI 121

DOWNING (continued),		DRAKE (continued),		DRURA, Elizabeth (?)	
William	QUE 37	Mathew	BCI 298		DOR 62
William H.	QUE 34	Willard	D.C. 80	George	SOM 139
DOWNS, --- (Mrs.)	D.C. 97	William	BCI 28	Stephen	SOM 128
Ann	BCI 279	DRANE, James	ALL 7	DRURY, Bennedict	CHA 204
Ann	PRI 232	James, Jun.	ALL 5A	Charles	ANN 289
Benjamin	QUE 26	Richard	ALL 7	Enoch	SAI 81
Benjamin	QUE 41	DRAPER, Elisha	CLN 89	Henry C.	ANN 262
Benjamin	WAS 83	Garretson	BCI 285	Henry C. of Chs.	ANN 263
C. (Dr.)-his quarter		Lewis	CLN 75	John C.	D.C. 160
	QUE 19	Margarett	CLN 100	Joseph, overseer of	
Charles	PRI 231	Sarah	BAL 186	Clement DORSEY	
Daphne	QUE 39	Thomas	FRE 162		SAI 81
Delila	D.C. 147	William	CLN 89	Journingham	ANN 280
Fanny	BCI 305	William	FRE 129	Leonarce?	WAS 135
Hawkins	QUE 27	William	FRE 161	Leonard	WAS 135
Hector (negro)	TAL 19	DRAUGH, Adam	FRE 198	Mary	SAI 66
Henery	BAL 99	DRAUGHBAUGH, Valentine		Mary	SAI 80
Isaiah	BCI 533		Bal 208	Mary	SAI 82
Jacob	WOR 206	DRAY, Margrett	BCI 275	Michael	SAI 79
Jacob (of ---)	WOR 206	Sesar	FRE 79	Peter	SAI 77
James	BAL 175	DREES, Nics.	D.C. 165	Peter, agent to	
James	BCI 88	DRENEN, Samuel	CEC 135	Emily BOWLING	SAI 78
Jesse	BAL 105	DRESSLER, Henry	FRE 150	Plato	ANN 274
John	BCI 504	Jacob	FRE 150	Plummer	ANN 262
John H.	D.C. 107	DREW, Martha	HAR 24	Samuel	ANN 274
Joseph	BAL 175	Mary	D.C. 162	Samuel	CAL 64
Joseph	BCI 304	Mary H.	BCI 127	William	ANN 268
Joseph	SAI 76	Nancy	D.C. 156	William	BCI 84
Joshua	BCI 195	Samuel	ANN 350	William	SAI 78
Joshua	WOR 206	Solomon	D.C. 176	DRYDEN, Ann	BCI 498
Jubie	TAL 8	Susan	D.C. 206	Isaac	WOR 218
Lyda	QUE 39	DREWETTS, William	BAL 246	Isaac (of Isaac)	WOR 180
Mary	D.C. 71	DREWRY, Samuel	D.C. 35	James	WOR 179
Mary	D.C. 148	William	SAI 90	John	SOM 156
Nathan H.	QUE 29	DRIDEN, James	SOM 128	John of S. (I.?)	WOR 217
Rebecca	WOR 206	Joshua	BCI 388	John of S. (J.?)	WOR 217
Robert	WOR 206	Mills	SOM 128	Joshua	WOR 212
Robert S.	BAL 214	DRIFF, Richard	BCI 411	Katy	SOM 155
Saml.	D.C. 167	DRIGGS, Nathaniel	BCI 148	Ruth	WOR 163
Soloman	BCI 457	DRIGGUS, John	CLN 79	Samuel	WOR 217
William	ANN 340	DRIK, David	D.C. 143	Sarah	SOM 155
William	SAI 76	DRILL, Andrew	FRE 122	Thomas	WOR 213
William, Sen.	WAS 83	Christian	FRE 127	William	WOR 209
William, Jun.	WAS 83	George	FRE 122	William	WOR 213
Zachariah	MON 150	Jacob	FRE 123	DUBARRY, ---	BCI 152
DOWSON, A. R.	D.C. 109	Joseph	FRE 128	DUBBERLY, Lacum	SOM 126
DOWYE, Willam	BAL 122	DRINKER, George	D.C. 181	DUBERNARD, William	
DOXEY, Joseph	SAI 56	DRISKELL, Roland	WOR 212		BCI 296
Josiah	SAI 56	DRISKILL, Aaron	WOR 215	DUBERRY, Mary	BAL 121
Mary	SAI 56	Benjn.	WOR 173	DUBLIN, George	BAL 123
DOXTON, Milley	SAI 97	Moses	WOR 215	Jahannah	ANN 292
DOXY, Bisco S.	BCI 94	Sally, Wd.	WOR 212	Joseph	KEN 91
DOYHER, Henry F.	BCI 192	DRITT, Joseph (?)	FRE 128	Mark	PRI 185
DOYL, James	BCI 502	DRIVER, Baccus	CLN 100	Michael-free	CAL 63
John G.	FRE 73	Henry	CLN 98	Rachel	BCI 295
Stephen	BCI 481	James	BAL 63	Richard	D.C. 51
DOYLE, George	WAS 114	John	DOR 12	DUBOIS, John (Revd.)	
James	BCI 149	Joseph	CLN 97	Prest. of St. Marys	
John	CEC 174	Matthew	CLN 88	Seminary	FRE 153
Mary	FRE 97	Sampson	CLN 96	DUBUCT, Marc	BCI 56
Patrick	BCI 5	DRONINBURGH, Jacob		DUCAN, John	BCI 25
Patrick	BCI 70		FRE 81	DUCAS, Peter	BCI 341
DOZSEY, William C. (?)		DROW, Thomas	QUE 41	DUCATE, Samuel	PRI 221A
	CEC 157	DRUBY, David	WAS 98	DUCATEL, --- (Doctr.)	
DRAGGON, Mary Ann		DRUDGE, Geo.	D.C. 106		BCI 466
	D.C. 188	James	PRI 185	Edme	BCI 231
DRAGGOU, Mary Ann (?)		DRUETT, James	D.C. 8	DUCATT, Samuel (?)	
	D.C. 188	DRUGER, Nancy	D.C. 53		PRI 221A
DRAIN, Anthony	PRI 194	DRULY, --- (?)	BCI 404	DUCK, Thomas	BCI 305
David	D.C. 68	DRUMM, Hugh	PRI 181	DUCKER, Fanny	MON 140
John	BCI 32	DRUMMER, Isaac	BAL 224	John T.	MON 139
DRAKE, Edward	ALL 24	DRUMMOND, Hugh (?)		Moses	D.C. 62
John	BCI 69		PRI 181	DUCKERY, Tom	QUE 15
Julia	D.C. 195	James	FRE 168	DUCKETT, Harkulus	
Julia	D.C. 197	Joseph	BCI 455		WAS 69

DUCKETT (continued),		
James	PRI	202
John	PRI	202
Richard	PRI	204
Richard	PRI	205
Ruthey	WAS	69
Sophia	PRI	205
DUCKHEART, Henry	BCI	177
DUCKWORTH, Alice	BAL	202
Aron	ALL	13
Geo.	D.C.	123
George	ALL	13
Henry	ALL	3
John	ALL	13
John	D.C.	94
Matthias	ALL	13
Uriah	ALL	13
William	ALL	13
DUDDERAR, Daved	FRE	220
Daver?	FRE	220
David	FRE	210
John	FRE	210
William	FRE	210
William	FRE	224
DUDDERO, Conrod	FRE	79A
DUDDLEY, Ann	KEN	115
DUDDRO, Benjamin	BAL	55
DUDDY, Henry	BCI	99
DUDELL, James	KEN	102
DUDERER, Frederick	FRE	173
John	FRE	174
DUDLELEY, John (?)	QUE	32
DUDLEY, Barbara	QUE	20
Dinah	D.C.	188
Elizabeth	KEN	90
Emanuel	QUE	11
James	D.C.	169
James	QUE	4
John	TAL	48
Julia	BCI	230
Nicholas	KEN	87
Rebeccah	KEN	93
Rebeccat?	KEN	93
Richard	TAL	5
Robert B.	TAL	8A
Thomas	TAL	52
Willm.	D.C.	187
Wm.	QUE	15
DUDROW, George	FRE	196
John	FRE	82
John	FRE	196
Philip	FRE	82
DUE, Jesse	CAL	64
Samuel	CAL	63
Thomas	CAL	65
DUEGAN, Pue	KEN	105
DUEL, Edward	BCI	277
DUER, John	BCI	379
Joshua	WOR	154
Samuel M.	SOM	128
DUESBERRY, Elizh.	BCI	173
DUFF, --- (Mrs.)	D.C.	78
Charles	ANN	299
George	BCI	167
Hector	ANN	310
James	D.C.	211
John	D.C.	77
John	HAR	40
Thomas	HAR	41
Wm.	BCI	223
DUFFENBARGER, John		
	WAS	67
DUFFEY, Tarence	CHA	214
DUFFIELD, John P.	WOR	170
DUFFIN, James	BCI	36
Susanna	FRE	100

DUFFY, Daniel	WOR	210
Eliza	WOR	212
Elizabeth	D.C.	53
George	D.C.	167
Jacob	WOR	219
James	BCI	452
John	CEC	122
John	D.C.	126
John	SOM	125
Mary	WOR	219
Sebastion	FRE	146
Soloman	SOM	133
Willm.	D.C.	166
DUFIEF, Sheridan	D.C.	46
DUGAN, Cumberland	BCI	243
Edward	WAS	136
George	BCI	436
John	KEN	103
Thomas	KEN	102
Wm. Y.	WAS	148
DUGAS, Lewis	BAL	197
DUGEN, John	WAS	151
DUGER, Hugh	CEC	135
DUGGINS, Henry	WAS	106
DUGLASS, George	BCI	131
George	BCI	268
DUGO, Edward (?)	BAL	23
DUHADWAY, Thomas	CLN	113
DUHAMEL, Ben.	QUE	12
Henry	QUE	12
Isaac	QUE	15
Juliet	QUE	4
DUHAMELL, Ann	QUE	34
James	QUE	34
Samuel	QUE	35
DUHAMOL, Ben. (?)	QUE	12
Henry (?)	QUE	12
DUHAZE, Joseph	ANN	265
DUHEN, Nancy (?)	WAS	150
DUKE, Basil	CAL	43
Bill-Negro	HAR	49
James	CAL	43
Joseph	BCI	309
William	CEC	135
DUKEATEL, Edmon	BAL	210
DUKEHART, John	BCI	251
Valerius	BCI	251
DUKEMAN, Peter	BCI	501
DUKEN, Nancy (?)	WAS	150
DUKER, Geo.	BCI	367
DUKES, Aaron	CLN	94
Connill (?)	WOR	210
Cornelius? (?)	WOR	210
Daniel	CLN	93
George	QUE	35
James	CLN	93
John	WOR	163
John	SAI	69
Levi	CLN	114
Melven	WOR	211
Nancy	WOR	217
Parker	WOR	174
Thomas	CLN	107
Thos.	WOR	161
William	CLN	105
Willson	CLN	106
DULAND, Risden	CLN	92
DULANY, Benjamin	CEC	135
Benjamin T.	CHA	212
Elizth.	D.C.	184
John	KEN	106
Joseph	HAR	23
Joshua	HAR	23
Judith	BCI	230
Mathew	D.C.	53
Moses	CEC	175

DULANY (continued),		
Thomas	D.C.	73
William	PRI	213
DULBY, William	BCI	64
DULEN, George	DOR	12
DULEY, Aquilla	MON	166
Barlon?	MON	166
Barton	MON	166
Bennedict H.	MON	150
Erasmus	MON	150
Jonathan	D.C.	26
Jonathan	MON	150
Joseph	MON	149
Thos.	MON	140
William	HAR	7
William	MON	150
DULIN, James	KEN	120
John	TAL	38
Reuben	CLN	73
William	BCI	314
DULING, Margarett	TAL	3
Samuel, Ovsr.	TAL	39
Thomas	TAL	2
DULL, Jacob	FRE	128
Jacob, Senr.	FRE	132
William	D.C.	63
DULLUM, Zachariah	BAL	121
DULOUS, M.	BCI	211
DULY, Jazeel	CHA	201
John	CHA	201
DUMAS, Peter	BCI	250
DUMBLETON, Jno.	D.C.	111
DUMBURG, Godfrey?	BCI	537
Goofrey	BCI	537
DUMEGIL, Jas.	BCI	219
DUMEST, Eliza.	BCI	512
DUMFRIES, Mary	BAL	221
DUMMERS, William	CEC	135
DUN, Arthur	BAL	196
Charles	QUE	46
George (?)	WAS	149
Jacob (?)	WAS	149
DUNADREW, Peter	BCI	218
DUNAN, Lewis M.	BCI	212
DUNAVANE, John	DOR	4
DUNAWAY, John	WOR	193
Polly	WOR	193
Sophia	WOR	193
William	FRE	100
DUNBAR, Alexander	D.C.	58
Charles	BCI	454
Edward	SAI	56
George T.	BCI	438
Henry	ANN	309
Jenny	D.C.	64
John A.	SAI	57
Peter	D.C.	201
William	CEC	122
William	SAI	56
William	SAI	89
DUNBARR, Andrew	CEC	175
DUNBROOK, Henry	BCI	55
DUNCAN, Alexander	KEN	87
Ben	WOR	192
Betsy	SOM	155
Deborah	ANN	275
James	ALL	23
James	BAL	52
James	HAR	59
James	WOR	201
Jas.	BCI	256
John	BCI	444
John	HAR	9
John Mason	BCI	259
Joseph	BAL	5
Joseph	WOR	195

DUNCAN (continued),			DUNNING (continued),			DURST (continued),		
Levi	WOR	200	Margaret	BCI	135	Jacob	ALL	9
Milby	WOR	185	Nathaniel	PRI	231	John F.	BCI	335
Thos.	WOR	175	Zacariah	PRI	223	DURUM, John	BCI	355
William	BAL	5	DUNNINGTON, Francis E.			DUSHANE, Cornelious		
DUNDAS, Eliza	D.C.	204		CHA	190		BCI	481
DUNDON, Christiana	WAS	109	James B.	CHA	189	John	BCI	370
DUNDY, Simon	QUE	16	John P.	CHA	190	DUSHIMA, --- (Widaw)		
DUNGAN, Charlotty	BAL	187	Jonathan F.	CHA	189		BCI	372
David	FRE	153	Margaret	CHA	196	DUSING, Philip	WAS	117
Henry	FRE	175	Nathan	CHA	191	DUSSINGER, John	WAS	93
Henry M.	D.C.	138	Peter	CHA	189	DUTEROW, Conrad	FRE	160
Wm.	BCI	412	Roger	CHA	196	DUTROW, Eliza	FRE	122
DUNCIN, Benjamin	SOM	147	Thomas	CHA	201	George	FRE	122
DUNHAM, Samuel	BCI	139	Walter W.	CHA	193	John	FRE	132
DUNKEL, E. (Doct.)	BCI	380	William W.	CHA	192	DUTTON, Anny (free		
DUNKIN, Benjamin	CEC	122	Wm.	BCI	535	negro)	SOM	118
Catherine	SOM	110	DUNNOC, John	DOR	28	Charles	DOR	42
Chris	BCI	519	Margret	DOR	28	Esther	SOM	133
Darah	CEC	122	Thomas	DOR	28	George	HAR	31
Henry	WOR	172	DUNNOCK, Samuel (?)			Guy	HAR	31
Peregrine	BCI	67		DOR	28	Hub	BAL	61
Solomon	BCI	141	DUNPHY, John	D.C.	89	James	CHA	200A
DUNKINSON, Robert	SAI	55	DUNSAN, William (?)			Jenny	SOM	135
DUNKLER, Ann	D.C.	121		BAL	5	John	BCI	90
DUNKLEY, Robert	BAL	2	DUNWOODY, Robert	BAL	107	John W.	BCI	87
DUNLAP, Henry	D.C.	12	DUPADEA, --- (Mrs.)			Lilly	DOR	42
James	FRE	155		BCI	455	Notley	CHA	201
James	MON	164	DUPLE, Jonathan	WAS	125	Robert	BCI	61
Willm.	D.C.	167	DUPORT, P. L.	D.C.	72	Roger	SOM	133
DUNLOP, Geo.	MON	135	DUPPIN, Ceasar	FRE	199	Rose	SOM	133
James	D.C.	39	DUPPING, John	D.C.	102	Silvah	DOR	42
James, jun.	D.C.	36	DUPPRA, Edward (?)			Stephen	SOM	137
Joseph	PRI	239		ANN	260	Thomas (?)	BAL	79
DUNMEAD, John	BAL	233	DURANG, John	BCI	175	DUVAL, Edwd. W.	D.C.	91
DUNN, Benjamin	BCI	91	DURBIN, Benjamin	ALL	23	Horace	D.C.	86
Charles	BCI	139	Elijah	ALL	17	Nathan	BCI	444
Daniel	BCI	150	Ephraim	FRE	198	Sarah	ALL	6
Darius	KEN	91	Honour	FRE	197	Washn.	D.C.	121
Edward	FRE	198	John	HAR	31	DUVALE, Amon	PRI	194
Elinor	BCI	23	John, Sen.	ALL	15	Charles	PRI	184
Ellen	D.C.	90	John, Jr.	ALL	16	Dennis (?)	PRI	181
George	ANN	401	Mary	FRE	191	Massum (?)	PRI	181
Hugh	D.C.	101	Nicholas	FRE	191	DUVALL, Abraham	ANN	342
James	D.C.	32	Samuel	ALL	23	Amon (?)	PRI	194
James	SOM	109	Susannah	FRE	188	Barton	PRI	186
John	ANN	388	Thomas W.	FRE	191	Beal	ANN	350
John	BCI	384	William	FRE	193	Beal	PRI	181
John	D.C.	122	William, Jr.	FRE	193	Benjamin	FRE	70
John	SOM	113	DURDEN, Charles	D.C.	96	Benjamin, of Lisha.	PRI	235
John	WAS	133	DURDING, William R.			Benjn.	HAR	6
Levi	DOR	61		KEN	87	Charles (?)	PRI	184
Moses	SOM	109	DURGAN, John	BCI	118	Cornelius	ANN	288
Patrick	ANN	394	DURGIN, James	BCI	70	Dennis	PRI	181
Rhoday (f.n.)	SOM	119	DURHAM, Abel	HAR	62	Eli	PRI	181
Richard, Senr.	SOM	114	Abraham	HAR	62	Elijah	FRE	211
Richard, Junr.	SOM	114	Ann	BAL	187	Elizabeth	ANN	303
Richardson	CEC	175	Hannah	SOM	149	F. J. L.?	PRI	181
Robert	BCI	386	Isaac	FRE	201	F. P. L.	PRI	181
Samuel	D.C.	19	John H.	SOM	110	Gabriel	PRI	185
Thomas	SOM	113	Mary	HAR	8	George	PRI	182
Thos.	D.C.	100	Saml.	BCI	480	Grafton	FRE	131
William	BCI	57	Sarah	HAR	63	Henry	ANN	313
William	BCI	177	Thomas	HAR	62	Henry	ANN	403
Wm.	BCI	375	Wm.	HAR	60	Howard	ANN	283
DUNNAC, Edward	DOR	35	Zechariah	BAL	210	Isaac	PRI	181
John (?)	DOR	28	DURILY, Natl.	D.C.	124	Isaiah	BAL	37
DUNNACK, Samuel	DOR	28	DURM, J.	BCI	413	James	FRE	69
DUNNAGAN, John	BCI	285	DURMUNN, Moses	BCI	429	Jemima	ANN	313
DUNNAM, Jacobb	BCI	29	DURNOTT, Francis	D.C.	213	John	CEC	157
DUNNAVAN, John	WAS	146	DURRIMPLE, Thomas			John	FRE	72
DUNNCK, Jeseph (?)	BAL	79		WAS	79	John	PRI	219
DUNNEK, Jeseph	BAL	79	DURRUM, Josiah	BCI	32	John, of M.	ANN	288
DUNNING, Butler	CHA	225	DURRY, Ignatius	WAS	83	John W.	ANN	393
John	D.C.	104	DURST, Christian	ALL	8A	Lewis	ANN	317
John H.	CHA	225	Henry	ALL	9	Lewis	ANN	390

EASTWOOD, John W.	PRI 212	
EATON, Anderton	CLN 113	
Curtis	DOR 64	
David	HAR 72	
Dennis	CLN 105	
Isaac	FRE 84	
James	TAL 45	
Jessee	CLN 109	
John	ANN 263	
John	CLN 94	
John	CLN 114	
John	FRE 87	
Juda	TAL 20	
Levi	CLN 95	
Levin	CLN 107	
Mary	DOR 64	
Mary	FRE 87	
Nancy	CLN 111	
Nathan	D.C.73	
Rachael	FRE 83	
Rebecca	BAL 97	
Richard	PRI 203	
EBAUGH, Conrad	BAL 151	
George, Esqr.	BAL 159	
Henry	BAL 148	
John (K.?)	BAL 143	
EBBERT, Geo.	FRE 126	
George	BCI 530	
EBBERTS, Jacob	FRE 225	
EBE, John	WAS 93	
EBERHARD, Conrad	BCI 458	
EBERT, George A.	FRE 97	
John	FRE 95	
John	FRE 102	
John	WAS 119	
Samuel	BCI 133	
EBERTS, Joseph	FRE 106	
Michael	FRE 106	
EBSWIRTH, Geo. D.	BCI 210	
ECCDES, Eliza	BCI 281	
ECCLESTON, James	DOR 60	
John H.	DOR 51	
Providence	KEN 100	
Thomas I.(?) H.	DOR 7	
Thomas J. H.	DOR 7	
Valentine	QUE 40	
William W.	DOR 64	
ECETOR, A. (Doct.)	BCI 521	
ECH, John (?)	FRE 180	
Peter (?)	FRE 180	
Theodore (?)	FRE 180	
ECHEL, Sarah	BCI 476	
ECHENRODE, John	FRE 172	
ECK, John	FRE 180	
Peter	FRE 180	
Theodore	FRE 180	
ECKARD, George	FRE 181	
ECKEL, P. P.	BCI 188	
ECKENRODE, John (?)	FRE 172	
ECKER, Christopher	FRE 201	
David	BAL 56	
Jacob, Sr.	FRE 199	
Jacob, Jr.	FRE 199	
John	FRE 192	
ECKERD, John	ALL 16	
ECKHART, Jacob	D.C.79	
ECXISS, Samuel	FRE 99	
ECKLE, Charles	D.C.45	
ECKLEBERGER, Elizabeth	BCI 140	
ECKLEBURGER, Frederick	FRE 196	
ECKLER, Uhlerick	FRE 186	
ECKLES, Richard	ALL 6	
Samuel	ALL 30	
ECKLOFF, Christr.	D.C.77	
ECKMAN, George	FRE 155	
John	FRE 156	
William	FRE 160	
ECKMON, William	FRE 199	
ECOFF, David	HAR 47	
ECTON, James	PRI 218	
John	PRI 230	
Leteclus	PRI 230	
EDDICK, Jarrett	BCI 425	
EDDY, Ralph	BCI 440	
Susan	BCI 146	
EDELEN, Alexlus	CHA 207	
Aloyslus	PRI 222	
Edward	CHA 200A	
Edward, Senr.	CHA 202	
Edward, Junr.	CHA 206	
Edward C.	PRI 235	
Elstan A.	CHA 207	
Fanny	PRI 222	
Francis	CHA 206	
Francis	CHA 213	
Francis	PRI 237	
George	CHA 213	
George	PRI 225	
George S.	CHA 214	
Horatio	CHA 203	
Jacob	PRI 227	
John B.	CHA 196A	
John J.	PRI 227	
Joseph	PRI 222	
Joseph T.	PRI 227	
Leonard	SAI 77	
Lewis	CHA 196A	
Mary Ann	PRI 227	
Oswell	CHA 202	
Raphel C.	PRI 222	
Richard	SAI 81	
Robert	PRI 225	
Stanislaus	CHA 196A	
Susanna	PRI 225	
Susanna	PRI 227	
Thomas	PRI 215	
William	CHA 206	
EDELIN, Barton	D.C.112	
George	CHA 222	
Igns.	D.C.93	
James	D.C.194	
Leonard	MON 172	
Samuel	D.C.58	
Walter	CHA 226	
EDEN, Cathran M.	SAI 93	
Jane	BCI 316	
EDER, Morris	MON 150	
EDES, Benja.	BCI 211	
Isaac	CAL 51	
John	D.C.25	
John	KEN 94	
EDGAR, Addam	KEN 104	
Ebenezar	BAL 43	
Elizabeth	TAL 25	
James	CEC 175	
Joseph	TAL 26	
Richard	TAL 4	
EDGELL, Eleoner	CLN 116	
Henry	CLN 107	
James	CLN 107	
Margarett	CLN 108	
Peter	CLN 105	
Thomas	CLN 108	
EDGEN, Prescilla	CLN 110	
EDGER, --- (Widaw)	BCI 412	
Arnold	DOR 32	
EDGER (continued)		
Baker	BCI 268	
Daniel	BCI 403	
Sally	DOR 31	
William	DOR 3	
William	DOR 35	
EDGIR, John	DOR 35	
EDICK, Juda	D.C.155	
EDILIN, Philip	MON 172	
EDIX, Charles	BAL 94	
EDLEING, James	ANN 381	
EDLEY, Henry	SAI 80	
EDMANSAN, James	DOR 23	
EDMANSON, Desius (?)	D.C.48	
Mosses (f)	DOR 21	
EDMASON, Brook	FRE 80	
EDMONDS, Charles	CAL 50	
Edmd.	D.C.151	
Richard	BCI 91	
Thos.	CAL 46	
EDMONDSON, Calep	CEC 157	
Sarah	D.C.85	
EDMONDSTON, William	BCI 88	
EDMONSAN, Samuel	DOR 23	
EDMONSON, Adam	DOR 7	
Basil	ANN 366	
C.	BCI 407	
Charlottee	TAL 10	
Desius	D.C.48	
Henry S.	DOR 49	
James (?)	DOR 23	
John	BCI 333	
John	TAL 8A	
Joshua	BAL 27	
Mingo	DOR 64	
Mosses (f) (?)	DOR 21	
Samuel (?)	DOR 23	
Thomas	D.C.49	
Thomas	FRE 69	
Thos. E.	BCI 351	
EDMONSTON, Archd., Senr.	PRI 184	
Archd., Junr.	PRI 184	
Brooke	D.C.92	
Eden	MON 137	
Francis	BCI 256	
James	PRI 183	
Mary	MON 150	
Nathan	PRI 184	
Polly	MON 150	
Richard	MON 150	
Robert	PRI 186	
Sarah	D.C.71	
Thos.	BCI 537	
Thos.	D.C.91	
EDMUNDSON, Joseph	BCI 462	
William	CHA 192	
EDWARD, Edward, L.	PRI 193	
John	BAL 217	
Phllis	ANN 336	
EDWARDL, Edward (?)	PRI 193	
EDWARDS, --- (Mr.)	BCI 462	
Aquila	BCI 171	
Benjamin	SAI 78	
Charles	SAI 90	
Daniel (?)	WAS 56	
Elchanah	SAI 90	
Elizth. & R. FRISBY	BAL 109	
Emory	KEN 93	
George (?)	WAS 57	
Gouvenier	BCI 454	
Ignatious	SAI 87	
James	FRE 196	

ELLIOTT (continued)
Statira	D.C. 22
Thomas	ANN 272
Thomas	BAL 204
Thomas, Jnr.	ANN 253
Thomas R.	QUE 47
Thos.	BCI 499
Thos.	BCI 504
Vin	QUE 19
William	HAR 72
Wm.	QUE 18

ELLIS, Artimissey KEN 90
Charles	BCI 3
Elijah	PRI 214
George	BCI 13
Hezekiah	D.C. 27
James	BCI 49
James	BCI 203
James	WOR 217
Jemima	HAR 44
John	BAL 174
John	BCI 340
John	PRI 213
John	WOR 164
Jos.	MON 173
Joseph	FRE 212
Joshua	D.C. 24
Josiah	WOR 157
Leonard	D.C. 12
Levi, Senr.	WOR 156
Philip	BAL 240
Philip	MON 175
Philips	D.C. 213
Richard	KEN 120
Robert	D.C. 7
Sarah	KEN 118
Thomas	BCI 113
Thomas	HAR 64
William	HAR 6
Wm.	WOR 157

ELLISON, Elijah	MON 162
Jno. L.	KEN 124
John	BAL 190
ELLISS, John	BCI 534
John	D.C. 87
Joshua	SOM 111
Saml. B.	D.C. 130
ELLIT, --- (Widaw)	BCI 404
ELLITT, Thos.	BCI 505
ELLIXON, --- (Mr.)	BCI 111
ELLOTT, Delia	BAL 90
ELMORE, James	BCI 34
ELMS, James	BAL 204
Joseph	MON 178
Thomas	BAL 207

ELNEIGHER, Daniel,
Jun.	WAS 73
ELSEROAT, Micl.	FRE 126
ELSEY, --- (Mrs.)	D.C. 4
ELSON, Henry	BAL 68
ELSROATE, George	BAL 18
John	BAL 18
ELSWORTH, Geo.	D.C. 81
ELVIN, Robert	FRE 99
ELVINS, William	FRE 68
ELVIS, Alfred	BCI 517
ELY, Amos	HAR 64
Daniel	FRE 106
David	HAR 45
Hugh	HAR 56
Isaac	CEC 175
Jacob	BCI 36
John	BAL 178
Thomas	BAL 178
Thomas	HAR 45
William	FRE 106

ELY (continued),
William	HAR 77
ELZEY, Arnold	SOM 106
EMACK, Will.	D.C. 105
EMBERSON, Henry	D.C. 191
John	QUE 40
EMBERT, Henry	CLN 80
EMERICK, Jacob	ANN 361

EMERSON, Acquilla D.
	D.C. 147
Harrison	D.C. 203
James	BAL 119
John	CHA 220A
John	WAS 85
John S.	D.C. 175
Smith	BAL 224
Thomas	WAS 85
EMERY, Samuel	CHA 202
Thomas	CHA 202

EMMERSON, --- (Mis?)
	BCI 383
--- (Mrs.)	BCI 383
Arthur	BCI 174
Edw.	D.C. 22
Jonan.	D.C. 22
P.	BCI 367
Peter	CAL 61
Samuel	CLN 112
William	CLN 77
William	CLN 91
EMMERSSON, Mary	CLN 97
EMMERT, Benjamin	WAS 87
Elizabeth	WAS 86
George	WAS 118
Michael	WAS 85
Nancey	WAS 81
EMMET, James	FRE 199
EMMIT, Josiah	FRE 153
EMMITT, Susanna	FRE 93
EMMONS, Ira	CEC 175
EMMORT, Henry	BAL 198
Philip	BAL 178
Thomas	BAL 178
William	BAL 178
EMONHIZAR, John	BAL 122
EMORY, Bryan	QUE 14
Gideon	QUE 40
Henry	QUE 33
James	QUE 38
John	CLN 91
John	TAL 10
John D.	QUE 38
John K. B.	QUE 40
Nicholas	ANN 331
Rachel	QUE 30
Richard	QUE 32
Samuel	CEC 122
Solomon	TAL 33
Stepney	QUE 13
Theadore	QUE 40
Thomas L.	BCI 279
William	QUE 15
William	QUE 30
EMPSON, David	ANN 391
EMRICK, Jacob	WAS 134[A]

ENDERSON (See also
ANDERSON),
Eliz.	BCI 337
ENDSLY, Thomas	ALL 15
ENGLAND, Amos	FRE 217
Catharine	FRE 104
Elisha	CEC 175
George	HAR 56
Isaac	CEC 175
James	BCI 47
James	BCI 399

ENGLAND (continued),
John	HAR 55
Joseph	CEC 175
Samuel	FRE 69
ENGLE, Adam	ALL 9
Barbary	FRE 219
Charles	FRE 197
Elizabeth	FRE 200
George	FRE 112
Jesse	FRE 72
John	FRE 176
John	FRE 197
Michael	FRE 182
Peter	FRE 113
Peter	FRE 198

ENGLEBRECHT, John
	FRE 99
Margaret	FRE 99

ENGLEBRIGHT, Elizabeth
	FRE 109
ENGLEMAN, John	FRE 191
ENGLER, Abraham	FRE 228
Daniel	FRE 200
David	FRE 200
David	FRE 200
Jacob	FRE 159
John	FRE 204
Mary	FRE 204
Peter	FRE 224
Philip	FRE 200
ENGLES, Abrahan	BCI 403

ENGLISH (See also IN-
GLISH),
Adam	BAL 129
Daniel	DOR 39
David	D.C. 39
David	D.C. 45
David	MON 178
James	D.C. 178
James	D.C. 195
James	D.C. 197
John	FRE 199
Levin	SOM 107
Matthew	D.C. 92
Rebecah	KEN 102
Rebecca	MON 150
Richard	FRE 101

ENLAWES (See also IN-
LOES, INLOWES),
James	BCI 411
Thomas	BCI 398
ENLOW, Jeremiah	ALL 5
John	ALL 6
ENNAL, Oxford (negro)	TAL 20
ENNALLS, Ann	DOR 60
Charles	CLN 111
Hager	DOR 44
Jobe	DOR 19
John	DOR 59
Joseph	DOR 44
Joseph	DOR 52
Joseph	DOR 57
Leah	DOR 22
Thomas (Col.)	DOR 49
William	BCI 86
ENNES, Philip	BCI 173
ENNIS, Anthony	ANN 266
Benjmn.	BCI 308
Betsey	BCI 475
Betsy	WOR 211
Elijah, Esqr.	WOR 214
George	FRE 128
Gregory	BCI 302
Jesse	WOR 169
John	ANN 397

ENNIS (continued),		
Joseph	WOR	186
Micajah	WOR	169
Outten	WOR	176
Samuel	ANN	266
Samuel	WOR	186
Stephen	WOR	176
William	ANN	256
William	ANN	280
Wm., Captn.	WOR	170
ENNISS, Joshua	BCI	67
ENO, David	CEC	175
Richard	D.C.	27
ENOX, Mary	BCI	25
ENSBARGER, Michael		
	WAS	87
ENSEY, William	D.C.	126
Wm.	BCI	507
ENSMINGER, George		
	WAS	132
ENSON, Abram	BCI	199
ENSOR, Darby	BAL	15
George	BAL	15
George	BAL	27
George	BAL	56
Joseph	BAL	153
Luke	BCI	111
Martha	BCI	60
Nathan (of George)		
	BAL	15
William	BCI	158
ENSSOR, Enoch	BAL	24
ENSTMINGER, Martin		
	WAS	79
ENT, George W.	FRE	98
ENTIRE, Francis W. (?)		
	BAL	67
ENTLER, Hannah	ALL	26
Philip	BCI	442
ENTRES, John	FRE	182
ENTSMINGER, Ludwick		
	WAS	82
Philip	WAS	140
ENTWISLE, Isaac	D.C.	148
Isaac, Jr.	D.C.	183
ENTZ, Andr.	BCI	480
EPPERLY, John	FRE	223
EPPERT, Henry	FRE	215
EPRON (See also APRON),		
Nichs.	BCI	221
EPWORTH, James	BCI	115
ERANS, Gamage (?)	WOR	196
ERAWMER, John	FRE	216
ERAWNRER, John (?)		
	FRE	216
ERB, Jacob	FRE	194
John	FRE	196
Joseph	ALL	15
Michael	ALL	14A
Peter	FRE	180
Peter	FRE	194
EREK, Casper	BCI	449
ERLOCKER, Francis	ANN	376
Joseph	ANN	376
ERNATHY, James	CEC	136
ERNSHAW, Benjamin		
	ANN	256
ERNST, Mathew	FRE	198
ERRELL, Michiel	KEN	122
ERRICK, George	WAS	126
ERRICKSON, Benjamin		
	QUE	47
Mary	BCI	58
Mary	QUE	47
Roderickson	QUE	47
Thomas	BCI	115

ERRICKSON (continued),		
William	QUE	47
ERSKINE, John	D.C.	90
Nancy	D.C.	33
ERUE, Pompy	CEC	175
ERVIN, John	FRE	194
Thomas	WAS	118
William	BAL	206
William	CLN	82
William	HAR	27
ERVING, John	ALL	7
ERWIN, Henry	D.C.	44
ERWING, John	BCI	133
ESCAVAILLE, Joseph		
	BCI	244
ESENBECT, William	D.C.	71
ESEX, Benjamin	CAL	59
ESGATE, Benjamin	TAL	4
James	TAL	19
Thomas	TAL	19
ESHOM, Sollemon	WOR	210
ESHON, Jas.	WOR	176
ESLING, George	D.C.	10
ESPANIEL, Peter	BCI	78
ESPELUY, Marey	BCI	388
ESPEY, John	D.C.	82
Wm.	BCI	184
ESRI, Benjamin (?)		
	ANN	318
ESSENDER, --- (Widaw)		
	BCI	417
James	BCI	385
John	BCI	385
ESSEX, Deboh.	D.C.	125
Isaac	CAL	41A
Samuel	CAL	51
Wm.	CAL	50
ESSUX, Eliza	BCI	480
ESTEP, Alexr.	D.C.	138
Benjamin	PRI	214
John	PRI	214
John	SAI	90
John J. (I.?)	CHA	224
Joseph	D.C.	133
Joshua	SAI	90
Margaret	CHA	223
Pricilla	PRI	214
Rebecca	SAI	90
Rezen	ANN	274
Richard	PRI	206
Thomas	SAI	98
ESTEPS, Zachariah	BAL	247
ESTING, George (?)		
	D.C.	10
ESTINGS, Isaac	CEC	175
ESTSTEP, John	BAL	155
ESWORTHY, James	FRE	218
ETCHBERGER, John		
	BCI	9
William	BCI	57
William	BCI	57
William	BCI	60
ETCHERSON, Fredk.		
	FRE	135
ETCHESON, James	PRI	221A
John B.	PRI	237
ETCHIS, Joseph	D.C.	177
ETCHISON, Elisha	MON	177
Ephraim	MON	177
Saml.	MON	177
Wm.	MON	177
ETERICH, Willm.	D.C.	119
ETHERINGTON, Bar-		
tholamew	KEN	87
Elenor	CEC	122
John	BCI	209

ETHERINGTON (continued),		
John W.	BCI	315
Joseph	CEC	122
William	CEC	122
ETHERTON, Willimam	DOR	28
Wm.	BAL	88
ETNEIGH, John	WAS	103
ETNEIGHER, Daniel,		
Senr.	WAS	73
Daniel, Jun.	WAS	73
George	WAS	89
Henry, Sen.	WAS	74
John	WAS	73
ETNUGHER, Henry, Senr.		
	WAS	74
John	WAS	73
ETNY POWDER MILL-		
Joseph JIMMISON		
& CO.	BAL	186
ETTER, Joseph	D.C.	75
Samuel	WAS	138
ETTING, Shirat	BCI	427
Solomon	BCI	427
ETZLER, Catharine	FRE	220
Daniel	FRE	216
Danl.	FRE	229
Mary	FRE	214
EULENSTEIN, Frederick		
	BCI	90
EULER, Conrad	BCI	309
Jacob	BCI	434
Nicholos	BCI	434
EUNICK, Thos.	BCI	339
EVANS, --- (See		
PHILIPS & EVANS?)		
--- (Mrs.)	BCI	436
--- (Mrs.)	BCI	452
--- (Mrs.)	BCI	460
Alexander	PRI	192
Amos	CEC	136
Amos	HAR	27
Amos	HAR	31
Andariah	WOR	185
Ann	D.C.	42
Ann C. (Mrs.)	CAL	48
Barbary	BCI	19
Basel?	BAL	206
Bazel	BAL	206
Cathe.	D.C.	84
Charles	BCI	281
Daniel?	BCI	16
Daniel	BAL	227
Daniel	BCI	7
Daniel (of Henry)	BCI	83
Darnil	BCI	16
David	ANN	338
David	BAL	55
David	BCI	195
David	D.C.	192
Denwood	SOM	129
Dolly	WOR	186
Drucilla	D.C.	144
Edward	HAR	25
Elijah	SOM	148
Elizabeth	BCI	83
Elizabeth	BCI	128
Elzy	SOM	152
Ephraim	D.C.	154
Evan?	QUE	34
Evan	D.C.	7
Evan	HAR	45
Eve	FRE	68
Ezekiel	FRE	198
Francis	SOM	152
Gamage	WOR	196
Geo.	D.C.	115

--- F ---

FABER, --- (Mrs.) BCI 407
FACE, Peter (?) BAL 166
FACKEY, Timothy BCI 217
FACKLER, John WAS 107
FACTORY-AVELIN ROL-
 ING & SLITING
 MILL & NAIL FAC-
 TORY, Nathaniel
 ELLICOTT & Co.,
 John DYKE, manager
                   BAL 192
FAER, John ALL 17
FAFAHONIER, Ann Clair
                   BCI 21
FAGAN, Cathe. D.C.85
 Daniel D.C.22
 Danl. D.C.71
 Hugh CEC 175A
 Joseph D.C.72
 Nichs. D.C.107
 Peter CEC 175A
FAGEN, George FRE 93
FAGG, George (?) D.C.26
FAGGETT, Benedict PRI 228
FAGLER, George FRE 112
FAGUE, George WAS 58A
 George, Senr. WAS 59
 Michael WAS 58A
FAHERTY, Martin BCI 461
FAHHAH, Henry BAL 216
FAHNESTOCK, Derick
                   ANN 379
 Derick BCI 441
 Peter BCI 442
FAHS, Henry FRE 154
FAHY, Mark D.C.32
 Murty ANN 283
FAIHERTY, Samuel ANN 281
FAILKNER, Resden CEC 158
FAIR, Charles HAR 21
 George BAL 146
 John BAL 146
 Joshua PRI 239
FAIRALE, Allica PRI 186
FAIRALL, Allica (?) PRI 186
 Benjamin PRI 184
 Horatio PRI 185
 Jason PRI 204
FAIRBANK, Daniel TAL 24
 David TAL 25
 Deborah TAL 22
 James TAL 27
 James, Jun. TAL 27
 Margarett TAL 25
 Mary TAL 25
 Noah CEC 158
 Samuel TAL 22
FAIRBANKS, Hester QUE 27
 John ANN 317
 William BCI 437
 William TAL 21
FAIRCHILD, Rob BCI 504
FAIRFIELD, Elizabeth
                   BCI 72
 Sarah BCI 101
FAIRHILL BOARDING
 SCHOOL MON 154
FAIRLY, Sarah CEC 158

FAIS, Nicholas BAL 162
FAITHFULL, Wm. BCI 527
FALCONAR, Saml. QUE 19
FALCONER, Elisha FRE 69
 Sarah BCI 485
FALCONOR, George W.
                   FRE 68
FALES, Benjamin BCI 123
FALKENROADS, George
                   WAS 97
FALKNER, Benjamin QUE 32
 Benjamin, Jn. QUE 29
 Caezar QUE 4
 William QUE 32
FALL, Ludwick BAL 156
FALLAN, Edwd. D.C.76
FALLEN, Henry SOM 110
FALLOWFIELD, William
                   KEN 102
 William QUE 34
FALLS, Moor BAL 10
 Stephen BAL 10
FANALL, Drusilla BCI 518
FANASON, Henry WAS 82
FANING, Zephiniah SAI 93
FANISFERRO, W. (?)
                   BCI 335
FANLEROY, William BCI 429
FANNEY, Patrick BCI 35
FANNING, Edmond BCI 515
FANT, John D.C.166
FANTHORP, Henry WAS 148
FAR, Edward MON 150
FARAN, Thomas BCI 137
FARD, James DOR 23
FARDELL, Ann KEN 93
 Solomon BCI 333
FARE, John FRE 171
 Michael FRE 170
 Peter BAL 166
 Peter FRE 172
FAREFAX, Chance BAL 29
 Chanie? BAL 29
 John BAL 29
FAREWELL, Jacob QUE 37
FARGESON, Addam QUE 41
FARHERTY, Micheal ANN 383
FARIBAND, Thomas BCI 376
FARIS, Aron WAS 145
FARLAND, John D.C.98
 Joseph TAL 27
FARLANE, Ann D.C.11
FARLING, John WAS 63
FARLOW, Benjamin WOR 201
 David WOR 202
 William TAL 22
 Wilta WOR 202
 Witta? WOR 202
FARMER, Benjamin CLN 95
 Nancy CLN 86
 Richard HAR 75
 William BAL 191
FARMMACE, James D.C.168
FARNANDIS, Saml. BCI 185
FARQUAR, Moses B.
                   FRE 176
 William P. FRE 176
FARQUHARSON, Chas.
                   BCI 254
FARR, James MON 140
 John B. CHA 202
 John B. SAI 86A
 Mary WAS 126
 Nicholas PRI 206
FARRAND, Hezekiah CHA 227
 John CHA 227

FARRAND (continued),
 Wm. (?) CHA 227
FARRATY, Mary D.C.89
FARRAUD, John (?) CHA 227
 William CHA 227
FARRE, Jacob FRE 116
 Jannarro S. MON 158A
FARREL, Charles O. BCI 153
FARRELL, Benjamin QUE 35
 Ed. QUE 10
 Eleanor BCI 46
 Grace QUE 17
 Jo. QUE 15
 John BCI 67
 John D.C.122
 John QUE 15
 Joshua QUE 15
 Sophia D.C.107
 Thomas BAL 38
 Wm. QUE 12
 Zephh. D.C.114
FARRIN, Susanna KEN 101
FARRINGTON, Theadore
                   SOM 104
FARRIS, John FRE 143
FARRISFERRO, W. (?)
                   BCI 335
FARROW, Charles WOR 209
 Hommett DOR 45
FARROWFIELD, Emory
                   CLN 77
 Jonas CLN 100
FARST, Jacob FRE 149
FARVER, John BAL 54
FARVOUR, George ANN 357
 Jacob ANN 357
FARWELL, Adam CLN 96
 Lydiea WOR 197
FASENBAKER, Elizabeth
                   ALL 13
 Jacob ALL 11
FASH, Casper BCI 229
FASSETT, Betsy WOR 193
 Elijah WOR 188
 George WOR 194
 Isaac WOR 196
 James, Jun. WOR 191
 Jas. (of John) WOR 177
 John of Jno. WOR 197
 Nelly WOR 191
 Thos., Doctor WOR 173
 William WOR 193
FASTER, Frances G. BCI 272
FAUBLE, --- (Mrs.) BCI 434
 Catharine BAL 158
 David BAL 162
 Frederick BAL 141
 George BAL 142
 John BAL 142
 John BAL 162
 John, of J. (l.?) BAL 141
 Melcher, Sr. BAL 149
 Melcher, Jur. BAL 151
FAUCKLER, Jacob WAS 103
FAUIN, Susanna (?) KEN 101
FAULK, --- (?) BCI 401
FAULKNER, Benjamin
                   ANN 312
 Burten CLN 79
 Daniel CLN 81
 Ephraim CLN 94
 Henry TAL 12
 Jacob TAL 49
 James CLN 106
 James TAL 13
 John TAL 28

FEW, John	HAR 64
FEYS, Jonathan (?)	WAS 99
FICKEY, Frederic	BCI 12
Harmon	BCI 3
FIDAMAN, Phillip	QUE 42
FIDDEMAN, Daniel	TAL 24
FIDLER, Samuel	CHA 204
FIEBUS, James	FRE 161
FIELD, Elizabeth	BAL 185
Henry	BCI 478
Joshua	BAL 44
Susan	BCI 525
FIELDER, Ann	SAI 67
FIELDS, Christ.	QUE 20
David	SOM 136
Edwd.	D.C. 123
George	SOM 136
Horace	D.C. 147
James	BCI 96
James	CLN 77
James A.	SAI 56
John	SOM 135
Jonnn.	D.C. 145
Mary	BCI 29
Stephen	QUE 38
Tamah	FRE 105
Thos.	SOM 136
William	WAS 77
Wilthe Ann	KEN 121
Wm.	MON 160
FIFE, Andrew H.	BAL 220
Robert	HAR 58
FIFELD, Ebeberr. O.	D.C. 196
FIFER, John	BCI 187
FIG, Daniel	FRE 148
FIGHLEY, Henry	WAS 123
John	WAS 122
Jonathan	WAS 98
Peter	WAS 116
Peter, Jun.	WAS 123
Samuel	WAS 122
William	WAS 98
FIGHTS, Elizabeth	FRE 194
FIKE, John, Sen.	ALL 7
John, Junr.	ALL 7
FILINGEN, John	KEN 93
FILINGIN, Mary	KEN 92
FILLER, Catharine	FRE 212
Jno.	FRE 126
John	FRE 228
FILLIGAN, Ann	WAS 115
Benjamin	WAS 96
FILLINGIM, Samuel	KEN 108
FILU, James	ANN 296
FIMESTER, Alx.	BCI 232
FIMPEL, John	BCI 98
FINAGAN, --- (Miss)	D.C. 76
FINCH, John	FRE 103
FINCKNAUR, Henry	BCI 178
FINDLAY, Oliver P.	D.C. 167
FINDLEY, George	QUE 37
FINDLEYS, --- (Mrs.)- plantation	D.C. 211
FINE, Frederick	FRE 217
John	FRE 217
Peter	FRE 76A
Philip	FRE 73
FINEFUCK, Daniel	WAS 67
FINEGAN, John, Jr.	BCI 500
Michael	FRE 175
FINEHOUR, Charles	ANN 369
FINFROCK, Henry, Senr.	FRE 179
Henry, Jun.	FRE 179

FINGSTROM, Peter (?)	FRE 110
FINICAN, James	BCI 450
FINK, Adam	BAL 7
George	WAS 63
Jacob	WAS 151
John	FRE 128
John, Jr.	FRE 132
Philip	FRE 132
Sebastin	BAL 93
FINKER, Francis	SAI 90
FINLAY, John	BCI 276
FINLEY, E. L.	BCI 511
Ebenezer	BCI 411
Hugh	BCI 210
John	BCI 50
Patrick	ANN 270
Thos.	BCI 514
FINLY, Michael A.	WAS 77
William	CEC 136
FINN, --- (See FINN & BILFERE)	
Ann	D.C. 23
Nathl.	BCI 223
William	BCI 256
FINN & BILFERE	BCI 408
FINNEY, Lewis H.	BCI 124
William	HAR 28
FIRBUSH, George	SOM 135
Joseph	SOM 135
FIRESTONE, Jacob	FRE 115
Susanah	WAS 96
FIRMAN, Michl.	D.C. 97
FIRNEY, Adam	BCI 314
FIRREY, Jacob	WAS 109
Hanry	WAS 134
John	WAS 134
FISCHER, Adam	FRE 96
FISH, Allen	BCI 312
John	CEC 175A
Lasurees	DOR 35
Linda	FRE 81
Richard	FRE 216
Robert	BCI 448
Susannah	FRE 84
Thomas	SAI 53A
William	FRE 135
FISHAUGH, Frederick	WAS 103
George	WAS 103
FISHER, Adam	CLN 90
Airy	ANN 367
Aquilla	MON 166
Artaxerxes	MON 167
Aza	ALL 20A
Basil	BCI 482
Benjm.	WOR 157
Benjn.	WOR 163
Chas.	D.C. 90
Denwood	QUE 29
Easter	FRE 78A
Elizabeth	BAL 161
Elizabeth	FRE 186
Elizabeth	SOM 123
Esau	WOR 160
Ezekiel	WOR 161
Francis	BCI 274
Gearge?	DOR 19
Geo.	BCI 168
Georg, Sener	BAL 19
George	BAL 147
George	DOR 19
George, Junur	BAL 19
Hannah	CLN 80
Henry	FRE 160
Henry	SOM 133

FISHER (continued),	
Henry M.	BCI 247
Isaac	BAL 229
Isaac	WOR 196
Jacob	FRE 95
Jacob	FRE 191
Jacob	WAS 82
Jacob	WOR 163
James	BCI 101
James	CEC 123
Jeremiah	ANN 340
John	ALL 16
John	BCI 273
John	CEC 158
John	CEC 158
John	D.C. 124
John	D.C. 137
John	FRE 186
John	HAR 73
John	MON 178
John	WOR 189
Joseph	BCI 185
Joseph	FRE 193
Keziah	CLN 73
Leonard	BAL 190
Magdelani	BAL 164
Margaret	FRE 187
Martin	ANN 318
Martin	MON 135
Martin	MON 136
Mary	BCI 71
Mary	BCI 191
Metter; C.M.	BCI 276
Michael	ALL 26
Michael	FRE 83A
Nancy	WOR 189
Nancy	WOR 196
Perygeren	ANN 379
Philip	FRE 115
Richard	DOR 61
Robert	BCI 271
Robt.	D.C. 159
Samuel	DOR 62
Sarah	BCI 30
Silas	CLN 72A
Sophia	ANN 366
Stephen	WOR 189
Susan	MON 163
Thomas	ANN 399
Thomas	BAL 205
Thomas	HAR 77
Thomas	WAS 65
Thoms.	MON 162
Tobias	BCI 455
William	ANN 279
William	BCI 53
William	HAR 77
William	MON 135
FISHOCK, --- (Mrs.)	BCI 434
FISHPAUGH, John	BAL 215
Thos.	BAL 3
FISHPAW, John	BAL 3
FISHU, Gearge (?)	DOR 19
George? (?)	DOR 19
FISK, Samuel	CEC 175A
FISSEL, Adam	BAL 81
FISTER, Henry, Senr.	MON 175
Henry, Junr.	MON 175
Henry	BCI 156
John	BCI 465
Joshua	BAL 117
Robert	BCI 371
William	BAL 116
William of Wm.	BCI 156
	BAL 113

82

INDEX TO THE 1820 CENSUS OF MARYLAND AND WASHINGTON, D.C.

FITCHER (See also PITCHER),		
James (?)	ANN	331
FITCHETT, Abel	DOR	44
John	DOR	57
Michael	DOR	44
FITCHUE, Edmonson	DOR	21
Ezekiel	DOR	18
Ezekiel	DOR	18
Levin?	DOR	18
Levin	DOR	18
Rosana	DOR	22
Sally	DOR	18
Sherton	DOR	18
Thomas V.	DOR	18
FITE, Adrew	BAL	194
Conrad (L.?)	BCI	399
Henry	BAL	195
John	BAL	194
John	WAS	133
Mary	BCI	376
FITSGERALD, Edward	BAL	47
FITSSIMONS, Samuel	PRI	230
FITZ, John	BCI	447
FITZGERALD, Austin	BCI	319
Edward	SOM	134
Edwd.	D.C.	89
Edwd.	D.C.	113
Geoge.	D.C.	209
Jas.	BCI	318
Jesse B.	SOM	123
John	BCI	318
Margaret	BCI	118
Maria	D.C.	35
Simon	HAR	70
FITZGERRALD, Jne.	MON	176
Jno.?	MON	176
FITZHUGH,---(Mrs.)	BCI	339
George	BAL	229
John	CAL	43
William	WAS	88
William	WAS	102
Wm. H.	D.C.	188
FITZ JEFFERY, Thomas	SAI	56
FITZPATRICK, John	BCI	307
Margaret	BCI	76
Nathaniel	BAL	240
William	CLN	77
William	PRI	229
FITZSIMMONS, Sam	D.C.	101
FLAGGS, Margaret	BCI	59
FLAHARITY, John	MON	150
FLAKE, Catharine	ALL	32
FLAMER, James	TAL	47
Sherry	QUE	41
William	TAL	46
FLANADY, Michael	QUE	14
FLANAGAN, Danl.	D.C.	123
Michl.	D.C.	89
Patrick	PRI	229
Thomas	FRE	105
FLANAYARD, William	ANN	301
FLANIGAN, Thos.	FRE	124
FLANNAGAN, James	ALL	9
FLANNAGIN, John	ALL	16
FLASHELL, Anthony	BCI	516
FLATER, George	BAL	9
John	BAL	9
Philip	BAL	9
FLAUGHERTY, Michael	FRE	157
FLAURENCE, Joseph J.		
(I.?)	PRI	214

FLAUT, George	FRE	148
Jacob	FRE	148
FLAX, Michael	BCI	157
FLAXCOMB, William	BCI	101
Wm.	BCI	200
FLEAGLE, David	FRE	172
John	FRE	173
John	FRE	193
FLECHER, Benjamin	WAS	119
Henry	WAS	111
FLECK, Adam	FRE	146
George	FRE	146
FLEEGLE, George	FRE	143
FLEEHARTY, John	HAR	57
John	HAR	73
Mary	QUE	29
Thomas	CEC	175A
Thomas	HAR	59
FLEET, Henry	D.C.	34
Sarah	D.C.	47
FLEETWOOD, Benjamin	BCI	78
Quality	HAR	29
William	BCI	21
William	BCI	95
FLEGLE, John, Jr.	FRE	197
FLEHARTY, John	CLN	109
Joseph	CLN	109
Richard	CLN	111
William	CLN	111
FLEMAN, Joseph	CEC	137
FLEMIN, Abraham	FRE	219
FLEMING, Cathe.	D.C.	170
James	BCI	138
John	FRE	72
John	TAL	12
Joshua	WOR	210
Littleton	WOR	163
Robert	FRE	143
Robert	WOR	210
Sarah	SOM	126
William	ALL	23
William	SOM	125
Willm.	BCI	203
FLEMINGS, Thomas	TAL	34A
FLEMMER, Philip	FRE	204
FLEMMING, Ann	FRE	72
Caleb	FRE	225
Fredk.	BCI	169
John	WAS	95
Joseph	FRE	114
Joseph of Arther	FRE	114
Mary	FRE	104
Philemon	BCI	55
Robert	WAS	83
Samuel	FRE	104
Samuel	FRE	114
Sarah	FRE	100
Thomas	WAS	103
Thomas	WAS	105
William	BCI	216
FLEMMINGS, John	FRE	225
FLEMMON, Francis	BCI	318
Robert	CLN	77
William	BCI	7
William	BCI	16
FLENNER, Daniel	FRE	168
FLETCHALL, James	MON	135
Walter W.	MON	130
FLETCHER, Ann Jane	WOR	169
Benjamin	HAR	28
Catherine	BCI	67
Charlotte	SAI	67
E.	DOR	15
Ellenor	D.C.	136

FLETCHER (continued),		
Henry	BAL	122
Henry	BCI	188
J.	BCI	382
James	BCI	201
James	DOR	60
Jas.	BCI	168
Jesse	D.C.	75
Jesse	D.C.	84
John	BCI	100
John	SOM	135
John	TAL	9
John	TAL	35
Joseph	DOR	57
Mary	D.C.	199
Michl.	D.C.	78
Noah	D.C.	92
Parriss	DOR	61
Peter	DOR	13
Philip	BCI	536
Samuel	SOM	111
Simon (f.n.)	SOM	119
Susan (f.n.)	SOM	119
Thomas	BCI	320
Walter	HAR	72
William	CHA	226
William	D.C.	12
FLEURRY, Elizabeth	CHA	197
William	CHA	192
FLEURY, Eli	D.C.	4
Paul A.	BAL	120
FLICK, George	D.C.	24
FLICKER, Lewis (?)	WAS	59
FLICKINGER, Andrew	BAL	144
Andrew	FRE	196
John	FRE	196
FLIGHT, John	FRE	128
FLING, James	MON	150
Owen	FRE	125
FLINN, Daniel	ANN	303
James	BAL	181
FLINT, J.	BCI	394
T.	BCI	244
William	DOR	3
FLINTHAM, Richard	CEC	123
FLITCHER, Roger	DOR	56
William	DOR	53
FLOARA, Conrad	WAS	103
John	WAS	102
Peter	WAS	104
Stuffele	WAS	103
FLOID, Charles	BCI	411
FLONEERY, Bartholoman (?)	DOR	30
FLOOD, James (?)	BCI	161
Philemond	ANN	365
FLOOK, Henry	FRE	128
FLOOKE, John, senr.	FRE	130
FLORENCE, Sebastian	FRE	190
FLOWER, Gustavus	SAI	65
Mary A.	SAI	76
Sarah	SAI	67
Susan	SAI	63
Sylvester	SAI	65
FLOWERS, Bartholoman	DOR	30
David	HAR	39
David	HAR	78
Frances	CHA	193
Gustavus	CHA	190
Henry	CLN	113
Henry	DOR	64
Jane	HAR	71

83

FLOWERS (continued),		FOLKER, Henry	FRE 180	FORD (continued),	
Jeremiah	WOR 212	Margaret	FRE 200	H. John	CEC 136
John (?)	BCI 501	Susannah	BCI 74	Henrietta	CHA 204
John	HAR 70	FOLKS, Charity	ANN 390	Hezekiah	CEC 123
Owen	DOR 7	Henry	BCI 150	Hugh	SOM 152
Solomon	FRE 118	FOLLIN, Basheta	D.C. 216	Ignatious	SAI 74
FLOWRER, John	WAS 127A	Willm.	D.C. 195	Ignatius	SAI 57
FLOYD, Elizabeth	SAI 82	Willm.	D.C. 197	Isaac	BAL 237
Ellen	BCI 268	FOLLOWBEE, Jos.	D.C. 111	Isack	BAL 44
Henry (?)	D.C. 44	FOLTZ, Philip	FRE 115	Jacob	KEN 107
Jesse, Jnr.	SAI 79	FONDERSMITH, John		James (?)	DOR 23
Joseph	BAL 218		BAL 243	James	CEC 158
Levi	D.C. 24	FONERDEN, Esther	BCI 250	James	PRI 213
Mary	TAL 4	FONKE, Robert	CHA 192	Jno., of Henry	SAI 57
Molly	SOM 134	FOOKS, Billa	WOR 202	John	ANN 259
Samuel	TAL 6	Charles	WOR 214	John	BAL 12
Thomas	BCI 160	Daniel	WOR 214	John	BCI 496
William	SAI 74	Daniell	WOR 206	John	BCI 521
Wm., Senr.	WOR 156	Eben	WOR 211	John	CEC 158
Wm., Junr.	WOR 156	Elijah, Capt.	WOR 200	John	CEC 158
FLOYED, Ellen	QUE 26	James, Capt.	WOR 215	John F.	SAI 79
FLUCK, Elie	ALL 27	James, of D.	WOR 202	John G.	D.C. 49
FLUHART, John	ANN 362	James, of Jesse	WOR 219	Joseph	CEC 122
FLUHARTY, Samuel G.		Jonithin, Capt.	WOR 206	Joseph	HAR 18
	DOR 54	Joseph	WOR 215	Joseph	PRI 186
James H.	DOR 55	Leah, Wd.	WOR 215	Joseph	WAS 132
FLUKE, David	FRE 130	Matta, Wd.	WOR 214	Joseph R.	BAL 116
Jacob	FRE 131	Mattee?, Wd.	WOR 214	Joshua	BAL 16
Jacob	FRE 133	William	WOR 215	Josiah L.	CEC 122
Mathias	FRE 133	FOOL (See also FOOT,		Josias (Overs.)	PRI 225
FLUNCK, Conrad	WAS 71	TOOL),		Josuwa	WAS 74
FLURRY, Gustavus	CHA 191	John (?)	BCI 179	Lambert W.	CEC 158
Matthew	CHA 189	Milly	BCI 140	Lewis	SAI 80
William	CHA 210A	FOOLKS, Levin	DOR 10	Lewis, overseer-	
FLYE, Henry	WAS 55A	FOOLMER, Martin	BCI 18	James HOWARD)	SAI 80
FLYN, Edward	TAL 45	FOORMAN, Lionhard		Lucy	PRI 225
FLYNN, Lawrence	D.C. 98		BCI 371	Margaret	D.C. 30
Thos.	D.C. 117	FOOSE, John	BAL 110	Martha	HAR 22
FLYS, Jonathan (?)	WAS 99	William	BAL 106	Martha	MON 173
FOARD, John B.	HAR 40	FOOT (See also FOOL,		Mary	CHA 196
John B., Junr.	HAR 57	FORT),		Mary	SAI 64
John R.	HAR 7	Ellen	BCI 131	Mary	SAI 82
Mary	HAR 77	Ester	BCI 529	Mary	WAS 123
FOBER, Peter	BAL 177	Milly (?)	BCI 140	Michd.	BCI 196
FOBES, Azariah	ANN 291	Westley	BCI 475	Nathaniel	PRI 211
FOBUS, Alexander	BAL 24	FOOTE, Henry	ANN 285	Nicholas	BCI 160
FOCKE, Frederick	BCI 241	Jim (negro)	TAL 23	Nicholaus	BCI 396
FOCKS, Charles	BCI 6	FOOTS, Peter	FRE 216	Patrick	BCI 396
FOGGET (See also POG-		FOPLOSS, Michael	BCI 186	Peggy	FRE 77
GET),		FORBA, Pea	BCI 521	Peter	FRE 77
Richard (?)	ANN 261	FORBES, Ellin	BAL 16	Philip	SAI 82
FOGLE, Baltzer	FRE 227	George	CHA 226	Philip J. (l.?)	CHA 215
Christian	FRE 82	James	BCI 2	Price	BAL 150
Henry of Bols.	FRE 223	FORCE, Abraham	WAS 115	Richard	BAL 219
Jacob	FRE 76	Peter	D.C. 85	Richard	BAL 224
Jacob	PRI 196	FORD, Abraham	BAL 209	Risden D.	TAL 49
John	FRE 227	Aley	CHA 224	Robert	BAL 236
John	FRE 229	Ann B.	CEC 123	Robert	BAL 236
Mathias	FRE 227	Benjamin	CLN 77	Samuel	BAL 12
Mathias	FRE 227	Benjamin	PRI 223	Samuel	BCI 140
Michael	FRE 169	Benjamin	SAI 63	Samuel	SOM 139
William	FRE 223	Catharine	BAL 12	Sarah	BAL 128
FOGLEMAN, George	BCI 376	Catharine	SOM 123	Sarah	KEN 101
FOGLER, Henry Senr.		Charles	BAL 198	Sarah	SAI 76
	FRE 105	Charles	CEC 158	Stephen H.	BCI 418
FOGLESONG, Jacob	FRE 189	Charles	SOM 152	Susanna	SAI 70
FOGWELL, Aquilla	QUE 4	Daniel	SOM 152	Thomas	BAL 224
Hannah	QUE 19	Edward	CEC 123	Thomas	BAL 238
Jas.	QUE 18	Edward	D.C. 26	Thomas	BCI 88
Jo.	QUE 19	Elias	BCI 195	Thomas	CLN 104A
Mary	QUE 19	Elizabeth	CEC 136	Thomas	HAR 44
FOLCK, John	ALL 24	Elizabeth	CHA 215	Thomas	WAS 81
FOLEY, John	ALL 31	Elzy	SOM 131	Walter	ALL 27
Nathl.	BCI 275	Francess	BCI 137	William	ANN 259
Timothy	BCI 66	George	CEC 122	William	DOR 7
FOLHER, Henry (?)	FRE 180	George	CEC 158	William	HAR 5

FORD (continued),		FORREST, Alexr.	D.C.138	FORWOOD (continued),	
William A.	CHA 212	Andrew	D.C.126	Saml.of Jac	HAR 41
Wm.	MON 134	Ann	SAI 81	Samuel	HAR 76
Wm.	MON 137	Archibald	CEC 175A	William	HAR 41
FORDE, Denham	BCI 296	Benjamin	ANN 331	William	HAR 72
Geo.	D.C.115	Carlton	ALL 38	FOSBENNER, Andrew	
James	D.C.85	David	D.C.73		BCI 314
John	BCI 167	Duley	MON 161	FOSDECK, Jno. M.	BCI 231
Josh T.	BCI 169	George	BCI 26	FOSEBY, --- (Widow)	
William	BCI 309	George	D.C.41		BCI 410
FORDER, Peter	BAL 242	Henry	D.C.11	FOSELEY, --- (Widow) (?)	
FORDICE, John	BCI 103	Henry	D.C.57		BCI 410
FOREMAN, --- (Mrs.)		James	SAI 62A	FOSLER, Jacob	BCI 81
	BCI 452	James	SAI 80	FOSS, --- (Widow)	BCI 405
Abraham	WAS 65	Jas.	D.C.138	George	BCI 454
Ann	QUE 30	Jeremiah	FRE 165	FOSSBANER, Peter	BCI 487
Christian	BCI 441	John	BAL 203	FOSSET, John	BCI 220
Daniel	SOM 115	John	BCI 348	FOSSETT, James	HAR 62
Edward	BCI 87	John	FRE 93	FOSTER, B. W.	BCI 415
Eliza	BCI 227	Joseph	D.C.5	Daniiel	DOR 35
Francis	BCI 439	Josiah	ANN 336	Edward	CEC 158
George	BAL 160	Lancelot	ANN 331	Elizabeth	D.C.9
Isaac	BAL 196	Richard	PRI 239	Elizh.	BCI 189
Jacob	BAL 145	Richd.	D.C.73	Francis	BCI 516
Jacob	FRE 195	Sarah	ANN 348	George	ANN 277
Jane	BCI 514	Shaderick	ANN 336	George	BCI 283
John	ANN 308	Stepney	D.C.112	George	CEC 136
Joseph	ANN 312	Umphrey	SAI 70	Hannah	ANN 336
Joseph	BCI 409	William	ANN 330	Isabella	BCI 61
Joseph	D.C.63	William	ANN 336	James	BCI 285
Leonard	ANN 306	FORRESTER, James	BAL 110	James	CEC 136
Lodwick	BAL 197	Rachel	KEN 123	John	BAL 165
Michael	BAL 144	Ralph E.	BCI 221	John	BAL 242
Philip	BAL 140	Reason	ANN 336	John J.	CEC 175A
Samuel	ANN 311	FORRIS, --- (Mrs.)	BCI 413	John M.	BCI 103
Thomas M.	CEC 123	FORRISTER, --- (Widow)		Mary	BCI 76
Valentine	BCI 454		BCI 387	Mary	BCI 345
Wm.	QUE 12	FORSCYTH, John,		Mary Ann	BCI 143
FORESCYTH, John,		Junr.	WAS 136	Mary J.	BCI 534
Senr.	WAS 136	FORSTER, Benadick	BAL 83	Meriah	TAL 36
FOREST, Jacob	FRE 129	Edwd.	D.C.127	Moses	HAR 79
Jonathan	FRE 192	James	SAI 91	Nancy	DOR 65
Jonathan, Jr.	FRE 199	John	BAL 85	Nathen	CEC 136
Leonard	BCI 141	Nicholas	BAL 93	Nelly	D.C.57
Owen	FRE 129	William	WAS 103	Peter	QUE 29
Peter	FRE 129	FORSYTH, Alexr.	BCI 241	Rebecca	BCI 242
Solomon	FRE 129	John	D.C.75	T. M.	BCI 396
FORESTER, Wm.	BCI 474	Thomas	ANN 381	Thomas	CEC 136
FORGUSON, John	FRE 183	William	BCI 461	Thomas	FRE 164
FORINGER, Henry	BCI 284	FORSYTHE, James	CAL 62	William	BCI 68
FORMALT, Daniel	FRE 188	Joseph	ALL 7	William	HAR 21
Jacob	FRE 202	Samuel	HAR 26	Willm.	D.C.153
John	FRE 193	Sarah	HAR 74	Willm.	D.C.160
Solomon	FRE 191	William	HAR 73	FOUBLE, Casper	FRE 155
FORMAN, Ezekiel	KEN 115	FORT (See also FOOT),		FOUCARD, John	D.C.144
Ezekiel	TAL 5	Benjamin	BAL 16	FOUCH, John	FRE 133
Geo.	KEN 115	Ellen (?)	BCI 131	FOUKE, George	WAS 110
Jacob	KEN 105	Joshua	BCI 272	FOULAC, Ann	BCI 135
John	QUE 6	FORT McHENRY	BCI 326	Anthony	BCI 123
Milisant	KEN 124	FORTESCUE, William		FOULDER, John	WAS 108
William	KEN 105		BCI 458	William	WAS 106
William	KEN 110	FORTNER, Ann	BCI 17	FOULER, John	PRI 206
FORMEY, Patrick	FRE 94	Benjamin	ANN 305	FOULK, Asher	MON 150
FORMSHAIL, John	BCI 187	FORTNEY, Henry	D.C.189	Lewis	BCI 509
FORNADIS, Walter	BCI 351	FORTUNE, Agnes	SOM 124	FOULKE, Lewis	BAL 227
FORNER, John	MON 142	Boston	FRE 112	FOUNTAIN, Anderton	
John, Senr.	MON 172	FORTY, John	ANN 400		CLN 99
FORNEY, Abraham	FRE 174	John	BCI 146	Casson	CLN 76
Danuel	BAL 19	T.	BCI 373	David	TAL 48
David	BCI 494	FORWARD, Dryden	ALL 28	Henry	SOM 153
John	FRE 173	FORWER, Nicholis	ALL 37	Isaac	CLN 106
Peter	BCI 460	FORWOOD, Jacob	HAR 41	Isaac	CLN 111
Saml. S.	FRE 170	Jacob	HAR 71	Jacob	CEC 136
FOROLL, William	SAI 93	John	HAR 41	James	CLN 73
FORQUHAR, Allen	FRE 74	John-B.smith	HAR 44	John	BCI 323
FORRDE, John	D.C.71				

FRANCIS (continued),			FRAUNFELTER, Felix			FREEMAN (See also TREEMAN),		
Natl.	D.C.	215		FRE	180	--- (Mr.)	BAL	124
Thomas	ANN	357	FRAY, George	KEN	92	--- (Mrs.)	BCI	381
Thomas	BAL	230	Jane	KEN	100	Abraham	KEN	89
FRANCISCUS, John	BCI	210	FRAYLEY, John	WAS	64	Anne	MON	140
FRANCOIS, --- (?)	BCI	432	FRAZIER, Charles	BCI	32	Athel	TAL	52
FRANER, John	WAS	115	Charles	DOR	14	Benjamin	CHA	203
Saml.	FRE	227	Charles	DOR	15	Chaney (Mrs.)	CAL	54
Sawl.?	FRE	227	Daniel R.	CHA	211	Charles	BCI	508
William	WAS	115	Ephraim	ALL	7	Constant	D.C.	5
FRANK, George	BAL	151	Ezekiel	DOR	55	Dennis	BCI	101
Johannah	BAL	161	Henry	FRE	123	Edward (?)	CAL	50
John	BAL	159	Henry	TAL	7	Edward, Ovsr.	TAL	6
John	D.C.	87	Horace	D.C.	117	Edwd.	BCI	493
Ludwick	BCI	321	Horatio	FRE	97	Eleanor (?)	D.C.	57
Philip	BAL	157	James	BCI	22	Ezekiel	BCI	436
FRANKENBARGER, Samuel (?)			James	BCI	219	Francis	BAL	109
	WAS	80	Jeremiah	ALL	6	Hannah	KEN	87
FRANKENBAYER, Samuel			Jeremiah	BCI	21	Henry	BCI	142
	WAS	80	Jeremiah	FRE	114	Henry	TAL	9
FRANKFORTER, Adam			John	BCI	46	Hetty	BCI	62
	BAL	141	John S.	FRE	135	Horace	ANN	287
Frederick	BAL	148	Jonathan	ALL	5A	Isaac	CLN	79
John	BAL	147	Joseph	BCI	132	Isaac	KEN	92
FRANKHAUSER, George			Levin	DOR	13	Isaac	KEN	121
	FRE	194	Maryland	FRE	126	John (?)	MON	143
FRANKLEN, Henry	WOR	188	Nanny	SOM	149	John	CLN	78
FRANKLIN, Anne	ANN	256	Otho	FRE	95	John	D.C.	17
Ben.	WOR	185	Penelope	CEC	175A	Martha	KEN	100
Benjamin	ANN	272	Peter	ANN	266	Mary (Mrs.)	CAL	44
Charles	FRE	210	Peter	BCI	166	Moses	WOR	190
Daniel	ANN	258	Richard	BCI	155	Nathaniel	CHA	226
Elkanah	CHA	196A	Robt.	D.C.	111	Philip	CLN	73
Garrett	BAL	110	Solomon	CLN	109	Saml.	KEN	125
Geo.	MON	143	Solomon	DOR	8	Samuel	CEC	122
Hezekiah	CHA	196	Solomon	DOR	10	Samuel	CEC	136
James	ANN	317	Therman	ALL	6	Sarah	BAL	120
James	BCI	19	Thos.	FRE	123	Sueilly?	D.C.	204
James	FRE	210	William	FRE	109	Sveilly	D.C.	204
John	ANN	260	FREBURGHER, Geo.			T. W.	CEC	158
Joseph	BAL	175		BCI	305	Thomas	SAI	57
Joshua	FRE	211	John	BCI	307	Thos. B.	CAL	45
Mary Ann	CHA	196	FREDDRICK, Peter	BAL	80	Wm.	BCI	65
Nichs.	D.C.	120	FREDERICK, David	BCI	301	Wm.	BCI	179
Rachel	ANN	273	Laurence	BCI	441	FREENEY, John	SOM	117
Resin	BAL	62	Michael	BCI	325	Joshua	WOR	205
Robert	ANN	259	Micheal	ANN	353	FREER, Peter	BCI	189
Robert	WOR	185	Peter	BCI	486	FREESE, George	FRE	161
Samuel	PRI	187	Sarah	D.C.	135	Samuel	BAL	228
Thomas	ANN	403	Saul	CHA	196A	FREEZE, Jacob	FRE	227
Thomas	BCI	426	FREDRICK, Aquila	BAL	96	John	FRE	155
Thomas	FRE	192	John	WAS	74	FREIZE, David	FRE	204
Thomas-[his] Slaves			Stephen	BAL	99	FRELAND, John	BAL	81
	ANN	256	FREE, Cornelias	WAS	147	FRELET, Joseph	BCI	244
Thos.	BCI	348	John	D.C.	68	FREMAN, William	CHA	203
Thos. L. B.	CHA	191	John B.	D.C.	68	FRENCH, Benjamin	CAL	61
William	CHA	190	Peter	BAL	81	Ebenezer	BCI	172
William	WOR	185	Sarah	D.C.	135	George	ALL	35
York	ANN	305	FREED, Laurance	BAL	146	George	D.C.	67
Zephaniah	CHA	196	FREEKS, Richard	KEN	87	J. C.	ANN	396
FRANKLIN PAPER MILL-			FREELAND, Alfred			Jacob	CAL	61
Laurence GRATERICK			(Capt.)	CAL	67	James	QUE	11
& Co.	BAL	185	Danuel	BAL	26	John	KEN	103
FRANKLIN WOOLEN MANU-			David	ANN	257	John B.	ALL	28
FACTORY-William			Edward	BAL	86	Marianna	D.C.	64
MARVIN	BAL	186	Elizabeth	TAL	9	Mary	BCI	34
FRANTOM, Mary	TAL	2	James	BAL	81	Mary	D.C.	37
Polly	TAL	34A	John	FRE	227	Matthew	BCI	209
FRANZONI, Jane	D.C.	97	Joseph	BAL	162	Nicholas	BAL	205
FRASER, John	D.C.	76	Michaja	BAL	98	Priscilla	ANN	389
FRASIER, Arcibald	PRI	207	Moses	BAL	156	Richd.	QUE	15
George	D.C.	189	Robert	CAL	52	Robert	ALL	7
John	BCI	452	Stephen	BAL	142	Sarah	D.C.	97
John, Senr.	KEN	87	Uriah	BAL	83	Simeon	BCI	85
Patk.	D.C.	78	Uriah	BAL	98	Thomas	D.C.	66
Willm.	D.C.	212	FREELEVE, John	BCI	527	Will	D.C.	107

FRENCH (continued),	FRISSLER, George	FRE 103
William ANN 372	FRITCHIE, John	FRE 93
William BCI 69	FRITHEY, Edward	ALL 26
FRESH, James BAL 10	FRITZ, Frederick	WAS 137
William BAL 19	Joseph	BCI 322
FRESHOUR, Catharine	Nicholas	WAS 95
FRE 106	FRIZE, Philip R.	BCI 340
FRESNEY, Joshua (?)	FRIZLE, Abraham	BAL 57
WOR 205	Absolm	BAL 56
FRETTE, Christian FRE 124	Edward	BAL 61
FREY, Daniel ALL 22	George	BAL 56
John BAL 111	Jacob	BAL 55
FREYCUD, Jos. (?) BCI 220	John, Senior	BAL 57
FREYEND, Jos. BCI 220	John, Junr.	BAL 57
FREYER, Henry BCI 191	Stephen	BAL 70
FRIBERGER, Henry BCI 454	William	BAL 57
FRIBURGHER, Henry G.	FRIZZEL, Nimrod	FRE 204
BCI 323	FROCK, Benjamin	FRE 188
FRICE, Jacob TAL 51	Daniel	FRE 197
FRICK, Charlott WAS 123	Henry	BAL 12
Peter BCI 210	Jacob	FRE 197
Rachel WOR 172	Jacob, of Mic.	FRE 197
William BCI 267	John	FRE 193
FRIDAY, Henry FRE 86	Michael	FRE 193
John C. BCI 438	Michael	FRE 196
FRIDINGER, Christian	Peter	FRE 197
FRE 158	William	FRE 196
FRIDLEY, Andrew WAS 88	FROMEY, Daniel	HAR 23
Andrew WAS 90	FROMFELTER, Jacob	
John WAS 90		FRE 197
FRIEND, Charles ALL 4	FRONK, Lewis	D.C. 6
Charles WAS 135	FRONSWA, Marey	BCI 395
Elizabeth WAS 140	FROOT, William	ANN 400
Gabriel ALL 5A	FROST, Bridget	SOM 140
Henry CLN 116	Isaiah	ALL 17
Henry, Jr. CLN 110	James	ANN 352
Isaac CLN 111	John	ANN 318
Jacob WAS 77	John	ANN 381
James D.C. 129	Joseph	BAL 177
Jane WAS 79	Josiah	ALL 17
John ALL 4	Mesheck	ALL 15
John ALL 5A	Nathanial	WAS 145
John CLN 107	FRUSH, Jacob	BCI 356
Joseph ALL 5A	FRUSHOUR, George	FRE 163
Lilley CLN 111	FRY (See also PRY,	
Robert T. WAS 78	VRY),	
FRIEZE, Simon CEC 175A	Andrew	FRE 147
FRIFOGLE, John BAL 5	Ann	BCI 115
FRIGER, Barbary (?)	Christr.	D.C. 186
WAS 60	Elizth.	D.C. 101
FRIJER, Barbary WAS 60	Isaac	FRE 112
FRINEY, Richard WOR 204	James	BCI 55
FRINGE, --- (See FRINGE	Jas.	D.C. 102
& MORRIS)	John	ANN 361
FRINGE & MORRIS BCI 342	John	FRE 113
FRINGER, George BCI 533	John	FRE 114
Jacob FRE 186	John	MON 139
Margaret BAL 22	John	WAS 96
Nicholas FRE 173	Jonathan	WAS 70
Stephen FRE 187	Joseph	FRE 156
FRIP (See also TRIP),	Leonard	PRI 236
Edwd. (?) BCI 340	Martha Ann	BCI 93
FRISBEY, Hanibel QUE 24	Olliver	PRI 198
FRISBY, Ashberry KEN 88	Osburn	PRI 236
Deborah QUE 12	Thomas	D.C. 24
George BCI 145	FRYATT, Susana	BCI 338
Manuel BCI 144	FRYE, John	ALL 6
R. (See Elizth. ED-	Nathaniel	D.C. 10
WARDS & R. FRISBY)	Saml.	BCI 515
BAL 109	FRYFOGLE, David	BAL 142
Richard J. (I.?) KEN 88	FRYMAN, John	WAS 125
Sandy KEN 92	FRYS, Jonathan (?)	WAS 99
Sandy KEN 93	FUGATE, Gustavus	D.C. 180
FRISE, John F. BCI 271	Martin	BAL 77
FRISSELL, Sharlottee	FUITT, Nicholas	D.C. 159
BAL 214	FULALOVE, James	D.C. 48

FULDWILER, George	WAS 118
FULFORD, Mary	BCI 8
William	HAR 18
FULK, William	WAS 127A
FULKER, Henry	FRE 191
FULKS, Elizabeth	ANN 399
Wm.	MON 165
FULLAR, Geo.	BCI 197
FULLARD, Henry	HAR 70
FULLER, Darious	BAL 188
James	HAR 75
Judithen	BAL 201
Nicholas	BAL 11
FULLERTON, James	HAR 8
Mary	BCI 61
FULLHART, Abraham	BAL 128
FULLON, John (?)	BAL 78
FULLOR, John	BAL 78
FULLTON, George	CEC 136
FULLWYTER, John	BCI 531
FULMAN, Henry	QUE 28
Jacob	QUE 33
FULMORE, Lewis	FRE 127
FULMYER, Francis	BAL 208
FULSOME, Joshua	D.C. 86
FULTON, Alexander	CEC 175A
Alexander	FRE 174
David	CEC 136
George	CEC 136
Hugh	CEC 136
James	BAL 176
James	CEC 137
James	HAR 6
James	HAR 9
James	HAR 38
John	BCI 497
Joseph	D.C. 180
Robert	FRE 225
Robt.	D.C. 146
Samuel, ng.	CEC 122
Thomas	CEC 175A
Thos.	BCI 499
William	CEC 137
William	HAR 38
Willm.	BCI 190
FULTZ, Henry	WAS 61
Henry	WAS 106
Jacob	BCI 486
John	BAL 144
John	WAS 140
William	WAS 135
FUNCK, Ann	WAS 98
Christiana	WAS 103
David	WAS 107
David	WAS 108
Henry	WAS 98
Henry	WAS 107
Isaac	WAS 86
Jacob	WAS 108
John	WAS 90
John	WAS 101
John	WAS 107
Michael	WAS 59
Mary	WAS 98
Peter	WAS 84
Samuel	WAS 86
FUNDABURG, David	FRE 222
FUNDENBURG, Henry	
	FRE 154
John	FRE 160
FUNK, Benedict	BCI 457
Elizabeth	FRE 156
George	FRE 219
Henry	FRE 161
Jacob	MON 177
FUNSTON, John	FRE 210

FURBUSH, James	SOM 117	
John	QUE 3	
Nelly	SOM 109	
FURDEN, --- (?)	DOR 32	
FURGERSON, Henry	SAI 88	
James	BCI 338	
Jonathan	SAI 92	
Margaret	DOR 3	
Wm.	BCI 340	
FURGURSON, Samuel	DOR 50	
FURGUSAN, David	D.C. 23	
FURGUSON, James	CHA 204	
James	TAL 6	
Jane	WAS 112	
Robert	CHA 197	
FURLONE, John (?)	BCI 5	
FURLONG, John E.	BCI 239	
Thomas	ANN 293	
William	BCI 103	
FURLOW, John	BCI 5	
FURLY, Wm.	FRE 223	
FURNACE, Willm.	D.C. 171	
FURNESS, William	WOR 192	
FURNEY, Jacob	BCI 35	
FURNISS, Josiah	SOM 153	
Littleton	SOM 139	
FURROW, Ben	WOR 197	
Joseph	WOR 170	
FURRY, Abraham	FRE 220	
John	WAS 65	
John	WAS 125	
Martin	WAS 64	
FURTNY, Samual	WAS 146	
FUSER, Elizabeth	FRE 179	
Jacob	FRE 172	
John	FRE 179	
FUSS, Daniel	FRE 169	
John	BCI 323	
John, Senr.	FRE 173	
John, Junr.	FRE 173	
Phillip	FRE 173	
William	FRE 174	
FUSSEL, Henery	BAL 86	
FUSSELL, Bartholomew	BAL 237	
Jacob	BAL 237	
Joseph	BAL 237	
FUSTOR, John	WAS 139	
FYE, Baltus	HAR 22	
FYFFE, John	MON 136	

--- G ---

GAARDE, Mary Ann	BCI 57	
GABBLE, Wm.	BCI 488	
GABLE, Elizabeth	BCI 325	
Mary A.	ANN 298	
GABRIEL, Wm.	BCI 536	
GABY, Joseph	WAS 97	
William	WAS 97	
GAD, Benjamin	DOR 24	
John	DOR 22	
Mahala	DOR 20	
GADOLDICH, Henry	FRE 117	
GADOLTICK, George	FRE 116	
GADSBY, John	BAL 191	
GAETZ, --- (Widaw)	BCI 376	
GAFFERD, Elisha	QUE 9	
Jas.	QUE 13	

GAFFERD (continued),		
Wm.	QUE 12	
GAFFORD, Benjamin	QUE 23	
James	QUE 3	
Jos.	BCI 226	
Joseph	HAR 7	
GAGE, Mathew	DOR 8	
GAHAGAN, Patk.	D.C. 73	
GAHAN, Henry (?)	BCI 401	
William	D.C. 86	
GAILER, Thomas	PRI 191A	
GAILEY, John	CEC 176	
GAILOR, Andrew	WAS 90	
GAILY, Daniel	KEN 92	
GAIMS, John	WAS 101	
GAINEE, Robert (?)	PRI 237	
GAINER, Robert	PRI 237	
GAINGER, Nathaniel	ANN 301	
GAINS, James	BCI 527	
Moses	CAL 44	
GAITER, Abraham	BCI 449	
GAITES, Benjamin	WAS 79	
Benjanin	WAS 79	
Charles	WAS 140	
Elenora	WAS 79	
GAITHER, Ann	ANN 288	
Beal	ANN 329	
Beal, Senr.	MON 143	
Beal, of Gerard	MON 177	
Benjn.	MON 137	
Edward	WAS 105	
Ephm. of Wm.	MON 144	
Ephraim S.	ANN 326	
Frdk.	MON 143	
G.	D.C. 85	
Geo.	MON 176	
Greenberry	ANN 370	
Henny	MON 143	
Henry	D.C. 59	
Henry C.	MON 143	
James	D.C. 7	
Jeremiah	ANN 339	
John	ANN 288	
John	ANN 370	
John	ANN 392	
John; of Rezin	ANN 288	
Josep	ANN 370	
Joshuas	ANN 343	
Mary	D.C. 95	
Rachel	ANN 288	
Rezin	ANN 370	
Samuel	ANN 379	
Samuel	PRI 181	
Sarah	ANN 373	
Susannah	ANN 344	
William	FRE 212	
Zakariah	WAS 101	
GALAWAY, Edward	FRE 105	
Lydia	BCI 121	
GALBREATH, James	CEC 176	
John	HAR 78	
GALE, Anthoy.	D.C. 128	
Charles (f.n.)	SOM 120	
Davy	SOM 155	
George	CEC 158	
Henry	SOM 110	
Isaac	KEN 109	
James	CEC 137	
James	KEN 88	
John (f.n.)	SOM 119	
John P.	SOM 110	
Leven	CEC 137	
Margret	CEC 158	
Martha	KEN 106A	

GALE (continued),		
Meriah	SOM 156	
Philip	KEN 91	
Rasin	KEN 106A	
Robert	ANN 290	
Rose (f.n.)	SOM 119	
Thomas	CEC 123	
Thomas	KEN 106	
Thomas	KEN 106A	
GALES, Jinny-free	CAL 60	
Joseph	D.C. 86	
GALL, Lusi	BCI 343	
Micheal	BAL 91	
GALLACER, Thomas	BAL 8	
GALLAGHER, Daniel	FRE 193	
Edward	BCI 458	
Gruce	BCI 133	
Michl.	BCI 166	
GALLAGHIR, Elizabeth	BCI 440	
GALLAHA, Edwd.	MON 160	
GALLAHAN, Susanna	PRI 231	
Thomas	PRI 231	
GALLAHER, John	CEC 137	
John	CEC 159	
John	D.C. 84	
Unity	CEC 176	
GALLAND, Jno. B.	BCI 210	
GALLARD, William	D.C. 87	
GALLAWAY, Aquilla	BCI 409	
Gas.	MON 160	
James	ANN 254	
Jehu	BCI 67	
Jos.	MON 163	
S.	BCI 371	
Thomas	BCI 22	
Thomas	BCI 82	
Willm.	D.C. 75	
GALLAWEY, Nancy	CAL 60	
Rebecca	CAL 60	
GALLEGA, Francis	BCI 4	
GALLESIO, Charles	FRE 107	
GALLINGER, John	BCI 514	
GALLION, Alexander	HAR 29	
Elizabeth	HAR 20	
Greenbury	HAR 28	
James	HAR 71	
Stansbury	HAR 25	
GALLIWAY, John	CAL 51	
GALLOWAY, Absalom	HAR 44	
Aquila	HAR 44	
Benjamin	WAS 118	
Henry	ALL 31	
Isaac	ANN 283	
Moses	BAL 130	
Moses	HAR 28	
Rachel	BCI 49	
Robert C.	BAL 115	
Sam	PRI 194	
Will.	D.C. 84	
William	PRI 194	
William H.	HAR 39	
GALLUP, Charles	HAR 23	
Gilbert	HAR 23	
Oliver	HAR 18	
Thomas, Senr.	HAR 23	
Thos. of Chs.	HAR 23	
GALLWORTH, John	WAS 60	
GALOWAY, James	BCI 145	
Rob	BCI 516	
GALT, Mathew	FRE 169	
Moses	FRE 171	
Peter	BCI 45	

GALT (continued)
Sarah FRE 180
Wm. FRE 224
GALVIN, Dorcas D.C.101
GALWORTH, Sary MON 163
GALWORTHS, Gabriel
MON 161
GAMBALL, John (?) BAL 228
GAMBLE, Benj. ALL 35
Darius KEN 92
Gideon CLN 106
Greensberry KEN 88
John BCI 121
Orange ANN 267
Polly ANN 400
Robert S. KEN 88
Samuel KEN 95
Thomas BCI 132
Will D.C.113
GAMBRALL, John BCI 196
GAMBRIAL, Richard ANN 338
GAMBRIEL, Henry TAL 34A
James, Ovsr. TAL 40
Levi TAL 34A
Peter ANN 336
Thomas ANN 304
GAMBRIELL, Augustin
ANN 342
Lidy ANN 342
Stephen ANN 342
GAMBRILL, Ann ANN 313
George G. ANN 334
John DOR 57
Richardson DOR 51
William ANN 300
GAMBY, David WAS 136
Mary FRE 77
Meshec DOR 13
Meshee? DOR 13
Primus DOR 13
GAME, Charles (f.n.)
SOM 119
George (f.n.) SOM 120
Henry (f.n.) SOM 120
Levin (f.n.) SOM 120
Sarah (f.n.) SOM 119
GAMES, Philip BAL 123
GANE, Jacab DOR 27
Jacob? DOR 27
GANNON, James D.C.65
James D.C.86
James TAL 52
John BCI 2
Memery TAL 4
Robert TAL 46
Sarah BCI 11
GANSEY, Joseph BCI 38
GANT, Christopher L.
ANN 287
GANTEAUME, James BIC 4
GANTT, Ann PRI 196
Benjamin L. PRI 196
Cath. D.C.106
Charles CAL 43
Daniel D.C.3
David PRI 196
Eliza D.C.13
Feelder PRI 194
Mary PRI 207
Mary H. CAL 62
Spencer D.C.26
Thomas CAL 62
Thos. (Doctr.) CAL 47
GANTZ, Adam BCI 490
GARACHT, Justus FRE 99

GARBER, Christian
FRE 189
John FRE 159
John FRE 171
Michael FRE 180
GARDENER, Alce QUE 38
George ANN 255
Isaac ANN 384
M. BCI 353
Richard QUE 47
Robert QUE 45
Willey ANN 274
GARDER, John ANN 300
GARDINER, --- (Mrs.)
D.C.108
Aloysius PRI 223
Caleb D.C.84
Charles CAL 63
Geo. BCI 302
George CHA 228
Ignatious PRI 223
Ignatius W. CHA 228
Isadore CHA 207A
James BCI 63
James CHA 228
James SAI 96
John BAL 59
John CHA 225
John F. CHA 224
Joseph CHA 226
Joseph A. CHA 225
Joshua N. PRI 219
Richard CHA 214
Richard B. CHA 227
Sylvester F. PRI 223
Thomas SAI 96
William BAL 58
William CAL 67
William CHA 223
GARDINOUR, Jacob
WAS 62
GARDNER, --- (Mrs.)
BCI 407
--- (Mrs.) D.C.14
Abraham ANN 335
Ann WAS 68
Cassander MON 162
Daniel BCI 2
Elias MON 143
Elizabeth FRE 93
Elizabeth FRE 98
Ephraim BCI 241
Gabriel CAL 45
George BCI 28
Honor MON 139
Ignatius MON 151
Isaac CAL 43
J. (I.?) L. (Lieut.)
D.C.45
James ANN 292
James BCI 29
John ANN 311
John BCI 36
Martha ANN 391
Mary BCI 75
Peter MON 140
Samuel ANN 311
Samuel BCI 129
Thomas ANN 399
Thomas D.C.54
Timothy BCI 59
William (?) ANN 306
William FRE 98
William KEN 86
William TAL 47
William P. D.C.15

GARDNER (continued),
Wm. C. D.C.177
Zachariah D.C.182
GARETSON, Jazan FRE 68
Jazar? FRE 68
GAREY, Ann D.C.47
Frederick ALL 25
George CLN 92
Gideon BCI 538
Jeremiah BCI 319
John ALL 20A
John TAL 46
Peter ALL 28
William G. BCI 145
GARIE, Hugh CEC 137
GARISH, Francis BAL 129
James BCI 309
GARLAND, John KEN 118
GARLETZ, Christian
ALL 9
GARLICK, Elizh. D.C.78
GARLINGER, Jacob WAS 93
GARLOCK, Henry WAS 110
GARLOUGH, Jacob WAS 148
GARMAN, Samuel WAS 60
GARNAND, Adam FRE 154
Jacob FRE 154
John FRE 154
William FRE 155
GARNAUD, John (?)
FRE 154
GARNER (See also
EARNER),
Ann PRI 216
Barnaby CEC 159
Benjamin PRI 216
Flin BAL 11
George FRE 200
Hannah (?) FRE 191
Harner BCI 308
Henry G. SAI 93
Ignatius F. PRI 212
James CEC 175A
Jesse D.C.41
John CHA 210A
John PRI 217
John WAS 68
John C. SAI 98
Joseph CHA 194
Joseph HAR 59
Margt. D.C.167
Michael PRI 217
N. BCI 398
P. BCI 398
Sarah PRI 215
Thomas CHA 210A
Tristram D.C.172
William CHA 196A
GARNETT, Geo. QUE 2A
Joseph FRE 112
Prince KEN 118
Robert KEN 108
Samuel CEC 123
GARNHART, Henry
FRE 102
GARNISH, Edward CEC 159
GARRATY, Patrick WAS 146
GARRAUD, Edward BCI 47
GARRAUGH, Jos. BCI 216
GARREL, William BAL 210
GARRET, Catharine
FRE 162
Christian FRE 190
Elizabeth BAL 98
Isaac BAL 93

GEORGE (continued),		
Joseph J.	QUE 39	
Parker	WOR 219	
Stephen	BCI 315	
W. E.	BCI 339	
William	CEC 123	
William	CEC 137	
GEORGETOWN, COL-		
LEGE OF	D.C.61	
GEPHARD, George	FRE 105	
John	FRE 95	
GEPHART, John	ALL 28	
John, Jun.	ALL 28	
Peter	ALL 29	
Peter	FRE 96	
William	ALL 28	
GERD, Eudocia	D.C.198	
GERE, Samuel (?)	BAL 60	
GERHEART, John	FRE 219	
GERMAN (See also JER-		
MAN, JERMEN, JER-		
MIN),		
--- (Widaw)	BCI 408	
A.	BCI 55	
Benjamin	BAL 217	
Benjamin	BAL 225	
David	BAL 121	
John	BCI 85	
Saml.	QUE 11	
Thomas	BAL 225	
William	BCI 301	
GEROM (See also JEROM),		
James	KEN 104	
GERRALD, Elijah F.	SOM 157	
Elisha	SOM 149	
Jessy	SOM 153	
GERRING, --- (Mr.)	BCI 369	
GERRY, James	CEC 176	
John S.	CEC 175A	
GERTY, Nancy	FRE 218	
GERVER, John	FRE 217	
GESABUNT, Jonathan		
	FRE 82	
GESS, Martha	FRE 74	
GESSFORD, Sarah	QUE 20	
GEST, Independant	FRE 146	
Richard	BCI 337	
GETS, John	FRE 187	
GETTIER, Jacob	BAL 138	
Jacob of Heny	BAL 138	
Peter	BAL 145	
Peter, of Hey.	BAL 142	
GETTINGER, Conrad	BAL 150	
Francis	BAL 10	
Jacob	BAL 10	
Jacob, Sener	BAL 10	
GETTINGS, Joseph	D.C.14	
Thomas	CHA 210A	
GETTIS, Francis	KEN 116	
GETTY, Anthoney	WAS 125	
Francis	BCI 245	
Jas.	BCI 293	
John A. (?)	WOR 188	
Robert	D.C.37	
GETTYS, James	D.C.49	
GETZ, Frederick	BCI 280	
GETZENDANNER, Alexander		
	FRE 113	
Henry	FRE 104	
Jacob	FRE 87	
Jacob	FRE 109	
John	FRE 111	
Mary	FRE 93	
GETZENDENNER, Thos.		
	MON 163	
GEUGAN, Henry	BCI 232	

GEW, Henry, Jnr.	ANN 372	
GEYER, John	BCI 166	
GEYMAN, Christopher		
	BAL 147	
GHEARHEART, Charine		
	WAS 105	
Daniel	WAS 108	
Jacob	WAS 128A	
GHEQUEIRE, Harriott		
	BCI 437	
GHER, Daniel	WAS 56	
GHERR, Andrew	WAS 99	
Daniel	WAS 135	
GHIRARDINI, Vincent		
	BCI 47	
GHISLIN, Reverdy	PRI 219	
GIANT, Sarah	KEN 106	
GIBB, David	BCI 285	
GIBBINS, John	MON 132	
Leah	SOM 145	
Wm.	CAL 47	
GIBBIONS, Thomas	BAL 206	
William	BAL 184	
GIBBON, Fiby	BCI 338	
GIBBONEY, John	WAS 133	
GIBBONS, --- (Mrs.)		
	PRI 196	
Alexander	PRI 215	
Benjamin T.	CHA 222	
Edward	D.C.22	
Elizabeth	PRI 214	
George	SAI 67	
George T.	PRI 216	
Jacob	FRE 110	
James H.	PRI 213	
John R.	PRI 214	
John R., Jr.	PRI 215	
Levin	SOM 123	
Mary	BCI 242	
Matthew	ALL 3	
Oswell	CHA 224	
Peter	SOM 155	
Robert	SAI 67	
Thomas	CAL 60	
GIBBONY, John	FRE 202	
GIBBS, Abraham	WOR 162	
Absalom	QUE 11	
Caty	QUE 14	
Eliza	QUE 13	
Hannah	CEC 137	
Huntley	D.C.208	
James	ANN 299	
James	BCI 513	
Jim	QUE 20	
John	BCI 445	
John	FRE 123	
John H.	D.C.193	
Mary	ANN 275	
Priscilla	BCI 62	
Thomas	ANN 253	
Varnal	PRI 196	
GIBISON, E.	CEC 137	
GIBS, Coffy	KEN 115	
William	BAL 190	
GIBSAN, John	D.C.59	
GIBSON, Andrew	CEC 137	
Ann	KEN 100	
Benjamin	HAR 39	
Bennett	SOM 129	
Charles	D.C.26	
Charles	TAL 47	
Cristopher (?)	TAL 52	
David	BCI 359	
Edward R.	TAL 6	
Eliza	DOR 19	
Elizabeth	FRE 68	

GIBSON (continued),		
Elizabeth	SOM 130	
Fayette	TAL 7	
Gabriel	BAL 130	
George	BCI 86	
George	CAL 64	
George	KEN 104	
Gerard	D.C.138	
Gustavus	D.C.185	
Hannah-f.c.p.	HAR 10	
Henny	TAL 49	
Hugh	BCI 190	
Ignatious	TAL 10	
Ignatius	HAR 22	
Isaac	CHA 224	
Isaac	D.C.194	
Jacob	TAL 9	
James	BCI 2	
James	CAL 67	
James	PRI 213	
James	QUE 24	
James	SOM 152	
James	TAL 39	
Jeremiah	SAI 88	
John (?)	D.C.59	
John	ANN 309	
John	BAL 221	
John	BCI 269	
John	CAL 60	
John	CAL 61	
John	CLN 73	
John	D.C.131	
John	SOM 128	
John	SOM 152	
John, Junr.	CAL 64	
Joseph	D.C.34	
Joshua	BCI 98	
Joshua	CEC 175A	
Leah	TAL 33	
Lewis	D.C.216	
Mary	CEC 158	
Mary A.	SAI 93	
Nathan	TAL 40	
Patrick	BCI 109	
Peter, Senr.	CAL 60	
Philemon	TAL 35	
Phoebe	D.C.84	
Pompy	TAL 36	
Rebecca	D.C.101	
Richard	D.C.61	
Richard	QUE 17	
Samuel	CAL 60	
Samuel	CAL 60	
Samuel	CAL 62	
Samuel	SAI 57	
Samuel of Rd.	CAL 62	
Sarah	TAL 4	
Sidney	CLN 96	
Thomas	CAL 58A	
W.	BCI 350	
William	BAL 129	
William	BCI 465	
William	CLN 78	
William	HAR 57	
William	QUE 42	
William	SAI 78	
William	SOM 130	
Wm.	BCI 188	
Wm.	CAL 49	
Woolman	QUE 47	
GIBSOR, Cristopher	TAL 52	
GIDDENS, John	D.C.137	
GIDDIER, Mary	BCI 449	
GIDDINS, Geo.	D.C.134	
GIDEON, Jacob, Jun.	D.C.86	
GIDINGER, George	WAS 104	

GIDLEY, Samuel	KEN 104	
GIFFEN, Ann	TAL 13	
GIFFIN, John	CEC 175A	
Robert	ANN 293	
GIFFORD, Alexander		
	BCI 99	
GILBECK, Chrs.	BCI 192	
GILBERT, Abner	HAR 26	
Amos	HAR 20	
Amos	HAR 26	
Ann	BCI 72	
Archillas	CEC 175A	
Charles	HAR 18	
Esiba.	D.C. 170	
Geo.	FRE 191	
George	BCI 70	
George	FRE 150	
George	FRE 226	
Henry	BCI 182	
Henry	FRE 174	
Henry	FRE 212	
Henry	HAR 26	
Henry	QUE 16	
Jacob	FRE 115	
Jacob	HAR 18	
James	BCI 416	
James	HAR 18	
James	HAR 26	
James	KEN 91	
Jervis	HAR 26	
Jesse	KEN 118	
John	BAL 69	
John	FRE 226	
Louis	KEN 94	
Martin	HAR 26	
Micah	HAR 26	
Michael	HAR 18	
Michael, of Wm.	HAR 45	
Peter R.	FRE 76A	
Rebecca	D.C. 13	
Reuben	FRE 132	
Rosetta	KEN 118	
Ruth	BCI 18	
Samuel	WAS 110	
Thomas	WAS 84	
William	HAR 25	
Wm.	QUE 9	
GILBERTHORP, William		
	BCI 70	
GILCHRIST, Andrew		
	WOR 153	
GILCOATE, John	FRE 75	
GILDEA, Daniel	HAR 7	
GILDENIER, Charles		
	BCI 90	
GILDHARDT, Frans. X.		
	BCI 219	
GILDS, Echard	FRE 114	
GILE, Honor (?)	BCI 500	
GILES, Easter	BAL 200	
Grace	BCI 427	
Hannah-Negro	HAR 50	
Jacob-Negro	HAR 80	
Jacob W.	BCI 123	
Jerry-free	CAL 62	
John	BAL 93	
John	D.C. 75	
Joseph	BCI 533	
Joseph	KEN 106	
Moses	DOR 11	
R. John	CEC 137	
Rhody	TAL 39	
Robert-Negro	HAR 80	
Sally	BCI 523	
Scipio-Negro	HAR 80	
Toby	BAL 128	
William	SOM 110	

GILES (continued),		
William	WAS 106	
Wm.	BAL 82	
Wm.	BAL 93	
GILESPIE, John	HAR 75	
GILHAM, Willm.	D.C. 143	
GILL, Benjamin	BAL 23	
Bennett	BCI 161	
Brison	BCI 538	
Charles	CHA 227	
Cristr	D.C. 107	
Edward	BAL 22	
Edward	BAL 27	
Ezekiel C.	BCI 184	
Gustavus	CHA 228	
Honor	BCI 500	
James	BAL 28	
Jas.	D.C. 118	
John	BAL 23	
John	BAL 27	
John	BCI 118	
John	BCI 122	
John	BCI 284	
John	BCI 286	
John	BCI 340	
John	BCI 379	
John	CLN 87	
Joshua	BAL 11	
Joshua	BAL 89	
Mary	SAI 54	
Nicholas	BAL 89	
Nicholas	BAL 214	
S. G.	BCI 401	
Selman	BAL 228	
Stephen	BAL 27	
Walter	FRE 133	
GILLAND, Margaret	FRE 142	
GILLARD, Nichl.	BCI 201	
GILLASPIE, John	BCI 285	
GILLASPY, Patrick	CLN 88	
GILLEN, Thomas	WAS 95	
GILLESPIE, Daniel	CEC 158	
Edward	ALL 33	
Frances	CEC 175A	
George	CEC 175A	
James	CEC 158	
John	BCI 121	
John	CEC 175A	
Mary	CEC 176	
Patrick	BCI 63	
GILLET, --- (Major?)		
	WOR 160	
John	WOR 154	
Major	WOR 160	
GILLETT, Marlain	BCI 413	
Martain?	BCI 413	
GILLEY, Caleb	BCI 159	
GILLIAS, Samuel	WAS 136	
GILLICK, Thomas	D.C. 105	
GILLIGAN, Michl.	D.C. 84	
GILLILAN, John	FRE 183	
GILLILAND, John	FRE 143	
Margaret	FRE 150	
GILLINGHAM, --- (Mr.)		
	BAL 234	
George	ANN 320	
James	BCI 374	
John	BCI 348	
Moses	CEC 175A	
Thomas	CEC 137	
Wm.	BCI 374	
GILLINGS, Jerremiah		
	FRE 125	
William	BCI 160	
GILLIS, Betsy	DOR 61	
George	D.C. 16	
Hamlet	BAL 68	

GILLIS (continued),		
Poshus	BAL 65	
Wm.	BAL 92	
GILLISPEE, Simon	MON 143	
GILLISPIE, Bolitha	D.C. 107	
Isaac	D.C. 126	
James	CEC 175A	
William	PRI 195	
GILLISS, Ezekiel	SOM 111	
Ezekiel McC.	SOM 123	
Joseph J.	WOR 171	
Josiah	SOM 103	
Levin J. (I.?)	PRI 206	
Rachael	SOM 105	
Thos. H.	D.C. 81	
GILLMYER, Catharine		
	FRE 142	
George	FRE 148	
GILLS, Sally (?)	BCI 523	
GILLUM, Thomas	D.C. 11	
GILLY, John	BCI 123	
GILMAN, E.	D.C. 89	
GILMOR, Robt., Sr.	BCI 244	
Robt., Jun.	BCI 243	
William	BCI 246	
GILMORE, --- (Mrs.)	BCI 352	
David	CEC 158	
Mary	BCI 26	
William	BAL 118	
GILMOT, Andrew J. (I.?)		
	BCI 229	
GILPIN, Bernard	MON 151	
George	BCI 16	
Jane	D.C. 159	
Thomas	CEC 137	
GILSON, Richard	FRE 180	
GILYUM, Thomas	D.C. 5	
GIMBALL, John	BAL 228	
GINAMAN, Paddy	BAL 197	
GINET, Cassandra	HAR 60	
GINKINS (See also JENKENS,		
JENKINS, JINKENS),		
Felex	FRE 84	
Henry	FRE 82	
Simon	FRE 83	
GINN, Elijah	WOR 161	
James	BAL 208	
John	CEC 137	
GINNAMAN, Giles	BAL 174	
GIPSEN, Wm.	BAL 4	
GIPSON, Benjamin	KEN 91	
Horatio	BAL 11	
GIRAUD, Jno.	BCI 241	
GIRD, Eudocia (?)	D.C. 198	
John	D.C. 143	
GIRTSIDE, Gabriel	BAL 231	
GISEBERT, Abraham	FRE 85	
Gisbert	FRE 85	
GISINER, John	HAR 48	
GIST, David R.	BAL 3	
Frances	DOR 3	
George W.	FRE 186	
James H.	QUE 46	
Joshua	FRE 198	
Mordica	BAL 8	
Ruth	BAL 9	
Thomas	FRE 230	
Thomas	FRE 234	
Thomas B.	BAL 143	
Thos. H.	BAL 3	
William	DOR 54	
Wm.	BCI 372	
GITCHELL, Suzanatt	CEC 137	
Suzannatt?	CEC 137	
GITHENS, Delaple.	D.C. 104	
GITON, Joseph	BAL 190	
GITT, Jacob	BAL 140	

GITTINGER, Elizabeth	BAL 158	GLASSGOW, W.	BCI 349	GODDARD (continued),			
Elizabeth	FRE 116	GLAYD, Jane	MON 137	Saml. B.	D.C.81		
John	FRE 116	GLAZE, George W.	ALL 36	Sollomin?	PRI 193		
GITTINGS, Archibald	BAL 239	Wm.	MON 173	Sollomon	PRI 193		
Berry	MON 167	GLAZER, Ricker?	D.C.9	Stephen	PRI 226		
Harriett	BAL 235	Ruker	D.C.9	Thomas	SOM 103		
James (Senr.)	BAL 235	GLAZIER, Jacob	BCI 190	Zacheriah	D.C.42		
Jerremiah (?)	FRE 125	Jacob	FRE 201	GODDART, --- (Mrs.)			
Joseph	MON 151	Jno.	BCI 240		BCI 453		
Mary	BCI 503	GLEAVES, Edward	QUE 2A	GODDERD, --- (Widaw)			
Richard	BAL 231	George	QUE 3		BCI 388		
Sarah	BAL 237	Jno. W.	QUE 5	CODFERY, Charles	WOR 206		
Stephen G.	BCI 112	Wm. F.	KEN 121	Samuel (?)	ANN 375		
Thomas	MON 150	GLEED, Comfort	BCI 16	GODFREY, Arther	WOR 193		
William?	BCI 160	GLEEN, John, Esqr.		Benjamin	BCI 111		
William	MON 151		BCI 268	John	BCI 534		
GITTY, John A.	WOR 188	GLEIM, Jacob	FRE 203	Josiah	WOR 193		
GIVANS, Ann	SOM 131	GLENDY, John	BCI 122	Samuel	ANN 375		
Ezekiel	SOM 123	GLENN, David	BCI 21	William	D.C.18		
Isaac	WOR 199A	Elias	BCI 493	GODFRY, Betsy-wd.	WOR 217		
John, Senr.	SOM 122	Elizabeth (?)	QUE 35	Henry	BAL 106		
Joshua	WOR 201	Hannah	FRE 201	William	WOR 219		
Nehemiah	SOM 132	James	BCI 175	GODMAN, Brutus	BCI 524		
Reubin	SOM 126	John	KEN 88	Humphrey	PRI 180A		
Robert; S.	WOR 217	Michael	KEN 87	Samuel	ANN 316		
Robert; J.	WOR 217	Nathan	HAR 59	GODSHALL, Andr. (?)			
Samuel	WOR 211	Robert	CEC 137		BCI 484		
Thomas	WOR 217	Robert	HAR 58	GODSHELL, Andr.	BCI 484		
William	WOR 199A	Robt.	D.C.204	GODWIN, George	QUE 16		
Zadoc	SOM 126	Saml.	BCI 166	James	QUE 46		
GIVENS, Isaac	SOM 156	Samuel	BCI 10	Jas.	QUE 6		
GIVERSON, Will.	D.C.104	Samuel	QUE 31	Jas.	QUE 16		
GIVIN, Thomas	D.C.79	William	HAR 58	Jeremiah	QUE 46		
GLACHAN, Daniel	CEC 176	William	QUE 26	John	QUE 26		
GLADDEN, Jacob	HAR 55	GLETTNER, Jacob	WAS 132	Kimmel	CLN 94		
John	HAR 64	GLISSAN, Charles	FRE 215	Saml.	QUE 18		
Polly	WOR 153	Saml.	FRE 215	Seth	CLN 74		
William	HAR 73	GLISSIN, John	FRE 219	Thomas	QUE 27		
GLADDIN, Edmond	WOR 154	GLISSON, James	MON 130	Thos.	QUE 3		
GLADEN, Susanna	D.C.152	GLOMDING, Jas., Ju.		Wm.	KEN 124		
GLADMAN, Hannah	BAL 69		QUE 6	GODY, Walter	D.C.32		
John	MON 150	GLOSSBRENNER, Adam		GOEN, Nat-f.c.p.	HAR 10		
Nancy	BAL 39		WAS 120	GOEY, James	D.C.107		
Thomas	BAL 39	Christiana	WAS 114	GOFF, Jacob	QUE 25		
GLAN, R. W.	BCI 80	GLOSSER, John	FRE 218	GOFLIN, Thomas	DOR 62		
GLANDEN, Shadrack	CLN 88	Philip	FRE 177	GOHAGAN, Robert	BCI 457		
Solomon	CLN 91	Philip	FRE 216	GOHAN, Henry	BCI 401		
Thomas	DOR 39	William	FRE 217	GOINARD, John	BCI 294		
GLANDING, Archd.	QUE 16	GLOVER, Charles	D.C.94	GOINGS, Benjn.?	D.C.213		
David	QUE 15	James	DOR 16	Binjn.	D.C.213		
James	QUE 9	Richard	D.C.29	George	FRE 80		
James	QUE 9	Thos.	D.C.187	George	FRE 87		
James	QUE 16	William	BCI 284	Jonston	D.C.217		
Jas.	QUE 16	GLOYD, Daniel	PRI 195	Joseph	D.C.188		
Jas.	QUE 20	Geo.	D.C.104	GOLD, James	DOR 44		
Jas., Ju. (?)	QUE 6	Jane (?)	MON 137	Peter	BCI 299		
GLANDON, Thomas	DOR 54	Samuel	PRI 195	GOLDEN, Daniel	ANN 363		
GLANVILLE, Jas.	QUE 10	William	D.C.64	Saml.	QUE 17		
John	BCI 446	GLUYES, --- (See		GOLDER, A.	BCI 381		
William	QUE 5	GLUYES & MAJOR)		R.	BCI 368		
GLAPES, Conrod	BCI 191	GLUYES & MAJOR	D.C.176	Robert	FRE 186		
GLARLINGER, Henry	WAS 90	GOBRIGHT, William	BCI 90	GOLDING, Andrew	WAS 145		
GLASCO, Charles	DOR 44	GODDARD, Benjamin		Chs.	QUE 19		
John	D.C.12		PRI 230	William	ALL 37		
GLASCOCK, Sarah	D.C.179	Edw.	D.C.42	Wm. R.	D.C.13		
Willm.	D.C.210	Edward B.	SAI 89	GOLDSBERRY, Benjamin			
GLASCOW, Sarah	WOR 158	George	SOM 104		SAI 64		
GLASGLOW, Theodore	PRI 223	James	SAI 77	Charles	SAI 70		
GLASGOW, Charles	DOR 60	Jeremiah	SAI 69	James	SAI 82		
James	HAR 41	John	D.C.25	William	SAI 76		
John	D.C.19	John	PRI 231	GOLDSBORAUGH, Ch. W.			
GLASS, John	BCI 69	John	SOM 106		D.C.7		
Peter	WAS 55A	John B.	D.C.41	GOLDSBORO, Charles			
Samuel	FRE 188	Nancy	SOM 112		DOR 12		
Vallentine	WAS 125	Nelly	D.C.205	GOLDSBOROUGH, Acahsah			
		Robert	HAR 79		ANN 389		

GOLDSBOROUGH (continued),
Charles TAL 14
Ephraim TAL 3
Greenbury TAL 39
Henry QUE 17
Herculus CLN 74
Honse? DOR 4
House? DOR 4
Howes HAR 18
Isaac QUE 18
James TAL 40
John BCI 426
John TAL 10
Joseph TAL 51
Nicholas TAL 38
Richard Y. D.C. 11
Robert H. TAL 8A
Sophiah TAL 9
Thomas CLN 76
William FRE 100
GOLDSBURY, Cornelius
SAI 56
Ignatius SAI 68
GOLDSMITH, --- (Widow)
BCI 395
James SAI 96
John D.C. 106
Sarah BCI 49
Townley CHA 225
GOLDTWARD, --- (Widaw)
BCI 389
GOLEE, James SOM 106
GOLER, James KEN 91
GOLEY, Elias CHA 191
GOLHICH, Richard BCI 483
GOLIBERT, Joseph BCI 3
GOLL, Christian F. WAS 114
John WAS 133
William A. E. WAS 94
GOLLAGER, Daniel WAS 63
GOLLAHAN, James TAL 48
GOLLEGER, Daniel FRE 219
GOLLEY, Catharine FRE 182
John FRE 182
GOLLICKKOFER, D. (?)
BCI 337
GOLT, James QUE 39
John QUE 33
Vachel QUE 33
William QUE 29
GOMBER, John FRE 102
GOMBLE, Polly FRE 189
GOMLY, Catharine BCI 521
GONDER, Jacob FRE 147
GONEGORE, Conwell PRI 229
GONSO, Jacob FRE 106
GONTZ, Stephen WAS 98
GONZER, John FRE 228
GOOD, Elizabeth CHA 223
Josiah WAS 55A
William CHA 223
William D.C. 26
GOODALL, Mathew BCI 508
Thos. D.C. 130
GOODBUN, James BCI 285
GOODD, Sarah BCI 78
GOODEN, Anthony BAL 91
George BAL 162
John BCI 217
Joshua BAL 153
Mary BAL 97
Philip BAL 85
GOODENBAGER, Andrew
BAL 6
GOODHAND, Christr. QUE 5
Jacob TAL 50

GOODHAND (continued),
James QUE 46
John QUE 46
William QUE 49
GOODIN, John CAL 44
GOODING, Ann BCI 120
Archibald CEC 138
Benjamin KEN 101
Frances BCI 121
Hellen BAL 48
Jacob BCI 349
John CEC 137
Lambert KEN 118
Lambert F.? FRE 98
Lambert T. FRE 98
Sarah KEN 120
William KEN 86
Zebidee KEN 103
GOODMAN, Clarissa
BCI 306
John KEN 94
Marmaduke QUE 46
Martha KEN 94
Moses BCI 508
Philip FRE 110
William ANN 394
William FRE 113
GOODMANSON, Peter
BCI 56
GOODRICH, Elijah CHA 201
George CHA 202
John CHA 203
Silvester CHA 202
Thos. D.C. 215
Willm. D.C. 215
GOODRICK, Ely BCI 52
Geo. D.C. 215
GOODS, Benjn. D.C. 195
Benjn. D.C. 197
GOODWIN, --- (Widow)
BCI 382
Alexander BAL 59
Caleb BAL 248
Caleb BCI 19
Edward BAL 248
Henry SAI 98
James D.C. 100
John BAL 248
John (farm) BAL 115
John R. WAS 123
Llyd BCI 270
Lyde BAL 112
Peter D.C. 192
Richard (overser
for Ann SAPPTON)
SAI 96
Rosanna BAL 109
T. BCI 401
GOODY, Arnet WAS 123
Arnett? WAS 123
William D.C. 22
GOODYER, Francis D.C. 14
Peter D.C. 18
Peter & Wm. MARAN
D.C. 14
GOOMS, Nathan BCI 308
William ANN 265
GOONE (See also GOORE),
George (?) DOR 19
Levin (?) DOR 19
Standly (?) DOR 18
GOORE (See also GOONE),
George DOR 19
Levin DOR 19
Standly DOR 18

GOOSTEN, Elizbeth (?)
DOR 19
GOOSTER, Elizibeth DOR 19
GOOSTOR, Amey DOR 19
GOOSTOX, Amey (?)
DOR 19
GOOTEE, Andrew S.
DOR 53
Edward DOR 31
Shedreck DOR 31
GOOTS, William BCI 86
GOOTY, Lurena ANN 404
GORCHAGE, Richard
BAL 161
GORDAN, George BCI 201
James BCI 194
Joseph BCI 450
William FRE 97
GORDEN, Ann D.C. 186
Ann HAR 58
Archabald CEC 137
Christopher CLN 93
Daniel (?) FRE 149
Jacob TAL 51
John HAR 42
Joseph BCI 33
Temperance HAR 42
William CLN 100
William DOR 45
William HAR 5
William HAR 43
GORDIN, Eli BCI 381
Frances BCI 381
GORDON (See also
PORDON),
--- (Mrs.) BCI 342
--- (Widow) FRE 169
Daniel FRE 149
Drusilla PRI [200]
Flora CEC 159
George QUE 32
John ANN 316
John BCI 119
John BCI 538
John D.C. 138
Jonathan QUE 16
Joseph BCI 71
Joseph N. KEN 103
Nathan BAL 237
Richard BCI 86
Samuel SOM 111
Wanton BCI 148
Wm. BCI 522
GORDY, Benjamin H.
SOM 118
Betsy-w. WOR 205
Isaac DOR 20
John P. WOR 202
Nathen, Esqr. WOR 202
Samuel WOR 204
Thomas WOR 202
William WOR 205
GORE, Amos, Junr. BCI 14
Austin, Ovsr. TAL 7
Barbary BAL 11
Charles BAL 84
David BAL 13
Drew BCI 65
Fanny CLN 91
George BAL 11
Isack BAL 14
John BAL 21
Michal BAL 2
Phillip BAL 46
Rachel TAL 37
Samuel BAL 60

GORE (continued),		
William	BCI	458
GORHAM, John	BCI	23
GORIDDSON, Aquilla	BCI	387
GORMAN, Edwd.	BCI	519
John	QUE	31
John B.	D.C.	144
Nichas	BCI	224
GORMERON, Michael	BCI	19
GORMLEY, Richard	BCI	125
GORRELL, Abraham	HAR	24
Avarilla	HAR	25
Crawford	HAR	74
Elizabeth	HAR	20
James	CEC	158
James	HAR	29
John	CEC	138
Thomas	HAR	74
William	CEC	158
GORSUCH, Benjamin	BAL	54
Benjamin	BAL	93
Charles	BAL	92
Charles	HAR	39
Charles of Dd.	HAR	59
David	BAL	87
Edward	BAL	95
Elisha	BAL	2
Elisha	BAL	87
Elizabeth	BAL	3
George	BAL	49
Jemima	BAL	247
John	BAL	49
John	BAL	91
John	BAL	95
John	BAL	232
John M. (farm)	BAL	128
Joseph	BAL	237
Joshua	BAL	236
Joshua	BCI	156
Keziah	BAL	90
Lovers	BAL	233
Mary	BCI	62
Nathan	BAL	49
Nathan	BAL	90
Nichalos	BAL	90
Niches	BCI	177
Pellecia	BAL	54
Pelluia?	BAL	54
Rob.	BCI	213
Robert, Junr.	BAL	112
Thomas	BAL	237
Thomas	BAL	243
William	BAL	244
William	BCI	451
GORSURCH, Charles	BAL	78
GORTON, Anthony	BCI	122
GOSHON, Oliver C.	FRE	157
GOSLEE, Betsy	SOM	138
Jacob (f.n.)	SOM	120
John	SOM	101A
John	SOM	138
Nelly	SOM	135
Thomas	SOM	105
Thomas	SOM	137
GOSLEN, William	BCI	159
GOSLER, John	D.C.	50
GOSLIN, Abednigo	BAL	220
Anna	FRE	104
Beal	BAL	68
Francis	BAL	82
Joseph	BAL	66
Lewis	PRI	228
Peter	BAL	66
Sarah	BAL	69
Thomas (?)	DOR	62
Thomas	DOR	50

GOSLING, Smith	DOR	55
GOSLLEE, Louday	SOM	104
GOSNELL, Amos	FRE	209
Casper	BAL	42
Charles	BAL	42
Charles	BAL	42
Greenbury	BAL	41
James	BAL	41
Jeremiah	BAL	42
Jesse	BAL	10
Lemuel W.	FRE	202
Martha	BAL	202
Mordicae	ANN	274
Moses	BAL	44
William	BAL	41
William	FRE	209
Wornell	BAL	44
GOSS, John	D.C.	129
GOSSAGE, Annanias	TAL	7
Charles	TAL	46
Daniel	TAL	39
Greenbury	TAL	19
John	BCI	19
Nicholas	TAL	37
Peter	TAL	23
Samuel	TAL	22
GOSSEN, Henry	TAL	11
GOST (see also DOR-		
SEN),		
Henry	PRI	191A
GOSWELLING, David		
	SOM	131
GOSWICK, Thomas	BAL	113
GOTHICH, Richard (?)		
	BCI	483
GOTHLUP, Richd.	BCI	482
GOTHROP, William	CEC	175A
GOTHTUP, Richd. (?)		
	BCI	482
GOTLICKKOFER, D. (?)		
	BCI	337
GOTROW, --- (Mrs.)		
	BCI	342
Julie	BCI	341
GOTT, Edward	BAL	226
Elenor	CAL	62
Elizabeth	ANN	260
Richard	BAL	218
Richard	MON	130
Robert	BCI	298
Samuel	ANN	268
Stephen	BCI	51
Susan J. (I.?)	ANN	269
Wm.	CAL	47
GOTTIER, Francis	CEC	137
John	CEC	137
GOUCHARD, Peter	BCI	54
GOUFF, John	WAS	70
John, Jun.	WAS	70
GOUGER, Anna	FRE	180
Jacob	FRE	179
Peter	FRE	180
GOUGES, Gustaves	BCI	281
GOUGH, Bennet	SAI	73A
Dorathy	SAI	65
Harry D.	HAR	40
James J.	SAI	73A
Jeseph	SAI	81
Peter (See Richard		
---, negro, slave		
of Peter GOUGH)		
Peter	SAI	63
Prudence	BAL	242
Prudence	BCI	179
Stephen	SAI	75
Thomas	SAI	76

GOUGH (continued)		
Thomas W.	SAI	77
GOULD, Alexr.	BCI	316
Ann	QUE	31
Frances	QUE	11
John	BCI	5
John	D.C.	179
John G.	BCI	282
John W.	QUE	35
Jos.	BCI	341
Paul	BCI	341
Peter	QUE	35
Rachel	QUE	35
Saml.	QUE	6
Stepney	QUE	3
Thomas	DOR	64
Wm.	QUE	3
GOULDEN, Darky	BCI	425
William	BAL	20
GOULDING, Fred.	D.C.	32
John	D.C.	91
John, Jun.	D.C.	90
Samuel	D.C.	54
Samuel	KEN	93
GOULDSBERRY, Robert		
	QUE	42
GOULDSBOROUGH, Richd.		
	BCI	294
GOULDSMITH, Rachel		
	BCI	522
Sarah	BCI	130
GOURAN, Isra	BCI	232
GOURDE, Lawrence	BCI	244
GOURDON, Fred.	BCI	357
GOURER, Adam	WAS	136
GOURLEY, Thomas	FRE	187
GOUSS, Jacob	WAS	55A
GOVEN, Daniel	BCI	156
GOVER, Anty. P.	D.C.	176
Ephraim S.	BCI	130
James-Negro	HAR	80
Margaret	HAR	24
Robert	HAR	41
Robert	HAR	71
Samuel	ANN	269
Tower-Negro	HAR	80
William	ANN	289
William A.	CAL	64
GOW, James	BCI	157
GOWER, John	WAS	126
Nicholas	ALL	3
GOWTY, Abel	CLN	107
James	CLN	93
Thomas	CLN	99
GOYER, Mary	FRE	104
GRABBLE, William	BAL	247
GRABEL, Philip	BCI	342
GRABER, Henry	FRE	186
GRABILL, John	FRE	217
GRABRIEL, Joseph	WAS	123
Josiah	WAS	134
GRACE, Alexandria	CEC	123
Ann	TAL	11
Charles	FRE	133
Elizabeth	CEC	159
Frances	FRE	96
Freeborn (?)	KEN	119
George	BCI	198
Henry	TAL	45
John	BCI	158
Joseph	DOR	5
Mary (negro)	TAL	23
Peter Boyer	BAL	110
Philip	FRE	101
Redman	BCI	527
Samuel	BCI	46

GRACE (continued),		GRAMMER (continued),		GRAVES (continued),	
Skinner	TAL 24	John	FRE 178	William	KEN 93
Standley	TAL 6	GRANDISON, Benj.	D.C.38	William	QUE 38
William	CEC 159	GRANGE, Will.	D.C.118	Zepheniah	SAI 79
William	TAL 12	GRANGER, Anthony	QUE 13	GRAY, --- (Capt.)	BCI 338
William	TAL 24	John	DOR 15	Alexander	CHA 189
GRACEY, John	BCI 133	Jonathan	MON 163	Ann	PRI 205
William	BCI 132	Nath.	BCI 344	Anna	BCI 75
GRACIE, Henry	BCI 103	Peregrine	QUE 26	Archabald	DOR 41
GRADY, Frances	CEC 158	Rebecca	DOR 62	Archlbald	CHA 212
GRAEFF, John	D.C.85	Thomas	KEN 92	Austin	BCI 117
GRAEFFE, Nichs.	D.C.137	GRANT, Alexander	HAR 81	Barnet	MON 151
GRAERY, Joseph	CEC 176	Benjamin	FRE 84	Benja. of Richd.	CAL 48
GRAF, Fred. C.	BCI 370	Charles	BAL 46	Benjamin	CLN 92
GRAFF, Francis (?)	BCI 410	Charles	BAL 64	Benjamin	CHA 204
George	MON 160	Edud.	MON 139	Benjamln	PRI 230
Jacob	BCI 45	Edwd.?	MON 139	Benjn.	D.C.117
Jacob	BCI 286	Elizabeth	BCI 279	Bisha	MON 166
Joseph	FRE 158	Fanny-Negro	HAR 79	Caley	WOR 192
GRAFLIN, Jacob	BAL 180	George	D.C.126	Catherine	PRI 237
GRAFTEN, Mark	BCI 388	Hannah	D.C.206	Cato	CLN 110
GRAFTON, Aquila	HAR 37	Henry	BCI 172	Chars.	BCI 348
John	HAR 37	Isaac	CEC 176	Christn.	D.C.105
Martin	HAR 37	Jacob	HAR 38	Conl. Benjamin	CAL 67
Nathan	BCI 316	James	MON 137	Daniel	ANN 364
Nathaniel	HAR 37	John	BCI 304	David	BCI 429
Samuel	HAR 37	John	BCI 443	David	WOR 189
William	HAR 37	John	BCI 449	David L.	WOR 193
GRAGERAY, E. N.	WAS 146	John	CEC 158	Edward	BAL 206
S. J.	WAS 146	John	MON 151	Edward B.	ANN 298
GRAHAM, Charles	BCI 97	Jos.	BCI 212	Elias	CHA 204
David	BCI 177	Joseph	CEC 175A	Elias	PRI 238
Edward	DOR 35	Margaret	CEC 158	Elijah	ANN 308
George	DOR 35	Priscilla	MON 167	Eliza	D.C.92
Griffin	D.C.205	Richard	KEN 87	Elizabeth	WOR 192
James	SOM 112	Thomas	QUE 28	Elizabeth (Mrs.)	CAL 45
Jas.	QUE 6	William	BAL 229	Ephraim	ANN 297
John	BCI 68	William	BCI 63	Geo.	D.C.138
John	CEC 176	William	BCI 118	George	CAL 51
John	D.C.98	William	D.C.44	George	CHA 193
John	D.C.102	Wm.	MON 163	George	D.C.41
John	MON 151	GRAOREY, Rebecca	CEC 159	George	PRI 208
John	SOM 107	GRAREY, Raney	D.C.191	George	PRI 228
John	TAL 28	GRASON, William	QUE 31	George	WOR 193
John (free negro)	SOM 118	GRASVENER, Daniel		Gregory	PRI 228
Moses	D.C.68		SOM 127	H. W.	BCI 232
Peter	SOM 106	GRATE, Jacob	BCI 525	Henry W.	BCI 94
Phillip	SOM 109	GRATERICK, Laurence		Hughriah	MON 171
Richard	CAL 62	& Co.-FRANKLIN		Isaac	CLN 94
Richd.	BCI 195	PAPER MILL	BAL 185	Isaac	CLN 98
Robert	BAL 191	GRAU, Michael	FRE 170	James	BCI 353
Salley	SOM 109	GRAUFT, Joseph	WAS 121	James	CAL 48
Samuel	ANN 319	GRAVE, Joseph	WAS 148	James	CLN 108
Samuel	CEC 175A	GRAVENOR, Benjamin (?)		James	DOR 41
Thomas	BCI 134		SOM 103	James	PRI 231
Thomas	TAL 23	Loudy	SOM 107	James	WOR 201
Wm.	BCI 170	Mary	SOM 111	Jane	CEC 137
Zachariah	CEC 159	William	SOM 111	Jane-Negro	HAR 80
GRAHAME, Elizabeth	BCI 146	GRAVENSTINE, Elizabeth		Jas.	QUE 17
Hamilton	BCI 114		BCI 103	Jno.	BCI 212
John	FRE 117	GRAVES, Alexr.	BCI 166	John	ANN 306
Mary Ann	BCI 137	Ann	SAI 87	John	BCI 8
Thomas	FRE 71	Dedrick	FRE 201	John	BCI 23
GRAIG, John	CEC 137	Geo.	D.C.125	John	BCI 53
GRAINGER, --- (Widaw)		Harry	KEN 91	John	CAL 46
	BCI 396	Henry	KEN 90	John	CAL 49
GRAITRAKE, Lawrence		James (?)	BAL 110	John	CLN 115
	BCI 511	James R.	SAI 78	John	D.C.65
GRAMBURGE, John	BAL 177	Jestinion	SAI 76	John	HAR 23
GRAMMAR, Gotleb J. (l.?)		John	D.C.58	John	PRI 204
	ANN 389	Milcah	KEN 90	John	PRI 228
John A.	ANN 312	Peregrine	SAI 78	John, Sen.	WOR 192
GRAMMER, Benjamin	FRE 205	Richard	KEN 86	John, Jun.	WOR 187
G. C.	D.C.74	Robert	BCI 78	John F.	CHA 191
Hanry	BAL 150	Rozetta	QUE 3	John M.	BCI 247
Jacob	FRE 187	Thomas	SAI 78	John T.?	CHA 191

GRAY (continued),
Johnson	WOR 191
Joseph	ANN 364
Joseph	BCI 297
Joseph	CAL 46
Joseph	CLN 109
Joseph	CHA 192
Joseph	HAR 19
Joseph	KEN 106A
Joseph	WOR 191
Joseph	WOR 195
Joshua	ANN 307
Joshua	TAL 37
Leah	TAL 13
Levi	PRI 227
Lewis	PRI 228
Littleton	WOR 194
Lucy	D.C. 108
Matilda	PRI 231
Mitchell	WOR 189
Monica	CHA 194
Nathaniel	ANN 326
Nathaniel	D.C. 61
Nicholas	BCI 60
Obadiah	MON 172
Otho	ANN 273
Peter	WOR 193
Philip	ANN 361
Rachael	FRE 94
Ralph	ANN 324
Ralph	ANN 346
Randol	SAI 78
Rebecca	BAL 129
Richard	ANN 310
Richard	ANN 393
Richard	SAI 78
Robert	BAL 123
Robert	CHA 192
Samuel	WOR 192
Senah	SOM 134
Siras	FRE 226
Somercett	CAL 45
Spencer	D.C. 150
Stephen	BCI 87
Stephen W.	D.C. 80
Sylvester	D.C. 132
Thomas	BAL 93
Thomas	WOR 201
Thomas, Senr.	DOR 64
Thomas, Junr.	DOR 49
Thos. S.	WOR 193
Tilley	BCI 524
Vincent	D.C. 162
Walter	CHA 205
Walton	BCI 113
Warrick	BCI 345
William	ALL 37
William	BCI 25
William	CLN 115
Wm. of James	CAL 42
Wm. of Richd.	CAL 47
Wm. D.	CAL 45
Zachariah	BAL 116
Zachariah	CEC 159

GRAYBILL, Moses, Senr.
	FRE 228A
Moses, Junr.	FRE 228A

GRAYHAM, Alexander TAL 13
Ann	CLN 80
Archable	TAL 3
David	BCI 488
George	BCI 506
Henry	CLN 106
James	ANN 375
John	BCI 217
John	CAL 48

GRAYHAM (continued),
William	ANN 278

GRAYLESS, Charles,
Ovsr.	TAL 7
James	CLN 106

GRAYSON, George D.C. 189
Polly	D.C. 11
Sally	D.C. 9

GRAYUM, Marcillus SAI 57
GREARSON, Andrew
	BCI 448

GREATE, Michel BAL 12
GREAVES, Edward CEC 137
Edward	CEC 137
Matthew	QUE 31
Richard	D.C. 40

GREEFIELD, John BCI 447
GREEG, Thomas BCI 456
GREEN, Abednego BAL 244
Abednego	SOM 122
Abraham	BAL 96
Andrew	BCI 199
Andrew S.	CLN 78
Ann	ANN 393
Ann	BCI 186
Ann	CHA 214
Armstead	BCI 210
Berry	TAL 32
Betsey	SOM 113
Catharine	D.C. 188
Catherine	ANN 354
Cato (negro)	TAL 19
Charles	BCI 156
Chas. R.	BCI 219
Clement	HAR 41
Conrod	FRE 129
Daniel	QUE 9
Dause	BAL 164
Easther	SOM 147
Edward	BCI 212
Edward	BCI 413
Edward	CEC 158
Elijah	BAL 190
Elisha	QUE 24
Eliza	MON 137
Elizabeth	ANN 384
Elizabeth	HAR 39
Elizabeth	SAI 56
Esther Ann	BCI 6
Frances	BCI 525
Francis	FRE 164
Geo.	MON 172
George	BCI 18
George	BCI 47
George	CEC 176
George	FRE 164
George W.	BCI 508
Hannah	D.C. 185
Harry	QUE 4
Henry	BAL 40
Henry	BCI 481
Henry	QUE 6
Hester Ann	QUE 6
Isaac	ANN 291
Isaac	BAL 222
Israel	BAL 247
Jacob	ALL 12
Jacob	ANN 290
James	QUE 35
James	QUE 36
James R.	CHA 217
Jane	FRE 74
Jere	BCI 232
John	ALL 13
John	ANN 258
John	ANN 343

GREEN (continued),
John	BAL 47
John	BAL 92
John	BAL 241
John	BCI 94
John	BCI 189
John	BCI 460
John	CEC 137
John	D.C. 146
John	FRE 156
John	QUE 28
John	SOM 105
John F.	D.C. 173
John H.	SOM 112
Joseph	CHA 213
Joseph	WAS 79
Joshua	BAL 141
Joshua	FRE 149
Joshua	HAR 20
Joshua	SOM 108
Josias	BAL 114
Laurence	D.C. 78
Leah	SOM 112
Leonard	MON 143
Leonard	MON 162
Lewis	FRE 103
Lucy	QUE 35
Mary	BCI 173
Mary	BCI 218
Mary	HAR 46
Mashach	BAL 248
Mathew	ANN 263
Michl.	D.C. 97
Patsey	ANN 354
Peregrine	BCI 86
Priscilla	MON 175
Rachael	SOM 113
Rachel	QUE 42
Rachel	TAL 47
Ralph	CEC 176
Rebecca-free	CAL 61
Rebert	BCI 5
Rezin	ANN 357
Richard	ALL 12
Richard	ANN 370
Richard	BAL 222
Richard	BCI 134
Richd.	MON 137
Robert	ALL 12
Robert	CLN 109
Ruth	BAL 106
Sally	BCI 351
Saml.	QUE 19
Samuel	ANN 344
Samuel	BCI 143
Samuel	BCI 151
Samuel	QUE 31
Sarah	CEC 159

Sarah-[her] slaves
	ANN 360
Shadric	BAL 97
Silva	ANN 332
Solomon	PRI 222
Solomon-f.c.p.	HAR 10
Stepney	QUE 39
Susana	BCI 149
Thomas	BAL 157
Thomas	D.C. 77
Thomas, of W.	BAL 157
Thos.	KEN 125
Thos.	MON 135
Thos. D.	BCI 178
Valentine	BCI 429
William	ALL 29
William	BAL 205
William	BCI 56

GRIFFIN (continued),			GRIFFITH (continued),			GRIMES (continued),	
Robert	DOR 53		Margaret	FRE 96		Ann	PRI 238
Samuel	QUE 34		Mary	BCI 102		Basil	ANN 367
Sarah	QUE 5		Mary	CEC 175A		Basil	FRE 72
Stephen	CEC 123		Mary	MON 175		Charles	FRE 159
Thomas	HAR 6		Matthew	BCI 136		Constantine	WAS 139
Thomas	KEN 115		Minar?	DOR 35		Cornelus	BAL 66
Thomas	QUE 27		Minor	DOR 35		Elias	FRE 168
Thomas	SAI 55		Nacy	MON 175		Elias	MON 133
Thomas B.	D.C. 35		Nancy	WAS 147		Frederick	FRE 75
Thos.	BCI 525		Nathan	CEC 175A		Greenburry	ANN 370
Walter	BCI 63		Noble	CLN 92		Igns.	MON 131
Wilks	QUE 27		Philamon	FRE 70		Isaac	PRI 219
William	BCI 455		Philamon, Jr.	FRE 70		James	BAL 8
GRIFFISS, Dorcas (Mrs.)			Phillip	FRE 177		James	BAL 22
	CAL 43		Philm.	MON 177		James	BAL 90
Edwd.	BCI 183		Richard	ANN 268		James	FRE 143
GRIFFITH, Abednigo	BAL 6		Richard	CEC 175A		Jas.	BCI 190
Abraham	CLN 86		Richard	DOR 35		Jno.	QUE 3
Abraham	CEC 138		Richard	PRI 195		John	BAL 180
Abraham	FRE 85		Richd.	MON 177		John	FRE 223
Abraham	FRE 113		Robert	ANN 334		John	PRI 216
Alexander	CLN 85A		S. (Widow)	BCI 389		Joshua	MON 177
Alfred	FRE 102		Salathiel	SOM 108		Joshua	WAS 58A
Ally	CEC 137		Sam. G.	BCI 339		Levi	BCI 63
Anna	FRE 115		Saml.	MON 163		Lewis	ALL 6
Basil	MON 176		Saml.	MON 177		Lloyd	ANN 366
Benjamin	ANN 268		Scott	HAR 25		Lot	FRE 168
Benjamin	BAL 6		Susanah	BCI 281		Martin	FRE 174
Camillus	D.C. 175		Sylus	DOR 54		Michael	D.C. 46
Catharine (Mrs.)	BCI 267		T. Samuel	CEC 137		Nicholas	BAL 117
Charles	ALL 7		Thomas	ANN 326		Rezin	BAL 237
Charles	ANN 327		Thomas	BAL 15		Richard	BCI 51
Charles	ANN 341		Thomas	BCI 439		Richard	BCI 161
David	BCI 11		Thomas	FRE 144		Robert	PRI 197
Dennis	ANN 334		Thomas W.	BCI 269		Samuel	ANN 366
Dorcas	CLN 115		Thos.	BCI 518		Samuel	FRE 163
Edward	BAL 49		Thos. H.	BCI 171		Sebastian	BAL 117
Edward	BAL 176		William	BAL 49		Stephen	BAL 117
Edward	DOR 32		William	CEC 175A		Thomas	ALL 35
Edward	HAR 26		GRIFFITHS, John	BAL 110		William	ANN 304
Edwd.	BCI 171		John	BAL 121		William	BAL 49
Edwd.	D.C. 177		Rebecca	D.C. 198		William	BAL 113
Elizabeth	CAL 65		Richd.	BCI 316		William	BAL 195
Evan	HAR 42		GRIFFITT, Anne	MON 143		William	BAL 237
Fadeus	CLN 91		GRIFFITTE, Greenby (?)			William	QUE 46
George	DOR 31			MON 137		Willm. (?)	D.C. 209
Greenbury	CLN 113		Howard (?)	MON 137		Wm., Senr.	FRE 228A
Greenby (?)	MON 137		GRIFFITTES, Greenby			Wm., Junr.	FRE 228A
Greenby	MON 137			MON 137		GRIMIS, Ann (?)	D.C. 206
Griffin	BCI 125		GRIFFITTS, Anne (?)			Willm. (?)	D.C. 209
H. B.	BCI 390			MON 143		GRIMS, John	WAS 82
H. P.	BCI 390		GRIFFY, John	FRE 130		Samuel	WAS 90
Hannah	HAR 28		GRIFINE, Sherita	BCI 347		GRIMSBY, Edwd.	D.C. 116
Haword, Jun.	BCI 418		GRIFITH, Henney	BCI 357		GRINACE, James	QUE 3
Henry	DOR 45		GRIGG, Alexander	BCI 116		GRINALDS, John (?)	D.C. 151
Henry, Sen.	MON 143		Richd.	BCI 510		GRINDAGE, Wm.	KEN 122
Henry, Jun.	MON 143		GRIGGS, George	SAI 88		GRINDAL, William	SAI 77
Howard	MON 137		James	BCI 115		GRINDALL, John	HAR 47
Israel	CEC 175A		GRIGS, William	BCI 137		Josiah	BCI 132
James	BAL 6		GRIGSBY, Jas.	D.C. 143		GRINDER, Michael	FRE 228A
John	ANN 333		John	D.C. 189		GRINDOLL, Philis	SAI 92
John	BCI 109		GRIM, Abraham	WAS 69		GRINER, John	BCI 324
John	DOR 28		Christopher	FRE 213		GRINN, Allen (?)	DOR 49
John	DOR 41		Daniel	WAS 67		GRINNAGE, Benjamin	QUE 32
John	KEN 104		David, Senr.	WAS 68		Jessee	QUE 49
John	MON 175		David of A.	WAS 69		John	CLN 80
John, Senr. of Jno.			Elxander	WAS 69		John	CLN 88
	ANN 276		Henry	WAS 68		GRINNALS, Francis	D.C. 32
John, Senr. of Jns.?			John	WAS 70		GRINNUM, Rachel	DOR 63
	ANN 276		Samuel	WAS 69		GRINWELL, Mary	FRE 129
John, Jnr.	ANN 269		GRIME, Allen	DOR 49		GRISESON, Michael (?)	
Joshua	BAL 232		GRIMES, Alex.	BCI 474			WAS 85
Kinsey	D.C. 164		Ann (?)	D.C. 206		GRISSUM, John (negro)	
Lemuel	FRE 70		Ann	ANN 299			TAL 47
Lewis	DOR 41		Ann	PRI 215			
Lyde	MON 177						

GRIST, John	CEC 176	GROVE (continued),		GRYMES, Guy	D.C.81
Peter	WAS 57	Barbara	FRE 104	Jeremiah	D.C.135
GRISWOLD, Levi	BCI 266	Caleb	D.C.156	GUARDNER, Wm.	BCI 527
GROBEWINE, Frederick		Catherine	WAS 56	GUDGEON, Richard	KEN 86
	BCI 402	Daniel	WAS 140	William	KEN 86
GROBEY, Anthony	BCI 318	David	WAS 61	GUE, Geo.	MON 139
GROBP, John, Revd.		David, Senr.	WAS 69	Henry	ANN 371
	FRE 170	David, Jun.	WAS 69	Rebecce	MON 140
GROCE, Daniel	CLN 76	Francis	FRE 180	Saml.	MON 141
David	CLN 73	George	FRE 180	GUEST, Basil	BCI 98
Jacob	CLN 90	Henry	BCI 501	George	BAL 82
James	CLN 95	Jacob	FRE 180	Job	BCI 96
Lucy (?)	BCI 140	Jacob	FRE 187	John	BAL 82
Nathan	D.C.98	Jacob	WAS 139	Joseph C.	BAL 62
Nathaniel	CLN 89	Jacob, Sr.	FRE 131	Moses	BAL 82
Patience	BAL 196	Jacob, Jr.	FRE 131	Penelope Die	BAL 245
William	CLN 87	Jamison	BCI 493	Robert	CHA 202
GROCHONG, Elias	FRE 155	John	WAS 55A	GUESTIER, P. A.	BCI 172
GROF, Fred. C. (?)	BCI 370	John	WAS 100	Peter A.	BAL 210
GROFF, Andrew	MON 144	John	WAS 139	GUFFIE, Mary	CEC 159
Christian	BCI 159	Peter	FRE 115	GUIBERT, Josephine	BCI 297
Francis	BCI 410	Philip	WAS 57	GUIGER, John	BCI 487
Henry	FRE 145	Ruben	FRE 106	GUILDA, Felix	BCI 518
GROGG, Jacob	BAL 150	Sarah	BCI 494	GUILLET, Peter	SOM 129
GROOFF, Sabastion	FRE 227	Wm. Hair (?)	QUE 3	GUINEA, Hannah	CEC 176
GROOM, Edwd.	BCI 490	GROVER, Ann	BAL 118	GUINN (See also QUINN),
James	KEN 105	Barbary	BAL 231	John	SAI 91
Samuel	TAL 13	George	FRE 140	John, Ovsr.	TAL 6
William	BCI 14	Jacob	BCI 341	John-[his] Slaves (?)
William	SOM 135	Martain	BAL 165		ANN 259
GROOME, John	CEC 137	Prissilla (Mrs.)	CAL 47	Micheal	ANN 364
Thomas	BCI 159	Robert	CAL 41A	GUISENDOFFER, John
GROOMS, Charles	KEN 118	Thomas	BAL 221		BCI 494
Emanuel	BCI 529	GROVERMAN, Cathe.		GUISHARD, Henry	FRE 188
James	MON 173		D.C.152	GUITON, Henry	WAS 106
GROSE, Charles	BCI 379	GROVERMON, Anthony		GULEN, James	TAL 48
GROSENICLE, Jno. of			BCI 504	GULL, Archibald	FRE 109
Jno.	FRE 129	GROVES, Abednigo	CHA 190	GULLATT, Willm.	D.C.193
Jno. of Peter	FRE 129	Charles	BCI 109	GULLETT, Daniel	TAL 2
GROSH, Frederick	WAS 124A	Gorden	CHA 217	William	SOM 117
Godlip	WAS 124A	Henry	BCI 123	GULLEY, Philip	D.C.4
GROSHONG, Abraham		Jacob	BCI 309	GUM, Elizabeth	MON 166
	FRE 158	Jacob	FRE 224	GUMERIE (See also
Abraham, of Jno.	FRE 159	John	CHA 192	MONTGOMERY)
John	FRE 158	Joshua	ANN 379	Henry	CEC 137
GROSS, Adam	ALL 21	Leander	CHA 192	GUMLY, Nancy	D.C.218
Charles	FRE 122	Peter	BAL 65	GUMMEL, George	BAL 146
Eleanar	D.C.55	Richard	CEC 123	GUMMER, Thomas	ANN 255
Elizabeth	WAS 116	Solon.	D.C.120	GUMP, Mary	FRE 150
George	TAL 50	Walter	CHA 226	Michael	WAS 69
Henry	BAL 163	William	ALL 12	GUNBY, Benja., Captn.
Henry	FRE 122	GRUB, Michael	BCI 408		WOR 163
Henry	WAS 138	Michael	BCI 461	David	SOM 147
Irvin	BCI 199	GRUBB, George	BCI 505	Elisha	SOM 145
Jack (negro)	TAL 23	John	D.C.183	George	DOR 64
Jacob	FRE 116	Joseph	CEC 159	Hannah	WOR 179
James	BCI 498	Rachel	CEC 176	Stephen	BCI 61
Jerry	CAL 50	Wm.	BCI 505	GUNN, Wm.	BCI 391
Jno.	FRE 126	GRUBER, John	WAS 114	GUNNCE, Ellen	D.C.8
John	BAL 156	Samuel	WAS 139	GUNTER, Thomas	D.C.4
John	BCI 180	GRUBY, Francis	HAR 64	GUNTON, William	FRE 95
John	BCI 181	GRUCHY, John D.	BCI 282	GUNTZ, --- (Mr.) (?)
John	D.C.43	GRUE, John A.	BCI 343		BCI 357
John-free	CAL 53A	GRUMBINE, John	FRE 187	M.	BCI 357
John, Junr.	CAL 53A	GRUMBLE, Alex.	D.C.12	GUPTON, Peter	SOM 113
Jonathan	CAL 52	Jas.	D.C.125	GURLEY, Joseph	CEC 158
Michael	WAS 103	GRUMPINE, Jacob	FRE 96	GURNES, James	BCI 141
Michl.	BCI 524	GRUNDY, George	BCI 465	GURNEY, John	SOM 140
Sampson	FRE 228	GRUPEY, Jacob	HAR 64	GUS, Cloe	D.C.200
Sarah	CAL 67	GRUSELL, Susan	BCI 341	GUSLER, Catherine	D.C.57
Thomas	D.C.28	GRUSH, Andrew	WAS 104	George	D.C.21
Thomas	FRE 117	Henry	WAS 139	John	D.C.57
Thos.	CAL 54	John	BCI 20	GUSLOR, John (?)	D.C.57
Wm.-free	CAL 53A	Michael	WAS 107	GUST, Richard W.	WOR 162
GROUARD, Geo. M.	D.C.93	GRUSHI, Elizabeth	BCI 55	GUSTA, Isaac	TAL 9
GROVE, Abraham, Jun.		GRUVER, John	D.C.178	GUSTAVUS, John	D.C.103
	WAS 69			Sutha	BCI 68

GUSTINE, J. (I.?) T.		HADFIELD, ---	D.C.88	
(Doc.)	D.C.56	Benjamin	BAL 66	
GUSTIS, Ruthy	BCI 304	Geo.	D.C.99	
GUSTY, Isaac	TAL 3	HADIN, Dennis	BCI 400	
Jacob	DOR 57	HADLEY, Athoney	BAL 180	
GUTHERY, Jesse	WOR 196	Elizabeth	QUE 35	
GUTHRIE, Willm.	D.C.158	George	QUE 8	
GUTHRY, --- (sister)		--- H ---	James	BAL 24
(See Jas. GUTHRY			Richard	WAS 149
& sister)	WOR 175	HAAFF, John	BCI 496	Samuel	BCI 58
Jas. & sister	WOR 175	Susan	D.C.53	HADS, Robert	D.C.21
GUTTREY, Sarah	CAL 46	HABBARD, Charles		HADSKEY, Nancy	BCI 512
GUY, Alexander	SAI 82		CLN 99	HAEFFER, JOel	BCI 526
Ann	SAI 80	HACK, John	BCI 501	HAELY, Michael	BCI 46
Bob	QUE 14	HACKE, Andrew	BCI 390	HAGAN, Adam	FRE 71
Bob-Negro	HAR 49	Nicholaus	BCI 412	Celetia	D.C.58
Debby	BCI 425	HACKET, B.	BCI 378	Charles	BCI 55
Elizabeth	CEC 158	Benja.	BCI 230	Francis	FRE 79A
John	CHA 211	Eliza	D.C.97	Henry F.	BCI 11
John	SAI 77	H. W.	BCI 372	Horatio	D.C.122
Mathew	CHA 222	J.	DOR 15	James	CEC 159
Samuel	CEC 158	Luwiser	SAI 89	Jeremiah	D.C.56
Susanna D.	PRI 224	Rachel	ANN 402	John	PRI 239
Thomas	DOR 59	Thomas	DOR 13	John B.	CHA 207
William	CHA 212	Thos.	KEN 123	Peter	FRE 110
GUYBERT, Elizabeth	SAI 94	William	ANN 351	HAGER, Conrad	ALL 24
GUYER, Henry	FRE 142	William	DOR 57	George	WAS 114
Samuel	FRE 69	HACKETT, --amuel		George, Sen.	ALL 23
GUYMAN, David	FRE 188		BCI 161	George, Jr.	ALL 24
GUYNN, William of Jno.		Adam	CLN 77	Jacob	ALL 24
	BCI 279	Benjamin	QUE 36	James	D.C.64
GUYTHER, William	SAI 66	Benjn.	D.C.77	John	ALL 22
GUYTON, Abraham	FRE 97	Charles	BCI 141	Jonathan, Sen.	WAS 113A
Benjamin	HAR 48	Dyannah	TAL 35	Jonathan, Jun.	WAS 113A
Edward M.	HAR 61	Eleonar	CLN 111	Samuel	WAS 74
Elisha	HAR 56	Harry	QUE 6	HAGERTHY, Martha	BAL 186
Henry	BAL 235	James	CLN 88	HAGERTY, John	BCI 450
Isaiah	BAL 237	Jno.	QUE 2A	Patrick	ALL 33
James	BAL 240	Mary	HAR 22	HAGGER, Benjn. K.	BCI 241
James	HAR 37	Richard	QUE 24	HAGGERTY, Ann	D.C.34
John	BAL 235	Sam	QUE 5	HAGGINS, Anne	MON 172
John	BAL 237	Sarah	QUE 16	HAGMER, Martin (?)	WAS 78
John	HAR 47	Thos.	QUE 7	HAGNER, Peter	D.C.7
Joshua	HAR 48	Tilghman	DOR 58	HAGON, Francis	D.C.180
Joshua, Junr.	HAR 48	William	BCI 159	HAGOR, Christian	WAS 112
Margaret	BAL 235	William	DOR 59	HAGTHROP, Edward	BCI 56
Mary (widow)	BAL 235	Wm.	QUE 7	Thos.	BCI 192
Sarah	BAL 235	HACKNEY, Barbary		HAGUE, John	QUE 7
Underwood	BAL 237		FRE 135	Michal	CEC 123
GWIN, James	CEC 158	Barton	FRE 124	Peregrine	KEN 110
Joseph	WAS 83	Samuel	ANN 393	William	KEN 87
Thomas	KEN 108	Wm.	BCI 533	HAHN, Daniel	BCI 397
GWINN, --- (?)	BCI 387	HADAWAY, James	KEN 90	Daniel	FRE 172
--- (?)	BCI 407	James	QUE 26	David	FRE 178
--- (Mrs.)	BCI 438	Oakley	TAL 14A	Elizabeth	FRE 203
Bill-f.c.p.	HAR 11	Robert	KEN 90	Henry	FRE 197
Chales	DOR 40	HADDAWAY, Daniel		Hugh	ALL 12
James	BAL 106		TAL 33	Jacob	FRE 158
James	BAL 106	Danl. L.	TAL 27	Jacob	FRE 181
James	DOR 39	Harrison	TAL 26	Jacob	FRE 182
Jamis?	BAL 106	Hugh	TAL 25	Jacob	FRE 197
Richard	FRE 175	James	TAL 3	John	FRE 197
Sandy	BAL 249	William	TAL 27	Joseph	FRE 172
Wm.	BCI 367	William W.	TAL 28	Peter	FRE 169
GWYNN, Bennete?	PRI 221A	HADDER, Elisha	WOR 171	Peter	FRE 170
Bennett	PRI 221A	John	WOR 190	HAIGER, John	BAL 22
Charles	BCI 253	Lemuel	WOR 171	HAIGHT, John	ANN 375
John	BAL 77	Thomas	WOR 186	HAIL, William	FRE 86
John H.	PRI 223	HADDOCK, Ebzey	WOR 175	HAIN, Nathen (?)	ANN 371
Thomas B.	PRI 221A	James	WOR 213	HAINES, Abraham	FRE 191
William	D.C.39	James	WOR 218	Alexander?	PRI 229
GYCINGER, Francis	FRE 134	Joseph P.	BCI 68	Alexander	PRI 229
GYER, John	ANN 362	HADEN, Charles	ALL 7	Daniel	FRE 216
GYTON, Vinson	FRE 82	Francis	CHA 222	David	FRE 209
		Jane	D.C.194	Elizabeth	FRE 199
		John	BCI 128	George	FRE 211

HAINES (continued),		HALES (continued),		HALL (continued),	
Henry	FRE 199	Statia	WOR 179	George	HAR 5
Henry	FRE 211	HALEY, James	BCI 215	George	SOM 151
Israel	FRE 177	John	BCI 218	George, Captn.	WOR 175
Job	CEC 177	Martha	KEN 101	Grafton	PRI 182
John	FRE 199	Matilda	D.C. 218	H.	BCI 409
John	FRE 199	Sam	QUE 20	Henery	BAL 91
Joseph	FRE 199	HALFPENNY, William		Henry	BCI 126
Mary	CEC 176		BCI 15	Henry	CAL 50
Mordecai	FRE 202	HALFTOWN, Peter	FRE 197	Henry	PRI 201
Nathan	FRE 200	HALIDAY, Thos.	D.C. 126	Henry	TAL 4
Reuben	FRE 202	HALKERSON, Robert		Henry A.	ANN 280
Samuel	FRE 177		CHA 228	Henry S.	ANN 393
Sarah	FRE 199	HALL (See also HALE),		Hez.	D.C. 117
Simon-Negro	HAR 79	---	BCI 271	Ignatius	D.C. 50
William	FRE 177	Adam	BCI 427	J.	BCI 409
William	FRE 203	Adam	CEC 123	Jacob, Senr.	BAL 201
HAINS, Adam	WAS 139	Airy Anne-[her]		Jacob, Junr.	BAL 201
Daniel	ANN 351	Slaves	ANN 264	Jacob, of Wm.	BAL 207
Daniel	ANN 371	Alxd.	CAL 45	James	BAL 201
Jacob	ANN 367	Andrew	BCI 269	James	BCI 24
Jacob	ANN 381	Andrew	CEC 139	James	FRE 170
John	WAS 71	Andrew	CEC 177	James	MON 161
John	WAS 137	Ann	ANN 390	James	QUE 31
Mathias	WAS 71	Ann	SAI 67	James	QUE 38
Nathen	ANN 371	Aquila	HAR 7	James	WOR 193
Sepher	WAS 65	Arin	BAL 236	James & Co. (of Jas.)	
HAIR, Jacob	BAL 152	Arthirr	TAL 49		WOR 153
Jacob	BAL 158	Augustin	KEN 119	James (of Levi)	WOR 153
Jacob	BAL 160	Barruck	FRE 81	Jane	CEC 160
John	BAL 155	Benedict	HAR 26	Jane	D.C. 107
Mary	BAL 164	Benedict E.	HAR 23	Jane	D.C. 109
Phebe	BCI 157	Benjamin	ANN 329	Jas. J.	QUE 6
Philip	BAL 165	Benjamin	FRE 74	Jere	WOR 217
Thos..	BCI 358	Benjn.	WOR 158	Jeremiah	WAS 69
HAIRGROVE, Wm.	QUE 3	Brice	D.C. 29	Jesse	BCI 168
HAIRNE, Betsy	WOR 203	Carlos A.	BCI 173	Jesse	SOM 147
Elijah	WOR 203	Carvel	CEC 159	Jno. B.	BCI 173
Isaac, Capt.	WOR 203	Cathn.	BCI 170	John	ANN 299
James	WOR 203	Cephus	ANN 325	John	ANN 360
Peter G.	WOR 203	Charles	BCI 502	John	CAL 45
Samuel	WOR 202	Charles	SOM 142A	John	CAL 47
HAIRS, Mary	BCI 139	Charles	SOM 146	John	CAL 64
HAISLIP, Henry	CHA 196	Charles G.	HAR 18	John	CHA 203
Hezakiah	CHA 194	Chrisr.	BCI 201	John	D.C. 162
John	CHA 194	Christopher	KEN 122	John	HAR 19
John (of Robt.)	CHA 196	Cuthbert	KEN 118	John	KEN 90
Samuel	CHA 195	Daniel	ANN 305	John	PRI 197
HAIT, Job	BCI 139	Dolly (?)	BCI 482	John	SAI 69
HAKESLY, John	BCI 201	Don Carloss	BCI 120	John	SAI 88
HALBACH, John	WAS 136	Dorcas	FRE 105	John	SOM 152
HALBACK, John (?)	WAS 136	Edward	ANN 270	John	TAL 23
HALDERMAN, Jacob	ALL 8A	Edward	BAL 94	John	WAS 95
HALE (See also HALL),		Edward	BCI 56	John	WOR 202
Caleb, Senr.	BCI 531	Edward	BCI 102	John-[his] Slaves	ANN 270
Caleb, Jr.	BCI 524	Edward	CHA 204	John S.	FRE 68
Charles	BAL 239	Edward	HAR 22	Jos.	MON 136
Dolly	BCI 482	Edward	PRI 181	Joseph	ANN 273
Elizabeth	PRI 184	Edward	QUE 25	Joseph	BCI 84
George	FRE 155	Edward, Jun.	QUE 26	Josiah	HAR 28
Henry	BAL 214	Edward C.	HAR 24	Lettetea	BCI 299
Isabella	ANN 399	Elenor	DOR 18	Levi	WAS 64
John	CEC 123	Elias	BCI 498	Levin	SOM 154
Ruth	BAL 247	Elisha	ANN 291	Lewis	CEC 159
Sarah	TAL 8A	Elisha	D.C. 26	Lewis	SAI 57
Stephen	BAL 193	Elisha I. (J.?)	BAL 9	Margaret	ANN 289
Thomas (?)	ANN 281	Elizabeth (?)	PRI 184	Martha	BCI 145
Thomas	PRI 184	Elizabeth	D.C. 9	Mary	ANN 265
Thomas	TAL 8A	Elizabeth	D.C. 192	Mary	CEC 139
William	ANN 404	Elizabeth	HAR 8	Mary	FRE 211
William	BAL 164	F. (Washingn tavern)		Mary	HAR 44
HALES, Benjamin	CHA 202		D.C. 163	Mary	SOM 155
Jeremiah	WOR 174	Favourite	D.C. 177	Mary Ann	BCI 429
John	WOR 174	Francis M.	PRI 205	Mortimer	CEC 159
John M.	CHA 217	George	BCI 22	Moses	BCI 491
Matthew	WOR 179	George	CLN 78	Nancy	BCI 428

103

HALL (continued),			HALLON, John	BAL 236	HAMILTON (continued),	
Nathan	ANN 298		HALLORAN, Mary	D.C.97	Jacob	QUE 28
Nathan	D.C.104		Will	D.C.88	James	BAL 37
Nicholas	FRE 72		HALLOWELL, Josh. T.		James	CEC 177
Patrick	BCI 188			D.C.167	James	CHA 210A
Peggy	SOM 146		HALN, Danl.	BCI 476	James B.	BCI 93
Philip	SAI 57		HALPHIN, Andrew	BAL 37	James B.	PRI 224
Phillis	BCI 334		HALSEY, Eanos	BAL 189	Jas.	BCI 232
Polly	WOR 194		HALVET, Charles	BCI 434	Job	BAL 38
Rebecca	WOR 153		HAM, John	BCI 224	Joel	BAL 36
Retty?	DOR 64		Martha	CEC 138	John	BAL 223
Richard	ANN 292		HAMAN, Lawrence	D.C.62	John	BAL 233
Richard	D.C.29		Mary Anne	MON 163	John	BCI 54
Richard	KEN 109		HAMANS, Benj.	D.C.16	John	CLN 116
Richard	QUE 38		HAMBLE, Robert	BAL 43	Joshua	BAL 40
Richard	SOM 145		HAMBLETON, Alfred		Josias	CHA 225
Richard H.	ANN 287			TAL 24	Louisa	QUE 30
Richard M.	BCI 280		Edward N.	TAL 39	Margaret	CEC 160
Richard T.	PRI 216		James	BAL 130	Matthew	BCI 8
Richard W., Doct.	BCI 268		John	BCI 23	Pliny	BCI 227
Ritty	DOR 64		John	FRE 191	Rhodey	CHA 217
Robert	BAL 236		John	TAL 32	Robert	BCI 124
Robert	KEN 101		Lydia	TAL 24	Robert	PRI 237
Robt.	D.C.167		Sarah	TAL 37	Robert M.	BCI 121
Sally	PRI 194		Sarrah	CEC 138	Saml.	D.C.72
Sally	WOR 184		Thomas	TAL 24	Samuel	BAL 37
Saml.	KEN 114		Thos.	MON 132	Susannah	PRI 207
Samuel	BAL 201		William	BAL 109	Thomas	BCI 253
Samuel	QUE 26		William	HAR 21	William	CHA 194
Samuel	SOM 152		William	KEN 92	William	CHA 210A
Sarah	BAL 13		William	TAL 25	William	QUE 29
Sarah	HAR 21		HAMBLIN, Marshell	WOR 206	William	WAS 82
Sarah (of Thos.)	WOR 178		HAMBURY, Thos. (?)		William C.	TAL 52
Sary	BCI 352			WOR 159	William G.	TAL 5
Shadrack	ANN 398		HAMBY, James	HAR 26	HAMLIN, Mary	BAL 41
Sharper	BAL 200		HAME, Overton (?)		HAMLITON, Henry	WAS 121
Soloman R.	BCI 442			FRE 222	HAMM, John	WAS 56
Solomon	ALL 35		HAMELL, Barbary	WAS 118	Joshua	KEN 123
Susan	BAL 217		HAMER, Martin	WAS 78	Margaretta	WAS 57
Susan	TAL 9		HAMERSLY, Henry	CHA 201	HAMMACKER, Peter	WAS 106
Susanna	BAL 239		HAMERSMITH, Peter		Samuel	WAS 106
Thomas (?)	BAL 127			CEC 177	HAMMAND, John	QUE 25
Thomas (?)	PRI 184		HAMES, Robert	DOR 31	Nathan	FRE 215
Thomas	ANN 281		HAMIL, Chs.	BCI 216	HAMMELL, Jacob	WAS 137
Thomas	WAS 95		HAMILL, Isaac	CEC 176	HAMMELTON, John	BCI 401
Thomas B.	WAS 95		Patrick	CEC 176	HAMMER, Ann	BCI 286
Thomas L.	SAI 57		HAMILLON, --- (Mrs.)		Augt.	BCI 342
Thomas W.	ANN 293			D.C.88	Jacob	FRE 143
Tilbury	WOR 178		Catherine (?)	D.C.157	Jacob	WAS 115
Vachel	ANN 286		HAMILTON, --- (Mrs.) (?)		HAMMERSLEY, Mathias	
Walter	ANN 375			D.C. 88		FRE 158
Walter T.	HAR 18		Absolam	D.C.194	HAMMET, James	FRE 154
Warfield	BAL 67		Alexander	HAR 75	John	SAI 95
Washington	BCI 485		Andrew	PRI 183	HAMMETT, Bennett	SAI 69
William	ANN 265		Benjamin	BAL 37	Enoch	SAI 64
William	BAL 112		Bennet	CHA 210A	Jeremh.	D.C.124
William	BAL 249		Catherine	D.C.157	Jesse	BAL 176
William	BCI 110		Chas. B.	D.C.114	John B.	D.C.174
William	PRI 202		Christian	WAS 71	Joseph	SAI 64
William	QUE 32		Christiana	D.C.95	McKelvie	FRE 104
William	SOM 152		David	D.C.116	Richard	SAI 63
William	WAS 99		Delia	PRI 227	Robert	SAI 63
William, Junr.	ANN 289		Edward	BAL 36	Samuel	SAI 63
Willm.	D.C.162		Edward	BCI 242	Wolford	WAS 127A
Winey-free	CAL 64		Edward	CHA 220A	HAMMILL, Mary	ALL 14
Wm.	BAL 94		Edward	DOR 7	HAMMILTON, Francis	
Wm.	BCI 233		Edwd. J. (I.?)	CHA 206		BAL 188
Zeb	D.C.187		Eli	BAL 203	Hugh	BCI 474
HALLAND, Littleton (?)			Elizabeth	BCI 65	James	BCI 511
	BCI 380		Elizabeth	CEC 160	James	BCI 516
HALLARD, Joseph	BCI 130		Ellen	D.C.157	John	BCI 497
HALLER, George W.	D.C.37		Ephraim	BAL 203	HAMMOM, Carral (?)	
Joseph	FRE 100		George	BAL 186		FRE 218
Joshua	FRE 73		George	HAR 56	John (?)	FRE 218
HALLERT, Joseph	BCI 76		Henry	DOR 14	Reason (?)	FRE 218
HALLIDAY, R. (?)	BCI 372		Henry	DOR 60		

HAMMON, Charles	ANN 327	HAMMS, Josep	WAS 55A	HANDS (continued),		
Deven	BCI 346	Joseph	WAS 63	William G., Esqr.	BCI 279	
Henry	BCI 340	HAMNER, George	WAS 113A	Wm.	BCI 509	
Jacob	WAS 59	HAMNUR, Isaac	WAS 105	HANDY, Ebbin (f.n.)		
Jesse	WOR 200	HAMONOM, Vachel	FRE 218		SOM 119	
John	WAS 146	HAMONOND, Vachel		Eliza	WOR 218	
Oliver	DOR 65		FRE 218	Elizabeth	SOM 129	
HAMMOND, Andrew	ANN 302	HAMPSHEAR, George		Elizh.	D.C. 75	
Benjn., Captn.	WOR 178		BAL 83	George	SOM 129	
Bowden	WOR 177	HAMPSHIER, John	BAL 162	George	WAS 120	
Carral	FRE 218	HAMPSHIRE, Casper		George D. S.	KEN 88	
Catharine	BCI 243		BCI 324	Hannah	SOM 151	
Charles	BCI 158	HAMPSON, Bryan	D.C. 144	Isaac	SOM 146	
Charles of Chs.	ANN 354	HAMPTN., Managers		James	SOM 156	
Denton	FRE 78	at	BAL 222	James H.	D.C. 16	
Denton	FRE 223	HAMPTON, John	FRE 76	John	SOM 146	
Eliza	ANN 333	John	QUE 49	John C.	WOR 169	
George	BCI 83	John B.	QUE 47	Joseph	SOM 147	
George	FRE 222	Roderick	D.C. 11	Levin	SOM 155	
Harriot (Miss)	BCI 280	HAMSLEY, James	BCI 173	Mary	SOM 156	
Henry	ALL 16	HANCE, Benja.	CAL 50	Mary	WOR 169	
Henry	ANN 300	Francis	CAL 66A	Michael	WAS 94	
Henry G.	WAS 114	Jacob B.	CAL 50	Nancy	WOR 181	
Isaac	WOR 172	James	BCI 245	Nelly	ALL 36	
Jacob	WAS 87	James	CAL 48	Philis	QUE 7	
Jacob	WAS 87	Kinsey	CAL 51	Richard H.	SOM 105	
James	ANN 348	Richd., Jun.	CAL 49	Saml., Senr.	WOR 170	
James	D.C. 178	Samuel	CAL 51	Saml., Junr.	WOR 180	
John	ANN 287	Sarah	CAL 64	Saml. U.	D.C. 72	
John	D.C. 121	Young D.	CAL 44	Thomas, (Gineral)	WOR 218	
John	FRE 218	HANCHOS, Chars.	BCI 338	Trustim	DOR 62	
John	TAL 3	HANCOCK, Absolem		Vilet	SOM 149	
John	WAS 87		BCI 90	W. W.	BCI 354	
John	WOR 194	Benjamin	ANN 299	William	SOM 151	
John L.	BCI 246	Francis	ANN 308	William	WOR 212	
Johnsey	FRE 201	Gustavus	CHA 222	William (Senr.)	SOM 104	
Joseph	BCI 319	James	CHA 221	HANE, Daniel	FRE 98	
Joshua	WOR 172	Jna.	BCI 218	David	FRE 68	
Larkin	ANN 337	John	D.C. 155	Gideon	KEN 89	
Lloyd T.	ANN 376	John R.	ANN 298	J.	BCI 387	
Lucretia	WOR 156	Nathan	ANN 308	John (?)	BCI 224	
Mary	ANN 362	Randolph S.	CHA 195	John	FRE 97	
Mathias	ANN 346	Sarah	CHA 207	HANEBURY, Thos.	WOR 159	
Michael	WAS 109	Walter	CHA 222	HANES, Thomas	ANN 339	
Molly (of Ewdd.)	WOR 175	William	BAL 200	HANESEY, John	BCI 323	
Nancy	ANN 304	William	FRE 157	HANESWORTH, Daniel		
Nancy	FRE 107	Zachariah	BAL 120		BAL 189	
Nathan	FRE 75	HAND, Abram	CEC 176	HANEY, --- (?)	FRE 163	
Nathan	FRE 78A	Ann	D.C. 74	Daniel	HAR 28	
Nathan, of Va.	FRE 78	Elizabeth	QUE 42	Gatty	WOR 170	
Nelly	WAS 84	John	BCI 70	Jane (?)	DOR 18	
Nicholas	TAL 8A	Moses	BCI 517	Jona.	BCI 271	
Ormand	FRE 78	HANDCOCK, Alce	CLN 96	Zedack	DOR 30	
Peter	WAS 60	Esther	WOR 192	HANHOOVER, Daniel	WAS 118	
Philip	WAS 67	Jas.	WOR 179	HANHUIK, Catharine (?)		
Philip, Senr.	ANN 338	Robert	BCI 114		FRE 219	
Philip, Junr.	ANN 332	Robert	WOR 162	HANKEY, Fredk.	BCI 166	
Phillip	MON 143	Sally	WOR 161	HANLES, Moses	D.C. 209	
Rachel	FRE 219	William	WOR 191	Zachariah	D.C. 209	
Reason	ANN 332	Wm. (of Wm.)	WOR 163	HANLEY, Denis	FRE 161	
Reason	FRE 218	HANDFORD, A. B.	TAL 50	John	FRE 163	
Rezin	ANN 355	HANDLEY, Abraham		HANLON, David	ANN 388	
Rezin, of Rn.	ANN 302		BCI 27	HANN, Abraham	FRE 180	
Samuel	FRE 107	Clinton	DOR 44	Catharine	FRE 182	
Sarah	BCI 512	John	D.C. 5	Henry	FRE 169	
Sarah H.	ANN 376	Planner	DOR 44	Mathias	FRE 176	
Susanna	FRE 102	HANDMON, William	TAL 48	Phillip	FRE 182	
Thos.	FRE 222	HANDS, Alexr.	BCI 196	William	FRE 173	
Upton	FRE 211	Alexander	TAL 13	HANNA, Alexander	HAR 43	
Vachel (?)	FRE 218	Beddingfield	KEN 101	Alexander B.	BCI 121	
Walter	FRE 78	Ben	QUE 18	Ann	BCI 60	
William	FRE 97	Ephraim	ANN 317	Elija	FRE 170	
William	WAS 82	James	CLN 97	Ellen	D.C. 107	
William	WAS 119	John	ANN 334	James	BCI 452	
Wm.	WOR 172	Nicholaus	BCI 398	John	BCI 301	
Wm. L.	BCI 245	Paul G.	BCI 171	John	PRI 229	

HANNA (continued),	
Richard	CEC 177
Robert	HAR 9
Thomas	TAL 23
William	HAR 18
William, Junr.	HAR 43
HANNAH, John	BCI 275
John	CEC 139
John	HAR 40
HANNAN, Jacob	WAS 56
Walter W.	CHA 212
HANNER, John	FRE 211
John	WAS 107
Mathias	FRE 228A
William (?)	BCI 223
HANNEY, Chars.	BCI 354
HANNIMAN, Henry	BCI 489
HANNON, George C.	BCI 48
John	BCI 168
Walter W.	PRI 222
Wm.	D.C.163
HANSE, William A.	BCI 100
HANSELL, Jacob	ALL 17
HANSEN, --- (?)	BCI 378
HANSHAW, Basil	ANN 308
Lloyd	ANN 308
HANSON, Benedict H.	
	HAR 23
Benjamin	KEN 93
Chars. A.	BCI 336
Dolly	CHA 195
Frank	D.C.19
George	BCI 9
George	WAS 123
George A.	KEN 91
Grace	ANN 400
H. W.	BCI 397
Isaac	CEC 124
Isaac	D.C.94
James	BAL 96
John	HAR 18
John	KEN 107
John D.	CHA 206
Luke	D.C.112
Maria	BCI 493
Mark	D.C.200
Matilda	PRI [200]
Moses	D.C.6
Nathaniel	BAL 93
Nicholas	BCI 192
Philip	BCI 492
Priscilla	ANN 319
Robert W.	CHA 190
Samuel	ANN 404
Samuel	CHA 190
Samuel, Junr.	CHA 190
Thomas M.	CHA 197
William	BCI 119
William	D.C.125
Wm.	BCI 250
HANSTRON, --- (Widaw)	
	BCI 415
HANTS, Georgs	KEN 105
HANWAY, Sarah	HAR 64
Washington	HAR 64
HANY, James	BAL 186
HAPE, Jacob (?)	FRE 174
HAPNER, John	FRE 96
HAPPY, Catharine	FRE 188
HARAGAN, Jonathan	CEC 177
Samuel	KEN 93
HARBACH, George	FRE 201
HARBAN, Thomas	BCI 454
HARBARGER, Leonard	
	FRE 113
HARBAUGH, Christian	
	FRE 162

HARBAUGH (continued),	
Ely	FRE 143
Ely (of Chr.)	FRE 147
Henry	FRE 149
Jacob	FRE 140
Jacob (of Jacob)	FRE 150
Jacob (of Jno.)	FRE 149
Jacob, of L.	FRE 150
John	FRE 149
John	FRE 149
John	FRE 154
Joseph	D.C.90
Joseph	FRE 150
Leonard	D.C.98
Thomas	WAS 118
Yost	FRE 150
HARBER, Thomas	BCI 402
HARBEST, John (Revd.)	
	BAL 140
HARBIN, Aquilla	CHA 226
George	PRI 228
Horo.	D.C.80
James	PRI 228
Naylor	PRI 230
Rapheal	CHA 220A
Rezin	CHA 221
Roswil	CHA 222
Walter	CHA 222
Zepheniah	CHA 228
HARBINE, Daniel	WAS 134
HARBISON, Robert	
	BCI 463
HARBOUGH, Benj.	BCI 514
HARCUM, Lee P.	SOM 138
HARDACRE, John	CAL 58A
HARDAN, Peter	FRE 229
HARDCASTLE, Mathew	
	DOR 49
Peter	CLN 82
Robert	CLN 82
Samuel	CLN 73
Simon	DOR 56
Thomas (?)	TAL 49
Thomas	CLN 72A
Thomas	TAL 50
Wm. W. E.	CLN 82
HARDEN, Elizabeth	
	BAL 226
Grace	ALL 21
Henry, Ovsr.	TAL 3
James	CLN 100
John	ALL 16
John	ANN 371
John E.	SAI 91
Joseph	BAL 60
Joseph, Sen.	ANN 382
Joseph, Jnr.	ANN 382
Letty	QUE 37
Mathew	ANN 382
Nicholas	ANN 381
Pepie	BCI 429
Samuel	BAL 177
Savil	ALL 15
Stephen	BAL 197
Thomas	ANN 326
Thomas	CLN 106
Thomas	TAL 7
William	ALL 27
Wm.	BCI 418
HARDESTER, Frederick	
	FRE 213
HARDESTY, Abraham	
	ANN 327
Ann	CAL 51
Benjamin	BCI 115
Benjamin	CAL 62
Benjamin D.	ANN 278

HARDESTY (continued),	
Daniel	CAL 68
Eleanor	CHA 205
Eleanor	MON 165
John	BAL 184
John	SAI 82
Joseph, Senr.	CAL 67
Joseph, Junr.	CAL 58A
Joshua	ANN 278
Mary	CAL 61
Mary	MON 132
Mathew	ANN 254
Nancy	CAL 59
Rezin	PRI 184
Richard	CAL 62
Thomas	ANN 256
Thomas	ANN 276
Thomas	QUE 28
William D.	CAL 60
William P.	ANN 267
Wm. H.	CAL 47
HARDEY, Prissella	BCI 495
Wm.	BCI 538
HARDGROVE, Charles	
	WOR 195
Ephraim	HAR 24
HARDICAN, Charles	DOR 9
Robert	DOR 9
HARDIN, Ignatus	BAL 48
Robert	CLN 106
HARDING, Absolem	DOR 41
Charles	BAL 85
Charles F.	FRE 80
Chrisr.	BCI 200
Christian	FRE 75
Edward	MON 151
Elias	MON 133
Elias H.	FRE 80
Garetson	DOR 41
Henry	MON 151
John L.	FRE 101
Lithy	DOR 41
Mary	BCI 6
Mathew	DOR 49
Nicholas	ANN 383
Nicholas	BAL 46
Nicholas	MON 161
Phillip	CEC 138
Sarah	FRE 82
Siris	CEC 138
Thomas N.	FRE 80
William	D.C.65
William	DOR 41
William	FRE 214
HARDISTER, Charles R.	
	BCI 316
HARDISTIN, Joseph	ANN 321
HARDISTY, Henry	BCI 152
John	KEN 87
HARDMAN, Abraham	FRE 217
George	FRE 225
Jane	CAL 44
Thos.	CAL 48
William	DOR 3
HARDON, Jas. T.	QUE 8
HARDT, Peter	FRE 101
HARDY, --- (Mrs.)	PRI 185
Barbary	FRE 223
Benjamin	PRI 198
Charles	D.C.61
George	BAL 208
Henry W.	CHA 226
Ignatious	PRI 239
Isadore	PRI 222
Marshall (f.n.)	SOM 119
Mary	BCI 281
Mary	PRI 240

HARDY (continued),			HARMAN (continued),			HARPER (continued),		
Mary Ann	PRI	223	George	FRE	191	James	HAR	59
Mary G.	PRI	231	Jacob	FRE	117	James K.	QUE	24
Nicholas	ANN	371	Jacob	FRE	176	John	BCI	133
Noah	PRI	229	Jacob	FRE	198	John	D.C.	153
Peter	ALL	37	Jacob	WOR	157	John	DOR	31
Thomas	SAI	62A	John	FRE	204	John	DOR	53
Thomas S.	PRI	226	John	FRE	223	John	WAS	64-65
HARE, John	BAL	85	Lazarus	WOR	176	Joseph	BAL	97
Julian	BCI	444	Levin	WOR	170	Joseph	D.C.	38
Morris P.	BCI	390	Mathias	WAS	150	Joseph	WOR	170
William	MON	129	Michael	FRE	223	Levin	DOR	35
HARER, Jacob	ALL	9	Nathanl.	WOR	176	Mary	BCI	153
Philip	ALL	8A	Philip	BCI	377	Matilda	BCI	214
HARFIELD, --- (See			HARMEN, Levin	WOR	219	Noah	CLN	99
HARFIELD & ROSE)			HARMER, Abraham	HAR	78	Richard	DOR	22
HARFIELD & ROSE	BCI	358	Amos	MON	151	Richard	FRE	212
HARFORD, John	BAL	234	HARMITAGE, Willm.	D.C.	158	Rob. G.	BCI	211
HARGADINE, Mary	QUE	41	HARMKIN, Aaron	BCI	515	Robert W.	PRI	230
HARGEST, James	BAL	108	HARMON, Andrew	ANN	347	Saml.	D.C.	184
HARGETT, Abraham	FRE	85	Ann	WOR	214	Samuel	HAR	63
Abraham, Jr.	FRE	85	Belsy?	WOR	210	Sarah	D.C.	186
John	FRE	86	Betsy	WOR	210	Stephen	CLN	74
Peter	FRE	86	Charlotte	WOR	181	William	BCI	255
HARGIS, John	WOR	159	Eve	ANN	347	William	DOR	60
Peter	WOR	176	Frederick	FRE	80	William	KEN	120
Stephen W.	WOR	156	George	ANN	336	William	QUE	24
Thomas M.	SOM	127	Henry	D.C.	189	William S.	DOR	50
HARGROVE, Ben	QUE	10	Henry	WOR	210	Willm., Senr.	D.C.	150
John	BCI	122	John	BCI	344	Willm., Junr.	D.C.	144
HARGROVES, Jane	D.C.	198	John	WAS	56	Willm. A.	D.C.	172
HARIGAN, John	CEC	139	Mary	ANN	347	Wm.	QUE	11
HARINGTON, Henry	DOR	19	Nicholas	FRE	83	Wm.	WOR	170
Richard	DOR	35	Peter	ANN	334	Wm. F., Dr.	QUE	3
HARIS, Levin	SOM	123	Samuel	CEC	139	HARPERS, --- (Mrs.)		
HARISSON, Joseph (?)			Southy	WOR	174		BCI	341
	KEN	107	Thomas	CLN	110	HARPS, Mary ann	BAL	66
HARKER, James	BCI	139	HARMONSON, Sarah			HARPST, Michael	FRE	147
John	BCI	201		WOR	186	HARR, Conrad	WAS	146
John, Jr.	BCI	160	HARMONY, --- (Mrs.)			Lydia	FRE	147
Willm.	BCI	201		BCI	444	Peter	BCI	195
HARKIN, Will	D.C.	104	HARN, John	ANN	299	HARRADER, Conrod	FRE	205
HARKINS, Aaron	HAR	56	HARNE, Caleb	FRE	211	HARRETY, Bridget	D.C.	96
Joseph	HAR	56	Denton	FRE	211	Timothy	D.C.	97
HARKNESS, Samuel	D.C.	8	Overton	FRE	222	HARREY, Jane	DOR	18
HARLAID, Thomas H.	BAL	89	HARNER, Christian	FRE	173	HARRIESS, Samuel (?)		
HARLAN (See also KAR-			Daniel	BCI	432		DOR	51
LAN),			Frederick	FRE	172	HARRIGAN, John	FRE	150
Esther	CEC	159	Jacob	FRE	140	HARRIMAN, George	BAL	233
Jeremiah	HAR	78	Michael	FRE	171	Mary	BAL	114
John	HAR	43	Michael	FRE	178	Nathl.	BCI	533
Joseph	CEC	177	Michael	FRE	180	Stephen	BAL	114
Joshua	FRE	227	HARNESS, Hannah	ALL	31	HARRIN, Elias (?)	D.C.	124
Lewis	CEC	177	Samuel	DOR	51	HARRING, Geo.	MON	142
HARLAND, Joswa	WAS	69	HAROVER, Hiram	D.C.	166	HARRINGTON, Edmand		
HARLAUGH, Christian			HARP, Caleb	D.C.	63		DOR	24
	FRE	149	Calob	D.C.	12	Edmond?	DOR	24
HARLEMAN, Conrad	WAS	69	Hezekiah	BCI	53	Ellen	BCI	300
HARLES, Thomas	DOR	9	Jacob	FRE	157	John	DOR	19
HARLEY, Ann	D.C.	156	Mary	D.C.	26	John, Senor	DOR	19
John (?)	D.C.	65	Sarah	BAL	186	Levin	DOR	16
Joseph	BCI	69	HARPEE, Robert W. (?)			Lydia	CLN	76
Joshua	FRE	128		PRI	230	Nathan	TAL	21
Pinneny (?)	DOR	42	HARPEN, Bethusia (?)			Peter	DOR	27
Smith	CHA	200A		DOR	31	Rachel	TAL	33
HARLIN, Elijah	FRE	122	HARPER, Allen	DOR	63	Richard	CLN	90
HARLOW, Clarissa	BCI	139	Anna	D.C.	23	Richard	TAL	22
David	BCI	325	Anne	MON	132	Sally	DOR	20
Rebecca	BCI	54	Bethusia	DOR	31	Timothy, Doct.	SAI	66
HARLY, Bartly	PRI	229	David	DOR	22	William	SOM	141
HARMAN, --- (Mr.)	BAL	244	Edward	MON	161	HARRIS, --- (Mrs.)	BCI	354
Abel	WOR	176	Elizabeth	WOR	155	--- (Mrs.)	BCI	435
Christian	FRE	156	Francis	MON	162	Alexander	BAL	151
Daniel H.	BCI	149	James	CLN	88	Amos	ALL	25
George	D.C.	68	James	D.C.	205	Ann	BCI	14
George	FRE	154	James	FRE	94	Ann	KEN	117

HARRIS (continued),		HARRIS (continued),		HARRISON (continued),	
Anthy.	D.C. 189	Pompey	D.C. 205	John	WAS 97
Barton	MON 158A	Pricilla	PRI 224	John	WAS 115
Benjamin	ANN 278	Rachel	BAL 77	John, Sen.	WAS 138
Benjamin	BCI 101	Richard	ANN 375	John, Jun.	WAS 138
Benona	CEC 138	Richard	BAL 141	Jonathan	BCI 249
Caleb	FRE 211	Richd.	QUE 14	Jos.	QUE 19
Charles	CEC 176	Robert	BCI 149	Joseph	ANN 346
Charles	CEC 177	Robert	BCI 304	Joseph	CHA 216
Daniel	BCI 22	Robert	QUE 34	Joseph	TAL 24
David	BCI 450	Sally	SOM 141	Joseph, Ovsr.	TAL 38
David	FRE 223	Sam.	BCI 347	Joseph of Jos.	TAL 22
David	FRE 228A	Sarah	QUE 3	Joseph of Rob.	TAL 22
Ed	QUE 3	Shoebrooks	QUE 35	Joshua	BCI 13
Edward	BCI 440	Solomon	TAL 32	Joshua	MON 160
Edward	QUE 32	Suky	D.C. 170	Kinsey	ANN 361
Edward-Negro	HAR 80	Tho. J. (I.?)	QUE 11	Kinsey	QUE 29
Elijah	CEC 176	Thomas	ANN 400	Margaret	BCI 110
Elisa	BCI 462	Thomas	BAL 152	Mary	BCI 28
Elizabeth	ANN 280	Thomas	BCI 378	Mary	TAL 24
Enos	BCI 67	Thomas	FRE 168	Mary A.	SAI 94
Franklin	FRE 173	Thomas	HAR 30	Nicholas	BAL 178
George	BCI 434	Thomas	KEN 95	Nicholas	TAL 34A
George	FRE 203	Thomas	QUE 30	Parraway	QUE 17
George	SOM 141	Thomas W.	CAL 65	Peter	BCI 51
Hannah-Negro	HAR 49	Toney	ANN 341	Peter	TAL 25
Henry	D.C. 149	Tubmon	WOR 212	Phebia	WAS 134[A]
Isaac	KEN 125	Turbott	QUE 32	Prissilla (Miss)	CAL 51
Isaac	SOM 136	W.	BCI 376	Rd. J.	QUE 6
Isaac	TAL 47	William	BCI 140	Richard	BCI 414
Isaac (of John)	SOM 126	William	FRE 173	Richard	D.C. 60
Isaac (of Spencer)	SOM 128	William	KEN 101	Robt.	D.C. 17
Isham	D.C. 25	William	SAI 93	Samuel	ANN 255
J. (I.?) W.	BCI 380	William	SOM 141	Samuel	BCI 30
Jacob	FRE 78A	William	TAL 38	Samuel	D.C. 17
James	BCI 29	William, Ovsr.	TAL 6	Samuel	TAL 28
James	D.C. 191	Willm.	D.C. 190	Sarah	TAL 27
James	KEN 104	Wm.	BAL 80	Solomon	QUE 27
James	QUE 33	Wm. C.	BCI 249	Sophiah	TAL 2
James	SAI 93	Zachariah	SAI 93	Stephen	TAL 25
James	SOM 115	HARRISON, Abraham		Thomas	CHA 226
James	SOM 131		HAR 80	Thomas	SAI 94
James, Jun.	KEN 92	Alexander	BCI 5	Thomas	TAL 23
Jane-Negro	HAR 80	Alexander B.	TAL 19	Thomas	TAL 26
John	BAL 118	Aquila	SAI 94	Thomas	TAL 38
John	BAL 188	Banjamin	SAI 92	Thomas, of Wm.	TAL 22
John	CEC 160	Benj.	D.C. 4	Thomas E.	SAI 94
John	CEC 176	Benjamin	ANN 256	Thomas S.	BCI 31
John	CEC 176	Benjamin	TAL 25	Uphama	WOR 170
John	CEC 177	Charles	ANN 258	William	BAL 220
John	D.C. 89	Charles	BCI 446	William	BAL 231
John	FRE 144	Daniel	BCI 58	William	BCI 130
John F., Esqr.	BCI 279	Edward	TAL 23	William	PRI 206
John G.	HAR 23	Elie	BAL 17	William	QUE 47
Jonathan	KEN 92	Elizabeth	BCI 55	William	SAI 93
Jonathan	TAL 20	Francis	CAL 52	William	TAL 38
Jos.	MON 133	Gustavus	D.C. 60	William of Jas.	TAL 22
Joseph	BAL 123	Hall	BCI 122	William of Robt.	CAL 51
Joseph	CAL 67	Henny	QUE 7	William D.	CHA 195
Joseph	D.C. 200	Isaac	WOR 190	William E.	DOR 50
Joseph	SAI 75	Jacob	BCI 7	Wm.	QUE 6
Josh.	D.C. 160	Jacob	CAL 48	Zepheniah	FRE 95
Levin (?)	SOM 123	Jacob	TAL 25	HARRISS (See also KAR-	
Littleton	SOM 137	James	ANN 260	RISS),	
Margaret	ANN 381	James	ANN 326	Aaron	DOR 39
Mary	BCI 114	James	BCI 22	Allice	SOM 109
Mary	CEC 177	James	BCI 31	Arthew	CAL 49
Mima	D.C. 161	James	CAL 50	Arthur?	CAL 49
Moses	BCI 141	James	FRE 76	Benja.	CAL 47
Moses-Negro	HAR 80	James	QUE 27	Edwd.	BCI 494
Nathan	CEC 176	James	QUE 37	Elizabeth	CLN 116
Nathan	D.C. 161	James	TAL 24	Ephraim	SOM 109
Ned-Negro	HAR 65	John	ANN 275	Ge.	FRE 218
Patty	BCI 446	John	DOR 20	George	TAL 8
Perdue	QUE 30	John	KEN 102	George	WOR 195
Philip	CEC 123	John	TAL 24	Henry	DOR 8

HARRISS (continued),		HARRY (continued),		HARTLOVE, John	D.C.10
Henry (of A.)	CLN 106	Sam	BCI 336	John	D.C.87
Henry (of Jno.)	CLN 107	Zekial	WAS 133	HARTMAN, Charles	D.C.6
Isaac	CLN 106	HARRYMAN, David	BCI 128	Christian	WAS 145
Isaac (negro)	TAL 20	Samuel	BAL 14	Fred.	D.C.8
James	CLN 77	Sarah	HAR 4	George	D.C.6
James	CLN 98	Thomas	BAL 123	Jacob	WAS 145
James	CLN 108	HARSH, Benjamin	FRE 118	Samuel	BAL 118
James	CHA 211	Frederick	WAS 97	Susannah	BCI 438
James	PRI 212	George	WAS 141	HARTMON, Benjamin	
James	PRI 215	HARSHBARGER, Henry			WAS 96
James W.	QUE 29		WAS 73	Catherine	WAS 57
John	CLN 95	Jacob	WAS 110	HARTNER, Fred.	BCI 537
John	CLN 98	HARSHEY, Christly		HARTS, Francis	FRE 105
John	CLN 114		WAS 85	Peter	FRE 115
Joshua	DOR 26	HARSHMAN, Henry	D.C.134	HARTSHORN, James	KEN 104
Lucretia	SOM 112	Susna	D.C.134	Mary	CEC 177
Margaret	DOR 8	HARSHNER, Jacob	BAL 81	HARTSHORNE, Susannah	
Mary	SOM 146	John	BAL 81		D.C.161
Meteus	CLN 91	HART, --- (brother)		HARTSOAK, David	FRE 212
Morgan (Doctr.)	CHA 218	(See Robert HART		John	FRE 212
Mosses	DOR 24	& brother)	HAR 45	Joseph	FRE 212
Nathan	CHA 203	Ann	BCI 322	HARTSOCK, Frederick	
Richard	CLN 86	Ann	CHA 196		ALL 33
Robert	CLN 110	Benjamin	BAL 235	Nicholas	FRE 216
Robert	TAL 24	Benjamin	DOR 36	Peter	FRE 161
Silvah	DOR 45	Daniel	ANN 391	HARTSOOK, John	ALL 31
Thos.	WOR 160	David	KEN 115	HARTT, Ben	QUE 16
William	CLN 85A	Elizabeth	FRE 100	HARTY, John	BCI 285
William	DOR 24	Ellis	FRE 218	HARTZSOCK, Daniel	
William	SOM 109	George	DOR 33		WAS 128A
William A.	CHA 206	George?	DOR 33	HARVEN, James	WAS 64
William S.	DOR 49	Henry	BCI 203	Robert	WAS 105
HARRISSON, Benjamin		Henry	BCI 251	HARVEY, Alexander	ANN 358
	CAL 61	Henry	BCI 417	Allen	ANN 345
Benjamin	DOR 25	J.	BCI 368	Andrew	CEC 139
Catharine	WOR 190	Jacob	BCI 450	Ann	BCI 46
Elizabeth	CAL 59	Jacob	WAS 145	Casandra	BAL 245
James	CAL 59	James	KEN 89	Charles	ANN 367
John D.	D.C.178	John	BCI 202	Eleanor	D.C.57
Joseph	CLN 97	John	D.C.58	Eliz.	BCI 354
Mary	CLN 96	John	HAR 45	George	WAS 147
Maryland	CAL 60	Joseph	BCI 174	Jacob	BCI 447
Richard	CAL 58A	Mary Ann	CHA 193	James	CLN 79
Robert	CAL 58A	Michael	BAL 139	James	D.C.43
William	BCI 316	Michael	FRE 129	James	D.C.101
William	CAL 59	Nicholas	CEC 160	James	HAR 73
Wilm.	D.C.215	Petsey	BCI 343	James	QUE 46
HARRISTER, Polly	D.C.11	Richard	ANN 347	James G.	PRI 212
HARRITT, John	FRE 140	Robert?	DOR 31	John	BCI 51
HARROD, Charles	HAR 46	Robert	BCI 82	John	D.C.135
Henry	BCI 24	Robert	CEC 160	John	HAR 42
John J.	BCI 266	Robert & brother	HAR 45	John	HAR 70
Sanny?-free	CAL 65	Robrt	DOR 31	Joseph	BCI 448
Sauny-free	CAL 65	Valentine	BCI 147	Leonard	PRI 216
Walter	HAR 41	William	FRE 155	Mary	CEC 138
William	HAR 56	HARTE, John D.	WAS 148	Nancy	CLN 99
HARROP, Jos.	BCI 340	Sara	WAS 145	Richard	BAL 227
HARROPS, Jos. (?)	BCI 340	HARTHORN, Jane	WAS 120	Richard	PRI 182
HARROW, John O.	WAS 99	HARTLE, George	WAS 99	Seth	MON 141
HARRY, --- (Mrs.)	D.C.25	Seboston	WAS 99	Thomas	CEC 159
--- (son) (See Mary		HARTLEY, Darcus	KEN 103	Thomas	PRI 183
HARRY & son)	HAR 43	James	BAL 48	Will.	D.C.130
Andrew	CEC 176	James	CEC 177	William	PRI 182
David	WAS 80	Jesse	HAR 46	William	PRI 194
David	WAS 116	Margarett	BCI 306	Zadoc	DOR 63
Evan	MON 151	Richard	KEN 105	HARVIN, Elias	D.C.124
George I. (J.?)	WAS 118	Samuel	BAL 36	Elisha	PRI 218
Isaac	FRE 154	Sarah	D.C.195	Thomas	PRI 218
John	HAR 55	Sarah	D.C.197	HARVY, Charles	FRE 75
John	WAS 121	Thomas	BAL 36	James	BCI 18
Mary	HAR 64	Thomas	BAL 48	Richard	FRE 133
Mary & son	HAR 43	Thoms.	ALL 35	Thomas	PRI 226
Richard	FRE 174	William	BAL 36	HARWICK, --- (Widow)	
Richd.	MON 165	William	CAL 66A		BCI 392
Sally	WAS 116				

HAWKINS (continued),		HAYDEN (continued),		HAYS (continued),	
James	PRI 237	Catherine	BAL 52	Bartholoman?	DOR 28
James	QUE 24	Charles	SAI 86A	Bartholomaw	DOR 28
James L.	BCI 250	George, Sen.	SAI 87	Cator	BCI 462
John	CLN 75	George, Junr.	SAI 88	Daniel	HAR 44
John	D.C. 42	Gerard	SAI 86A	David	CEC 123
John	HAR 46	Harac H.	BCI 358	Esater	BAL 174
John-free	CAL 63	Henritta	SAI 93	Elizabeth	BAL 184
John-Slave	CAL 61	James	BCI 523	Elizabeth	HAR 45
John L.	CHA 207	James	SAI 86A	Emelia	FRE 129
Joseph	ANN 315	John	SAI 94	Fielder	PRI 196
Joshua	ANN 330	Jonathan	SAI 89	Geo. B.	MON 130
Joshua	BAL 54	Joseph	SAI 98	George	CEC 123
Levin	TAL 51	Peregrine	SAI 92	Hannah-Negro	HAR 50
Mary	BCI 287	Samul	SAI 92	James	CEC 124
Mary	BCI 287	HAYDON, Bennet	SAI 77	John	ALL 26
Mary	HAR 45	James	SAI 76	John	BCI 383
Mary	HAR 57	Joseph	SAI 79	John	CEC 123
Matthew	QUE 31	William	SAI 76	John	FRE 104
Perry	QUE 18	William, of Richd.		John	QUE 17
Peter	MON 133		SAI 79	John	WAS 60
Ralph	ANN 315	HAYES, A. Hannah	CEC 138	Joseph	FRE 169
Robert	HAR 28	Abram S.	MON 132	Joseph G.	FRE 219
Rose	KEN 101	Chas.	MON 138	Leonard	MON 130
Saml.	BCI 320	Elizabeth	MON 151	Leven	WAS 136
Samuel	ANN 273	James	WOR 155	Manliff	CEC 124
Samuel	CEC 159	Joell	CEC 139	Nathl. W. S.	HAR 48
Samuel	CEC 159	John	BAL 38	Rebecca	CHA 224
Samuel	CHA 221	John	BCI 80	Robert	BCI 267
Sidney	DOR 15	John	KEN 115	Robert	CEC 123
Solomon	D.C. 101	Mary	D.C. 178	Saml.	MON 132
Thomas	ANN 330	Mary	QUE 20	Samuel	DOR 30
Thomas	BAL 98	Reverdy	BCI 152	Simon	BCI 529
Thomas	CHA 226	Robert	D.C. 89	Theodoca	WAS 57
Thomas	FRE 123	Samuel	CEC 138	Thomas	FRE 140
Thomas	HAR 70	William	BCI 133	Thomas A.	HAR 47
Thos.	D.C. 128	William	CEC 138	Walter C.	BCI 95
Walter	D.C. 28	HAYGHE, Joseph J. (I.?)		William	BCI 97
William	ANN 320		BCI 38	Wilson	FRE 129
William	BAL 120	HAYLE, Hannah	WOR 205	Wm.	BCI 414
William	D.C. 40	Jacob	D.C. 65	HAYSE, Fanny	SOM 116
William (Mrs.)	BCI 265	Stephen	WOR 216	Micheal	ANN 359
HAWKSWORTH, Thos.	KEN 124	Thomas	BCI 517	HAYWARD, Arthur	SOM 140
HAWLAND, John M.	BCI 440	HAYLEY, Robert-f.n.		David	WOR 205
HAWLEY, Francis H.	CLN 91		SOM 120	Esther	WOR 205
Wm. (Rev.)	D.C. 15	HAYLIE, Bob	SOM 132	George	WOR 180
HAWMAN, Peter	FRE 155	Sally	SOM 133	John	BCI 476
HAWN, Christiana	WAS 123	HAYLY, Jno.	KEN 124	John	DOR 34
David	WAS 57	HAYMAN, Ballard	SOM 125	John E.	WOR 180
Eve	WAS 78	Caspar	D.C. 157	Margaret	KEN 102
George	WAS 123	Charles	WOR 216	Thomas	TAL 39
Jacob	WAS 96	Cornelus	WOR 217	William	ANN 320
John	WAS 99	Ephraim	SOM 132	William	TAL 5
Mary	WAS 122	Isaiah	SOM 132	HAYWOOD, Isaac	BCI 477
Michael	FRE 225	Milly	SOM 126	Jane	DOR 8
Thomas	WAS 119	Randal	SOM 133	Jno.	MON 130
William	BCI 97	Rilly	SOM 132	John	SAI 68
HAWON, Grafton D.	PRI 195	Tabitha	SOM 118	Joseph	DOR 44
HAWS, Ann (?)	PRI 212	HAYMON, Handy	WOR 214	Joseph	SAI 63
Charles	SOM 149	John; S.	WOR 215	Joseph H.	DOR 58
HAWVER, Daniel	FRE 164	William	WOR 216	Mary	PRI 195
George	FRE 149	HAYNE, Harah	WOR 205	Thomas	DOR 60
George, Junr.	FRE 164	HAYNES, Cathe.	D.C. 96	William	D.C. 55
Peter	FRE 164	Daniel	BAL 56	HAYWORTH, Jonathan	
HAY, Cynthia	HAR 7	Daniel	D.C. 23		BAL 36
David	BCI 316	Frances	BAL 144	HAYYARD, Mary (?)	KEN 104
Edwd.	WOR 175	Henry	CLN 98	HAZARD, George	BAL 20
Elizabeth	CLN 77	Job	FRE 176	John	BAL 28
Jacob	BCI 512	John	DOR 60	HAZEL, Ann	SAI 89
John	BCI 483	John	KEN 106A	William	SAI 97
John A.	WOR 175	William	TAL 11	Zach.	D.C. 107
Martha	BCI 176	HAYON, Richard	SAI 78	HAZELETT, Edward	HAR 43
HAYCOCK, Solomon	HAR 24	HAYRE, John	D.C. 100	HAZZARD, Benjamin	CAL 60
HAYDEN, Bartholomew		HAYS, Abraham	HAR 63	Cord.	WOR 184
	SAI 88	Abram.	BCI 194	Grant	WOR 179
Basil	FRE 187	Archer	HAR 46	Matthew	QUE 48

HEAD, Cecelius	FRE 103	HEBBERN, Barnet	BCI 150	HELFENSTEIN, Alfred	
James	FRE 192	HEBIN, Jacob	BCI 346		BCI 244
John	FRE 146	HEBREW, --- (?)	BCI 397	Jonathan	FRE 99
Nathan	FRE 203	--- (Mrs.)	BCI 401	HELFLEICH, Catherine	
William B.	FRE 159	HEBREWS, Wm.	BCI 529		WAS 116
HEADLEY, James	BAL 91	HEBS, Lewis	BCI 400	Peter	WAS 114
Job	D.C. 17	HECH, Peter	FRE 169	HELLEN, Jacob	CAL 43
Samuel	MON 151	HECK, Christian	WAS 59	Joseph J. (I.?)	CAL 45
HEADLY, Thomas	BAL 79	Henry	WAS 58A	HELLER, Barbary	WAS 136
HEADRICK, John	WAS 57	Jacob	FRE 182	Daniel	WAS 139
Joseph	WAS 57	John	FRE 181	Jacob	WAS 83
HEAFLING, Daniel (?)	FRE 173	Peter (?)	FRE 169	HELLIN, John I. (J.?)	
HEAIRN, John	BCI 21	Peter	WAS 59		CAL 44
HEALD, William	BCI 124	Peter	WAS 85	HELLIOUS, John	BCI 460
HEALEY, Daniel	HAR 72	HECKMAN, Christopher		Thomas	BCI 462
Elizabeth	HAR 72		FRE 101	HELLRICLE, Jacob	D.C. 151
HEALY, Henry	BCI 90	William	FRE 146	Philip	PRI 228
HEAP, James	BAL 186	HECKROTE, Aron G.		HELLY, Benjamine P. V.	
HEAPS, Arthur	HAR 73		ALL 9		SOM 104
C.	BCI 176	William	BCI 249	HELM, Richd.	BCI 321
John	HAR 58	HECTOR, John	TAL 3	HELME, Daniel	CLN 89
Mary	HAR 78	HEDDINGER, Michael		HELMER, John W.	WAS 101
Robert	HAR 58		BCI 100	HELMLING, Anth.	BCI 338
William	HAR 73	HEDDINGTON, Nicholas		John	BCI 434
HEARD, Benidict, J.	SAI 89		BAL 52	HELMS, David (?)	BAL 10
Charlotte	SAI 69	William	BAL 51	L.	BCI 378
Edmond	SAI 76	HEDEN, Ellen	D.C. 173	Samuel	BCI 33
Edward J. (I.?)	CHA 207A	HEDGE, Isaac	FRE 115	HELMSWORTH, Jeremh.	
Elendor	SAI 80	Isabella	FRE 115		D.C. 131
Glending (See Jenny		Julian	FRE 101	HELPHNER, Henry	FRE 227
---, Negro, slave of		Shedrick	FRE 130	HELRIGLE, Barbary	D.C. 160
Glending HEARD)		HEDGES, Hanson	BCI 477	George	PRI 192
Ignatious	SAI 98	Joseph	FRE 228A	Gurge?	PRI 192
John	BCI 28	Moses	FRE 226	HELSBY, Ann	DOR 45
Joseph	SAI 80	Richard	D.C. 37	James	DOR 7
Joseph of James	SAI 80	HEDLEY, George	BAL 246	James	TAL 35
Matthew	SAI 57	HEDRICK, George	WAS 66	John	TAL 35
HEARN, Benjamin	SOM 117	Jacob	WAS 90	John, Jr.	TAL 31
Calib	ANN 374	Peter	BAL 145	Sarah	DOR 8
Cesar (f.n.)	SOM 119	Thomas	BCI 114	Thomas	TAL 33
Ebenr.	WOR 154	HEDRICKS, William	HAR 45	William	TAL 33
Edward	SOM 144	HEDROCK, Jacob	BCI 531	HELSLING, Jacob	BAL 21
Harriot	BCI 33	HEDROR, George	CEC 124	HELTER, Little	FRE 159
Isaac	ANN 375	HEERHEART, Nicholas		Litte?	FRE 159
John	ANN 375		BAL 82	HELTERBRACK, Jacob	
Spencer	SOM 105	HEFFLEY, John	FRE 192		FRE 209
William, Senr.	SOM 110	Peter	FRE 193	HELTERBRIDLE, Jacob	
HEARSY, Philip	D.C. 71	Peter	FRE 205		FRE 191
HEART, Josias	BAL 94	Stephen	FRE 203	Jacob	FRE 224
HEARTHERTON, George		HEFFNER, Catharine		Jacob, of Jno.	FRE 192
	WAS 100		FRE 114	John	FRE 201
HEARTTE, Isaac T.	BCI 166	Frederick	FRE 116	Rachel	FRE 219
HEATER, John	MON 165	Frederick, Jun.	FRE 116	Solomon	FRE 203
HEATH, Conny	D.C. 180	Jacob	FRE 116	HELTON, John	ANN 297
James	KEN 116	John	FRE 116	Samuel	MON 129
James P.	BAL 181	Michael	FRE 116	HEMICK, Jacob	BCI 298
Jassa	ANN 337	Michael	FRE 116	HEMIS, Frederick	BCI 100
John B. M.	SOM 123	HEFNER, Danl.	MON 131	HEMMELL, Jacob	FRE 102
Richard (Genl.)	BCI 273	HEGAN, Anthony	BCI 119	HEMP, Frederick	FRE 122
Richard K.	BAL 193	HEGGINS, Elizabeth (?)		Henry	FRE 163
Robert	ANN 312		MON 151	Philip	FRE 161
Samuel	SOM 132	HEGHEN, Susan	WAS 66	HEMPHILL, Joseph	CEC 138
Sarah	CEC 123	HEIBNER, Frederick		Mary	CEC 138
Thomas	CEC 159		D.C. 33	HEMPSTON, Townley	MON 130
William	SAI 69	HEICHLEY, Henry	FRE 97	Wm.	MON 132
HEATHERS, Samuel	QUE 23	HEINER, Henry	FRE 171	HEMSLEY, Alexander	TAL 22
HEATON, John	HAR 59	John	FRE 182	James	BCI 11
HEBB, Bennet	SAI 79	Peter	FRE 183	James T.	QUE 33
Caleb	SAI 63	HEINZ, Hen.	BCI 339	Philemon W.	TAL 46
Edward T.	FRE 83	HEIRD, Benedict J.	CEC 124	Samuel	QUE 42
Elizabeth	SAI 63	HEIS, Emous	BCI 346	Thomas	QUE 38
James	SAI 62A	HEISE, John C.	PRI 195	William	QUE 40
John	QUE 46	HEISON, Nicholas	BCI 109	HENCOCK, John	BCI 385
John	SAI 69	HEITTON, Abram	BCI 346	HENCY, Perry	FRE 75
William	PRI 237	HELDEBRAND, Conrad		Philip	FRE 70
HEBBARD, Wm. B.	FRE 170		WAS 89		

HENDCOCK, Daniel	WOR 199A	HENDS, Jacob (?)	WAS 56	HENRY (continued),			
William	WOR 200	HENEMON, Isue	BCI 110	Thos.		MON 141
HENDERICKSON, Joseph		HENESTOFLE, Ann	BAL 158	Thos.		MON 143
	CEC 139	Samuel	BAL 148	William		BCI 432
HENDERSON, Alexr.	D.C.202	HENING, Henry	FRE 217	HENSAN, Richard (?)		
Ann	D.C.201	HENISON, William	QUE 41			D.C.60
Benjn.	BCI 516	HENKEY, Fredk.	BCI 71	HENSEN, --- (?)		BCI 383
Charles	WOR 158	Isaac	FRE 143	HENSEY, William		BAL 65
David	BCI 217	HENLEY, Eleanor	BCI 68	HENSHAW, I. P. K.		BCI 357
Frisby	CEC 138	Fred	BCI 476	HENSON, Ann		BCI 295
Geo.	D.C.97	Jane	D.C.174	David		BCI 275
George	ANN 383	Patrick	MON 163	Ellen		D.C.188
George	HAR 18	Wm.	MON 167	Hannah		ANN 303
H. Andrew	CEC 138	HENNEBARGER, Christian		Horrace		ANN 376
Hanah	BAL 19		WAS 99	Jacob		ANN 296
Jacob	WOR 176	John	WAS 116	James		BCI 339
James	FRE 169	HENNEMAN, Gabael		Jeremiah		BCI 97
James	WAS 84		BAL 63	John		BCI 277
James	WOR 169	HENNERLY (See also		Judy		WAS 70
Jane	BCI 173	KENNERLY),		Mary		D.C.33
Jas.	WOR 157	Whittington	SOM 112	Nace		BCI 433
Jessee	D.C.188	HENNESTOFLE, Henry		Richard		D.C.60
John	ANN 381		BAL 156	William		BAL 210
John	BAL 201	John	BAL 156	HENWOOD, Mary		ANN 299
John	BCI 239	HENNICK, Barbary	BAL 177	HENY, James		BCI 436
John	CLN 113	George	BAL 178	HEPBURN, Alex		D.C.109
John	CEC 138	Joseph	BAL 195	Ann		D.C.102
John	CHA 190	HENNIMAN, Jb.	BCI 240	John		D.C.37
John	HAR 43	HENNING, --- (Widaw)		Peter		D.C.71
John (of Saml.)	WOR 158		BCI 392	HEPRON, John		KEN 107
John P.	D.C.62	Bennett	SAI 68	Thomas, Ser		KEN 107
- Joseph	WOR 156	Frederick	SAI 62A	HER (See also ILER),		
Josiah	CLN 113	George	D.C.116	Conrod		FRE 227
Lemuel	WOR 204	John	FRE 146	Jacob		FRE 222
Lemuel	WOR 216	Priscilla	D.C.116	John, of Conrod		FRE 223
Levi	SOM 155	Thomas	BCI 406	Peter		FRE 227
Levi	WOR 156	Thomas	FRE 149	HERAUT, --- (Mrs.)		
Levin	WOR 158	HENNISS, John	ALL 29			BCI 388
Moses	D.C.13	HENNISTOFLE, Tobias		HERBER, Ignatius		BCI 197
Noah	WOR 156		BAL 144	HERBERT, Benedict		HAR 23
Peter	BCI 513	HENNON, Stephn.	D.C.129	Charles		BCI 310
Robert	BCI 154	HENOS, Jacob	WAS 56	Charles		WAS 74
Robert T.	HAR 61	HENRIELE, Jacob	BCI 298	Frances		SAI 75
Sally	WOR 189	HENRIX, Danl.	BCI 405	Francis		D.C.113
Sarah	HAR 61	HENRY, Aaron	FRE 71	Francis		HAR 45
Sarah	MON 174	Daniel	WAS 134	George		HAR 45
Susan	BCI 484	David	BCI 323	Hannah		D.C.66
Thos. (Doc.)	D.C.38	Doroth	SOM 104	James		CHA 217
William	BCI 99	Edward	WOR 186	James		SAI 87
William	WOR 218	Ester	CEC 138	James B.		HAR 45
Wm. (of John)	WOR 156	Henry S.	SOM 129	Jeremiah		CHA 201
HENDLEY, George	TAL 9	Isaac	HAR 78	John		CHA 203
James	SAI 54	Jacab	DOR 25	John		D.C.57
Richd.	D.C.90	Jacab?	DOR 25	John		D.C.95
HENDON, Joshua	BAL 232	Jacob	BAL 122	John		HAR 45
Sophia	HAR 38	Jacob	WOR 197	John		PRI 240
HENDRAKESON, Pergrin		James	DOR 11	John		WAS 79
	CEC 123	John	BAL 222	John C.		PRI 186
HENDRICK, Edwd.	BCI 226	John	BCI 462	Joseph		D.C.123
Thomas	BCI 20	John	BCI 483	Joseph		HAR 26
HENDRICKS, James	BCI 455	John	BCI 532	Noblett		D.C.169
HENDRICKSON, William		John	D.C.121	Perry		FRE 130
	BCI 139	John	DOR 19	Philip		SAI 89
HENDRIX, Chs.	QUE 7	John C.	DOR 6	Robert		SAI 95
Elizabeth	FRE 175	John W.	DOR 10	Samuel M.		CHA 220A
Henry	FRE 87	Joshua	CLN 93	Sarah		D.C.166
Henry	QUE 6	Kassey	TAL 34A	Soln.		D.C.89
Isaac	BAL 86	Lucy	PRI 194	Thomas		D.C.16
Lodia	QUE 7	Martha	D.C.154	Thomas		HAR 25
Nathan	FRE 177	Nancy	DOR 49	Thomas		SAI 55
Thomas	BAL 86	Nelly	DOR 7	Thos., Senr.		D.C.169
Thomas	TAL 14A	Peter	BAL 165	William		SAI 54
HENDRIXON, James	ALL 26	Peter	DOR 52	HERBET, Joseph		FRE 82
Thomas	ALL 35	Robert J.	SOM 155	HERCULEES, Adam		TAL 36
HENDRY, Thomas J. (I.?)		Robert J. (I.?)	WOR 185	Benjamin		TAL 36
	ANN 395	Saml.	TAL 52			

HERD, Joshua	FRE 76A	
William	FRE 76A	
William B.	WAS 77	
HERINGTON, Elizabeth		
	QUE 40	
Samuel	WOR 219	
Thomas	BCI 138	
Thomas	WOR 218	
HERIS, Henery (?)	BAL 88	
HERLER, Dorotha	BCI 453	
HERLEY, John	WAS 93	
HERLY, Daniel	FRE 80	
Moses	WAS 89	
HERMANGE, Marger.	BCI 357	
HERN, John M.	D.C. 135	
Mathias	BAL 68	
Rixham	TAL 2	
HERNER, John	BCI 402	
HERON, Henry	QUE 40	
James	SOM 108	
Thos.	BAL 2	
HERONIMUS, Mary	D.C. 77	
HERR, David	WAS 87	
John	WAS 78	
John P.	WAS 117	
Rudalp, Sen.	WAS 140	
Rudalp, Jun.	WAS 137	
HERRING, Adam	FRE 134	
Casper	FRE 134	
Charles	HAR 22	
David	BCI 414	
David	QUE 8	
Elizh.	BCI 168	
George	ALL 6	
Henry	BAL 15	
Henry	BCI 114	
Henry	FRE 134	
Jacob	BAL 143	
Jacob	FRE 134	
John	BCI 182	
John	FRE 124	
John	KEN 110	
Mary	D.C. 48	
Patrick	BCI 181	
Thomas	BCI 28	
HERRINGTON, David	CLN 94	
Henry	BCI 37	
Henry	CLN 94	
John	BAL 42	
John	CLN 76	
John	SOM 114	
Otis (See Otis HERRING-		
TON R. Taney SMITHS)		
	BAL 126	
Richard	QUE 26	
Shepherd	SOM 114	
HERRON, Thomas	BCI 286	
HERSCH, Elizabeth	BCI 321	
HERSEY, Solomon	CEC 177	
HERSH, Betsey	FRE 174	
John	FRE 174	
HERSHBERGER, Henry		
	FRE 183	
HERSHEY, Andrew	WAS 85	
David	WAS 86	
Jacob	WAS 109	
John	WAS 117	
John	WAS 133	
HERSPERGER, John	FRE 123	
HERST, John	BCI 222	
HERTZOCK, George	BCI 432	
HERTZOG, Jacob	BCI 177	
HERVEY, Nicholas	BAL 3	
Robert	BCI 98	
HESELGROOM, William	PRI 229	
HESH, Charles	BCI 523	

HESHER, Zepheniah		
	WOR 209	
HESS, Charles	FRE 172	
Danl.	FRE 229	
David	WAS 67	
George	FRE 200	
Henry	FRE 169	
John	FRE 201	
Joseph	BCI 448	
Mary	WAS 126	
Samuel	FRE 180	
William	WAS 121	
HESSA, Thomas	CEC 123	
HESSANS, John	FRE 224	
HESSER, Caleb	BCI 410	
HESSEY, Archc.	BCI 523	
John	QUE 28	
HESSILIUS, Mary	BCI 243	
HESSON, Abraham	FRE 181	
Baltzer	FRE 179	
Balzer	FRE 179	
Daniel	FRE 179	
Daniel	FRE 181	
Jacob	FRE 178	
Peter	FRE 179	
Peter	FRE 182	
Wendel	FRE 179	
William	BAL 141	
HESTAND, Daniel	WAS 69	
HESTER, --- (Negro		
Woman) (?)	BAL 242	
HESTERLINE (See also		
AESTERLINE),		
Catharine (?)	FRE 189	
Henry	FRE 190	
HESTIN, Joseph	BAL 16	
HESTON, Conrad	BCI 535	
John	BCI 254	
Joseph	D.C. 194	
HETHERINGTON, Jas.		
	D.C. 169	
HETSER, George	WAS 149	
HETSLER, John	BCI 139	
HETZER, John	WAS 78	
HEUES, John (?)	D.C. 36	
HEUING, John (?)	KEN 110	
HEUISLER, Margarett		
	BCI 312	
HEUITT, William	D.C. 93	
HEVSER, James	MON 166	
HEWBAR, --- (?)	BCI 382	
HEWELL, John	BCI 501	
HEWES, Evan	BAL 16	
J.	BCI 435	
John	D.C. 160	
Richd.	D.C. 180	
Robert	CEC 139	
Samuel	CEC 138	
HEWET, William	FRE 156	
HEWETT, Benjamin	SAI 66	
Daniel	WAS 105	
Increse	FRE 222	
Jacob	WAS 105	
Jacob	WAS 107	
Jacob R.	QUE 4	
John	SAI 69	
Robert	BAL 42	
Robert	WAS 59	
HEWING, Henry	BAL 109	
HEWINGS, John	SAI 97	
HEWIT, Elbert	BCI 114	
Jacob	ANN 356	
James	SOM 130	
William	BCI 112	
HEWITT, Eli	BCI 377	
Elisha-Negro	HAR 65	

HEWITT (continued),		
Ellen	ANN 394	
Rebecca	CEC 138	
Thos.	QUE 16	
William (?)	D.C. 93	
William	CEC 138	
HEWLETT, Henry	BCI 412	
HEWS, Edward	MON 159	
John	ANN 274	
John	D.C. 36	
Levi	DOR 59	
Levin	DOR 42	
Samuel	BAL 11	
HEYER, Frederick	ALL 30	
HEYSER, Ann	WAS 120	
William	WAS 109	
William	WAS 117	
HIBBANS, Jeramia	WAS 148	
HIBBERD, Benjamin	FRE 72	
Joseph	FRE 73	
HIBBERT, Allen	FRE 192	
Jane	FRE 192	
Silas	FRE 201	
HIBS, Lewis (?)	BCI 400	
HICHEW, David	FRE 141	
John	FRE 159	
William	FRE 158	
HICKENBATHAM, Ralph		
	BCI 391	
HICKEY, Alexander	CHA 223	
Danl.	D.C. 126	
James	BCI 525	
Mark	D.C. 97	
Mary	D.C. 100	
Owen	BAL 37	
Timothy	HAR 71	
William	CHA 223	
HICKLEY, Robert	BCI 450	
Sabastian	BCI 215	
Thomas I. (J.?)	FRE 181	
HICKMAN, Ann	D.C. 101	
Benjamin F.	WAS 56	
David	BAL 111	
Isaac	CLN 100	
Jacob	CLN 98	
John	BAL 105	
Josh	MON 130	
Josiah, Captn.	WOR 177	
Margaret	MON 135	
Margaret	PRI 196	
Mary	QUE 5	
Mary A.	MON 136	
Nicholas	CLN 98	
Sally	WOR 187	
Thos.	MON 136	
Thos.	WOR 195	
Willm.	D.C. 133	
Wm.	MON 134	
Wm.	MON 167	
HICKS, Ann	BCI 310	
Ann	DOR 55	
Elijah	BCI 155	
Eliza	DOR 50	
Elizabeth	CLN 107	
Geo.	D.C. 103	
George (?)	BCI 156	
George	BCI 176	
George	PRI 192	
Giles	CLN 92	
Gurge	PRI 192	
Henry	PRI 239	
Henry C.	DOR 50	
Henry W.	DOR 50	
John	BCI 155	
John	BCI 227	
John	CLN 94	

HICKS (continued),		HIGINS, James L.	FRE 75	HILL (continued),	
John S.	DOR 52	HIGNUT, Emanuel	CLN 98	James	CHA 196
Levin	CLN 94	HIGNUTT, Archibald		James	D.C.147
Mary	ANN 292		QUE 37	James	PRI 218
Mary	CLN 92	John	BCI 493	James	SOM 117
Nancy	CLN 95	Rebecca	CLN 74	Jeremiah	CEC 176
Nehemiah	D.C.206	William	CLN 86	John	ALL 25
Thomas	DOR 56	HILBERT, Barbary	BCI 325	John	ANN 373
Thomas	DOR 57	Henry	BCI 344	John	BAL 36
Wm.	BCI 482	HILBITCH, Joseph	BCI 130	John	BAL 173
Wm.	BCI 530	HILBREATH, Thomas		John	BCI 32
HICKSENBAUGH, William			BCI 444	John	BCI 339
	ALL 18	HILBURGH, William	BCI 267	John	BCI 426
HICKSON, George	BCI 68	HILBUS, Jacob	D.C.58	John	CEC 139
HICKTON, Robert	BCI 368	HILBUSH, William	FRE 70	John	CEC 160
HIDE, Jonathan	FRE 209	HILDEBRAND, Christian		John	DOR 64
Jos.	BCI 222		BCI 438	John	FRE 148
HIDLEBACK, John	BCI 478	Jacob	BAL 159	John	MON 151
HIED, George	BCI 265	Jacob	FRE 112	John	MON 162
HIELER, Charles	FRE 143	John	BAL 157	John	SAI 82
HIERICK, --- (Widaw)		John	FRE 81	John B.	D.C.152
	BCI 407	Joseph	FRE 112	John H.	BCI 323
HIGDEN, Noyer	BCI 97	HILDERBRANDT, Andrew		John H.	WOR 174
HIGDON, Anna	D.C.27		BCI 307	John S.	SOM 104
Francis, Senr.	CHA 207A	HILERMAN, Jacob	CEC 139	Johnson	WOR 176
Francis, Junr.	CHA 202	HILKEY, George	FRE 86	Joseph B.	PRI 221A
Gusts.	D.C.130	HILL, Aaron	HAR 5	Joshua	SOM 138
John	D.C.22	Alexander	ANN 275	Josiah	WOR 186
John	D.C.178	Alx.	BCI 223	Jushua	BCI 475
Richard.	BCI 355	Anthony	FRE 225	Laurence	D.C.151
Sarah	CHA 207	Arthur	BCI 280	Lethe	D.C.45
Thomas E.	PRI 202	Barbara	FRE 110	Lettie?	D.C.45
HIGENBOTHAM, Thos.		Benedict	HAR 5	Levin, Jun.	WOR 196
	BCI 473	Benjn.	MON 162	Lewis	FRE 109
HIGGERTY, Willm.	D.C.213	Catherine	WOR 155	Margarett	DOR 39
HIGGINS, Benjamin	MON 151	Ceaser	CEC 177	Mary	BCI 283
Charles	PRI 203	Charity	CHA 206	Milkey	SOM 116
David	DOR 4	Charles	ANN 352	Morgan	ANN 274
Ebenzer	QUE 31	Charles	BCI 213	Nancy	D.C.53
Elizabeth	MON 151	Charles	PRI 202	Patience	BCI 85
Francis	DOR 50	Charles	PRI 238	Peggy	WOR 197
George	TAL 9	Charles	PRI 239	Peter	FRE 130
George W.	ANN 289	Clement	FRE 177	Polly	WAS 69
James	TAL 33	Cristopher	FRE 163	Purnell	WOR 157
James B.	MON 166	Daniel	CLN 75	Purnell	WOR 196
James H.	MON 151	Daniel	DOR 39	Richard	ANN 274
John	PRI 185	David	BCI 253	Richard	BCI 459
John S.	TAL 32	David	D.C.176	Richard	CEC 176
Margaret	MON 143	Dorathy	BCI 21	Richard	D.C.36
Mary	ANN 312	Elenor	BCI 512	Richard	SAI 90
Matthew	TAL 32	Eligah	CEC 139	Roberson	DOR 9
Nehemiah	TAL 6	Eliger	CEC 138	Robert	ALL 16
Samuel	DOR 40	Elijah?	CEC 139	Sally	WOR 187
Sarah	TAL 35	Elijer?	CEC 138	Samuel	BCI 179
Susan	BCI 243	Elizabeth	WAS 70	Samuel	CHA 216
HIGGINSON, Mary	SAI 57	Elizebeth	DOR 18	Sarah	ANN 344
HIGGON, William	DOR 18	Elizth.	D.C.149	Scarboro	DOR 53
HIGGS, Alexander	CHA 205	George	BCI 95	Stephen	BCI 493
Barrot	CHA 205	George	D.C.7	Stephen	WOR 160
Hanson	CHA 205	Gilbert	WOR 191	Susan	BCI 430
James	D.C.131	Giles	PRI 184	Temperance	SAI 90
John T.	CHA 206	Godard	D.C.206	Theodore	CHA 216
Thomas	WAS 61	H. V.	D.C.101	Thomas	DOR 53
HIGH, Frederick	FRE 219	Hannah	BCI 183	Thomas	MON 151
James	BCI 530	Hannah	FRE 183	Thomas F.	DOR 7
James	BCI 538	Harriet	D.C.42	Thos.	BCI 351
Susan	BCI 513	Henny	QUE 28	Tower	SAI 97
Wm.	BCI 486	Henry	FRE 163	Tower-Negro	HAR 79
HIGHBARGER, Adam	WAS 56	Henry	PRI 218	Towes (?)	SAI 97
David	WAs 55A	Henry	SAI 68	William	BAL 40
David of A.	WAS 56	Henry	SAI 90	William	BCI 24
John, Sen.	WAS 56	Jacob	BCI 346	William	DOR 39
John, J.	WAS 56	Jacob	WAS 70	William	PRI 202
HIGHFIELDS, Athey	CHA 197	Jacob	WOR 197	William	SAI 93
HIGHTON, John	MON 163	James	ANN 316	William	WOR 190
HIGINBOTHOM, William		James	BAL 179	William E.	CEC 177
	BCI 8	James	CEC 177		

HILL (continued),		HINA, Henry	FRE 224	HINSON (continued),	
Wm.	BCI 488	HINCHE, John	BCI 375	Joseph	BCI 143
Wm.	CAL 43	HINCHIN, Charles	CEC 176	Joseph	BCI 145
Wm.	WOR 169	HINCK, Wm.	BCI 397	Joseph	CEC 138
Wm. (of Stephen)	WOR 174	HINCKLE, John	ANN 402	Joseph	TAL 2
HILLARD, Christopher		HINCLE, John	BAL 13	Peregrin	CEC 123
	WAS 115	HIND, George	WAS 65	William	CLN 79
Jos.	MON 130	HINDES, Wm.	BCI 286	HINTERLING, John	FRE 197
HILLEARY, John, Senr.		HINDIMAN, Casar	ANN 296	HINTON, Abraham (free	
	FRE 124	HINDLE, James	ANN 384	negro)	SOM 118
John, Junr.	FRE 122	Noble	D.C. 47	Fanny	ANN 277
Joseph P.	ALL 21	HINDMAN, Elizabeth (?)		Gilbert	CAL 43
Margarett	PRI 208		TAL 51	John	ANN 384
Perry	FRE 123	James	BCI 258	Joseph	ANN 292
Ralph	ALL 23	Joseph	WAS 119	Joseph	CAL 43
Ralph	ANN 372	Robert	CEC 177	Robert	D.C. 95
Thos.	MON 131	Samuel	CEC 177	Ruth	PRI 180A
Waller H.	PRI 194	HINDS, John	BCI 305	Walter	MON 151
William	ALL 21	Moses	BCI 240	HINTZE, Chs.	BCI 211
Wm. (Doctr.)	FRE 123	Solomon	BCI 318	HIPKINS, Elizabeth	HAR 6
HILLEN, John	BCI 128	Thomas	CEC 138	Lewis	D.C. 175
Solomon	BAL 222	HINDSLEY, Peter	CLN 77	HIPLEY, Joshua	BAL 79
Thomas	BAL 222	HINDSMAN, Andrew		HIPSLEY, Caleb	FRE 200
HILLERY, Clement T.			ANN 300	Charles	ANN 359
	FRE 84	Casar (?)	ANN 296	Charles G.	ANN 356
Lewis	D.C. 37	HINE, John	WAS 67	John	BAL 63
Margaret	D.C. 38	HINEKER, Frederick		Joseph	BAL 63
Rignald	D.C. 50		BCI 239	HIRES, Henery	BAL 88
Thomas	FRE 84	HINER, Jacob	BCI 140	HIRST, Edward	SOM 112
HILLET, John	BCI 58	HINES, Abraham	D.C. 8	HISE, Wm.	BCI 495
HILLIARD, Jos.	MON 172	Charity	D.C. 8	HISER, Frederick	BAL 146
Saml.	MON 133	Daver?	FRE 218	John	BCI 296
Thos., Senr.	MON 129	David	FRE 218	HISS, --- (See HISS	
Thos., Junr.	MON 134	Edwd.	KEN 115	& AUSTON)	
HILLIARY, Tilghman	PRI 193	Elizabeth	CEC 159	Jacob	BAL 248
Virlinda	PRI 194	Frederick	D.C. 8	Jacob	BCI 114
HILLIRY, James	FRE 82	George	CEC 159	Joseph	BCI 266
HILLMAN, Ignatius	FRE 118	George	QUE 30	HISS & AUSTON	BCI 380
William	SOM 136	Henry	D.C. 15	HISSEY, Archibald	BCI 319
HILLOCK, Joseph	CEC 139	Isaac	KEN 125	Charles	BAL 194
HILLON, John (?)	D.C. 54	Isaac	QUE 31	Henry	BAL 193
HILLS, Samuel	D.C. 28	Jacob	D.C. 8	James	BAL 194
HILT, Nicholas	BCI 320	John	ANN 375	William	BAL 177
HILTEBEITEL, John	FRE 181	John	BCI 369	HISTLER, Clement	FRE 73
HILTEBRITEL, John (?)		John	D.C. 53	HITCH, Adam	SOM 137
	FRE 181	John	FRE 197	Ezekiel	SOM 105
HILTON, Abraham	BAL 242	Patrick	FRE 195	Garey	CLN 114
Abraham	BCI 296	Peter	FRE 78A	Isaac-f.n.	SOM 120
Abraham-f.c.p.	HAR 10	Philemon	QUE 30	John	SOM 132
Benn. R.	MON 131	Philip	D.C. 16	Leah	SOM 132
Clement	FRE 71	Philip	FRE 220	Levin	WOR 205
David-f.c.p.	HAR 11	Samuel	BCI 109	Mary	SOM 103
E.	BCI 406	Susan	D.C. 111	Polly	SOM 103
George W.	BCI 265	Thomas	CEC 159	Robert	SOM 134
Grace	ANN 338	William	HAR 62	Sovren	CLN 114
James	BAL 224	William	KEN 94	William	SOM 117
James	MON 131	HINEY, Philip (?)	FRE 70	HITCHCOCK, Aquila C.	
John	D.C. 54	HINGSTON, Nics.	D.C. 154		ANN 350
John	HAR 44	HINKEL, Nicholas	WAS 134	Asael	HAR 62
Leonard	MON 139	HINKLE, Alpheus	ALL 21	Claudius	BCI 148
Lydia	BCI 147	David	ALL 22	Elisha J.	CEC 160
Mary	BAL 4	Eli	BAL 176	Elizabeth	HAR 58
Mary	SAI 92	George	BAL 147	Isaac	HAR 59
Peregrine	D.C. 56	George P.	ALL 21	Isaac of Jno.	HAR 63
Saml.	D.C. 130	Jesse	ALL 22	Jesse	BAL 243
Saml.	MON 143	William	BAL 147	Jesse	BCI 187
Thos.	MON 139	HINKS, William	ANN 322	Milley	HAR 58
William	SAI 53A	William	ANN 357	Nicholas	HAR 6
Willm.	D.C. 149	HINLAN, Laurence	CHA 211	Nimrod	HAR 62
Wm.	MON 142	HINMAN, Ralph	WOR 155	Robert	BAL 107
Wm., Senr.	MON 134	HINNER, Michael	WAS 118	Robert J.	HAR 4
Wm., Junr.	MON 134	HINSON, C.	BCI 371	Toader	BCI 224
HIM, John (?)	WAS 67	Frisby-Neg.	CEC 123	William	BAL 240
HIME, David	FRE 110	Jacob	CEC 138	William	HAR 59
HIMES, Isaac	WAS 68	James	BAL 125	HITCHENS, James	DOR 52
Susanah	WAS 134[A]	James	CEC 123	Sarah	WOR 195
		John	CLN 80		

HOGG (continued),		HOLLAND (continued),		HOLLIDAY (continued),	
John	WAS 77	Isaac	WOR 194	Jacob	MON 151
Samuel	CEC 160	Isaac, Jun̲.	ANN 395	James	FRE 141
HOGGE, Isaac	WOR 178	James	ANN 396	Joshua	BCI 529
HOGGINS, Anne	MON 172	James	BAL 217	Mary	ANN 253
Richard	FRE 97	James	CLN 98	R.	BCI 372
HOGMIRE, Jonas	WAS 82	James	DOR 64	Rob	BCI 209
HOGNER, George	BCI 510	James	SOM 147	Thomas	ANN 253
John	BCI 313	James	WOR 169	Urban	CEC 177
William	BCI 483	Jas.	BCI 211	William	D.C.40
HOGSTEN, James	HAR 73	Jas̲.	QUE 14	Wm.	BCI 392
HOGWELL, George	WAS 138	Jas. (of Wm.)	WOR 177	HOLLIDAYOAKE, John	
HOHN, Daniel (?)	BCI 397	Jas. (of Wm.)	WOR 177		ANN 259
HOHNE, Christopher	ANN 397	Jesse	BAL 238	HOLLIDAYORKE, Ann	
HOHY, William	CEC 138	John	BCI 190		ANN 398
HOISLER, Joseph A.	BCI 494	John	MON 151	HOLLIFIELD, Joseph	BAL 178
HOKE, Peter	HAR 18	John	SOM 156	HOLLING, Rach.	BCI 339
HOLADAY, Clement	PRI 216	John	WOR 155	HOLLINGBAUGH, John	
Nat.	FRE 127	Jos̲.	MON 174		BAL 161
HOLBERD, Daniel	WAS 149	Joseph	ANN 376	HOLLINGER (See also	
John	WAS 149	Joseph	BCI 252	KOLLINGER).	
HOLBERT, Samuel	BAL 235	Joseph	BCI 295	Jacob (?)	ALL 11
Thomas	WAS 133	Kendal	WOR 195	William	BCI 69
HOLBROOK, Frederick		Levi	WOR 214	HOLLINGSHEAD, Margt.	
	CLN 107	Levin	WOR 173		D.C.28
Jno. T.	D.C.102	Littleten	BCI 380	William	HAR 59
Joseph	BCI 122	Lyddia	MON 174	HOLLINGSWERTH, Francis	
Thomas, Jun.	SOM 126	Margt.	D.C.90		BCI 276
HOLBRUNER, John	FRE 226	Mary	BAL 239	HOLLINGSWORTH, Horatio	
HOLDBROOK, Mary	BCI 148	Mary	MON 133		BAL 21
HOLDEN, Catherine	BCI 76	Mary	MON 140	Isaac	BCI 183
Peter	CLN 88	Mason-free	CAL 67	Jacob	ANN 353
HOLDER, Daniel	BCI 433	Michael	WOR 172	Jacob	BCI 381
William	SOM 105	Milby	WOR 210	Jane	CEC 138
HOLDING, Caleb	QUE 11	Milly	BCI 428	Jno.	QUE 2A
James	QUE 10	Moses	ANN 322	Levi	BCI 278
Jas̲.	QUE 17	Nathan	MON 151	Margt.	QUE 6
John̲	QUE 13	Nehemiah	WOR 155	Nathl̄.	HAR 42
Singo	QUE 19	Nero	FRE 222	Robert	HAR 59
Wm. (of Jno.)	QUE 13	Noah	SOM 157	Thomas	HAR 8
Wm. (of Wm.)	QUE 16	Peter, Doctr.	WOR 162	Zeb	BCI 502
HOLDSON, Sarah	KEN 109	Pleasant	WOR 180	HOLLINGWORTH, S.	BCI 358
HOLEBARGER, Mathias		Rachel	BAL 224	HOLLINS, Wm.	BCI 473
	FRE 200	Saml. (of Jno.)	WOR 163	HOLLINSBERRY, John	
HOLEN, George	BCI 22	Solomon	MON 159		D.C.185
HOLF (See also KOLF,		Thomas	PRI 212	HOLLIS, Affa	DOR 45
WOLF),		Thomas	SOM 142A	Amos	HAR 22
Pressilla (?)	BAL 98	Titus	QUE 26	Clark	HAR 22
HOLIDAY, James T.	BCI 155	Tony-f.c.p.	HAR 11	Henny	DOR 39
HOLINGSHEAD, James	CAL 49	William	BCI 444	James	CHA 211
HOLIVER (See also		William	SOM 146	John	CHA 191
OLIVER),		William	WOR 189	P.	BCI 451
John	D.C.105	Wm.	MON 141	Richard	ALL 25
HOLLADAY, Peola	BAL 19	Wm.	WOR 173	Richard F.	HAR 5
HOLLAMAN, Joseph	BCI 65	Wm., Captn.	WOR 163	Sarah	DOR 45
HOLLAN, John	DOR 39	HOLCANDS, John	BCI 287	HOLLIVY, Ephraim	BCI 305
Joseph	DOR 12	HOLLAR, Barbara	FRE 98	HOLLMON, John H.	WAS 79
HOLLAND, --- (Mrs.)	BCI 284	Elizabeth	FRE 98	HOLLON, Charles	WAS 58A
Aaron	BAL 238	Henry	FRE 98	Joseph	FRE 69
Archibald	HAR 5	Jacob	FRE 98	HOLLOR, Charles (?)	
Asa	MON 174	Peter	FRE 93		WAS 58A
Benjamin	FRE 154	HOLLARN, Jas.	D.C.92	HOLLORD, John	WAS 124A
Benjamin	HAR 38	HOLLAWAY, Hannah	ANN 307	HOLLOWAY, Adam	WOR 188
Daniel	SOM 149	HOLLEN, Conner	DOR 39	Ananias	WOR 196
Delilah	ANN 400	Thomas	DOR 39	Gilligate	HAR 24
Dennis	BCI 217	HOLLENBECK, Wm.	D.C.9	Jacob	WOR 189
Edward	ANN 259	HOLLER, Daniel	FRE 127	James	WOR 191
Edwd.	D.C.86	Fredk.	FRE 130	Kendal	WOR 191
Esther	BCI 160	HOLLEWAY, Joshua	WOR 204	Levin	WOR 190
Fanny	CAL 52	HOLLEY, James	D.C.57	Levin	WOR 191
George	BAL 237	HOLLICE, Thomas	CEC 123	Milby	WOR 194
George (Jun.?)	CAL 51	HOLLIDAY, --- (?)	BCI 406	Richard	HAR 22
Henry-[his] Slaves	ANN 263	Ben	BCI 520	Robt.	BCI 180
Henry S.	ANN 284	Betsy	BCI 321	Thomas	WOR 189
Isaac	SOM 144	Chas.	BCI 177	William	HAR 24
Isaac	WOR 175	David	BCI 343		

HOLLOWDAY, Henry	DOR 7	HOLTON, James	ANN 353	HOODS, Elizth. (See	
Henry	DOR 51	John	ANN 380	Hester & Elizth.	
Thomas	DOR 51	John	BCI 34	HOODS)	ANN 287
HOLLY, Airy	KEN 106A	John	SAI 66	Hester & Elizth.	ANN 287
Ann	CHA 217	Robert	SAI 66	HOOE, James H.	D.C. 208
Hannah	SAI 65	William	BCI 78	HOOFER, Nancy	BCI 317
Hilleary H.	FRE 94	William	SAI 68	HOOFF, Laurence	D.C. 167
Joseph	SAI 64	York	CEC 138	HOOFFS, Laurence-	
Sarah	HAR 22	York	CEC 139	[his] farm	D.C. 218
Sarah	HAR 22	HOLTRY, John	FRE 171	HOOFMAN, Christian	HAR 27
Sary	SAI 90	HOLTSMAN, George	D.C. 46	Christly	WAS 99
Thomas	SAI 65	HOLTZ, Christian	BCI 73	Jacob	D.C. 183
William	ALL 28	Jacob	FRE 225	Mathias	WAS 99
HOLLYDAY, David	FRE 118	Jacob	FRE 230	Peter	HAR 27
Henry	TAL 6	Jacob	FRE 234	Philip	BAL 111
Isaac	QUE 41	John	FRE 225	HOOICE, Adam (?)	FRE 143
John	SOM 116	Michael	FRE 116	HOOK, Andrew	BCI 301
Susan	QUE 31	Nicholas	FRE 114	Conrod	BAL 184
HOLLZMAN, Eli (?)	D.C. 42	Peter	BCI 134	Fred	BCI 528
HOLMAN, John	D.C. 125	Peter	BCI 157	Fred. C.	BCI 534
HOLMEAD, Anthony	D.C. 137	HOLTZAPPLE, Daniel	FRE 114	Frederick	BAL 174
Jas. B.	D.C. 91	HOLTZINGER, Jane	BCI 82	Jacob, of Rudolph	BAL 182
John	D.C. 67	HOLTZMAN, Charles	ALL 15	James	ALL 29
HOLMES, Allen	TAL 32	Eli	D.C. 42	John	FRE 122
Ann	BCI 319	Elizabeth	FRE 161	John S.	ALL 30
Ann	D.C. 114	John	ALL 15	Joseph	BAL 2
David	BCI 298	John	D.C. 40	Joseph	BCI 503
Henry	TAL 49	Saml.	D.C. 74	Joseph, Sen.	BCI 503
James	BCI 257	William	D.C. 96	Josiah	BAL 222
James	FRE 187	HOMAN, Danl.	D.C. 104	Michael	BCI 394
John	BCI 32	Michael	D.C. 52	Rezin	ALL 29
John	TAL 40	HOMES, Abraham	BAL 149	Rudolph	BAL 174
Joseph	BCI 7	Archibold	WAS 68	Soloman	BAL 174
Levy	BCI 503	David	WAS 64	Susannah	BAL 173
Mary	BAL 92	Ephraim	DOR 64	Thomas	BAL 173
Mary	TAL 11	Henry	WAS 64	HOOKER, Mary	BAL 7
Norman	SAI 54	Jonathan	BAL 149	Shok	BCI 218
Peter	ANN 401	Martin	WAS 64	HOOKES, Jacob	D.C. 157
Robert	FRE 141	Peter, Senr.	WAS 64	HOOKS, Sarah	BCI 298
Samuel	D.C. 8	Robert (?)	DOR 31	HOOPEN, Comfort	DOR 27
Samuel	D.C. 51	Robert	BCI 171	John (?)	DOR 29
Thomas	BCI 68	William	WAS 64	HOOPER, Abraham	HAR 6
Thomas	TAL 32	HOMRICKS, John	FRE 224	Alexr.	D.C. 98
William	CHA 207	HOMSHIER, Henry	BAL 157	Cesar	DOR 23
William	MON 151	HONE, John (?) (See		Comfort (?)	DOR 27
William	TAL 34	John HOUE &		Eliza	DOR 7
William J. (I.?)	CEC 160	John LYNCH)		Elizh.	D.C. 118
HOLMS, David	BAL 10	HONEWELL, Sam.	BCI 349	Frances?	DOR 8
Jacob	WAS 136	HONEY, Amus	BCI 406	Francis	DOR 8
John	WAS 136	Henry	QUE 24	Henry	ANN 315
HOLSEMAN, Mary	FRE 126	John	MON 178A	Henry	DOR 29
HOLSESOCKLE, Abrm.	FRE 132	Tom	QUE 20	Henry	DOR 55
HOLSLINGWORTY, Thos. H.		William	BAL 61	James	BCI 54
	BCI 334	HONEYWELL, James	D.C. 65	James	DOR 29
HOLSTE, Peter C.	BCI 267	HONGER, Lewis	BCI 521	Jemes	BCI 333
HOLSTEIN, John (of Wm.)		HOOCKEN, Joshua (?)		John	DOR 23
	WOR 163		BAL 78	John	DOR 29
Michael	BCI 450	HOOCKER, Joshua	BAL 78	John	DOR 56
HOLSTON, John	WOR 171	HOOD, Benjamin	ANN 356	John	FRE 78
Sarah	BCI 179	Charles	CEC 123	John	FRE 97
HOLT, Andrew	CEC 160	Edward	ANN 341	John	WAS 84
Elizabeth	SAI 93	Isaac	ANN 284	John	WOR 170
Ennals	D.C. 98	James	ANN 361	Mary	FRE 199
Enoch	BAL 109	James	BAL 64	Michael	HAR 39
Francis	CAL 59	James	BAL 194	Rebecca	D.C. 180
Isaac	CEC 139	James	BAL 195	Rebuca?	D.C. 180
James	CAL 58A	John	ANN 340	Richard	DOR 53
James	CEC 138	John	FRE 213	Roger	DOR 49
James	SOM 104	John	MON 174	Stephen	BAL 130
Jesse	FRE 156	Robert	ANN 328	Theanar (f.n.)	SOM 119
John	D.C. 50	Sarah	ANN 367	Thomas	BCI 68
John	SAI 93	Sarah	ANN 380	Thomas	FRE 199
Phillip	CAL 58A	Thomas	ANN 380	Thomas, Capt.	WOR 207
Robert	SOM 107	William	ANN 337	Thomas H.	DOR 3
Thomas	CEC 138	William, Junr.	ANN 337	Thos.	D.C. 98
HOLTER, George	FRE 85			William	BCI 89
Margaret	FRE 86			William	BCI 97

119

HOOPER (continued),		HOPKINS (continued),		HOPPEN, Lewis	ANN 347
William	BCI 160	Jerrard	PRI 180A	HOPPER, Ann	QUE 42
William	DOR 53	Joel	ANN 317	Benjamin	FRE 79A
Wm.	BCI 170	John	BAL 234	Daniel C.	QUE 42
HOOPPER, Abriham	CAL 45	John	BCI 3	Philemon B.	QUE 26
Benja.	CAL 46	John	CEC 159	Thomas W.	QUE 25
Isaac	CAL 42	John	CEC 176	William	QUE 42
James	CAL 42	John	D.C.138	HOPPY, Justis	BCI 391
Wm.	CAL 47	John	HAR 77	HOPS, James	CEC 160
HOOPS, Abraham	WAS 64	John	SAI 55	HOPWOOD, John	FRE 72
HOOSTON, John, Doct.		John	SOM 116	Joshua	FRE 79
	WOR 207	John	TAL 14A	Joshua	MON 139
HOOT, Samuel	D.C.8	John	TAL 24	HORDEN, --- (Widow)
HOOVER, Adam	ALL 31	John	TAL 33		BCI 384
Adam	BAL 143	John C.	SOM 110	H.	BCI 392
Adam	FRE 103	Johnsey	BAL 234	HORINE, Tobias	FRE 132
Adam	WAS 109	Johnze	PRI 205	HORLEY, John	D.C.65
Christian	FRE 144	Jonathan	TAL 8A	HORN, Abraham	FRE 122
Cornelius A.	ALL 35	Joseph	DOR 12	Henry	BCI 385
Daniel	BAL 143	Joseph	HAR 20	John	BCI 118
David	D.C.34	Joseph	HAR 75	Philip	BAL 210
Easter	WAS 99	Joseph J. (l.?)	ANN 289	HORNBURY, Margaret
George	FRE 189	Josiah, Captn.	WOR 177		CHA 225
Henry	BAL 152	Lambert	TAL 5	HORNE, Thomas	BCI 136
Henry	BCI 491	Levin	BAL 27	HORNER, Abel	BCI 315
Henry	FRE 132	Mary	ANN 392	Ann	BCI 520
Ignatious	BCI 492	Mary	BAL 229	Benjamin	ANN 308
John	D.C.34	Matthias D.	SOM 113	Benjamin	SOM 141
John	FRE 129	Philip	ANN 325	Ephraim	DOR 52
John	FRE 147	Philip	HAR 27	James	CEC 176
John	WAS 128A	Philip	MON 151	James	SOM 141
Michl.	D.C.87	Philip Ho.	ANN 291	John	D.C.129
Motelene	FRE 144	Philomon	FRE 117	John	D.C.143
Peter	WAS 102	Rachel	KEN 123	Joseph	CEC 176
HOPE, Danl.	BCI 378	Rezin	ANN 317	Levin	SOM 114
David	D.C.81	Richard	ANN 316	Moses	DOR 58
George	BCI 257	Richard	BCI 130	Moses	SOM 141
Jacob	FRE 174	Richard	PRI 216	Thomas	BCI 454
James	HAR 59	Richard	TAL 13	Traverse	SOM 129
Richard	D.C.209	Richard, Senr.	ANN 290	HORNEY, Benjamin	TAL 6
Thomas	HAR 62	Rigby	TAL 21	Nancy	TAL 25
HOPEWELL, Amaza	TAL 12	Risin	CAL 64	Philemon	TAL 48
Angellaca	SAI 64	Robert	TAL 14	Sarah	QUE 29
David	WAS 55A	Saml.	D.C.80	Thomas	BCI 31
Moses	BCI 295	Saml.	TAL 50	William	TAL 25
HOPKING, John	BCI 345	Samuel	ANN 368	William, Jr.	TAL 26
HOPKINS, Amanuel	DOR 51	Samuel	HAR 26	HORNICKER, Peter	FRE 143
Ami	SOM 115	Samuel	HAR 74	HORNISH, John	WAS 111
Benj. B.	WOR 180	Samuel	HAR 78	HORRACE, Milly	BCI 141
Benjamin	TAL 31	Samuel	SOM 115	HORRICK, Elias	BAL 146
Charles	ANN 328	Samuel G.	ANN 338	HORRINE, Adam	WAS 90
Charlotte	SAI 55	Samuel S.	ANN 290	George	WAS 104
Daniel	MON 151	Sarah	ANN 344	John	WAS 106
Danl.	MON 139	Sarah	BCI 129	HORRIS, --- (?)	BCI 382
David	BAL 42	Sarah	SOM 115	HORSE, Frederick	BCI 430
David	BAL 199	Sarah	TAL 36	Frederick	FRE 228
David	HAR 46	Soloman	BAL 208	HORSEKINS, Benjamin
Elias	TAL 51	Solomon	TAL 12		WAS 62
Elijah	SOM 139	Solon.	D.C.138	Rachael	WAS 62
Elizabeth	TAL 11	Stephen	SOM 109	HORSEMAN, Arnald	DOR 43
Elizabeth	HAR 77	Stephen	SOM 125	Constantine	SOM 114
Ephraim	HAR 29	Thomas	ANN 319	Elijah	DOR 41
Ephraim G.	HAR 80	Thomas	CLN 99	Henry	DOR 42
Esther-Negro	ANN 343	Thomas	DOR 30	Jason	DOR 42
Evan	HAR 29	Thomas	TAL 12	Job	DOR 42
Frances	SOM 113	Thomas-Negro	HAR 79	John	DOR 42
George	ANN 289	Thomas-Negro	HAR 80	Livina	DOR 43
Gerrard R.	BCI 122	Thos.	SOM 141	Luke	SOM 109
Grace	BCI 145	William	ANN 253	Mary	SOM 106
Greenbury	ANN 285	William	CLN 97	William	DOR 42
Isaac H.	ANN 287	William	CEC 159	HORSENEST, Catherine
Isaiah	BCI 374	William	CEC 177		WAS 65
J. T.	QUE 45	William	TAL 10	HORSEY, Ande	SOM 144
James	TAL 5	William (of Jno.)	SOM 106	Benjamin	CEC 139
James	TAL 26	William (of Levi)	SOM 106	Charles	SOM 108
James M.	D.C.52	HOPP, Elizabeth	D.C.38	Edward	SOM 144
Jared					

HORSEY (continued),			HOUCK (continued),			HOW, Bernard	SAI 95
Elizabeth	SOM	123	Jacob	FRE	110	James	FRE 81
Isaac	SOM	144	John	BAL	157	John	ANN 326
John	SOM	104	John	FRE	101	John B.	SAI 87
John	SOM	142A	John	FRE	111	Joseph	BCI 129
Levin	WOR	163	Michael	FRE	116	Mary	HAR 78
Mary	WOR	170	Nancy	ALL	30	Pompey	BAL 125
Outabridge	SOM	107	William	ALL	29	Robert	BAL 123
Outherbridge?	CEC	123	William	BAL	144	Samuel	BCI 81
Outhertridge	CEC	123	HOUCKS, Jacob	BAL	60	Scas-Negro	HAR 49
Sally	SOM	123	HOUE (See also HONE),			HOWALL, James	CEC 123
Samuel S.	SOM	142A	John & John LYNCH			HOWARD, --- (?)	BCI 464
Sarah	BCI	176		BAL	108	--- (Coll.)-[his]	
Stephen	SOM	146	HOUEL, Israel	FRE	74	Farm	BAL 129
Thompson	CLN	88	HOUGH, George S.	D.C.	199	--- (Doct.)	BCI 438
William	SOM	142A	John	ALL	23	--- (Mr.)	BAL 223
HORSLER, Joseph A. (?)			Sarah	ANN	323	Abner	SOM 128
	BCI	494	HOUK, Peter	FRE	190	Absolom	SOM 128
HORSSELTON, Christiain			Philip	FRE	190	Amelia	D.C. 106
	WAS	70	HOULTZEY, Emanuel			Ann	BCI 183
HORTEN, William	BAL	68		WAS	80	Ann	BCI 502
Wm. L.	BCI	174	HOUP, Henry	FRE	133	Anthoney	WAS 110
HORTON, James	BCI	246	Jacob	FRE	131	Archabald	BAL 105
Thomas	CEC	177	Nicholas, Sr.	FRE	131	Arnold	SOM 128
William	BCI	450	Nicholas, Jr.	FRE	132	Beal	ALL 28
HORWELL, Richd.	D.C.	148	HOUPER, Jacob	BCI	333	Beal	D.C. 218
HORZE, Wm.	BCI	371	HOUR, John H.	FRE	76	Beal	MON 151
HOSAMAR, William	DOR	59	HOUSE, Andrew	FRE	131	Beall	D.C. 181
HOSGOOD, William	ANN	369	Anna	ALL	33	Benj.	BCI 368
HOSHEL, John	BAL	96	Caleb	FRE	127	Benjamin	ANN 400
HOSHELL, Isaac	BAL	100	Charles	ALL	5A	Benjamin	BCI 270
Jesse	BAL	100	David	D.C.	179	Benjamin	KEN 107
HOSHER, Hannah	WOR	173	David	CEC	177	Brice W.	ALL 26
John	WOR	171	Elitha	FRE	124	Catharine	PRI 207
John	WOR	219	Enoch	ALL	33	Charles	ANN 353
Joshua	WOR	174	Geo.	FRE	127	Charles	FRE 70
HOSIER, Saml.	WOR	179	James	BCI	343	Chloe	BCI 258
William	KEN	88	Jesse	BCI	126	Cornelious	FRE 71
HOSKINS, Peter	D.C.	90	John	FRE	127	Cornelius	SAI 55
HOSKINSON, Geo. B.	MON	132	John	FRE	224	Cornelus	BAL 46
Nathan	MON	151	Michael	WAS	119	Daniel	WAS 141
HOSKYNS, Ann	BCI	252	Sam	BCI	338	Dennis	FRE 212
HOSLET, Wm. (?)	BCI	386	Stephen	FRE	128	Dorcus	FRE 82
HOSPELHORN, Henry	FRE	141	Valentine	ALL	33	Edward	FRE 69
HOSS, Henry	WAS	111	William	ALL	33	Edward	SOM 153
Jacob	WAS	128A	William	FRE	96	Edward A.	BAL 121
Jacob	WAS	134	William	FRE	127	Elisha	FRE 82
Mary	WAS	123	HOUSEMAN, John	D.C.	94	Elisha	MON 131
Peter	WAS	101	HOUSER, Jacob	WAS	63	Elizabeth	MON 163
Peter	WAS	123	HOUSHOLDER, Catherine			George	ANN 323
Philip	WAS	98		WAS	79	George	ANN 353
William	WAS	105	Jonothan	WAS	145	George	SOM 154
HOSSEFROSS, Jno.	BCI	167	Philip	WAS	111	George	WAS 140
HOSSELBACH, John	BCI	381	HOUSMAN, Jacob	FRE	156	Gibson	KEN 106A
HOSSELBAUGH, John	FRE	85	HOUSTON, Hannah	KEN	100	Greenby?	MON 178
HOSTETTER, Samuel	BAL	141	Isaac	WOR	180	Greenly	MON 178
HOSTMAN, John	BCI	27	Isaac	WOR	210	Gusts.	D.C. 111
HOTRIL, Thomas	ANN	276	James	CLN	86	H.	BCI 404
HOTT, J.	D.C.	152	James F.	FRE	103	Hannah	ANN 259
John	CAL	50	Levin	WOR	217	Henry	BCI 248
HOTTE, Philip	D.C.	127	Levin B.	WOR	156	Henry	BCI 274
HOTTER, Margaret (?)			Sarah	WOR	156	Henry	BCI 300
	FRE	86	Susan	KEN	91	Henry	D.C. 50
HOTTRY, John (?)	FRE	171	William	WOR	159	Henry	MON 140
HOTTSMAN, George (?)			HOUTON, Michael	FRE	160	Ignatious	SAI 75
	D.C.	46	William-free	CAL	65	Ignatious	WAS 147
HOUCK, Anthony	BAL	58	HOVEIS, John (?)	BAL	150	Jacob	BCI 536
Barnet	BAL	161	HOVER, Mary	FRE	225	Jacob	DOR 52
George	BAL	155	Peter	D.C.	13	Jacob	TAL 36
George	FRE	106	HOVERMEAL, John	WAS	66	James	BAL 207
George	FRE	118	HOVERS, John	BAL	150	James	BCI 474
George	FRE	142	HOVERSTEK, Daniel (?)			James	SOM 139
George, Junr.	FRE	147		WAS	103	James (See Lewis	
Jacob	BAL	155	HOVERSTOK, Daniel			FORD, overseer-	
Jacob	FRE	68		WAS	103	James HOWARD)	
Jacob	FRE	106	HOVICE, Adam	FRE	143	Jane	ANN 392

HUDSON (continued),		HUGHES (continued),		HULL (continued),	
Thomas (?)	D.C. 65	Jesse	SOM 116	John	TAL 10
Thos.	QUE 14	John	BCI 84	Joshua	SOM 144
Thos.	WOR 188	John	BCI 133	Peter	FRE 179
William	CEC 139	John	D.C. 74	Rachel	BCI 36
William	HAR 57	John	FRE 110	Sarah	D.C. 56
William	WOR 189	John	FRE 214	Susan	KEN 103
William	WOR 194	John	HAR 26	Thomas	BAL 127
William (of H.)	WOR 185	John	HAR 60	HULLEBERGER, Peter	
Wm.	KEN 123	Jonas	ANN 301		FRE 181
Wm. (of Wm.)	WOR 164	Joseph	FRE 140	HULLENBARGER, William	
Zepporah	WOR 192	Levi	FRE 117		FRE 177
HUFF, --- (Widaw)	BCI 374	Mary	D.C. 80	HULSE, John	BCI 81
Abraham	HAR 62	Nathanl.	HAR 25	HUMBERSON, George	
Abraham	HAR 78	Osborne	D.C. 120		ALL 15
Daniel	CEC 139	Robert	WAS 103	William	ALL 17
Edward S.	BAL 188	Samuel	HAR 27	HUMBERT, Adam	FRE 197
Elisha	ALL 34	Samuel	WAS 114	George	FRE 195
Frederick	ALL 6	Scott	HAR 19	Michael	FRE 132
Michael	HAR 78	Simon	CEC 160	William	FRE 162
Morgan	ALL 16	Solomon	BAL 118	HUMBY, Solomon	DOR 22
William N.	D.C. 55	Taylor	HAR 60	HUME, John	D.C. 93
HUFFER, Abraham	WAS 68	Theophs.	D.C. 137	Robt.	D.C. 176
Jacob	WAS 70	Thomas	BAL 131	HUMER, Grace	DOR 8
John	WAS 70	Thos.	D.C. 94	HUMERE, Comfort	DOR 8
Joseph	FRE 131	Will	D.C. 112	HUMERICKHOUSE, Fredeick	
HUFFINGTON, Eleanor		William	BCI 321		WAS 115
	SOM 111	William	HAR 44	Peter	WAS 115
John	DOR 59	William	WOR 185	HUMES, John	BCI 203
Jonathan	SOM 139	Zenas, Jr.	HAR 58	Thos.	BCI 183
Joshua	KEN 108	HUGHEY, William	CLN 107	William	BAL 175
Mary	SOM 112	HUGHEZ, John (?)	FRE 214	HUMMER, Andrew	FRE 159
Patience	SOM 111	HUGHLET, John	DOR 29	Francis	ALL 18
William	SOM 107	Joseph	DOR 29	Henry	FRE 159
HUFFMAN, Francies W.		HUGHLETT, Richard	CLN 74	John	FRE 159
	WAS 90	William	CLN 75	HUMPBERT, John	FRE 195
Henry	WAS 99	HUGHS, Alexander	TAL 9	HUMPHIES, Hugh	BCI 257
Jacob	WAS 61	Edward	TAL 12	HUMPHISS, Joshua	SOM 112
Jacob	WAS 134	Geo. L.	BCI 172	Thomas	SOM 108
John	WAS 60	Henny	DOR 10	HUMPHREYS, Ellin	BCI 522
John E.	WAS 115	James	CLN 75	Joe.	D.C. 213
Nicholas	WAS 87	James	DOR 3	John	D.C. 159
Wm.	FRE 220	James	DOR 37	John	KEN 85
HUFFMANGLE, John	BCI 85	James	WOR 155	Joshua	PRI 191A
HUFFMASTER, Christian		John	BCI 181	Kerr	BCI 49
	WAS 65	John H.	BCI 532	Mary	D.C. 170
John	WAS 65	Josiah	SOM 114	Wat.	D.C. 17
HUFFORD, Daniel	FRE 84	Ledia	BCI 36	William	BCI 73
John	FRE 84	Samuel, Ovsr.	TAL 33	HUMPHRISS, Elijah	SOM 104
Solomon	FRE 163	William	DOR 9	Zacheus	SOM 103
HUFNAGLE, John	FRE 195	William	DOR 56	HUMPHRY, John B.	PRI 224
HUGATE, Joseph	D.C. 111	HUHGS, George	FRE 68	HUMPHRYS, Mathias	BCI 314
HUGES, Janes	BCI 354	HUINGTON, Mary	QUE 38	Richard L.	PRI 226
Leusa	BCI 347	HUKFORD, ---ry	BCI 161	HUMRICH, John-?	FRE 183
HUGGINS, James	HAR 60	HUKILL, Wm.	QUE 5	HUNGERFORD, Benja.	
Thomas	CEC 159	HUL, Nancy (?)	WOR 179		CAL 45
HUGHES, --- (Widow)	FRE 171	HULETT, Richd.	BCI 197	Edward	CAL 46
Aquila	BCI 444	HULL, Abraham	FRE 196	John B.	CHA 203
Aram	HAR 60	Andrew	FRE 171	Wm. E.	CAL 41A
Belinda	BCI 248	Andrew	FRE 195	HUNNAYMAN, George	
Caleb	SOM 116	Beauchamp	SOM 105		WAS 148
Christopher, Sen.	BCI 325	Benjamin	FRE 225	HUNNINGTON, Ignatius	
Edward	CEC 176	Brittingham (Senr.)			CHA 205
Elizabeth	BAL 120		SOM 103	HUNT, Benj.	ALL 38
Everitt	HAR 19	C. John	CEC 139	Benjn.	BCI 172
Frank	CEC 159	Daniel	FRE 226	Caleb	CHA 221
George	ALL 27	David	FRE 225	Dawson	TAL 25
George	HAR 60	George	ANN 399	Eli	CHA 217
Henry	BAL 118	Jacob	FRE 222	Elijah	CHA 205
Hugh	BCI 140	Jacob	FRE 226	Enoch	BAL 80
James	BAL 131	Jessee	TAL 47	James	TAL 25
James	DOR 50	John	FRE 101	Jessee	BCI 440
James	FRE 141	John	FRE 181	Job	WAS 115
James	SOM 137	John	FRE 196	John	BCI 111
Jehu	BCI 438	John	FRE 225	John	BCI 219
Jeremiah	ANN 395	John	TAL 3	John	CLN 91

HUNT (continued),		HURDLE, Basel	MON 166	HURXTHAL, Ferdinand	
John	D.C.172	Clemment	WAS 81		BCI 412
John	WAS 133	George	D.C.40	Lewis	BCI 412
Johnsey H.	BAL 246	John	D.C.91	HUSBAND, James	BAL 117
Josias	PRI 212	Laurence	MON 168	Joseph	HAR 46
Judson	CHA 225	Robert	ANN 398	Joshua	HAR 41
Judson W.	ANN 254	Robert	MON 164	Samuel E.	ANN 347
Nino	DOR 8	Thos.	D.C.103	Sarah	FRE 112
Samuel	BAL 241	HURDMON, T---? (?)		HUSE, Daniel	BAL 94
Samuel	TAL 25		CAL 51	Maryann	BAL 90
Susan	CHA 222	HURLEY, Aaron	DOR 45	Samuel	BAL 85
Sylvester	PRI 215	Alexander	DOR 40	HUSH, Elizabeth	BAL 200
Thomas	BAL 80	Aljah	DOR 40	John	BAL 196
Thomas, Junr.	BAL 80	Andrew	DOR 9	William	BCI 239
William	BAL 79	Arnald	PRI 184	HUSLER, Joseph	D.C.20
William	BAL 115	Elijah	DOR 42	William	CEC 138
William	BAL 131	Ezekiel	DOR 43	HUSS, David	FRE 228A
William	CHA 221	George	DOR 43	HUSSELBAUGH, ---	
William	SAI 77	Gilbert	DOR 43	(See TSCHUDY &	
Willm.	D.C.93	Jervas	DOR 41	HUSSELBAUGH)	
Wilson	SOM 123	Job	DOR 43	HUSSEY, --- (Mrs.)	BCI 439
HUNTER, --- (See		Jobe	DOR 6	Asahal	BCI 427
HUNTER & FERRETTS		John	DOR 40	Eunion	BCI 94
QUARTER)	D.C.213	John	MON 162	Grace	BCI 83
Alexander J.	BCI 47	Joseph	DOR 42	Joseph	BCI 111
Alexr.	D.C.213	Keene	DOR 8	William	BCI 83
Andw.	D.C.102	Levi	DOR 43	HUSTER, Cutlip	BCI 492
Ann	D.C.185	Levi	MON 175	HUSTING, Elizabeth	BCI 62
Catharin	WAS 146	Mark	DOR 42	HUSTON, James	HAR 24
David	BCI 70	Mark	DOR 43	HUT, Nancy (?)	WOR 179
Eliza.	BCI 228	Mary	D.C.121	HUTCHEDSON, Charles	
Henrietta	D.C.158	Mary	DOR 42		WAS 134
James	ANN 392	Patrick	DOR 43	HUTCHENS, Isaac(k)	
James	BAL 100	Pinneny (?)	DOR 42		CAL 59
James	FRE 175	Rebecca	MON 163	John	CAL 67
John (?)	ANN 284	Reuben	DOR 42	Jos.	QUE 14
John	BAL 235	Rhoda	DOR 34	Michael	CAL 67
John	D.C.152	Robert	DOR 43	HUTCHERSON, Benjamin	
Lewis J.	BCI 154	Shadrick	DOR 42		BCI 113
Nancy	D.C.157	Zebulon	DOR 42	Theodore (?)	PRI 218
Nathan	CLN 76	HURLOCH, William	DOR 63	HUTCHESON, Andrew	
Nathaniel	BAL 94	HURLOCK, Elkanah			CEC 138
Peter G.	BAL 91		QUE 15	HUTCHINGS, Aquilla	
Phinahas	BAL 2	Jacob	KEN 124		CLN 111
Pollard	QUE 39	James	DOR 49	Francis	CAL 48
Rebeca	BCI 335	Saml.	KEN 121	Rebecca (Mrs.)	CAL 49
Robt.	D.C.156	Thomas	DOR 53	Samuel	BCI 15
Robt.	D.C.160	William (?)	DOR 63	Sewel	CAL 50
Samuel	BCI 147	HURLY, Cornellus	PRI 238	Thomas	CLN 100
William	BAL 50	Salem	PRI 238	Thos. G.	CAL 48
William	HAR 4	William	PRI 238	HUTCHINS, Ann	QUE 40
William	HAR 4	HURRY, John	SAI 77	Benedict	D.C.54
HUNTER & FERRETTS		HURST, Basil	BAL 84	Bennett	SAI 69
QUARTER	D.C.213	Benidick	BAL 100	Charity	D.C.25
HUNTERMAN, Dedrick		Bennet	ANN 394	Esther	QUE 35
	BCI 302	E.	BCI 250	Henry	QUE 35
HUNTINGTON, John	CHA 204	Elijah	ANN 403	Jacob	BAL 85
John, Senr.	CHA 205	G. D.	BCI 253	James	BCI 142
Luke	CHA 204	James	DOR 60	James	QUE 30
HUNTSBERRY, Fredk.	FRE 132	Lydia	BCI 116	Jane	BCI 59
HUNTT, Barbara	CAL 61	Samuel	DOR 3	Jarrett	BAL 90
Daniel	D.C.37	Samuel	DOR 9	Jarrett	BAL 92
Jeremiah	D.C.8	Samuel	DOR 61	John	BCI 51
John, Senr.	CAL 65	Shadrach	BCI 192	John	CLN 105
John W.	CAL 64	Thos.	D.C.118	John	D.C.55
Mary	CAL 61	William	BCI 134	Joshua	BAL 90
Phillip	CAL 61	HURSTON, John	CEC 138	Moses	D.C.174
Thomas	CAL 65	HURT, Edwd.	KEN 116	Richard	BAL 77
William	CAL 66A	Henry	KEN 125	Richard	BAL 79
HUNTZBURRY, Henry	WAS 139	Jacob	KEN 125	Richard	HAR 61
HURBERT, Sleward	WAS 120	John	KEN 123	Samuel	CLN 88
HURBIT, Charles	BCI 500	John D.	BCI 127	Samuel	QUE 36
HURD, Enoch	D.C.26	Saml.	KEN 122	Thomas	BAL 123
William	CLN 75	Thos.	KEN 119	Thomas	HAR 61
William	CLN 96	HURTT, John	KEN 89	William	BAL 237
		Richard	KEN 86	Wm.	BAL 77

HUTCHINS (continued),		**HYATT (continued),**		**IBO, Leah**	DOR 49		
Wm.	BAL 79	Isaac	CLN 104A	ICHELBERGER, Jacob			
HUTCHINSON, Ann	D.C.135	John	BCI 179		BAL 24		
Benjn.	D.C.121	Philip	MON 171	ICKES, --- (Widow)	FRE 168		
E.	DOR 55	Sarah	PRI 182	--- (Widow)	FRE 171		
Edwd.	D.C.132	Seth	D.C.94	ICRUASS, Robert	FRE 218		
Fanny	D.C.50	Seth	PRI 184	IGLEHART, Anne	ANN 370		
Geo.	D.C.135	HYDE, Daniel T.	ANN 395	Edward	ANN 382		
James	DOR 52	Francis	BCI 270	James	ANN 270		
James	MON 164	George	CHA 226	Jesse	ANN 374		
John	WOR 155	James	D.C.51	John	ANN 271		
Nathan	PRI 203	Saml. G.	BCI 271	John	ANN 374		
Samuel	D.C.15	Samuel G.	BCI 254	Micheal	ANN 379		
Waller	D.C.134	Sarah	ANN 395	Richard	ANN 335		
Walter?	D.C.134	Thomas	D.C.40	William	ANN 352		
William	PRI 202	HYDER, Christopher		IGLEHEART, James	MON 152		
Willm.	D.C.124		FRE 183	Leonard	ANN 285		
HUTCHIRSON, Theodore		Elizabeth	FRE 223	IGO, Joshua	BAL 6		
	PRI 218	Jacob	FRE 223	IIAMES, Gassaway	ANN 255		
HUTCHISON, --- (?)	BCI 406	John	FRE 201	IIAMS, John (?)	ANN 332		
John B.	SAI 92	Mary	FRE 223	IJAMS, John, Jr.	FRE 69		
Joseph	WOR 169	HYER, Jane	D.C.102	John, Jr.	FRE 74		
HUTCHSION, Catherine		HYETT, Jose	FRE 212	Plummer	FRE 72		
	WAS 127A	HYLAND, Eliga	WAS 78	ILER (See also HER),			
HUTCKEDSON, Charles (?)		Elisabeth	KEN 102	John, Senr.	FRE 223		
	WAS 134	Henry	SOM 116	ILEY, John	HAR 41		
HUTJESON, Thomas	WAS 58A	Jacob	CEC 160	ILGRANTFRITZ, John			
HUTLZE, Henry F.	BCI 301	James	KEN 86		BAL 215		
HUTSON, Adam	BCI 153	Jane	CEC 124	ILLER, Stephen	CEC 139		
Benj.	WOR 177	John	CEC 160	ILOT, George	MON 151		
Edward	BAL 93	John	WAS 140	IMBERT, James E.	CLN 80		
Elizabeth	BCI 10	Johnson	CEC 139	IMES, John	BCI 136		
Hooper	CLN 76	Joshua	CEC 139	IMMORH, Fredk.	D.C.146		
James	DOR 30	Lambert	SOM 125	IMMORT, Fredk. (?)	D.C.146		
Jane	CLN 99	Moses (f.n.)	SOM 119	IMPEY, Comfort	ANN 307		
John	CLN 76	Nicholas	CEC 139	Davy	ANN 307		
John, Jr.	CLN 76	Nicholas	CEC 160	Jacob	BCI 77		
Michael	BCI 461	Sally	SOM 126	Jane	FRE 94		
Richard	CLN 89	Stephen	CEC 160	Sarah	ANN 306		
Samuel	HAR 7	HYMAN, Charles	BCI 73	IMPY, Amos	FRE 78		
Silvah	DOR 41	HYME, Andrew	FRE 93	INCH, Philip	D.C.126		
William	BCI 24	HYMES, Abigail	FRE 94	ING, Edwd.	BCI 225		
William	BCI 120	John	FRE 126	INGERSAL, John	WOR 215		
William	DOR 49	Rachael	FRE 105	INGERSOLL, Richard	SOM 139		
William	DOR 62	HYNSON, Benjamin	KEN 87	INGHAM, John	BAL 12		
HUTT, Henry	WOR 180	Betty	KEN 103	John	BCI 8		
Rachell	WOR 213	Henry	KEN 106	INGHRAM, Chary	WAS 64		
Soln.	WOR 181	Henry	KEN 120	INGLE, Andrew	ALL 37		
HUTTON, Calep	CEC 177	Isaac	KEN 115	George	WAS 141		
Elijah	BCI 152	John C.	KEN 89	Henry	D.C.102		
Enos	FRE 69	Joseph	KEN 89	Kiah	BCI 76		
George	FRE 147	Levin	CLN 81	Mary	D.C.163		
Jacob	D.C.75	Moses	KEN 106	Will.	D.C.103		
Jas.	BCI 231	Nathaniel	BCI 94	INGLEMAN, Catherine			
John	FRE 148	Nathaniel	KEN 101		WAS 116		
Jonathan	ANN 397	Nathaniel	QUE 28	INGLER, John	FRE 176		
Joseph	D.C.87	Nicey	KEN 124	Joseph	FRE 177		
Joseph	PRI 206	Thomas	KEN 89	INGLIS, James	BCI 259		
Rhody	DOR 4	Thomas B.	KEN 89	Margaret	BCI 74		
Richard G.	ANN 274	Wm.	KEN 122	INGLISH (See also EN-			
William	ANN 276	HYSER, Nichl.	BCI 519	GLISH),			
HUTZEL, Ann	BCI 307	HYSON, Charles	BCI 157	Thomas	ANN 356		
HUTZELL, Jacob	WAS 70	Solomon	BCI 277	INGMAN, Ambrose	FRE 69		
John	WAS 89	HYTH, James	BCI 339	Amelia	FRE 73		
HUTZENTUNER, Adam	WAS 62	HYTHE, Charles	DOR 7	Henry	ALL 3		
HUZZA, John	BCI 124			Luke	FRE 76A		
Joseph	TAL 11			INGRAM, Hannah	BCI 81		
Robert	TAL 14			John	HAR 75		
HYAM, Abm.	BCI 209			Joseph	WAS 88		
HYATE, Elijah	PRI 180A			Rachel	KEN 106		
HYATT, Asa	MON 173	--- I ---		INLOES (See also EN-			
Christopher	WAS 125			LAWES, INLOWES),			
Elijah (?)	PRI 180A	I (J.?), August	WAS 119	Abraham	BCI 450		
Elisha R.	MON 173	IAMS, John	D.C.37	David	BCI 383		
Ely	FRE 73	IAQUET (See also JAQUET),		Elizabeth	BCI 54		
Ezra	FRE 76	John (?)	D.C.135	James	HAR 38		

INLOES (continued),		IRVIN, Alexander	BCI 441	IVY, John	KEN 86
Jane	BCI 483	Bridget	WAS 115		
Samuel	BAL 190	Elizabeth	BCI 437		
William	BCI 40	Gideon H.	WAS 117		
INLOWES (See also		James	MON 137		
ENLAWES, INLOES),		John	WAS 123		
Abraham	HAR 38	John	WAS 125		
INMAN, John	BCI 112	Jonathan	WAS 125	--- J ---	
INNMORE, Peter	BCI 275	Saml.	BCI 474		
Peter	BCI 276	Thos.	D.C. 186	J, August (?)	WAS 119
INSLEY, Denwood	SOM 114	Walte	WOR 201	J--NES, Vila	FRE 87
Elijah	DOR 62	IRVINE, John	CLN 75	JAAL, James	QUE 17
Esau	DOR 32	John	HAR 59	JABINE, John	CHA 226
James	DOR 36	IRVING, Handy H.	SOM 104	JAC---, --- (?)	FRE 87
John	DOR 34	John	BCI 157	JACH, John	WAS 136
John	SOM 114	John	SOM 123	JACK, Ann	BCI 256
Keene	DOR 37	William	SOM 109	James	CEC 177
Levi	DOR 31	IRWIN, Abner	CEC 161	James	D.C. 167
Lucresia	DOR 36	James	BAL 36	Jeramia	WAS 144
Merulas	DOR 37	Joseph	D.C. 167	John (?)	WAS 136
Theafphilus	DOR 34	IRWINE, John	CEC 161	John	BCI 519
Thomas	DOR 62	John	CEC 178	Saml. C. S.	CHA 214
Valentine	DOR 37	ISAAC, Edward	CAL 51	JACKSAN, Emanuel	BCI 426
William	SOM 114	Elizabeth	BCI 32	Murray	BCI 432
William	SOM 114	Joseph	PRI 184	Urias	BCI 426
INSLEYE, Bazel	DOR 36	Pharo	BAL 117	William	BCI 426
INSLY, Habby	DOR 42	Richard	PRI 182	JACKSON, --- (See	
INSOR, Abham., Snr.	BAL 89	Richard, Senr.	PRI 182	JACKSON & PEACOCK)	
Abraham	BAL 88	Shadarac	WOR 164	--- (Captn.)	D.C. 159
John	BAL 88	Susanna (Mrs.)	CAL 51	--- (Major?)	BAL 124
John	BAL 89	ISAACKS, Joseph	BCI 511	--- (Mrs.)	BCI 350
John	BAL 95	ISAACS, Bill (negro)		Aaron	CLN 75
John, of Abram	BAL 89		TAL 26	Abel	BAL 91
John, Junr.	BAL 88	Cupid	ANN 345	Abner	D.C. 19
William	BAL 218	Gabl.	BCI 231	Alexander	BCI 497
IONCHEREZ (See also		John	ANN 353	Ann	ANN 389
JONCHEREZ),		Saml.	D.C. 163	Ann H.	PRI 186
Ann (?)	D.C. 28	ISABELL, Wm.	D.C. 145	Benj.	BCI 335
IRELAND, --- (?)	BCI 404	ISARAL, Gilbert (?)	BAL 5	Benjamin	BAL 197
Edward	BAL 47	ISAREIL, Gilbert	BAL 5	Betsey	BAL 64
Georg	CAL 44	ISBIE (See also JSTICE),		Bridget	D.C. 55
James	CAL 46	Sarah	FRE 220	Charles	CEC 178
Jessee	KEN 109	ISBURN, Sarah	BCI 193	Chester	QUE 19
John	CAL 42	ISEHART, Jacob	ALL 23	Christeener	BCI 273
John	CAL 65	ISELING, Frederick	BCI 492	Christopher	ANN 285
John	KEN 121	ISENTRAGER, Anna	FRE 106	Clement	SAI 64
John C.	CAL 42	Peter	FRE 115	Daniel	BAL 119
Joseph	KEN 87	ISETT, Adam	BCI 403	Daniel-f.n.	SOM 120
Joseph (Doctr.)	CAL 43	John	BCI 377	David	QUE 13
Mary	CAL 65	ISGRIG, William	BAL 123	Dina	ANN 389
Nathan	BCI 318	ISHMEL, Samuel	WOR 157	Edward	CEC 160
Nathan	QUE 32	ISLER, John	BCI 129	Edward	D.C. 79
Rhoda	CLN 100	ISONBIE, Peter	KEN 106	Edward	HAR 9
Richard	CAL 44	ISONS, Francis (?)	QUE 38	Elihu	SOM 113
Richard	CAL 63	ISRAEL, Beal	BCI 484	Elihu, Senr.	SOM 117
Richard	QUE 38	Fielder	BCI 513	Elisha	BAL 18
Sarah	CAL 64	Jacob	BCI 474	Elizabeth	D.C. 200
Stephen G.	CAL 62	ISREAL, Dorsey	BAL 62	Elizabeth	QUE 17
Susannah	BCI 246	Gilbert	BAL 53	Emanuel	DOR 6
Thomas, col'd.	BAL 215	ISSAR, Joh. J.	BCI 340	Ezekiel	TAL 27
Thos. C.	CAL 47	ISSEMINGER, George		Fanney	TAL 5
William	BCI 142		WAS 125	George	BCI 141
Wm. P.	KEN 121	Michael	WAS 126	George	CEC 178
IREN, Peter	FRE 218	ISSIMBARGER, Nicholas		George W.	SOM 153
IRGRUM, James	FRE 216		WAS 123	Greenbury	TAL 26
IRIMES (See also JRIMES),		IVEINGTON, Jerimiah		Hannah	BCI 123
James	WAS 82		PRI 223	Hannah	BCI 133
IRIVING, Jacob	BCI 126	William	PRI 223	Hannah	D.C. 157
IRON, Ann	KEN 107	IVERY, Isaac	CEC 139	Harriet	PRI 197
IRONS, Francis	QUE 38	William	CEC 139	Harriett	D.C. 149
John	ALL 4	IVES, James	BCI 230	Henry	BCI 461
Michael	FRE 161	IVIL, Adam	CEC 139	Henry	CHA 213
Rebecca	FRE 177	IVINGS, Joseph	BAL 82	Henry	D.C. 177
Thomas, Sen.	ALL 21	IVORY, ---	BCI 457	Henry	SOM 112
Thomas, Jr.	ALL 21	Francis	FRE 124	Henry	TAL 38
IRONSIDE, Geo.	D.C. 98	Francis	FRE 136	Hester	D.C. 150

JACKSON (continued),		JACKSON (continued),		JACOBS (continued),	
Hugh	CEC 160	Sophia	BCI 77	Saml.	BCI 232
Hugh of J.	CEC 160	Sophia	D.C.104	Thos.	D.C.181
Isaac	DOR 39	Stephen	BCI 37	William	ANN 284
J. E.	BCI 436	Stephen	DOR 57	Wm.	QUE 3
Jackson	WAS 94	Stephen	HAR 31	JACQUES, Arther	WAS 144
Jacob	FRE 130	Stephen	WOR 186	Lancelot	WAS 144
Jacob	FRE 225	Tack	QUE 48	Lancelot	WAS 145
James	ANN 398	Thaddeous (Inn-		JACQUET, William	BCI 58
James	BCI 370	Keeper outside		JACSON, Thos.	BCI 333
James	CEC 139	fort)	BCI 326	JADUN, Daniel	FRE 151
James	CEC 160	Thomas	BAL 128	JADWIN, Susan	ALL 38
James	CEC 177	Thomas	BAL 219	Thomas	ALL 38
James	PRI 237	Thomas	BCI 297	JAGART, Jesse	BCI 202
James	QUE 38	Thomas	CHA 201	JAIL-ALEXANDRIA	D.C.147
James, Sn.	CEC 161	Thomas	CHA 212	JAIL, BALTR. COUNTY	
Jamima	BAL 158	Thomas	D.C.49		BCI 203
Jaseph	D.C.26	Thomas	QUE 31	JAKES, Fredreck	BCI 267
Jo.	QUE 5	Thomas H.	HAR 24	JAMART, Michal.	BCI 221
John?	BCI 136	Thos.	BCI 345	JAMASON, --- (Doctr.)	
John	BAL 115	Tubman	SOM 104		BCI 387
John	BAL 217	W. B.	PRI 195	--- (Mr.)	BCI 370
John	BCI 413	William	ANN 311	JAMBERS, John	BCI 368
John	CEC 160	William	BAL 206	JAMES, --- (Widaw)	BCI 400
John	CEC 160	William	BCI 58	Abraham	WAS 83
John	FRE 225	William	BCI 459	Adam	CLN 107
John	HAR 60	William	CLN 74	Amos	BCI 299
John	KEN 117	William	CEC 124	Amus	BCI 373
John	SOM 117	William	DOR 60	Ann	ALL 11
John	WAS 63	William	TAL 24	Archibald	DOR 50
John	WAS 139	William G.	PRI 219	Daniel	BCI 56
John	WOR 174	Wm.	BCI 252	Daniel	FRE 75
John, Ju.	CEC 160	Wm.	BCI 497	Edward	WAS 66
John K.	SAI 66	Wm.	QUE 5	Eli	FRE 125
John R.	D.C.157	JACKSON & PEACOCK		Elizabeth	BCI 54
Johnathan	SOM 110		QUE 14	Elizh.	D.C.75
Joseph?	D.C.26	JACOB, Ge.	BCI 397	Frances W.	SOM 104
Joseph	BAL 115	James	ANN 288	Frank	BCI 510
Joseph	BCI 459	John J. (I.?)	ALL 31	Frederick	HAR 64
Josias	CHA 218	Mary	D.C.199	Hannah	BCI 463
Julius A.	SAI 65	Riddle	PRI 182	Henry	BCI 138
Leah	WOR 211	William	ANN 288	Isaac	ANN 377
Leven	QUE 39	JACOBS, Adam	FRE 76A	Jack (?)	CEC 177
Major	BAL 124	Anna	ANN 396	Jacob	SOM 104
Margt.	D.C.79	Arcady	DOR 59	Jacob	WOR 204
Maria	D.C.1u0	Arnold	QUE 6	James	ALL 5A
Mary	DOR 13	Daniel	WAS 95	Jane	BCI 188
Mary	TAL 26	Daniel P.	ANN 270	Jese	BCI 282
Milly	ANN 303	Delinda	ANN 308	John	BAL 190
Milly	D.C.167	Elias	BCI 148	John	BCI 240
Minty	DOR 42	Eliza	BCI 122	John	FRE 170
Moses	WAS 63	Elizabeth	ALL 13	John	FRE 202
Nace	ANN 299	Gabriel	ALL 12	John	TAL 35
Nancy	ALL 31	George	FRE 117	John	WAS 63
Nathan	QUE 7	George	PRI 181	Joseph	HAR 27
Nathan	QUE 12	George	WAS 111	Joseph	TAL 38
Nicholas	BAL 40	Hannah	ANN 299	Joseph	TAL 51
Patience	PRI 197	Henry	D.C.20	Joseph, col'd.	BAL 216
Perre	CLN 80	Ignatius	FRE 118	Ledgwick?	HAR 75
Perrigrine	DOR 7	Jacob	ALL 10A	Levi	BCI 27
Peter	BCI 319	Jane	BCI 50	Lodgwick	HAR 75
Philip	D.C.7	Joel	FRE 127	Luiza	SOM 104
Prudence	CLN 74	John	FRE 82	Mary	BCI 297
Rachel	BCI 475	John	FRE 97	Mary	BCI 354
Ralph	QUE 13	John	FRE 112	Mary	WAS 83
Richd.	QUE 5	Mathias	WAS 136	Meriah	TAL 8
Robert	CEC 160	Matthias	ALL 10A	Nancy	D.C.194
Robert	CEC 178	Michael	FRE 160	Peach	BCI 357
Rose (free negro)	SOM 118	Muda	CLN 114	Peggy	DOR 61
Saml.	D.C.40	Philip	BCI 110	Peter	BCI 88
Samuel	ALL 12	Philip	FRE 76A	Peter	FRE 228A
Samuel	PRI 184	Presley	D.C.163	Rebecca-Negro	HAR 80
Samuel	TAL 12	Rachael	BAL 51	Rezson	WAS 84
Sarah	CLN 87	Richard	ALL 31	Samuel	BAL 121
Sarah Ann	ALL 27	Richard	WAS 68	Samuel	BCI 117
Simon	PRI 193	Robert	ANN 273	Samuel	BCI 463

JAMES (continued),		JANVIER, Joseph	BCI 152		JEFFERICE, Isaac-negro			
Samuel	D.C.68	P.	BCI 113				CEC 124	
Samuel	SOM 110	JAQUES, Henry	CLN 95		JEFFERIES, John	KEN 93		
Sarah	DOR 51	JAQUET (See also			Joseph	ALL 21		
Sarrah	BAL 150	IAQUET),			JEFFERRY, Rachel	BAL 199		
Sedgwick	HAR 78	John	D.C.135		JEFFERS, Jacob	QUE 14		
Thomas J. (I.?)	KEN 88	JAQUIN, Paul	BCI 215		John	D.C.135		
Watkins	WAS 82	JARBEO, James	SAI 65		William	ANN 317		
William	BAL 6	John	MON 151		William	QUE 29		
William	BCI 51	Robert F.	SAI 69		JEFFERSAN, Henry	DOR 18		
William	CEC 124	JARBO, Bennet	D.C.77		JEFFERSON, Ahollybamma			
William	D.C.17	Lutecia	ANN 399			PRI 225		
William	QUE 6	Matthew	D.C.114		Ammy	BCI 275		
William, Senr.	ALL 33	JARBOE, Alexander	FRE 81		Basil	CAL 49		
William, Jr. (?)	ALL 33	Benedict	CAL 46		Ben	FRE 177		
JAMESON, Amelia	CHA 222	Catharine	FRE 81		Benjn.	D.C.146		
Ann	CHA 207B	Francis	FRE 126		James, Ovsr.	TAL 38		
Ann	CHA 222	Henry	FRE 124		Jessie	DOR 59		
John	CHA 202	John B.	SAI 86A		John	TAL 23		
Leonard	CHA 221	Joseph	SAI 76		John	TAL 39		
Luke	CHA 212	William	D.C.33		Sarah	D.C.165		
Rapheal	CHA 222	Willam, of Jos.	FRE 85		Thomas	TAL 21		
Richd.	D.C.138	William B.	FRE 81		Thomas	TAL 22		
Samuel	CHA 220A	JARDELLI, Frans.	D.C.104		William	BCI 275		
Sarah	CHA 226	JARMAN, Ananias	WOR 185		William	TAL 22		
JAMIESON, Andn.	D.C.173	Benjamin	WOR 197		Wm.	BCI 231		
Andw.?	D.C.173	Henry	WOR 190		JEFFERY, Cassandra	HAR 48		
Robert	BCI 243	Henry (of Ans.)	WOR 185		Mingo	BCI 147		
William	D.C.31	James	WOR 186		Samuel	ANN 336		
JAMISON, --- (Widow)		Lydiea	WOR 186		Thomas	HAR 19		
	FRE 168	Robert	CLN 80		Thomas Fitz (?)	SAI 56		
Baker	FRE 124	JARMON, Sally	WOR 199A		Vincent	HAR 48		
F.	MON 132	JARONE, Thos. (?)	QUE 5		JEFFREY, Henry	BCI 12		
George	CEC 140	JARRELL, Garrettson			Thomas	BCI 294		
Henry	FRE 123		CLN 75		JEFFREYS, Joseph	BCI 112		
Jane	CEC 140	Richard	CLN 76		Mathias	D.C.15		
Jno.	BCI 170	JARRETT, Abraham	HAR 18		William	BCI 161		
John	BCI 73	Abraham	SOM 115		JEFFRIES, Benjamin	PRI 203		
John	FRE 168	Abraham, Jr.	HAR 62		Caleb	PRI 229		
P.	D.C.168	Jesse	HAR 62		JEMASON, Leonard	FRE 85		
Saml.	FRE 124	John	BCI 300		JEMINY, George	D.C.170		
Samuel	CEC 140	Samuel	BCI 446		JEMISON, Ausburn	FRE 87		
JAMMESON, Joseph	BCI 212	Susanna	BAL 240		Ignatious	FRE 83		
Saml.	BCI 218	JARRICE, Martha	WOR 191		JEMISSON, William	BAL 51		
JAMPER, Thomas	BAL 22	JARVER, Joseph	BCI 26		JENIFER, Chloe	CHA 194		
JAMS, John (?)	D.C.37	JARVIS, Amos	BAL 188		Daniel	CHA 191		
William, Jr.	ALL 33	James	CEC 178		Polly	MON 152		
JANDINE, Rose	BCI 294	Jane	D.C.27		Thomas	CHA 191		
JANE, Mary	BCI 528	John	HAR 43		JENKENS, David	CEC 178		
JANES (See also JONES),		Joseph	BCI 413		Jobe	FRE 122		
Daniel (?)	DOR 34	L.	BCI 391		JENKINS (See also			
Jacob, Senor	DOR 27	Mary	ANN 403		GINKINS, JINKENS),			
Jane (?)	BCI 219	Nancy	BCI 444		Archibald	PRI 203		
John	DOR 34	Nancy	BCI 459		Asa	CHA 202		
Joseph	DOR 33	Orman	BCI 303		Benedict	BCI 87		
Lamuel	DOR 34	Phenehas	BCI 519		Charles	CHA 207		
Martha (?)	DOR 19	Sarah	BCI 74		Charles	PRI 227		
William	DOR 19	Thomas	D.C.127		Clarissa	D.C.52		
Zebulan	DOR 34	Wm.	BCI 381		David	BCI 530		
JANNEY, Casmillia	D.C.203	JAUFFREL, John B.	BCI 149		David	BCI 536		
Eli	CEC 160	JAURNEY, John	D.C.56		David	SOM 136		
George	BCI 123	JAY, Anthony	BAL 108		Ebenezer	CEC 160		
George	MON 151	Benadick	FRE 84		Edward	BCI 241		
Isabella	BCI 127	Benjamin	CEC 177		Elleanor	PRI 197		
Israel	D.C.199	Caeser-Negro	HAR 79		Felix	BCI 248		
Jacob	ANN 338	Joseph	BCI 242		Francis	CHA 195		
James	CEC 178	Martha	HAR 24		Francis	D.C.51		
Jesse	CEC 160	Saml.	BCI 482		Francis	D.C.116		
John	CEC 140	Thomas	HAR 71		Francis	PRI 227		
John	D.C.199	William	ALL 32		Francis J. (I.?)	BAL 235		
Jonathan	D.C.200	William	MON 129		George	CLN 97		
Joseph	D.C.163	JEAN, George	BAL 38		George	CHA 218		
Sarah	BCI 247	JEANES, Joseph	PRI 187		George	KEN 93		
Thomas	CEC 177	JEANS, John	PRI 182		George	TAL 34		
Thos.	D.C.161	Wm.	MON 160		George, Overs.	PRI 232		
William	CEC 177	JEEDEN, John (?)	BCI 530		Grace	KEN 90		

JOHNSON (continued),		JOHNSON (continued),		JOHNSON (continued),	
Christr.	D.C.96	Isaac	BCI 187	Josiah	HAR 71
Clara	BCI 52	Isaac	D.C.42	Josiah	SOM 145
Claricy	TAL 36	Isaac	D.C.103	Lacom	WOR 154
Clemt.	D.C.91	Isaac	SOM 151	Lawson	CHA 195
Daphney	D.C.202	Isaac	TAL 34	Leah, wd.	WOR 203
David	BAL 240	Isaac	WOR 190	Leonard	PRI 195
David	BCI 63	Isaac, Senr.	WOR 176	Leven	CHA 228
David	BCI 85	Isaac, Junr.	WOR 176	Levi	CEC 140
David	BCI 120	Isaac J. (I.?)	WOR 162	Lloyd	ANN 299
David	CEC 140	James	BCI 2	Lloyd	ANN 302
Davy	SOM 148	James	BCI 219	London-Negro	HAR 49
Dick	D.C.63	James	BCI 492	Loyd	CHA 228
Dider	CLN 116	James	CAL 48	Lucy	ANN 305
Duke	FRE 195	James	CLN 86	Lydia	BCI 63
Edward (?)	DOR 26	James	CEC 140	M. John	CEC 139
Edward	BCI 253	James	CEC 160	Martha	SOM 144
Edward, Esqr.	BAL 248	James	CEC 178	Martha	WOR 187
Eleanor	SOM 133	James	CHA 217	Mary	ANN 298
Elijah	ANN 310	James	FRE 156	Mary	ANN 350
Elijah	BAL 194	James	PRI 211	Mary	ANN 394
Elijah	BCI 189	James	SAI 91	Mary	ANN 402
Elijah	SOM 142A	James	SOM 105	Mary	BCI 71
Elijah, Sen.	SOM 149	James	SOM 146	Mary	BCI 475
Elijah, Jun.	SOM 144	James (Junr.)	WOR 179	Mary	BCI 514
Elijah C.	SOM 104	James W.	BAL 221	Mary	CLN 87
Elisha J. (I.?)	BAL 14	Jane (?)	D.C.59	Mary	CEC 161
Eliza	BCI 501	Jane	ANN 284	Mary	CHA 224
Eliza (See William		Jane	BCI 85	Mary	D.C.129
LOCK (of Eliza		Jane	D.C.114	Mary	D.C.133
JOHNSON))		Jas.	D.C.104	Mary	D.C.205
Elizabeth	ANN 316	Jas., Senr.	WOR 177	Mary	SAI 88
Elizabeth	BAL 38	Jemima	SOM 144	Mathew (Revd.)	CAL 60
Elizabeth	BCI 90	Jeremiah	CEC 161	McMurray	SOM 106
Elizabeth	HAR 40	Jesse	SOM 145	Michael	HAR 5
Elizabeth	TAL 4	John	ALL 23	Milly	D.C.21
Ellen	BCI 294	John	ANN 370	Mithias	DOR 26
Erasmus	FRE 118	John	BAL 41	Nancy	CLN 91
Esther	SOM 137	John	BAL 182	Nancy	DOR 31
Eve	CLN 86	John	BAL 239	Nathan	BCI 62
Ezekiel	DOR 22	John	BCI 9	Nathan (Patterson's	
Fanny	PRI 224	John	BCI 499	Farm)	BAL 122
Fayett	BAL 27	John	CAL 43	Nelley	CEC 178
Flora	BAL 226	John	CEC 139	Nelly	BCI 483
Flora	BAL 239	John	CHA 223	Nicholas	ANN 305
Frances	HAR 24	John	D.C.187	Nicholas	ANN 312
Francis	BCI 301	John	DOR 35	Nicholas	BCI 499
Francis	CEC 140	John	HAR 4	Nicholas	QUE 20
Frank	QUE 38	John	HAR 23	P.	BCI 230
Fred.	BCI 498	John	PRI [200]	Patsey	FRE 107
Gaberal	WOR 176	John	SAI 88	Peggy	WOR 180
Georg	BCI 333	John	SOM 113	Peter	BCI 226
George	ALL 20A	John	SOM 114	Peter	BCI 324
George	BCI 500	John	WAS 136	Peter	BCI 334
George	D.C.68	John, Sen.	ALL 22	Peter	BCI 347
George	D.C.152	John, Senr.	WOR 173	Peter	CLN 89
George	D.C.166	John, J.	ALL 22	Peter	CEC 177
George, Senr.	WOR 176	John (of Hezekah)		Peter	D.C.9
George (of John)	WOR 173		WOR 155	Peter	FRE 68
George W.	BAL 14	John (of Jas.)	WOR 164	Peter	FRE 199
Gerard	BCI 255	Jonatn.	BCI 177	Peter C.	WOR 164
Gillis P.	WOR 211	Jos.	BCI 349	Phebe	BCI 222
Grace	ANN 388	Joseph	ALL 13	Philip	ANN 309
Greenbury	CLN 107	Joseph	BAL 225	Philip	BAL 110
Hambilton	DOR 32	Joseph	BAL 238	Philip	BCI 484
Hambleton	SOM 142A	Joseph	BCI 299	Philip A.	CHA 206
Hannah	CEC 140	Joseph	BCI 504	Priscilla	ANN 296
Henry	BCI 49	Joseph	CEC 139	Purnell	WOR 209
Henry	BCI 61	Joseph	CHA 222	Rachael	ANN 381
Henry	D.C.38	Joseph	CHA 224	Rachel	D.C.43
Henry	PRI 213	Joseph	D.C.92	Rachel	QUE 47
Henry	WOR 216	Joseph	D.C.116	Randolph	SAI 94
Henry (f.n.)	SOM 119	Joseph	FRE 199	Rebecca (See Re-	
Henry A.	ANN 303	Joseph A.	FRE 80	becca JOHNSON	
Hickman	BAL 14	Joseph W.	FRE 84	& Mary WILLIAMS,	
Humphrey	CEC 178	Joshua	FRE 117	C.P.)	BCI 274

JOHNSON (continued),		
Rebecca	CLN 73	
Rebecca	CLN 81	
Rebecca	FRE 93	
Rebecka	DOR 22	
Rebuka?	DOR 22	
Reuben	D.C.154	
Reverdy	BCI 273	
Richard	BAL 234	
Richard	FRE 84	
Richard	FRE 85	
Richd.	BCI 502	
Richmd.	D.C.117	
Rob	BCI 510	
Rob-f.c.p.	HAR 11	
Robert	ANN 303	
Robert	ANN 310	
Robert	CEC 139	
Robert	WOR 161	
Roderick	ANN 262	
Roger	FRE 81	
Sally	SOM 151	
Sally	WOR 175	
Sam.	BCI 346	
Sam	HAR 30	
Sam	HAR 31	
Saml.	BCI 489	
Saml.	BCI 490	
Saml.	BCI 521	
Saml.	FRE 215	
Saml., Senr.	WOR 174	
Samuel	ANN 378	
Samuel	BCI 86	
Samuel	CEC 124	
Samuel	CEC 177	
Samuel	DOR 40	
Samuel	KEN 93	
Samuel (Doctor)	FRE 160	
Samuel A.	CAL 48	
Sarah	BCI 71	
Sarah	D.C.93	
Sarah	DOR 31	
Sary F.	SAI 93	
Seladdy	QUE 12	
Selby	WOR 155	
Shepard	WOR 209	
Simon	CLN 81	
Solomon	ANN 310	
Sophia	D.C.40	
Stephen	FRE 203	
Stephen	WOR 178	
Stephen	WOR 213	
Steven	BCI 348	
Susan	D.C.195	
Susan	D.C.197	
Thomas	BAL 112	
Thomas	BAL 174	
Thomas	BAL 190	
Thomas	BCI 103	
Thomas	D.C.3	
Thomas	D.C.5	
Thomas	D.C.15	
Thomas	FRE 72	
Thomas	FRE 83A	
Thomas	WAS 128A	
Thomas	WOR 218	
Thomas of Bart	HAR 37	
Thomas R.	SAI 66	
Thomas W.	FRE 230	
Thomas W.	FRE 234	
Thos.	BCI 475	
Thos.	D.C.98	
Thos. of Mos.	HAR 41	
Thos. (of Saml.)	WOR 173	
Tilghman (Assistant Deputy Marshal of Maryland for Caroline County)	CLN 82	
JOHNSON (continued),		
Timothy	ANN 353	
Trusty?	KEN 106A	
Tuisty	KEN 106A	
Vachel	ANN 391	
W.	BCI 344	
Walter	PRI 207	
Washington	FRE 83	
William	ALL 4	
William	ANN 256	
William	ANN 330	
William	BAL 124	
William	BAL 206	
William	BCI 63	
William	CEC 139	
William	CHA 217	
William	D.C.96	
William	DOR 18	
William	DOR 25	
William	FRE 85	
William	FRE 156	
William	FRE 213	
William	HAR 6	
William	HAR 38	
William	HAR 79	
William	QUE 27	
William (of Letec?)	SOM 149	
William (of Leten?)	SOM 149	
William (of Leter?)	SOM 149	
William P.	SOM 108	
William T.	FRE 81	
Wm.	BCI 349	
Wm.	QUE 4	
Wm.	WOR 154	
Zachariah	ANN 306	
Zachariah	ANN 310	
Zachariah	ANN 394	
JOHNSTAN, Robert	BCI 426	
JOHNSTEN, Susan	BCI 445	
JOHNSTON, Anna	BCI 436	
Benjn.	DOR 8	
Betsey	BCI 158	
Charles	BCI 447	
Charles	CEC 161	
Clark	BCI 133	
Columbas	BCI 462	
Curril	BCI 143	
Francis	BCI 140	
Hannah	KEN 120	
Harmon	BCI 159	
Iliza	BCI 148	
Jacob	DOR 11	
James	BCI 137	
James	MON 151	
James	SAI 81	
James H.	SAI 73A	
Jeremiah	MON 152	
Jethro	CEC 161	
John	BCI 401	
John	BCI 427	
John	SOM 137	
John	WAS 146	
John, of Lee	SAI 77	
Joseph	SAI 75	
Levin	DOR 11	
Lyddea	MON 172	
Mary	DOR 50	
Mary	MON 133	
Mary	WAS 144	
Nancy	BCI 430	
Philip	SAI 74	
Purnell	DOR 61	
Rachel	DOR 50	
JOHNSTON (continued),		
Rachel	DOR 58	
Rachel	SOM 136	
Rewbin	DOR 57	
Richard	DOR 56	
Richd.	MON 176	
Rose	DOR 3	
Samuel	BCI 132	
Samuel	BCI 151	
Samuel	MON 152	
Simon	BCI 161	
Sophy	BCI 159	
Thomas	SOM 132	
Thos.	MON 140	
Thos. B.	MON 172	
William	BCI 464	
William	WAS 61	
Wm.	MON 133	
Wm.	MON 167	
Wm.	WAS 149	
Wm. A.	MON 136	
Wm. J. (I.?)	MON 130	
JOHONES, John	BCI 511	
JOICE, Aaron	BCI 473	
Anne	ANN 256	
George	ANN 265	
J.	BCI 417	
John	ANN 375	
Jonas	BCI 141	
Joseph	CEC 161	
Richard	ANN 265	
Sarah	ANN 305	
Sarah	ANN 315	
Stephen	BCI 494	
Zachariah	ANN 304	
JOINER, Benjamin	BCI 153	
Benjamin	BCI 284	
Daniel?	QUE 48	
Samuel	KEN 93	
William	QUE 49	
William, Senr.	KEN 86	
William, Junr.	KEN 89	
JOINES, Benjamin (?)	BCI 153	
Daniel	DOR 34	
Henry of Wm.	MON 163	
Leonard	BCI 92	
Samuel	QUE 45	
William	WOR 156	
JOISE, Edward	BAL 18	
JOLI, Glaude	BCI 340	
JOLLICKKOFER, D.	BCI 337	
JOLLY, Grace	BCI 144	
Henry	DOR 13	
James	ALL 31	
John	QUE 37	
Mathew	DOR 4	
Peter	ALL 35	
Peter	CLN 105	
Thomas	DOR 43	
JONAS, Bill	HAR 30	
JONCHEREZ (See also IONCHEREZ),		
Ann	D.C.28	
JONCKHEERE, Francis	BCI 46	
JONCKHEEVE, Francis (?)	BCI 46	
JONDEN, Jerome	BCI 24	
JONES (See also JANES, JOANES, JOANS),		
--- (Leutn.)	BCI 341	
--- (Major?)	WOR 159	
--- (Widaw)	BCI 383	
Aaron	ANN 388	
Aaron	D.C.12	
Aaron	D.C.179	

JONES (continued),

Aaron	DOR 23	David	BCI 493	Horaica	DOR 25
Aba	SOM 140	David	CLN 109	Horatio	D.C. 51
Abner	HAR 43	David	D.C. 74	Horatio	FRE 83A
Abraham	ANN 272	David	KEN 91	Huller (f.n.)	SOM 119
Abraham	BAL 204	Dennis	BCI 317	Ignatius	FRE 96
Abraham	FRE 219	Dennis	D.C. 24	Isaac	ANN 253
Abraham-free	CAL 59	Denwadd	DOR 22	Isaac	ANN 317
Abram	MON 130	Dorsey	BCI 447	Isaac	ANN 345
Agnes	ANN 319	E. (Mrs.)	PRI 185	Isaac	BCI 425
Alexander	PRI 195	Edward	ANN 255	Isaac	PRI 229
Alexander	SOM 128	Edward	ANN 269	Isack	BAL 10
Alfred	QUE 24	Edward	CAL 42	J.	BCI 407
Amon	BAL 147	Edward	CHA 214	Jacob	BAL 202
Amon	BAL 243	Edward	D.C. 38	Jacob	BCI 39
Amos	ANN 350	Elan	BCI 122	Jacob	BCI 139
Amos	HAR 38	Eleanor	MON 167	Jacob	KEN 105
Amos	HAR 72	Eleanor	SOM 140	Jacob	KEN 106A
Amos	QUE 12	Elects.	D.C. 127	Jacob	KEN 120
Ananias	WOR 186	Elenor	D.C. 120	Jacob	KEN 123
Andrew B.	BCI 463	Elisabeth	KEN 105	Jacob	MON 151
Ann	BCI 69	Elisha	ANN 350	Jacob, Senor (?)	DOR 27
Ann	SAI 56	Elisha	BAL 202	Jahn	DOR 28
Ann	SAI 90	Elisha	BCI 322	Jahon, Jur.	DOR 22
Ann	TAL 46	Elisha	FRE 187	James	ALL 4
Aquilla	BCI 478	Elisha	WOR 209	James	BCI 85
Aquilla	MON 167	Elisha (Senr.)	WOR 161	James	BCI 139
Arnold E.	SOM 139	Eliza	BCI 533	James	BCI 309
Arthur	BCI 37	Elizabeth	BAL 21	James	BCI 459
Arthur	QUE 34	Elizabeth	BCI 241	James	BCI 529
Arthur T.	KEN 85	Elizabeth	CAL 63	James	CAL 62
Barney	BCI 28	Elizabeth	FRE 101	James	CAL 65
Bartholemew	QUE 30	Elizabeth	FRE 113	James	D.C. 96
Basil	SAI 55	Elizabeth	PRI 230	James	FRE 83A
Benedict	KEN 125	Elizabeth	PRI 231	James	HAR 5
Benj. O.	MON 130	Elizabeth (Farm)	BAL 129	James	HAR 24
Benjamin	BAL 131	Enick	WAS 140	James	HAR 76
Benjamin	PRI 193	Ezekiel	DOR 18	James	KEN 116
Benjamin	SOM 129	Ezekiel	DOR 42	James	MON 159
Benjamin G.	HAR 39	Ezekiel	HAR 57	James	QUE 34
Benjamin J. (I.?)	SOM 116	Ezekiel	HAR 71	James	SAI 89
Bennett	TAL 13	Evan, of Evan	MON 178A	James	SOM 130
Betsey	BCI 520	Evan, of Nathan	MON 167	James	SOM 134
Betsey	D.C. 22	Fanny	HAR 74	James	SOM 136
Betsey	D.C. 171	Felis	BCI 482	James	TAL 23
Betsy	SOM 127	Fender	SOM 124	James	TAL 25
Betsy	SOM 130	Flora	SOM 130	James	WOR 155
Betsy	SOM 135	Francis	BCI 428	James	WOR 161
Brookes	MON 129	Frank	DOR 27	James-free	CAL 52
C. L.	D.C. 31	Frederick	D.C. 51	James, Ovsr.	TAL 7
Caleb	SOM 130	George	CEC 139	James B.	TAL 19
Caleb	WOR 157	George	CEC 178	James C.	MON 177
Caleb M.	SAI 54	George	D.C. 144	Jane	BCI 219
Cassius	BCI 110	George	PRI 236	Jas.	D.C. 133
Charles	ANN 263	George	SOM 136	Jason	ANN 311
Charles	BAL 220	George	SOM 149	Jeremiah	ANN 345
Charles	BCI 62	George (of Geo.)	SOM 129	Jeremiah	DOR 42
Charles	BCI 130	George (of Robt.)		Jerimiah	FRE 77
Charles	CEC 124		SOM 133	Jerimiah M.	ANN 350
Charles	HAR 77	George P.	SOM 134	Jesse	KEN 94
Charles	MON 151	George W.	SOM 114	Jesse	WOR 173
Charles	SOM 123	George W.	WOR 171	Jessee	CLN 115
Charles C.	MON 164	Giles	WOR 162	Jo.	QUE 5
Clement	BCI 29	Hanbury	MON 135	Job (f.n.)	SOM 119
Comfort	WOR 195	Harry	DOR 44	John (?)	DOR 34
Cotter	SOM 103	Hatton	PRI 227	John	ANN 298
Daniel	DOR 10	Henry	ANN 254	John	ANN 301
Daniel	HAR 5	Henry	ANN 379	John	BAL 13
Daniel	QUE 12	Henry	CLN 110	John	BAL 116
Daniel (of Danl.)	WOR 157	Henry	DOR 32	John	BAL 131
Darius	KEN 94	Henry	QUE 24	John	BAL 205
David	ANN 378	Henry, of Wm.	MON 134	John	BCI 8
David	BAL 12	Hetty (f.n.)	SOM 119	John	BCI 134
David	BAL 127	Himlet	ANN 352	John	CEC 124
David	BAL 156	Hintson	TAL 25	John	DOR 12
David	BAL 223	Hiram	KEN 85	John?	DOR 28

JONES (continued),		JONES (continued),		JONES (continued),	
John	FRE 79	Marey	BCI 393	Richard	D.C. 27
John	FRE 117	Margarett	CLN 81	Richard	HAR 6
John	FRE 131	Margl.	BCI 226	Richard	PRI 181
John	FRE 175	Margt.?	BCI 226	Richard C.	PRI 186
John	FRE 195	Marshal	KEN 89	Richard C.	PRI 195
John	HAR 23	Martha	DOR 19	Richard I. (J.?)	QUE 38
John	HAR 74	Mary	ANN 270	Richard J. (I.?)	ANN 401
John	KEN 92	Mary	ANN 320	Richard J.	QUE 48
John	KEN 104	Mary	BAL 202	Richard M.	ANN 351
John	MON 151	Mary	BCI 57	Robert	BAL 42
John	PRI 202	Mary	BCI 179	Robert	CEC 160
John	SOM 129	Mary	BCI 458	Robert	PRI 183
John	SOM 136	Mary	CLN 81	Robert	QUE 39
John	SOM 137	Mary	PRI 181	Robert	SOM 124
John	TAL 22	Mases?	D.C. 60	Robert	TAL 26
John	TAL 52	Matilda	D.C. 65	Robert	TAL 46
John	WAS 145	Matthias	SOM 139	Robert (of Robert)	
John	WOR 186	Mehaly	DOR 28		SOM 107
John	WOR 196	Memory	TAL 37	Robinson	BCI 196
John, Senr.	SOM 129	Merican	ANN 350	Roger	DOR 18
John, Senr.	SOM 141	Michael	MON 151	Ruben	QUE 12
John, Junr.	SOM 129	Milly	WOR 176	Sally	SOM 141
John, Junr.	SOM 141	Mordica	SAI 55	Saml.	D.C. 87
John (of Benjamin)	SOM 114	Moses	D.C. 60	Saml. E.	CHA 195
John (of Elisha)	WOR 177	Moses	DOR 44	Samuel	ANN 255
John, of Evan	MON 137	Moses	FRE 200	Samuel	ANN 335
John (of Jas.)	SOM 114	Moses	MON 131	Samuel	BAL 110
John (of John)	WOR 158	Moses	QUE 12	Samuel	BAL 174
John (of Nathan)	MON 167	Moses U.	WOR 158	Samuel	PRI 223
John B.	SAI 89	Nancey (f.n.)	SOM 120	Samuel	PRI 237
John G.	D.C. 13	Nancy	BCI 481	Samuel	QUE 34
John H.	CLN 112	Nancy	DOR 8	Samuel	SOM 130
John N.	BCI 26	Nancy	DOR 22	Samuel C.	SAI 56
John W.	SOM 132	Nancy	DOR 39	Samuel G.	BCI 248
Jos. J. (I.?) W.	MON 134	Nancy	TAL 37	Sarah	ANN 307
Joseph (?)	DOR 33	Nancy, Wd.	WOR 215	Sarah	ANN 307
Joseph	BAL 98	Nathan	D.C. 93	Sarah	BCI 71
Joseph	BCI 4	Nathan	QUE 34	Sarah	BCI 81
Joseph	BCI 426	Nathaniel	ANN 345	Sarah	MON 160
Joseph	FRE 125	Nathen	CEC 140	Selvey	WAS 79
Joseph	HAR 74	Nelly	BCI 135	Senah	BCI 437
Joseph	PRI 193	Nicholas	ALL 3	Sewal	SOM 140
Joseph	SAI 57	Nicholas	BAL 246	Silvya	ANN 400
Joseph J. (I.?)	PRI 183	Nichs. S.	BCI 180	Solomon	DOR 5
Joseph M.	ANN 350	Noah	BCI 325	Spencir?	CEC 160
Joshua	BAL 15	Obed	WOR 209	Spenen	CEC 160
Joshua	BAL 120	Oliver	D.C. 190	Stephen	CEC 124
Joshua	BCI 505	Oliver	D.C. 203	Stephen	HAR 48
Joshua	FRE 131	Owen	BCI 21	Sterling	WOR 186
Joshua	SOM 134	Patk.	BCI 257	Susannah (of Giles)	
Joshua	WOR 212	Patty	KEN 103		WOR 157
Joshua, Es.	FRE 209	Peggy	SOM 112	Talbat	BCI 397
Josiah	ANN 337	Peggy	SOM 126	Tho.	FRE 219
Josiah	MON 151	Peter	KEN 103	Tho.	QUE 14
Josiah	WOR 186	Peter	SOM 130	Thomas	ANN 372
Kendal	WOR 185	Philip	CLN 76	Thomas	BAL 112
Kiturah	BAL 20	Philip	FRE 111	Thomas	BAL 182
Kizzia	SOM 129	Philip	FRE 187	Thomas	BAL 196
L.	BCI 393	Phillamon	PRI 181	Thomas	BCI 55
Labin	DOR 56	Planner	DOR 42	Thomas	BCI 99
Lamuel (?)	DOR 34	Priscilla	DOR 40	Thomas	CAL 52
Leuty.?	BCI 341	R. H.	BCI 355	Thomas	CLN 82
Levin	DOR 44	R. L.	D.C. 30	Thomas	CLN 99
Levin	DOR 64	Rachael	BCI 438	Thomas	CEC 161
Levin D.	SOM 109	Rachel	BCI 50	Thomas	CHA 189
Levy	BCI 217	Rachel	QUE 29	Thomas	D.C. 53
Lewe	SOM 132	Rachel	SOM 136	Thomas	DOR 19
Lewin	PRI 227	Raphael	D.C. 89	Thomas	FRE 73
Lewis	ANN 302	Rebecca	WOR 155	Thomas	FRE 217
Lewis	BAL 106	Rebecca	WOR 217	Thomas	HAR 4
Lewis	SOM 110	Reuben	HAR 72	Thomas	PRI [200]
M.	BCI 389	Reuben	HAR 74	Thomas	PRI 231
Mahlon	BCI 452	Reuben	TAL 24	Thomas	SAI 53A
Major	WOR 159	Richard	ANN 328	Thomas	SOM 104
Marcellus	SOM 109	Richard	CEC 140	Thomas	SOM 135

KAILER, Abraham	FRE 201	
KAILOR, John	ALL 24	
KAIN (See also CAIN, CAINE, CANE),		
--- (Mrs.)	D.C. 88	
Edward	HAR 40	
Henry	FRE 190	
Patrick	D.C. 111	
Robert	CEC 179	
KAINE, George	WAS 70	
KAIS, Elizabeth	BCI 102	
KAISER, Michael	WAS 100	
KALBFAUS, Wm.	BCI 99	
KALFFOUSE, Danl.	BCI 533	
Lewis	BCI 533	
KALKMAN, C. F.	BCI 519	
KALL, Mann F.	BCI 370	
KALLER, Frederick	WAS 126	
KAMICUM, Jacob (?)	WAS 138	
KANE (See also CAIN, CAINE, CANE),		
Daniel	BCI 84	
Devonshire	BCI 81	
Henry	BCI 53	
Thomas	WAS 68	
KANEY, --- (?)	FRE 163	
KAPP, Catherine	WAS 113A	
Michael	WAS 116	
KARAGAN, Joseph	CHA 194	
KARLAN (See also HARLAN),		
Joshua (?)	FRE 227	
KARNABY, James	BAL 3	
KARNEY, Thomas	ANN 388	
KARNICUM, Jacob	WAS 138	
KARNYHAN, John	MON 132	
KARRISS (See also HARRISS),		
Joshua (?)	DOR 26	
KARTOHER, Frederick	ANN 347	
KAUDERER, Geo.	BCI 311	
KAUFFMAN, Danl.	BCI 274	
Jona.	BCI 521	
KAUFMAN, --- (Widaw)	BCI 370	
Abraham	BAL 225	
Conrad	FRE 107	
George	FRE 198	
Henry	FRE 102	
KAUFT, Jacob	WAS 117	
KAUSLER, Jacob	WAS 98	
John	WAS 118	
KAWLINGS (See also RAWLINGS),		
Thos.	MON 160	
KAY, John	CEC 179	
KAYLOR, Danl.	BCI 217	
Geo.	BCI 227	
KEADLE (See also CADEL, CADLE, KADEL),		
Humphrey	PRI 206	
Wiseman G.	PRI 236	
KEAGLER, Jno.	D.C. 119	
KEALEY, Daniel	D.C. 132	
Danl.	D.C. 125	
David	D.C. 138	
KEALHOOFER, Christopher	WAS 117	
Henry	WAS 118	
John	WAS 113A	
KEAN, Augustus	HAR 31	
Elizabeth	D.C. 6	
John	ALL 36	
John	CEC 140	

KEAN (continued),		
John	HAR 41	
John (of Patk.)	HAR 62	
Patrick	HAR 46	
Robert	HAR 44	
William	ALL 38	
Wm.	BCI 505	
KEARMAN, James	D.C. 78	
KEARN, John	D.C. 29	
Robert	D.C. 30	
KEARNEY, Alexr.	D.C. 87	
Ann	D.C. 133	
KEARNS, Levi	HAR 46	
KEATH, Alexander	BAL 162	
James	WAS 63	
John	BAL 157	
William	BAL 163	
KEATING, George S.	ANN 388	
Henry S.	BCI 187	
Mary	D.C. 168	
Mary Ann	D.C. 168	
William	KEN 119	
KEATLY, John	CEC 140	
Nathen	CEC 140	
KEATTY, --- (Mrs.)	BCI 336	
KEBLINGER, Saml.	BCI 397	
KEBY, Mary	ANN 258	
KEDWELL, John	QUE 37	
KEECH, Elizabeth	CHA 206	
James	SAI 94	
John E.	SAI 90	
Mary	SAI 93	
Philemon	CHA 227	
Samuel	SAI 90	
KEEDY, Daniel	WAS 65	
George	WAS 66	
Henry, Senr.	WAS 66	
Henry, Jun.	WAS 70	
Henry of A.	WAS 72	
Jacob	WAS 66	
Jacob	WAS 74	
Jacob of G.	WAS 72	
John	WAS 87	
John, of A.	WAS 73	
KEEFER, David	FRE 187	
Elizabeth	FRE 198	
Frederick	WAS 147	
George	FRE 148	
George	FRE 180	
Henry	FRE 175	
Jacob	FRE 175	
Lewis	FRE 154	
Phil.	FRE 130	
KEEFFER, Christian (Jun.)	FRE 87	
Christian, Jur.	FRE 87	
Henry	FRE 87	
Henry	FRE 105	
Jacob	FRE 87	
Peter	FRE 102	
Philip	FRE 105	
Samuel	FRE 100	
KEEFOVER, George	WAS 71	
KEEHOFFER, Jno.	FRE 135	
KEEN, Job	CLN 78	
John	FRE 172	
Timothy	HAR 18	
Zachra.	BCI 227	
KEENAN, Charles	BCI 400	
KEENE, Benjamin	DOR 24	
Betsey	D.C. 193	
Capiwil	DOR 24	
Catherane	DOR 35	
Charles	DOR 18	

KEENE (continued),		
Charllotte W.	DOR 30	
Draper	DOR 20	
Elizebeth	DOR 24	
Ezekiel	DOR 8	
Ezekiel	DOR 46	
Fancy	DOR 18	
Faney?	DOR 18	
Hannah	DOR 18	
Henry	DOR 28	
Henry, Senor	DOR 24	
Isaac	DOR 32	
James	CLN 92	
Jas.	QUE 13	
John	KEN 103	
John	QUE 11	
Levin	DOR 30	
Levin C.	DOR 24	
Margret	DOR 21	
Nancy	DOR 30	
Nany	DOR 30	
Newton	D.C. 176	
Richard C.	DOR 50	
Saml. C.	QUE 10	
Saml. (of E.)	DOR 8	
Samuel	DOR 35	
Samuel (of Benj.?)	DOR 27	
Samuel of Bey.	DOR 27	
Sarah	DOR 21	
Shedreck	DOR 24	
Vatchel	DOR 22	
William	DOR 24	
William	MON 152	
Wm. R.	QUE 16	
KEENER, Ann	BCI 209	
Christian	BCI 136	
Christian	BCI 418	
David	BCI 268	
John	BCI 240	
Peter	BCI 526	
Susan	BCI 534	
KEENES, Joseph	DOR 60	
KEENRIGHT, John	BAL 200	
KEENS, Jacob	BCI 411	
Michael	FRE 77	
KEEPER, Joseph	D.C. 122	
KEEPERS, Alexander T.	FRE 142	
Hellen	FRE 144	
KEER, Jacob	BCI 315	
KEERL, John	BCI 320	
KEERLE, George H.	BCI 439	
Henry	BCI 439	
KEERSE, Ezekiel (?)	DOR 46	
James	DOR 46	
KEESE, Thomas	BCI 149	
KEETH, Jas., Senr.	D.C. 152	
William	ANN 370	
KEETHE, --- (?)	QUE 2A	
KEETLY, Richard	CEC 179	
KEETS, John	QUE 40	
William	CLN 90	
KEFFER, Joseph	BCI 46	
KEFLER, George	FRE 85	
KEFOVER, John	WAS 71	
KEHO, Daniel	BCI 202	
KEHOE, Michl.	D.C. 100	
KEIFER, George	FRE 192	
Henry	WAS 104	
Isaac	WAS 101	
KEIFLE, Henry	BCI 434	
Nicholas	BCI 438	
KEIM, Jacob	FRE 199	
KEINER, John	WAS 119	

KEINEY, John	FRE 216	KELLEY (continued),			KELLY (continued),		
Wm.	FRE 217	Patk.	D.C.126		Thomas	CLN 106
KEINYMAN, Perrygrine		Pattrick	BAL 143		Thomas	CEC 161
	DOR 63	Thomas	BCI 286		Thomas	HAR 41
KEIRL, Math.	BCI 355	Thomas	D.C.107		William	BAL 42
KEIRLE, John W.	BCI 241	William	HAR 57		William	BAL 207
KEISENDERFFER, --- (Mrs.)		William	SOM 110		William	BCI 146
	BCI 397	Wm.	BCI 406		William	CLN 77
KEISER, John	WAS 104	KELLINGER, Henry			William	CLN 85A
KEISINDEFFER, John	D.C.201		BCI 448		William	BCI 427
KEISLER, John	BCI 28	KELLISON, William	FRE 126		KELPAN, Thomas	WOR 163
KEITH, Jas., Junr.	D.C.200	KELLUM, Henry (f.n.)			KELPIN, Handy	WOR 163
John	BAL 28		SOM 119		KELSEY, Elijah	BAL 232
Mary	BCI 70	John	SOM 108		William	BAL 240
Susanna	D.C.174	KELLY, --- (Widaw)			KELSO, Ann	BCI 187
KEITHLEY, James	TAL 23		BCI 396		John	BAL 173
Nancy	TAL 23	--- (Widaw)	BCI 413		John R.	BCI 248
Richard	TAL 23	Anna	SOM 130		Mary	ANN 315
Thomas	CEC 161	Bartholw.	BCI 310		Thos.	BCI 193
Thos.	D.C.133	Bassel	BAL 156		KELSON, John	BCI 158
KEITLY, Henry	CEC 161	Benjamine P. V. (?)			KELTING, James	KEN 119
Thomas	CEC 161		SOM 104		KELTY, Frank	CAL 50
KELBAUGH, Christian	BAL 138	Branson	CLN 115		KEMMEY, Sarah (?)	DOR 63
Christian, Jur.	BAL 140	Cables	ANN 328		KEMP, --- (Widaw)	BCI 379
Henry	BAL 143	Caleb	DOR 53		Abraham	FRE 113
KELIER, John	FRE 135	Catherine	BCI 73		Andrew	BCI 320
KELL, Abraham-Negro		Charles	CEC 161		Ann	FRE 123
	HAR 50	Christian	BCI 24		Benjamin	TAL 4
Absolum	WAS 127A	Dennis	CLN 109		Christian	FRE 87
Isaac	D.C.183	Edward	WAS 136		Daniel	FRE 109
Jacob	HAR 29	Edwd.	BCI 201		David	FRE 225
Moses	HAR 29	Elizh.	BCI 189		Dorothy	FRE 113
Thomas	BCI 131	Hannah	CLN 99		Frederick	FRE 113
Thomas (farm)	BAL 126	Hannah	QUE 17		Georgo	FRE 198
KELLAR, John	D.C.87	Henry	KEN 106A		Gilbert	FRE 228
KELLEN, David	FRE 190	Henry	WOR 180		Hannah	TAL 32
KELLENBERGER, Geo.		Isaac	BAL 122		Henry	FRE 85
	D.C.24	James	ALL 26		Jacob	MON 152
John	FRE 142	James	BCI 149		Jeremiah (on John
Peter	FRE 148	James	BCI 167		& Robert OLIVER's
KELLER, --- (Widaw)	BCI 390	James	D.C.153		farm)	BAL 129
Abraham	BAL 155	James	KEN 106A		John	BAL 29
Catharine	FRE 104	James	QUE 29		John	DOR 50
Charles	FRE 104	James	SOM 130		John	FRE 203
Christian	BCI 259	John	BAL 10		John	KEN 101
Conrod	BCI 283	John	BAL 187		John	TAL 27
Conrod	FRE 78	John	D.C.26		John, Junr.	TAL 27
Elizabeth	WAS 70	John	DOR 60		Joseph	FRE 112
Frederick	FRE 118	John	KEN 106A		Joseph	TAL 12
George	BCI 358	John	MON 136		Joseph	TAL 22
George	WAS 111	John	SOM 137		Joshua	BAL 29
Henry	FRE 125	Joseph	BAL 7		Lewis	FRE 85
Henry	WAS 111	Levi	CLN 77		Margaret	FRE 104
Henry	WAS 118	Martin	BAL 208		Margt.	QUE 17
Henry T.	FRE 73	Mary	CEC 161		Mary	FRE 113
Jacob	FRE 73	Mary	FRE 144		Matthias	SOM 141
Jacob	FRE 96	Matthew	BCI 64		Nancy	TAL 23
Jacob	FRE 122	Moses	ALL 3		Robert	TAL 51
Jacob, Jr.	FRE 70	Nicholaus	BCI 402		Samuel	TAL 39
John	BAL 200	Oliver	D.C.211		Samuel T.	TAL 11
John	BCI 489	Patrick	BAL 53		Sarah	MON 152
John	FRE 97	Patrick	BCI 380		Shadrack	BAL 15
John	WAS 107	Patrick	BCI 462		Solomon	FRE 72
Joseph	BAL 28	Peregrine	KEN 89		Thomas	TAL 26
Margaretta	WAS 111	Peter	CLN 109		Thomas	TAL 51
Michael	FRE 128	Philip	PRI 229		Thos.	QUE 20
Philip	WAS 118	Rachl.	BCI 197		William, Ovsr.	TAL 40
KELLEY, Adn.	BCI 499	Richard	ANN 300		Wm. A. C.	TAL 49
Benjamin	KEN 90	Robert	ANN 328		KEMPE, James	PRI 201
Henry	FRE 105	Saml.	QUE 14		KEMPF, Gilbert (?)	FRE 228
James	HAR 6	Samson	SOM 134		KEMPTON, Saml. A.
Jane	BCI 474	Samuel	BAL 52			BCI 270
John	ANN 356	Thomas	ALL 6		KEN, Samuel	KEN 108
Julian	BAL 148	Thomas	BAL 28		KENADAY, Peter	QUE 28
Lurena	HAR 70	Thomas	BCI 223		KENADY, Daniel	FRE 74
Mord.	BCI 480	Thomas	BCI 393		KENARD, John	KEN 105
					Joseph	D.C.198

137

KERTTY, Jonathan	CEC 161	KIDD (continued)		KILLY (continued),	
KERTZ, Benjamin	WAS 116	John	BAL 234	Torrence	BCI 462
KERWIN, Fredrick	DOR 41	Joshua	BAL 218	KILMAN, Thomas	BCI 18
Thos.	BCI 182	Pencely	HAR 63	KILMAND, Thos.	BCI 168
KESHER, George (?)	BAL 87	Rebecca	CEC 178	KILMON, Thomas	ANN 342
KESLER, ---	BCI 431	Samuel	CEC 179	KILPATRICK, John	BCI 462
Andrew	FRE 135	KIDMORE, William	D.C.25	KILRIGHT, Michael	D.C.199
Frederick	BCI 119	KIDRAL, William L.		KILTY, William	ANN 393
Jacob	FRE 222	KIDWELL, Dory	D.C.100	KIMBALL, John	D.C.182
John M.	BCI 83	Elizth.	D.C.186	KIMBERLY, Jacob	ALL 17
Rachael	FRE 125	Fieldee	PRI 238	John	ALL 35
KESLERING, Michael	FRE 182	Fielder	PRI 238	John, Jr.	ALL 9
Wendle	FRE 179	Francis	MON 158A	John, of M.	ALL 9
KESLEY, William	BCI 446	George	PRI 215	Nathl.	BCI 250
KESLY, Henry	BCI 335	Heziciah	WAS 135	William H.	BCI 46
KESSECKER, Jacob	WAS 111	James	PRI 216	KIMBLE, George	QUE 16
Philip	WAS 111	Jas.	D.C.157	Jas.	QUE 6
KESSINGER, Jacob	WAS 127A	John	CHA 216	John	HAR 22
Michael	WAS 78	Joseph W.	PRI 218	William	QUE 36
KESSLER, Chis	BCI 478	Kemiah?	PRI 218	Zachariah	HAR 22
David	FRE 96	Leonard	PRI 215	KIMBOLL, Catharine	
George	FRE 103	Nemiah	PRI 218		FRE 95
Jacob	BAL 141	Robert C.	BCI 84	KIMBRIDGE, Edward	
Jacob	FRE 101	Theodore	D.C.116		TAL 9
Michael	FRE 222	Thomas C.	PRI 218	KIMES, Thos.	BCI 334
KETCHENER, Fredk.	D.C.194	Thomas T.	PRI 218	KIMMEL, Michael	BCI 381
KETTING, James (?)	KEN 119	KIERNAN, John	ANN 298	KIMMELL, Michael-	
KETTMOCKER, John	WAS 72	John	BCI 80	[his] farm	BAL 116
KEW, James	PRI 228	KIERSTED, Luke	BCI 6	KIMMERLY, Michl.	BCI 490
KEWTER, Elias	WAS 97	KIGER, Leonard	FRE 158	Nichl.?	BCI 490
KEY, Ann (Mrs.)	D.C.38	KIGGS (See also		KIMMEY, Saba	CLN 112
Edmond	PRI 217	RIGGS),		Sarah	DOR 63
Francis	SAI 94	Remus	MON 177	KINARD, Joseph (?)	
Francis S.	D.C.26	KIGHT, Henry, Sen.			D.C.198
Frank	FRE 180		ALL 11	Samuel	BCI 59
Henry G. S.	SAI 75	KIGLAR, Nancy	BCI 312	KINCAID, G. W.	FRE 226
James	QUE 16	KILBAUGH, Henry (?)		George	D.C.202
John Ross	FRE 173		BAL 143	James	D.C.37
Richd.	FRE 229	KILBURN, Russel	BCI 23	Jas.	BCI 182
Sophiah	SAI 92	Saml.	BCI 503	Samuel	HAR 79
William	FRE 177	KILDAY, Catharine		KINCHY, --- (See	
KEYLER, Henry	BCI 479		FRE 142	KINCHY & CO.)	
KEYNE, Bridget	D.C.90	KILE, George	D.C.24	KINCHY & CO.	D.C.82
John	D.C.89	George	WAS 150	KINDALL, John	D.C.98
KEYS, Edward	D.C.17	Marke	WAS 149	KINDER, Horrice	BCI 209
Hary	CEC 161	Robert	ALL 22	KINDLE, Davolt	WAS 109
Hugh	BCI 386	KILEHOLTZ, Philip		Henry	KEN 124
Jehu	CEC 179		FRE 150	James	WAS 124A
John	BCI 228	KILER, Daniel	FRE 212	William	WAS 106
John	DOR 8	KILGORE, Alexander (?)		KINDLER, Azariah	MON 171
Joseph	D.C.212		D.C.27	John	MON 171
Joseph	DOR 59	Edward (?)	D.C.27	KINDLEY, George F.	
Levin	DOR 49	James	CEC 140		FRE 72
Precilla	DOR 9	William	CEC 140	KINEMONT, Hopkins	
Rachael	FRE 204	KILGOUR, Carles J.			QUE 27
Robert	DOR 50		MON 158A	Samuel	QUE 31
Thomas	DOR 9	Jno. A. T.	MON 159	William	QUE 34
William	BAL 217	John	SAI 94	KING, --- (Mrs.)	D.C.4
William	DOR 39	William	SAI 87	Abner	BCI 116
KEYSER, Derrick	BCI 378	KILGOW, Alexander		Abraham	BAL 238
George	BCI 440		D.C.27	Adam	D.C.59
Samuel	BCI 441	Edward	D.C.27	Adam	FRE 175
KEYSOR, Wm.	BCI 378	KILKENNY, Jane	MON 132	Adraham	WAS 121
KEYWORTH, Robt.	D.C.85	KILLAN, David	KEN 118	Agness	HAR 74
KIBBLE, Polly	SOM 137	KILLEN, Henry	CEC 140	Ambrose	D.C.64
Rozy	SOM 133	KILLEY, Henry	WOR 178	Ann	BCI 396
KICHELL, Michael	WAS 135	Henry; S.	WOR 212	Ann	PRI 231
KICKELL, Michael (?)	WAS 135	William	WOR 219	Anne (Mrs.)	PRI 202
KICKMAN, Samuel	KEN 103	KILLIAM, Henry	SOM 153	Ben., Jun.	D.C.120
KID, David	BAL 92	KILLIAN, Philip	FRE 95	Benjamin	CAL 58A
Henery	BAL 91	KILLIM, Wm.	WOR 180	Benjn.	D.C.132
Joshua	BAL 92	KILLISON, William	KEN 107	Benjn.	MON 142
Moses	BAL 92	KILLMAN, Noah	TAL 23	Catharine	BCI 443
Thomas	ANN 309	KILLY, George	WOR 209	Cathe.	D.C.93
KIDD, Andrew	CEC 178	Samuel	WOR 217	Cathe.	D.C.96
George	CEC 179			Cathe.	D.C.113

KING (continued),			KING (continued),			KINSEY (continued),		
Charles	D.C.	34	Sarah	FRE	83A	Levy	MON	152
Charles	D.C.	49	Susannah (Mrs.)			Zenis	D.C.	205
Charles	D.C.	126		CAL	60	KINSLEY, Barbara	HAR	19
Chas.	D.C.	173	Thomas	ALL	37	Ben.	D.C.	123
Daniel	TAL	3	Thomas	ANN	260	KINSOLOW, John	CEC	140
David	MON	152	Thomas	ANN	334	Robert	CEC	140
Edmund	SAI	65	Thomas	BCI	416	KINSTRICK, William	WAS	67
Edward	BCI	434	Thomas	D.C.	96	KINT, Abraham	FRE	181
Elias	ALL	4	Thomas	PRI	204	KINTZ (See also KURTZ),		
Eliza	FRE	129	Thomas E.	CAL	58A	George (?)	BCI	521
Elizabeth	FRE	165	Vinsan	D.C.	65	John (?)	D.C.	46
Elizabeth	WAS	109	Vinson?	D.C.	65	Peter (?)	D.C.	48
Enoch	D.C.	20	Whittington	SOM	123	KINZAR, Ann (?)	FRE	223
Ezekiel	D.C.	4	Will	PRI	185	John	FRE	217
Fitz	BCI	4	William	ALL	10A	KINZER, Jacob	FRE	227
Francis	PRI	185	William	ANN	326	KIPER, George	WAS	134
Geoge. S.	D.C.	210	William	CAL	62	KIRBEY, Samuel	QUE	36
George	BCI	347	William	CEC	179	KIRBY (See also CURBY,		
George	D.C.	48	William	D.C.	30	KERBY),		
George	D.C.	60	William	D.C.	55	Abner	TAL	48
George	WAS	149	William	FRE	129	Benjamin	TAL	3
George W.	BCI	110	William	SOM	155	Betsy	WOR	196
Gideon	BCI	277	William (of Jesse)			Charles	TAL	21
Henry	ANN	269		SOM	128	Cloudsbury	TAL	8A
Henry	CAL	43	William R.	FRE	84	Clowdsberry	TAL	45
Ignatius	D.C.	58	Wilm.	D.C.	145	Cornelius	SAI	66
Isaac	PRI	197	Wm. W.	MON	174	Daniel	TAL	45
Jacob	BCI	455	Zadock	MON	133	Edward	TAL	46
Jacob	FRE	196	KINGEICK, Christian			Elizabeth	SAI	63
Jacob	WAS	120		WAS	66	Francis	PRI	226
James	ALL	37	KINGREY, Jacob	WAS	66	George	PRI	225
James	ANN	344	KINGSBURY, Horatio			Henry	DOR	10
James	BCI	16		D.C.	98	J. (I.?) B.	D.C.	135
James	D.C.	162	James	PRI	203	Jacob	TAL	47
James	PRI	197	KINGSMORE, John S.			James	ANN	311
James C.	BCI	181		BAL	124	James	BCI	314
James S.	CAL	58A	Richd. S.	BCI	198	Jane	SAI	64
Jane	D.C.	154	KINGSTON, Thos.	D.C.	173	Jessee	TAL	45
Jesse	FRE	110	KINKADE, Alexander			Jim (negro)	TAL	22
John	BCI	446		CEC	140	Joseph	DOR	64
John	CAL	61	William	CEC	140	Josiah	TAL	3
John	D.C.	33	KINKEL, Adam	WAS	119	John	D.C.	208
John	D.C.	88	KINKELL, Henry	WAS	119	John	DOR	12
John	D.C.	136	KINKLEY, Mary	FRE	99	John	DOR	62
John	MON	136	KINNAMON, Sorden			Luther	CLN	79
John	PRI	208		CLN	91	Mary	SAI	54
John	PRI	226	William	CLN	108	Nichls.	MON	171
John	SOM	131	KINNAMONT, Jonathan			Oliver	TAL	47
John, Docr.	SOM	122		TAL	9	Rebecca	ANN	403
John D.	MON	172	KINNAN, Patk.	D.C.	92	Richd.	D.C.	217
John H.	D.C.	40	KINNARD, Nathaniel			Thomas	DOR	61
John S.	BCI	351		BCI	92	Thomas	TAL	12
John W.	SOM	145	KINNEMAN, Parker Y.			Thomas	TAL	51
Jos.	BCI	349		CHA	212	Vachel	ANN	308
Joshua	SAI	65	Nehemiah S.	CHA	213	William	TAL	12
Josias W.	D.C.	74	KINNEMONT, Hopkins			KIRCHNER, John C.		
Leonard	D.C.	213		TAL	7		BCI	438
Margarel?	BCI	490	KINNER, George (?)			KIRDAL, George	D.C.	6
Margaret	BCI	490		D.C.	146	KIRE, Easter	DOR	8
Mary	D.C.	89	KINNEY, John	WAS	136	Jeremiah	DOR	59
Mary	D.C.	97	Josiah	SOM	117	John	DOR	4
Monarchy	FRE	220	KINNICK, Mary	CHA	222	Stephen	DOR	4
Nancy	CAL	58A	KINNIS, Richard	TAL	32	Stephen	DOR	59
Nancy	CAL	61	KINSBURY, Cath.	BCI	532	KIRK, Abner	CEC	178
Nicholas	FRE	132	KINSELL, Enock B.			Allen	CEC	179
Peggy	SOM	128		WAS	118	Amelia	CEC	178
Philip	CHA	205	F. B. O.	WAS	119	Ann	CEC	179
R. J. (I.?), Doc.	SOM	128	Jacob	WAS	119	Eli	CEC	179
Richard	HAR	78	Martin	WAS	132	Elisha	CEC	178
Richd.	BCI	528	KINSEY, Christian (?)			Elisha	CEC	179
Richd. H.	D.C.	202		FRE	218	Howell	CEC	178
Robert	D.C.	3	Ezra	D.C.	205	James	SAI	55
Samuel	ANN	335	George	FRE	221	John	HAR	23
Samuel	BCI	156	Henry	FRE	178	Mahlon	MON	152
Samuel	FRE	211	Henry	FRE	221	Mary	BCI	126
Samuel	SOM	133	Joseph	MON	152	Mary	CEC	178

KIRK (continued),		
Polley	CEC	179
Rachel	CEC	179
Reuben	D.C.	203
Saml.	BCI	231
Saml.	D.C.	146
Violett	D.C.	150
William	BAL	107
William	CEC	178
William	CEC	179
William M.	CEC	178
KIRKLAND, --- (Mrs.)		
	BCI	451
Alexander	BCI	239
Edward	ANN	283
KIRKLEY, John	D.C.	106
KIRKLIN, David	BCI	374
KIRKMAN, Elizabeth	BAL	81
Nimrod	CLN	105
Pompey	DOR	13
KIRKPATRICK, James	BCI	337
John	CEC	140
KIRKWOOD, Jabez	HAR	72
John	HAR	61
Robert	HAR	61
Sarah	D.C.	50
William	HAR	59
KIRLEY, J. (I.?) (See		
Wm. & J. (I.?)		
KIRLEY)	BAL	69
Wm. & J. (I.?)	BAL	69
KIRSHAW, Francis	CAL	48
KIRWAN, Elliott	SOM	141
Jacob	SOM	140
John	DOR	32
John	SOM	141
Methias	DOR	31
Peter	DOR	30
Solomon	DOR	30
Thomas	DOR	32
Zebulan	DOR	24
KISER, Martin	WAS	135
KISS, John	BCI	372
KISSER, Ludwick	WAS	59
KISSICK, --- (Mrs.)	D.C.	123
KISSINGER, Catherine		
	WAS	71
George	WAS	107
KISWICK, Thomas V. (?)		
	SAI	74
KITCHEN, Caleb	D.C.	204
KITE, Henry	ALL	12
John	ALL	11
Joshua	ALL	11
KITELY, Jo-f.c.p.	HAR	11
KITHS, Reuben	BCI	342
KITLEN, Lydia	PRI	230
KITNEY, --- (Widaw)	BCI	413
KITTS, Barnet	BCI	144
KITZMILLER, Elizabeth		
	FRE	204
Elizabeth	WAS	86
Jacob	WAS	88
John	FRE	218
John	WAS	85
KIZAR, Ann	FRE	223
Sarah	BAL	119
KIZER, Philip	FRE	116
KIZNER, Frederick	ALL	3
KLASSEN, Charles	BCI	392
KLEE, John	BCI	457
KLEIBER, George	D.C.	90
Jacob	D.C.	87
KLEIN, E. F.	BCI	100
KLICE, Frederick	FRE	114
John	FRE	115

KLINE, Andrew	WAS	134
Daniel	FRE	193
David	WAS	94
Elizabeth	BCI	14
Elizabeth	WAS	98
Frederick	FRE	113
Geo.	BCI	367
George	WAS	73
George	WAS	124A
Godlep	WAS	71
Henry	FRE	112
Henry	WAS	115
Jacob	BCI	4
Jacob	WAS	66
John	WAS	73
John	WAS	133
Joseph	FRE	110
Michael	FRE	114
Philip	WAS	78
Philip	WAS	83
Stephen	FRE	110
Wm.	WAS	145
KLINEDINST, John	WAS	69
KLINEFELTER, Nichs.		
	BCI	192
KLINEHART, Francis		
	FRE	103
KLINEHAUR, --- (Widaw)		
	BCI	410
KLINK, George	WAS	117
KLIPSTINE, Lewis F.		
	ALL	14
KLOCKGATHER, Didrich		
	BCI	408
KLUGE, John Peter		
(Rev.)	FRE	154
KNABLE, George	WAS	134[A]
KNAPP, John	BCI	89
Mary	D.C.	5
KNAUF, Jacob	FRE	105
KNEEDY, Jacob	WAS	103
John	WAS	137
KNEGS, John	ALL	8A
KNELLER, George	D.C.	95
KNIGHT (See also		
NIGHT),		
Abraham	HAR	21
Ann	HAR	28
Aquilla	BAL	127
George W.	BAL	219
Isaac	BAL	197
J. (I.?) B.	BAL	39
John	BAL	183
Joseph	ANN	355
Joshua	BAL	39
Margarett	BCI	318
Nace	BAL	40
Nathaniel	BCI	45
Peter	D.C.	77
Philip	ALL	24
Prudence	CEC	179
Thomas	CEC	178
Thomas	HAR	23
Will.	D.C.	88
William	ANN	350
William	CEC	140
William	PRI	195
Wm.	KEN	125
KNIGHTON, Gassaway		
	ANN	273
John	ANN	273
Nicholas	ANN	273
Richard	ANN	259
William	ANN	259
KNIGT, Thomas	CEC	140

KNIPPLE, Barbara	FRE	190
Christopher	FRE	190
David	FRE	190
John	FRE	189
KNOBLOCK, John	D.C.	6
KNOCK (See also NOCK),		
Benjamin	CEC	124
Jesse	KEN	116
Phillip	KEN	103
Wm.	QUE	19
KNOCKS, Margaret	FRE	142
KNODE, George	WAS	69
Henry	WAS	103
Jacob	WAS	58
Jacob	WAS	67
Jacob	WAS	85
Jacob	WAS	94
Jacob	WAS	119
Jacob	WAS	134
John	WAS	61
John	WAS	84
John	WAS	124A
Samuel	WAS	56
William	WAS	109
KNODLE, John	WAS	57
John	WAS	82
Jonathan	WAS	82
Samuel	WAS	82
KNODT, John	BCI	323
KNOK, Edwd.	WOR	169
Henry	ANN	363
KNOLL, James	BCI	247
KNOT, Cement	PRI	223
Prissy	DOR	57
KNOTT, Caleb	FRE	145
Charles	CHA	218
Edward	FRE	80
Elizabeth	PRI	230
Francis	SAI	96
Jane	SAI	87
John	CHA	200A
John B.	CHA	204
John B.	SAI	91
John T.	MON	172
Lewis	MON	129
Nathanial	SAI	81
Philip	MON	172
Richard	PRI	229
Richard	PRI	230
Sarah	CHA	207B
Stanis L.	MON	132
William	SAI	87
Wm.	MON	172
KNOTTS, Andrew	QUE	5
David	CLN	90
Emory	QUE	45
Henry	QUE	36
Isaac	CLN	79
John	KEN	91
John	QUE	33
Kitty	QUE	38
Lydia	QUE	15
William	KEN	103
William	QUE	32
KNOUFF, Greenbury		
	FRE	140
John	FRE	158
KNOWELL, Elizabeth	PRI	219
KNOWELS, John	TAL	37
KNOWF, Henry	FRE	83A
KNOWFEN, George	FRE	83
KNOWLAN (See also NOWLAND)		
Thomas	D.C.	45
KNOWLES, Ann	BCI	10
David W.	D.C.	32

KNOWLES (continued),		KRAFFT, Edwd. De (?)		KUHNS, Abraham	
Henry	D.C.31		D.C.85		FRE 171
John	BCI 40	William B.	D.C.41	Henry	FRE 171
John	D.C.31	KRAGER, Fred	BCI 510	Jacob	FRE 170
John	D.C.210	KRAMER, Andrew	ALL 27	KUM, Jacob	WAS 102
Thomas	D.C.31	Christian	BCI 495	KUMMER, Frederick	BCI 379
William	D.C.16	George	ALL 30	KUMP, Frederick	FRE 195
Wm., 2d.	D.C.32	KRAUSE, Jacob	WAS 104	KUMPS, Catherine	BCI 513
KNOX, Basil	BAL 66	John	WAS 115	KUNCLE, John	FRE 96
Charles	WOR 177	Peter	WAS 104	KUNE, Adam	WAS 63
Edwd.	WOR 178	KRAUSS, Barnard	CEC 178	Christian	WAS 63
Elijah	CHA 195	Leonard	CEC 178	John	WAS 64
Henry	ANN 377	KREAGER, Barbary		Newton (?)	D.C.176
Isaac	WOR 172		WAS 122	Peter	WAS 63
James	WOR 169	Barbary	WAS 123	KUNES, Joshua	QUE 34
John	ANN 367	Daniel	WAS 119	Ruthey	WAS 122
Joseph	FRE 124	Henry	WAS 122	KUNS, Nancey	WAS 122
Nehemiah	WOR 177	John	WAS 121	KUNSE, Peter	WAS 112
Reynolds	BCI 439	John	WAS 123	KUNTZ, Catharin	BAL 139
Sarah	D.C.66	Mariah	WAS 121	George	BCI 461
William	FRE 169	William	WAS 134	KURTZ (See also	
William	PRI 185	KREAGLOE, Jacob	FRE 171	KINTZ),	
Wm.	BCI 499	John	FRE 171	--- (Widaw)	BCI 375
KNULLY, George	WAS 122	KREBS, Samuel	BAL 193	Abraham	FRE 188
KNUP, Abraham	BCI 430	Wm.	BCI 492	Daniel	BCI 253
KNUT, Adam	BCI 402	KREIGH, Jacob	WAS 135	Daniel	D.C.59
KNUTT, John	BCI 496	KREMER, Frederick		David	D.C.33
KOCH, Catharine	FRE 175		BAL 208	Eliza	MON 140
KOLB, Daniel	FRE 96	Fredk.	BCI 309	Henry	D.C.116
David	FRE 163	KREMMER, Adam	FRE 81	John	BCI 458
Elizabeth	FRE 107	KREPPS, Christian	ALL 27	John	D.C.46
George	FRE 97	K[R]EPS, Michael (?)		John	FRE 183
Isaac	FRE 155		WAS 77	Michael	WAS 147
William	FRE 105	KREPS, George	BCI 84	Michl.	BCI 474
KOLENBURG, Frederick		Jacob	BCI 84	Peter	D.C.48
	FRE 70	Jacob	WAS 133	KUTH, Jas., Senr. (?)	
Henry	FRE 70	William	WAS 97		D.C.152
Justice	FRE 70	William	WAS 118	KYLE, Adam B.	BCI 352
KOLF (See also HOLF,		KRICK, Catherine	WAS 137	KYLER, Danl.	BCI 355
WOLF),		George	WAS 116		
Pressilla (?)	BAL 98	Jane	WAS 116		
KOLLINGER (See also		Sophia	WAS 116		
HOLLINGER),		KRIDLER, John	BAL 160		
Jacob (?)	ALL 11	KRIGH, Catherine	WAS 134[A]		
KOLLOCK, Samuel	BCI 310	Nicholas	WAS 134[A]	--- L ---	
KOME, Daniel	BCI 174	Philip	WAS 135		
KONIG, Elizabeth	BCI 125	KRIL, John G.	BCI 333	LABACH, Adelade	BCI 520
Fred	BCI 510	KRISE, Daniel	FRE 164	LABARD, Francis	BAL 108
George	BCI 496	Peter	FRE 146	LABARER, Nicholas	BCI 294
KONTZ, John	FRE 147	KRITLER, Jacob	FRE 140	LABE, Jacob	FRE 93
KOON, George	FRE 164	KRITZER, John	BCI 477	LABELLE, Lewis	D.C.12
KOONE, John	WAS 85	KROFT, Christ.	BCI 531	LABOO, Michael	TAL 52
KOONES, David	PRI 222	Jacob	BCI 534	LABOY, Thomas	BCI 150
Frederick	D.C.198	Michl.	BCI 520	LABROQUERE, Bernard	
KOONS, Madaline	BCI 521	William	BAL 198		BCI 239
KOONTZ, George	FRE 196	William	BAL 200	LACER, Elizabeth	SAI 98
Henry	ALL 17	KRONTZ, George	BAL 140	LACKEY, John	BCI 177
Henry	FRE 96	KROUSE, Ann	BCI 485	LACKLAND, Dennis	MON 130
Jacob	FRE 130	Jacob	BCI 495	George	MON 166
Jacob, Sen.	ALL 16	John	D.C.60	James	CEC 179
Jacob, Jr.	ALL 12	KRUG, Henrietta E.		James	MON 163
John	ALL 18		FRE 101	Nathan	CEC 162
John	FRE 80	KRUMER, Adam	BAL 192	LACKNAN, John	BCI 497
Magdalaine	FRE 196	KRUMPS, Danl.	BCI 497	LaCOMB, --- (Madam)	
Rebecca	ALL 26	KRUSE, George	BCI 505		BCI 518
KOPHER, Christopher	WAS 96	KUBY, Joseph (?)	KEN 107	LACY, Benj. H.	ALL 29
KOPLINGER, Michael	BCI 161	KUGLAR, John	FRE 172	Hanah	BCI 491
KOPP, Andrew	FRE 142	KUGN, Augustus	BCI 138	Joseph (?)	KEN 107
KORN, Henry	ALL 29	KUHN, Christian	FRE 158	LADD, John H.	D.C.182
KOROWFEN, George (?)		Elizabeth	FRE 205	Josh. B.	D.C.145
	FRE 83	Henry	FRE 103	LADDY, Nathan	KEN 94
KOUNZS, Mary	BCI 309	Henry, of Chris.		LADLOE, Joseph	BCI 88
KOUTZ, Elizabeth	BAL 160		FRE 158	LADY, Elizabeth	ALL 4
KOYL, David	BCI 517	John	FRE 187	Henry	WAS 95
KRABER, Martin	BCI 517	Zebulon	FRE 163	Wm.	BCI 414

LANE (continued),	
Susan	QUE 27
Thomas	BCI 136
Thomas	BCI 257
Thomas	PRI 206
Thomas	SOM 117
William	SOM 118
William P.	FRE 199
Zadock	CLN 112
LANG, Caty	QUE 17
Charlotte	BCI 62
Eleanor	D.C. 25
Eliza	QUE 15
John	BCI 220
William	D.C. 35
LANGDON, Chs.	QUE 2A
Elizth.	D.C. 160
Giles	CEC 179A
Peter	CEC 179A
William	BAL 110
William	CEC 179A
LANGFITT, Francis	DOR 63
Revel	DOR 63
LANGFORD, Charles	DOR 40
Frances	BCI 21
Jemima	BAL 111
Obediah	BAL 127
Sharlottee	DOR 39
LANGLEY, Athaneus	CHA 225
Battaniel	SAI 55
Charles	D.C. 132
Eleanor	CHA 221
George	D.C. 170
Henry	PRI 207
Hezah	D.C. 74
Hezekiah	BCI 73
Ignatius	SAI 53A
James	PRI 218
John	CHA 222
Lexers	SAI 90
Pilip	SAI 54
Walter	D.C. 130
Walter	SAI 55
William	PRI 211
William	SAI 56
LANGLY, Cornelius	PRI 224
LANGNEL, Asia (?)	DOR 32
LANGRALL, Job	DOR 42
LANGREL, Asia	DOR 32
LANGRELL, James	DOR 43
LANGSDALE, Elizabeth	SOM 108
Huet	SOM 113
Isabella	SOM 116
John	SOM 107
Joshua W.	SOM 110
LANGTON, Thos.	MON 131
LANHAM, Aquilla	MON 164
Bartheba	PRI 231
Cloe	PRI 227
Eleanor	MON 152
Elisha	D.C. 116
George	PRI 232
Georges H.	PRI 226
Henry W.	PRI 226
Horatio	PRI 225
Ignatius	PRI 214
John	D.C. 125
John	D.C. 178
John, Senr.	D.C. 149
Julia	PRI 226
Lewis	PRI 184
Lloyd	MON 152
Verlinda	D.C. 104
William	D.C. 81
William	FRE 80

LANHAM (continued),	
William	PRI 183
LANIUS, Jacob	BAL 87
LANK, Israel (f.n.)	SOM 120
Phillip (f.n.)	SOM 120
LANKFORD, Abram	SOM 145
Anny	SOM 153
Benjamin (of N.)	SOM 156
Betsy	SOM 153
Binjamin, Senr.	SOM 151
Coulbourn	SOM 151
David	SOM 144
Easter	SOM 154
Elijah	SOM 112
Esther	SOM 117
Henry	SOM 146
John	SOM 101A
John	SOM 124
John	SOM 142A
John	SOM 156
John P.	SOM 145
Jonah	SOM 127
Jonithin	WOR 203
Joshua	SOM 147
Josiah (?)	SOM 127
Killam	WOR 154
Stephen M.	SOM 142A
Thomas	SOM 154
Tubman	SOM 124
William	SOM 156
William H.	SOM 124
LANNAY, Peter	BCI 316
LANNUM, --- (Sarg.)	
(rendz.)	D.C. 4
Elisha	D.C. 47
LANNY, Lewis J. (l.?)	BAL 183
LANPHIER, Elizth.	D.C. 186
Robt.	D.C. 181
Willm.	D.C. 161
LANPONTIER, Lewis B.	BAL 183
LANSDALE, Cesar	MON 152
Charles	MON 163
Henry	MON 163
Isaac	MON 152
John	MON 158A
Wesley	MON 152
William M.	HAR 18
LANTERN, David	ANN 363
Elizabeth	MON 164
LANTHORN, George	WAS 107
LANTOR, Elijah	PRI 229
LANTZ, Christian	WAS 96
George	ALL 37
George	WAS 96
Henry	WAS 68
John	FRE 126
Margaret	ALL 36
Peter	ALL 36
Peter	FRE 202
Samuel	WAS 99
LANY, Laurence (?)	DOR 26
LANZ, Conrad	D.C. 18
LAPHAM, Oliver	D.C. 148
LAPHAN, Patk.	D.C. 153
LAPOLE, Val.	FRE 126
LAPOURAIL, Pier	BCI 341
LAPPING, Samuel	BCI 73
LAPY, David	WAS 93
LARABY, Danl.	BCI 405
LARACY, Michael	BCI 122
LARAMORE, James	ANN 254

La RARENTREE, J.	BCI 493
LARCUM, John	D.C. 93
LARD, Isaac	SOM 146
John	SOM 147
LAREW, James	BCI 242
John	WAS 147
LAREY, Mary	QUE 40
Philemon	CLN 93
LARIMORE, Nicholas	TAL 40
LARK, Greenbury	ANN 311
LARKEN, Will---	ANN 399
LARKIN, John	FRE 220
L. James	D.C. 30
Wm.	BCI 372
LARKINS, John	FRE 76A
John	WAS 62
LARKUM, William	BCI 99
LARMAN, James	FRE 148
LARMER, Martha	ANN 398
LARMORE, Jonah (?)	SOM 135
Josiah	SOM 135
LARMOUR, Elizabeth	SOM 109
Saml. B.	D.C. 164
LARMOURE, Ebbin	SOM 114
Elijah	SOM 114
James	SOM 113
John	SOM 114
Mary	SOM 113
Reuben	SOM 114
LARNDER, Saml.	D.C. 98
LARNED, Jas.	D.C. 75
LARNER, Bryan	MON 152
Michl.	D.C. 92
Thomas	D.C. 90
LAROUGE, Jno. M. (?)	BCI 232
LAROUNG, James	ANN 333
LAROUQE, Jno. M.	BCI 232
LARRIMORE, Alexander	TAL 26
Jacob	QUE 41
Jonathan	TAL 25
Robert	QUE 40
Robert	TAL 25
Thomas	CLN 87
Thomas	TAL 21
LARRY, Lawrence	DOR 26
LARSH, Charles	BAL 19
George	BAL 107
John	BCI 487
LARWOOD, Jacob	KEN 109
LARY, Joseph	KEN 107
LASAGE, Thomas	QUE 36
LASELL, William C.	KEN 102
LASHEAR, Elias	MON 152
Gassaway	MON 141
Henry	MON 141
Jacob	MON 141
Ruth	MON 142
LASHLEY, Arnold	MON 152
John	ALL 32
Robert	ALL 32
LASKEY, John	D.C. 116
LASLICK, Elizabeth	WAS 64
LASSLEE, George, Jun.	CEC 179
LASSLIE, George, Senr.	CEC 179A
LATCHEM, Isaiah	WOR 195
John K.	WOR 189
Joseph	WOR 196
LATE, Catharine	FRE 85
Elizabeth	FRE 85
George	FRE 159

LATE (continued),	LAVALEN, Jas. BCI 228	LAWSON (continued),
John FRE 85	LAVALL, --- (Colonel)	Isaac (of Hance) SOM 144
Michael FRE 85	D.C. 4	Isaac (of Saml.) SOM 150
LATEN, Nichols TAL 11	LAVE, Sarah (?) D.C. 65	James SOM 150
LATERODOUS, Joseph A.	LAVEILLE, Abriham CAL 51	Jas. MON 141
BAL 116	James CAL 41A	John D.C. 176
LATHAM, Joseph FRE 170	LAVELL, Joseph (Doc) (?)	Richd. BCI 172
Mathew SAI 79	D.C. 62	Samuel SOM 150
William SAI 78	LAVELY, Jacob FRE 210	Stepn. D.C. 213
LATHROM, Thomas SAI 91	John S. BCI 512	Thomas D.C. 28
LATHRUTH, --- (Mrs.)	LAVENDER, John R.	Thomas PRI 215
BCI 342	PRI [200]	William SOM 150
LATIMER, Archd. QUE 5	LAVIELLE, Uriah CAL 45	LAWTON, Jesse BCI 246
Catharine BCI 255	LAVIGNAC, Matthew BCI 73	LAWVER, Jacob WAS 101
Hannah E. CHA 202	LAVY, James BCI 2	LAWYER, Anna FRE 188
Henry QUE 2A	LAW, Adam D.C. 27	Casper FRE 188
Thomas CHA 201	Anthony BCI 443	Jacob FRE 188
Thomas PRI 222	Elijah WOR 203	John FRE 188
Walter CHA 207A	G. William CEC 141	LAY, Richard D.C. 52
LATIMORE, James BCI 277	Hannah FRE 172	LAYFIELD, Betsy SOM 124
LATIN, James WOR 218	James BCI 513	Ezekiel SOM 124
LATONRAUDER, Josa. A.	John D.C. 94	George SOM 123
BCI 283	Thomas PRI 238	Isaac WOR 158
LATOUR, John BCI 509	LAWDER, Benjamin BAL 108	James SOM 123
LATOURAUDAIS, Elijah	LAWELL, J. BCI 395	Jesse SOM 110
ANN 397	LAWN, Edwd. BCI 194	John SOM 125
LATOURAUDER, Josa. A. (?)	LAWRANCE, John CAL 59	Robert SOM 111
BCI 283	John QUE 28	Saul WOR 205
LATOURNAU, J. (I.?) B. M.	John S. (Capt.) FRE 214	Sollimon WOR 203
BCI 48	LAWRASON, Elizth. D.C. 205	Thomas SOM 126
LATSHAW, Wm. BCI 507	James D.C. 205	Thomas SOM 131
LATTIMER, John D.C. 63	LAWRENCE, Adam FRE 134	William WOR 212
Sylvester ALL 30	Charles KEN 92	William; S. WOR 202
LATTIN, Thomas P. ANN 254	David WAS 148	LAYMAN, Elizabeth CHA 208
LATTY, Joseph BCI 3	Elijah BCI 125	George BCI 534
LATURITE, John P. D.C. 163	George W. CAL 58A	Jacob BCI 532
LAUB, John D.C. 47	Hammond (?) ANN 369	Jacob FRE 161
LAUBINGER, George M.	Jacob FRE 134	John MON 142
ALL 36	James BAL 223	Joshua BAL 205
LAUDEMAN, Frederick	James W. CAL 62	Nicholas BAL 184
BCI 56	John D.C. 11	LAYN, James KEN 110
LAUDENSLAGER, George	Joseph D.C. 23	LAYNE, John CLN 91
BAL 17	Mary CEC 161	LAYPOLE, John WAS 146
LAUDER, William HAR 23	Moses ANN 312	LAYPORT, John ALL 12
LAUDERMAN, George BAL 51	Peter BCI 6	LAYTON, Andrew O.
LAUDERSLAGLE, Frances	Richard BCI 13	TAL 48
BAL 165	Richard BCI 239	Asher MON 141
Solomon BAL 149	Richard PRI 239	Asher, of Uriah MON 174
LAUDUBAUGH, John WAS 98	Robert BCI 11	Daniel CLN 78
LAUGHLIN, Jonathan ANN 255	Sarah BCI 34	Daniel DOR 62
LAUGHRY, Mary HAR 41	LAWRENCES, John-	James DOR 60
LAUNAN, M. BCI 216	plantatn. D.C. 214	Peter DOR 61
LAURANCE, Francis ANN 329	LAWRENSON, Philip	Thomas CLN 110
John SAI 63	BCI 272	Uriah MON 141
John, Jun. SAI 63	LAWREY, Henry WAS 102	William DOR 41
Patsy SAI 63	James CEC 162	LAZENBY, Cephas MON 152
LAURENCE, Calib ANN 369	John CEC 162	James MON 152
Hammond ANN 369	Robert CEC 162	LEA, Charles BCI 297
Jas. D.C. 127	LAWRY, Mary D.C. 9	Joshua (?) BAL 95
John D.C. 164	LAWS, Elijah of Wm. WOR 216	Susannah BAL 199
John M. ALL 30	John SOM 134	LEACH, Ann BCI 8
Joseph BCI 92	Joshua D.C. 170	Ann QUE 40
Joseph SAI 88	Joshua WOR 217	Benjamin BAL 80
Larkin ANN 369	Robert SOM 108	Elizabeth SAI 76
Nathan SOM 104	Robert SOM 137	Henry BCI 25
Otho WAS 114	Thos. CAL 48	Hetty SOM 152
Ruth BCI 75	William; S. WOR 216	James HAR 8
Sarah BCI 93	William M. CEC 124	John ANN 368
Thomas R. ANN 267	LAWSER, Walter BCI 355	John BCI 202
Upton WAS 118	LAWSON, --- (?) BCI 404	John D.C. 106
William BCI 450	Charles CEC 162	John SAI 54
William SAI 98	Edward BAL 152	Mary D.C. 162
LAURIE, James D.C. 76	Elijah SOM 144	Moses D.C. 89
LAUS, Isaac H. WOR 186	Hance SOM 150	Peggy SOM 153
James WOR 195	Henrietta CHA 207	Philemon D.C. 56
LAVALA, M. BCI 216	Henry (?) BCI 273	Ralph ANN 359

LEACH (continued),		
Samuel	SAI	55
Susan	D.C.	124
Susana	SAI	76
Thomas	ANN	269
Thomas	BCI	159
Thomas	PRI	182
Thomas O.	TAL	13
William	PRI	203
William	SAI	74
LEADAN, John	ANN	382
LEADDY, Sandy	BCI	415
LEADEE, John	BCI	439
LEADLY, Jacob	BCI	487
LEAF, John	BAL	195
LEAFF, Jonsey	BCI	19
LEAGUE, Ann	BCI	251
Luke	BCI	134
William	BCI	227
LEAGUR, Benjamin	BCI	110
LEAK, Joseph	D.C.	68
Reasin	PRI	227
LEAKE, Adam	BCI	300
Saml.	BCI	306
Samuel	BCI	304
LEAKEN, Andw. T.	BCI	173
Thos. J.	BCI	173
LEAKIN, Danl.	FRE	122
John	FRE	122
Margarett	FRE	122
Sheppard C.	BCI	48
LEAKY, John	DOR	49
LEAMANS, Thos.	BCI	180
LEAMMON, Electious	BAL	141
LEANHART, --- (Mrs.)		
	BCI	435
LEAP, Jacob	D.C.	146
LEAPELY, George	FRE	83
LEAR, B. L.	D.C.	9
LEARNED, Joseph D.	BCI	260
LEARS (See also SEARS),		
James	BCI	248
LEARY, Andw.	D.C.	148
Jas. P.	QUE	15
Peter	BCI	45
LEASE, Abraham	BCI	79
George	FRE	105
Henry	FRE	76A
Jacob	FRE	73
Jacob, Jr.	FRE	76A
Nicholas	FRE	105
Philip	FRE	203
William	FRE	76A
LEASER, John	FRE	74
LEASHER, Leash	WAS	98
LEATH, Saml.	BCI	500
LEATHBURY, John	WOR	195
LEATHER, George	FRE	109
John, Sr.	FRE	86
John, Jr.	FRE	86
LEATHERBURY, Asa	SOM	106
James (f.n.)	SOM	119
Jolly W.	SOM	141
Levin	SOM	137
Lidia	KEN	103
Robert	SOM	141
Samuel	SOM	137
LEATHERMAN, Danl.		
	FRE	129
Frederick	FRE	157
Godphrey	FRE	129
Henry	FRE	107
John	FRE	154
Joseph	FRE	144
Peter	FRE	130
LEATHERWOOD, John		
	ALL	10A
John	BCI	225
Mary	ANN	320
Saml.	FRE	210
LEATHRLAND, Wm.	CAL	42
LEATTO, John	BCI	465
LEAVERTON,, John	TAL	49
LEBER, Christian	D.C.	6
LEBON, Lewis	BCI	222
LEBRANTHWAIT, James A.		
	BCI	46
LEBRUN, Solomon	BCI	66
LECATES, James	WOR	192
LECHE, David	BCI	245
Le CHEMINANT, Nicholas		
	BCI	296
LECKRONE, Jacob	WAS	95
Jacob	WAS	99
John	WAS	105
LECLAR, George	BCI	465
LECOMPT, Jas.	WOR	169
McKerrnny	WOR	153
Wm.	WOR	169
LECOMPTE, B. W.	DOR	4
Ben	DOR	60
Benjamin	DOR	39
Caleb	DOR	12
Charles	DOR	44
Charles	DOR	45
Charles	DOR	52
Charles B.	DOR	54
Daniel	DOR	6
Edmand	DOR	34
Edward	DOR	11
Hugh	DOR	9
James	DOR	50
John	DOR	12
Joseph	DOR	7
Joseph	DOR	45
Joseph	DOR	51
Joseph T.	DOR	16
Lee	DOR	6
Moses	DOR	51
Peter	DOR	7
Philemon	CLN	95
Risdon	DOR	12
Samuel	CLN	92
Samuel	DOR	4
Samuel	DOR	42
Samuel	DOR	45
Stephen	DOR	44
Thomas	DOR	3
Thomas	DOR	63
William	DOR	55
William W.	DOR	49
LECOUMT, --- (Mrs.)		
	BCI	396
LECTOR, Chs.	BCI	519
LEDDON, Benjn.	BCI	166
Perry	BCI	184
LEDENHAM, Edward	TAL	4
Garrison	TAL	25
John	TAL	22
Joseph	TAL	10
Noah	TAL	4
Sally	TAL	22
Shadrach	TAL	24
LEDLEY, Isaac	BAL	121
LEDNUM, Ignatius	CLN	88
LEDRINGER, Henry (?)		
	BAL	217
LEDRUM, Ignatius	CLN	88
LEDSINGER, Elizabeth		
of Gow.	BAL	109
Elizabeth of Wm.	BAL	109
LEDSINGER (continued),		
Henry	BAL	217
Joseph	BAL	215
LEDWIDGE, John	FRE	229
LEE, --- (Mrs.)	BCI	337
Abraham	BCI	116
Allen	KEN	118
Amos	QUE	5
Basil	MON	152
Benedict	BCI	473
Benjamin	PRI	201
Caesar-Negro	HAR	80
Charles	ANN	307
Charles	CEC	179A
Charles	DOR	40
Charles	DOR	59
Charles (Mount)	FRE	145
Charles G.	SAI	88
Charles H.	WAS	110
Christopher	KEN	106A
Daniel	MON	152
David	CEC	179
David	D.C.	120
David	HAR	38
Draper	DOR	11
E.	BCI	398
Edmd. J. (I.?)	D.C.	192
Edward	HAR	76
Elias & Saml. R.		
BIDDLE	BAL	113
Eliza	BCI	521
Elizabeth	HAR	46
Elizabeth	MON	164
Elizabeth	TAL	35
Emanuel-Negro	HAR	49
Frederick	ALL	4
Gabl.-f.c.p.	HAR	11
Geo.	D.C.	121
Geo. W.	D.C.	80
George	BAL	165
George	BAL	183
George	BCI	171
George	CEC	140
Harry	DOR	46
Henry	DOR	3
Jacob	ALL	4
Jacob	BCI	52
Jacob	BCI	143
James	ALL	4
James	BAL	37
James	BAL	106
James	BCI	53
James	CAL	67
James	D.C.	172
James	HAR	8
James	HAR	72
James	MON	152
James	MON	167
Jan M.	BCI	356
Jno.	FRE	124
Joanna	D.C.	114
Jobe	CEC	140
John	ALL	4
John	BCI	50
John	BCI	63
John	CEC	141
John	D.C.	177
John	MON	131
John	QUE	9
John	TAL	35
John (of Wm.)	BAL	4
Joseph	DOR	22
Joseph	SAI	97
Joshua	BAL	59
Joshua	BAL	95
Judia	BAL	165

LEE (continued),		LEFEVER, Christiana		LEKINS, Dennis	FRE 222	
K--- (?)	DOR 57		WAS 83	LELLY, Sarah (?)	BCI 452	
Lancastee	PRI 239	David	CEC 140	LELOUP, Lewis Francis		
Lancaster	PRI 239	George	WAS 83		BCI 316	
Levi	TAL 48	John	FRE 141	Le MATE, Renang	BCI 51	
Levi	WAS 69	LEFLER, Geo.	BCI 323	Le MILLARD, Joseph		
Lloyd	HAR 8	LEGARD, Joseph	BCI 197		BCI 54	
Louis	D.C. 191	LEGARE, John	D.C. 121	LEMISON, Richard	FRE 156	
Margaret	ANN 271	LEGG, Basil	QUE 29	LEMMON, Alexis	BAL 107	
Marshall	HAR 28	Benjamin	KEN 85	George	HAR 60	
Mary	BCI 243	Eli	D.C. 217	Martha	D.C. 38	
Minte	D.C. 113	Harris	QUE 45	Mosses	BAL 164	
Mitaway-Negro	HAR 80	John C.	QUE 45	Nancy	SOM 108	
N.	BCI 411	John C., Jnr.	QUE 45	Peter	BAL 235	
Nancy	BCI 518	Lemuel	QUE 48	Richard	BAL 191	
Nancy	D.C. 188	Matthew	QUE 48	Richard	BCI 436	
Nancy	D.C. 204	Moses	QUE 36	Sarah	BCI 302	
Parker H.	HAR 46	Richard	QUE 33	Thomas	BAL 154	
Peter	D.C. 131	Ruthy	QUE 41	Thomas	SAI 79	
Philip	BCI 425	Samuel	QUE 33	LEMMOND, Susannah		
Philip	D.C. 55	Silas	KEN 94		BAL 193	
Phylis	D.C. 188	William	ANN 269	LEMMONS, Eliza	MON 171	
Rachael	BAL 57	William	QUE 45	LEMON, Elizabeth	BAL 25	
Ralph	HAR 39	LEGGETT, Jerremiah		Nicholas	FRE 186	
Ralph S.	HAR 6		WAS 60	Rebecca	FRE 187	
Rebecca	D.C. 169	Sarah	WAS 61	LEMOND, John	WAS 137	
Richard	QUE 48	LEGH, Margart	BCI 475	LEMONS, John	BCI 115	
Richard D.	HAR 46	LEGO, Spencer	HAR 7	LEMORE, Christn.	MON 178	
Richd. B.	D.C. 118	LEGORE, Jacob	FRE 211	L'ENFANT, P. Chas.		
Richd. H.	D.C. 173	LEGRAND, Samuel D.			PRI 228	
Robert	WOR 161		BCI 98	LENMAN, Isaiah	D.C. 14	
Robert	WOR 154	LEHAULT, Joseph	D.C. 20	LENNARD, Mary	BCI 283	
Samuel	ANN 296	LEHAY, John	BCI 34	LENNIX, --- (Widaw)		
Samuel	BCI 463	Morris	BCI 58		BCI 387	
Samuel	CEC 179A	LEIDY, Henry	WAS 101	LENOX, Peter	D.C. 83	
Samuel	D.C. 12	LEIGH, Elizabeth	SAI 53A	Richd.	BCI 169	
Sarah	D.C. 132	Elizabeth	SAI 54	LEOHR, Frederick	FRE 102	
Sarah	DOR 5	Jacob	SAI 56	George	FRE 97	
Stephen	ANN 275	Jeremiah	SAI 64	LEONARD, --- (Mrs.)		
Susana (Mrs.)	BCI 357	John	SAI 75		BCI 337	
Susanna	BCI 134	Joseph	SAI 67	Amey (f.n.)	SOM 119	
Thomas	ANN 317	Lewis	SAI 81	Benjamine	SOM 106	
Thomas	BAL 59	Nicho.	BCI 473	Daniel	TAL 21	
Thomas	DOR 6	Philip	SAI 56	Ebenezer	WOR 205	
Thomas	DOR 15	LEIGHT, Barhart B.		Eleanor	TAL 19	
Thomas	HAR 45		WAS 97	Eusibius?	TAL 49	
Thomas	TAL 32	Benjamin	WAS 118	Geo.	QUE 6	
Vincent	QUE 10	Catherine	WAS 123	Henry	TAL 40	
William	ALL 38	John	WAS 120	Isaac	SOM 103	
William	BAL 37	LEIGHTER, Abraham		Jacob	WAS 116	
William	CEC 124		WAS 134	John	D.C. 86	
William	D.C. 15	Abraham	WAS 135	Jonathan	TAL 37	
William D.	HAR 46	Andrew	WAS 96	Jonathan	TAL 51	
William T.	SAI 88	Henry	WAS 74	Joseph	WOR 207	
Wm.	FRE 124	Jacob	WAS 96	Joseph, Senr.	SOM 110	
Wm.	QUE 5	John	WAS 101	Joshua	SOM 118	
Wm., Senr.	QUE 20	Joseph	WAS 73	Joshua	TAL 19	
LEECH, Azel	CHA 223	Juliana	WAS 97	Jseph	TAL 8	
Elizabeth	CHA 223	Samuel	WAS 97	Macy	BCI 430	
Jesse	MON 159	LEILUK, John (?)	D.C. 67	Margaret	TAL 20	
John	CEC 141	LEINGELER, Mary	BCI 274	Nathan	TAL 8	
LEEDS, James	BCI 466	LEIPY, George	BAL 9	Richard	FRE 86	
LEEF, Henry	BAL 15	LEISTER, Abraham	BAL 7	Samuel, Ovsr.	TAL 4	
LEEK, Henry	MON 140	Conrod	FRE 195	Stephen	ALL 30	
Jesse	MON 139	David	FRE 194	Thomas	TAL 4	
John	MON 140	John	FRE 193	William	CEC 141	
Saml.	MON 162	LEISURE, John	ANN 375	William	TAL 36	
Samuel	MON 152	Richard	ANN 375	William A.	TAL 49	
LEEKE, Nicholas	BCI 15	LEITCH, Benja.	CAL 51	Woolman	TAL 8	
LEEKINS, Joshua (?)	BCI 410	Eliza.	CAL 62	LEONI, Gaspar	BCI 79	
William	FRE 209	James	CAL 66A	LEONOX, John	FRE 212	
LEESIER, Daniel	FRE 132	John	CAL 58A	LEOPARD, Jacob	WAS 147	
Zack	FRE 132	Mary	CAL 58A	LEPELLIER, Francis	BCI 321	
LEESON, John	BCI 306	LEITH, John	CLN 82	LEPO, John	WAS 134[A]	
LEESTON, Gracy	BCI 430	LEIZER, Jonathan	WAS 104	LEPOARD, Adam	WAS 116	
LEEWIS, Jerem.	MON 176	LEIZURE, John	ALL 25	LEPOLD, Philip	WAS 74	

LEPPO, Catharine	FRE 191	LEWIS (continued),		LEWIS (continued),	
Jacob	BAL 22	Abra J.	BCI 493	Robt.	D.C.209
Le PREUX, Lewis	D.C.15	Abraham	ANN 328	Ruben	DOR 28
LEPT, Christopher (?)		Abraham	BAL 184	Saml.	D.C.74
	BAL 65	Abriah	QUE 48	Samuel	ANN 312
LEREW, James	BCI 189	Ann	BCI 9	Samuel	CEC 179
LERMIN, John	KEN 115	Ann	KEN 93	Samuel	D.C.3
LERNED, Sarah	FRE 125	Benedick	FRE 83A	Samuel	FRE 220
LERRIE, Allen (?)	PRI 228	Catherine	D.C.71	Solomon	WOR 191
LERRY, Thomas	BCI 93	Daniel	PRI [200]	Stephen	MON 175
Le SOURD, John	HAR 61	Duncan	BAL 25	Susanna	MON 160
Joseph	HAR 61	Edward	CEC 125	Thomas	BAL 112
LESSONBY, John	QUE 13	Edwd.	D.C.117	Thomas	CEC 162
LESTER, Mary	BAL 184	Elisha	DOR 10	Thomas	MON 152
LESURD, Daniel	BAL 86	Elizabeth	BAL 188	Thomas	PRI 218
John	BAL 85	Elizabeth	BCI 85	Washington	FRE 73
Peter	BAL 87	Erastus	DOR 21	Wheeler	CHA 195
LETCHAN, Christ.	BCI 519	Fredercik?	D.C.16	William	BAL 230
LETHERBERY, Ann	KEN 120	Frederick	D.C.16	William	WAS 120
LETHERBURY, Pere	QUE 20	George	BAL 197	Willm.	D.C.204
LETHERWOOD, John	BAL 65	George	BCI 350	Willoughby	BCI 137
LETSINGER, Wm.	BCI 526	Harry	CHA 207B	LEYPOLD, Fredk.	BCI 252
LETT, Judy	WAS 65	Henry	DOR 29	LEYSTER, Daniel	BAL 155
Obediah	ANN 369	Henry	WAS 114	LEYTH, Polly	BCI 446
LETTER, Thomas	BCI 154	Hooper	DOR 41	LIAS, James	KEN 100
LETTICE, Mary	BCI 427	Isaac	BAL 127	LIAUTIEN, Lawrance	
LETTON, Brice	MON 167	Isaac	WOR 201		BCI 188
LEUSARE, Nathan	QUE 38	Isaiah	DOR 41	LIAVIS, William	BAL 239
LEVALLEN, John	ALL 13	J. N.	BCI 383	LIBBY, Richd.	D.C.159
LEVELEY, John	BAL 69	Jacob	CLN 82	LICHLITER, Henry	FRE 113
LEVELY, Elizabeth	BCI 82	James	BCI 136	LICHTENWALTER, Abraham	
LEVER, Henry	D.C.33	James	BCI 412		FRE 168
LEVERAGE, Benajah	CEC 124	James	QUE 49	LICKLIGHTER, Coonrad	
LEVERING, Aaron	BCI 485	James-Negro	HAR 79		FRE 162
Aaron R.	D.C.35	James, Jnr.	QUE 49	George	FRE 224
Enoch	BCI 437	Jas.	D.C.109	LICKLITER, Peter	ALL 30
Jessee	BCI 437	Jeremiah	DOR 63	Peter	FRE 117
John	BCI 485	Jesse	BAL 186	LIDAMOR, Edward	SAI 56
Nath.	BCI 355	Jobe	DOR 21	LIDAY, James	WAS 145
Thos.	D.C.93	John	BCI 181	LIDDARD, Moses	BAL 112
LEVERKNICHT, Christian (?)		John	BCI 312	LIDDY, John	BCI 464
	WAS 150	John	BCI 343	LIDERSTICK, Elizabeth	
LEVERTON, Andrew	QUE 7	John	DOR 41		WAS 107
Daniel	CLN 104A	John	FRE 124	LIDEY, Samuel	ALL 9
Isaac	QUE 33	John	MON 152	LIDIARD, John	ANN 380
Jacob	CLN 111	John	MON 175	LIDIE, Jacob	FRE 155
James	CLN 96	John	PRI 228	Judith	FRE 156
Jessee	CLN 104A	Joseph	KEN 124	Margaret C.	FRE 156
Moses	CLN 88	Joseph	MON 152	LIEATIRD, Dennis	BCI 484
Thomas	TAL 46	Joshua	MON 152	LIELUK, John	D.C.67
LEVI, Ann	CHA 227	Levi	BCI 311	LIEN, W.	BCI 354
Jos.	BCI 349	Levin (See Major		LIGGETT, James	WAS 56
Lazarus	BCI 68	& Levin LEWIS-		John	BCI 96
Theodore	CHA 224	N.C.)	DOR 40	LIGHT, Mary	DOR 54
LEVINGSTON, Benjamin		Levin (Guined?)	DOR 40	Thomas	DOR 54
	WOR 215	Levin (Gurnid)	DOR 40	William	BCI 296
George	WOR 214	Lewis D.	BCI 173	LIGHTBODDY, John	BCI 135
James	SOM 110	Lucy	BCI 434	LIGHTER, Barbary	WAS 96
LEVIRTON, Isaac	DOR 64	Major & Levin-N.C.		Henry	FRE 110
LEVIS, William	D.C.36		DOR 40	LIGHTFOOT, Ann	D.C.202
LEVRIE, Allen	PRI 228	Mannen	DOR 41	LIGHTHISER, Henry	
LEVY, --- (Mrs.)	BCI 381	Margarett	CLN 115		BAL 197
Andrew	BCI 66	Margaretta	WAS 125	Joshua	BAL 196
David	FRE 215	Mary	QUE 49	LIGHTNER, George	CEC 141
John	HAR 20	Mathew	DOR 29	Isaac	FRE 221
Leonard	FRE 95	Nathan	MON 152	Isaac F.	BCI 178
LEW, Ann	CEC 140	Nicholas	CEC 162	James	FRE 114
LEWES, John	WOR 204	Philip	ANN 376	Jno.	BCI 190
Joseph	WOR 201	Philip	BCI 182	Jno.	BCI 197
Levi	WOR 200	Phillip	FRE 154	Nathl.	CEC 179
LEWIN, John	HAR 77	Rachel	ANN 300	LILBURN, Robert	SAI 54
LEWIS, --- (Major) (?)		Rebecca	QUE 49	LILIS, Paterick	WAS 139
(See Major & Levin		Richard	BCI 110	LILLE, John (?)	D.C.27
LEWIS-N.C.)	DOR 40	Robert	CLN 74	LILLEY, Henry	CEC 162
Aaron	DOR 37	Robert	CEC 124	Joseph	ALL 21
Abel	DOR 30	Robert	WOR 201	Joseph	D.C.6

147

LONG (continued),		
Ann	HAR 60	
Ann	WOR 158	
Arth.	BCI 342	
Catharin	WAS 144	
Charles	SAI 91	
Charles	SAI 93	
Christian	BAL 149	
Christiana	FRE 190	
Clawson	ALL 31	
Conrad	ALL 22	
Conrad	BAL 149	
Cornelius B.	BCI 48	
Coulbourn	SOM 117	
Daniel	WAS 110	
David	D.C. 72	
David	WAS 139	
David, Senr.	WOR 154	
David, Junr.	WOR 153	
Duke	SOM 131	
Elisa S. (Mrs.)	CAL 47	
Elizabeth	BCI 124	
Elizabeth	PRI 238	
Elizabeth	WOR 179	
Ester	ANN 359	
Ester	ANN 360	
Fredk.	D.C. 158	
George	ANN 305	
George	ANN 361	
George	FRE 164	
Henry	BCI 181	
Henry	BCI 214	
Henry	DOR 12	
Henry	FRE 164	
Henry K.	SOM 133	
Isaac	WAS 85	
Isaac, Jun.	WAS 83	
Jacob	FRE 214	
Jacob	WAS 70	
Jacob	WAS 83	
James	SAI 92	
Jeremiah	SAI 91	
Jesse	SOM 140	
Jesse	WOR 153	
John	ANN 327	
John	CHA 207A	
John	D.C. 95	
John	SAI 88	
John	WAS 84	
John	WAS 110	
John, Senr.	FRE 124	
John of Jere	SAI 97	
John W.	WOR 154	
Jos.	BCI 337	
Joseph	WAS 79	
Joseph	WAS 83	
Joseph M.	SAI 89	
Josias	SAI 89	
Josseph	SAI 89	
Kennedy	BCI 465	
Leah	SOM 128	
Levin	WOR 156	
Limas (f.n.)	SOM 119	
Littleton	SOM 140	
Ludwick	BAL 149	
Martin	FRE 190	
Mary	BCI 8	
Mary	BCI 156	
Mary A.	SAI 89	
Peter	BAL 219	
Peter	BAL 229	
Peter	FRE 211	
Peter	WAS 110	
Philip	ALL 22	
Richard	BCI 130	
Richard	KEN 105	

LONG (continued),		
Robert C.	BCI 392	
Sally	WOR 153	
Saml.	WOR 173	
Samuel	BCI 158	
Samuel	FRE 191	
Samuel	SOM 156	
Samuel	TAL 33	
Samuel	WAS 112	
Sarah	CHA 207A	
Sewal	SOM 123	
Sophia	CLN 97	
Susannah	BCI 78	
Thomas	BCI 47	
Thomas	BCI 128	
Thomas, Sen.	SAI 96	
Tubman K.	CAL 54	
William	CEC 179	
William	FRE 143	
William	SOM 137	
William	SOM 156	
William	TAL 37	
William	WAS 98	
Zadock	SOM 128	
LONGANAKER, David		
	WAS 144	
LONGDON, John	D.C. 163	
LONGFELLOW, Gidion		
	CEC 124	
John	CLN 78	
Nathan	QUE 13	
William	KEN 87	
LONGLEY, John	BCI 318	
William	BAL 13	
LONGLY, Samuel	BAL 176	
LONGMAN, Jacob	FRE 132	
John	WAS 71	
Joseph	WAS 71	
LONGPOINT, Nancy		
	DOR 60	
LONGSWERTH, Lucey		
	BAL 68	
LONGSWORTH, Basil		
	FRE 75	
Saml.	FRE 211	
LONGUE, Joshua (?)		
	BAL 8	
LONGWELL, Thomas		
	BAL 190	
LOOCKEBAUGH, Henry		
	WAS 99	
LOOCKERMAN, Jacob		
	TAL 8A	
Lydia	CLN 87	
Richard	CLN 114	
LOOKABAUGH, John		
	BAL 165	
Peter	BAL 158	
Peter	BAL 165	
LOOKART, John (?)		
	BAL 43	
LOOKENBEAL, Peter		
	FRE 196	
LOOKINBEEL, Saml.		
	FRE 210	
LOOKINGBEEL, John		
	FRE 214	
LOOKINGLAND, David (?)		
	FRE 155	
LOOKINGLAUD, David		
	FRE 155	
LOOMAN, Elizabeth	ALL 24	
LOONDER, Lucy	ANN 296	
LOOPER, James	KEN 119	
LOOS, Jacob	BAL 177	
LOPER, Anthony	QUE 14	

LORANCE, Thos.	BCI 386	
LORD, Adam	DOR 52	
Andrew	BCI 85	
Andrew	CLN 107	
Aron	SOM 150	
Betty	SOM 146	
Cratcher	CLN 73	
Erasm A.	BCI 536	
Frans. B.	D.C. 95	
Henry	DOR 62	
Jesse	SOM 139	
Lenard	DOR 60	
M.	BCI 406	
Stephen	SOM 149	
Thomas	SOM 149	
LORE, Andrew	FRE 195	
LORIMER, --- (Widow)		
	FRE 168	
David	FRE 168	
LORMAN, William	BCI 111	
LORO, Adam	FRE 195	
LORRANCE, John	BCI 465	
LORRETT, Joseph	CEC 141	
LORSHBAUGH, Elizabeth		
	WAS 119	
John	WAS 119	
LORTON, Elizabeth	ANN 308	
LORTY, Sarah	SAI 62A	
LORY, Francis	BCI 321	
Peter	BCI 319	
LOTHER, Moris.	BCI 491	
LOTHERS, William	ANN 349	
LOTZ, Henry	BCI 14	
LOUDERMAN, Ann	BCI 64	
LOUDESLAGER, Henry		
	WAS 89	
John	WAS 89	
LOUDON, Peter	D.C. 180	
LOUGUE, Joshua	BAL 8	
LOUIE, Eliza	FRE 135	
Peter	FRE 106	
LOUIS, Samuel	FRE 228	
LOURER, John	WAS 79	
LOUROR, John	WAS 111	
LOURY, Samuel	CEC 141	
William	CEC 141	
LOVDAY, Esther	TAL 7	
Nicholas	TAL 13	
Thomas S.	TAL 10	
LOVE, Bennet	HAR 40	
George	BCI 18	
Jacob	CEC 179	
James	BCI 478	
John	BCI 175	
John	D.C. 104	
John	HAR 41	
John	TAL 45	
Margaret	HAR 40	
Peregrine	BCI 49	
Philip	BAL 151	
Robert	CEC 179	
Samuel	CEC 179	
Samuel	CEC 179	
Samuel C.	CHA 204	
Sarah	D.C. 65	
Solomon	TAL 5	
Thomas	BAL 91	
William	HAR 38	
William	TAL 13	
LOVEALL, Enoch	BAL 151	
Jahu	BAL 156	
Luther	BAL 149	
Susan	BAL 149	
LOVEDAY, Charles	TAL 51	
LOVEGROVE, James	BCI 247	

LOVEJAY, Zedekiah (?)	D.C.56	
LOVEJOY, John	D.C.81	
Zedekiah	D.C.56	
LOVELACE, Elijah	MON 164	
John	CHA 213	
Samuel	CHA 213	
William	PRI 238	
LOVELESS, Basil	PRI 227	
Ignatious	PRI 231	
Thomas H.	PRI 207	
William	D.C.20	
LOVELL, Joseph	D.C.4	
Joseph (Doc)	D.C.62	
Sarah	BCI 311	
Wm.	BCI 254	
Wm.	BCI 415	
Wm., Jur.	BCI 415	
LOVELY, William	D.C.49	
LOVERING, Will.	D.C.101	
LOVERKNICHT, Christian (?)	WAS 150	
LOVETT, Jonas	ALL 12	
LOVITT, John	BCI 256	
LOVMAN, William	BCI 266	
LOVYER, Hugh	WAS 90	
LOW, --- (Capt.)	BCI 339	
Alley	MON 133	
Ann (?)	CEC 140	
Anne	MON 143	
Asel	BAL 81	
Bennet	PRI 196	
David	BAL 13	
Elijah	WOR 206	
Elizabeth	BCI 57	
Elizabeth	PRI 197	
George	WAS 133	
Hendersan P.	BCI 449	
John	BAL 13	
John	FRE 75	
John	WAS 67	
John W.	MON 171	
Joseph	BAL 203	
Joshua	ANN 352	
Joshua	BAL 87	
Margaret	BCI 112	
Nathaniel	PRI 196	
Nehemiah	MON 176	
Nicholas	BAL 12	
Thomas	CEC 162	
Thomas	PRI 197	
LOWDENSLYGER, Jacob	BCI 35	
LOWDERBAUGH, Conrad	ALL 29	
LOWE, Aaron	QUE 27	
Abrlham	CAL 49	
Arther	DOR 50	
Barbara	D.C.111	
Celia	FRE 140	
Charles	DOR 58	
Christiana	D.C.206	
Christlana	FRE 100	
Elizabeth	CEC 179A	
Henry	FRE 99	
Henry	QUE 25	
Isaac	DOR 49	
Isaac of I. (J.?)	DOR 64	
Isabella	FRE 105	
James	DOR 58	
Jas.	D.C.167	
Jeremh.	D.C.105	
John	DOR 5	
John	SOM 106	
John M.	FRE 99	
Joshua	CEC 179A	
Judah	TAL 34	
LOWE (continued),		
Loyard M.	PRI 232	
Loyd M.	D.C.78	
Mary	FRE 104	
Michael	ANN 317	
Nichs.	D.C.75	
Nichs.	D.C.76	
Patrlck	FRE 140	
Ralph	SOM 105	
S. P.	D.C.113	
Samuel	SOM 101A	
Solomon	TAL 14	
Thos.	D.C.187	
William	DOR 50	
William	FRE 212	
William	TAL 27	
William G.	DOR 62	
Willm.	D.C.187	
Wrightson	TAL 26	
LOWER, Sarah A.	D.C.149	
LOWERY, Jacob	QUE 25	
Margarett	QUE 49	
Samuel	QUE 47	
LOWES, Tubman	SOM 113	
LOWMAN, Emory	BAL 123	
Jacob	MON 172	
Jacob	WAS 81	
Jacob	WAS 86	
James	WAS 110	
John	ANN 341	
John	FRE 210	
John	MON 172	
John	WAS 86	
Michl.	D.C.128	
Reason	ANN 333	
LOWN, Elizabeth	WAS 124A	
LOWNDES, Francis	D.C.22	
LOWNDS, Ann	PRI 195	
Richard T.	PRI 192	
LOWNS, John	WAs 133	
John	WAS 134[A]	
Joseph	ANN 351	
LOWREY, Henry	WAS 115	
John	WAS 106	
Robert	BCI 247	
Solomon	WAS 127A	
LOWRY, Agness	BCI 221	
Allen	D.C.83	
Herculas	D.C.29	
James	SOM 117	
James	TAL 25	
John	BCI 111	
Joseph	TAL 26	
Margarett	TAL 34A	
Mary Ann	D.C.50	
Salvadire	BCI 223	
William (Colo.)	BCI 271	
Willm.	D.C.103	
LOWS, Bella	SOM 138	
LOWSS, Ann	SOM 108	
LOX, Alexander	BCI 502	
Jacob	BCI 77	
John	BCI 77	
Summerset	BCI 78	
LOY, Frederick	FRE 158	
Frederick	FRE 163	
George	FRE 158	
Jacob	FRE 158	
LOYD, Adam	D.C.127	
Frisby P.	CEC 124	
John	BCI 23	
Sarah	CHA 196	
LOYDE, Jamima	BAL 27	
John	BAL 25	
John	BAL 25	
LUBUSH, John	BCI 23	
LUBY, Ruslin	BCI 521	
LUCAS, Adam	PRI 218	
Ann	BCI 294	
Basil	BAL 48	
Benjamin	ANN 330	
Benjamin	CEC 124	
Bennett	D.C.63	
Bowen	D.C.131	
Charles	ANN 286	
Fielding, Junr.	BCI 280	
Henry	D.C.62	
Jas.	D.C.108	
Joanna	PRI 224	
John	ANN 333	
John	D.C.10	
John	KEN 102	
John	QUE 25	
John R.	CHA 221	
Joshua	DOR 58	
Michael	DOR 3	
Peter B.	BCI 64	
Preciella	BAL 42	
Robert	BAL 58	
Samuel	BCI 256	
Samuel	CLN 111	
Sarah	BCI 153	
Stephen, Sr.	CLN 95	
Thomas	CLN 88	
Thomas	CLN 89	
William	ALL 24	
William	BCI 201	
William	D.C.25	
William-Overseer, Poor House	CLN 99	
William, Jr.	CLN 110	
LUCASS, Thomas B.	BCI 506	
LUCAST, Ignatius	D.C.6	
LUCIUS, George	PRI 239	
LUCKET, Elizabeth	CHA 210A	
Samuel	CHA 218	
Thomas L.	CHA 213	
LUCKETON, Benjamin	WAS 83	
LUCKETT, Clary (Miss)	FRE 122	
Jane	CHA 207	
Lloyd	FRE 122	
Nelson	FRE 122	
Nina?	WAS 64	
Niner	WAS 64	
Notley	CHA 206	
Paul F.	D.C.150	
S.	FRE 122	
Saml.	FRE 122	
Sophia	D.C.154	
Thomas, Senr.	CHA 218	
LUCKEY, George (Revd.)	HAR 61	
LUCKITT, John	D.C.116	
LUCTON, Will.	D.C.107	
LUCUS, Daniel	BAL 81	
Henry	FRE 209	
LUCUST, Thomas	BAL 125	
LUDLOW, Ebenezar	BCI 297	
LUDWICK, George	FRE 133	
Jacob	FRE 131	
Samuel	WAS 107	
LUDY, John	FRE 133	
Nicholas	FRE 132	
Susanah	WAS 59	
LUFBOUROUGH, Nathan	MON 164	
LUFFBORAUGH, Nat. (?)	D.C.67	
LUFFBOROUGH, Nat.	D.C.67	
LUGENBEEL, John	FRE 211	
Peter	FRE 211	

MABURY, Catharine	BAL 14	
Mark (?)	BCI 481	
MACABEE, Elizabeth	BAL 203	
MACATEE, Elizabeth	HAR 76	
Henry	HAR 73	
MACAULEY, John	ANN 324	
Joseph	ANN 317	
Thomas	ANN 317	
MACBIE, Calib	ANN 358	
MACCA, Richard	PRI 195	
MACCABLESTER, Wm.	FRE 217	
MACCALLUM, Wm.	FRE 217	
MACCARDLE, John	MON 162	
MACCAULEY, John	MON 153	
William	BCI 130	
MACCUBBIN, Moses	BCI 181	
MACDANEIL, George	D.C. 25	
MACDANIEL, George (?)		
	D.C. 25	
George	D.C. 9	
John	D.C. 43	
MACDANIL, James	FRE 212	
MACE, Ann	BCI 24	
Ann	DOR 18	
Charles R.	BAL 110	
George	WAS 88	
Jacob	DOR 12	
John	D.C. 123	
John	DOR 18	
Moses	ANN 258	
Moses	DOR 11	
Rebecca	DOR 5	
Richard	ANN 257	
MACER, Ann	DOR 18	
MACFADDON, Francis	ANN 321	
MACGILL, Patrick	ANN 323	
MACHEN, Lewis H.	D.C. 83	
MACHERARY, John	D.C. 216	
MACHIN, William	BAL 13	
MACK, Margaret	BCI 69	
Natl.	BCI 499	
MACKAL, Benja. H.	CAL 44	
MACKALL, Benja. of		
Benja.		
Benja.	CAL 50	
Benja. B.	CAL 47	
Benjamin	D.C. 44	
Henry	CAL 43	
James G.	CAL 48	
John, of Benj.	CAL 43	
John G.	CAL 45	
Margaret (Mrs.)	CAL 47	
Martha D. (Miss)	CAL 48	
Moses	BCI 295	
Richard	BCI 336	
Richard	CAL 44	
MACKELFRESH, David	BAL 23	
John	BAL 5	
Margaret	BAL 19	
MACKENHEIMER, Catharine		
	BCI 156	
John	BCI 156	
MACKENHIMER, --- (Mrs.)		
	BCI 409	
MACKENTIRE, Andrew		
	CEC 141	
Peter	BCI 395	
MACKERY, James	CLN 94	
MACKETTIE, Thomas	WAS 86	
MACKEY, Catherine	CEC 142	
David	CEC 143	
Henry	CLN 97	
Jack	FRE 141	
James	BCI 74	
James	CEC 143	
James	D.C. 130	
James	TAL 40	

MACKEY (continued),		
John	BCI 369	
John	CEC 143	
John	D.C. 62	
Phillip	TAL 40	
Robert	BCI 18	
Samuel	CLN 74	
Thomas	TAL 35	
Will	D.C. 121	
William (?)	D.C. 39	
William	CEC 143	
William	TAL 51	
William, Jr.	TAL 35	
MACKINTERE, David		
	BCI 394	
MACKINZE, Calib	ANN 349	
MACKLEROY, John	BCI 35	
MACKREY, Isaac	TAL 32	
Levin	TAL 32	
MACKUBIN, Elizabeth		
	ANN 399	
George	ANN 397	
Mary	ANN 395	
MACKURHIMER, --- (Widaw)		
	BCI 399	
MACLIN, Rives	TAL 13	
MACNUSE, Benjn. (?)		
	TAL 47	
MACNUZE, Benjn.	TAL 47	
MACON, Charles	DOR 58	
MACUBBIN, --- (Mr.)		
	BCI 382	
Zachr.	MON 159	
MACUM, Leonard	D.C. 46	
MADAM, Spencer	WAS 62	
MADARA, Andrew	FRE 79A	
MADARY, Jacob	BCI 335	
MADCAP, Chloe	MON 139	
MADDEL, Cooper	BCI 324	
MADDEN, Elias	MON 160	
Elizabeth	CEC 180	
George	TAL 51	
Hannah	CLN 99	
James	HAR 60	
John	HAR 48	
John	MON 160	
Keel	ALL 21	
MADDEX, William T.		
	SAI 74	
MADDIN, Jacob	TAL 46	
John	BCI 325	
William	BAL 209	
William	BCI 325	
MADDINGER, Chris.		
	BCI 193	
Jacob	BAL 107	
MADDON, S.	BCI 398	
MADDOX, Edward	SAI 95	
Elizabeth	CHA 217	
Francis	PRI 206	
Frederick	CHA 210A	
Isaac	CHA 190	
John	CHA 203	
John	SAI 88	
Joseph	CHA 194	
Lauson	SAI 88	
Mary	CHA 194	
Notley	PRI 224	
Notley	PRI 225	
Notley	PRI 238	
Samuel	SAI 95	
Sarah	CHA 208	
Thomas	BCI 67	
W. R.	D.C. 111	
William	CHA 194	

MADDUX, Benja.	WOR 162	
Comfort	SOM 148	
Danl.	WOR 170	
Elzy	SOM 155	
George	SOM 157	
Harry	SOM 131	
Henry	SOM 105	
Henry	SOM 153	
Isaac	WOR 161	
John	SOM 103	
John	SOM 131	
John	SOM 153	
Lazarus	SOM 127	
Lazarus	SOM 153	
Levin	SOM 127	
Littleton D.	SOM 153	
Lizzy	SOM 147	
Priscilla	SOM 131	
Stoughton	SOM 105	
William	SOM 110	
William	SOM 153	
Zippora	SOM 113	
MADEIRA, Treacy	FRE 81	
MADIGAN, Biddy	BCI 239	
MADISON, Mary	QUE 37	
MADKIN, Kneelia	DOR 19	
MADOCKS, John	BCI 180	
MADORE, Francis	ALL 28	
MADOX, Edwd.	BCI 402	
Equlor	WAS 79	
MADSION, William	WAS 84	
MAEUSOT, Cafmiere	BCI 221	
Casmiere?	BCI 221	
MAFFITT, Charles	CEC 163	
John	CEC 163	
S. John	CEC 142	
William	CEC 163	
MAGAR, John	SAI 68	
MAGARITY, John	BCI 251	
MAGEE, Absolem	BAL 22	
Aquila	BAL 22	
Charles	SAI 74	
Robert	ALL 27	
Wm.	SAI 77	
MAGEIRER, Hugh (?)		
	DOR 22	
MAGER, R.	BCI 379	
MAGERS, Greenberry		
	FRE 191	
MAGGINE, Jos. F.	BCI 183	
MAGGS, Jane	BCI 252	
MAGILL, Charles	SAI 80	
John	FRE 103	
Mary	BCI 486	
Mathew	SAI 82	
Rachael	ALL 30	
Samuel	ALL 26	
MAGINIS, Rhodalph	MON 130	
MAGINNIS, Abigl.	BCI 219	
MAGLOTTEN, Ann	DOR 6	
MAGNESS, James	HAR 9	
James	HAR 44	
John	BAL 119	
John	BAL 238	
Thomas	HAR 39	
William	HAR 6	
William	HAR 39	
MAGNIER, Thos.	D.C. 98	
MAGNOR, John	KEN 101	
MAGO, John	BCI 195	
MAGRATH, ---	D.C. 82	
MAGRUDEE, Dennis (?)		
	PRI 230	
MAGRUDER (See also		
O'MAGRUDER),		
Alexander C.	ANN 388	

MAGRUDER (continued),			MAHONY (continued),			MALOY (continued),		
Alxd. H.	CAL	44	Thomas	MON	166	Patrick	BCI	7
Ann	PRI	197	MAIL, Uriah	BAL	119	MALRY, John	BCI	34
Burgess	ALL	28	MAILS, William	BAL	26	MALSBY, Morris	HAR	40
Dennis	PRI	230	MAIN, George	WAS	112	MALSHAM, Thomas	BCI	67
Edward	PRI	194	John W.	WAS	128A	MALTER, John A.	HAR	24
Eleaner?	MON	137	MAINLEY, John	CEC	163	MALTZELL, Thomas	BCI	51
Eleanor	MON	137	William	CEC	163	MALVY, John (?)	BCI	34
Fielder	PRI	194	MAINLY, John	CEC	141	MAMAKEE, William	MON	153
George	D.C.	51	Nicholas G.	CEC	163	MAMILY, Poor	TAL	37
George	MON	166	MAINSTER, Jacob	BCI	100	MAN, John H.	WAS	148
Hannah	D.C.	79	MAINYARD, Elizabeth			Ths.	BCI	233
Henderson	PRI	208		FRE	112	U. H.? (Leut.)	BCI	224
James A.	D.C.	37	MAIRS, Ceasar	FRE	110	W. H. (Leut.)	BCI	224
Jane	BCI	536	MAITLAND, James	D.C.	6	MANAGERS AT HAMP-		
Jas.	MON	161	MAIZE, George	BAL	127	T'N.	BAL	222
Jas.	MON	177	Jeremiah	BAL	230	MANAHAN, Beal	ANN	382
Jne. B.	MON	176	MAJILL, Mathew (?)	SAI	82	Thomas	FRE	210
Jno. B.?	MON	176	MAJOR, --- (See			William	BAL	66
John B.	MON	167	GLUYES & MAJOR)			MANAHORN, William (?)		
John R.	PRI	203		D.C.	176		BAL	66
John R., J.	PRI	219	John	D.C.	92	MANAKES, William	ANN	369
John S.	PRI	202	Peter	DOR	41	MANAWELL, Adam	CEC	141
Lauisa	PRI	207	Peter	DOR	59	MANDELL, John C.	D.C.	186
Lewis	D.C.	52	MAJORS, Acsha	BAL	185	MANDERS, Joseph	DOR	43
Lloyd	MON	165	Nathan	ALL	16	MANDEVILLE, Elizth.		
Louisa	PRI	207	Richd.	BCI	478		D.C.	168
Martha	MON	140	William	ALL	15	Josh.	D.C.	165
Mary	PRI	215	MAJOS, John	BCI	118	MANE, Frederick	FRE	132
Mary A.	MON	167	MAKAL, Benje.	BCI	479	MANEALY, Agness	BCI	212
Nathaniel B.	ALL	14	MAKEL, Benje.	BCI	486	M'ANERELL, Hugh	CEC	141
Nathl.	MON	163	Thos.	BCI	475	MANERY, John	D.C.	170
Otho	MON	165	MAKER, Nohoma (?)	BCI	138	MANEY, Thos.	BCI	495
Richard	PRI	198	MALABRE, Jacob	FRE	95	MANGILLON, Jeremiah		
Richard B.	BCI	268	MALAVE, Francis	FRE	101		ANN	317
Rignal O.	PRI	193	MALBROUGH, Abraham			MANGLES, Catherine	BCI	54
Robert	PRI	212		BCI	150	MANGUN, Henry	PRI	211
Robt. P.	MON	160	MALCOMB, George	SOM	105	John	MON	166
Saml.	MON	162	William	ALL	32	Jonas G.	PRI	211
Thomas	PRI	198	MALE, Wilmurah	ALL	4	Sarah	PRI	217
Walter	MON	167	MALIANI, Petr.	BCI	379	Zachariah	PRI	207
Warren	MON	166	MALLALIEW, --- (See			MANIFOLD, Henry	HAR	76
William	ALL	25	MORTON & MALLA-			William	HAR	59
William B.	BCI	433	LIEW)	BAL	173	MANING, Richard	BAL	9
Wm.	PRI	194	MALLAN, George	D.C.	195	Samuel	BAL	9
Zachariah	ALL	11	George	D.C.	197	MANKEY, Solomon	FRE	87
MAGUIRE, Hugh (?)	D.C.	102	MALLANEE, Josias	BAL	95	MANKIN, Chas.	D.C.	195
John	BCI	215	Wm.	BAL	79	Chas.	D.C.	197
William	DOR	24	MALLERSON, Aron (?)			Isaiah	BCI	36
MAHAN, Edward	CEC	142		BAL	23	MANKINS, Betsey	D.C.	187
Elisha	CEC	142	MALLET, Elizabeth	HAR	58	David	D.C.	146
George	CEC	141	MALLION, Vindora	D.C.	105	MANLAY, Martha	BCI	212
James	HAR	22	MALLISON, Obed	BCI	485	MANLEFF, Mark	CEC	125
James	HAR	23	MALLONEE, Leonard			MANLEY, Harrisson	D.C.	161
Jeremiah	CEC	142		ANN	332	Margt. B.	D.C.	146
John	HAR	27	MALLONEY, James	FRE	170	Matw.	D.C.	172
Joseph	CEC	141	MALLONY, Eliza	BCI	67	MANLO, Charlotte	KEN	120
Moses	CEC	142	MALLSEED, Samuel	BAL	242	Maria	KEN	121
Richard	CEC	142	MALON, Moses	BAL	7	Rosetta	KEN	119
Stephen	CEC	142	MALONE, George	SOM	134	MANLY, Elizh.	D.C.	114
Stephen, Senr.	CEC	142	James	WAS	87	Lilly?	WAS	83
William	CEC	141	Muncy	WAS	87	MANN, ----	BCI	460
William	CEC	143	Peter?	SOM	138	Abraham	KEN	118
MAHANY, John	BCI	86	Robert	SOM	136	Anthony	BCI	197
MAHAR, Patrick	BCI	524	William	ALL	31	Charles (Revd.)	CHA	206
MAHN, George	FRE	112	William	SOM	137	Fredk.	BCI	187
Jacob	FRE	112	William	WAS	78	Geo.	QUE	12
John, Junr.	FRE	116	William, Jun.	SOM	138	George	BAL	235
MAHON, Andrew	D.C.	118	MALONY, Denis	BAL	29	Hannah	BCI	484
Philip	D.C.	97	George	BAL	15	Henry	D.C.	5
MAHONEY, Barney	FRE	86	MALOONY, Eleanor	QUE	39	Isaac	KEN	115
Robert	ANN	301	MALOOT, Daniel	WAS	82	Joseph	KEN	117
MAHONY, Barney	D.C.	106	MALOTT, Benjamin	WAS	85	Julius	BCI	251
Charles	D.C.	96	MALOY, Catharine	BCI	119	Nathan	ANN	306
Daniel	ANN	310	Charles	BCI	5	Piercy	ANN	308
George	D.C.	58	John	D.C.	100	Sarah	D.C.	114

MARR (continued),			MARSHALL (continued),			MARTEENEY (continued),		
James	CHA	191	Elizabeth	BCI	26	George, Junr.	WAS	120
Jno.	BCI	239	Elizabeth	BCI	32	MARTEN, ---	BCI	434
John	CHA	190	Elizabeth	DOR	10	Chayne	WOR	211
William	BAL	197	George	BCI	453	Ennels, Junior	TAL	46
MARRAN, Richard	BAL	221	Greenbury	TAL	21	Joh. B.	SAI	66
MARRATT, William	BAL	36	Handson	PRI	202	MARTHENY, Mary	D.C.	116
MARRE, Allaxd.	BCI	335	Henry	DOR	11	MARTIAG, John	BAL	106
MARRENDER, --- (Major?)			Isaac	BAL	152	MARTIAQ, John (?)	BAL	106
	WOR	177	Isaac	WOR	191	MARTIENCY, John (?)		
Major	WOR	177	James	DOR	11		WAS	115
MARRETT, James	WOR	181	Jane	CHA	205	MARTIN, Adam	WAS	93
Sarah	WOR	180	John	BCI	79	Alexander	FRE	145
MARRICK, --- (Mrs.)	BCI	400	John	CEC	180	Ann	BCI	274
MARRIOT, Joshua	BAL	204	John	CHA	203	Barbary	FRE	146
MARRIOTT, Achsah	ANN	286	John	D.C.	120	Benjamin	SAI	68
Caleb	ANN	339	John	DOR	60	Caleb	PRI	225
Ephraim	ANN	293	John	FRE	95	Charles	BAL	21
James H.	ANN	333	John	WAS	68	Christian	FRE	158
John	ANN	286	John B.	BCI	446	Daniel	DOR	21
Joseph	ANN	346	John P.	WOR	186	Daniel	SOM	131
Joseph	BAL	64	John P.; Doc.	SOM	137	Daniel	TAL	40
Joshua	BCI	435	Jonathan	DOR	39	David	FRE	86
Richard, Doctr.	ANN	297	Jonathan	DOR	59	David	FRE	94
Thomas	ANN	326	Josias	D.C.	130	David	FRE	144
William, of Thos.	ANN	333	Leona	D.C.	190	David	FRE	169
MARRIS, Betsey	D.C.	193	Levin	DOR	53	David	WAS	111
James	D.C.	200	Levin	TAL	22	Edward	BCI	133
John (?)	DOR	19	Matthias	DOR	15	Edward	SOM	154
Lewis	D.C.	200	Meredith	TAL	21	Edward	TAL	40
MARROCE, John	FRE	85	Nicholas	DOR	15	Elijah	MON	153
MARS, Rebecca	CEC	163	Nicholas	TAL	22	Elizabeth	SAI	63
MARSDEN, James	BAL	193	Nicholas, of Jos.	TAL	21	Elizabeth	WOR	170
William	BAL	38	Perry	TAL	26	Ennals	TAL	11
MARSELLAS, Jno.	BCI	233	Peter	FRE	145	Fanny	BCI	431
MARSH, Barbury	BAL	28	Philip S.	BCI	86	Geo.	WOR	192
Barnet	BAL	80	Priscilla P.	CHA	203	George	ANN	402
Benedick	BAL	99	Richard	TAL	21	George	BCI	132
Benedict	BAL	229	Robert	ANN	307	George	FRE	86
Benidict	BAL	81	Robert	PRI	235	George	SAI	70
Calab	BAL	89	Robert	WOR	153	George	TAL	10
David	BAL	229	Samson	WOR	160	George	WAS	84
Elijah	FRE	190	Samuel	HAR	62	Greenbury	TAL	39
Ellen (?)	BAL	5	Skinner	DOR	39	Hannah	TAL	39
George	BAL	96	Thomas	CHA	211	Henry	FRE	129
Grafton	BAL	218	Thomas	DOR	60	Henry	HAR	5
Henry H.	FRE	214	Thomas	HAR	57	Henry	PRI	225
James	BAL	97	Thomas	WAS	63	Henry	WAS	90
James	WOR	174	Thos.	D.C.	113	Honore	MON	158A
Joel	FRE	98	William	DOR	5	Isaac	FRE	158
John	BAL	89	William	PRI	222	Isack	NAL	9
John	BAL	97	William	SOM	131	Isack	BAL	18
John	BAL	209	William	SOM	134	Jacob	ALL	37
Jonathan	SAI	55	Zadok	WOR	196	Jacob	FRE	125
Joshua	BAL	229	MARSHEL, Arther	TAL	4	Jacob	FRE	173
Nathanal	BAL	38	Jesse (?)	BAL	98	Jacob	TAL	9
Peter	WOR	180	Wm.	BAL	84	Jacob	WAS	88
Wm.	BAL	81	MARSHELL, Elizabeth			Jacob	WAS	103
Wm.	BAL	89		TAL	35	James	BCI	50
MARSHAL, Daniel	BCI	25	Jeremiah	TAL	37	James	BCI	247
Isaac	BAL	84	Robert N.	SOM	154	James	BCI	250
James	CAL	43	Thomas	SOM	147	James	D.C.	8
John	BAL	82	MARSHTELLER, George			James	D.C.	104
Joseph	TAL	21		WAS	62	James	D.C.	133
Samuel	ANN	369	John	WAS	62	James	KEN	95
Thomas	BAL	82	MARSOLLETTI, Vincent			James	KEN	118
Thomas	WOR	161		D.C.	185	James Noland	FRE	141
Vallent	DOR	16	MARSON, John	MON	153	Jane	CEC	142
MARSHALL, Adrian	SOM	132	MARSTELLER, Henry			Jane	WOR	218
Archibald	TAL	21		WAS	89	Jesse	FRE	141
Bennett	TAL	25	S. A.	D.C.	148	Joannah	BCI	93
Barba.	D.C.	115	MARSTLLER, John	WAS	89	John	BCI	157
Catherine	BCI	88	MARTAIN, Peachey	BAL	151	John	BCI	273
Charles	TAL	21	Peter	BAL	151	John	BCI	451
Denton	TAL	23	MARTEENEY, George,			John	BCI	476
Elijah	DOR	7	Senr.	WAS	120	John	BCI	518

MARTIN (continued),		MARTINO, Reubin	DOR 60	MASON (continued),	
John	BCI 528	MARTON, Hugh	CAL 51	Rebeckah	SAI 65
John	CHA 211	MARTZ, Danl.	FRE 226	Richard	BCI 451
John	D.C. 89	George, Senr.	FRE 113	Richard B.	SAI 66
John	D.C. 115	George, Junr.	FRE 113	Richard C.	BCI 451
John	FRE 93	MARVIN, Ann	BCI 138	Richd. C.	D.C. 175
John	FRE 95	William-FRANKLIN		Samuel	CLN 78
John	FRE 142	WOOLEN MANUFAC-		Simon	D.C. 97
John	FRE 161	TORY	BAL 186	Sinah	WOR 162
John	FRE 177	MARY, Mary	BCI 68	Solomon	D.C. 91
John	FRE 224	MARYANN, Mary	BCI 520	Thompson F.	D.C. 175
John	HAR 57	MARYLD. PENITEN-		Upshaw	WOR 157
John	PRI 228	TIARY	BCI 203	William	BCI 15
John	SOM 141	MARYMAN, Ann	SAI 78	William	CLN 95
John S., Doctr.	WOR 169	Elizabeth	BAL 175	William	CHA 193
John T.	SAI 66	James	SAI 96	William	KEN 119
Joseph	BCI 484	Joseph	SAI 77	William	WOR 155
Joseph	TAL 40	Lydia	SAI 77	William (of Wm.)	CHA 194
Lennox J. (I.?)	ANN 354	MARZAN, Charles	MON 164	Wm.	CAL 46
Lenox	ALL 34	MASEMORE, George		MASONHEIMER, Elizabeth	
Levin	QUE 28		BAL 147		FRE 196
Luther	BCI 300	Leonard	BAL 156	MASS, Christian	BCI 117
Luther	CEC 180	MASEN, --- (?)	BCI 382	John	BCI 451
Margaret	CEC 163	Peter	BCI 373	MASSAP, James	DOR 63
Martha	BCI 68	MASEY, Daniell	WOR 202	MASSARD, Amy	BCI 212
Mary	FRE 182	MASHER, James	BCI 266	MASSEE, Josiah	WAS 126
Mary	MON 160	James, Junr.	BCI 278	MASSEY, Alexander	WOR 190
Michael	CHA 214	MASK, Willm.	BCI 195	Aquila	HAR 74
Miley	CHA 207	MASLIN, Jacob	KEN 88	Benjn.	KEN 120
Nancy	BCI 504	John	KEN 93	Charles	SAI 96
Nathaniel	WAS 111	M. M.	BCI 440	Isaac	HAR 77
Nicholas	TAL 40	Titus	KEN 93	James	QUE 36
Oxford	KEN 92	MASON, Andrew	CLN 79	James	WOR 206
Patrick	D.C. 54	Ann	SAI 96	John	CEC 179A
Peter	FRE 80	Ann-free	CAL 61	John	WAS 73
Peter	FRE 224	Arcibald	ANN 340	Josias	KEN 116
Rachael	WAS 56	Arthur	QUE 27	Kendal	WOR 191
Richard	ANN 328	Bagwell	WOR 213	Margaret	KEN 101
Richard	BCI 429	Benjamin	SAI 65	Nicholas	CEC 125
Richd., Senr.	MON 163	Catharine	BCI 7	Purnell	WOR 190
Richd., Junr.	MON 163	Danl., Senr.	WOR 163	Robt.	D.C. 152
Robert	CHA 211	Danl., Junr.	WOR 157	Sally	WOR 197
Robert	HAR 76	Ebbin H.	SOM 107	MASSICOT, Wm.	BCI 170
Robina	FRE 187	Elijah	WOR 213	MASSIE, Francis	D.C. 199
Robind?	FRE 187	Eliza	FRE 69	Saml.	D.C. 215
Saml.	D.C. 134	Elizabeth	FRE 69	MASSOCK, Jacob	WAS 101
Saml.	MON 159	Elizabeth	SAI 97	MASSY, David	QUE 11
Samuel	CHA 216	Geo.	QUE 18	Geo.	QUE 11
Samuel	WAS 121	George	CHA 194	Jacob	QUE 14
Samuel B.	BCI 15	Henry	BAL 184	James	QUE 21
Sarah	CEC 181	Henry	CLN 81	Joshua W.	QUE 14
Sarah	D.C. 101	James	BAL 95	Joshue J. (I.?)	QUE 4
Sarah	HAR 26	James	BCI 536	Lydia	QUE 17
Sarah	SAI 76	James	QUE 36	MASTERS, Nathan	PRI 193
Slephey	WAS 100	James	TAL 13	Patrick	BCI 298
Sollomen	BAL 22	James	TAL 49	Willm.	D.C. 193
Stephen	SAI 67	James	WOR 163	MASTERSON, Laughlin	
Susannee	BCI 178	Jeramia	WAS 149		D.C. 156
Thomas	PRI 214	Jno.-Island & farm		MASTIN, Saml.	KEN 119
Thomas	SOM 138		D.C. 213	MATCHET, James	FRE 198
Thomas	SOM 141	Jno. D.	BCI 228	MATCHETT, George	BCI 9
Thomas	TAL 34A	John	CLN 76	Richard	BCI 269
Thomas	TAL 40	John	HAR 6	MATDKIN, Zebulon	DOR 19
Thomas	WAS 122	John	MON 137	MATGOY, Susan	BCI 513
Thos. (of George)	WOR 180	John	SAI 63	MATHARD, James	FRE 218
Thos. L.	D.C. 164	John	SOM 152	MATHER, Joseph	BCI 220
Tobias	D.C. 128	John	WOR 156	Michael	HAR 8
Walter	HAR 56	John (Gen.)	D.C. 60	MATHERS, Sarah	D.C. 153
William	ANN 347	John T.	CLN 78	MATHES, Sally	DOR 27
William	ANN 347	John T.	WAS 135	William C.	CEC 125
William	BCI 309	Joseph	D.C. 158	MATHEW, Daniel	ANN 304
William	KEN 95	Joseph	SAI 67	MATHEWAY, Thomas	
William	TAL 35	Kesiah	QUE 17		ANN 318
William	TAL 37	Lehanna	MON 153	MATHEWES, Eliza	BCI 489
William B., Esqr.	DOR 6	Lot	CHA 193	John	BCI 476
Willm.	D.C. 125	Matthew	CLN 79	Richard	BCI 484
Wm.	BCI 373	Michael	BAL 182		

MATHEWS, Ann	CHA 227	MATTHEWS (continued),		MATTINGLY (continued),		
Benjamim	FRE 213	Ann	CHA 195	John	ALL 15	
Chloe	ANN 303	Ann Maria	BCI 158	John	D.C.115	
David	CEC 142	Benjamin	BAL 81	John	SAI 96	
Dinah	DOR 52	Benjamin	KEN 90	John, Senior	SAI 91	
Edmond	ANN 367	Casandra	ANN 399	John, Jr.	ALL 17	
Edmond	ANN 378	Daphna	BCI 53	Margt.	D.C.128	
Elizabeth	HAR 44	Edward	BAL 98	Monica	CHA 206	
Ephraim	WOR 178	Edw'd.	BAL 84	Philip	CHA 205	
Franceis	WAS 70	Eli	BAL 93	Samuel	ALL 17	
George	SOM 147	Eli	WOR 153	William, Sen.	SAI 86A	
Henry	ANN 258	Elizabeth	ANN 396	William, Jr.	SAI 88	
James	CEC 142	Elizabeth	WOR 154	Zach.	D.C.111	
James	CEC 142	Francis	QUE 42	Zachariah of Luke	SAI 87	
James	D.C.20	Garrettson	CLN 88	MATTINLEY, Ann	D.C.29	
James	TAL 51	George	SOM 114	MATTINLY, Francil	SAI 93	
James	WOR 218	Henry	SOM 124	MATTISON, Obed (?)		
James B.	ANN 366	Jacob	BCI 136		BCI 485	
Jerry (negro)	TAL 27	James	FRE 147	MATTOCK, Simeon (?)		
Jesse	FRE 135	Jarrett	BAL 83		D.C.101	
John	ANN 296	John	ALL 10A	MATTOCKS, George	BCI 277	
John	BAL 209	John	ALL 18	MATTON, Jane	BCI 214	
John	BAL 245	John	BCI 202	MATTOX, Erasmus	PRI 196	
John	CHA 207B	John	CLN 74	George	BAL 43	
Josiah	HAR 22	John	FRE 201	John	BAL 114	
K.	BCI 400	John	SOM 137	Thomas	BCI 313	
Kate	PRI 186	Joseph	CLN 76	Wm.	MON 163	
Levi	SOM 147	Joshua	ANN 389	MATTS, John	FRE 130	
Mary	ANN 346	Levi	SOM 128	MATTUX, George	WOR 205	
Nathan	BAL 61	Mary	CLN 74	Lazeris	WOR 216	
Nelly	ANN 346	Mordacai	BAL 94	MAUGAURIN, J. (I.?) C.		
Nicholas	TAL 47	Philip	FRE 148		BCI 441	
Pheby	ANN 327	Polly	CHA 192	MAUGAVRIN, J. (I.?) C. (?)		
Rachel	BCI 512	Rebecca	QUE 29		BCI 441	
Robert	WOR 169	Robert	BCI 462	MAULDEN, Benjamin	CEC 163	
Sollomon	PRI 186	Saml.	BCI 178	John	CEC 163	
Stephen-Negro	HAR 49	Sarah	BCI 435	Zebulon	CEC 163	
William	ALL 35	Thomas	BAL 93	MAULSBY, David	HAR 4	
William	ANN 346	Thos.	BCI 176	David	HAR 8	
William	BAL 162	Thos.	QUE 5	Israel D.	HAR 48	
William	BAL 199	William	CLN 87	Wheeler	HAR 6	
William	BAL 210	William	CHA 227	MAURAN, James	BCI 124	
William	BAL 245	William	D.C.87	MAURER, Paul	FRE 209	
William P.	BAL 207	William	SOM 132	Peter	BCI 430	
Wm.	WOR 174	William	TAL 33	MAURO, P.	D.C.93	
Zachariah	SOM 154	William (Taylor)	SOM 124	MAURS, P. (?)	D.C.93	
MATHIAS, Daniel	FRE 163	William B.	TAL 5	MAUSE, Jacob	FRE 179	
Francis	FRE 205	Wm.	BAL 84	MAUTE, James	BCI 24	
Griffian	FRE 224	Wm.	BAL 93	MAVOIS, John	BCI 343	
Jacob	FRE 187	Wm., Dr.	QUE 4	MAXFIELD, Charles	BAL 214	
Joseph	FRE 188	MATTHIAS, David	BAL 146	John	BCI 197	
Mary	FRE 188	George	BAL 147	MAXMELL, Thomas	FRE 227	
Peter	FRE 171	Jessee	BAL 153	MAXVILL, Alexander		
MATHIS, John	FRE 78A	John	BCI 465		QUE 27	
MATHY, Betty	ANN 326	Joseph	BCI 52	James	QUE 28	
MATINGLY, Gabriel J.		MATTICKS, Leah	DOR 61	MAXWELL, Adam	BCI 527	
	FRE 81	MATTIE, Rachel	CLN 74	Alexander, Jr.	CLN 88	
Thomas	PRI 222	MATTINGLEY, Allouisa		Elizabeth	BAL 139	
MATKIN, Levin	DOR 19		SAI 78	Elizh.	BCI 171	
Standly	DOR 22	Clemant	SAI 78	George	D.C.77	
MATLACK, John	BCI 432	Edward	SAI 80	James	CEC 180	
Samuel T.	BCI 433	John	D.C.21	John	CEC 143	
MATLICKS, Leah (?)	DOR 61	Joseph	SAI 77	John	KEN 108	
MATLOCK, Simeon	D.C.101	Lewis	D.C.10	N.	BCI 270	
MATNEY, Thos.	D.C.216	Stephen	D.C.12	Nathl. Greene	BCI 280	
MATOX, William	BCI 312	Sylvester	SAI 78	Robert H.	CLN 87	
MATSON, Thomas	HAR 70	William	D.C.24	Samuel	BCI 145	
MATTELESSOE, --- (Mrs.)		Zachariah	SAI 80	Thomas (?)	FRE 227	
	BCI 461	MATTINGLY, Alexander		William	CEC 143	
MATTEN, Joseph	DOR 30		SAI 87	William	HAR 22	
MATTER, George	BAL 139	Edwd.	D.C.111	William	KEN 109	
John A.	HAR 24	Eliz.	D.C.127	MAXY, Virgil	ANN 271	
Mary	BAL 139	Elizabeth	SAI 88	MAY, Benjamin	BAL 209	
MATTERSON, Aron	BAL 23	Elizh.	D.C.126	Catharine	FRE 128	
MATTHEOT, George	BCI 128	Hen.	D.C.123	Daniel	WAS 114	
MATTHEWS, Aaron	DOR 40	Henry	ALL 16	Edwd. W.	D.C.148	
Allen	CHA 195	Ignatious	SAI 92	Francis B.	CHA 201	

MAY (continued),		M CLEAN, John	CEC 181	M NAME, Frances	CEC 181
Fredk.	D.C.102	M CLELAND, Robert		M'NAMEE, Hannah	CEC 142
Geo. U.?	D.C.94		CEC 181	Mary	CEC 142
Geo. W.	D.C.94	M CLELEHAN, John	CEC 180	M'NEVAIN, Maneys	BCI 348
James	BCI 379	M CLELLAND, James		Marreys?	BCI 348
James	WAS 86		CEC 180	M'SPARIN, Eligah	CEC 143
John	QUE 33	M'CLENHAN, James	CEC 142	Elijah?	CEC 143
John	SAI 73A	William	CEC 142	M VAY, Amy	CEC 163
Jonn C.	D.C.145	M'CLERRY, John	CEC 143	Benjamin	CEC 179A
Thomas	D.C.27	M CLUER, Christopher		James	CEC 180
Wm. F.	QUE 4		CEC 163	James of Ed	CEC 162
MAYBERRY, Justinian		M COLE, Neal	CEC 181	Mary	CEC 163
	FRE 93	M.CONIKIN, William (?)		William	CEC 163
Thomas	FRE 110		QUE 46	M'VEA, Benjamin	CEC 142
MAYBIN, Edward	CEC 143	M'CONNELL, James	CEC 143	Pasmore	CEC 142
MAYBURY, Willoby	FRE 156	Samuel	CEC 141	McADOW, Andrew	HAR 39
MAYDWELL, John	BCI 216	M'CONRAORS, William		McAFEE, Archibald	FRE 164
MAYER, Christ.	BCI 511		CEC 142	Marke	WAS 148
Henry	ANN 297	M CORKLE, John	CEC 181	Mary	BAL 186
MAYERS, Greenberry	(?)	M CORMICK, James	CEC 180	McAFFERY, Bartholomew	
	FRE 191	M'COY, John	CEC 142		FRE 141
William	QUE 26	M CREA, Robert	CEC 162	McAGLANON, Willm.	D.C.161
MAYFIELD, Benj.	D.C.28	M'CRERRY, Jane	CEC 143	McALISTER, Daniel	FRE 141
Henry	D.C.82	Jesse	CEC 142	Hugh	QUE 32
Thomas	BCI 461	Sarrah	CEC 143	John	FRE 175
William	D.C.28	M'CRUE, Samuel	CEC 142	McALLEN, Robert	WOR 212
MAYHALL, Jas.	D.C.152	M CUE, Lanty	CEC 180	McALLIN, Arthur	WOR 209
MAYHAN, Patrick	WAS 87	Susan	CEC 179A	McALLISTER, Jehue	
MAYHEW, Edward	WAS 106	M CULLOUGH, Alexander			BAL 183
Heziciah	WAS 101		CEC 180	Jno.	BCI 190
James	WAS 90	Andrew	CEC 179A	Loyd	BAL 183
John	WAS 99	Henry	CEC 179A	Margt.	D.C.151
John	WAS 127A	James	CEC 180	Mary	BCI 76
Nicholas	FRE 70	John	CEC 179A	Richard	BCI 91
MAYHUE, John	PRI 207	John	CEC 180	Sarah	BCI 219
MAYNADIER, Wm. N.	D.C.152	Jonathan	CEC 180	McARDLE, Henry	BCI 428
MAYNARD, Foster	TAL 20	Joseph	CEC 180	McATEE, Benjamin	CHA 215
Henry	FRE 213	Robert	CEC 180	James	FRE 70
Nathan	FRE 78A	Samuel	CEC 179A	Mary	FRE 82
Quincy	BCI 314	Samuel	CEC 180	Samuel	HAR 76
Samuel	ANN 396	William	CEC 163	Walter	ALL 37
Thomas	FRE 78A	M CUMMINGS, Joseph		William	CHA 203
MAYNE, Adam	D.C.46		CEC 180	Wm.	MON 139
MAYNIARD, Ephraim	FRE 221	M'FERRIN, Allexander		McATEER, Mary	FRE 144
MAYO, Geo.	BCI 218		WAS 148	McAUCHON, Jacobine	
Joseph	ANN 255	M GAR, John	CEC 162		D.C.193
Simon	BCI 21	M'GILTON, James	CEC 142	McBEE, Hez.	BCI 477
William	D.C.17	M GLEUEGLIN, Robert		McBLAIR, Michael	BCI 274
MAYOR, Lewis	BCI 270		CEC 163	Michael	BCI 465
MAYRE, Augustus	BCI 273	M GOLDRICK, John	CEC 181	McBRIDE, Barney	BCI 518
MAYS, James	BAL 88	Patrick	CEC 181	Edward	FRE 141
John	BAL 97	M GOWAN, John	CEC 180	Eliza	WAS 114
Simon (?)	BCI 21	M GRADY, Enoch	CEC 180	Phil.	FRE 128
MAYTERRY, William	WAS 62	John	CEC 162	McBRYDE, Elizabeth	SOM 104
MAZANT, John	BAL 126	M GRAW, James	CEC 181	McBRYETY, Anthony	
MAZINE, Cathe.	D.C.86	M'GREGOR, James	CEC 142		BCI 302
MAZINGER, William	D.C.12	M'GREW, Thomas	CEC 142	McBUOIN, --- (Widaw)	
MAZOE, Robt.	CAL 41A	William	CEC 142		BCI 416
M'ANERELL, Hugh	CEC 141	M GRORY, John	WAS 128A	McCABE, Ednd.	WOR 194
M'ANNELL, Hugh (?)	CEC 141	M HEIRD, Isaac-negro		Garrisson	WOR 194
M'CABE, James	CEC 141		CEC 125	Obed.	WOR 195
John	BCI 342	M'KEAG, James	CEC 143	Sarah	QUE 37
Robert	CEC 142	M KENNEY, Stephen		McCAFFETY, Catharine	
M CARTNEY, John	CEC 180		CEC 163		FRE 205
M'CASLIN, Robert	CEC 141	M KENNY, Benjamin	CEC 163	McCAFFREY, Will.	D.C.105
M'CAULEY, Wm.	WAS 148	Daniel	CEC 163	McCAIN, John	BCI 119
M'CAULLY, Daniel	CEC 142	John	CEC 163	John	BCI 152
Daniel	CEC 143	John	CEC 179A	McCALASTER, James	
Elizabeth	CEC 143	M KINLEY, Henry	WAS 145		BCI 161
Henry	CEC 143	M'KINSEY, Benjamin,		McCALEB, John	FRE 171
James	CEC 141	Senr.	CEC 142	McCALENDER, Patrick	
James	CEC 142	Benjamin, Jr.	CEC 142		DOR 61
John	CEC 143	M MULLEN, James	CEC 162	McCALL, John	FRE 143
Thomas?	CEC 142	Joseph	CEC 163	Sarah	BCI 296
M CAY, James	CEC 162	Thomas	CEC 163	Susan	ANN 277
M CLAY, William	CEC 162	M.MULLIN, John (?)		McCALLA, Wm.	BCI 189
William	CEC 163		QUE 48		

McCALLESTER, --- (Mrs.)		McCLAIN (continued),		McCLUSKEY, Wm.	BCI 179
	BCI 460	Chs. W.	BCI 485	McCLUTCHEY, John G.
McCALLISTER, Christopher		D.	BCI 240		BCI 132
	BAL 120	George	FRE 111	McCOBB, John	D.C. 196
McCAMBRIDGE, Francis (?)		James	WAS 139	McCOBS, Barnett	CLN 80
	ALL 7	John	BAL 109	McCOLESTER, Allen	DOR 58
McCAN, William	BCI 147	John	BCI 112	Andrew	DOR 54
McCANAN, Ann	BCI 279	John	BCI 387	David?	DOR 58
McCANDLESS, Esther	HAR 46	John	WAS 139	David	DOR 40
McCANE, John	BCI 377	Joseph	FRE 149	James	DOR 54
McCANN, Arthur	D.C. 54	Peter	FRE 149	James	DOR 55
Catharine	BAL 239	William	KEN 103	Nancy	DOR 54
Charles	BCI 276	McCLAIR, John (?)	BAL 109	Nathan	DOR 63
Charles	CHA 208	McCLAISH, James	HAR 4	Samuel	DOR 5
Charles	HAR 71	McCLAKEN, John	BCI 342	Samuel	DOR 40
John	FRE 111	McCLALAND, John	WAS 146	McCOLLINS, Patrick	BCI 98
John	FRE 148	McCLANE, Charles	BAL 184	McCOLLOCH, Edward	FRE 146
Thomas	BCI 221	James	SOM 153	McCOLLY, John	FRE 134
William	BCI 276	Robert	BCI 376	McCOLM, Mathew	BCI 241
McCANNON, James	BAL 126	McCLANNAN, John	D.C. 78	McCOLTER, Hezekier	DOR 11
William H.	FRE 187	McCLARE, John	HAR 57	McCOMAS, Aaron	HAR 5
McCARDEL, Mary	WAS 121	McCLAREN, Duncan	D.C. 40	Alexr. of Aql.	HAR 60
McCARDLE, Eliz.	D.C. 100	McCLAREY, Andrew	ALL 28	Amos	HAR 63
John	CEC 181	John	BCI 523	Aql. of Jas.	HAR 57
McCARGAN, James	BAL 179	McCLARY, Jas.	D.C. 75	Aquila	HAR 7
McCARNISH, David	CEC 163	John	WAS 143[A]	Aquila of Ed.	HAR 57
McCARRY, Elizabeth	WAS 125	Robert	ALL 27	Barnet	HAR 6
McCARTY, Alexander	WAS 149	McCLASKEY, David	HAR 19	Elizabeth	HAR 5
Isaac	ALL 10A	Edward	BAL 206	Elizabeth	HAR 9
Jacob G.	HAR 27	James	HAR 45	Frederick	BCI 138
James	CLN 87	William M.	HAR 45	James	BAL 92
John	D.C. 103	McCLAY, Thomas	WAS 133	James	HAR 8
Mary	D.C. 171	McCLAYLAND, Alexander		James P.	HAR 58
Sarah	BCI 52		TAL 33	James S.	HAR 9
McCASKEY, Mary	HAR 21	John	TAL 41	John (Bush)	HAR 4
Mc CATTEN, Joseph	DOR 22	William	TAL 50	John W.	HAR 9
McCAUFERTY, Dennis	WAS 84	McCLEAN, Billy	D.C. 205	Nathaniel	HAR 7
McCAUGHAN, Davis	BCI 6	Danl.	D.C. 183	Preston	HAR 40
McCAULEY, Elijah	ANN 290	Saml.	D.C. 183	Sarah	BCI 231
Elizh.	D.C. 127	McCLEARIN, Andrew		Solomon	HAR 5
Hugh	WAS 83		D.C. 71	Wm.	BCI 505
James	CEC 163	McCLEARY, Andrew		McCOMB, John	BAL 149
James	WAS 114		FRE 100	McCOMBS, James	CLN 93
Patrick	BCI 210	Robert	FRE 100	McCOMMICK, Thomas	WAS 120
Samuel	WAS 94	William	BCI 245	McCOMMONS, Sarah	HAR 29
William	D.C. 62	McCLEDEN, Isaac	BCI 192	McCOMMUS, Zacariah	WAS 121
Zachariah	ANN 374	McCLEERY, Peter	ALL 15	McCOMRICKS, Joseph	
McCAUSLAND, George	HAR 70	McCLEIRY, John (?)			WOR 189
Marcus	BCI 254		CEC 141	McCOMSKEY, John	BAL 153
Robert	HAR 70	McCLEISH, Jas.	D.C. 146	Mary	BAL 145
Wm.	BCI 221	Martha	D.C. 169	McCOMUS, Solomon	BCI 20
Wm.	BCI 229	Willm.	D.C. 169	McCON, Roseann	BAL 187
McCAUSLIN, James	BAL 205	McCLELLAN, Jennette		McCONCHIE, Lucey	CHA 195
McCAWLEY, Caleb	BAL 204		BCI 448	Thomas	CHA 190
McCAY, Dorcas (Mrs.)		John	BAL 117	McCONCKY, William	BCI 113
	BCI 272	Maria (Mrs.)	BCI 268	McCONKEY, James	HAR 6
Elijah	SOM 137	McCLELLAND, Geo.	SAI 63	John	BCI 117
Elizabeth	ANN 267	John	SAI 66	McCONLEY, James	BCI 221
George	KEN 116	Robert	SAI 65	McCONNEL, Mary	BCI 31
John	BCI 129	McCLELLEN, Saml.	BCI 370	McCONNELL, Elija	BCI 214
Joshua	KEN 118	McCLENAHAN, Wm.	BCI 250	Samuel	HAR 40
Martha	QUE 17	McCLENAN, Frans.	D.C. 167	Thomas	BCI 283
Saml.	BCI 283	McCLENNON, Mathew		McCONNICK, Alexr. (?)	
McCEMRICKS, Joseph (?)			BAL 117		D.C. 105
	WOR 189	McCLERRY, John	CEC 141	McCONNIKIN, Elias	QUE 6
McCENDLEY, Ths.	BCI 219	McCLESTER, John	SOM 106	McCOOBERY, William	BAL 226
McCENEY, Benjamin	ANN 262	McCLEUN, Arthur	BCI 538	McCORDELL, Thomas	WAS 109
Joseph	ANN 269	McCLISTER, Henry	BCI 223	McCORGAN, Paul	HAR 46
Martha	ANN 272	McCLOSKY, Charles	BCI 73	McCORKLE, Jos. P.	D.C. 3
McCEW, Edward N.	BCI 145	Will	D.C. 104	McCORMICK, Thos.	BCI 480
McCHESLEY, Daniel	D.C. 46	McCLOUD, John	D.C. 94	McCORMICK, A. T.	D.C. 101
McCHOLESTER, Nathan		McCLUNG, Robert	HAR 58	Alexr.	D.C. 105
	SOM 113	Samuel	HAR 58	Duncan	BCI 213
McCLAHANAN, Mathew		McCLURE, John	BCI 280	James	BAL 227
	WAS 102	Mary	BCI 302	James	BCI 136
McCLAIN, Ann	BCI 111	William G.	BCI 442	James	BCI 299
Charles	BCI 447	William G.	HAR 56	Jas.	D.C. 154

McCORMICK (continued),
John	BCI 211
John	BCI 227
John	BCI 460
Saml.	BCI 322
Samuel	BAL 17
William	BCI 154

McCORMIKIN, Elias (?)
| | QUE 6 |

McCOSH, Esther	QUE 32
Samuel	QUE 32
McCOSLIN, Tho.	D.C. 97

McCOTTER, Annanias S.
	CLN 113
Hezekier (?)	DOR 11
James	CLN 113
McCOULL, Robert	BCI 137
McCOY, Alexander	PRI 194
Alexr.	BCI 320
Andrew, Senr.	WAS 58
Andrew, Jun.	WAS 58
Daniel	WAS 138
Edmond	WAS 89
Elizabeth	ANN 313
Elizabeth	BCI 26
Elizabeth	WAS 58
G.	D.C. 75
James	KEN 101
James, Senr.	WAS 94
James, Junr.	WAS 93
Jane	BCI 10
Lavinia	ANN 286
Michael	WAS 58
Moses	WAS 80
Patsey	ANN 306
Precilla	BCI 430
Rachl.	MON 137
Robt.	D.C. 80
Samuel	BCI 448
Stephen	BCI 98
Thomas	BCI 464
William	HAR 76
William	WAS 60

McCRACKEN, Alexander
	BCI 130
Jno.	D.C. 113
Sarah	HAR 76
Um.?	BCI 216
Wm.	BCI 216
McCRACKIN, Thomas	CLN 92
McCRACKING, James	HAR 26
McCRADAN, James	HAR 64
McCRADY, Andrew	DOR 42
James	DOR 40
John, Senr.	DOR 43
John, Junr.	DOR 43
McCRAY, Charles	BCI 375
McCREA, --- (Mrs.)	BCI 444
Cathe.	D.C. 167
Elizth.	BCI 255
Thompson	FRE 171
McCREADY, Isaac	SOM 154
John	SOM 154
Solomon	SOM 154
McCREARY, Benjamin	HAR 55
McCREEDY, Danl.	BCI 231
McCRERY, M.	BCI 351
Nancy	BCI 343
Robert	WAS 120
McCREY, Catherine	WAS 94
McCRISTAL, John	BCI 73
McCROSSIN, Mary	BCI 53
McCROSSOM, Thomas	ANN 402
McCUBBIN, Ann	ANN 302
Elizabeth	ANN 306
Henry	ANN 306

McCUBBIN (continued),
James	ANN 297
Jane	ANN 306
Joseph	BAL 119
Linghan	PRI 222
Lloyd	BAL 120
Samuel	ANN 253
Samuel	BCI 161
McCUBBINS, John	BAL 127
William	BAL 120
McCUBIN, William	BCI 22
McCUE, Ann	BAL 53
Harriett	D.C. 171
Owen	D.C. 125
Susanah	CEC 142
McCULLER, James	BAL 87
McCULLEY, Robert	BCI 283
McCULLICK, Samuel	WAS 126
McCULLOAH, James	ANN 275
McCULLOCH, James	BCI 458
James H.	BCI 465

McCULLOCK, James W.
	BCI 354
McCULLOH, Duncan	BCI 87
George	ALL 15
James W.	BAL 192
Joseph	ALL 26
Samuel	BAL 197
William	ALL 14A

McCULLOUGH, Samuel
	CEC 162
McCULLY, John J. (I.?)	
	FRE 93

McCUMPSEY, Marggaretta
	WAS 134
McCUMSEY, John	WAS 134[A]
William	FRE 204
McCUNE, James	HAR 42
McCURDY, Cammel	FRE 159
Dennis	D.C. 12
Sarah	BCI 69
McCURLEY, Felix	BCI 528
McCURTY, John	BCI 397
McCUTCHEN, Geo.	BCI 311
James	BCI 47
John	D.C. 30
McDADE, Peter	FRE 128
McDANALD, Richard	
	WAS 122
McDANIEL, Allen	PRI 223
Ann	CHA 217
Arian	QUE 36
Cain	BCI 151
David	SOM 152
Edward	TAL 49
Ezekiel	D.C. 137
Frances	FRE 214
Francis	BAL 182
Horatio	CHA 224
James	TAL 26
John	BAL 225
John	PRI 195
Lymus	QUE 39
Oswell	CHA 206
Thomas	CHA 213
Thop.	D.C. 134
Willen	SOM 107
McDANIELL, John	SOM 110
John	SOM 139
Marcy	SOM 125
McDANIELLS, Danl.	BCI 320
McDANN, John (?)	BCI 60
McDANNAH, Patrick	BAL 84
McDANNEL, Elizabeth	
	FRE 150
Henry	FRE 155

McDANNEL (continued),
Jacob	FRE 155
John	FRE 150
McDANNELE, John	KEN 114
William	KEN 114
McDANNELL, John (?)	
	KEN 114
William (?)	KEN 114
McDANNIEL, Thomas	ANN 263
McDANNILL, Risdon	WOR 210
McDARGLE, Francis	BCI 463
McDAVID, Watt	WAS 84
McDENNICK, James (?)	
	D.C. 144

McDERMOT, Catharine
| | BAL 112 |
| Jane | BCI 12 |

McDERMOTT, Charles
	CEC 163
Peter	D.C. 36
McDINNICK, James	D.C. 144
McDIVITT, John	MON 171
McDONAL, --- (See
McDONAL & RIDGELY)
Alex.	BCI 414
Barnard	BCI 415
John	BCI 383
John	BCI 416
Lenney	BCI 344
Solomon	BCI 343

McDONAL & RIDGELY
| | BCI 343 |
| McDONALD, --- (Widaw) |
	BCI 399
Alex.	BCI 405
Alexander	FRE 98
Alexr.	D.C. 78
Asa	ALL 22
Catherine	BCI 75
Chas.	BCI 197
Eliza.	ANN 401
Hariet	D.C. 53
Henry	WAS 150
Isabel	D.C. 76
J.(I.?) G.	D.C. 105
Jas.	BCI 228
Jno.	D.C. 113
John	ALL 37
John	BCI 405
John	FRE 106
Margt.	D.C. 168
Nelly	D.C. 60
Nelly	WAS 121
Patk.	BCI 254
Sarah	WAS 99
Timy.	D.C. 117
William	D.C. 38
Willm.	BCI 169
Wm., Shff.	CLN 99
McDONAUGH, John	BCI 439
McDONNALD, Francis	
	CEC 180
John	BCI 6

McDONNEL, Alexander
| | BCI 16 |

McDONNELL, Alexander
	BCI 49
Henry	BCI 2
Hugh	BCI 4
James	BCI 71
McDONNER, Joseph	BAL 179
McDONNOH, James	BAL 199
Peter	BAL 200
McDONOUGH, Jno.	QUE 7
McDORMAN, Geo.	SOM 126
Lewis	SOM 129

McDORMAN (continued),		McFERRAN, John	BCI 244	McGLUE, Owen	D.C.90
William	SOM 130	McFUNN, David	CEC 180	McGOODING, Thomas	
McDOUEL, Samuel	BCI 51	McGAHAN, Eliza.	D.C.44		BCI 491
McDOUGAL, Mary	D.C.165	McGAIN, Elizabeth	FRE 81	McGOWAN, Andrew	BCI 273
McDOWELL, Geo.	BCI 250	McGAREY,Michl.	BCI 511	Ann	D.C.80
Hamilton	BCI 143	McGARRATY, James	CEC 179A	Hugh	FRE 197
James C.	CEC 180	McGARY, Jno.	BCI 215	John	D.C.76
Jas.	D.C.164	McGAW, James	HAR 9	Patk.	D.C.104
John	PRI 229	John	HAR 9	McGOWEN, Daniel	WAS 125
Joseph	D.C.103	Ritchard	BAL 90	George	WAS 87
Maxwell (Doctr.)	BCI 269	McGEE, Elizabeth	D.C.8	McGRAIN, Mary	BCI 523
Samuel	CEC 163	George	D.C.14	McGRANE, John	WAS 58A
Thomas	CEC 179A	Hugh	FRE 134	McGRATH, Benj.	D.C.32
Thos.	KEN 124	James	CEC 180	Daniel	D.C.85
William	CEC 163	James	SOM 124	David	SOM 116
Willm.	D.C.131	John	BCI 281	David G.	SOM 125
McDUELL, John	D.C.92	John	WOR 191	John	D.C.80
McDUGALL, James	D.C.12	John	WOR 196	Levin	SOM 115
McECHREN, Margt.	D.C.151	Mary	BCI 59	Sarah	SOM 139
McELDARY, Hugh	BCI 133	Nasha	WOR 195	Tubman	SOM 141
McELDERY, Horatio C.		Patrick	BCI 459	William	SOM 124
	CHA 207B	Peter	SOM 126	McGRAW, Arthur	SOM 138
McELFISH, David	ALL 33	Samuel	WOR 200	Benjn.	KEN 116
John	ALL 32	Sarah Ann	D.C.32	Levin	DOR 8
Thomas	ALL 32	Thomas	CLN 86	William	WOR 216
McELFRESH, Charles	FRE 81	McGEERY, Felix	FRE 159	McGREAVY, Patrick	BCI 485
Henry	FRE 69	James	FRE 141	McGREERY, James	D.C.64
Jane	FRE 74	McGIBBON, Jas.	BCI 173	McGREGOR, Jno.	KEN 125
John	FRE 219	McGILE, George	WAS 121	McGREVY, James	BAL 105
John H.	FRE 97	McGILL, Basel	MON 178	McGRIGER, William	WAS 66
Philamon	FRE 81	Benidict	SAI 88	McGRIGOR, William	WOR 186
Philip	FRE 72	G.	BCI 403	McGRUDER, Jno. R.	
Sarah	FRE 72	James	D.C.105		FRE 133
McELHINEY, Robert	HAR 77	James	PRI 184	Louisa	FRE 133
McELROY, John	BAL 181	John	PRI 204	McGRUSHA, Joseph	BCI 536
John	BCI 464	Nancy	PRI 184	McGUICE, Edw. (?)	D.C.11
Saml.	BCI 166	Patk., Senr.	FRE 125	McGUIER, Sarah	BCI 303
McELWEE, Jane	BCI 68	Patk., Jr.	FRE 123	McGUIN, James	BCI 275
John	D.C.77	Robert	WAS 62	McGUIRE, Edw.	D.C.11
McENERNY, John	D.C.138	Thomas	ANN 383	James	D.C.167
McENTIRE, Francis	BAL 67	Tower	BCI 475	James	QUE 18
James	DOR 6	Willm.	D.C.131	Mary Ann	BCI 57
McENTYRE, Daniel	SOM 116	McGILLEN, Jas.	BCI 193	Michael	BCI 256
James	SOM 116	McGILLY, Edward	BCI 70	Redmond	BCI 255
McEVERS, Daniel	BAL 181	McGILTON, Danl.	BCI 494	Thomas	CLN 72A
McEVOY, James	BCI 198	McGIN, R.	BCI 150	Wm.	KEN 124
McEWEN, William	D.C.34	McGINN, James (?)	BCI 275	McGUIRK, John	BCI 525
McEWIN, Robert	PRI 229	McGINNATOR, Mary	BCI 191	Peter	BCI 530
McFADAN, Sam	BCI 226	McGINNIS, Casparas		McHANNEY, Solomon	
McFADAR, C.	BCI 382		KEN 120		BAL 138
McFADDEN, James	HAR 71	Geo.	KEN 123	McHANY, Mathias	D.C.155
John	HAR 71	Nathl.	KEN 123	McHENNEY, Spencer	
John	WOR 162	Robert	FRE 174		BAL 162
John, Jr.	HAR 73	Sarah	CLN 95	McHENRY, Dennis	BCI 443
William	HAR 44	McGINNY, Nathaniel	BCI 92	Francis D.	BCI 388
McFADDON, Neil	BCI 275	McGINSEY, Fanny	BCI 506	Henry	FRE 140
McFADGEN, Michael	FRE 147	McGINTLY, Margaretta		John	ALL 4
McFADGEON, Denis	FRE 142		WAS 106	Wm.	WOR 155
McFADON, John	BCI 249	McGINTY, Robert	WAS 126	McHENRY, FORT	BCI 326
McFAIEL, Eneas	BCI 455	McGIOCH, Andrew	BCI 138	McHERRAN, Duncan	BCI 302
McFALL, Catherine	WAS 123	McGIRK, John	BCI 514	McIHOY, Elizth.	BCI 248
Danl.	BCI 499	McGIRR, James	ALL 3	McILHANEY, --- (Mr.)	
Mariah	WAS 117	McGITTON, Betsy	BCI 347		BCI 382
McFANN, David (?)	CEC 180	McGLASHAN, Isabella		McILHENNEY, John	WAS 114
McFARAN, John	BCI 115		BCI 295	Joseph	WAS 117
McFARLAND, Geo.	D.C.129	McGLENAN, Mary	BCI 307	McILHENNY, Alexandria	
George	ALL 26	McGLENEN, James	BCI 339		FRE 204
Ignatius	D.C.215	McGLENN, Shadrack		McILLVANE, William	BAL 142
Walter	BCI 498		CLN 78	McILVAIN, Robt.	BCI 186
William	MON 153	McGLOCHLIN, Danl. (?)		Sarah	BCI 284
Wm.	D.C.17		KEN 124	McILVAIRE, Sarah (?)	
McFARLIN, William	BCI 25	Geo.	KEN 115		BCI 284
McFARLING, Joseph	WAS 61	Thomas	KEN 115	McILVEY, James	BCI 52
McFEE, Robert	CEC 163	McGLOCKLIN, Danl.		McINTIRE, Alex.	D.C.16
McFEELY, Jno.	BCI 166		KEN 124	Charles	BCI 25
Patrick	CLN 77	McGLOLLEN, John	DOR 51	David	ALL 2

McINTIRE (continued),			McKESSICK, John	FRE	150	McLAUGHLIN, Alexander		
James	ALL	11	William	FRE	149		PRI	228
James	D.C.131		McKEWEN, James	BCI	516	Daniel	BCI	62
John	BCI	117	McKEWIN, Ann	BCI	71	Daniel	BCI	91
Saml.	D.C.7		McKEY, Abner	KEN	123	Daniel	FRE	148
McINTOSH, Daniel	ALL	3	Richd.	D.C.154		Edwd.	BCI	181
Daniel	FRE	107	McKILLIP, John	FRE	170	Edwd.	D.C.166	
Mary	ALL	29	McKIM, --- (Mrs.)	BCI	356	Fransec	BCI	518
Thos.	D.C.105		Alexander	BCI	114	George	HAR	41
McIVER, James	BCI	217	Isaac	BCI	125	Henry	WAS	112
John	D.C.203		Jno., Jr.	BCI	252	Irwin	ANN	349
McJILTON, W. A.	D.C.131		John	BCI	135	James	HAR	39
William	HAR	77	John, Junior	BAL	116	John	D.C.3	
McKAFFERTY, John	BCI	515	Mary	BCI	197	John	D.C.72	
McKAMAN, --- (Mrs.)			Saml.	BCI	233	John	WAS	112
	BCI	334	Wm. D.	BCI	259	Joseph	BCI	100
McKAMARE, William	DOR	4	McKIMLEY, Ann (?)			Mathew	HAR	79
McKANE, Elizabeth	WAS	121		BCI	439	Michael	HAR	21
McKANRIC, Orphenia			McKINALEY, Lenorad			Michael	HAR	38
	BAL	36		WAS	89	Michael H.	HAR	70
McKAY, Benjamin	SAI	64	McKINLEY, James	ALL	21	P.	BCI	239
Cornels.	D.C.89		McKINNEY, David	QUE	12	Patrick	HAR	18
Hugh	BCI	215	John	CAL	45	Susanah	WAS	112
John	SAI	62A	McKINNY, John	FRE	156	William	ALL	34
Mattw.	D.C.123		William (?)	DOR	53	William	BCI	457
Patty	BCI	446	McKINSEY, Aron	ALL	15	McLAUGLIN, Math.	BCI	351
Stephen	SAI	64	Aron	ALL	22	McLAWCE, Robert	CEC	162
William	D.C.10		Caleb	ALL	17	McLEAN, Corns.	D.C.72	
Willm.	BCI	189	Daniel	ALL	9	McLEOD, Danl.	D.C.164	
McKBEE, Edward	ANN	384	Daniel	ALL	22	John	D.C.81	
McKEAN, Elizh.	BCI	193	Daniel	BAL	202	McLEVY, Henry	BCI	229
McKEARNAN, Peter	FRE	101	Gabriel	ALL	18	Jos.	BCI	226
McKEE, George	D.C.6		Jesse	ALL	16	McLIN, James	WOR	219
James	PRI	215	Joseph	BCI	527	McLOCHLAN, Michl.		
John	D.C.215		Joshua	ALL	18		MON	130
John	MON	162	Moses	ALL	17	McLONE, Lancelot	CEC	162
John	WAS	73	Moses	ALL	23	McLOUGHLIN, Francis		
John	WAS	112	Richard	ALL	21		BAL	129
Mary	WAS	109	Samuel	ALL	16	Mary	BCI	224
McKEEL, James	TAL	11	Samuel	ALL	22	McLUNG, Joseph	BAL	85
Thomas	TAL	13	Samuel	WAS	86	Joseph	BAL	89
McKEHAN, George	FRE	147	William	DOR	53	McMACIN, Benjamin	ANN	349
McKELBY, William	WAS	64	McKINSTRY, Evan	FRE	177	McMAHAN, Daniel	TAL	36
McKELDEN, Ellin	BCI	474	Jesse	BAL	236	James	TAL	33
Jos.	BCI	478	McKINSY, Elizabeth			John	TAL	32
McKELDON, Margt.	D.C.15			FRE	199	John H.	TAL	32
McKELDRIN, William	CHA	197	McKINZIE, Aaron	ANN	352	Richard	TAL	32
McKELVEY, Alexander			Catherine	ANN	352	Richard	WAS	133
	FRE	98	Colen	BCI	210	Solomon	TAL	36
McKENAL, John	BCI	393	John	SOM	137	Thomas	TAL	33
McKENESTY, Jane	BCI	353	Oster	FRE	187	William	TAL	32
McKENLEY, Elize.	BCI	520	McKIRNLEY, Ann	BCI	439	Wm.	FRE	123
James	BCI	527	McKISSICK, James	WAS	100	McMAHON, Abagail	D.C.87	
McKENNA, Jas. L.	D.C.166		McKLEE, Edward (?)			Peter	ALL	28
McKENNEY, --- (Mrs.)				ANN	384	William	ALL	27
	BCI	403	McKLEFISH, William			McMAIN, George	BCI	439
Elizabeth	KEN	115		ANN	378	McMANUS, Owen	BCI	339
John	HAR	21	McKLING, William	WAS	78	McMASTER, Samuel	CEC	180
John	HAR	47	McKNEW, --- (Mrs.)			McMASTERS, Samuel		
Peter	HAR	20		PRI	185		WOR	156
Rose	D.C.80		Peter	PRI	185	McMATH, William	HAR	43
Samuel	CEC	163	McKNIGHT, Chas.	D.C.196		McMEAL, Daniel (Capt.)		
McKENNY, Bensn.	D.C.108		John	D.C.198			FRE	140
Saml.	D.C.40		McKONNAL, Hugh	WAS	80	McMECHEN, Hugh	BAL	45
Thomas L.	D.C.65		McKOY, Andrew	ALL	16	John	BAL	207
William	D.C.59		McKUBBIN, Eleanor			Samuel	BAL	181
McKENSTRAY, Thos.	BCI	535		ANN	300	Thomas	BAL	193
McKENZIE, Alexr.	D.C.160		Richard	ANN	290	William	BAL	45
James	BCI	110	McKUCHEAN, Wm.	FRE	226	William, Esqr.	BAL	248
James	D.C.174		McKUMPSEY, John	WAS	134	Wm.	BCI	259
Maria	BCI	76	McLAIN, Jane	BCI	23	McMECHIN, William	BAL	206
McKEOWN, James	CEC	163	Mary	FRE	87	McMECHUM, Saml. (?)		
Samuel	CEC	163	William	TAL	37		D.C.16	
Samuel, Sr.	CEC	163	McLANE, Charles	BCI	10	McMECKUM, Saml.	D.C.16	
McKERDEY, John	WAS	116	McLARY, Mary	CEC	179A	McMELLON, William	BAL	199
McKERLIE, Isabella	BCI	65	McLASKY, Ann	MON	175	McMICHAEL, William	DOR	43

McMILLEN, John FRE 94
McMILLION, Sary PRI 224
McMULLEN, Martis BCI 26
Stephen BCI 437
McMULLIGAN, Patrick BCI 315
McMULLIN, Francus WAS 95
Hugh ALL 5A
Hugh FRE 101
James ALL 5A
James BCI 250
James FRE 114
John ALL 6
Margurett BCI 317
Robert WAS 79
McMURPHY, John BCI 119
McMURRY, Samuel BAL 55
McNABB, Daniel HAR 44
Isaac HAR 45
James HAR 76
John D.C.171
McNABL, John (?) D.C.171
McNAIR, William D.C.40
McNALLY, Peter BAL 204
McNAMARA, Francis CEC 180
Pat. D.C.17
Sarah D.C.18
McNAMARE, Rebeca DOR 5
McNAME, Alee WAS 68
George WAS 94
Moses WAS 94
McNANTZ, Neal D.C.107
McNEAL, Gary TAL 36
Harrisson BCI 317
Henry TAL 40
James BCI 24
James TAL 36
Jas. BCI 239
John BCI 216
John BCI 378
John TAL 38
McNEAR, George BCI 284
William BCI 109
McNEILL, John ALL 30
John WOR 192
McNEIR, George ANN 394
William ALL 14A
McNELTY, Catharine BCI 277
John HAR 27
McNEMANE, Patience (?) DOR 35
McNEMARE, John S. DOR 32
Patience DOR 33
Thomas DOR 33
McNEMARNE, Henry DOR 33
John DOR 33
Levin DOR 33
Thimothey DOR 33
McNESH, William CLN 87
McNEW, Jeremiah ANN 366
Nathan PRI 180A
Thomas D.C.32
McNEWS, Nathan (?) PRI 180A
McNICHOLS, Jacob BCI 425
McNICKLE, Isaac BCI 488
McNIEL, Farniah CEC 125
McNIELL, George WOR 211
McNIER, Thomas ANN 291
McNIGHT, John BCI 386
John DOR 30
McNMARNE, Nancey DOR 33
McNOLTY, Thos. D.C.126
McNUTT, David WAS 85
William HAR 75
McNUTTY, Thomas WAS 55A
McOANN, John BCI 60
McORMICK, Samuel BAL 82

McOY, Isaac BAL 215
McPARLIN, William ANN 391
McPARTRIDGE, Alexander CEC 162
McPHALE, Danl. BCI 384
McPHERSAN, Samuel D.C.31
McPHERSEN, Isaac BCI 445
McPHERSON, --- (Miss)
(of Charles County)-
her slaves PRI 223
Alexander FRE 98
Benny CHA 210A
Dolly D.C.58
Elisha B. CHA 211
Filinda D.C.213
Gustavus D.C.63
Henry CHA 213
Henry D.C.30
Henry PRI 214
Henry T. CHA 211
James FRE 111
John CHA 224
John D.C.25
John FRE 87
John FRE 102
Jonas BCI 386
Mary CHA 221
Patience PRI 239
Robert G. FRE 109
Thomas ANN 268
Thomas CHA 212
W. T. D.C.133
William BAL 124
William CHA 211
William D.C.11
William FRE 109
McQUANN, John D.C.206
McQUAY, John BAL 238
John TAL 24
Patrick BAL 54
Patrick TAL 24
Thomas TAL 45
McQUIN, Alexander PRI 229
Kelly BCI 357
Patrick PRI 231
Philip BCI 374
McQUINN, Wm. BCI 167
McREA, John ALL 38
McREADY, Stephen WOR 209
McREDING, Edwd. D.C.85
McREIGHLER, Stephen (?) D.C.20
McREIGHTER, Stephen D.C.20
McROBY, Elijah ALL 2
William ALL 3
McSOARLEY, Patrick BCI 66
McSTATOM, Mary BCI 344
McSWEENEY, Patrick BCI 417
McTIER, Alexander BCI 266
Wm. BCI 347
McVAY, Benjamin CEC 163
McVEIGH, Michl. D.C.95
McVEY, James HAR 38
McVICAR, Elizabeth FRE 95
Hetty D.C.8
McVICKER, Lucy ALL 23
McWATTERS, Adam D.C.129
McWICKER, Hetty D.C.19
McWILLIAM, Wm. BCI 285

McWILLIAMS, Alexr. D.C.122
Clemt. D.C.91
Edwd. W. D.C.109
George SAI 78
James SAI 98
MEAD, Benjamin BCI 102
James PRI 202
John SAI 70
Samuel ANN 391
Walter C. CAL 64
Watter C.? CAL 64
Zachariah CAL 64
MEADE, Bridget D.C.89
Theodore D.C.184
MEADS, Benjamin ANN 276
Betsey BCI 506
Hannah HAR 60
James HAR 60
Pheby BCI 496
Uriah ANN 276
MEALY, Michael FRE 69
Michael, Jr. FRE 74
MEANLEY, Edward WAS 77
MEANS, Philip WAS 149
Thos. WAS 149
MEARS, Harrison DOR 11
Mary CLN 113
Robert FRE 209
MEASLE, Jacob FRE 116
Rosanna FRE 113
MECHEM, Francis HAR 40
John HAR 40
MECHEN, Hugh W. (?) BAL 45
William W. (?) BAL 45
MECKLIN, John D.C.15
MECONIKIN, Thomas TAL 13
William E. QUE 42
MEDARD, Jos. BCI 354
MEDCALF, Abraham BCI 7
Ann BCI 50
Enos FRE 80
George ANN 388
John FRE 204
Joshua FRE 193
Thomas FRE 178
Thomas FRE 203
W. M. BCI 127
MEDDIS, John DOR 39
MEDDOWS, Jno. KEN 125
MEDFORD, James ANN 398
Jas. QUE 19
Lemuel DOR 60
McCall KEN 107
Nathaniel DOR 50
Peter DOR 54
Robert CLN 110
Robert DOR 52
William DOR 55
MEDLEY, Clare SAI 81
Elijah MON 178
James CHA 211
Philip SAI 98
MEDLICAUFF, Christian WAS 67
MEDLICOAT, Samuel BAL 144
MEDSTIFF, John BCI 480
MEDTARD, John BCI 359
MEDTART, Jacob FRE 102
MEECH, Thos. BCI 172
MEECHER, James (?) DOR 13

MEECKENS (See also	
MUCKENS),	
Jacob (?)	DOR 27
John (?)	DOR 26
John (?)	DOR 29
Joshua (?)	DOR 26
Levin (?)	DOR 26
Mary (?)	DOR 26
Rebeka (?)	DOR 29
Robert (?)	DOR 30
Thomas (?)	DOR 25
MEECKER, James	DOR 13
MEECKINS, Richard (?)	
	DOR 28
Robrt (?)	DOR 30
MEEDS, Abraham	BCI 9
Henry	CLN 91
Joshua	QUE 5
Mallakiah	CLN 73
Nicholas N.	QUE 33
Parry	CLN 82
Richard	QUE 30
Samuel	BCI 25
Samuel	QUE 29
William	QUE 23
MEEK, James	ANN 306
John	ANN 286
MEEKENS, John D.	DOR 27
Mathew	DOR 27
MEEKINGS, Benjamin	CEC 125
MEEKINS, Isaac	DOR 11
Joseph S.	ANN 289
MEEKS, Ann	KEN 102
C.	BCI 411
David	ANN 329
James	KEN 124
St. Leger	KEN 104
Thomas	HAR 45
William	KEN 109
MEFFERD, John	FRE 154
MEGAR, Peter	BCI 300
MEGEE, Charles	CEC 125
MEGINNEY, Daniel	TAL 34A
Daniel	TAL 37
Levin	TAL 37
MEGINNIS, William, Ovsr.	
	TAL 39
MEHIM, --- (Dr.?)	BCI 254
Dl.	BCI 254
MEIGS, Josiah	D.C.74
MEKINS, Joshua	KEN 117
MELBURN, Samuel	BCI 462
MELEASE, John	BCI 217
MELEER, Wm.	BCI 232
MELINDER, John	CEC 143
MELISEAS, Frederick	BAL 54
MELLER, Henry	WAS 98
Martin	WAS 93
MELLHOOF, Daniel	WAS 134[A]
MELLIN, William G.	ANN 356
MELLOCK, John	ANN 307
MELLON, Joseph	BCI 513
MELONEY, William	CLN 88
MELOYD, Thos.	QUE 8
MELSON, Benjamin, Capt.	
	WOR 202
Betsy	WOR 191
William	SOM 103
William	SOM 126
MELTON, James	KEN 90
John	SAI 66
MELVIN, Avra, Revd.	WOR 158
Betsy	WOR 194
Charity	WOR 160
Elisha	WOR 163
James	D.C.34

MELVIN (continued),	
James	WOR 159
John	QUE 38
Joshua	CLN 96
Polly-w. (of Isaac)	
	WOR 163
Samuel	QUE 40
Thomas	CLN 96
Thomas	SOM 131
Wm. Handy	WOR 158
MENGER, Moses	PRI 215
MENNITT, Wm.	CAL 51
MENOONEY, James	TAL 14
MENSIES, James	BCI 444
MENTZEL, Henry	BCI 13
MENTZER, Conrad	WAS 103
John; S.	WAS 97
John, Jun.	WAS 96
MEQUAY, Jeremiah, Ovsr.	
	TAL 6
MERAN, Jerimiah	DOR 26
MERCER, Andrew	ANN 356
Elizabeth	CEC 125
Francis	ANN 380
George	CEC 179A
George-negro	CEC 125
Henry	ANN 319
Henry	ANN 320
Henry	ANN 390
Isaiah	ANN 349
James	BAL 198
John	ANN 271
John	ANN 357
John	CEC 125
John F., Senr.	ANN 271
Joshua	ANN 356
Luke	ANN 359
Rachel	D.C.105
Samuel	FRE 75
Thomas	ANN 380
William	ANN 362
MERCES, John	CEC 125
MERCHAND, Peter	BCI 267
MERCHANT, Archibd.	
	D.C.190
James	TAL 3
Noah	QUE 4
Thos.	D.C.180
MERCIER, Archabald	
	ANN 356
R. T.	BAL 64
Richard	ANN 356
Richard	BAL 64
MERE, John	CEC 125
MEREADY, Norris	FRE 178
MEREDETH, --- (Mrs.)	
	BCI 456
Jno.	BCI 170
MEREDITH, Abram.	QUE 20
Ben	QUE 9
Benjamen R.	CLN 91
Francis	CLN 73
James	KEN 116
James	QUE 31
Job	KEN 94
John	CHA 208
John	QUE 16
Levi	FRE 218
Rachel	CLN 77
Samuel	QUE 27
Thomas	ANN 297
Thomas	ANN 364
Thomas	BCI 441
William	QUE 25
William	TAL 50

MERICAN (See also	
AMERICA, MARICA,	
MERICHA, MERRICA),	
Henry	WAS 127A
MERICHA, Boston	BAL 189
MERICK, Michl.	MON 177
MERIDITH, James, Jnr.	
	QUE 32
John	KEN 108
John	QUE 30
Mary	DOR 36
Moses	QUE 33
William B.	QUE 24
MERIT, Abel	FRE 87
MERITT, Samuel	FRE 219
MERIWEATHER, Nicholas	
	ANN 370
Thomas	ANN 366
MERKLE, ---	BCI 458
MERNLL, Philip (?)	PRI 213
MERPHY, James	TAL 37
William	TAL 7
MERRICA (See also	
AMERICA, MARICA,	
MERICAN, MERICHA),	
George	BAL 105
MERRICK, Ezekiel	QUE 9
Herietta	TAL 13
James	TAL 24
John	DOR 54
Joseph J.	WAS 118
Rachel	TAL 41
Solomon	CLN 109
William	DOR 40
William D.	CHA 203
MERRIDETH, John	DOR 8
MERRIDITH, Levi	WAS 59
Samuel	BAL 87
Thomas	BAL 87
MERRIDY, John	BCI 408
MERRIKEN, John	ANN 297
Mary	ANN 296
Richard	ANN 303
William D.	ANN 289
MERRIL, Joseph	HAR 6
MERRILL, Jeremiah	ANN 318
John	WOR 156
Levin	WOR 158
Philip	ALL 15
Philip	PRI 213
Stephen	ALL 17
Thos., Senr.	WOR 156
Thos. (of Scarborough)	
	WOR 159
MERRIS, John	CEC 179A
MERRIT, James	CEC 141
Rachel	ANN 303
Sh---rick	BCI 160
MERRITT, Araminta	KEN 125
Benjn.	KEN 122
Edwd.	D.C.129
James	KEN 120
John	BCI 313
Joseph	CEC 125
Samuel, Sen.	KEN 91
Samuel, Jun.	KEN 91
Wm.	KEN 125
MERRY, William	PRI 228
MERRYMAN, Ann	FRE 222
Augusta M. O. D.	
	BAL 245
Caleb	ANN 264
Caleb	BAL 175
Fanny	BAL 224
Fanny (col'd.)	BAL 217
George	BAL 152

MILES (continued),		MILLEMAN, John	BAL 230	MILLER (continued),	
Henry	SAI 97	MILLER, --- (father)		Henry	BAL 173
Henry W.	SOM 129	(See Henry MILLER		Henry	CEC 141
Isaac	SOM 156	& father)	FRE 157	Henry	CEC 162
Jacob	SOM 150	--- (Mrs.)	BCI 462	Henry	D.C.92
James	PRI 195	--- (Widow)	BCI 405	Henry	FRE 157
John	BCI 371	Abner	FRE 74	Henry	FRE 178
John	FRE 112	Abraham	FRE 155	Henry	HAR 20
John	SOM 145	Abraham	WAS 67	Henry	MON 178
John (of Wm.)	SOM 131	Adam	BAL 17	Henry	WAS 94
Levin D.	SOM 126	Andrew	BCI 451	Henry	WAS 121
Lucy	PRI 187	Ann	BCI 18	Hezekiah	D.C.60
Martha	ANN 375	Ann	QUE 26	Isaac	ALL 14A
Mary	SOM 150	Ann	TAL 4	Isaac	BAL 97
Matthias, Senr.	SOM 126	Ann	WAS 120	Isaac	BAL 205
Matthias, Junr.	SOM 126	Anthony	FRE 181	Isaac	BCI 382
Nacy	FRE 78	Augs.	BCI 242	Isaac	KEN 116
Nathan	MON 140	Baltzer	WAS 102	Isaac	KEN 125
Nathaniel	BCI 96	Betsey	BCI 495	Jacob	ALL 12
Nicholas	CHA 228	Catharine	BCI 225	Jacob	ALL 29
Peter	PRI 187	Catharine	CHA 210A	Jacob	BAL 166
Polly	BCI 479	Catherine	WAS 57	Jacob	BCI 93
Rachel	SOM 144	Catherine	WAS 109	Jacob	BCI 180
Rebecca	CEC 141	Ceaser	CEC 179A	Jacob	BCI 412
Richard	WAS 137	Charles	BCI 85	Jacob	BCI 531
Richard H.	SAI 96	Charles	BCI 397	Jacob	FRE 128
Robert	ALL 35	Charles	BCI 446	Jacob	FRE 131
Robert	WAS 136	Chas.	D.C.133	Jacob	FRE 151
Samuel	SOM 149	Christ.	BCI 340	Jacob	FRE 164
Samuel	WAS 136	Christian	FRE 125	Jacob	FRE 224
Sarah	D.C.113	Christian	WAS 93	Jacob	MON 137
Stephen	SOM 151	Christian	WAS 98	Jacob	PRI 186
Thomas	BAL 234	Christopher	MON 129	Jacob	WAS 55A
Thomas	HAR 61	Christopher, Sen.		Jacob	WAS 95
Whitington	DOR 32		ALL 12	Jacob	WAS 145
William	D.C.103	Christopher, Jr.	ALL 14	Jacob, Sen.	WAS 99
William (Sen.)	SOM 144	Conrad	BCI 463	Jacob, Junr.	WAS 66
William (of Horif?)	SOM 146	Conrad	WAS 112	Jacob, Junr.	WAS 95
William (of Horis?)	SOM 146	Dampier-Negro	HAR 80	Jacob, of Chr.	ALL 12
William (of Saml.)	SOM 146	Daniel	FRE 118	Jacob F.	WAS 65
William (of Wm.)	SOM 149	Daniel	FRE 157	James	BCI 111
William; P.N.	SOM 153	Daniel	FRE 183	James	BCI 154
Wm.	BCI 482	Daniel	WAS 134[A]	James	CLN 93
MILHOLLAND, Daniel	ALL 8A	Daniel	WAS 137	James	D.C.27
Stephen	ALL 8A	Daniel	WAs 144	James	QUE 36
MILHORN, Chasper	BAL 161	Dick-f.c.p.	HAR 10	James	WAS 79
John	BAL 53	Edward	CEC 125	John	ALL 12
MILIWAY, Polly	SOM 140	Edward	HAR 22	John	ALL 30
MILL-BELLONA POWDER		Edwin	ANN 359	John	ANN 310
MILL, John YOUNG,		Eli	BAL 195	John	ANN 391
manager	BAL 182	Elijah	BAL 180	John	BAL 160
MILL-ETNY POWDER MILL,		Elizabeth	WAS 74	John	BAL 201
Joseph JIMMISON &		Fredeick	WAS 115	John	BAL 237
CO.	BAL 186	Frederick	BAL 147	John	BCI 38
MILL-FRANKLIN PAPER		Frederick	WAS 95	John	BCI 75
MILL-Laurence		Frederick, Junr.	WAS 65	John	BCI 186
GRATERICK & CO.		Frederick W.	FRE 105	John	BCI 195
	BAL 185	G. W.	BCI 375	John	BCI 198
MILL, & NAIL FACTORY,		Geo. W.	ANN 305	John	BCI 221
AVELIN ROLING &		Geo. W.	BCI 219	John	BCI 457
SLITING-Nathaniel		George	BAL 48	John	CAL 52
ELLICOTT & CO.-		George	BAL 49	John	CHA 220A
John DYKE, manager		George	BCI 82	John	FRE 74
	BAL 192	George	BCI 146	John	FRE 100
MILLAGEN, Michael	CEC 141	George	BCI 448	John	FRE 116
MILLAN, James	D.C.181	George	BCI 520	John	FRE 133
MILLANEY, William	KEN 115	George	D.C.57	John	FRE 149
MILLARD, Edward	SAI 79	George	D.C.73	John	FRE 151
Enoch J.	SAI 74	George	FRE 97	John	FRE 158
John L.	SAI 79	George	FRE 112	John	FRE 169
Jonathan	CEC 179A	George	FRE 203	John	FRE 194
Joseph Le (?)	BCI 54	George	WAS 110	John	FRE 210
Joshua (See Ambrose		George	WAS 114	John	FRE 224
---, negro, slave of		Godfrey	ALL 12	John	FRE 228
Joshua MILLARD)		Henry	ANN 349	John	FRE 228A
Joshua	D.C.84	Henry	ANN 349	John	HAR 22

MILLER (continued),			MILLER (continued),			MILLS (continued),		
John	PRI	185	Richard	KEN	87	Chas.	MON	139
John	WAS	57	Robert	BCI	121	Cornelius	ANN	292
John	WAS	71	Robt.	D.C.	75	David	DOR	3
John	WAS	89	Sam	WOR	196	Edward	BCI	158
John	WAS	96	Saml.	BCI	277	Elenor	SAI	94
John	WAS	112	Saml.	D.C.	128	Elizabeth	WAS	127A
John	WAS	138	Samuel	BAL	208	Elizabeth D.	SAI	92
John, Senr.	WAS	67	Samuel	BCI	57	Ezekiel	BCI	209
John, Senr.	WAS	116	Samuel	BCI	57	Fanny	BCI	346
John, Senr.	WAS	118	Samuel	CEC	141	George	BCI	30
John, Junr.	ANN	389	Samuel	CEC	142	Gillet	WOR	156
John, Junr.	BAL	140	Samuel	HAR	25	Handy, Senr.	WOR	174
John, Jr.	FRE	194	Samuel	WAS	132	Handy, Junr.	WOR	156
John, Junr.	WAS	61	Sarah	KEN	85	Hannah-f.c.p.	HAR	10
John, Junr.	WAS	118	Sophia	BCI	483	Henry	SOM	127
John of George	WAS	96	Susannah	BAL	174	Henry C.	MON	130
John, of MI.	BAL	157	Thomas	BAL	60	Isaac	SOM	116
John D.	BCI	442	Thomas	BAL	92	James	D.C.	193
John G.	WAS	58A	Thomas	CLN	105	James	SOM	151
John P.	FRE	159	Thomas	CEC	142	Job B.	D.C.	15
John S.	FRE	102	Thomas	HAR	25	John	ALL	38
John W.	FRE	102	Thomas	HAR	63	John	BCI	339
Jonathan	FRE	83	Thomas	KEN	85	John	CAL	45
Joseph	ANN	334	Thomas	QUE	33	John	DOR	25
Joseph	BAL	86	Titus	QUE	31	Jonathan	DOR	36
Joseph	HAR	57	Walter M.	CHA	192	Jonathan	SOM	127
Joseph	WAS	94	William	ALL	23	Joseph	SAI	75
Lawrence	D.C.	72	William	CEC	143	Joseph	WAS	89
Leonard	FRE	133	William	D.C.	53	Leonard	CAL	45
Levin	SOM	123	William	FRE	106	Letcia	CEC	125
Lewis	BCI	185	William	HAR	9	Levin	SOM	101A
Lewis	CEC	141	William	HAR	25	Lewis	SAI	79
Lydia	BAL	115	William	KEN	94	Margaret	BCI	138
Margaret	ANN	318	William	WAS	104	Margery	D.C.	195
Margurett	BCI	313	William C.	CEC	163	Margery	D.C.	197
Martin	FRE	162	William F.	HAR	41	Nancy	WOR	196
Mary	BCI	532	Wm.	FRE	224	Nicholas	SAI	82
Mary	CLN	76	Wm.	KEN	124	Patiance	WOR	204
Mary	D.C.	113	Wm. T.	BCI	226	Patrick	CAL	44
Mary	QUE	6	MILLERMAN, George			Rabert?	DOR	25
Merritt	KEN	106		BCI	518	Rabrt	DOR	25
Michael	BAL	140	MILLESTOCK, George			Rebecca	D.C.	151
Michael	BAL	146		HAR	62	Richard	BCI	87
Michael	FRE	93	John	HAR	62	Richard	CEC	141
Michael	KEN	85	MILLHOLLAND, Robert			Richard	FRE	94
Michael	KEN	105		BCI	49	Robert?	DOR	25
Michael	WAS	73	MILLHOOF, John	HAR	21	Robert	BCI	276
Monness	WAS	96	MILLHOUSE, Amoss			Robert	WOR	160
Mordecai	D.C.	200		HAR	28	Robrt?	DOR	25
Muritt?	KEN	106	MILLICAN, James	DOR	61	Robt. A.	D.C.	181
Nehemiah	ANN	339	P.	BCI	399	Saml., Junr.	WOR	159
Nicy	SOM	135	Whalen	DOR	9	Samuel	ANN	316
Peregrine	KEN	119	MILLIGAN, George B.			Samuel, Senr.	WOR	158
Peter	ANN	285		CEC	125	Selby	SOM	101A
Peter	BAL	144	Joseph	D.C.	39	Stephen	SOM	101A
Peter	FRE	71	MILLIKEN, Thomas	HAR	71	Stephen	WOR	217
Peter	KEN	85	MILLIKIN, Richard	PRI	194	Susanna	D.C.	158
Peter	WAS	67	MILLIMAN, George	BCI	131	Susanna	MON	171
Peter	WAS	69	MILLINBARGH, Anthony			Susannah	BCI	26
Peter	WAS	110		BCI	486	Theodore	WAS	85
Phebe	DOR	6	MILLINGTON, Geo. I.			Thomas	BCI	465
Philip	ALL	12		BCI	193	Thomas	DOR	11
Philip	FRE	189	William	CLN	89	Thomas	FRE	72
Philip	PRI	191A	MILLIRON, Samuel	BAL	176	Thomas	HAR	47
Philip Cron	BCI	3	MILLIS, Leven	TAL	48	Thomas	SOM	127
Phillip	FRE	168	Richard	TAL	4	Thos.	WAS	150
Phillip	FRE	169	William	CLN	72A	Walter	CAL	44
Precella	BAL	62	MILLIUM, Moses	BCI	72	William	DOR	22
Priscilla	KEN	119	MILLROY, John	BCI	491	William	DOR	33
Priscilla	KEN	121	MILLS, --- (See			William	HAR	47
Priscilla	QUE	4	MURRY & MILLS)			William, Senr.	SOM	111
R.	BCI	357	Adam	D.C.	11	Willm.	D.C.	174
Richard	ANN	341	Andr.	BCI	496	Wm. N.	D.C.	184
Richard	BAL	152	Archible S.	BCI	17	Wm. P.	BCI	217
Richard	BCI	11	Benjamin	SOM	101A	York	BCI	527

MILLS (continued),		
Zachariah	ANN 332	
MILLS, & NAIL MANU-		
FACTORY, PATAPSCO		
ROLING & SLITING-		
ELLICOTT & CO.		
	BAL 205	
MILS, David	WOR 203	
MILSON, Elijah	WOR 205	
Samuel	WOR 204	
MILSTEAD, Barton	D.C. 115	
Edward	CHA 196	
George K.	CHA 189	
Matthew	CHA 194	
Peter	CHA 196	
Samuel	CHA 194	
Thomas	CHA 194	
Walter	CHA 194	
MILTON, Elizabeth	SAI 87	
MIMM, --- (Mrs.)	D.C. 36	
MINCE, Daniel	BCI 76	
Joseph	BCI 77	
Seth	BCI 143	
MINCHIN, Patience	D.C. 102	
MINEER, George	BAL 40	
MINEQUINN, Martin	BAL 110	
MINER, John	WAS 96	
MINES, Marcus	BCI 97	
MINETT, Ann	BAL 181	
MINGLING, Frederick		
	CEC 142	
MINGO, Daniel	KEN 123	
John	BCI 431	
Sally	BCI 429	
MINICH, Michl.	BCI 524	
MINICK, John	BCI 524	
MINISTER, RUSSIAN		
	D.C. 12	
MINKEY, John	BAL 139	
MINNER, Joshua, Jr.		
	CLN 82	
Solomon	CLN 96	
MINNIS, John	ANN 287	
Sarah	D.C. 135	
MINOKEN, Thomas	DOR 26	
MINOR, Ann	D.C. 92	
Daniel	D.C. 186	
Hugh W.	D.C. 216	
Nace	D.C. 191	
Smith	D.C. 216	
Willm.	D.C. 216	
MINSKEY, Ann M.	ANN 298	
MINT, William	WAS 60	
MINTER, Martain	BAL 139	
MINTUS, Hope	BCI 52	
MINTY, Mary	FRE 142	
MINZIES, James	D.C. 129	
MIRES, Ebinezer	KEN 109	
Jacob	FRE 221	
John	FRE 79A	
Sally	FRE 78	
William	CEC 125	
MIRROR, Michael	WOR 153	
MISENER, Jacob	FRE 79	
MISER, Mary	WAS 145	
MISHOLLY, His.	BCI 224	
MISKEL, Patrick	BAL 12	
MISKIMMON, Samuel	HAR 61	
Wm.	BCI 242	
MISKIMMONS, Hanna	WAS 147	
Nelson	WAS 147	
MISKIMMUNS, Joseph		
	WAS 147	
MISSER, W.	BCI 337	
MISSERSMITH, Francis		
	BCI 267	

MISSLE, Casper	FRE 161	
MISTER, Abraham	BCI 315	
Anny	BCI 335	
Londry?	DOR 32	
Loudry	DOR 32	
Severn	SOM 130	
MITCHAEL, Adam	FRE 84	
Andrew	FRE 84	
Ignatious	FRE 80	
Jacob, Sr.	FRE 84	
Jacob, Jr.	FRE 84	
MITCHEAL, Thomas	ANN 266	
Thomas	ANN 366	
MITCHEL, Charles	FRE 106	
Franc. J.	BCI 400	
Henry	BCI 301	
Isaac	ANN 284	
Jacob	BCI 317	
John	BCI 373	
John	BCI 378	
M.	BCI 392	
Rebeckah	DOR 42	
Thomas	FRE 85	
MITCHELD, Kelly	BCI 351	
W.	BCI 350	
MITCHELE, Singleton		
	PRI 193	
MITCHELL, ---	PRI 207	
Aaron	DOR 3	
Alexander	ANN 279	
Alexander	PRI 203	
Alexr.	BCI 175	
Andrew	WAS 57	
Andw. C.	D.C. 7	
Arthur	BCI 185	
Benj.	WOR 181	
Benjamin	CEC 180	
Catherine	D.C. 193	
D. Abram	CEC 143	
Drusilla	PRI 203	
Dymoch	WOR 213	
Edward	CAL 60	
Edward	HAR 29	
Edward	HAR 42	
Elijah	HAR 45	
Elisha	BCI 18	
Elizabeth	CAL 62	
Elizabeth	CHA 210A	
Evan	HAR 45	
Ezekiel	HAR 20	
Frederick	HAR 45	
Gabriel	HAR 19	
Gedding	BAL 55	
George-Colo.	CEC 143	
Henry	DOR 44	
Henry	HAR 29	
Howel	HAR 76	
Hurlah	PRI 181	
Isaac	WOR 218	
Jacob (negro)	TAL 23	
James	ANN 271	
James	BCI 254	
James	CEC 125	
James	QUE 12	
James	WOR 206	
James H.	WOR 206	
Jeffrey	DOR 60	
Jeremiah	PRI 185	
Jesse	WOR 205	
John	BCI 116	
John	HAR 25	
John	PRI 203	
John	PRI 204	
John	WAS 57	
John	WOR 206	
John W.	DOR 5	

MITCHELL (continued),		
Joseph	CEC 162	
Joseph	KEN 86	
Joseph	PRI 206	
Js. (Captn.)	D.C. 155	
Judson	D.C. 12	
Kent	HAR 29	
Leven	DOR 41	
Levin	DOR 15	
Lucey	ANN 260	
Mary	CEC 141	
Mary	WOR 184	
Mary Ann	CHA 192	
Michael	DOR 14	
Michiael	SOM 140	
Nathan	PRI 181	
Nicholas	BAL 192	
Oliver	CLN 98	
Oliver	CEC 141	
Peg	WOR 187	
Peggy	D.C. 177	
Peggy	SOM 153	
Pelly	WOR 206	
Ralph	DOR 44	
Rector	PRI 207	
Reubin	DOR 15	
Richard	BCI 116	
Richard	CLN 85A	
Richard	CHA 210A	
Richard	HAR 19	
Richard B.	BAL 125	
Richard B.	BCI 272	
Robert	HAR 26	
Robert	WOR 185	
Sally	SOM 127	
Samuel	PRI 211	
Samuel	WAS 63	
Sarah	DOR 3	
Sarah	HAR 25	
Sarah	HAR 26	
Singleton (?)	PRI 193	
Steven	WOR 202	
Susan	QUE 18	
Theedere	PRI 193	
Thomas	ANN 265	
Thomas	BCI 27	
Thomas	HAR 19	
Thomas	PRI 206	
Thos.	D.C. 127	
Thos.	FRE 122	
Thos. L. (?)	PRI 191A	
Tubmond	SOM 151	
Walter	D.C. 134	
Walter	MON 132	
Walter D.	FRE 135	
Washington	ANN 301	
William	HAR 29	
William	WOR 215	
Wm. B.	WOR 180	
Zebidee, Jr.	DOR 15	
Zebidee, of J. (I.?)		
	DOR 14	
Zeph.	PRI 182	
Zepheniah	PRI 205	
MITCHER, John, Esqr.		
	BCI 281	
MITCHILL, Richard	DOR 14	
Thos. L.	PRI 191A	
MITEN, William	FRE 97	
MITTEN, James	FRE 186	
Job	HAR 40	
William	FRE 186	
MITTING, John	BAL 142	
Miles	BAL 155	
Thomas	BAL 150	
MIUS, Ebinezer (?)	KEN 109	

MOODY (continued),
Isaac	BCI 131
John	D.C. 126
John	KEN 87
Robt.	BCI 189
Roger	D.C. 136
Samuel	BCI 151
Sarah	QUE 5
Stephen	QUE 35
Thomas	ANN 317
Thomas	BAL 118
Thomas	BCI 466
William	BCI 22
William	BCI 252
MOOLER, Mary	SAI 79

MOOLOCK (See also MORLOCK),
Isaac (?)	DOR 57
Samuel (?)	DOR 49
MOON, Henry	MON 142
Jacob	ALL 4
Richard	BCI 21
Thomas	ALL 4
MOONEY, Cornelius	BAL 202
Edward	BCI 310
James	BCI 490
Mary	D.C. 164
Patrick	BCI 255

MOONSHOWER, Nicholas
	FRE 168
MOONY, James	DOR 61
MOOR, George	BAL 143
Harvey	CEC 180
Henry (?)	MON 142
John	D.C. 156
Joseph	CEC 181
Martha	CEC 181
Thomas	BCI 215
William	CEC 181

MOORE, --- (Mrs.)
	BCI 453
--- (Mrs.)	BCI 463
--- (Widaw)	BCI 384
Adam-f.n.	SOM 120
Alexander	CEC 141
Alexander	CEC 143
Alexander	HAR 43
Alexander C.	D.C. 8
Allexander	WAS 150
Andrew (negro)	TAL 23
Ann	BCI 51
Ann	BCI 487
Ann	CEC 125
Ann	DOR 53
Ann	KEN 120
Archd.	BCI 179
Aron	BCI 133
Barbary	D.C. 183
Benj.	FRE 122
Benjamin	SOM 106
Benjamin D.	CHA 216
Benjn.	BCI 417
Biddy-f.c.p.	HAR 10
Bill	HAR 29
Charles	D.C. 31
Charles	FRE 117
Christopher	CLN 114
Clenas	HAR 30
Daniel	SAI 53A
David	CEC 179A
Duglass	BCI 192
Elijah	DOR 61
Elizabeth	D.C. 14
Elizh.	BCI 183
Enoch	ALL 24
Ezekiel	DOR 42
Fielder	ANN 286

MOORE (continued),
Gabriel	ALL 6
George	ALL 30
George	BCI 464
George	CEC 180
George	FRE 98
George	HAR 20
George	HAR 70
George	SAI 66
Gods Grace	CAL 66A
Hannah (negro)	TAL 26
Harriet	BCI 82
Henry	BCI 383
Henry	CHA 214
Henry	CHA 216
Henry	HAR 74
Henry	SOM 145
Horatio	PRI 222
Isaac	DOR 36
Isaac	DOr 42
Isaac	DOR 56
Isaac	MON 153
Isaac	SOM 150
Isaac B.	SOM 145
James	ALL 23
James	CHA 216
James	D.C. 120
James	DOR 37
James	DOR 59
James	FRE 140
James	HAR 74
James	MON 133
James	QUE 13
James	SOM 112
James, Senr.	D.C. 138
James, Junr.	D.C. 85
James, Jr.	DOR 3
Jane	D.C. 181
Jason	HAR 47
Jesse	FRE 94
Joe (negro)	TAL 19
John (?)	DOR 33
John	ALL 13
John	BCI 135
John	BCI 409
John	CLN 82
John	CEC 141
John	CEC 142
John	CEC 163
John	D.C. 37
John	D.C. 114
John	DOR 53
John	FRE 176
John	HAR 71
John	QUE 6
John (free negro)	SOM 118
John C.	PRI 226
John D.	FRE 132
John O.	WAs 144
Johnathan	SOM 109
Joseph	ALL 6
Joseph	CEC 179A
Joseph	D.C. 53
Joseph	HAR 37
Joseph	MON 153
Levi	DOR 5
Levi	SOM 150
Levin	DOR 25
Lucy	CHA 216
Lydia	BCI 498
Marcus	ALL 22
Margt.	D.C. 207
Maria	D.C. 143
Mary	BCI 487
Mary	DOR 34

MOORE (continued),
Mary	DOR 37
Matthew	CHA 226
Matthew	WOR 186
Mordaica	D.C. 28
Mordica J.	PRI 212
Moses	BAL 205
Moses	CEC 180
Nancy	DOR 59
Nancy	SOM 131
Nathan	D.C. 8
Nathaniel	MON 153
Neley	CEC 180
Nicholas E.	SOM 109
Phillip	BCI 94
Phoebe	BCI 161
Reuben	DOR 51
Rob	BCI 511
Robert	DOR 37
Robert (Doctor)	FRE 140
Ruth	CEC 180
S. (Mrs.)	BCI 387
Saml.	BCI 301
Saml.	MON 144
Saml. L. (Doctor)	
	BAL 241
Samuel	ALL 13
Samuel	HAR 29
Sarah	BCI 503
Sarah	FRE 148
Stephen	CEC 125
Stephen	SAI 54
Stephen	SOM 149
Stephen H.	BCI 255
Susan	DOR 25
Syrus	BCI 487
Thomas	ANN 318
Thomas	BCI 77
Thomas	BCI 265
Thomas	CEC 142
Thomas	DOR 25
Thomas	MON 153
Thomas	PRI 237
Thomas T.	SAI 69
Thos.	QUE 13
Toney	BCI 466
Warring F.	SAI 74
William	ALL 28
William	BAL 63
William	BCI 134
William	CEC 143
William	CEC 180
William	DOR 41
William	DOR 53
William	HAR 20
William	SOM 105
William	SOM 149
William	WOR 187
William, Jun.	WOR 195
William S.	BCI 249
William W.	SOM 145
Wm.	BCI 493
MOOREHEAD, John	BCI 466
Turner	BCI 417
MOORES, John	HAR 47
William A.	BCI 16
MOORHEAD, Robert	FRE 160
MOOSE, Henry	FRE 194
MOOTE, George	BCI 187
MOPPS, Adam	ALL 28
William	BAL 246
MORAIN, Ally	DOR 45
Ellinder	DOR 45
John	DOR 61
Mary	DOR 61

MORAN, Alexander	CHA 222	MORGAN (continued),		MORGIN (continued),	
Charles	CHA 227	Ann	D.C.190	Jaal?	BCI 386
Edward	CHA 205	Ann	SAI 97	Joal	BCI 386
Edward B.	CHA 228	Charles	CLN 73	MORLAND, Stepney	TAL 6
Elijah	CHA 223	Charles	D.C.130	MORLING, Mary	TAL 47
Elkanah	CHA 223	Charles	SAI 86A	MORLOCK (See also
Gabriel	BCI 347	Daniel	CLN 105	MOOLOCK),
Henry	CHA 223	Dani.	KEN 123	Isaac	DOR 57
James	PRI 193	David	BAL 203	Samuel	DOR 49
James D.	PRI 191A	David	FRE 129	MORNINGSTAR, Henry
James G.	CHA 228	David G.	TAL 35		BAL 148
Jerimiah (?)	DOR 26	Edward	BCI 131	John	FRE 221
Jesse	PRI [200]	Edward	CEC 141	Philip, Jr.	FRE 160
John	CHA 227	Hamilton	HAR 71	Phillip	FRE 160
John	D.C.137	Henry	TAL 33	MORR, Mathias	BCI 295
Joseph	D.C.52	Hopey	SAI 94	MORRASON, Andrew	WAS 150
Luke	CHA 227	Ignatious	SAI 95	Wm.	WAS 150
Mary	CHA 222	Isaac-negro	HAR 79	MORRICE, Mary	WAS 125
Mary	FRE 163	Jacob	D.C.170	MORRICKS, Jacob	BAL 15
Meberal	CHA 222	James	BAL 204	MORRIN, Blair	WAS 79
Meberal H.	CHA 227	James	CEC 125	MORRIS, --- (See
Michal	BAL 16	James	SAI 63	FRINGE & MORRIS)
MORAND, Willm.	D.C.137	Jane	SAI 63	Abel	CEC 180
MORANE, Henry	DOR 36	Jeremiah	SAI 98	Ailcy	DOR 13
MORANG, Samuel	BCI 62	Jessee	BCI 434	Benjn.	WOR 173
MORDICA, Isaac	BCI 177	John	BAL 84	Caleb, Revd.	WOR 176
MORDOCH, Ann	FRE 142	John	BAL 195	Ceazer	WOR 195
MORE, Abreham	WOR 213	John	BCI 356	Charles	D.C.159
Benjn.	D.C.127	John	CLN 92	Clement	TAL 49
Catherine	WAS 115	John	CEC 162	David	CLN 86
Charles	D.C.78	John	D.C.30	Edward	BAL 86
Daniel	KEN 117	John	D.C.144	Edward	DOR 60
James	BAL 92	John	FRE 95	Edward	WOR 213
James	D.C.85	John	QUE 9	Elijah	CLN 95
James D.	WAS 138	John	SAI 65	Ellinor	BCI 5
John	CEC 181	Jonathan	CAL 48	George	BCI 268
John	FRE 198	Joseph	ANN 377	Isaac	CEC 179A
John	KEN 106	Joseph	SAI 86A	Isaac	WOR 216
John	SAI 73A	Joseph	WAS 111	Isack	BAL 11
Joseph	WAS 96	Kiturah	BAL 2	Jacob, Sen.	SOM 132
Josias	D.C.135	Margaret	D.C.24	Jacob (of John)	SOM 132
Morran	BCI 343	Mary	ANN 402	James	ANN 383
Nancy	QUE 48	Mary	CLN 109	James	WOR 216
Richard	CEC 125	Mordica	CAL 44	Jeptha	WOR 216
Richard	WAS 57	Nancy	TAL 48	Jeremiah	CLN 92
Robert	ANN 273	Ned-negro	HAR 65	Jesse	BCI 257
Robert	TAL 38	Nelly	D.C.193	Jesse	KEN 124
Samuel	TAL 14	Patty	CEC 141	Jethro	WOR 219
Stephen	WOR 172	Philip	D.C.115	John	BAL 145
Tobias	FRE 198	Philip-Negro	HAR 80	John	BAL 192
Tolly	ANN 263	Raphael	SAI 79	John	CHA 217
Verlinda	D.C.82	Rebecca	CLN 111	John	DOR 19
William	KEN 106A	Rob. C.	BCI 220	John	WOR 200
William W.	TAL 12	Robert	HAR 78	John of J. Ho.	WOR 214
MOREAN, Zacchus	KEN 87	Samuel	WAS 84	John (of Jacob)	SOM 132
MOREGROUND, Ceasar		Sarah	KEN 89	John B.	BCI 245
	ANN 255	Solomon	CLN 78	John H.	SOM 136
MOREHAUSE, Wm.	BCI 409	Thomas	ANN 404	Joseph	BAL 81
MOREHEAD, John	BCI 499	Thomas	BCI 129	Joseph, Junr.	BAL 81
MOREHOUSE, Thomas	D.C.64	Thomas	HAR 27	Joshua	WOR 187
MORELAND, Elias	PRI 202	Thomas W.	FRE 97	Joshua	WOR 216
George	D.C.169	W.	BCI 355	Leah	SOM 139
Levin	SAI 92	William	CLN 89	Leah	WOR 162
Mary	PRI 230	William	CEc 125	Levin	PRI 237
William	FRE 151	William	D.C.31	Levin	SOM 133
MORELL, John	BCI 47	William	D.C.72	Lloyd	HAR 40
MORELOCK, Michael	FRE 204	William	HAR 71	Mary	QUE 20
MOREMVILLE, John	BCI 40	William	QUE 39	Masan	D.C.60
MORETON, Robert	SOM 115	William	WAS 72	Mason?	D.C.60
MORFORD, John	BAL 241	William, Senr.	WAS 73	Milly	SOM 132
MORGAGE, Nancy	CLN 81	William, Jr.	CLN 99	Nancy	SOM 138
MO[R]GAN, Philimon (?)		Willm.	D.C.167	Nathan	D.C.42
	TAL 51	Wm.	FRE 226	Nathan	PRI 208
MORGAN, --- (Mrs.)	BCI 415	Wm. L.	D.C.176	Noah	DOR 64
Aires	SOM 131	MORGIN, --- (Widaw)		Owen	BCI 445
Alexander	BAL 231		BCI 403	Peter	WOR 219

MORRIS (Continued),		
Philip, Captn.	WOR	177
Rattiff	WOR	216
Reuben	ALL	4
Saml.	WOR	181
Sarah	QUE	20
Shadarac, Junr.	WOR	177
Shaderack (Senr.)	WOR	178
Thomas	BAL	106
Thomas	SOM	133
Thomas, of J.	WOR	214
Thomas B.	PRI	196
Thomas C.	BCI	6
Vincent	CLN	93
William	CHA	217
William	HAR	42
William ˅	HAR	58
William	KEN	119
William	SOM	133
MORRISON, Alexander		
	WAS	62
Andrew	ALL	14
Arthur	ALL	22
Arthur	FRE	228
Daniel	FRE	151
David	BCI	443
David	FRE	146
H.	BCI	251
James	BCI	132
James	BCI	499
James, Sen.	ALL	14
Jas.	D.C.	122
Jas.	FRE	124
Job	CEC	180
John	BCI	50
John	FRE	116
John	FRE	146
John	HAR	7
John	HAR	74
John	WAS	62
Mathew	HAR	74
Peter B.	BCI	169
Robert	CEC	180
Sammuel	BCI	31
Samuel	WOR	153
William	HAR	6
William	WAS	66
MORRISS, Charles	SOM	120
Joseph	SOM	118
Richd.	BCI	478
Walter	CHA	207
MORRISSON, Michl.	D.C.	157
Wm.	BCI	187
MORRISTON, George	CLN	89
MORROSON, Phibea	WAS	84
MORROW, Archibald	FRE	151
Fanny	BAL	20
James	D.C.	162
James	D.C.	210
John	CAL	63
Mary	BAL	243
William	BCI	56
MORS, Joseph	CEC	125
MORSE, Charles	FRE	81
Charles	CEC	162
Orlando	BCI	58
MORSEL, Joseph	TAL	32
MORSELE, John C.	PRI	184
Richard J. (I.?) (?)		
	PRI	198
MORSELL, --- (Widaw)		
	BCI	403
Benjamin K.	PRI	182
James	CAL	63
James, Senr.	CAL	66A
James S.	D.C.	25

MORSELL (continued),		
John	CAL	60
John	DOR	9
John C. (?)	PRI	184
Margaret (?)	PRI	181
Richard J. (I.?)	PRI	198
William	FRE	71
Wm. S., Esq.	CAL	50
MORSH, John (?)	BAL	89
MORSHEL, Jesse	BAL	98
MORT, Elizabeth	FRE	162
George	FRE	173
Peter	FRE	169
Peter	FRE	200
Wm.	FRE	221
Wm.	FRE	224
MORTER, Andrew	FRE	178
Jacob	FRE	126
Jacob	WAS	117
John	WAS	121
Vallentine	WAS	109
MORTHLAND, Robert		
	BAL	244
MORTIMER, Hetty	D.C.	213
John	BCI	132
Sarah	D.C.	205
Thomas	ANN	305
Wm.	D.C.	212
MORTIMERE, --- (Widaw)		
	BCI	375
MORTOM, Robert	BAL	90
MORTON, --- (See		
MORTON & MAL-		
LALIEW)		
--- (Mrs.)	BCI	410
George	CHA	224
George	PRI	213
Henry	PRI	214
J., Jun.	BCI	270
Jacob	BAL	48
James	CHA	227
John	BCI	61
John B.	CEC	125
Joseph	ANN	276
Joseph	CHA	224
Lettitia	BCI	149
Samauel	BAL	173
Samuel	BAL	173
Samuel	SAI	90
William	D.C.	41
MORTON & MALLALIEW		
	BAL	173
MOSART, John G.	D.C.	18
MOSBERGH, Andrew		
	FRE	82
MOSBURGH, Jno.	MON	135
MOSER, Benj.	FRE	130
Henry	FRE	160
John	FRE	156
Leonard	FRE	162
Leonard, Jr.	FRE	162
MOSGROVE, Geo.	BCI	181
William	BCI	58
MOSHER, Archibald	BCI	415
Daniel	ALL	2
Jacob	BAL	247
MOSHO, Christiana	BCI	461
MOSIL, P.	BCI	371
MOSLEY, George-f.n.		
	SOM	120
MOSS, Christopher	ALL	6
Chs.	BCI	225
David	BCI	48
Henry	WAS	56
James	ANN	297
Philemon	D.C.	125

MOSS (continued),		
Samuel	BCI	88
William	QUE	3
MOTH (See also MOTT),		
Benjamin	KEN	104
John	KEN	104
Levi	KEN	108
Pue	KEN	104
MOTHERS, Corod	FRE	215
MOTHEWES, --- (?)	BCI	398
MOTON, J. (I.?) H. B.		
	DOR	5
MOTT (See also MOTH),		
John (?)	KEN	104
Levi (?)	KEN	108
MOTTE, Isaac	QUE	12
Jeffrey	D.C.	121
MOTTER, George	FRE	134
George	FRE	179
Henry	FRE	134
Lewis	FRE	141
Michael	FRE	134
MOTTERN, Philip (?)		
	FRE	109
MOTTLEMIRE, John	FRE	128
MOTTOW, Francis	BAL	181
MOTTS, Ben	QUE	13
MOTZ, Christopher	FRE	217
MOUDEY, John	WAS	80
MOUDY, Casper	WAS	137
George	WAS	78
George	WAS	140
Michael	WAS	138
MOULDEN, Jacob	ALL	38
MOULDER, John M.	D.C.	9
MOULDING, Eliza	D.C.	80
MOUND, William	WAS	61
MOUNT, Adam	CEC	141
John	MON	142
Thos.	D.C.	163
Thos.	MON	173
MOUNTAIN, Ceasar-free		
	CAL	59
Susan	QUE	16
MOUNTICUE, John	CLN	79
William	CLN	76
MOUNTS, John	D.C.	31
MOUNTZ, Jacob	D.C.	37
MOUREN, Patrick	WAS	55A
MOURER, John	WAS	89
MOUREY, Henry	FRE	187
MOURRER, Martin	WAS	68
MOUSE, George	FRE	180
Jacob	WAS	149
John	FRE	146
Ludwig	FRE	173
Peter	WAS	149
Robert	BAL	25
MOWBERRY, Henry E.		
	BCI	94
MOWBRAY, Ann	BCI	303
MOWLAND, Richd.	D.C.	26
MOWTON, James	BCI	274
John	BCI	275
MOXLEY, Ann	D.C.	177
Basil	HAR	22
Benjn.	D.C.	158
Chas.	MON	142
Daniel	PRI	237
Ezekiel	MON	142
Jacob	MON	142
Jane	D.C.	167
Nehemiah	ANN	325
Nehemiah	ANN	374
Nehemiah	D.C.	32
Rezin	ANN	374

MOXLEY (continued),			MULLEN (continued),			MUMFORD (continued),		
Richard	D.C.	194	Owen	BCI	29	Sarah	WOR	178
Samuel	D.C.	25	Thos.	BCI	190	Shadrick	WOR	213
Sarah	D.C.	187	William	FRE	141	Thomas	FRE	213
Spencir	WAS	101	MULLER, Lewis	BCI	222	MUMIRET, Nichol.	BCI	386
Thomas	BCI	459	MULLICAN, Delia	BCI	81	MUMLEY, Robert (?)		
Wm.	MON	142	Edward	BCI	138		D.C.	48
MOXNEY, John	ANN	325	Eliza	MON	176	MUMMA, Christian	BAL	108
MOYER, Daniel	WAS	125	Jas.	MON	161	Mary	FRE	110
Peter	WAS	100	John	MON	153	Samuel	BAL	217
Rudolph	FRE	109	Jonathan	MON	153	William	BAL	108
MOYERS, Abraham	WAS	100	Marey	BCI	392	MUMMAW, Jacob	FRE	126
Henry	WAS	95	Mary	MON	132	MUMMEY, Joshua	BCI	425
Jacob	WAS	121	Thos.	MON	160	Thomas	BCI	379
John	WAS	108	Walker	MON	153	MUMMO, James	BAL	60
MOZIER, John	BCI	193	MULLIGAN, Joseph	D.C.	134	MUNA, John	WAS	66
Samuel	D.C.	31	MULLIKEN, Basil	ANN	339	MUNAY, Jabah (?)	BAL	52
William	D.C.	13	Benjamin	ANN	333	MUNCASTER, John	D.C.	149
MRIDITH, Vatchel	DOR	34	Osburn	ANN	344	MUNDEE, Thadues	FRE	164
MUCHALREY, Richd.	D.C.	208	MULLIKIN, Bazel D.			MUNDELL, Thomas	PRI	226
MUCHETT, Walter	BCI	273		BCI	276	MUNDER, C. F.	BCI	375
MUCK, Conrad	WAS	107	Edward P.	TAL	35	MUNDORF, Casper	BCI	461
Henry	FRE	133	Elizabeth	TAL	38	MUNEKIZAR, Jacob	BAL	120
Jacob	WAS	106	Frans.	D.C.	136	MUNGAN, John	BAL	173
John	WAS	73	Jeremiah	PRI	205	MUNGER, Lacky	BCI	466
MUCKENS (See also			John	PRI	206	MUNJAR, Joseph	KEN	90
MEECKENS),			John	TAL	34	MUNKS, Thomas	BCI	377
Jacob	DOR	27	Lydea	TAL	32	MUNN, John	BCI	317
John	DOR	26	Lydia	TAL	37	MUNNETT, Abriham	CAL	50
John	DOR	29	Maria	PRI	206	Moses	CAL	48
Joshua	DOR	26	Mary	TAL	38	MUNNITT, Thomas	ALL	35
Levin	DOR	26	Nancy	TAL	41	MUNRO, Isabella	FRE	146
Mary	DOR	26	Patrick	CLN	78	J.	BCI	358
Rebeka	DOR	29	Solomon	TAL	34	Mad.	BCI	358
Richard	DOR	28	Thomas	PRI	226	Nath.	BCI	358
Robert (?)	DOR	30	William	CLN	100	MUNROE, Alexander	CHA	215
Robrt	DOR	30	William	PRI	196	Ann	ANN	394
Thomas	DOR	25	William	TAL	34	Danl.	D.C.	122
MUDD, Ann	CHA	214	MULLIN, Abrom	SAI	91	Jane	SAI	66
Ann	PRI	223	Barnabas	ALL	36	John	BCI	78
Benett	PRI	218	Basil	PRI	204	John	PRI	223
Bennett	D.C.	53	Daniel	CEC	141	John	PRI	232
Dianna	PRI	226	John	CEC	141	Theodore	CHA	215
Edwd.	D.C.	129	John M. (?)	QUE	48	Thomas	D.C.	15
Eliza	CHA	207B	Joseph	PRI	197	Thomas	PRI	223
Francis L.	CHA	214	Maz.	CLN	114	MUNSON, --- (Widaw)		
Henry L.	CHA	225	Richard	ANN	265		BCI	369
Igns.	D.C.	74	Sam.	BCI	338	Ann	KEN	87
Josiah	CHA	214	Thomas	ANN	258	Henrey	BCI	413
Leonard	CHA	226	MULLINDORE, John			Munday	KEN	89
Mary	CHA	226		WAS	68	MUNTAGUE, Rachael		
Michael	CHA	214	MULLING, Bryan H.				D.C.	153
Theodore	CHA	225		PRI	231	MUNTZ, Wm.	BCI	73
Thomas J. (I.?)	D.C.	46	MULLON, John	FRE	187	MURAY, Ann-(C.W.?)		
Thomas N.	PRI	221A	MUMA, Henry	WAS	72		BCI	281
MUDGE, William	BCI	300	Jacob	WAS	67	MURCHEN, Charity	BAL	244
MUER, Joseph	SOM	131	Jacob, Senr.	WAS	61	MURDOCH, Mary	ALL	28
MUGG, Peter	SAI	74	John	ALL	29	MURDOCK, Alexander		
MUIR, Henry	SOM	128	Joseph	WAS	61		CHA	189
Jas. (Revd.)	D.C.	155	MUMAW, Catharine	ALL	23	Benjamin	FRE	70
Mary	D.C.	158	David	ALL	23	Edward	CHA	193
Robert	SOM	124	MUMBY, Robert	D.C.	48	Elenor	FRE	99
Susanna	D.C.	147	MUMFORD, Alisha	WOR	187	Francis	CHA	217
Unice	SOM	139	David	WOR	178	Gilbert	ANN	396
MUKER, Nohoma	BCI	138	David	WOR	181	James	CHA	190
MULES, Isaac	ANN	278	Eleenar	WOR	185	James, Jnr.	CHA	192
Isaac	CAL	60	James	FRE	213	Jno.	QUE	11
MULHORN, Barbara	FRE	107	James	WOR	190	John	CHA	193
MULIKIN, Elizabeth	PRI	239	Jesse	WOR	193	John	D.C.	64
Rignal	BCI	302	John	FRE	163	Mariann	D.C.	64
MULINASE, John	FRE	213	John	WOR	189	Mary Ann	CHA	193
MULINIX, Robert	FRE	75	John	WOR	191	Muncaster	CHA	195
MULLEN, James	FRE	174	John E.	WOR	187	Pliny	CHA	195
James	WAS	61	Littleton	WOR	171	Richard	BCI	451
John	CEC	162	Riley	WOR	196	Samuel	CHA	196
Mary	BCI	450	Risden	WOR	177	Tho.	QUE	5

MURDOCK (continued),		MURRAH, John	DOR 6	MURRY (continued),	
William	CHA 192	Leah	DOR 63	John, Senr.	BAL 143
MURE, James	DOR 13	MURRAN, Thos.	BCI 202	John, Junr.	BAL 143
James	WAS 140	MURRAY, Amey	CLN 94	John R.	WAS 150
John	DOR 14	Connoway	BCI 175	Joshua	FRE 74
Robert	DOR 6	Daniel	ANN 280	Josias	BAL 151
MURET, James	FRE 103	Daniel	HAR 29	Mary Ann	FRE 198
MURETT, William	WAS 67	David	BCI 445	Mathew	FRE 161
MURMOOD, Yarrow	D.C. 53	Dinah	CLN 114	Mathew	WAS 114
MURNEY, Michael	BCI 519	Dorothea	D.C. 62	Perry	BCI 298
MURPHEY, --- (Mrs.)		Elizabeth	BCI 50	Samuel W. (?)	BAL 55
	BCI 402	Elizabeth	HAR 76	William	BAL 148
Christopher	WAS 118	Francis	BCI 158	William	WAS 104
Daniel	DOR 52	George	D.C. 166	William of J. (I.?)	
Ellick	DOR 63	Hugh	CHA 217		BAL 145
Ephraim	MON 153	Ibby	SOM 135	MURRY & MILLS	BCI 394
Gilbert	HAR 40	Ignatius	D.C. 205	MURTH, Philip	BCI 340
James	CHA 228	Jabah	BAL 52	MURTS, Chrisn.	BCI 167
James	FRE 79A	James	D.C. 168	MURY, Denne	WOR 219
Jemima	ANN 374	James	MON 134	John	WAS 110
John	MON 153	James	SOM 123	MURYAR, Matthew	SOM 126
John	QUE 4	James M.	CHA 215	MUSE, Joseph E.	DOR 5
John B.	CHA 207	Jenny	SOM 127	MUSEATER, Alexd.	FRE 215
Joshua	ANN 374	John	BAL 107	MUSETTER, Catharine	
Oswell	CHA 202	John	CLN 72A		FRE 78
Owen	CEC 163	John	D.C. 118	Christan, Sr.	FRE 73
Priscilla	D.C. 66	Mathew	BAL 105	Christian, Jr.	FRE 73
Robert	BAL 153	Owen	BCI 239	Pheby	FRE 77
Saml.	KEN 120	Patience	DOR 63	MUSGROVE, Andrew	
Thomas	KEN 109	Peter	BAL 247		HAR 18
Thomas	QUE 24	Rachael	BAL 56	Benjamin	BAL 187
Titus	ANN 365	Richard	ALL 38	Nathan	MON 143
William	DOR 33	Sam (negro)	TAL 21	Peter	WAS 86
William	FRE 79A	Samuel	D.C. 13	Priscilla	BAL 186
William	QUE 23	Sarah	ANN 401	Samuel	FRE 172
William B.	DOR 51	Severn	WOR 194	Stephen	ANN 366
Wm.	BCI 529	Thomas	BAL 116	Stephen	ANN 367
Wm.	BCI 531	Thomas	SOM 123	Thomas	CEC 179A
MURPHY, Anne	MON 178	Thos.	D.C. 119	Zachr.	MON 174
Banzila?	DOR 33	Thos.	D.C. 132	MUSHETT, Mungo	CHA 196A
Barzila	DOR 33	Thos.	D.C. 161	Philip	CHA 196A
Benjn.	D.C. 124	Thos.	D.C. 202	MUSKETT, Susannah	
David	BCI 500	William	ANN 272		BCI 4
Edwd.	D.C. 131	Wm.	BCI 202	MUSLIN, Thomas (?)	
Elleanor	BCI 64	MURRELL, John, Jr.			D.C. 37
Francis	MON 172		ALL 26	MUSSELMAN, Christopher	
Frans.	D.C. 164	MURREY, Alexander			ALL 15
George	FRE 79A		BCI 120	MUSSER, Christian	ALL 7
Isabel	D.C. 101	M.	BCI 367	Nicholas	ALL 7
James	ALL 13	Matthew	BCI 3	MUSSLEMAN, Samuel	
James	D.C. 68	Susan	CEC 180		CLN 79
Jerimiah	WOR 204	MURRIL, Mary	SOM 138	MUSTIN, Thomas	D.C. 37
Jesse	BCI 199	MURRO, Francis	BCI 178	MUTT, Nathen	ANN 272
Jno.	BCI 212	MURROW, George	ALL 28	MYERLY, Benjamin	BAL 139
John	BCI 15	George	ALL 35	Jacob	FRE 188
John	BCI 138	Robert	ALL 35	Solomon	BAL 139
John	DOR 41	MURRY, --- (See		MYERS, --- (Widow)	
John	HAR 18	MURRY & MILLS)			FRE 173
Jos. A.	MON 134	Benj.	BCI 397	Adam	BCI 199
Levin	CLN 98	Christian	BAL 23	Adam	FRE 214
Micheal	ANN 374	David	DOR 43	Adam	WAS 62
Patric	FRE 79A	David	PRI 228	Adam	WAS 150
Philip	MON 164	David	PRI 230	Alla	BCI 123
Robt.	D.C. 101	Elizabeth	WAS 141	Andrew	FRE 192
Sally	WOR 170	Francis	BAL 206	Augustus	BAL 200
Singleton	MON 137	Henry	QUE 39	Bair	WAS 57
Thomas	BAL 17	Isaac	QUE 36	Catharine	BCI 293
Thomas	BCI 244	Ishmael	BAL 18	Catharine	FRE 117
Thomas	WOR 203	Jacob	BCI 26	Catharine	FRE 144
Thomas L.	BCI 13	James	BAL 203	Cathn.	BCI 188
Thos.	BCI 174	James	BAL 216	Christly	WAS 97
William	ALL 28	James	BCI 385	Christopher	FRE 103
William	BCI 125	James	BCI 407	Daniel	FRE 196
William	D.C. 13	John	BCI 40	Daniel	FRE 204
William	DOR 33	John	FRE 198	Daniel	WAS 127A
MURRAH, John	DOR q	John	SAI 68	David	CEC 162

MYERS (continued),			MYERS (continued),			NAILOR (continued),	
David	FRE 147		Nicholas	BCI 70		Thomson	D.C.209
David	WAS 70		Perry	BCI 456		NAIRING, James	PRI 229
Elizabeth	FRE 160		Peter	FRE 175		NAIRN, Jas.	WOR 180
Elizh.	BCI 180		Peter	FRE 193		NAIRNE, Robert	WOR 210
Francies	WAS 90		Peter	WAS 65		NALE, Catharine	FRE 189
Frederick	D.C.27		Philip	BAL 160		Daniel	FRE 189
Frederick	WAS 65		Philip	WAS 57		Jacob	FRE 194
Frederick	WAS 134[A]		Richd.	BCI 345		Peter	FRE 194
Geo.	FRE 198		Robert	BCI 92		NALL, Jessee	DOR 42
George	BAL 193		Saloma	D.C.95		Susannah	BCI 69
George	BCI 510		Samuel	MON 153		William	BCI 61
George	WAS 97		Stephen	BCI 444		NALLEY, Bennet	CHA 221
Godfrey	BCI 244		Thomas	FRE 229		James	CHA 214
Henry	ALL 12		William	ALL 22		Lavina	CHA 195
Henry	BAL 66		William	BCI 113		Raphael	CHA 207
Henry	BCI 50		William	FRE 182		Zachariah	CHA 192
Henry	BCI 87		William	FRE 215		NALLY, Aaron	D.C.3
Henry	BCI 151		Willian	BAL 28		Charity	D.C.113
Henry	BCI 531		MYLES, Abraham	WAS 136		John	SAI 66
Henry	HAR 20		Zacoria	BCI 412		Joseph	PRI 194
Henry	WAS 66		MYRES, Benjamin	PRI 185		NAND, Francis (?)	BCI 223
Isaac	FRE 197		Mary Ann	BCI 31		NANKIN, James	D.C.6
Isreal	FRE 113		Samuel	FRE 77		NANTZ, John	BCI 116
Jacob	BCI 46					NAPP, Joseph	BCI 27
Jacob	BCI 192					Rebeca	BCI 30
Jacob	BCI 255					Thomas	BCI 64
Jacob	BCI 278					NARDIN, Baptiste	D.C.77
Jacob	BCI 526					NARE, Jacob (?)	BAL 17
Jacob	FRE 197					NARMAN, Richard L.	
Jacob	FRE 214		--- N ---				PRI 207
Jacob	WAS 137					NARTH (See also	
Jacob, Senr.	WAs 62		N. Yd. TENDER (?)	D.C.133		NORTH),	
Jacob, Junr.	WAS 61		NABB, Charles W.	TAL 10		Hicks (?)	DOR 23
James	BCI 391		James	TAL 46		Jacob (?)	DOR 28
James	WAS 97		John	BCI 91		Jobe (?)	DOR 21
Jane	BCI 119		John	QUE 41		Richard (?)	DOR 25
Jeremh.	D.C.118		John, Jur.	QUE 41		Sidney (?)	DOR 23
John	ALL 21		Joseph	QUE 26		NARVILL, Robert	CLN 80
John	BAL 227		Joseph, Jur.	QUE 32		NASE, Henry (?)	BAL 161
John	BCI 194		NACE, Adam	BAL 83		Jacob	BAL 17
John	BCI 374		Barnet	BAL 144		NASH, Chars.	BCI 347
John	CAL 42		John	BAL 142		Ephraim	BCI 314
John	D.C.40		Peter	BAL 141		Jane	D.C.164
John	D.C.131		William (Colo.)	BAL 139		John	TAL 33
John	D.C.162		NACEBOCK, Jacob	FRE 131		Patrick	BCI 318
John	FRE 77		NAFE, Henry	BAL 161		NASON, David	ANN 375
John	FRE 113		NAGHLE, Francis	BCI 32		William	ANN 349
John	FRE 161		NAGLE, Catharine	BCI 492		NATH, M.	BCI 342
John	FRE 182		Joseph	BCI 489		NATHEN, Charles	ANN 380
John	FRE 192		NAGLEY, Henry	WAS 139		NATS, Heney? (negro)	
John	FRE 197		NAIL, Christian	FRE 183			TAL 50
John	WAS 100		Samuel	FRE 170		Henry? (negro)	TAL 50
John	WAS 135		William	FRE 181		NATT, William (?)	BCI 61
John	WAS 150		NAIL FACTORY, AVE-			NATTALI, Joseph	BCI 301
John, Senr.	WAS 65		LIN ROLING &			NAUD, Francis	BCI 223
John, Junr.	WAS 65		SLITING MILL &,			NAUGHTON, John	D.C.126
John J.	BCI 176		Nathaniel ELLICOTT			NAURSE, Michael	D.C.62
John W.	BCI 383		& Co., John DYKE-			NAVE, Abraham	WAS 56
Jonathon, Jr.	WAS 150		manager	BAL 192		Abraham	WAS 57
Jonothan	WAS 150		NAIL MANUFACTORY,			David	WAS 100
Joseph	ALL 16		PATAPSCO ROL-			George	WAS 113A
Joseph	BCI 400		ING & SLITING			John	WAS 124A
Joseph	FRE 204		MILLS-ELLICOTT			NAVIL, Patrick	BAL 198
Joseph	FRE 217		& Co.	BAL 205		NAVY, James	DOR 12
Joseph, Jr.	FRE 204		NAILER, Benjamin	D.C.54		Thomas	DOR 23
Lewis	WAS 134		Martha	D.C.54		NAYLOR, George	PRI 215
Marey	BCI 404		Pere	QUE 20		Hannah-old free woman	
Margarel?	BCI 484		Sampson	KEN 106			CAL 60
Margaret	BCI 90		NAILING, James	PRI 230		Isaac	PRI 215
Margaret	BCI 484		NAILOR, Aquila	BAL 27		James	PRI 214
Martin	WAS 135		Darby	BCI 100		James; of George	PRI 213
Mary	BCI 334		Gorge	BCI 490		Jetson	PRI 239
Mary	D.C.149		John	FRE 155		Joshua	PRI 212
Mary	FRE 194		Louisa	BCI 70		Margaret W.	CHA 225
Michael	ALL 6		Thomas	HAR 42		Thomas	PRI 223

NAYLOR (continued),		NEBERT, Eliza	BCI 196	NELSON (continued),	
Verlinda	D.C.134	NED, John	ALL 26	James	HAR 61
NEAD, Dennis	BCI 226	NEED, Henry	FRE 140	James	KEN 109
NEADET, Julian	BCI 377	NEEDHAM, Ann	BCI 4	James T.	SOM 116
NEAL (See also		NEEDLES, --- (Widaw)		Jane	BCI 213
O'NEAL),			BCI 369	Jessey	BAL 56
Abiner	BCI 266	John	BCI 356	John	BAL 88
Charles	KEN 91	Tristram	TAL 11	John	BAL 92
David O.	MON 168	Vincent	TAL 45	John	FRE 103
George	KEN 88	William	TAL 4	John	FRE 149
Hannah	BCI 307	NEEL, Jos.	MON 176	Joseph	BCI 141
Harriet	BCI 133	NEELAN, Joseph H.	CEC 164	Joseph	BCI 155
James	BCI 318	NEELD, John	MON 153	Juda	MON 173
James	TAL 32	Richd.	MON 137	Mary	WOR 175
John	BCI 140	NEFF, Benjamin F.	ANN 264	Mary M.	CHA 197
John	BCI 172	Eve	FRE 134	Nathan	HAR 61
John	BCI 251	Hannah	BAL 50	Nathaniel W.	CHA 192
John G.	BCI 500	Henry	BAL 52	Obediah	SAI 75
Joseph	TAL 3	Jacob	ALL 28	Paris	TAL 9
Mary	DOR 56	Jacob	FRE 132	Robert	CEC 181
Nevills	DOR 56	John, Sen.	ALL 14A	Robert	FRE 210
Peter	DOR 11	John, Jur.	ALL 16	Saccah?	SOM 149
Rachael	BCI 446	Peter	ALL 10A	Saceah	SOM 149
Rebecah	DOR 45	NEGRO, Elizabeth (?)		Samuel	BCI 39
Richard	BAL 177		QUE 7	Thomas	BAL 188
Richard	PRI 237	Patt. (?)	QUE 12	Thomas, Senr.	SOM 149
Rodger	BCI 130	NEGROES whose Master		Thomas, Jun.	SOM 149
Saml.	BCI 255	resides in a dif-		William	HAR 59
Samuel	DOR 62	ferent district	PRI 204	William	SOM 122
William	PRI 192	NEGROES whose Master		William	TAL 13
NEALE, Catherine	BCI 82	resides in the ad-		Willm.	D.C.215
Charles	D.C.116	joining district		Wm.	MON 144
Charles, of Jas.	SAI 78		PRI 207	NELTY, John	HAR 28
Charles (Revd.)	CHA 217	NEHEMIAH, John	FRE 116	NENNINGER, John	BCI 278
Christr.	D.C.182	NEIELD, James (?)	DOR 18	NEPPARD, Geo.	BCI 196
David	CLN 105	NEIGH, John	FRE 101	NEPTUNE, John	ALL 13
Elenor	SAI 98	NEIGHBORS, Nathan		NERRIS, --- (Mrs.)	BCI 387
Enoch	CAL 52		FRE 115	NERTH, Richd.	BCI 317
Francis	ANN 394	NEIGHBOURS, Elizabeth		NESBAM, John	FRE 77
Francis (Revd.)	CHA 207B	(& suple)	BAL 128	NESBITT, Alexander	
George	SAI 98	Henry	BCI 18	(Esqr.)	BAL 243
George W.	CHA 196A	Tristram	TAL 32	John	CEC 181
George W., Captain		NEIILD, James	DOR 18	Moses	CEC 181
of George Morgan		NEIL, Alexander	WAS 117	Samuel	CEC 181
and The H Mster		Issibella	WAS 112	NESMITH, Ann	D.C.126
Schooner Sally	SAI 80	James	WAS 78	NESSMITH, Ann	FRE 72
Henny	D.C.41	Jonathan	WAS 97	NESWANDER, Daniel	
Henry	SAI 77	NEILD, Hugh	DOR 18		WAS 89
Henry A.	CHA 196A	NEILDS, --- (Major)		NETH, Lewis	ANN 395
Henry C.	D.C.77		DOR 25	Lewis (Primrose)	ANN 284
Jane	SAI 97	Major	DOR 25	NETHGEN, Christian	
John	CLN 82	NEILL, John	D.C.144		ALL 4
John	D.C.44	NEILLE, --- (Mr.)	BCI 358	NETT, Peter	BCI 499
Joseph	CHA 228	NEILSON, James	BCI 254	NETTLE, James	CHA 201
Joshua	SAI 75	Joel	WOR 174	John	CHA 201
Mary	SAI 97	John	BCI 192	Matthew	CHA 201
Raphael	SAI 97	Josh.	BCI 183	NETTLES, Harry	BAL 106
Richard	BCI 89	O. H.	BCI 336	James	ANN 276
Richd.	D.C.136	Robert	BCI 271	John	BCI 346
Robert	FRE 174	Thos. N.	BCI 170	NEUGENT, Neal	BCI 229
Samuel	CLN 113	NELAN, Richard	BCI 154	NEVERSON, George	D.C.46
Sary	SAI 94	NELLSON, Cyrus	SOM 108	NEVETE, William (?)	
Thomas G.	SAI 95	Frances D.	SOM 110		PRI 222
William	BCI 85	John (Senr.)	SOM 108	NEVETT, William	PRI 222
William	CLN 106	NELSON, --- (Widaw)		NEVIL, Francis	SAI 89
William of James	SAI 97		BCI 409	Jona	QUE 4
William H.	CHA 204	Ann	D.C.163	Nathan	QUE 9
NEALLE, Solomon	TAL 49	Aquila	HAR 24	NEVILL, Ann	HAR 71
Turbett	TAL 46	Benjamin	FRE 215	John (?)	D.C.54
NEAT, Christopher	FRE 215	Burgis	FRE 209	John	HAR 75
NEAVILL, John	QUE 38	Elisha	FRE 78A	Joseph	D.C.66
Martha	QUE 33	Eliza	FRE 103	Joseph	D.C.67
Samuel	QUE 23	Frederick	CHA 191	William	HAR 70
Thomas	QUE 36	Henry, Sr.	FRE 78A	NEVIS, John S.	D.C.45
NEAVITT, Joseph	TAL 25	Henry, Jr.	FRE 78A	NEVITT, Ann	D.C.120
Thomas (?)	QUE 36	J. (I.?) S.	D.C.117	John	D.C.18

NEVITT (continued),			NEWNAM (continued),			NICHELS, Jacob	FRE	82
John	D.C.	54	Edward	BCI	33	NICHILSON, Izabella	PRI	206
Joseph (?)	D.C.	67	Edward	TAL	3	NICHODEMAS, Conrad		
Joseph	D.C.	196	Edward	TAL	36		WAS	72
Nace	MON	167	Garritt	KEN	117	NICHODEMUS, Felly	WAS	72
NEWBERRY, John	CHA	228	Geo. N.	QUE	9	NICHOELS, Mathias	FRE	164
NEWCOM, James	BCI	348	Henrietta	BCI	8	NICHOL, David	BCI	348
NEWCOMB, Edward	QUE	2A	J. S.	QUE	19	Thos.	BCI	185
Eliza	QUE	12	James	TAL	38	NICHOLAS, Henry	WAS	64
Elizabeth	SOM	153	Jas.	QUE	10	Sarah	D.C.	12
Jno.	KEN	121	Jas.	QUE	13	NICHOLASON, John	ANN	268
Jno., ju.	KEN	121	John M.	KEN	117	Joseph	ANN	270
Thos.	KEN	119	John S.	KEN	116	Mary	ANN	270
NEWCOMER, Andrew; J.			Jonathan	KEN	121	NICHOLDSON, Charles		
	WAS	88	Jos.	QUE	10		BCI	150
Christly	WAS	99	Mary	QUE	14	Joshua	BCI	130
Christly	WAS	104	Nathl.	QUE	9	Robert	WAS	78
David	WAS	110	Peter	TAL	34A	NICHOLLS, Archd., Senr.		
Emanuel	WAS	83	Robert (negro)	TAL	27		MON	174
Henry	WAS	107	William	KEN	114	Bennony	PRI	207
Isaac	WAS	89	NEWNEMOCKER, Samuel			Camden R.	MON	173
Jacob	WAS	83		WAS	122	Cephas	MON	165
Joel	WAS	86	NEWNHAM, Hannah	TAL	52	Cinta	DOR	9
John	WAS	102	John	TAL	47	Curta?	DOR	9
Jonathan	WAS	88	Peter (negro)	TAL	47	Eliz.	BCI	506
Martin	WAS	104	NEWPORT, Catharine			Isaac	D.C.	32
Peter	WAS	83		FRE	97	Jas. B.	D.C.	199
Peter	WAS	86	John	FRE	77	Jeremiah	BCI	76
Peter	WAS	87	NEWSER, Eli	D.C.	44	John S.	PRI	204
Peter	WAS	102	NEWSON, Abraham	WAS	133	Lewis	BCI	55
Rebecca	CEC	181	James	WAS	108	Saml.	MON	165
Samuel	FRE	183	Jane	WAS	140	Thos.	MON	160
NEWELL, Elenor	BCI	477	Joseph	WAS	135	Thos. C.	MON	143
Perry	BCI	536	Thomas	WAS	139	William J. (1.?)	ANN	391
Robert	D.C.	62	NEWTAN, Walter (?)			Wm. S.	D.C.	36
NEWENS, Thomas	FRE	93		D.C.	60	Zachariah	D.C.	144
NEWEY, John	FRE	150	NEWTON, Anthony	BCI	246	NICHOLS, --- (Mrs.)		
NEWFER, William	FRE	86	Athe	SAI	98		BCI	270
NEWGENT, Fanny	MON	141	Augustine	D.C.	199	Ann	TAL	39
NEWHAM, Benidick	TAL	49	Clement	D.C.	23	Charles	TAL	35
NEWKIRK, Henry	BCI	202	Clement	PRI	180A	Daphney	KEN	89
NEWLAND, David	MON	176	Edward	DOR	55	Edward	BCI	396
Syres	TAL	36	Enos W.	CLN	91	Elizabeth	TAL	12
NEWLEE, George	CLN	77	Ignatious	DOR	53	Enos	FRE	69
James	CLN	76	Ignatius	D.C.	46	Francis W.	HAR	48
NEWMAN, Ann	DOR	11	Igns.	D.C.	73	Henry	BAL	105
Catharine	BCI	478	Isaac	BCI	496	Isaac	ANN	261
Elizabeth	CHA	203	James	SAI	77	James	BAL	123
George	D.C.	207	Jeremiah	PRI	195	James	KEN	89
George, Jr.	ALL	8A	John	BCI	109	James	TAL	9
George A.	ALL	8A	John	DOR	53	John	FRE	150
George B.	ALL	9	Josias	KEN	116	John	TAL	9
James	BCI	388	Nancy	D.C.	24	Levi	WOR	219
James	PRI	224	Nimrod	BAL	207	Lloyd	TAL	4
John	ALL	9	Selby	WOR	210	Nelson	ANN	397
John	D.C.	113	Walter	D.C.	60	Parthina	ANN	374
John	PRI	224	William	DOR	55	Person	BCI	495
John	SOM	137	Zedechia	KEN	120	Peter	FRE	99
John	SOM	150	NEYHOFF, Catharine			Pompy	TAL	4
John	WAS	112		FRE	117	Sam.	BCI	336
Joshua	ALL	21	Catharine	FRE	117	Samuel	ANN	275
Lawson	BCI	111	NEYMYER, Herman	BCI	428	Sealy	QUE	40
Nathanl.	BCI	454	NIAL, Mary (?)	DOR	56	T.	BCI	369
Rebecca	WAS	78	NIBBLETT, Henry	WOR	207	William	BAL	19
Richard	KEN	115	NIBERT, John	WAS	62	William	FRE	150
Richard	QUE	24	NIBLET, James	WOR	203	NICHOLSAN, N.	BCI	453
Robert	ALL	36	William	WOR	203	NICHOLSON, Adam	BCI	515
Robert N.	D.C.	56	NIBLOCK, S. Sarrah			Anne	MON	176
Samuel	WAS	119		CEC	143	Catharine	KEN	89
Verlinda	PRI	197	NICE, Abraham	BAL	174	Charity	D.C.	128
William	ALL	36	David	TAL	12	Charlotte	QUE	39
William	PRI	223	John	TAL	5	Charlotte	QUE	48
William	SOM	129	NICEWANGER, Christian			Chrs.	BCI	213
NEWMON, Thomas	PRI	198		FRE	131	Chs. R.	QUE	3
NEWNAM, Ann	CLN	111	NICHALLS, Isaac (?)			Edward	KEN	106A
Daniel	QUE	25		D.C.	32	Elisha	MON	175

NICHOLSON (continued),		
Frederick	BCI	19
Henry	D.C.	169
Henry	D.C.	170
Henry	SOM	117
James	TAL	11
Jno., Senr.	MON	174
John	BCI	218
John	BCI	300
John	BCI	414
John	SOM	112
John, Junr.	MON	172
John B.	ANN	284
Joseph	WOR	210
Mary	KEN	121
Nancy	D.C.	22
Nancy	WOR	193
Peter	D.C.	120
Sarah	ANN	398
Sarah	BCI	496
Thos.	BCI	174
Thos	BCI	482
Thos.	D.C.	24
NICHOLSS, Andrew	ANN	284
NICHOSON, Eliza	QUE	19
Jacob	QUE	10
Jas.	QUE	20
Jno. L.	QUE	11
John	QUE	11
Lambt	QUE	20
Thos.	QUE	11
Wm.	QUE	8
Wm.	QUE	9
NICKELLS, Noah	CEC	143
NICKELOW, Frederick		
	ALL	7
NICKELS, Aaron	SAI	94
John	FRE	83A
Ralph	FRE	80
Richard	FRE	83A
NICKELSON, Asa	FRE	80
NICKENS, Harry	CEC	181
Rose	D.C.	155
NICKERSON, James	WAS	78
James	WOR	206
NICKESLEY, Phelix	D.C.	12
NICKLE, Warren L.	CAL	44
NICKOLS, Joseph	FRE	83A
NICKOM, Peter	FRE	131
NICKSDORFF, Tobias		
	D.C.	49
NICKSON, Richd.	QUE	18
NICKUM, Jacob	FRE	146
John	FRE	142
Mary	FRE	146
Samuel	FRE	148
NICODEMUS, Andrew		
	FRE	191
Elizabeth	FRE	182
Henry	FRE	192
John	FRE	193
Mary	FRE	198
Philip	FRE	198
Valentine	FRE	198
NICOLL, Archibald	CEC	181
David	BCI	79
William	CEC	181
NICOLLS, Henry	DOR	54
James	DOR	56
Jeremiah	DOR	62
John	DOR	62
Joseph	DOR	54
Levin	CEC	181
Thomas	BCI	83
William	CEC	181

NICOLS, Edward	CLN	113
Henry	CLN	98
Isaac	CLN	112
Isaac	SOM	104
James	CLN	105
James	DOR	44
Jeremiah	KEN	100
John, Capt.	SOM	110
Lambert	CLN	111
Margaret	CLN	96
Paris	CLN	109
Paris	CLN	111
Richard	CLN	95
Rody	SOM	124
Thomas	CLN	114
NIEL, H. G. O.	FRE	134
NIER, John M.	BCI	349
NIESSER, --- (Mr.)	BCI	396
NIGH, Elizabeth	WAS	126
NIGHMAN, Henry	WAS	59
NIGHT (See also		
KNIGHT),		
--- (Widaw)	BCI	382
Benjamin	WAS	147
James	BCI	40
Michael	BCI	135
Moses	FRE	164
Perigine	BCI	415
Peter	FRE	198
Robert	BCI	524
NIGHTING, Thomas	BCI	145
NIGHTINGALE, Bristo		
	BCI	79
Samuel	BCI	251
NIHUFF, Nicholas	BAL	199
NIKARK, George	WAS	87
Henry	WAS	67
John	WAS	111
Michael	WAS	140
NILES, Hesekiah	BCI	124
NILSON, B.	BCI	353
NIMAN, Mary	D.C.	127
NIMEY, Rachael	WAS	60
NIMMO, R. (Reverend)		
	BCI	375
NIND, James	BCI	210
William	CEC	125
NINDE, Isaac	TAL	13
NINDICK, Abraham	FRE	228
NINE, Conrad	ALL	3
NIPLEY, Solomon	D.C.	12
NIPPARD, George	BCI	100
Mary	BCI	100
NIRNAN, Mary (?)	D.C.	127
NISBET, John	DOR	58
Jonathan	WAS	135
NISWANDER, Abraham		
	WAS	134[A]
Catherine	WAS	134[A]
John	WAS	137
NITZELL, John	WAS	78
NIVING, Thomas	BCI	33
NIWELL, Robert (?)	D.C.	62
NIX, Chas.	D.C.	188
NIXDORFF, Henry	FRE	94
NIXON, Richard	MON	153
NIXSON, Edwd.	BCI	497
Isaac	ALL	35
NOAH, Timothy	BCI	28
NOAKES, Gilbert	D.C.	53
NOALS, William	WAS	138
NOAT, Martha	BCI	430
NOBLE, Alexander	BCI	73
Basil	BCI	417
Charles	CEC	181
James	HAR	22

NOBLE (continued),		
James	SOM	124
Levin	DOR	39
Mark	HAR	27
Nancy	SOM	117
Thomas	SOM	139
NOBLET, --- (Mrs.)	BCI	452
NOCK (See also KNOCK),		
Henry	ANN	364
NOCKEN, E.	BCI	418
NOEL, --- (Mr.)	BCI	352
Blassius	FRE	179
John	FRE	140
Mary	CLN	98
Peter	FRE	179
NOKE, William	QUE	27
NOKES, James	KEN	119
Richard	FRE	107
NOLAN, Michael	PRI	229
NOLAND, James, Jnr.		
	KEN	106A
James. L.	KEN	107
NOLL, --- (Mrs.?)	BCI	160
Abraham	FRE	169
Michael	FRE	175
Saml.	FRE	169
NOLLS, Rachel	FRE	184
NOOMAN, George	TAL	49
NOON, --- (Mrs.)	BCI	400
Patrick	BCI	382
NOOSBAUM, Abraham		
	FRE	216
Catharine	FRE	215
NOOSBON, John	FRE	209
NOOSBOOM, Susanna	FRE	228A
NOOSE, John	WAS	62
NORBERRY, Geo.	BCI	390
NORFOLK, Isaac	CAL	59
Isaac A.	CAL	67
James	PRI	247
James H.	CAL	66A
Jas.	D.C.	160
John, Sen.	CAL	67
John, Junr.	CAL	45
John T.	CAL	67
Margarett	CAL	58A
Sceny	CAL	59
Thomas, Sen.	CAL	67
Thomas W. L.	CAL	67
William, Sen.	CAL	68
William, Jun.	CAL	67
NORGET, James	DOR	9
NORMAN, ELsey	D.C.	43
Henry	DOR	58
Henry	MON	161
HOrace	FRE	112
Jessee	CLN	98
Kitty	BCI	488
Rose	DOR	53
Samuel	ANN	274
Theophilus	ANN	259
Thomas W.	BCI	273
Walter	ANN	259
William	ANN	257
William	BAL	180
NORRARD, Thomas	ANN	331
NORRID, James	BCI	146
NORRINGTON, Martha		
	HAR	60
Sarah	HAR	41
NORRIS, --- (?)	BCI	385
--- (Mrs.)	BCI	387
--- (Mrs.)	BCI	447
Aaron	HAR	62
Abraham	HAR	74
Alexander	HAR	58

NUSZ (continued),		O'CONNOR, Catherine		OGLE, Benjamin	PRI [200]
Jacob	FRE 104		BCI 52	Horace	D.C. 50
Michael	FRE 105	Danl.	BCI 225	John	FRE 158
NUTT, James	D.C. 143	Thomas	HAR 78	John	FRE 217
Jemima	D.C. 181	Willm.	D.C. 167	Joseph	FRE 144
NUTTALI, Joseph (?)		ODAFFER, Henry	WAS 135	Joseph, of Thos.	FRE 158
	BCI 301	O'DEAR, Sally	SOM 125	Mary	FRE 157
NUTTER, Charles	BCI 300	ODEER, Kendal	SOM 125	Peter	FRE 183
Dover-f.n.	SOM 120	O'DELL, Abraham	BAL 39	Rebecca	FRE 101
Ephraim	SOM 136	Anny	BAL 40	Samuel	BCI 151
Frahk	DOR 15	Henry	BAL 41	Samuel	FRE 144
Henry-f.n.	SOM 119	Isaiah	BAL 40	Thomas	FRE 159
Henry-f.n.	SOM 119	Walter	BAL 39	Thomas	FRE 214
Phillip	SOM 119	William	BAL 39	William	BCI 433
William	WOR 219	ODEN, Benjamin	PRI 202	OGLEBAY, Chrispin	ALL 36
NUTTHRAL, Charles	SAI 67	John	PRI 222	John	ALL 27
NUTTLE, Charles	QUE 33	Josiah	MON 139	OGLEBY, Pheby	BCI 294
Margarett	CLN 99	Nathan	MON 137	OGLEMAN, George	FRE 219
William	CLN 99	ODONAL, Columbus	BCI 356	OGLETON, Richard	D.C. 22
NUTWELL, Levi	D.C. 9	John	ANN 365	OGTON, Janathan	BCI 384
Samuel	CAL 42	O'DONELL, Bernard		O'HAGAN, Sarah	D.C. 41
NYMAN, Jacob	BCI 473		BCI 229	O'HARA, William	ANN 271
NYSOR, Thomas	BCI 40	O'DONIVAN, Eliz.	BCI 505	O'HARRA, Carey	BAL 241
		O'DONNEL, Columbus		O'HAYRE, Richd.	D.C. 131
			BCI 36	O'HEW, Dinah	BCI 490
		Thos.	BCI 169	OHLER, Frederick	FRE 147
		O'DONÑELL, Barney		George	BCI 532
--- O ---			D.C. 105	George	FRE 146
		John	BCI 323	George Adam	FRE 146
OAKEY, Edwd.	D.C. 100	John	HAR 47	Hannah	FRE 182
OAKLEY, Charles	CHA 202	Patk.	BCI 256	Jacob	BCI 532
John	CHA 200A	Patrick	BCI 227	John	FRE 147
Richard	CHA 205	Sarah C.	BCI 503	Lawrence	FRE 146
OAROUKE, James (?)		ODRICKS, Robert	D.C. 83	Peter	BCI 532
	ANN 340	OEHLER, Andrew	CHA 227	Philip	BCI 532
OARS, Thos.	WAS 145	OFARRAL, John	WAS 147	Thomas	FRE 146
OBERHOFF, Frederick		O'FARREL, Charles (?)		OHR, Micheal	ANN 360
	BCI 96		BCI 153	OIESTER, Henry (?)	WAS 97
OBOIL, Rhoda	FRE 77	OFERRY, Dennis	CEC 143	OILER (See also AILER),	
OBOLD, Joseph	FRE 145	OFF, Leonard	FRE 191	Amon (?)	BAL 13
Sebastlon	FRE 145	OFFER, Deborah	ANN 272	George (?)	BAL 20
O'BRIAN (See also		OFFLEY, Jno.	QUE 4	Mathias (?)	BAL 19
BRIAN),		OFFUTT, Aaron	MON 160	Nancy	WAS 98
Briget	BCI 29	Andrew	MON 161	OILLER, David	WAS 56
Dennis	BCI 451	Basil	MON 161	OLAHAM, Edward, Sr.	
John	D.C. 90	Charles	FRE 170		CEC 126
Mary	D.C. 124	Colmore	MON 167	Edward, Jr.	CEC 126
Michl.	D.C. 133	John	MON 162	O'LARY, Edward	QUE 26
Prina	HAR 31	Margaret	MON 162	OLDFIELD, G. S.	BCI 535
Susan	D.C. 83	Osgood	MON 162	Wm. G.	BCI 391
Terrance	FRE 227	Thomas B.	MON 162	OLDHAM, Charles	CEC 126
William	BAL 235	Thos. L.	MON 162	Cyrus	CEC 182
William	PRI 193	Thos. W.	MON 162	Elizabeth	CEC 182
OBRIAN, Daniel	FRE 228	Washington	MON 161	James	BCI 217
O'BRIEN, Daniel	ALL 16	Wm. of John	MON 167	John	BCI 241
Eliza	D.C. 39	Wm. M.	MON 167	John	CEC 143
Josephus	D.C. 23	Zadoc, of Wm.	MON 166	Joseph	BCI 283
Mary	HAR 43	OFMAN, Isaac	DOR 53	Milcah	CEC 182
Owen	HAR 20	OGBERN, Caleb	FRE 72	Nancy	CEC 164
William	HAR 48	OGBURN, Benjamin	FRE 177	Nathaniel	CEC 182
OBRINE, Terrance	FRE 215	OGDEN, Joseph	CEC 143	OLDSON, Robt.	QUE 9
OBWIN, Daniel?	FRE 72	Nathan J.	BCI 139	OLDUM, Jacob	BCI 340
OCCONNOR, Wm. O. (?)		William	D.C. 38	OLDVINE, Richd.	BCI 186
	MON 162	William	D.C. 40	OLDWINE, Barney	WAS 121
OCCUMY, Aaron	TAL 5	OCDON, James	CAL 49	Charles	WAS 120
David	TAL 9	Joseph J.	BCI 512	O'LEARY, Humphrey	D.C. 96
OCHER, Christian	FRE 145	Wm.	CAL 49	O'LECHLAN, Catharine	
OCKERMAN, George	BAL 180	Wm.	CAL 53A		BCI 159
George	BCI 3	OGG, Benjamin	BAL 51	OLEPHINT, George	WOR 218
OCKMAN, George	BCI 53	Charles	BCI 257	OLEWIN, Daniel	FRE 72
O'CONNELL, Patk.	D.C. 126	George, Senr.	BAL 51	OLIIER, Robert	BCI 246
O'CONNER, Ann	BCI 15	George, Junr.	BAL 51	OLIPHANT, Jane	BCI 175
Danl.	BCI 324	James	BAL 49	OLIVAR, James	CHA 217
		William, of George		OLIVER (See also	
			BAL 51	HOLIVER),	
		William H.	BAL 51	--- (Negro) (?)	BAL 234

OLIVER (continued),		ORAM (continued),		ORRICK, Daniel	BAL 88
--- (Widow)	FRE 176	John	BCI 50	Edward	BAL 77
Benjn.	D.C.92	John	BCI 393	James	BAL 90
Elizabeth	D.C.31	John	BCI 528	ORRIN, Archabald (?)	
Francis	ANN 357	Saml.	BCI 396		FRE 80
George	KEN 90	Samuel	BAL 182	ORRIS, Stephen	D.C.54
Henry	CHA 207	Thomas	BAL 178	ORRISON, Annanias	ALL 12
Jacob	ANN 344	William	BAL 123	Jacob	CEC 182
James	BCI 436	Zachariah	ANN 353	John	ALL 12
James	BCI 489	ORBIN, Thomas	BCI 536	ORRM, Archabald	FRE 80
James	KEN 89	ORDE, James	D.C.107	ORROK, John W.	BCI 310
Jo	QUE 14	ORDNER, Peter	FRE 94	ORSBERN, William	BCI 39
John and Robert		ORE, William	CEC 126	ORSBORN, Joseph	ANN 342
(farm)	BAL 129	O'REILLY, Elizth.	D.C.217	Joshua	ANN 342
Joshua	D.C.137	Margaret	BCI 254	ORSBURN, Saml. G.	KEN 114
Lucy	ANN 332	OREL, Samuel	BCI 203	ORSHAMAN, Henry	FRE 128
Noah	BCI 18	OREM, Andrew	TAL 20	ORSLER, Greenbury	BAL 8
Robert (?)	BCI 246	Hugh	TAL 20	John	BAL 9
Robert (See John &		Hugh S.	TAL 36	John	BAL 40
Robert OLIVER		James	DOR 53	Stephen	BAL 9
(farm)	BAL 129	John	DOR 53	William	BAL 8
Thomas	BCI 34	John	TAL 25	William	BAL 45
William	CHA 222	Robert S.	DOR 54	ORSTER, Soloman	BAL 89
OLLER, Joseph	FRE 149	Spedden	TAL 20	ORTMAN, Jacob	FRE 135
OLLINGER, Daniel	WAs 96	Thomas	TAL 19	ORTNER, John	FRE 104
OLLINNEE, M.	PRI 219	ORETHARD, Willm.	BCI 195	ORTZ, Abraham	FRE 131
OLLIPHANT, Hugh	SOM 117	ORFORD, Charles	D.C.25	OSBERN, Basil	QUE 46
OLLIVER, John	WAS 146	Reisin B.	D.C.56	John	QUE 47
Nace	MON 162	ORIELLY, John A.	ANN 280	Samuel	QUE 46
O'LOCHLING, Dennies (?)		Patrick H.	ANN 280	OSBORN (See also AUS-	
	WAS 78	O'RILEY, Michael	BCI 401	BOURN),	
O'MAGRUDER (See also		ORLIS, Richd.	MON 174	Amos	HAR 25
MAGRUDER),		ORLY, Richd. (?)	MON 174	Ann	HAR 25
Rignal (?)	PRI 193	ORM, Mary	D.C.91	Aquila	HAR 25
OMARR, John	BAL 210	ORMAN, Andrew	FRE 96	Christ.	BCI 345
OMEY, Benjamine	QUE 49	ORME, Betsy	PRI 196	Cyrus	HAR 19
OMNY, Chloe	DOR 46	George N.	D.C.11	David	HAR 22
O'NEAL (See also NEAL),		James	MON 153	E.	BCI 395
Charles	ALL 21	Jesse	MON 153	Jas.	BCI 214
Charles	BCI 166	Patrick	MON 153	Jason	ANN 308
David	MON 168	Reusin	D.C.37	John	HAR 29
Theodore	D.C.40	Richd. J. (1.?)	MON 137	Johna	PRI 203
Walter	D.C.136	Thomas	D.C.29	Joseph	BCI 495
William	D.C.14	ORMS, Moses	ANN 255	Joshna?	PRI 203
Wm., of John	MON 163	ORMSBY, John	BCI 66	Levi	PRI 203
ONEAL, Barney	CEC 126	ORNDORF, Abraham		Richard	D.C.30
Charles	CEC 164		FRE 179	Sam-Negro	HAR 50
Ferdinand	FRE 210	Eve	FRE 188	Sarah	BCI 479
Henrietta	MON 135	John	FRE 178	Sarah	MON 153
Henry	HAR 77	Peter	FRE 184	Soloman	BAL 3
James	ANN 354	Peter, Senr.	FRE 168	Solomon (See Solo-	
John	BAL 109	ORNDORFF, Susanah		mon OSBORN &	
John	HAR 21		WAS 120	BATTEN)	BAL 247
Margaret	MON 137	ORNER, Samuel	FRE 209	Thos.	BCI 502
Wm., Senr.	MON 159	OROURKE, Thomas	ANN 264	William	HAR 22
O'NEALE, Jas.	D.C.104	ORPHAN, John	D.C.57	OSBORNE, Archibald	
John	D.C.19	ORPITT, William	BAL 56		D.C.67
John	D.C.86	ORR, Andrew	DOR 51	David	D.C.57
Laurence	WAS 59	Andrew	DOR 59	Dennis	D.C.130
ONEALE, Mary	PRI 217	Ann	FRE 151	Jas.	D.C.106
William	PRI 217	B. G.	D.C.108	John	D.C.121
ONEILL, Patrick	FRE 78A	Henry	WAS 124A	William	BCI 312
O'NIEL, H. G. (?)	FRE 134	Jacob J. (1.?)	WAS 124A	OSBOURN, Charles C.	
O'NIELL, Robert	BCI 443	James	CEC 182		PRI 223
ONION, Corbin L.	HAR 39	Jane	CEC 182	John	ANN 342
ONIONS, Ann	PRI 195	John	D.C.88	Thomas	PRI [200]
Elizabeth	BAL 121	Mary	CEC 182	OSBOURNE, Francis	ANN 341
Stephen	PRI 194	Mordecai C.	HAR 75	OSBURN, Alvin	PRI 227
ONIUN, Juliot	BCI 149	Robert	CEC 143	Archibald	D.C.213
ONWENS, Samuel	PRI 186	Robert	HAR 77	James H.	HAR 19
O'OCCONNOR, Wm.	MON 162	William	CEC 164	John	CHA 216
OPPERMAN, Geo. L.	BCI 220	William	FRE 150	John	D.C.214
O'QUEEN, William	ALL 37	ORRELL, ELizabeth	KEN 121	Joseph	BAL 23
ORAM, Benjamin	BCI 447	Robert	CLN 95	Joseph	BAL 23
Cooper	BAL 122	William	CLN 87	Joseph	CHA 226
Elizabeth	BAL 130			Michael	BAL 249

PACKLET, --- (?)	BCI 382	PALLAS, Joshua	BCI 81	PARIMORE, Peter	WOR 180
PACKWOOD, James	BCI 55	PALLERSON, Richard		PARIS, James	ALL 14
PACUM, Saml.	D.C.136		DOR 4	Peter	D.C.178
PADD, Robert	D.C.17	PALMATARY, John H.		PARISH, James	KEN 102
PADDING, John	WAS 126		BCI 209	John	BAL 13
PADDY, John	PRI 213	PALMEE, Elial	PRI 236	John	FRE 149
Robert	PRI 213	Elizabeth (?)	PRI 231	William	ANN 398
PADEN, John	DOR 27	John (?)	PRI 231	William	BCI 125
Polly	SOM 141	PALMER, Abraham	BAL 228	PARK, Mary	BCI 338
Susan	SOM 155	Daniel	D.C.82	PARKE, Rebecca	QUE 14
PADER, Domk.	BCI 519	Edwd.	BCI 336	PARKEE, Samuel (?)	
PADGET, Aaron	CHA 216	Eliakim	D.C.19		PRI 181
Elizabeth	CHA 215	Elial (?)	PRI 236	PARKER, Alexander	BCI 528
Henry	CHA 215	Elizabeth	PRI 231	Alley	ANN 273
Hezekiah	CHA 216	George	CEC 183	Andrew	ANN 290
Jas.	MON 135	George	QUE 8	Anne	ANN 273
Jonathan	CHA 226	Jas. W.	DOR 12	Ayres	WOR 200
Josiah	PRI 203	John	D.C.18	Bacon	ALL 31
Moses	MON 163	John	KEN 103	Benjamin	ALL 27
Sarah	CHA 215	John	PRI 231	Benjamin	BAL 99
Susanna	CHA 225	John	TAL 49	Billa of E.	WOR 203
Thomas	CHA 216	Joseph M.	FRE 103	Billa; of J.	WOR 207
Violet	D.C.124	Philip	WAS 144	Charles, Capt.	WOR 213
Walter B.	CHA 215	Richard	CEC 182	Charles-free	CAL 67
William	CHA 216	Susanna	D.C.81	Chas.	BCI 176
PADGETT, Ann	D.C.175	Thomas	BCI 385	Daniel	D.C.8
Benjamin	PRI 206	Thomas	HAR 38	David C.	D.C.65
Benjamin D.	PRI 223	Wilson L.	TAL 49	Derick	KEN 116
William	FRE 84	Wm.	KEN 125	Elisha	ANN 321
PADGIT, William	BAL 209	PALMOR, Elijah	BAL 94	Elisha	WOR 203
PAGAN, Henry (?)	DOR 23	PALMORE, Christly	WAS 84	Elizabeth	CAL 62
PAGE, Chas.	D.C.143	Gearge	BAL 94	Fanny	CAL 61
Daniel	BCI 167	Jacob	WAS 85	Fielder	PRI 183
Danl.	D.C.122	John	WAS 85	Gabriel	BCI 79
E.	BCI 340	PALMOUR, Susanna	SOM 104	George	BCI 459
Francis	MON 131	PALSAN, Joseph	BCI 396	George	BCI 533
George	PRI 194	PAMBLETON, John	BCI 432	George	CAL 59
Henry	KEN 86	PAMPEL, Frederick	FRE 112	George	D.C.83
James	BCI 121	PAMPHILION, Thomas		George	D.C.166
John	BCI 500		BCI 9	George	SOM 124
John	DOR 55	Thomas	TAL 39	George, Senr.	D.C.207
Lucy	D.C.26	PAN, Nicholas (?)	WAS 67	George, Senr.	SOM 110
Lydia	D.C.171	PANCOAST, Samuel	FRE 82	Gilderry	DOR 59
Maria	KEN 91	Will	D.C.107	Henry	BAL 141
Milly	D.C.204	PANCOST, John	FRE 68	Henry	BCI 522
Shederick	ANN 371	PANE, Eliza	ANN 341	Henry	CHA 222
Silus	BCI 91	Peter	FRE 221	Isaac	WAS 116
PAGETT, Benedict	ANN 254	Sally	BCI 37	Jacob	WOR 203
PAGGET, John	BCI 283	PANEBAKER, Peter	BAL 147	James	ALL 16
PAGON, Henry	DOR 23	PANEBAST, Calib	ANN 358	James	ALL 22
PAIN, Amos	PRI 186	PANNELL, Edward	BCI 245	James	ANN 290
Jacob	QUE 36	Hugh	CEC 165	James	BCI 480
Richard	BCI 396	James	HAR 46	James	KEN 104
PAINE, Benjamin	HAR 57	William	CEC 164	James	KEN 115
Betsy	D.C.186	PANNON (See also CAN-		James, Senr.	ANN 290
Francis	D.C.214	NON),		Joel	BAL 43
Grace	D.C.168	Comphart (?)	DOR 34	John	BAL 91
James	D.C.213	PANNUM, Benj.	D.C.14	John	BAL 162
James (negro)	TAL 46	PANTER, Samuel (?)		John	BCI 351
John	D.C.214		BAL 197	John	CAL 51
Lackin	D.C.167	PANTRY, Jeremiah	SAI 89	John	CAL 67
Larkin?	D.C.167	PAPER MILL, FRANK-		John	D.C.103
Peter	BCI 239	LIN-Laurence		John	KEN 123
Samuel	CLN 74	GRATERICK & Co.		John	SOM 124
Thos.	D.C.107		BAL 185	John; S.	WOR 207
William	WAs 136	PAR, Nicholas (?)	WAS 67	John of Elisha	WOR 202
Wm.	WOR 155	PARASH, Elizabeth	BAL 28	John of H.	WOR 199A
PAINTER, Jacob	CEC 144	PARDEE, E. S.	QUE 21	John T.	WOR 207
John	MON 141	PARDOE, Ann (Mrs.)		Jonathan	PRI 195
Mary	BCI 52		CAL 46	Jonithin	WOR 207
Melker	WAS 141	John	CAL 43	Joseph	HAR 76
Ratcliff	WOR 176	Wm.	CAL 42	Joshua	DOR 51
Samuel	BAL 157	PAREDICE, Wm.	WOR 162	Juliet	SAI 98
PAIR, Charles	ANN 279	PAREWAY, Cornelius?		Levin	CAL 62
PAIRO, Thos. W.	D.C.74		BCI 144	Levin	CLN 109
PAISLEY, Barthollomew (?)		Cornetius	BCI 144	Lewis	D.C.124
	KEN 105				

PARKER (continued),		PARKS (continued),		PARROT, Henry	BCI 125
Margaret	ANN 275	Frederick	BCI 70	John	ANN 258
Marsham	CAL 44	George	D.C. 180	Richard	BCI 6
Mary	ANN 275	Henry	SOM 152	Thomas	ANN 270
Mary	PRI 223	James	TAL 50	Thomas	CAL 64
Mary; Wd.	WOR 217	John	QUE 33	William	BAL 187
Nancy	ANN 287	John	SOM 147	PARROTT, George	TAL 50
Ned-free	CAL 67	John	SOM 152	Isaac B.	TAL 50
Pavis	FRE 71	Joseph	SOM 115	James	BCI 312
Resin	CHA 196A	Joshua	BAL 247	James	TAL 10
Richard	DOR 29	Matty	SOM 152	James	TAL 13
Robert	ALL 29	Maybury	BCI 154	James	TAL 38
Robert	BCI 439	Peter	BAL 246	James	TAL 40
Sam.	D.C. 180	Rachel	DOR 8	John	BCI 82
Sampson	CEC 164	Richard	CEC 164	John	TAL 37
Samson	SOM 135	Roger	BCI 389	Joseph	TAL 11
Samuel	BAL 240	Ruben	SOM 152	Peter	TAL 51
Samuel	HAR 7	Ruth	BAL 124	Richard	D.C. 65
Samuel	PRI 181	Thomas	DOR 29	Stephen	CEC 127
Samuel	WOR 203	Thomas	SOM 130	Thomas	TAL 14A
Scarborough	WOR 204	Thomas	WAS 88	William	TAL 5
Selby	WOR 210	William	BCI 83	PARROWAY, Charles	
Selby	WOR 217	William	KEN 92		BAL 188
Southey	D.C. 5	William	SOM 152	William	BAL 189
Susan	ANN 273	William, Jr.	BCI 84	PARRY, Edward	BCI 438
Susan	ANN 287	William T.	SOM 107	Mary	CEC 164
Susanna	CHA 223	Zebulon	SOM 145	Stephen	D.C. 122
Thomas	BCI 12	PARLET, Benjamin	BCI 138	PARSHANEY, Charles	
Thomas	BCI 102	Hannah	BAL 114		WAS 115
Thomas	BCI 272	PARLETT, William	BAL 227	PARSLEY, Bartholomew	
Thomas	CEC 183	William	BAL 248		KEN 105
Thomas	PRI 186	PARLIT, William	BAL 191	James	MON 153
Thomas	SOM 124	PARMER, Ann	FRE 82	Jonas	MON 158A
Thomas	WOR 200	B.	BCI 368	PARSON, John	WAS 64
Thomas L.	BCI 30	Joseph	WAS 109	PARSONETT, Lovering	
Tobias	ANN 281	Perry	WAS 85		QUE 38
Will.-free	CAL 68	PARMERLY, P. H.	BCI 417	PARSONS, Barney	D.C. 108
Williaim (?)	DOR 29	PARNELL, John	BAL 115	Betty; wd.	WOR 202
William	ALL 29	PARNHAM, Ann	CHA 204	Calob T.	WOR 202
William	ANN 263	John	CHA 205	Daniel	BAL 47
William	ANN 274	PARR, David	BCI 240	Elijah	SOM 104
William	BAL 42	Elisha	BCI 98	Elizth.	D.C. 182
William	BAL 114	PARRAMO, Ebbin	CAL 63	Francis	D.C. 147
William	BAL 118	PARRAN, Alxd.	CAL 46	George	CAL 64
William	BCI 20	Benja.	CAL 43	George of G.	WOR 203
William	D.C. 14	John	CAL 66A	Harry	KEN 91
William	DOR 46	Richard S.	CAL 42	Hiram	BCI 445
William	DOR 62	Richard T.?	CAL 42	Isaac-f.n.	SOM 120
William	WOR 218	Young	CAL 42	James of G.	WOR 215
William A.	WOR 185	PARRIS, Edward	BAL 94	Jehu	SOM 106
William C.	DOR 29	PARRISH, Benjamin		Job	WOR 202
Wm.	BCI 512		BAL 57	John	BCI 506
Zipporah	WOR 187	Edward	BAL 13	John	HAR 42
PARKERHORN, Richd.		Eleanor	BCI 101	John, of John	WOR 200
	BCI 348	Elizabeth	BAL 6	John, of John	WOR 207
PARKERSON, Abraham		Eqiller	FRE 213	John, of S.	WOR 203
	ANN 259	James	BAL 59	John of Z.	WOR 203
	ANN 267	James	FRE 216	John W., Capt.	WOR 203
William	SOM 129	John	ANN 257	Johnathan S.	SOM 107
Nathan	BCI 26	John	ANN 258	Jordan	WOR 203
Williaim	DOR 29	John	BAL 50	Joseph	BCI 306
PARKINSON, Ann	BCI 77	John	BAL 51	Joseph	D.C. 135
John	CLN 72A	John	BCI 177	Joseph	FRE 176
Richard	ANN 399	John	BCI 196	Joseph	HAR 38
Robt.	D.C. 111	Joshua	BAL 48	Joseph	KEN 107
PARKMAN, --- (See		Mary	ANN 258	Levin	SOM 104
RIGHT & PARKMAN)		Moses	BAL 47	Michael C.	BAL 41
PARKS, --- (Mrs.)	BCI 386	Nicholas	BAL 245	Moses-Negro	HAR 50
Abel	SOM 147	Nicholas	QUE 31	Peter	WOR 202
Abraham	BCI 85	Prudence	BAL 13	Thomas	BAL 48
Archibald	BCI 84	Richard	BAL 50	Thomas	D.C. 89
Arthur	SOM 135	Stephen	BAL 50	Thomas	TAL 39
Betsy	DOR 45	Thomas	BAL 49	Thomas D.	BCI 52
Charles	SOM 152	Zebediah	BAL 50	Thos.	BCI 489
Davis B.	BAL 100	PARRIT, John	WAS 148	Vice, Wd.	WOR 203
Elisabeth	BCI 392	Nicholas	WAS 146	William	D.C. 49

PAYNE (continued),		PEARCE (continued),		PECK (continued),	
Wrexham	WOR 163	Josiah	FRE 193	William	BCI 32
PAYSON, Henry	BCI 343	Kitty	BCI 483	PECKER, Ceasar (?)	
PAYTON, Yelverton T.		Levy	BCI 538		ANN 404
	ANN 396	Logan	BAL 24	PECKHAM, Rachel	QUE 28
PEA, Jim (negro)	TAL 23	Mathew	CEC 126	William	D.C. 45
PEABODY, John	D.C. 28	Milcah	KEN 92	William	TAL 52
PEACH, Bennett	WAS 102	Pere	QUE 34	PECKMAN, George	WAS 83
Fender	PRI 187	Phillip	BAL 77	Joseph	WAS 95
Saml.	D.C. 196	Richard	BAL 243	PECKUM, Elizabeth	D.C. 43
William E.	PRI 185	Richard	KEN 92	PEDDICORD, Jasper	ANN 367
PEACO, Samuel	ANN 402	Robert	BCI 495	Jasper	MON 162
PEACOCK, --- (See		Sarah	D.C. 30	Thomas	ANN 381
JACKSON & PEA-		Thomas	BAL 87	William	ANN 357
COCK)		Thomas	FRE 198	William	ANN 367
George	PRI 221A	Thomas, of Wm.	BAL 89	William	ANN 380
Ingram	BCI 281	Thos.	BAL 78	Zacharia	ANN 357
Jacob	BAL 176	William	CEC 126	PEDDICORRD, Carllon	
Mary	BCI 525	William	CEC 183		MON 162
Nancy	WOR 159	William	FRE 198	Carlton?	MON 162
Paul	SAI 75	William M.	BAL 247	PEDEN, David	ANN 384
Thomas	KEN 114	Wm.	BAL 92	PEDICOARD, Allen B.	
William	ANN 306	PEARCY, George	DOR 40		PRI 206
William	KEN 110	PEARE, L. (?)	BCI 399	PEDICORD, Adam	BAL 8
Zachariah	SAI 75	PEAREE, Sarah (?)	D.C. 30	Adam	BAL 178
PEACOK, Sarah	SAI 75	PEARL, Daniel	D.C. 71	Humphrey	BAL 9
PEACRE, Henny	QUE 41	PEARRIE, James	FRE 210	John	BAL 196
PEAK, Annastatia	SAI 76	PEARS, L.	BCI 399	PEDINGER, --- (See	
Gustavus	SAI 81	William	BCI 126	SMITH & PEDINGER)	
John	SAI 82	PEARSAN, Edward	DOR 35	PEDRICK, Thomas	TAL 36
Joshua	SAI 62A	PEARSE, Julious	BCI 506	PEDUZI, Peter	BCI 49
Ruth	FRE 99	PEARSEY, Richard	DOR 44	PEED, James	D.C. 161
Wilfred	SAI 79	PEARSON, Benjamin		William	DOR 58
PEAKE, Elizh.	D.C. 129		CEC 182	PEEKER, Ceasar	ANN 404
Humphry	D.C. 182	Charles	BAL 107	PEEKINS, Susanna	KEN 101
Ignatius	CHA 204	Charles	CEC 182	PEERCE, Elizabeth	MON 153
Joseph	PRI 205	Edward (?)	DOR 35	Henrietta	MON 153
Peter	SAI 68	Enoch	HAR 77	John	PRI 191A
Thos.	D.C. 121	Jacob	ANN 301	Richard	MON 154
Thos.	D.C. 179	Joseph	BCI 80	PEERMAN, Charles	FRE 68
PEAL, Elizabeth	BCI 28	Joseph	D.C. 138	PEERS, Acquilla	D.C. 215
John	BCI 196	Laban	DOR 31	PEEVERS, John	ALL 34
Samuel	BCI 20	Lawson	D.C. 127	PEGG, Randolph	PRI 229
PEALE, Charles	D.C. 40	Naah	DOR 31	PEIRCE, Margarett	PRI 214
Hannah	D.C. 14	Noah?	DOR 31	William	BCI 142
James	ALL 14	Thomas	CLN 89	PELCHER, Levi	WOR 157
Rembrandt	BCI 253	William	BCI 300	Moses	WOR 157
Teresa	D.C. 55	PEARTREE, John	HAR 76	PELGRINE, Nathen	BCI 387
PEAN, Fredireck	BCI 456	PEAS, James	ANN 348	PELL, Wm.	BCI 368
PEARCE, Benjamin	CEC 144	John	ANN 398	PELLETT, Isaac	BCI 487
Benjamin	CEC 144	PEASE, Adrel (?)	BCI 356	PELTER, Sarah	D.C. 178
Charles	KEN 92	Adul	BCI 356	PELTON, Enoch	D.C. 166
Drucilla	BAL 131	Alfred	D.C. 116	PELZER, Elizabeth	BCI 53
Edward	BAL 112	Christ.	BCI 514	PEMBARTON, Joshua	
Edward	BAL 232	PEASELEY, Ithream	FRE 71		BAL 38
Enos	ANN 349	PEBBLE, Peter	BCI 490	PEMBERTON, William G.	
George	BAL 230	PECHART, Daniel	FRE 170		CHA 192
Gideon	SOM 129	PECHER, John	FRE 151	PEN, John	FRE 72
Hester	KEN 89	PECHIN, William	BAL 185	PENBROOKS, Robert	
Isaac	D.C. 67	PECHTLE, Christian			QUE 37
Israel	BAL 113		FRE 147	PENCE, Catharine	BCI 153
James	CLN 76	PECK, Charles	BAL 179	PENDERGRASS, Charles	
James	KEN 88	David	BCI 32		HAR 21
James	KEN 92	David	FRE 102	PENDLETON, Daniel	
James	KEN 93	Elizabeth	FRE 106		BCI 486
James	KEN 116	Elizabeth	TAL 5	Edmund	WOR 196
John	BAL 25	Francis	BCI 93	Mary	BCI 74
John	BAL 77	Henry	BCI 491	PENDRID, Saml.	D.C. 201
John, of Josp.	BAL 78	Henry	FRE 75	PENELL (See also	
Joseph	ANN 349	Henry	QUE 40	PONELL, POWELL),	
Joseph	BAL 91	Hiel	PRI 192	Henry (?)	WOR 190
Joseph	KEN 91	John	BCI 17	Jesse (?)	WOR 186
Joseph, Senior	BAL 78	Nicholas	BCI 473	Peter	WOR 191
Joseph, Junior	BAL 78	Saml.-Negro	HAR 79	PENEWELL, Milby?	WOR 219
Joseph of Thos.	HAR 61	Samuel	CEC 164	Milly	WOR 219
Joshua	BAL 94	W.	BCI 344	Sarah	WOR 219

PENEWILL, Milby	WOR 199A	PENNINGTON (continued),		PERKINS (continued),	
PENICK, Solomon	CEC 144	Wm.	KEN 124	Sally	WOR 189
PENIN, Benjn.	MON 174	Wm.	QUE 20	Samuel	PRI 237
PENINGTON, Abraham		PENNOCK, Benjamin		Samuel-negro	CEC 126
	CEC 126		CEC 165	Sarah	BCI 174
Ann	CEC 164	Robert	CEC 164	Susanna (?)	KEN 101
Benedict	CEC 164	William	CEC 164	Thomas	BCI 54
Benedict	KEN 117	William	CEC 165	Thomas	BCI 111
Edward	CEC 126	PENNY, Alexander	BAL 12	Thomas R.	QUE 25
Elias	CEC 183	Ann	CHA 197	William	KEN 110
Elizabeth	CEC 126	Henry	BAL 42	William	KEN 115
Elizabeth	CEC 126	Sarah	CHA 197	William	SOM 155
Hyland B.	CEC 126	Thomas	BAL 42	PERKS, Susan	D.C. 66
Hyland (L.?)	CEC 126	PENNYBAKER, Samuel		PERMARR, James	CLN 87
John	CEC 126		FRE 73	Rachel	CLN 73
Josiah	BAL 8	PENNYFIELD, Thos.		PERNELL, Lemuel	QUE 38
Robert	CEC 144		MON 162	PERREGROY, Moses	BAL 51
Robt., Sn.	CEC 127	PENNYVILLE, Thos.		PERREL, Philip	FRE 80
Robt., Jr.	CEC 127		WOR 176	Thos.	FRE 122
William	CEC 144	PENTZ, Daniel	BCI 99	PERRELL, Thos. (?)	FRE 122
PENITENTIARY,		Henry	BCI 99	PERRIE, Ann	CHA 224
MARYLD.	BCI 203	John Joseph	BCI 99	Hugh	CHA 228
PENIWELL, Milby	WOR 217	PENTZER, Daniel	FRE 154	James A.	CHA 224
PENN (See also JENN),		Valentine	FRE 154	Lemuel	FRE 211
Edward	BAL 198	PENWILL, Thomas	WAS 104	Susanna	CHA 224
Edward	PRI 182	PEOPLE, Rebecca	ANN 277	Thomas D.	CHA 224
Edwd.	MON 140	PEPE, Littleton	WOR 211	PERRIGO, Benjamin	BAL 156
Francis	BAL 198	PEPER, George	WOR 212	Benjamin	BAL 215
Henry	CHA 200A	Levi	WOR 212	Daniel	BCI 21
Ignatius	CHA 201	PEPPER, Ann (of		Edward	BAL 153
Jacob	BCI 481	Saccer)	WOR 157	George	FRE 216
John (?)	BCI 501	Catharine	BCI 121	John	BAL 153
John	CHA 202	Frances	BCI 523	Joseph	BAL 153
John O.	CHA 206	Jacob	BCI 125	Joseph	BAL 244
Joshua	ANN 373	Peter P.	WOR 210	Moses	BAL 95
Joshua	FRE 209	PEPPLE, Abraham	FRE 181	N.	BCI 393
Mary	FRE 68	PERDEL, Peter	BCI 358	PERRIL, Anna P.	FRE 109
Stephen	MON 140	PERDEW, Labom?	BAL 77	Prissillah	FRE 84
Walter	CHA 194	Laborn	BAL 77	PERRILL, Charles	ALL 35
Walter	CHA 206	Walter	BAL 77	PERRINTON, Draper	DOR 65
William	BAL 196	Wm.	BAL 77	PERRUR, Thomas	ALL 33
William	CHA 202	PERDUE, Eli	WOR 203	PERRY, Alexander	MON 133
William	CHA 203	James W.	WOR 203	Alexr.	D.C. 176
Wm. G.	MON 177	John K.	WOR 203	Alexr., Junr.	D.C. 201
PENNELL, Jonathan	WAS 63	PEREGOY, Caleb	BCI 456	Ann	BCI 37
PENNENTON, John	BCI 349	James	BCI 455	Ann	D.C. 124
PENNER, John	WAS 99	Rob	BCI 508	Apellonia	SAI 74
Peter	FRE 164	PERIELEY, Samuel	ANN 306	Benjn.	MON 166
PENNEVILL, Purnell		PERICO, Charles	BCI 399	Burdit R.	CHA 190
	WOR 171	James	BAL 20	Charlott	WAS 56
PENNEWILL, Isaac	WOR 185	John	ANN 317	Edward-Negro	HAR 49
John	WOR 187	Joseph	BCI 32	Elbert	MON 163
Leu?	WOR 194	Moses	BAL 25	Elias	MON 153
Levi	WOR 194	PERIGOY, Joel	BAL 184	Elisha	PRI 202
PENNIMAN, Silas	BCI 249	Joseph	BAL 184	Erasmus	MON 154
PENNINGTON, Daniel		PERINE, David M.	BCI 418	Frances	BCI 3
	BAL 50	E.	BCI 389	Gassaway	MON 159
Diner	CLN 78	Malden	BCI 138	Hannah	BCI 185
Elijah	ANN 397	Margarett	BCI 433	Herman	BCI 111
Eliza.	BCI 526	Richd.	BCI 531	Hugh	PRI 216
Henry	BCI 152	Wm.	BCI 532	James	BAL 128
Isaac	HAR 39	PERKINS, Affa	WOR 176	James	D.C. 93
James	BCI 110	Benjamin	BAL 45	Jeremiah	BCI 283
Jas.	QUE 17	Daniel	BCI 114	John	BCI 134
Jno. H.	KEN 123	Easter	WOR 159	John	BCI 184
Jno. J.	QUE 11	Ebenezer	BCI 114	John	CLN 107
Jno. W.	QUE 8	Ed.	QUE 7	John	D.C. 213
John	QUE 13	Elisha	BCI 513	John, Senr.	CHA 190
Joshua	QUE 8	Francis	PRI 197	Levin	DOR 44
Julia	BCI 511	Jeremh.	D.C. 123	Messer	CEC 144
Levi	ANN 301	Jno. D., Dr.	QUE 4	Milley	D.C. 171
Nathaniel	ANN 388	John	FRE 174	Nathaniel	CLN 105
Robert	BCI 28	John	PRI 184	Priscilla	MON 168
Robert B.	KEN 125	Lotty	WOR 186	Rebecca	TAL 2
Samuel	BAL 119	Nancy	WAS 94	Robt.	QUE 12
William	BAL 59	Peter	KEN 117	Roger	ALL 27

PERRY (continued),		PETERSON (continued),		PHILIP, Denton	WAS 138
Rubin	TAL 36	Margarett	BCI 303	PHILIPS, --- (?)	BCI 395
Ruth	PRI 216	Tobias	CEC 144	--- (See PHILIPS	
Samuel	ANN 301	PETERY, John	WAS 94	& EVANS?)	
Sarah	CLN 110	Philip	WAS 89	Austin	DOR 28
Sineca	ANN 355	PETHERBRIDGE, Jno. C.		Benjamin	DOR 27
Sophia	CEC 144		BCI 175	Charles	BCI 400
Thomas	CHA 190	PETIT, Charles	D.C.93	Corsey	QUE 10
Thomas J.	ALL 27	William	D.C.30	Denard	DOR 28
Thos.	MON 174	PETRY, J. (I.?) B.		Elijah	QUE 5
William	CLN 92		D.C.73	Elizebeth	DOR 28
William	CEC 144	PETTER, Cuff-negro		Elizebeth	DOR 30
William	CHA 190		CEC 126	Ely	FRE 83
William	FRE 93	George	ANN 353	Fanney	DOR 30
Wm.	QUE 13	PETTIBOONE, Charles		Geo.	D.C.101
PERRYMAN, Isaac	HAR 18		ANN 300	Harry-f.c.p.	HAR 10
PERSON, Henrietta	DOR 13	PETTICHORD, Greenburry		Hatten	DOR 28
PERVAIL, John	HAR 79		FRE 144	Hattur?	DOR 28
PERVESS, Thomas	BCI 14	PETTICOAT, John	BCI 187	Hilly	DOR 28
PESE, Louis	BCI 275	PETTICORD, Moris?	BAL 4	Isaac	ANN 401
PETER, --- (Mr.)		Mosis	BAL 4	Isaac	BCI 466
(negro)	BAL 111	William	WAS 122	James	D.C.190
Boslin	WAS 120	PETTIGO, James	HAR 39	James	WOR 159
Geo.	MON 136	PETTIGREW, Jas.	D.C.82	Jas.	BCI 170
George	D.C.38	Theophs.	D.C.102	Jason	FRE 83
George	MON 160	William	CEC 183	Jesse	MON 134
John	D.C.10	PETTIT, Samuel, Captn.		John	ANN 309
John	D.C.25		WOR 174	John	ANN 402
John	D.C.86	PETTY, Jesse	WOR 192	John	ANN 402
Sarah	D.C.45	PEUKE, Robert	BAL 122	John	BAL 2
Thomas	D.C.45	PEVERS, John, Sen.		John	D.C.187
W.	BCI 338		ALL 34	John	D.C.199
William	D.C.112	PEW, Hatha	BCI 356	John	D.C.203
PETERBENNER, John		Jonathan	HAR 38	John	MON 171
	WAS 90	PEWLEY, J. (I.?)	BCI 407	John	QUE 17
PETERBRENNER, Henry		PEYTON, Ann	D.C.196	John B.	D.C.152
	WAS 59	Ann E.	D.C.95	John H.	D.C.203
PETERKIN, Jacob	DOR 29	Benjamin	ALL 8A	Levy	MON 173
PETERMAN, George	WAS 79	Craven T.	D.C.184	Margret	DOR 27
Jacob	FRE 149	Francis	D.C.217	Moses	D.C.83
John	FRE 142	James	ALL 8A	Nany	DOR 30
PETERS, ASbury	QUE 8	PFALDZ, William	BAL 112	Noah	FRE 224
Charles	FRE 99	PHAREALL, Walter	ANN 343	Peter	ANN 398
Charles-free	CAL 64	PHEBUS, James	SOM 122	Robert	KEN 91
Christian G.	BCI 248	Lewis	SOM 122	Saml.	QUE 8
Daniel	BCI 404	Thomas	SOM 125	Samuel	KEN 87
Geo.	BCI 412	PHELAN, John	BCI 218	Samuel	PRI 196
George	FRE 171	PHELIX, John Jarvis		Samuel	TAL 24
George (f.n.)	SOM 119		BAL 229	Soloman	DOR 28
Harry	CEC 182	PHELPS, Abm.	BCI 217	Solomon	BAL 150
Henry	BCI 473	Archd., Senr.	MON 174	Stephen	D.C.92
Henry	BCI 511	Cammel	ANN 321	Thos. H.	MON 135
Jacob	BAL 224	Ezekiel	ANN 325	Trestram	QUE 10
James	CLN 98	Ezra	D.C.64	Vatchel	DOR 28
Jane	BAL 234	Greenbury	BCI 142	William	BCI 445
John	BCI 167	Isaiah	MON 172	Willm.	D.C.187
John	BCI 503	Jacob	BCI 145	Wm. H.	D.C.204
John S.	MON 129	James	ANN 329	PHILIPS & EVANS?	
Joseph	CEC 164	Jesse	D.C.204	(See also Philips	
Micl.	FRE 134	Jesse	PRI 226	V. EVANS)	ANN 265
Pere	QUE 19	Joseph	ANN 393	PHILLIPE, Joseph	BCI 246
Priscilla	QUE 16	Joshua	BCI 84	PHILLIPS, Ann	D.C.77
Priss	QUE 19	Richard	ANN 329	Asa	SOM 109
Richard	PRI 196	Samuel	ANN 353	Benjamin	WOR 202
Ruth	D.C.218	Sarah	ANN 338	Benjamin	WOR 206
Sam-f.c.p.	HAR 11	Sophia	ANN 321	Charity	ANN 275
Samuel	FRE 106	Walter	ANN 329	Day G.	SOM 108
Samuel	WAS 56	Walter, of Chas.		Elihu	SOM 135
Susan	SOM 138		ANN 329	Elizabeth	QUE 48
Thomas	BAL 249	William	ANN 341	Ennalls	DOR 56
Thomas	BCI 88	William	ANN 344	Ennalls	DOR 65
William F.	CLN 92	Zachariah	ANN 292	George	BCI 49
Wm.	QUE 18	PHENISEY, James	D.C.213	Handy	SOM 107
PETERSON, Cezar	PRI 186	PHIFFER, Dederick G.		Handy	WOR 163
John	BAL 247		BAL 163	Harman	CEC 144
John	BCI 72	PHILINGIM, George	CEC 127	Henry	KEN 101

INDEX TO THE 1820 CENSUS OF MARYLAND AND WASHINGTON, D.C.

PIPER, Daniel	WAS 61	PLANTER, Israel	SOM 132	PLUNKETT, James	D.C.207
Hugh	D.C.204	Samuel	BAL 197	PLYMOUTH, John	CEC 182
Jacob	WAS 55A	PLAPOT, John	FRE 203	John	CEC 183
Jacob	WAS 69	PLATENBURG, Christian		POCHON, Charles	BCI 436
James	BCI 276		BCI 155	POCKLINGTON, John	
John	WAS 61	PLATER, Charles	QUE 40		D.C.33
Margaretta	WAS 56	George	SAI 74	POCOCK, Abel	ANN 317
Michael	WAS 67	John	BCI 144	Daniel	HAR 60
Philip	BCI 490	John R., Sen.	SAI 75	David	HAR 61
Susan	BCI 372	John R., Jr.	SAI 81	Elijah	HAR 61
PIPPIN, Darius	CLN 77	Nace	FRE 122	George	ANN 316
Elijah	CLN 80	Sarah	CEC 182	Jesse	BAL 86
George	CLN 81	Thomas	D.C.36	John	BCI 96
James	CLN 81	PLATOE, Judah	TAL 6	Robert	BAL 85
Perre	CLN 77	PLATT, Christian	FRE 156	Sutton	BCI 201
Sol.	QUE 18	PLEASANTS, James		Thos.	BCI 201
Tristram	QUE 18		MON 153	POE, Jacob	FRE 225
PIPPINGER, Danl.	FRE 224	John P.	BCI 271	Thomas	ANN 316
James	FRE 224	Ned	D.C.156	Thomas	BCI 169
Jeremiah	FRE 224	PLEASONTON, Stephen		POFFENBARGER, Adam	
Saml.	FRE 223		D.C.5		WAS 86
PIPPINGERS, John	FRE 223	PLOTTINGBERGER, Joseph		Andrew	WAS 124A
Rachel	FRE 223		BAL 243	Christian	WAS 72
PIPPINS, Sally	QUE 19	PLOUGHMAN, John		Christian	WAS 86
PIPSECO, John	D.C.179		BAL 87	Henry	WAS 71
PIRKENCE, Lambert	TAL 9	PLOWDEN, William H.		Henry	WAS 85
PIRTLE, Leah	DOR 26		SAI 97	Jacob	FRE 132
PITCHER (See also		PLOWMAN, Hannah	BAL 161	Jacob	WAS 71
FITCHER),		James	BAL 157	John	WAS 60
Agness	WOR 160	James	FRE 205	Simon	WAS 71
Eliza	BCI 224	Jessee	BAL 143	POFFENBERGER, Henry	
James	ANN 331	Johnston	BAL 161		FRE 128
John	WOR 163	Joshua	BAL 149	Jacob	FRE 128
Sarah	WOR 160	Nicholas	BAL 142	John	FRE 130
Stephen	WOR 157	Richard	BAL 148	POGGET (See also	
Walter	CAL 43	Thomas	CLN 112	FOGGET),	
Young	CAL 49	PLUCK, Jacob	CEC 144	Richard	ANN 261
PITCOCK, Benjn.	HAR 6	PLUMER, Jeremiah	ALL 24	POGUE, --- (Mrs.)	BCI 440
PITT, Abarilla	BCI 86	Mary	BCI 143	John	BCI 503
Jane	HAR 29	Notly	BCI 138	POINTER, George	D.C.64
John	BCI 347	Sam	BCI 349	Peter	WOR 201
Mary	DOR 4	PLUMM, Lewis W.	D.C.206	Thomas	CLN 96
Richard	BCI 12	PLUMMER, Allen	TAL 38	POINTIER, Mary	BCI 251
Stephen	KEN 89	Betsey	MON 178A	POINTS, James	HAR 48
Thomas	KEN 103	Cesar	MON 154	POJEY, George (?)	CAL 42
Thomas (Col.)	DOR 3	Christopher	QUE 32	POKETY, Ritty	DOR 56
William	BCI 134	Eli	KEN 87	POKITIY, John	DOR 5
William	BCI 175	Elkaneh	QUE 5	POLAND, Aron	ALL 12
PITTENGER, John	FRE 154	Gerard	D.C.193	John	ALL 12
PITTET, --- (Mrs.)	BCI 395	Isaac	FRE 79	John	ALL 14
PITTMAN, Cathe. A.		James, Jr.	TAL 6	Margaret	ALL 13
	D.C.198	James, Ovsr.	TAL 7	Samuel	ALL 13
PITTS, Benson-negro		Jesse	FRE 78	William	ALL 20A
	WOR 197	Jno.	MON 133	POLK, --- (Miss)	D.C.72
Edee	BAL 27	John	ANN 271	Aaron-f.n.	SOM 120
Eder?	BAL 27	John	ANN 328	Alec	WOR 205
Hannah	D.C.28	Jonathan	FRE 74	Amey (free negro)	
Hillary, Sen.	WOR 187	Jonathan	TAL 21		SOM 118
Hillary, Jun.	WOR 197	Jos.	MON 133	Benjn.	WOR 164
James	WOR 187	Joseph	MON 133	Casey-f.n.	SOM 120
John	FRE 72	Mordica	ANN 270	David	BCI 130
John P.	WOR 189	Nicholas	CEC 127	David	BCI 285
Lewis	BAL 27	Perry	TAL 21	Isaac	SOM 124
William	D.C.48	Philemon	CLN 87	James	CEC 144
William	WOR 187	Philip	CEC 127	James	SOM 138
PITZEL, Henry	FRE 157	Philln.	MON 144	Jane	SOM 126
PLACENE, Jas.	BCI 226	Samuel	FRE 74	John	CEC 144
PLACID, Paul	BCI 222	Solomon	TAL 12	Joshua	CLN 112
PLAIN, George	ANN 393	Solomon	TAL 39	Josiah F.	SOM 132
Jacob	FRE 158	Sophiah	FRE 75	Olivia	SOM 108
PLANE, Catharine	FRE 200	William	ANN 328	Philip	WOR 154
David	FRE 74	William	FRE 68	Saml.	SOM 126
PLANK, Jacob	ALL 35	William	FRE 84	Whittington	SOM 127
PLANNATE, William	BAL 141	Wm.	MON 174	POLKE, Levin (f.n.)	
PLANT, Horatio	MON 153	Yale (?)	FRE 70		SOM 120
Nathaniel	D.C.71	Yate	FRE 70		

191

POLLARD, Horatio	WAS	83
James	ANN	293
Seth	BCI	89
Thomas	ALL	27
POLLETT, Nemiah	BCI	71
Thos.	SOM	125
POLLICK, James T.	WAS	73
POLLIT, Jos.	BCI	203
POLLITT, George	SOM	132
James S.	SOM	108
John	WOR	216
John, Senr.	SOM	132
Jonithin	WOR	215
Joshua	WOR	204
Levin	SOM	129
Levin G.	SOM	104
Stephen	WOR	215
Thomas	WOR	211
William, Senr.	SOM	122
William T.	BCI	282
POLLOCK, Samuel	BAL	117
Samuel T.	BCI	135
POLMEN, John	FRE	132
POLMORE, Joseph	WAS	84
POLOCK, Elias	BCI	177
POLSTON, Valentine	BAL	119
POLTER, James	WAS	78
POLTON (See also POTTON),		
Aara	ANN	324
Charles	ANN	331
Thomas	ANN	325
Zachariah	ANN	324
POMEROY, Willm.	D.C.	203
POMPY, Richd.	CAL	46
PONCET, Lewis	BCI	231
POND, Caleb	WOR	163
PONDERS, Nathan	WOR	191
Ruel	WOR	185
PONELL (See also PENELL, POWELL),		
Ebenezer (?)	WOR	190
Eli (?)	WOR	190
Elijah (?)	WOR	191
Elisha (?)	WOR	192
Handy (?)	WOR	184
Jehue (?)	WOR	190
Jesse (?)	WOR	191
Jesse	WOR	195
John (?)	WOR	193
Keziah (?)	WOR	189
Zadok (?)	WOR	185
Zeno (?)	WOR	191
POODER, Abraham	BAL	69
POOL, Adam	FRE	77
Albinus	FRE	199
Beal	ANN	358
Charles	ANN	368
Charles, Jnr.	ANN	368
Denton	ALL	38
Henry	FRE	79A
Henry	FRE	94
James	ANN	364
John	CLN	113
John	MON	141
John	SOM	154
John, Senr.	MON	133
Joseph	BCI	480
Levin	CLN	112
Lloyd	ANN	376
Marshal	ANN	319
Philemon	ALL	31
Rebecca	WAS	78
Rezin	BCI	250
Samuel	ANN	361
Thomas	FRE	191
Vacheal	ANN	355

POOL (continued),		
Walter	FRE	117
Warner	ANN	361
William	FRE	200
William H.	FRE	75
Zachariah	ANN	368
POOLE, Achsah	FRE	214
Amos	BAL	60
Ann	D.C.	38
Benjn.	MON	135
Dennis	FRE	213
Henry	FRE	212
Jacob	FRE	221
James	BAL	66
John	D.C.	205
Jos.	MON	135
Joshua	BAL	65
Lewis A.	D.C.	79
Mathew	BAL	49
Saml.	MON	135
William	BAL	66
William	FRE	135
Wm.	MON	135
POOLL, Richard	ANN	328
POOR, Edward	CAL	62
John	CLN	81
John, Senr.	D.C.	75
John, Junr.	D.C.	75
John H.	BCI	272
Mamily (?)	TAL	37
Mary	D.C.	67
Moses	D.C.	83
Saml.	BCI	168
William	CLN	79
POORE, Dudley	BCI	514
POORMAN, Abraham		
	FRE	164
Henry	FRE	149
Jacob	FRE	164
POPE, David	BCI	433
Ellenor	D.C.	127
Folger	BCI	241
Francis John	BCI	67
Fredk.	D.C.	130
George	BCI	526
John	HAR	78
John	PRI	239
Littleton	WOR	214
Nathaniel	ANN	335
Nathaniel	MON	162
William	FRE	96
POPLIN, Thomas	MON	154
POPP, Charles	BCI	447
POPPIN, William	ANN	259
POPPLEIN, --- (See POPPLEIN & BROTHERS)		
POPPLEIN & BROTHERS		
	BCI	441
POPPLIN, George	BCI	200
PORDON (See also GORDON)		
Wanton (?)	BCI	148
PORHETT, Michail (?)		
	WAS	137
PORKETT, Michail	WAS	137
PORRERGER, Frank		
	PRI	185
PORT, Teany	QUE	39
PORTER, Alexander		
	BAL	66
Allen	ANN	349
Andrew R.	CEC	182
Ann	QUE	39
Archabald	BAL	5
Arthur	TAL	26

PORTER (continued),		
Augustin	BCI	39
Bartholomew	ALL	16
Benjamin	TAL	45
Charles	D.C.	92
David (Com.)	D.C.	62
Edward	CHA	202
Edward	MON	153
Eleanor	CEC	183
Elizabeth	BCI	31
Elizabeth	CEC	183
Gabriel M.	ALL	14A
George	SOM	133
George	TAL	33
George W.	SOM	126
Hart	CEC	183
Henry	ALL	17
Hetty	SOM	110
Hugh	HAR	61
Hugh	SOM	114
Isaac	WOR	169
Isaiah	D.C.	27
Isaiah	D.C.	32
James (?)	WAS	78
James	BAL	69
James	CEC	126
James	SOM	140
James, Ovsr.	TAL	6
James B.	CEC	182
James L.	CEC	182
Jenny	SOM	128
John	ALL	15
John	ANN	320
John	BCI	95
John	FRE	102
John	HAR	40
John	TAL	21
John; of S.	ALL	16
John R.	WAS	79
Jonathan	CLN	75
Joseph	DOR	5
Joseph	KEN	110
Joseph	SOM	126
Joshua	KEN	118
Joshua	WOR	179
Kendal	WOR	185
Laurance	CLN	95
Levi, Senr.	WOR	163
Levi, Junr.	WOR	164
Margaret	CEC	183
Mary	CEC	144
Michael	ALL	16
Michael	BCI	433
Moses	ALL	17
Nathan	BAL	46
Nathan	MON	153
Nathan	QUE	16
Nathan	QUE	49
Nathan	TAL	26
Nathaniel	ANN	377
Nathaniel	FRE	213
Neoma	WOR	170
Pegy, Wd.	WOR	215
Peregrine	BAL	125
Perry	TAL	23
Philip	CLN	78
Priscilla	SOM	128
Purnell	WOR	173
Ralph	BCI	60
Richard B.	SOM	105
Robert	CLN	75
Robert	HAR	44
Robert L.	BCI	38
Robert L.	BCI	89
Sally (of Jas.)	WOR	164
Saml.	WOR	175

PORTER (continued),			POTTER (continued),			POWEL (continued),		
Samuel	FRE	76	Kelita	ALL	13	Levin (of Levin)	WOR	160
Sarah	D.C.	93	Martin	BAL	107	Philip	SAI	81
Shadrack	BAL	10	Nathl., Doctr.	BCI	267	Samuel	MON	153
Susanna	BAL	125	Stephen	CLN	87	Thomas	BCI	38
Thomas	ALL	15	Thomas	BAL	219	William	FRE	194
Thomas	BCI	8	Valentine	CLN	107	Wm., Junr.	WOR	175
Thomas	WAS	66	Vere	TAL	48	POWELL (See also		
Thomas, of M.	ALL	16	William	CLN	89	PENELL, PONELL)		
William	ALL	17	POTTINGER, Thomas B.			Abraham	CEC	144
William	BCI	137		D.C.	59	Adam	D.C.	106
William	BCI	157	POTTON (See also			Alfred	D.C.	170
William	BCI	241	POLTON),			Ann (?)	D.C.	57
William, Ovsr.	TAL	6	Aara (?)	ANN	324	Ananias	WOR	197
Wm.	MON	140	Charles (?)	ANN	331	Andrew	WAS	148
Wm.	QUE	5	Thomas (?)	ANN	325	Burr	PRI	230
Wm. W. (of Purnell)			Zachariah (?)	ANN	324	Dafney	BCI	498
	WOR	175	POTTS, --- (Mrs.)	BCI	346	Davis	BAL	240
Woolman, Ovsr.	TAL	7	Aron	WAS	147	Ebenezer	WOR	190
PORTZ, Jacob	WAS	87	Charles	WAS	138	Edward	SOM	113
John	BAL	143	Daniel	TAL	32	Eleaner	CLN	94
POSEY, Benjn.	D.C.	172	Edward	QUE	33	Eleanor	D.C.	59
Burdit, Senr.	CHA	190	Elenor	FRE	102	Eli	WOR	190
Burdit, Junr.	CHA	190	Elizabeth C.	FRE	104	Elijah	WOR	191
Cathe.	D.C.	82	George	HAR	38	Elijah	WOR	209
Charles	CHA	223	Hannah	TAL	35	Elisha	WOR	192
Frances	D.C.	77	Isaac	CLN	78	Elizabeth	ANN	300
Francis	CHA	196	John	D.C.	8	Elizabeth	BCI	69
Hanson H.	CHA	190	John	QUE	14	Handy	WOR	184
Harrison	SAI	93	Peter	BCI	203	Henry	ANN	357
Henley	CHA	193	Pompy	QUE	14	Henry	BCI	257
Henry	CHA	196	Richard	FRE	100	Henry	WOR	190
James	CHA	193	Robert	WAS	96	Howell	TAL	31
Jesse	CHA	197	Saml.	QUE	15	Howell, Jr.	TAL	41
John	CHA	190	Samuel	D.C.	45	James	CLN	77
Laurence	CHA	206	Shadrick	QUE	29	James	SOM	125
Margaret	CHA	202	Thomas	CLN	77	James	WAS	111
Nathl.	BCI	195	Thos.	D.C.	148	Jehue	WOR	190
Richd.	D.C.	81	William	BAL	193	Jesse (?)	WOR	195
Roger	CHA	190	POULSON, Cornelius			Jesse	WOR	186
Stephen	BCI	481		FRE	192	Jesse	WOR	191
Vincent	CHA	201	John	BCI	357	John	BAL	190
William	DOR	24	John	FRE	193	John	WOR	172
POSOM, Danuel	BAL	26	POULSTON, John	CEC	144	John	WOR	193
POSSEY, Edison	BCI	339	POULTNEY, Thomas	BCI	266	John	WOR	211
POSSTLY, Ben	WOR	187	POUMARANT, John	BCI	211	John; of Elij.	WOR	206
Jacob	WOR	187	POW, Adam	MON	154	John H.	CLN	77
Job	WOR	191	George	WAS	96	Jos.	QUE	18
POSSTTY, Ben (?)	WOR	187	POWABLLE, Kenddal (?)			Joseph	CEC	182
POST, Thomas	WAS	121		WOR	201	Kenddal	WOR	201
POSTETTER, David	WAS	108	POWDER, Andrew	FRE	186	Keziah	WOR	189
POSTIN, Fielding	D.C.	11	Jacob, Sr.	FRE	186	Levin	SOM	155
POSTLEHORN, George			Jacob, Jr.	FRE	186	Levin	WOR	156
	ALL	37	POWDER MILL, BEL-			Mary	D.C.	14
POSTLEWAIT, Henriette			LONA-John			Matilda	SOM	156
	QUE	42	YOUNG, manager			Milby	WOR	201
POSTON, Bartholw.	D.C.	105		BAL	182	Nathan	ALL	10A
Francis	D.C.	184	POWDER MILL, ETNY-			Nathaniel	CLN	77
Thomas	BCI	257	Joseph JIMMISON			Percey	SOM	117
POTEE, Peter	BCI	487	& Co.	BAL	186	Peter (?)	WOR	191
POTEET, James	HAR	62	POWDERS (See also			Peter R.	WOR	178
Jesse	BCI	157	PONDERS),			Rezin	BCI	295
John	HAR	63	Nathan	WOR	191	Sarah	CLN	113
Thomas	HAR	59	Ruel.	WOR	185	Sarah	SOM	139
Thomas, Junr.	HAR	62	POWEL, --- (Mrs.)	BCI	404	Sarah	WOR	213
William	HAR	41	Charles	MON	153	Soloman	WOR	176
POTTENGER, Mary	WAS	116	Ebenz., Junr.	WOR	173	Thomas	BCI	7
POTTER, David	ALL	13	Elisha	WOR	179	Thomas	BCI	295
David	ANN	404	Elizabeth	BCI	39	Thomas	FRE	134
David	SOM	157	Hesster	FRE	194	Thos.	BCI	481
Elijah	SOM	144	Jacbo	FRE	198	Thos. (of Thos.)	WOR	175
George	SOM	147	Jacob	MON	153	Upton	WAS	88
Henry	CLN	107	James	SAI	80	William	BAL	250
James (?)	WAS	78	Jas. (Sherriff)	WOR	175	William	BCI	112
James	BCI	308	Jesse (of Levin)	WOR	160	William	WAS	100
John	BCI	486	John	BAL	157	Willm.	D.C.	145
John	WAS	68	John	FRE	198	Wm., Sen.	WOR	171

POWELL (continued),		PRATTIS, Isaac	CLN 106	PRICE (continued),	
Zadok	WOR 185	Rachel	CLN 106	Andrew	CEC 126
Zadok of Elij.	WOR 209	PRAUL, Cornelius	CEC 183	Archelon	ALL 13
Zeno	WOR 191	PRAUT, --- (?)	BCI 414	Archibald	SAI 63
POWER, Edward	D.C. 53	M.	BCI 374	Archilus	TAL 50
Elizabeth	D.C. 43	S.	BCI 396	Aron	CEC 183
Henry J. (I.?)	ANN 357	PREAST, Clement	D.C. 162	Avarilla	BCI 176
Isaac N.	SAI 68	PRENTICE, Alexander		B. Thomas	CEC 144
Jesse	SAI 87		BCI 246	Barbary	WAS 90
Michael	BCI 240	PRESBURY, --- (Mrs.)		Bazel	QUE 10
Michl.	BCI 172		BCI 129	Beal	BAL 93
Sam	BCI 336	Geo. G.	BCI 210	Benedict A.	SAI 86A
Thos.	D.C. 149	George	HAR 5	Benjamin	ANN 338
POWERS, Abraham	ALL 32	Greenbury	HAR 8	Benjamin	BAL 18
Cornelia	BCI 10	James	HAR 20	Benjamin	KEN 107
David	BCI 464	James L.	HAR 7	Benjamin	WAS 148
Elizabeth	BCI 63	Joseph	BCI 67	Benjamin-negro	CEC 126
James	BCI 416	Mary	BAL 130	Calep	BAL 152
James	BCI 478	Ned-f.c.p.	HAR 11	Charles	CLN 79
James	BCI 507	Stephen-Negro	HAR 65	Charles	HAR 6
John	BCI 310	William	HAR 5	Charles	TAL 32
John	BCI 514	PRESGROVES, James		Charles N.	CLN 94
Philip	D.C. 137		BCI 97	Christopher	QUE 32
Richard	PRI 230	PRESSLE, Michael	FRE 158	Corns.	QUE 6
Robert	CHA 189	PRESTIN, Diana	BCI 173	Daniel	BAL 95
Thomas	BAL 184	PRESTMAN, Ann	BCI 302	Daniel	BAL 96
Thomas	PRI 207	Thomas	BCI 69	Danl.	MON 134
POWHATTON COTTON		PRESTON, Ann	D.C. 75	David	BCI 286
MANUFACTORY-		Barnet	HAR 39	David	CEC 126
Philip WILSON,		Charles	FRE 113	David	D.C. 195
manager	BAL 188	David	HAR 43	David	D.C. 197
POWLASS, Jacob	WAS 120	Darby-Negro	HAR 49	Elijah	BAL 94
POWLOES, Henry (?)	WAS 94	Frederick	FRE 74	Elijah	FRE 81
POWTER, Elijah	FRE 210	George	ALL 16	Elizabeth	QUE 39
POXTER, James (?)	WAS 78	Harry-Negro	HAR 49	Elizabeth H.	CEC 126
PRACTIER, Nicey	DOR 21	Jacob	BCI 334	Elonara	WAS 60
Vicey?	DOR 21	James	HAR 39	Ephriam	DOR 33
PRASER, Masy	BCI 341	James-f.c.p.	HAR 11	Evan	MON 143
PRATER, Friend	WAS 144	Jno.	MON 132	Francis	TAL 40
PRATHER, Bazel	WAS 138	Jonas	CEC 182	Fredus	CEC 126
Benjamin	PRI 184	Joseph	CEC 182	George	CEC 127
Benjn.	MON 167	Joshua	FRE 81	George	CLN 94
Henry	WAS 136	Keziah-Negro	HAR 65	George	FRE 170
James	ALL 31	Margt.-Negro	HAR 50	George	TAL 40
James	WAS 138	Mary-Negro	HAR 49	Gouldsborough	QUE 32
John C.	PRI 183	Milly-Negro	HAR 49	Henereta	BAL 27
Josiah	PRI 184	Moses	HAR 44	Henry	ANN 396
Ruthey	WAS 135	Peter	ALL 14A	Henry	BCI 358
Samuel	WAS 138	Rebecca	HAR 40	Henry	TAL 32
Thomas	PRI 202	Samuel-Negro	HAR 80	Hezekiah	BCI 278
Walter	PRI 193	Samuel-Negro	HAR 80	Howell	BCI 82
William	PRI 183	Thomas	CEC 182	Hyland	CEC 182
Wm.	MON 167	Thos.	D.C. 148	Isaac	CLN 92
Zephaniah	PRI 193	Will.	D.C. 100	Isaac	WAS 148
PRATT, Alexander	ANN 276	William	BCI 451	Isaac-negro	CEC 126
Charlotte	QUE 38	William	CEC 183	Isaac B.	BCI 113
Christopher	CLN 87	PRETELOW, John	BCI 524	Isabela	BAL 15
Darkey-free	CAL 63	PRETTYMAN, David		Jacob	CEC 182
Edwin W.	QUE 27		D.C. 152	Jacob	WAs 108
Fredk.	BCI 230	PREUSS, Augustus W.		Jacob-f.c.p.	HAR 10
George	QUE 16		PRI 231	James	CEC 144
Henry	WAS 104	PREWET, William	BCI 19	James	HAR 45
Henry R.	QUE 24	PREWILL, John (?)	HAR 57	James	QUE 30
James	CLN 81	PREWITT, Fisher	WOR 181	James	TAL 10
James R.	QUE 33	John	HAR 57	James-Negro	CEC 126
Joshua	CLN 74	PRIAN, Margaret	BCI 10	Jane	SAI 54
Martha	BCI 248	PRICE, --- (?)	BCI 416	Jas. W.	QUE 5
Mary	QUE 16	--- (Widaw)	BCI 414	Jeremiah	D.C. 148
Nancy	CLN 90	Abraham	BAL 70	Jesse	BCI 188
Perregrine	CLN 87	Abraham (Captn.)		Joabb	FRE 81
Rachel	D.C. 38		BAL 245	John	BAL 64
Thomas	ALL 38	Abrahame	DOR 33	John	BAL 151
Thomas	CLN 90	Absolomn	WAS 83	John	BCI 3
William	CLN 77	Ambrose	CEC 126	John	BCI 38
William	QUE 39	Ammon	FRE 74	John	BCI 317
		Andrew	BCI 273	John	CEC 144

PRICE (continued),		PRICE (continued),		PRITCHARD (continued),	
John	HAR 45	William	ALL 14	Stepn.	D.C. 161
John	MON 143	William	BAL 29	PRITCHET, Betsy	DOR 33
John	QUE 46	William	BAL 115	Elijah	DOR 32
John	SAI 63	William	BAL 223	Samuel	HAR 18
John	WAS 84	William	BCI 2	PRITCHETT, Abraham	
John	WAS 86	William	CLN 78		CLN 109
John	WAS 148	William	FRE 163	Arthur	DOR 33
John, Jnr.	QUE 48	William	HAR 6	Benjn.	MON 175
John B.	CEC 126	William	HAR 25	Colleson	CLN 98
John H.	BCI 369	William	PRI 240	Edward	CLN 86
John P.	CLN 98	William	QUE 31	Elias	MON 163
John R.	CEC 126	William	WAS 86	Elizebeth	DOR 37
Joseph	BAL 96	William	WAS 118	Jabez	SOM 131
Joseph	HAR 44	William P.	SAI 53A	Jahn?	DOR 33
Joseph	KEN 106A	Wm.	BAL 29	John	DOR 33
Joseph	KEN 107	Wm.	BCI 538	Lavinia	BCI 60
Joseph (free negro)		Wm.	MON 144	Lott	CLN 104A
	SOM 118	Wm.	QUE 18	Thomas	DOR 33
Joseph W.	KEN 119	Wm., Jun.	QUE 11	Zebulan	DOR 33
Joshua	CEC 126	PRICHARD, Acquilla		Zebulan	DOR 33
Joshua	KEN 107		CEC 164	PRITMAN, John	WAS 107
Josiah	WAS 134[A]	Greenberry	QUE 36	PRIZE, William (?)	BAL 29
Kibble	SOM 135	John	QUE 32	PROBY, Elizabeth	FRE 95
Louther	SOM 138	Thomas?	QUE 35	PROCTER, Armour	WAS 99
Loyd	PRI 185	William	ANN 264	PROCTIER, Nicey (?)	
Margaret	BCI 117	PRIDEAUX, Joshua	WOR 188		DOR 21
Margaret	MON 135	Whittington	WOR 179	Vicey? (?)	DOR 21
Mary	FRE 95	PRIER, James	WOR 203	PROCTOR, Alexius	CHA 222
Mary A.	SAI 98	James	WOR 219	Alexr.	D.C. 97
Mordacai, of M.	BAL 96	John	WOR 218	Ann	D.C. 115
Mordecai	BAL 93	Josep	BCI 408	Augustus	PRI 216
Nehemia	BAL 56	PRIEST, Richard	CLN 79	Basil	CHA 226
Nicholas	CEC 126	William	KEN 107	Elenor	D.C. 91
Nicholas	CEC 144	PRIESTLEY, Edwd.	BCI 226	Isaac	PRI 224
Nicholas	CEC 144	PRIGG, Edward	HAR 70	James	HAR 21
Nicholas	TAL 34	Edward	HAR 76	John	D.C. 91
Peter	BAL 193	John	HAR 71	John	PRI 224
Priscilla	QUE 11	Joseph	HAR 78	Migl?	FRE 88
Rachell	WOR 218	Mark-Negro	HAR 79	Nancy	BAL 236
Richard	BAL 227	William	HAR 72	Priscilla	BAL 118
Richard	CHA 196	William-Negro	HAR 80	Raphael	PRI 217
Rudolph	WAS 147	William-Negro	HAR 80	Rebecca	BCI 433
Saml.	BCI 311	William (Tanr.)	HAR 77	Sarah	DOR 16
Saml.	KEN 122	PRIM, Thomas	FRE 157	Thomas	BAL 249
Saml.	MON 178A	PRIMROSE, Hannah	KEN 118	Thomas	HAR 70
Samuel	BAL 93	Wm.	QUE 7	William	BCI 48
Samuel	BAL 215	PRIMUS, Simon	CEC 164	William	D.C. 98
Samuel	CLN 92	PRINCE, Casper	BCI 4	PROEBSTING, T. C.	
Samuel	CEC 126	Elizabeth	BCI 109		BCI 378
Samuel D.	WAS 62	PRINE, Ann	HAR 64	PROSBURY, James	BCI 52'
Sarah	TAL 51	Edward	BAL 217	PROSSER, David	BAL 16;
Sarrah	CEC 144	John	CEC 144	Isaac	BAL 83
Simon	CLN 76	William	BAL 214	PROTZMAN, Ann Maria	
Skelton	BAL 97	William	KEN 110		WAS 113A
Solomon	BAL 157	PRINGLE, Mark M.	BCI 279	Daniel	WAS 137
Sophia	BAL 245	PRIOR, Fanny	D.C. 48	Franceis	WAS 102
Stephen	ANN 328	Jo.	QUE 11	Loudwick	WAS 99
Steven?	TAL 51	Josep (?)	BCI 408	PROUD, David	BCI 478
Stevus	TAL 51	Peggy	SOM 133	John S.	ANN 323
Susanah	WAS 125	Sandy	SOM 133	Richard	BCI 109
Tabitha	BAL 29	Thomas	CEC 165	PROUDFOOT, John	BCI 274
Thomas	ANN 288	Thomas	SOM 133	PROUGH, Frederick	BAL 55
Thomas	ANN 384	PRISE, William (?)	BAL 29	PROUSE, George	CLN 109
Thomas	BAL 93	PRITCHARD, Charles		John, Sr.	CLN 95
Thomas	BAL 152		DOR 53	John, Jr.	CLN 85A
Thomas	CEC 144	Elijah	BCI 147	Seth	CLN 106
Thomas	KEN 94	James	SOM 105	PROUT, Ann	CAL 60
Thomas	QUE 36	James	TAL 31	Arther	BCI 477
Thomas, Senr.	CHA 193	John, Ovsr.	TAL 40	Edward	BCI 52
Thomas, Junr.	CHA 193	Levin	BCI 143	Isaac	FRE 118
Thomas S.	CEC 126	Mary	BCI 75	Jane	ANN 392
Thomas S.	CEC 127	Richard	TAL 33	John	BCI 426
Thos. T.	BCI 333	Robt.	D.C. 109	John	D.C. 77
Violette	CLN 97	Saml.	D.C. 127	M. (?)	BCI 374
Walter L.	ANN 395	Sarah	DOR 5	Robert	BCI 308

PROUT (continued),		
Robert	BCI	431
S. (?)	BCI	396
William	FRE	106
Willm.	D.C.	124
Wm.	BCI	346
PROVOST, Francis	BCI	519
PRUCHEE, John	FRE	214
Michael	FRE	213
PRUETT, Elijah	SOM	150
Wm. (of Elijah)	WOR	176
PRUIT, Charles	WOR	171
Rebecca	WOR	163
Sevirn	WOR	155
Walter	WOR	161
PRUSIA, Sam	QUE	7
PRUTER, William	D.C.	37
PRUTSMAN, Mary	FRE	159
PRUTT, Rachel (?)	D.C.	38
PRUTZMAN, Elizabeth		
	FRE	161
Henry	FRE	158
Jacob	FRE	163
Ludwick	FRE	154
PRY (See also FRY,		
VRY),		
Geo. (?)	FRE	123
Philip	WAS	66
PRYER, Edward	BCI	209
Hannah	FRE	129
Peter	FRE	129
PRYOR, James	ANN	380
Jo	QUE	20
William	KEN	120
PUCKHAM, George (f.n.)		
	SOM	119
Levin (f.n.)	SOM	120
PUCKHET, Elijah (?)	DOR	32
PUCKUM, Lemuel	WOR	214
Severn	SOM	125
Suckey	SOM	136
Thomas	WOR	216
PUCKYTY, Benjamin	BAL	88
PUE, Caleb	HAR	42
Mary	BCI	269
PUFF, Henry	HAR	56
PUGH, Elizabeth	BCI	90
Jesse	ALL	36
John	MON	178A
Joseph	CEC	164
Umphrey	CEC	127
PUICHEE, Michael (?)		
	FRE	213
PUKINS, Susanna (?)		
	KEN	101
PUKREN, John	DOR	22
PULLET, John	DOR	62
PULLY, James	TAL	26
PULTON, Randall	BCI	114
PUMFREY, Roy	D.C.	56
PUMPHREE, Moses	MON	154
PUMPHREY, E.	BCI	410
Edward	ANN	298
Jas.	D.C.	118
Jessey	ANN	333
John	PRI	202
Margaret	ANN	307
Sarah	ANN	298
Susanna	ANN	309
Thomas	ANN	305
Thomas	BAL	209
Walter	ANN	310
Will.	D.C.	134
William	ANN	299
William	ANN	330

PUMPHRY, William	ANN	376
William	PRI	240
William E.	PRI	227
PUMPREY, Vachel	FRE	77
PUNCH, Mary	BCI	518
Nancy	BAL	224
PUNNY, Henry	QUE	41
PURDAM, Zadock	MON	133
PURDOM, John	MON	139
John, Ju.	MON	137
Josh.	MON	141
Levi B.	MON	139
Mordecai	MON	141
PURDY, Charles	FRE	71
Edmond	FRE	71
Elizabeth	ANN	253
James	ANN	287
John	ANN	284
John	BCI	169
Richard	CHA	194
Sarah	BAL	206
William	ANN	292
Wm.	MON	173
PURIGHT, Lewis	BCI	439
PURKEYPILE, Henry		
	BAL	145
Jacob	BAL	145
PURKINS, William	KEN	102
PURMAN, Charles (?)		
	FRE	68
PURNELL, Amelia H.		
	WOR	177
Amos	WOR	177
Benjamin	WOR	206
Benjn.	WOR	172
Catharin (her		
Quarter)	WOR	181
Chesed (her		
Quarter)	WOR	181
Clarasy	CLN	82
Elizabeth	WOR	171
Frederick	CLN	79
George-f.n.	SOM	120
George W.	WOR	187
Gertrude	WOR	188
Henriette (of John)		
	WOR	178
Jacob	WOR	176
Jacob	WOR	217
James	CEC	144
Jesse	SOM	132
John F.	WOR	173
John J. (I.?)	WOR	189
Josa.	WOR	181
Lantie?	WOR	170
Levin	WOR	181
Littleton R.	WOR	178
Lot	WOR	181
Mathew	WOR	200
Mathias	CEC	144
Matthew	WOR	177
Moses	WOR	175
Richard W.	BAL	188
Robert J. H.	WOR	184
Rouse	WOR	177
Sarah (of Elisha)	WOR	174
Stephen	WOR	186
Thomas of Wm.	WOR	187
Thos. (of Milby)	WOR	173
Thos. of Walter	WOR	196
Thos. M.	WOR	179
Thos. M.	WOR	185
Zadock	WOR	179
Zadok	WOR	191
PURPER, --- (Widow)		
	BCI	372

PURS, William (?)	TAL	50
PURSLEY, James	TAL	22
PURTLE, John	DOR	41
PURVES, Adam	BCI	128
PURVIANCE, John	BCI	210
Robert	BCI	336
PURVIENCE, William	BCI	272
PUSEY, George, Senr.		
	FRE	177
George, Jr.	FRE	200
Joel	FRE	176
PUTEN, Leonard	BCI	417
PUTNAM, Caleb	D.C.	48
PUTNEY, David	FRE	86
PUZEY, Denard	WOR	211
Isaac	SOM	123
Isaac	WOR	211
John	SOM	125
John; S.	WOR	216
Lankford	WOR	211
Parker	SOM	125
Planner	SOM	125
Purnell	WOR	211
Purnell	WOR	216
PYE, Allsep	WAS	137
Edward	CHA	208
Henry	BCI	319
Olivia	CHA	212
Sarah	CHA	212
PYFER, Philip	FRE	97
PYKE, Abraham	BCI	380
PYLE, Amos	HAR	74
Herman	HAR	40
Isaac	HAR	40
John	HAR	40
Nathan	HAR	71
Ralph	HAR	40
Stephen	HAR	43
William	HAR	40
William, Junr.	HAR	40
PYNE, William	ALL	20A
PYONHEIDT, Alexandria		
	FRE	187
PYOTT, James	FRE	94

--- Q ---

QUADE, Verlinda	CHA	195
QUAIL, Robert	BCI	286
QUAILES, John	BCI	250
QUANDRILL, Thomas	WAS	115
QUARRY, Edward	BAL	112
William	BAL	2
QUARY, Danl.	MON	163
QUASH, Ailsy	DOR	6
Ellen	KEN	120
QUAY, Patrick W. (?)		
	BAL	54
Thomas	BCI	98
William	BCI	16
QUEEN, Ambros	ANN	283
Anthany	D.C.	42
Anthony	BCI	309
Anthony?	D.C.	42
Catherine	ANN	369
Chas. J. (I.?)	D.C.	137
Dennis	BCI	430
Dennis	D.C.	57
Eleanor	ANN	343
Eliza	D.C.	94
Elizabeth	ANN	287

REED (continued),		
Joseph	BCI	255
Joseph	BCI	528
Joshua	WOR	177
M.	BCI	214
Major	WOR	155
Mary	D.C.	203
Michael	WAS	134[A]
Mingo	DOR	43
Mitchel	WOR	163
Nelson	BCI	466
Pennington	QUE	12
Philip	WAS	58A
Philip, Senr.	KEN	94
Pierce (Lizard Island?)		
	WOR	154
Pierce (Tizard Island)		
	WOR	154
Richd.	QUE	18
Saml.	BCI	169
Samuel	BAL	185
Samuel	HAR	59
Silas	D.C.	164
Thomas	QUE	25
Thomas, Jnr.	QUE	27
Upton	BAL	119
Walter	WOR	162
William	ANN	363
William	QUE	28
William F.	BCI	440
Wilmer	CLN	79
Wm.	QUE	7
Wm.	QUE	15
Wm.	WOR	177
REEDENSTINE, John M.		
	BCI	284
REEDER, Alaxander W.		
	SAI	73A
Christopher	FRE	127
Franceis	WAS	71
Henson	WAS	134[A]
John	D.C.	41
Kenullum B.	WAS	135
Magdelan	WAS	148
Maria	SAI	81
Mary	WAS	136
Mary Ann	BCI	81
Nancey	WAS	73
Philip	WAS	70
Richard	SAI	75
Thomas	D.C.	50
Thomas H.	CHA	195
William	SAI	81
REEDY, Willm.	D.C.	131
REELE, John (?)	BAL	98
REELER, Saml.	D.C.	177
REEM, Josiah	BCI	457
REES, Harry	BCI	64
Jacob	BCI	64
REESE, Andrew	FRE	191
Ann	BAL	159
Benjamin	BAL	15
Cornelius	FRE	214
Danl. E.	BCI	178
David	BCI	155
David	HAR	71
David M.	BCI	152
Edmd. J.	BCI	174
Elizabeth	BCI	95
Elizabeth	CLN	105
Garrettson	CLN	105
Henry	BCI	199
Jacob	FRE	116
Jacob	FRE	187
Jacob	QUE	34
Jesse	HAR	72

REESE (continued),		
Jno. T.	KEN	114
John	BAL	155
John	BCI	397
John	FRE	114
John	HAR	47
John L.	BCI	313
John S.	BCI	128
Mary	BCI	448
Phebe	FRE	116
Thomas	CLN	104A
Thomas L.	MON	154
William	TAL	2
REESIDE, James	ALL	27
REEVER, Frederick	FRE	175
George	FRE	172
Henry	D.C.	24
Joseph	FRE	184
Phillip	FRE	171
Ulery	FRE	173
REEVES, Alexander	BCI	3
Benedick	D.C.	55
Hesekiah T.	D.C.	186
Horatio	CHA	226
James	CHA	216
John	BCI	2
John	BCI	20
Mary	CHA	221
Mary	D.C.	91
Robert	KEN	125
Thomas	CHA	206
Thomas C.	CHA	226
Ubgate	CHA	226
William	BCI	18
William	BCI	46
William	FRE	95
Wilson	CHA	221
REGGO, Clement (?)		
	BCI	53
REGGS, Clement	BCI	53
REGISTER, Samuel	BAL	108
Wilson	QUE	16
REIBLE, Andrew	BAL	156
REICH, John	FRE	98
REICHARD, Henry	FRE	149
Jacob	FRE	144
John	FRE	172
REICHLEY, Fredk.	BCI	212
REID, Andrew	FRE	143
Eliza	MON	133
Francis	ALL	32
Geo.	MON	132
George	FRE	188
Hanson	MON	133
Jas. B.	MON	134
Jne. M.	MON	132
Jno. M.?	MON	132
John	ALL	32
Leonard T.	MON	133
Margaret	FRE	170
Nelson	MON	134
Patrick	FRE	141
Patrick (of Alex.)		
	FRE	141
Thomas	CEC	145
Thos.	MON	133
Upton S.	FRE	169
William	ALL	32
Zachr.	MON	134
REIDER, Jacob	FRE	198
REIFSNEIDER, David		
	FRE	171
John	FRE	170
REIGERT, Philip	BCI	152
REIGLE, Adam	FRE	200
Henry	FRE	188

REIGLE (continued),		
John	ANN	285
REIHL, Elizabeth	FRE	93
Frederick	FRE	97
REILEY, Basil (?)	BAL	60
Charles	D.C.	28
Henry	FRE	200
Stephen	WOR	179
William	WOR	161
REILLY, Elizth. O.	D.C.	217
REILY, Daniel	FRE	192
Patrick	BCI	214
William	D.C.	72
Wm. F.	WOR	173
REINDINGER, Lewis	BCI	34
REINTZEL, Daniel	MON	154
REINTZELL, Daniel	D.C.	34
Samuel	D.C.	51
REISTEAU, Abraham	BAL	128
REISTER, Eve	BAL	19
Philip	BAL	19
REISTON, George	BCI	511
REITER, William	BCI	56
RELEY, John	CEC	183
Thomas	PRI	186
RELL (See also BELL),		
Henry (?)	WAS	57
Joseph	WAS	57
REMMY, Henry	BCI	97
REMSBERGER, S.	MON	135
REN (See also WREN),		
Catharine	FRE	87
RENALDUE, John (?)		
	D.C.	143
RENAULT, John	BCI	61
RENCH, Daniel	WAS	82
John	WAS	82
RENCHER, Esther	SOM	141
Moses	SOM	132
Priscilla	SOM	141
Saml.	SOM	141
William	SOM	106
RENCK, Margaretta	WAS	112
RENICK, William	WAS	101
RENNELLS, Isaac	BCI	229
RENNELS, Collen	BCI	28
RENNER, Adam	FRE	160
Adam	WAS	62
Daniel	D.C.	51
Henry	WAS	104
Jacob	FRE	223
Jacob	FRE	224
Jacob	WAS	119
John	BCI	461
John	FRE	115
John	FRE	179
Michael	WAS	56
Philip	WAS	94
Solomon	FRE	114
RENNERD, William	FRE	127
RENNIX, Rob	BCI	535
RENNOE, William	CHA	191
RENNOLDS, Nicholas	BAL	191
RENNOUS, John, Jun.		
	BCI	453
RENOLDS, Benjn.	KEN	122
RENSBURGH, John	FRE	113
Mary	FRE	113
Stephen	FRE	113
RENSHAW, Elizabeth	HAR	64
Jas.	BCI	176
John	HAR	40
Joseph	HAR	59
Wm.	MON	165
RENTSFORD, Hugh	BCI	54

REP, Jacob	WAS 102	REYNOLDS (continued),		RIBLET, Daniel	WAS 121
John	WAS 71	Leanord	CEC 184	RICAUD, Joseph	KEN 90
REPLOGAL, Henry	WAS 147	Lewis	BAL 144	Mary Ann	BCI 132
REPOLD, --- (Mrs.)		M. William	CEC 145	Thos.	BCI 380
	BCI 355	Noah	CEC 184	RICE, Abraham	HAR 30
REPP, George	WAS 106	Reason	ANN 329	Andrew of A.	ALL 24
Jacob	FRE 214	Richard	CEC 184	Anntty	TAL 51
Michael	WAS 100	Sally	BCI 52	Charles	WAS 78
REPPERT, Geo.	BCI 324	Saml.	BCI 490	Christian	WAS 119
Jacob	BCI 325	Samuel	CEC 184	Clefford	FRE 122
Lewis	BCI 324	Sarah	CEC 184	Daniel	TAL 49
RESCANIER, Peter	BCI 294	Taylor	CEC 184	Edmund	D.C.114
RESHER, George	BAL 87	Thomas	CEC 184	Frederick of A.	ALL 21
RESIDE, Wm.	BCI 525	Thos.	CAL 51	Frederick of J.	ALL 21
RESIDES, Edward	BAL 230	Thos.	D.C.132	George	D.C.160
RESINER, Martin	FRE 212	Tobias	ANN 329	George	FRE 106
RESINGER, George	BCI 499	Walter	D.C.104	George of Jno.	ALL 25
RESLAY, John	WAS 148	Warner	CEC 165	Gouldsborough (?)	
RESON, Abraham	CEC 145	William	ANN 260		QUE 32
RESSLER, Mary	D.C.153	William	CEC 165	Henry	WAS 127A
RETAICEL, Francis	BAL 220	William	D.C.13	Hugh	TAL 13
RETICHER, Jacob (?)		William	WAS 87	Jacob	ALL 21
	DOR 5	Willm.	D.C.155	Jacob	WAS 90
RETICKER, Jacob	DOR 5	Wm.	CAL 51	James	BAL 109
RETIKER, Adam	BCI 15	REYNOLSON, Robert		James	FRE 210
RETLEDGE, Ephriam			MON 154	Jane	HAR 29
	BAL 86	REZIN, Wm. D.	HAR 24	Jas. of Benj.	FRE 122
RETSLECK, Sarah	BCI 224	RHEA, George	CEC 184	John	ALL 21
REUD, Mary	BCI 295	Jean	CEC 166	John	ANN 286
REUSTIM, George (?)		Nathl.	D.C.81	John	WAS 105
	BCI 436	Stephen	FRE 186	John of A.	ALL 25
REUSTINE, George	BCI 436	RHEAM, George	FRE 69	John of Fred.	ALL 21
REVELL, William	SOM 123	George	FRE 221	Patk.	D.C.103
REVERE, D.	BCI 391	RHINE, John	FRE 222	Perry	FRE 127
REVILL, Charles	SOM 138	RHINEHEAT, Jacob		Sam	HAR 29
Curtis	SOM 149		BAL 83	Sam-f.c.p.	HAR 10
REX, Robert Ribbon		RHINICKER, Elizabeth		Sharlot	BCI 144
	BCI 91		FRE 112	Shields	BCI 92
REYLAND, Joseph P.		RHOADES, Phillip	BCI 306	Sophia	CEC 165
	CEC 165	RHOADS, Andrew	HAR 21	Thomas	D.C.86
REYMOLDS, Lucy	WAS 85	George	FRE 86	William	ALL 22
REYNER, Stephen	TAL 33	RHODE, Elisha	FRE 135	William	BCI 302
REYNHOLD, Jacob	CEC 145	RHODEN, Betey	TAL 34	William	D.C.34
REYNOLD, Christopher		Eve	TAL 35	RICH, --- (Miss)	D.C.16
	BAL 143	RHODENHISER, George		Arthen?	DOR 5
Mary	WAS 104		KEN 92	Arthur	DOR 5
REYNOLDS, Alex.	D.C.13	RHODES, Anty.	D.C.145	Daniel	CLN 95
Allen	ANN 329	Cath.	D.C.77	James	CLN 72A
Benjamin	CEC 184	Catharine	FRE 136	Matthew	BCI 171
Calep	WAS 80	Daniel	ALL 11	Peter	CLN 96
David	D.C.151	George	FRE 124	William	CLN 75
Dolly	WOR 179	Ignatious	TAL 39	RICHARD, Edward L.	
Eli	MON 154	Isaac	CAL 49		PRI 211
Elijah	CEC 166	Jacob	ALL 11	John	BAL 218
Elisha	CEC 165	James	CAL 49	John	BAL 228
Enoch	D.C.81	Jas.	D.C.133	Jos. R.	BCI 342
Esther	CEC 184	Jeremiah	CLN 88	Joshua	BAL 214
Hannah	CEC 184	John	CAL 49	Timothy	BCI 186
Harry	CEC 145	John	FRE 122	RICHARDS, Abraham	
Henry	CEC 184	Jos.	BCI 231		FRE 186
Hugh	ALL 11	Lewis	CLN 87	Andrew	BAL 157
Israel	CEC 183	Peter	D.C.157	Ann	FRE 70
Jacob	CEC 184	Rachel	CLN 97	Ann	PRI 218
James	ANN 329	Sarah	FRE 125	Arthur	BAL 144
Jo. W.	CAL 59	Thos.	CAL 48	Benedict	BCI 126
John	ANN 291	Valentine	FRE 114	Benjamin	ANN 288
John	BCI 453	William	DOR 59	Caleb	D.C.216
John	CEC 184	Zachariah	BAL 120	Catherine	BCI 56
John	D.C.46	RHODIER, Philibert		Elizabeth	WOR 172
John	WAS 117		D.C.34	Gabriel	PRI 203
John	WAS 120	RHODRICK, John	FRE 221	George	BAL 156
John H.	D.C.166	RHYNEA, Joshoa	CEC 166	George T.	PRI 217
Jonathan	CEC 184	RIAL, Elizabeth	BCI 252	Hagar	ANN 312
Joseph	BAL 44	Henry	FRE 177	Harry	BCI 66
Joseph	CEC 184	Henry	SOM 136	Isaac	CEC 184
Joseph	WAS 150	RIBLE, Susanah	WAS 90	Isreal	ANN 372

RICHARDS (continued),		
Jacob	CEC	183
Jacob	CEC	183
Jacob	CEC	184
Jacob	CLN	114
Jacob	WOR	209
James	BCI	29
James L.	CHA	216
Jenny	WOR	188
John	D.C.	184
John	D.C.	216
John C.	BCI	267
Jonathan	BCI	68
Joseph	SOM	127
Judea	CLN	108
Leonard	CHA	225
Lott	CLN	114
Mary	BCI	170
Mary	PRI	215
Mary Anne	MON	159
Mathias	FRE	125
Michl.	MON	173
Nancy	CLN	113
Nicholas	BAL	144
Paul	BCI	32
Paul S.	CHA	225
Resin	CHA	216
Richard	BAL	150
Richard	CHA	215
Richard	D.C.	6
Sabina-Negro	HAR	65
Sarah	ANN	397
Stephen	BAL	143
Thomas	BAL	160
Thomas	BAL	215
Thomas, Senr.	CEC	184
Wm.	WOR	173
RICHARDSAN, John	BCI	452
Trustun	DOR	25
RICHARDSEN, Charlotte		
	WOR	185
RICHARDSON, Adam		
	TAL	21
Allison	PRI	239
Anne	MON	159
Benj. Senr.	WOR	176
Benj. T.	WOR	175
Benjamin	BAL	224
Benjamin	BAL	247
Benjamin	TAL	24
Benjn.	HAR	46
Benjn. (Revd.)	HAR	42
Charles	WOR	188
Chs. (Doctor)	BCI	301
Clem.	D.C.	153
D. Peter	CLN	100
Daniel	BCI	118
Daniel	TAL	20
Daniel	TAL	22
David	FRE	81
David, Capt.	WOR	213
Easter	D.C.	124
Edward	HAR	72
Elijah	BAL	57
Elizabeth	BCI	24
Elizabeth	HAR	79
Elizth.	D.C.	158
Ellen	BCI	347
Esme	WOR	169
Ezekiel	DOR	3
George	BAL	182
George	WOR	174
Henry	BAL	18
Henry	CEC	166
Henry	CHA	195
Henry	TAL	26

RICHARDSON (continued),		
Isaac	ANN	378
Jacob	WOR	218
James	BCI	54
James	BCI	140
James	BCI	209
James	CLN	86
James	PRI	213
James	QUE	29
James	QUE	47
James	SAI	55
Jas. S.	BCI	214
Jesse	D.C.	13
Jesse	TAL	25
John	ANN	349
John	BCI	159
John	WOR	203
John; S.	WOR	216
John (of M.?)	WOR	205
John T.	ANN	264
Joseph	BAL	216
Joseph	CEC	166
Joseph	CLN	99
Joseph	SAI	53A
Joseph P. W.	CLN	88
Joshua (?)	WOR	218
Joshua	ANN	306
Joshua	TAL	26
Joshua	WOR	206
Levi	WOR	176
Luke	D.C.	118
Mark	CHA	213
Mary	BAL	19
Mary	BAL	221
Mary	KEN	120
Mary	WAS	139
Mary (of Jos.)	WOR	175
Mary Ann	BCI	75
Maryann	BCI	498
Mathew	WOR	206
Morgan	HAR	75
Nancy	SOM	138
Nancy	TAL	36
Nancy	WOR	160
Nath.	BCI	216
Nathanal	BAL	62
Noah	DOR	6
Perry	BCI	18
Peter	SAI	53A
Peter	WOR	171
Priscilla	ANN	391
Rachel	BCI	481
Rebecca	BCI	73
Reuben	CLN	94
Richard	FRE	163
Rob. R.	BCI	493
Robert	BCI	68
Robert	HAR	47
Saml. P.	MON	173
Samuel	WOR	169
Sarah H.	HAR	48
Solomon	CLN	86
Standly	DOR	25
Stephen	KEN	115
Thomas	BCI	20
Thomas	CEC	165
Thomas	CEC	183
Thomas	PRI	214
Thomas	QUE	33
Thomas	TAL	26
Thomas	WOR	212
Thos.	D.C.	132
Thos. T.	BCI	102
Toby	D.C.	162
Whittington	WOR	171
William	ANN	264

RICHARDSON (continued),		
William	BCI	31
William	CEC	165
William	CEC	166
William	CHA	213
William	DOR	18
William	HAR	47
William, Esq.	CLN	109
William, Sr.	HAR	47
William (of Jno.)	CLN	97
Wm.	BCI	533
Wm.	QUE	16
Wm., Senr.	HAR	57
Wm. (of Whittington)		
	WOR	175
Wm. H.	BCI	511
RICHART, John	BAL	142
John, Junr.	BAL	151
RICHASON, --- (?)	BCI	382
David K.	BCI	396
James	WAS	146
RICHEY, Archibold	WAS	62
John	HAR	72
RICHLER, Catharine (?)		
	BCI	482
RICHMON, Samuel	BAL	185
RICHMOND, Augustus		
	BCI	81
Elizabeth	QUE	39
Francis	FRE	134
James	BCI	17
RICHORD, Wm.	MON	143
RICHTER, Catharine		
	BCI	482
Elizabeth	BCI	482
Fred.	BCI	483
Mary	D.C.	164
RICHTSTENE, M.	BCI	390
RICHTSTINE, John	BCI	374
RICKARD, Daniel	WAS	111
Frederick	ALL	17
James	WAS	98
RICKER, James	BCI	111
RICKETS, Lovering M.		
	BCI	95
Nathan	HAR	70
Philip G.	KEN	86
Rachel	KEN	120
RICKETT, Robt.	MON	160
RICKETTS, Abram	MON	162
Anne	ANN	371
Anne	MON	173
Anthony	MON	166
Basil	MON	138
Benjamin	BCI	143
Benjn.	MON	160
David	BAL	179
David	CEC	145
George	CEC	145
Henrietta	MON	165
Hugh	BCI	450
John	CEC	145
Marchand	MON	160
Nathan	MON	178
Nicholas	MON	160
Samuel	HAR	7
William	CEC	145
RICKEY, Mary	BCI	168
RICKITTS, Winston	CEC	165
RICKORD, Wm. (?)	MON	143
RICKSECKER, Henry		
	FRE	154
RIDDLE, Ann	DOR	59
Carnelius	QUE	30
Jacob	PRI	182
Jacob, Senr.	PRI	182

RIDDLE (continued),			RIDGELEY (continued),			RIDINGER (continued),		
James R.	D.C.	196	John	PRI	205	Peter	FRE	181
John	CEC	165	Lucy	BCI	428	RIDLEY, Joseph	BAL	221
John	HAR	75	Noel	BCI	353	RIDMAN, Jesse K.	(?)	
John	WAS	125	William	D.C.	56		MON	144
Joshua	D.C.	151	RIDGELY, --- (See			RIDOUT, Hager	CLN	87
Lawsin	ANN	376	McDONAL & RIDGE-			Horatio	ANN	297
Robert	CEC	165	LY)			John	QUE	46
William	CEC	166	--- (See RIDGELY			Jos.	FRE	126
William	D.C.	72	LUX & CATOR)			Samuel	ANN	388
RIDDLEMOSOR, Michl.			--- (Gen.) at Hn.			RIELY, James	D.C.	66
	BCI	527		BAL	222	William	ALL	4
RIDELL, Lemuel	PRI	204	Charles	ANN	333	RIENHART, George	ALL	4
RIDENBAUGH, Fredk.			Charles	ANN	397	RIENICKER, Geo.	BCI	379
	FRE	126	Charles; of Ham.	BCI	253	RIFE, Daniel	FRE	146
RIDENHOUR, Adam	FRE	155	David	ANN	396	Jacob	FRE	146
Jacob	FRE	155	Elias	ALL	9	RIFFLE, George	MON	164
RIDENOUR, Adam	WAS	103	Eliza	BCI	117	RIFFLES, Margaret	D.C.	53
Benjamin	WAS	103	Greenbury	BCI	117	RIFFORD, William	CEC	166
Benjamin	WAs	123	Jacob	HAR	30	William	CEC	184
Daniel	WAS	133	John	ANN	395	RIGAN, James	BCI	20
Elizabeth	WAS	89	John	BAL	113	RIGBEE, Robert	BCI	412
Frederick	WAS	140	Nicholas	ALL	21	RIGBEY, John	QUE	26
George	WAS	103	Nicholas	BCI	129	RIGBY, Arthur	TAL	20
Henry	WAS	136	Nicholas O.	BAL	116	Aseneth	ANN	391
Isaac	WAS	109	Richard	ANN	396	Charles	KEN	89
Jacob	WAS	104	Thomas	FRE	110	Flora-Negro	HAR	80
Jacob	WAS	123	William	ALL	14A	Henry	BAL	230
Jacob (Mount)	FRE	164	William	BAL	241	James	HAR	62
John	WAS	108	William	BAL	244	James J. (I.?)	BCI	56
John	WAS	122	RIDGELY LUX &			Mary	TAL	19
Martin	WAS	117	CATOR	BAL	222	Matilda	D.C.	165
Michael	WAS	108	RIDGEN, William	BCI	96	Stanislas	D.C.	111
Nicholas	WAS	134	RIDGEWAY, Jesse	MON	164	RIGDEN, Joseph	D.C.	59
Nicholas, Ju.	WAS	140	Jessee	D.C.	55	William	BCI	114
Samuel	WAS	117	Johnathan	PRI	204	RIGDON, Baker	HAR	74
RIDEOUT, Catharine	FRE	148	Joseph	D.C.	55	Baker, Jr.	HAR	79
Jeter (negro)	TAL	20	Levi	PRI	203	Benjamin	HAR	72
Mary	FRE	158	Levin	D.C.	64	Samuel	HAR	55
Moses	WAS	64	Mordecai	PRI	205	Stephen	HAR	38
Nancy	DOR	43	Oden	D.C.	25	Stephen	HAR	76
Stephen	BAL	110	W. C.	DOR	59	Thomas	HAR	73
Susan	WAS	123	William	BCI	226	William	HAR	76
Thomas	TAL	52	RIDGLEY, Achsah	ANN	370	RIGELEY, Thoss.	BCI	355
RIDER, Charlotte	BCI	23	Beal	ANN	372	RIGEN, Lemuell	WOR	214
Danuel	BAL	17	Charles	BAL	56	Levi	WOR	214
Edward	BAL	243	Charles C.	ANN	382	Lowda	WOR	211
Frederick	FRE	154	Charles G.	ANN	382	Mary	WOR	218
Geo.	FRE	134	Charles St.	ANN	377	Puzey	WOR	215
James	CEC	145	Greenberry	FRE	126	RIGGAN, John	SOM	112
James	SOM	105	Henry	ANN	374	RIGGIN, Elisha	SOM	150
John	SOM	111	John	ANN	369	George	SOM	141
Joseph	CEC	145	Mary	BAL	175	Henry	SOM	154
Noah	SOM	110	Nicholas	ANN	369	Isaac	SOM	154
Thomas	BAL	245	Philemon	ANN	363	Jacob	WOR	154
Thomas	BAL	246	Rheuben	ANN	370	James	DOR	64
William	CEC	145	Richard	ANN	377	James	WOR	154
Willm.	D.C.	116	Richard	FRE	127	John	SOM	150
RIDGAWAY, Henry	TAL	20	Samuel	ANN	379	John (M.)	SOM	154
James	CLN	78	Samuel of Nich.	ANN	369	John, Senr.	SOM	151
James	QUE	27	Sarah	ANN	382	Joseph	WOR	156
Joseph (?)	D.C.	55	Stephen	ANN	322	Levi	BCI	309
Perre	CLN	76	William	ANN	372	Levi	SOM	147
Perry	TAL	31	RIDGWAY, Jesse	D.C.	135	Nehemiah	SOM	147
Richard	QUE	23	Joseph	DOR	5	Noah	DOR	32
William P.	TAL	28	Mary	PRI	237	Noah	SOM	154
Zedekiah	QUE	27	Rebecca	D.C.	131	Obed	SOM	146
RIDGE, Cornelius	FRE	156	Ruth Ann	PRI	239	Pearce	SOM	125
Ephraim	FRE	163	William	ANN	271	Robert	SOM	154
RIDGEAN, William	KEN	107	RIDGWEY, Thomas M.			Ruben	DOR	35
RIDGEAWAY, James	TAL	51		CAL	60	William	BCI	441
RIDGEL, Edmund	SAI	68	Walter J.	CAL	60	William	SOM	150
Jonathan	SAI	68	RIDING, William	D.C.	27	Wm.	WOR	155
Richard	SAI	68	RIDINGER, Barbary D.			RIGGINS, Israel	BCI	314
RIDGELEY, Dennis R.				FRE	215	RIGGS (See also KIGGS),		
	FRE	71	John	FRE	182	Alexander	FRE	210

RIZER (continued),		
Martin of M.	ALL	26
Mary M.	ALL	26
ROACH, Ann	BCI	80
Bridget	BCI	48
Cecelia	BCI	154
Charles	WOR	218
Esther	SOM	140
Gusts.	D.C.	128
Homard	CEC	166
Jacob	CEC	166
James	BCI	98
James	WOR	204
James	WOR	216
John	BCI	131
John	BCI	222
John	BCI	231
John	D.C.	156
John	SOM	144
Morris	DOR	53
Nemiah	SOM	155
Pheby	BCI	508
Stephen	SOM	145
Stephen	WOR	189
Thomas	CLN	99
William	BAL	210
William	SOM	150
William H.	BCI	113
ROACK, George	BCI	491
ROAD, John	D.C.	4
Joseph	BCI	431
ROADS, Eli	MON	154
Frederick	BAL	158
Geo.	MON	173
George	BAL	190
Jacob	WAS	68
John	ANN	370
John	MON	175
Peregrine	KEN	117
W.	BCI	355
ROAF, Pompey	KEN	90
ROAN, Adam	D.C.	100
ROB, John	CEC	145
ROBACH, William	WAS	55A
ROBACK, Henry	WAS	65
Jacob	WAS	57
John	WAS	65
William (?)	WAS	55A
ROBAY, John	WAS	147
Wm.	WAS	147
ROBB, Adam	MON	159
John	BCI	114
John	D.C.	54
Michael	FRE	189
ROBBERTS, George	BAL	166
William	BAL	159
ROBBINS, Benjamin	BAL	118
Isaac	D.C.	181
Samuel	DOR	36
Zina	BCI	77
ROBBIRE, John	MON	136
ROBBISON, William	BAL	141
ROBENSON, Wm.	BCI	510
ROBERD, William	WOR	219
ROBERDEAUX, Isaac (Maj.)		
	D.C.	61
ROBERDS, Levin	WOR	218
ROBERSON, Benjamin		
	CEC	127
Brice	BAL	13
Charles	BAL	27
Geo.	WOR	191
George	BCI	20
James	BCI	39
Joseph	WOR	189
Maria	CEC	127

ROBERSON (continued),		
William	WAS	135
William T.	WAS	135
ROBERT, Geirge	BCI	352
George	BCI	27
P.	BCI	350
ROBERTS, Amos	ALL	32
Ann	FRE	201
Anthony	BCI	307
Ben	QUE	4
Benja.	TAL	52
Benjamin	BAL	231
Benjamin	SOM	141
Betsy	BCI	458
Caleb	DOR	37
Dude	KEN	119
E. F.	BCI	413
Edmond	DOR	44
Edward	TAL	45
Ell	D.C.	188
Eliza	ALL	32
Elizabeth	BCI	439
Ellen	KEN	119
Esther	DOR	54
George	ALL	32
George	BCI	167
George	BCI	458
Hannah	DOR	44
Haratio	QUE	8
Henry	BAL	159
Henry	BCI	304
Henry	CHA	217
Henry	MON	161
Jacob	BCI	176
Jacob	FRE	140
Jas.	QUE	4
John	ALL	32
John	ANN	317
John	BAL	190
John	BAL	191
John	BCI	65
John	BCI	302
John	BCI	532
John	CEC	127
John	CEC	145
John	D.C.	86
John	D.C.	183
John	HAR	7
John	SOM	130
John	WOR	157
John, Sen.	ALL	32
Johnathan	BAL	3
Jos.?	QUE	4
Joseph	QUE	32
Joshua-Negro	HAR	65
Joshua B.	SOM	104
Josiah	BCI	31
Kizzy	SOM	130
Lemuel	ALL	34
Lewis	CEC	127
Lucretia	QUE	49
Marry	BAL	231
Mary	FRE	220
Mary-ngro.	CEC	127
Moses	ALL	32
Nathaniel	ALL	33
Peggy	WOR	159
Perry	TAL	10
Peter	BCI	153
Rachel	BCI	300
Richard	FRE	69
Richd.	CAL	53A
Sally	WOR	160
Samuel	BAL	231
Samuel	TAL	6
Sarah	BCI	293

ROBERTS (continued),		
Sarah	TAL	50
Severn	WOR	190
Severn	WOR	192
Sewell	QUE	4
St. George E.	DOR	53
Thomas	BCI	438
Thomas	CLN	105
Thomas	CEC	145
Thomas	QUE	26
Thomas	SOM	130
William	ANN	399
William	BAL	106
William	BCI	440
William	D.C.	20
William	FRE	216
William	SOM	141
William, Sen.	ALL	22
Willm.	D.C.	157
Wm.	BCI	227
Wm.	MON	160
Wm.	QUE	5
Woody	SOM	130
Zachariah	ANN	368
Zachariah	BCI	198
ROBERTSAN, Charles (?)		
	DOR	34
Clement (?)	DOR	34
Elias	DOR	34
Jahn?	DOR	34
John	DOR	34
William (?)	DOR	30
William (?)	DOR	34
ROBERTSON, Alexander		
	FRE	157
Alexander, Ju.	FRE	161
Ann	BCI	186
Charles (?)	DOR	34
Charles	ANN	350
Charles	BAL	16
Charles	FRE	143
Clement (?)	DOR	34
Dorathy	SOM	116
Ducci	SOM	155
Eli	SOM	110
Elias	SOM	116
Elijah	SOM	107
Elizabeth	SOM	107
Emelia (?)	DOR	24
Geo.	D.C.	77
George	CHA	196
George	SOM	116
George	SOM	123
Gerard	CHA	190
Guy	FRE	106
James	CAL	48
James	CHA	196
James	CHA	215
James	FRE	99
James	FRE	157
James	KEN	122
Jane	FRE	153
John (?)	MON	144
John	BAL	115
John	CHA	194
John	D.C.	20
John	SOM	105
John	WAS	117
John (Muddy Hole)		
	SOM	115
John-S.town	SOM	113
John (Taylor)	SOM	116
John, Junr.	WOR	163
John (of Chas.) (?)		
	DOR	33
John (of Isaac)	SOM	112

ROBERTSON (continued),		ROBINETT, Amos	ALL 33	ROBINSON (continued),	
John D.	SOM 103	Ann	ALL 33	James	DOR 9
Joseph (?)	DOR 24	Asa	ALL 33	James	HAR 42
Joseph	CAL 47	Elijah	ALL 33	James	PRI 226
Kitty	CHA 196	Elijah	ALL 33	James S.	BCI 245
Mary	BAL 197	Elijah, Sen.	ALL 33	Jane	BCI 265
Mary	D.C.38	Elizaphen	ALL 33	Jas.	D.C.145
Mary	D.C.85	George of N.	ALL 33	Jas.	QUE 10
Mary	SOM 116	Jasper	ALL 32	Jesse	TAL 21
Mary (Mrs.)	CAL 49	Jeremiah	ALL 33	John	ALL 15
Mihala (?)	DOR 24	Jesse	ALL 24	John	ALL 37
Nichls.	MON 137	Jesse	ALL 33	John	BCI 60
Nichls.	MON 178A	Joseph	ALL 32	John	BCI 241
Peggy	D.C.24	Levi	ALL 34	John	BCI 377
Rachel	HAR 27	Moses	ALL 32	John	BCI 400
Rachel	MON 154	Nathan	ALL 33	John	BCI 404
Richard	CEC 145	ROBINS, Dinah	BCI 17	John	BCI 406
Samuel	ANN 351	Edward	WOR 187	John	D.C.29
Samuel	SOM 103	James B.	WOR 181	John	HAR 72
Samuel (Muddy H.)		Rich	WOR 187	John	KEN 103
	SOM 116	Rick?	WOR 187	John	PRI 231
Sarah	ANN 254	Robert	BCI 298	John	QUE 9
Sophia	SOM 113	ROBINSON, Abraham		John W.	CHA 226
Stephen	CEC 127		BCI 520	Jonathan	HAR 73
Stephen	MON 143	Aldridge	CEC 166	Joseph	BCI 33
Thomas	BAL 202	Alexander	ALL 37	Joseph	BCI 271
Thomas	BCI 15	Alexander	BCI 490	Joseph	CAL 59
Thomas	BCI 17	Ann	BCI 119	Joseph	D.C.185
Thomas	D.C.63	Ann	D.C.102	Joseph	HAR 47
Thomas	SOM 147	Anthony	DOR 50	Joseph, Jun.	HAR 37
Thos.	CAL 50	Antony	ANN 302	Keziah E.	PRI 223
Thos.	D.C.42	Arthur	BCI 415	Lake	CLN 85A
Thos.	D.C.75	Benj.	ALL 32	Leah	DOR 62
Tolis	CEC 127	Benjamin	PRI 212	Lear	BCI 229
Vachel	MON 131	Bill	QUE 10	Levi	DOR 55
Verlinda	CHA 213	Charles	ANN 303	Lewis	BAL 53
Walter	FRE 162	Charles	ANN 310	Lewis	BCI 140
William (?)	DOR 30	Charles	HAR 61	M. (Mrs.)	ANN 389
William (?)	DOR 34	Charles	KEN 101	Margen	BCI 349
William	BAL 194	Chas.	BCI 170	Margt.	D.C.112
William	CEC 166	Daniel	BCI 61	Mary	D.C.78
William	D.C.56	Daniel	BCI 81	Mary	QUE 48
William	SOM 115	Daniel	CLN 80	Matthias	ANN 390
William	WAS 125	Daniel	DOR 10	Matw.	D.C.145
William M. (?)	DOR 20	Danl.	BCI 372	Mexandria	FRE 78
ROBERTSOR, John (?)		Darkey	QUE 48	N. N.	BCI 129
	MON 144	David	ANN 311	Nace	QUE 47
ROBESON, Isaac	WAS 144	David	CLN 90	Oneal	ANN 306
Wm.	WAS 149	DEnnis	ANN 309	O'Neil	BAL 42
ROBETS, Caleb	DOR 21	E. (Widaw)	BCI 394	Pere	QUE 48
ROBEY (See also BOBEY),		Edwd.	D.C.184	Peter	BCI 346
Alexander, Senr.	CHA 217	Eleanor	ANN 307	Rach	BCI 343
Alexander, Junr.	CHA 217	Elijah	BAL 47	Rachael	BAL 43
Ann	CHA 221	Elijah	D.C.114	Rebecca	ALL 13
Aquilla	CHA 217	Elizabeth	ANN 311	Rebecca	BCI 427
Baruk	D.C.130	Elizabeth	BCI 344	Richard	ANN 302
Caleb	CHA 217	Elizabeth	QUE 49	Richard	TAL 35
Charles	CHA 202	Elizabeth	TAL 38	Robert	BCI 23
Cornelius	CHA 212	Ely	BCI 80	Robt.	BCI 184
Elias	CHA 215	Fendall	CHA 216	Saml.	BCI 378
Isaac	D.C.137	Fendel	PRI 231	Samuel	D.C.5
James	CHA 227	Frank-free	CAL 61	Samuel	TAL 20
Jesse	CHA 217	George	ANN 293	Sarah	D.C.103
John	CHA 221	George	DOR 41	Seth	D.C.125
Josiah	CHA 213	George	HAR 38	Stanly	TAL 5
Malachi	CHA 215	Handy	DOR 62	Stepn.	D.C.211
Peter	CHA 208	Hannah	KEN 101	Suckey	BAL 64
Samuel	CHA 215	Henny	DOR 10	Susanna	PRI 238
Theodore	CHA 221	Henrey?	DOR 10	Thomas	BCI 147
Thomas	CHA 215	Henrietta M.	DOR 3	Thomas	BCI 385
Thos.	D.C.132	Henry	BCI 257	Thomas	TAL 4
Townley	CHA 213	Henry	BCI 265	Thomas, Ovsr.	TAL 36
William	ALL 38	Henry	KEN 85	Thos.	BCI 196
Willm.	D.C.123	Henry B.	D.C.48	W.	BCI 337
Zacheriah	D.C.41	Isack	BCI 345	William	CLN 80
ROBIN, Charles	KEN 94	James	BCI 47	William	CEC 145

ROBINSON (continued),			ROCK (continued),			ROE (continued),		
William	CEC	145	John, Capt.	WOR	210	Abner, Jr.	CLN	94
William	HAR	38	Richd.	D.C.	148	Angel	CLN	78
William	TAL	40	ROCKEFIELD, John	WAS	66	Ann	CLN	79
William C.	QUE	29	Martin	WAS	107	Benjamin	CLN	91
Wm.	BCI	526	ROCKETT, Edward	PRI	216	Benjamin	QUE	26
Wm., Senr.	HAR	42	ROCKEY, Henry	BAL	142	Cuff	QUE	15
Zachariah	ANN	310	ROCKHOLD, Charles			Eleanor	ANN	326
ROBISON, John	FRE	198		HAR	57	Elizabeth	HAR	77
ROBONSON, Ephrain			Edward	BAL	86	Elizth.	D.C.	148
	BCI	507	Elijah	ANN	299	George	SOM	130
ROBRTSAN, Charles			Elijah	HAR	61	Henry	CHA	214
	DOR	34	Jacob	BAL	86	James	CLN	81
Clement	DOR	34	John	HAR	39	James	QUE	28
Jahn	DOR	34	Sarah	HAR	48	John	CLN	80
John?	DOR	34	Thomas	ANN	302	John	CLN	93
William	DOR	30	ROCKWELL, John	WAS	149	John	CHA	212
William	DOR	34	Moses	BAL	228	Nancy	QUE	41
ROBRTSON, Charles (?)			RODBIRD, Absalom	D.C.	96	Parrott	CLN	79
	DOR	34	RODDY, Hugh	FRE	148	Parrott	TAL	47
Clement (?)	DOR	34	William	ANN	364	Richard	BAL	111
Emelia	DOR	24	RODE, Henry (?)	FRE	221	Saml.	SOM	129
John, of Chas. (?)			RODEN, Peter	BAL	131	Samuel	CLN	81
	DOR	33	RODENHEISER, Philip			Samuel	CLN	93
Joseph	DOR	24		HAR	6	Statia	QUE	36
Mihala	DOR	24	RODENISER, Henry	FRE	157	Susan	CHA	211
William (?)	DOR	30	RODENMAYER, Geo.			Thomas	CLN	79
William (?)	DOR	34		BCI	192	Thomas	CLN	87
William M. (?)	DOR	20	Geo.	BCI	195	Thomas	CLN	90
ROBSON, Joseph	BCI	25	RODEPOUCH, Peter	FRE	194	William	CLN	93
Thomas	TAL	4	RODERICK, Benj.	FRE	127	William	PRI	224
Thomas	TAL	7	Danl.	FRE	131	William, Sr.	CLN	89
ROBY, Anne	MON	139	Josuwa	WAS	69	William, Sr.	CLN	94
Berry	MON	154	Saml.	FRE	128	ROFLER, John C. (Doctor)		
Charles	PRI	222	RODES, Denny	QUE	45		FRE	154
Edward (Overs.)	PRI	230	John	WAS	73	ROFNER, John M.	WAS	63
James H.	MON	154	John	WAS	138	ROGAN, Charles	BAL	199
John; J.	ALL	35	Simon	BCI	294	ROGERS, Alexd.	BCI	343
John H.	PRI	223	RODGERS, Binah	BAL	226	Aron	BAL	43
Leonard S.	PRI	225	Elisha	BCI	124	Barney	BCI	447
Mary Ann	PRI	238	George	BAL	234	Benjamin	HAR	75
Thomas (?)	MON	164	James	FRE	182	Catharine	CEC	184
Thomas H.	PRI	227	Jesse	WOR	197	Drew	DOR	25
William	ALL	7	John	ANN	264	Edward	BCI	96
Zadok	ALL	7	John	D.C.	118	Elizh.	BCI	176
ROCARD, Benjn. (Mrs.)			John	D.C.	196	George	BAL	83
	BCI	269	John	HAR	73	George	BCI	89
ROCH, Abraham (?)	FRE	182	John	HAR	73	Henry	BAL	176
David	WOR	158	Joseph	BAL	127	Jacob	BCI	245
Mary	WOR	159	Joseph	HAR	76	Jacob	CEC	184
ROCHE, Catharine	D.C.	199	Joseph	HAR	78	Jeremiah	CEC	184
Jame	BCI	191	Nathan	KEN	91	John	BCI	180
John	BCI	168	Patk.	D.C.	95	John	BCI	229
John P.	BCI	200	Rachel	FRE	182	John	FRE	114
Patrick	BCI	167	Rebecca	BCI	72	John	FRE	225
ROCHESBURRY, William			Robert	BCI	120	John H.	BCI	488
	WAS	123	Rowland	BCI	156	Joseph	BCI	306
ROCHESTER, Abm.	QUE	15	Samuel	D.C.	5	Mage	BCI	357
Ann	QUE	2A	Samuel	HAR	73	Moses	BAL	40
Ann	QUE	13	Solomon	WOR	189	Nicholas	BAL	178
Francis A.	QUE	6	Thomas	BCI	122	Patrick	BCI	22
Horatio	QUE	7	Thos.	QUE	17	Patrick	BCI	406
Joseph	QUE	2A	William	SAI	77	Patrick	FRE	140
Leticia	QUE	4	William	SAI	81	Phillip	BCI	36
Martha	KEN	121	William	WOR	189	Rowland	HAR	39
Sarah	CLN	81	RODMAN, John	BCI	135	Samuel	BCI	250
ROCHFORD, Bartw.	D.C.	178	RODNESS, James	QUE	49	Stephen	ANN	338
ROCK, --- (Mr.)	BCI	368	John	QUE	46	Thomas	BCI	220
Abraham	FRE	182	RODNISER, John	FRE	157	Thomas-Negro	HAR	80
Charles	BCI	282	John (son of John)			William	BCI	325
Charles	SAI	89		FRE	157	William	CEC	184
Francis	CEC	127	RODRICK, Daniel	WAS	69	Wm.	BCI	240
George	CEC	166	Ludwick	ALL	37	Wm.	BCI	248
James	SAI	97	ROE, Abner	CLN	75	ROGERSON, Thomas	CHA	213
John	CEC	127	Abner	QUE	18	ROGGE, Charles	BCI	247
John	SAI	95	Abner, Sen.	CLN	93	ROHBACK, George	BCI	518

ROHM, Conrod	WAS 149	
ROHN, Joseph	WAS 111	
ROHR, Catharine	FRE 103	
Christian	FRE 85	
David	FRE 81	
George	FRE 100	
Jacob	FRE 95	
John	FRE 83A	
Philip	FRE 103	
ROHRBOCK, Christian		
	FRE 195	
ROHRER, Abraham	WAS 109	
Christian	WAS 71	
David	WAS 70	
David	WAS 101	
Elizabeth	WAS 66	
Elizabeth	WAS 118	
Frederick	WAS 117	
Frederick, S.	WAS 71	
Frederick, Jun.	WAS 70	
Jacob	WAS 70	
Jacob	WAS 118	
Jacob, Sen.	WAS 102	
Jacob, Jun.	WAS 102	
John	WAS 72	
John, Sen.	WAS 71	
John, Jun.	WAS 71	
Samuel	WAS 70	
Samuel	WAS 93	
ROISTEN, Henry	BAL 14	
ROISTER, John	BAL 20	
ROLAND, William	CHA 211	
ROLENTSON, John, of Chas.		
(?)	DOR 33	
William M. (?)	DOR 20	
ROLERTSAN, Charles (?)		
	DOR 34	
Clement (?)	DOR 34	
Jahn (?)	DOR 34	
John? (?)	DOR 34	
William (?)	DOR 30	
William (?)	DOR 34	
William (?)	DOR 34	
ROLERTSON, Charles (?)		
	DOR 34	
Clement (?)	DOR 34	
Emelia (?)	DOR 24	
John, of Chas. (?)		
	DOR 33	
Joseph (?)	DOR 24	
Mihala (?)	DOR 24	
William (?)	DOR 30	
William M. (?)	DOR 20	
ROLES, Charles	KEN 119	
John	BCI 528	
Joseph J.	BCI 510	
ROLEY, Thomas	MON 164	
ROLING & SLITING		
MILL & NAIL FAC-		
TORY, AVELIN-		
Nathaniel ELLICOTT		
& CO., John DYKE-		
manager	BAL 192	
ROLING & SLITING		
MILLS & NAIL		
MANUFACTORY,		
PATAPSCO-ELLI-		
COTT & CO.	BAL 205	
ROLINGSON, Ben	QUE 10	
ROLINSON, Charles	KEN 122	
James	QUE 24	
Jesse	QUE 3	
John	CEC 127	
ROLISON, Richd.	BCI 509	
ROLLE, John	TAL 24	
ROLLENS, Jacob	BAL 224	
ROLLES, Richard	SAI 92	

ROLLINGTON, John	FRE 98	
ROLLINS, Edward	BAL 123	
James	BCI 88	
John	D.C.80	
John	D.C.132	
John	PRI 228	
John G.	CHA 225	
Joshua	D.C.80	
Lucy	D.C.91	
Luke	D.C.115	
Robert	PRI 237	
William	D.C.49	
ROLLINSAN, John	DOR 25	
ROLLINSON, Levin	KEN 94	
ROLPH, Ed	QUE 21	
James	QUE 8	
Jno.	QUE 5	
John	QUE 39	
O'Niell	QUE 8	
Susanna	QUE 21	
Thos.	QUE 4	
Zachariah	QUE 9	
RONCKENDORFF, Fredk.		
	D.C.94	
RONEY, Hugh	BCI 149	
James	BCI 457	
Mary	BCI 504	
Patrick	BAL 199	
William	BCI 213	
RONINSON, Zepheniah		
	BCI 284	
ROOF, Grace (?)	SAI 82	
Peter	BCI 93	
ROOK, George	WAS 96	
ROOKE (See also		
BOOKE),		
Thomas D.	BCI 77	
ROOKER, Saml.	BCI 497	
ROOKERS, --- (Mrs.)		
	BCI 353	
ROOP, Christian	FRE 193	
Grace (?)	SAI 82	
Jacob	FRE 199	
John	FRE 203	
Joseph	FRE 201	
Joseph	FRE 221	
Joseph, Jr.	FRE 199	
Peter	WAS 140	
ROOSTER, James	D.C.134	
ROOT, Grace	SAI 82	
Margaret	FRE 220	
Richard	FRE 220	
Willm.	BCI 196	
ROPER, Eliza	D.C.211	
ROPP, Susanna	FRE 110	
ROSANNE, --- (Captain)		
	BCI 49	
ROSCOE, David C.	WAS 60	
ROSCROP, Jacob	D.C.107	
ROSE, --- (See		
HARFIELD &		
ROSE)		
Arthur	ALL 26	
Chars.	BCI 199	
Elizabeth	FRE 103	
George	BCI 316	
John	BAL 80	
John	BCI 499	
John	DOR 40	
John, Sen.	D.C.127	
John P.	BCI 94	
Mary	FRE 106	
Robt.	D.C.125	
Stephen P.	BAL 218	
William	DOR 40	
William	DOR 61	
William	TAL 3	

ROSE (continued),		
Wm.	BCI 244	
ROSEL, Anna	BCI 346	
ROSENBURY, John	BCI 526	
ROSENPLATTE, Charlotte		
	FRE 170	
ROSENSTEAL, Henry	FRE 203	
ROSENSTEEL, George		
	BCI 517	
ROSH, And.	BCI 333	
ROSHER, John	BAL 99	
Wm. (?)	BAL 100	
ROSHMAN, Sally	D.C.194	
ROSIN, Thomas	CEC 127	
ROSINBERRY, Jno.	BCI 178	
ROSLER, John C. (Doctor)		
(?)	FRE 154	
ROSLRER, Wm.	BAL 100	
ROSS, Aaron	ANN 293	
Abraham	DOR 53	
Andrew	D.C.35	
Ann	ALL 28	
Anthony	TAL 40	
Aquilla	CAL 49	
Archibald	CLN 106	
Archibald	PRI 206	
Bassille	CLN 106	
Benja. C.	BCI 232	
Benjamine	CAL 64	
Charles (?)	DOR 25	
Charles	ANN 308	
Charles B.	FRE 72	
Daniel	DOR 52	
David	SOM 130	
Elenor	FRE 164	
Hariet	D.C.56	
Henry	ALL 14A	
Henry	CLN 78	
Henry	DOR 29	
Henry (negro)	TAL 50	
James	ALL 2	
James	BCI 24	
James	CLN 112	
James	FRE 171	
Jerna?	DOR 11	
Jesna	DOR 11	
John	BCI 22	
John	BCI 28	
John	CLN 100	
John	CEC 184	
John	D.C.175	
John	SOM 155	
Joseph	WAS 138	
Lettice	BCI 295	
Levin	SOM 139	
Lewis	DOR 55	
Mary	BCI 150	
Mary	SOM 156	
Maryland	CAL 51	
Milcah	KEN 89	
Nace	MON 154	
Noah	CLN 104A	
Noah	SOM 146	
Oward	BCI 340	
Peggy	DOR 11	
Reubin	BCI 120	
Richard	MON 154	
Richard	QUE 37	
Robert	ALL 13	
Robert C.	QUE 29	
Samuel	WAS 80	
Solomon	QUE 40	
Thomas	BCI 285	
Upton	CAL 51	
Walter	D.C.185	
William	ALL 13	
William	ANN 397	

ROSS (continued),			ROW (continued),			RUARK, Comfort	DOR 28
William	BCI 310		Margaret	FRE 141		Daniel	WOR 210
William	D.C.54		Michael	FRE 142		Edward	DOR 25
William	D.C.56		Michael	FRE 148		Elget	WOR 210
William	DOR 32		ROWE, Absalom	D.C.8		Isaac	WOR 218
William	FRE 100		Edward	D.C.44		James	DOR 29
William	PRI 181		Frederick	BCI 27		James	WOR 209
William	PRI 191A		Hager	TAL 7		John (?)	WOR 204
William L.	SOM 131		John	ALL 29		John	DOR 29
Wm.	WOR 159		Thos.	D.C.157		John; S.	WOR 218
Wm. B.	BCI 373		ROWEÑGS, John	DOR 58		John of J.	WOR 218
ROSSELL, Ennalls	DOR 55		William	DOR 58		Joseph	WOR 204
George (?)	BCI 515		ROWINGS, Dawson	DOR 63		Nancy	WOR 204
Syrus	DOR 5		Francis	DOR 64		Sally, Wd.	WOR 214
ROSSER, Ed.	QUE 20		William	DOR 64		Seth	WOR 210
ROSSITY, Thos.	BCI 335		ROWLAND, Christly			William	DOR 29
ROSTON, James	MON 154			WAS 89		RUB, Phillip (?)	BAL 83
ROSWELL, Joseph	CEC 145		Christty?	WAS 89		RUBB, Henry	BAL 147
ROTH (See also WROTH),			David	WAS 106		RUBBEY, Henry	BAL 151
--- (Mr.)	D.C.74		Edwd.	BCI 495		RUBY, John, Sen.	ALL 34
ROTHAUGH, John	WAS 95		Elizabeth	WAS 85		Thomas	ALL 35
ROTHRICK, Ruth	BCI 79		Henry	WAS 85		RUCKLE, David	ALL 4
ROTHROCK, John	BCI 466		Henry	WAS 145		George	BAL 42
Phillip	BCI 298		Isaac	WAS 85		John	BCI 355
ROUGH, Henry	WAS 108		Jacob	WAS 85		Patrick	BCI 399
John	WAS 100		James	CEC 183		Paul	BCI 440
Peter	WAS 135		John	WAS 85		Thomas	BCI 400
ROULASON, Thomas			John	WAS 145		RUD (See also REED),	
	BCI 150		Jonothan	WAS 145		Hosanna	KEN 105
ROULET, William	WAS 62		Samuel	CEC 183		James (?)	FRE 219
ROUNDS, Hezekiah	D.C.19		Samuel	WAS 134[A]		John (?)	WOR 177
Jacob	WOR 219		ROWLES, Elie	ANN 353		John	KEN 103
James	WOR 200		Elihu	CEC 184		Joshua (?)	WOR 177
John	D.C.83		Isaac	ANN 353		Wm. (?)	WOR 177
Joshua, Esqr.	WOR 215		Joshua	ANN 328		RUDD, Willm.	D.C.151
Opha	D.C.19		Nehemiah	ANN 328		RUDDOCK, Joseph	BCI 432
Rachel	SOM 145		R.	BCI 113		RUDICILL, Michael	WAS 108
William	WOR 211		Rezin	HAR 18		RUDISELL, Ludwig	FRE 169
ROUNK, Barbary	WAS 87		William	BAL 207		RUDISIL, George	FRE 180
ROUNSAVELL, Andw.			ROWLEY, Catherine			RUDLEY, William	CEC 183
	D.C.147			WOR 163		RUDOLPH, Daniel	FRE 197
ROUP, Elizabeth	WAS 134[A]		James	D.C.103		Harmond	BCI 299
ROURKE, --- (Mrs.)			Jas.	D.C.122		John C.	WOR 193
	BCI 402		John	WOR 155		RUDULPH, Martha	CEC 145
Mich.	BCI 215		Sally	BCI 74		Tobias	CEC 145
ROUSBURRY, Ailcy	DOR 60		Saml.	WOR 180		Zebulon	CEC 145
ROUSE, Anna	BCI 52		Sarah	WOR 180		RUDY, Christian	FRE 135
Benjamin	BCI 96		William	BCI 77		Christian	FRE 136
Charles	CLN 75		ROWLINGS, Catharine			Emanuel	WAS 81
George	BCI 429			PRI 213		Fredk.	FRE 131
James	BCI 80		Daniel	PRI 214		George	WAS 61
John	BCI 418		Henry T.	PRI 215		George	WAS 133
John	HAR 6		John B.	PRI 213		Jos.	FRE 131
Pere	CLN 91		Richard S.	PRI 215		RUE, James	TAL 12
Robt.	QUE 9		William C.	PRI 214		Southy	DOR 46
William	CLN 72A		William J. (I.?)	PRI 215		RUFF, Andw.	BCI 257
ROUSKALPH, Samuel			ROWLINSON, Richard			Henry	HAR 47
	WAS 117			TAL 20		Henry P.	HAR 19
ROUTSONG, Adam	FRE 129		ROWZER, Daniel	FRE 157		James	HAR 44
Christian	FRE 122		Jacob	FRE 163		John	HAR 19
Daniel	FRE 127		Margaret	FRE 154		Richard	HAR 9
George	FRE 132		ROY, John	BCI 115		Samuel-Negro	HAR 80
Henry	FRE 135		ROYER, Mathias	WAS 128A		RUGGS, Thomas	CLN 112
Jacob	FRE 130		Peter	FRE 203		RUHEN, Englehard	BCI 517
Jacob	FRE 133		ROYLAND, Abraham			RULE, John	BAL 98
Jacob, Sr.	FRE 134			WAS 98		Phillip	BAL 83
Lewis	FRE 129		Abraham	WAS 118		Rachl	BAL 82
ROW, Charles	WAS 82		ROYSTEN, Samuel	BAL 63		RULER, Saml. (?)	D.C.177
Frederick	FRE 142		ROYSTON, John, Senr.			RULEY, Benjn.	KEN 120
George	FRE 143			BAL 91		RULING, Elizabeth	BCI 315
Jacob	FRE 106		John, Junr.	BAL 91		RULLETT, Thomas	WAS 64
Jacob	FRE 147		Robert	BAL 240		RULY, Benjamin	CEC 127
John	FRE 102		Thomas	BAL 98		Samuel	CEC 127
John C.	BCI 523		ROZELL, George	CLN 93		RUMBLE, Charlotte	TAL 9
John K.	BCI 338		RUANN, John	CEC 145		RUMBLER, Barbara	FRE 189
Joseph	FRE 142		Joseph	CEC 145		George	FRE 189

RUMBLER (continued),		
Peter	FRE	189
RUMBLEY, Levin	DOR	9
RUMBLY, Aaron	DOR	34
Deborah	DOR	41
Dolly	DOR	41
Dolly	DOR	59
Edward	DOR	42
RUMBOLD, John	CLN	106
RUMENSNIDER, Geo.	BCI	212
RUMLBY, Thomas	DOR	33
RUMLEY, John	D.C.	15
RUMLLEY, Thomas (?)		
	DOR	33
RUMMEL, Ludwick	FRE	159
T. A.	BCI	397
RUMMELLS, Stephen	ANN	398
RUMMEY, Robert	BCI	101
RUMSEY, Charles	HAR	8
Henry C.	HAR	8
John	HAR	9
RUNKELS, John	FRE	79
RUNKLE, John (Doctor)		
	FRE	140
William (Revd.)	FRE	140
RUNKLES, Jacob	FRE	213
Joseph	FRE	213
RUNLEY, John	BCI	494
RUNMER, Lambert	QUE	27
RUNNALS, Rutha	BCI	30
RUNNELLS, Alice	FRE	114
Elenor	FRE	96
Samuel	FRE	111
William	WOR	186
RUNNELS, John	BCI	15
RUNNER, John	FRE	87
Michael	FRE	134
Philip	FRE	134
RUNNUEL, Ludwick (?)		
	FRE	159
RUPARD, Rob?	BCI	74
Role	BCI	74
RUPP, George	BAL	138
RUSCUP, John	BCI	137
RUSEL, Comfort	WOR	195
James	BCI	345
RUSH, Arnold	HAR	43
Benjn.	D.C.	88
Daniel	ALL	12
Elizabeth	BCI	89
Jacob	ALL	10A
John	ALL	12
Joseph	WAS	141
Lewis	ALL	10A
Rebecca	KEN	121
Stephen	ANN	331
RUSK, David L.	BCI	491
Geo.	D.C.	117
George	BCI	97
John, Sr.	BCI	100
Robert	BCI	99
Samuel	BCI	184
Thomas	BCI	97
William	BCI	99
RUSS, Rebecca	D.C.	125
RUSSEL, Aljah	SOM	107
Allen	BCI	203
Andrew P.	TAL	33
Ann	CHA	193
Elzey	SOM	112
Enock	CLN	89
Hezekiah	MON	135
James	SOM	111
James	SOM	132
Jane	PRI	194
Jennet	BCI	181

RUSSEL (continued),		
John	CHA	193
Mary	ANN	341
Mary	DOR	61
Thomas	BCI	319
Walter	BCI	201
William	CHA	207
William	PRI	203
William B.	CHA	202
RUSSELL, Abel	FRE	74
All	BCI	335
Ann	BCI	71
Char.	BCI	189
Charles L.	SAI	78
David	WAS	66
Elijah	CLN	93
Elinathan	ALL	26
Emory	CLN	92
Fred. A.	D.C.	33
George	ANN	321
George	BCI	515
Gilbreth	BCI	478
Hugh	HAR	25
Isaac	D.C.	68
Jacob	WAS	66
Jeremiah	SAI	74
John	CEC	165
John	FRE	74
John H.	SAI	78
Joseph	BCI	408
Joshua F.	D.C.	4
Mary	CEC	166
Mary	D.C.	128
Michael	BAL	228
Milly	D.C.	176
Philip	SAI	95
Richard	BCI	295
Robert	CEC	145
Robert G.	ALL	26
Saml.	BCI	167
Samuel	BCI	303
Sarah	FRE	74
Solomon	DOR	57
Theophilus	KEN	103
Thomas	CEC	145
William	BCI	436
William	CEC	145
William	D.C.	87
William	HAR	19
William	HAR	21
William	SAI	78
RUSSIAN MINISTER		
	D.C.	12
RUSSILL, John B.	SAI	74
RUSSLE, Richd.	QUE	3
RUSSOM, Seth	CLN	98
RUSSUM, Mary	TAL	49
William	SOM	105
RUST, Mary	BAL	198
Paul	BAL	198
Samuel	BCI	139
RUSTEN, Joseph	SAI	90
RUSTIN, John	D.C.	191
RUTE, Jacob	WAS	87
RUTH, Christr.	QUE	9
Elizabeth	WAS	89
Garroll?	QUE	47
Garrott	QUE	47
Gilderoy	CLN	95
Harriott	QUE	37
John	HAR	26
John R.	CLN	104A
Margaret	FRE	101
Richard	CLN	80
Thomas	QUE	6
Thos.	QUE	18

RUTHERFORD, Alex.	D.C.	21
Benjamin	FRE	96
John	CEC	184
Josh	D.C.	153
Willm.	D.C.	117
RUTLEDGE, Abraham	BCI	437
Abraham	HAR	64
Edward	HAR	64
Jesse	BAL	221
John	BAL	240
John E.	BAL	80
Joshua	HAR	63
Shadrach	HAR	61
Shadrach, Jr.	HAR	60
Thomas	BAL	80
Wm.	BAL	99
RUTLEGE, John P.	WOR	175
RUTTER, Catherine	WAS	104
Charles	CEC	165
Edmond	WAS	83
Edwd.	KEN	123
Jno.	KEN	122
John	BCI	465
John	CEC	165
John	CEC	166
John	FRE	85
Josias	BAL	180
Martin	WAS	94
Philip	BAL	129
Pompey	KEN	106
Richard	BCI	31
Richard	CEC	165
Robt.	D.C.	203
Samuel	CEC	165
Solomon (Capt.)	BAL	220
Thomas	CEC	145
Thomas J.	BCI	465
Thos. R.	BCI	507
William	BCI	159
RUTTLE, Samuel	WAS	55A
RUVASTICO, James Smith		
	SOM	104
RYAN, Amos	BAL	20
Fielder	PRI	211
Fielder P.	PRI	212
Henry	D.C.	87
James	MON	165
John N.	CEC	165
Joseph	BAL	9
Joseph C.	CEC	165
Margarett	PRI	205
Nicholas	CHA	204
Samuel	BAL	26
Thomas	BCI	123
Thomas	PRI	194
William	FRE	156
RYDER, Thos.	BCI	202
RYE, Christian	FRE	227
John	CHA	191
Margaret	CHA	192
Warren	CHA	228
William	CHA	192
William	D.C.	121
Willis	CHA	192
RYEHOUSE, Eliza	BCI	497
RYEN, Thos. (?)	WOR	194
RYLAND, John	ALL	6
Mary	BCI	96
Sylvester	ALL	6
Will.	D.C.	78
RYLEY, Adam	BCI	185
Catharine	BAL	221
John	BAL	83
John	BCI	508
Lawrence	BCI	202
Samuel	BAL	99

SANVICTER, --- (Mr.) (?)		SATTERFIELD (continued),		SAWNERY, John	BCI 537		
	BCI 415	William	CEC 128	SAWVILL, Solomon	BAL 161		
SANVICTON, --- (Mr.)		SATTERWHITE, Rachael		SAWYER, Adam	FRE 106		
	BCI 415		D.C. 186	Charles	PRI 230		
SANWALT, George	BCI 348	SATTIN, David	KEN 109	David	BCI 151		
SANWATT, George (?)		SAUBERE, Samuel	BCI 271	William	D.C. 94		
	BCI 348	SAUCER, John	BCI 32	SAX, Joseph	D.C. 173		
SAP, Isaac	CLN 80	SAUGHTON, Thomas (?)		SAXON, Bennet	CHA 202		
SAPER (See also SAS-			TAL 50	SAXTON, Joseph	SAI 74		
SER),		SAULSBERRY, James		Joseph	SAI 88		
Milly (?)	PRI 217		TAL 47	SAY, Henry	BCI 430		
Underwood (?)	PRI 217	SAULSBURY, Charles		John	BAL 19		
William, Jr. (?)	PRI 216		CLN 87	R.	BCI 378		
SAPINGTON, Francis B.		Eli	CLN 96	SAYERSON, Charlot	BCI 498		
	FRE 219	George	BCI 54	SAYLER, Daniel	FRE 217		
Thomas	FRE 219	Gove	CLN 95	Daniel	FRE 221		
SAPP, Christiana	ALL 31	John	CLN 99	Solomon	FRE 217		
Daniel	BCI 39	Matthew	CLN 93	SAYLOR (See also TAY-			
Frederick	BCI 35	Nancy	CLN 94	LOR),			
George	BCI 134	Nehemiah	CLN 94	Jacob	ALL 28		
Henry	BCI 39	Noah	CLN 93	John	FRE 228A		
Isaac	ALL 31	Thomas	CLN 88	Saml. (?)	SOM 136		
Jacob	ALL 31	SAUMS, Barbary	FRE 212	SAYMAN, Toby	BCI 502		
John	ALL 34	SAUNDERS, Aaron	DOR 20	SAYRE, John B.	BCI 314		
John	BAL 128	Elizabeth	HAR 5	SAYRES, Mount	BCI 29		
Joseph	ALL 18	James	HAR 20	SCADER, Thomas	BAL 145		
Oliver	BCI 35	John	HAR 5	SCAFF, George	BCI 274		
William	BAL 112	John	HAR 7	William	BCI 36		
SAPPINGTON, Caleb	ANN 338	Levin	DOR 24	SCAGGS, Isaac	KEN 116		
George	QUE 23	Mary	DOR 20	James	PRI 180A		
John	ANN 332	Obediah	BCI 132	Leonard	FRE 135		
John	CEC 128	Walter	FRE 234	Susanna	D.C. 50		
John	KEN 93	William	ALL 23	SCALLION, Peter	CHA 205		
Jonathan	ANN 304	William	ANN 279	SCAMEHORN, John	WAS 64		
Lambert	KEN 120	SAUNER, George	BCI 436	SCANTLIN, James	CEC 128		
Mary	ANN 326	SAURWEIN, Daniel	BCI 453	SCANTLING, Mary	BCI 478		
Nathaniel	KEN 108	Peter	BCI 450	SCARBOROUGH, Edwd.			
Richard	HAR 18	SAUVAGE, Jane	BCI 149		WOR 174		
Saml. L.	QUE 12	SAUXTON, T.	BCI 258	John	CEC 147		
William	BAL 114	SAVAGE, Evan	ALL 4	John	CEC 185		
SAPPTON, Ann (See		James	PRI 208	Kendal	WOR 176		
Richard GOODWIN,		James	QUE 31	SCARBROUGH, Euclidus			
overser for Ann		Lemuel	ALL 5A		HAR 78		
SAPPTON)		Robinson	ALL 4	Hezekiah	HAR 78		
SARDE, John	DOR 55	Robinson T.	ALL 4	John	HAR 71		
M.	D.C. 82	SAVARY, Rachel	KEN 106	John, Jr.	HAR 72		
Sally	DOR 50	SAVEARE, Peter	QUE 27	Saml.	HAR 71		
SARDO, M. (?)	D.C. 82	SAVERY, Peter	BCI 518	Saml. of Jos.	HAR 71		
SARGENT, Allen	BCI 143	SAVIDGE, Babel	WOR 200	Thomas	HAR 74		
Saml.	BCI 314	Babet?	WOR 200	William	HAR 73		
SARINSON, --- (Widaw)		Levin	WOR 213	SCARF, Jno. L.	BCI 211		
	BCI 405	SAVIGE, --- (Mrs.)	BCI 351	SCARFF, David	PRI 181		
SASSER (See also SAPER),		SAVILLE, John	BAL 187	Edmund T.	HAR 56		
Benjamin	SOM 122	SAVIN, Ann	CEC 128	Hannah	HAR 56		
Elizabeth	SOM 122	Catherine	CEC 127	Henry	HAR 61		
Mary	SOM 140	John	CEC 128	John	HAR 56		
Milly	PRI 217	Samuel	CEC 128	William	BCI 442		
Thomas	PRI 203	Thomas L.	CEC 166	SCART, Patrick	BCI 463		
Underwood	PRI 217	SAVINGTON, T.	D.C. 117	SCATT, Jessee	TAL 46		
William	PRI 203	SAVOILE, Basil	BCI 345	SCEEHEFUSS, Abraham			
William, Jr.	PRI 216	SAVOIR, Charles	ANN 286		WAS 128A		
SATCHEL, John	TAL 38	SAVORY, Elias	BCI 7	SCELL, Daniel	FRE 148		
SATCHELL, John	DOR 59	Wm.	BCI 174	SCENEY, Joseph	BCI 525		
SATERFIELD, Hezekiah		SAVOUR, Jane	ANN 283	SCERCH, William	ANN 369		
	TAL 10	SAVOY, Barbara	BCI 427	SCHAED, M. G.	BCI 49		
SATTER, J.	BCI 416	Boss	ANN 379	SCHAEFFER, Charles	BCI 375		
SATTERFIELD, Elijah	CLN 85A	Darkey	ANN 348	F. G.	BCI 253		
Emory	QUE 29	Francis	CHA 216	Frederick	BCI 82		
Greenberry	QUE 15	Lydia	D.C. 112	Michael	BCI 379		
Henry	QUE 15	Samuel	FRE 79	SCHAEFFLER, Geo. F. (?)			
Hosea	CLN 86	Stephen	ANN 322		D.C. 105		
James	CLN 107	Thomas	PRI 217	SCHAEFFTER, Geo. F.			
James	CLN 114	SAWDER, George	BAL 145		D.C. 105		
John	CLN 76	SAWKINS, William	BCI 113	SCHAFER, Jacob	WAS 132		
Jos.	QUE 9	SAWL, Edward	D.C. 27	John	WAS 134[A]		
Nathl.	QUE 15	SAWN, William	CLN 79				
Thomas	QUE 29						

SCOTT (continued),		**SCOTTEN** (continued),		SEE, Banjamin	CEC 128	
John	CLN 75	Stephen	ANN 346	SEEARS, Benjamin	CAL 62	
John	CEC 146	William	CLN 81	Henry, 1st	CAL 62	
John	CEC 146	SCOTTON, Jno.	QUE 4	Henry, 2nd	CAL 62	
John	CEC 185	SCOUR, Rob.	BCI 529	Jesse	CAL 63	
John	D.C.118	SCOWDRICK, Mary Ann		Richard	CAL 62	
John	FRE 174		CLN 108	William	CAL 62	
John	SOM 126	SCRAGGS, John	BCI 442	SEEGAR, Arthur	QUE 7	
John	TAL 48	SCRIBNER, Mary	D.C.54	Jemimah	QUE 14	
John	TAL 48	SCRIVENER, Benjamin		Jo	QUE 19	
John (of John)	WOR 172		ANN 371	John	QUE 14	
Joseph	BCI 167	John	ANN 278	SEEKINS, Jesse (?)	BAL 79	
Joseph	BCI 446	Mary Anne	ANN 278	SEEMAN, Arthur	MON 133	
Joseph	WOR 212	William	ANN 370	SEEMORE, Jacob	BCI 489	
Leonard	ANN 396	SCRIVNER, Francis	CAL 59	SEEMOUT, David	BCI 492	
Leslie	BCI 257	George-free	CAL 65	SEENEY, David	QUE 17	
Margaret	MON 161	Jas.	QUE 18	Jona	QUE 9	
Margt.	D.C.184	Nelly-free	CAL 65	SEESKNAP, Adam	BCI 461	
Martha	BCI 130	William-free	CAL 65	Adam	BCI 461	
Mary	CEC 146	SCRIVONER, Horatio	QUE 28	SEESS, Henry (?)	FRE 218	
Mary	SAI 87	SCROGGIN, Martha	CHA 206	SEEVERE, William, Ovsr.		
Moses	CEC 146	SCROGGS, John (?)	BCI 442		TAL 7	
Moses	CEC 147	SCUFFEON, Charles	WAS 87	SEGAN, Anna	FRE 100	
Nancy	ANN 302	SCULLY, Darky	QUE 39	SEGAR, Ben	QUE 4	
Ned-f.c.p.	HAR 11	SCUREMAN, Peter	D.C.5	Mary	CEC 167	
P.	BCI 368	SCURRY, Augustine	CEC 127	SEGERS, Mary	CEC 146	
Patty	BAL 130	SCYNSTACK, Henry	WAS 121	SEGUIN, --- (See		
Peggy	TAL 14	SEABROOKS, Henry	FRE 156	SEGUIN & SMITH)		
Peter	WOR 194	SEAFERS, Dumbo	D.C.135	SEGUIN & SMITH	BCI 379	
Priscilla	BAL 174	SEAGMOND, John D.	SAI 64	SEIGHTER, Joseph(?)	WAS 73	
Rachel	ANN 343	SEAL, Martin	QUE 9	SEIGLER, Michael	BAL 195	
Rebecca	D.C.132	SEALS, Susan	D.C.204	SEIPS, John	BAL 195	
Richard	ANN 366	Thos.	WOR 190	SEISS, George	FRE 161	
Richd. K.	PRI 201	SEARAE, Jacob	D.C.169	SEITZ, John	WAS 119	
Richd. M.	D.C.169	SEARLY, James	BCI 27	SELBEY, Joseph	PRI 184	
Robert	KEN 93	SEARS (See also LEARS),		Mortify?	BAL 64	
Roster	BCI 152	C. L.	D.C.89	Mortigy	BAL 64	
Sabret	D.C.22	Caleb	ANN 284	SELBY, --- (Major?)	SOM 109	
Sabret E.	D.C.31	Edward	TAL 27	--- (Mrs.)	BCI 406	
Samuel	BAL 174	George	BCI 443	Adam	BCI 503	
Samuel	BAL 221	James (?)	BCI 248	Azeriah	WOR 175	
Samuel	BCI 86	James	D.C.183	Benj.	WOR 162	
Samuel	FRE 87	John	TAL 27	Betsy, Wd.	WOR 212	
Samuel	KEN 93	Mary	HAR 20	Brice	MON 159	
Samuel	PRI 192	Moses	CEC 166	Eleanor	MON 155	
Samuel-Negro	HAR 80	Simon	CEC 166	James	BAL 204	
Sarah	BCI 491	William	MON 155	James	WOR 195	
Solomon	QUE 33	William	TAL 27	James (Senr.)	WOR 180	
Solomon, Ju.	KEN 110	Wm., Junr.	MON 166	James (of Micajah)	WOR 180	
Stephen J.	CEC 185	SEASS, George	ALL 22	Jas.	MON 174	
Susan	ANN 362	SEATON, ---	D.C.86	Jesse	PRI 213	
Thomas	ANN 323	Rachael	FRE 194	John	MON 155	
Thomas	BAL 95	Robert	BCI 183	John, Senr. (Captn.)		
Thomas	HAR 43	Will.	D.C.99		WOR 173	
Thomas B.	MON 163	SEAVER, Elizabeth	FRE 100	John of L.	WOR 211	
Thomas C.	FRE 84	William	D.C.81	John (of Parker)	WOR 181	
Thos.	MON 161	SEBERRY, --- (Mrs.)		John O.	WOR 155	
Thos. (of John)	WOR 172		BCI 410	John S.	PRI 211	
Tilghman	PRI 202	SEBOLD, Peter	FRE 172	Joseph (?)	PRI 184	
Violet	CEC 146	SEBRESE, John	SOM 103	Joseph	FRE 83A	
Watkins	PRI 192	SECAFOOSE, Jno.	FRE 126	Levin	WOR 170	
Will. A.	D.C.107	SECEFORCE, Daniel	WAS 135	Levin (of Micujah)		
William	ANN 365	SECHRIST, John	FRE 165		WOR 170	
William	CEC 146	Mary	FRE 147	Lloyd	ANN 360	
William	CEC 185	Jones	FRE 144	Major	SOM 109	
William	FRE 125	SEDDEN, Wm.	BCI 505	Mary	WOR 184	
William	KEN 104	SEDDON, James	BAL 120	Mary (of John)	WOR 164	
William	TAL 3	SEDERS, William	ANN 297	Obadiah	FRE 175	
Wm.	BCI 485	SEDGWICK, Benjamin	MON 167	Parker	WOR 174	
Wm.	BCI 522	Cassa	MON 154	Peter	WOR 177	
Wm.	MON 166	SEDGWICKS, Thos.	MON 176	Philip	D.C.133	
Wm. (of Jos.)	WOR 175	Wm.	MON 132	Richd.	MON 177	
Wm. B.	SAI 75	SEDWICK, Barbara (Mrs.)		Richd.	MON 178	
Zachariah	CHA 193		CAL 50	Sampson	WOR 189	
SCOTTEN, Mezzy	QUE 17	Joshua	CAL 46	Thomas	ANN 379	
Squire	HAR 77	William	BAL 67	Thos.	WOR 195	

SELBY (continued)		SENTZ, Catharine	BAL 154	SEWELL (continued),	
Walter	ALL 23	Peter	BAL 150	Fanny	BCI 81
William	WOR 195	SENYARD, Abram (?)		Francis	TAL 24
Wm., Jun.	WOR 196		BAL 94	Henry	ALL 31
Wm. (of Zadock)	WOR 174	SEPHAS (See also		Jacob	TAL 5
Wm. F. (Doctor)	WOR 175	CEPHAS),		James	ANN 327
Zelpha	WOR 157	Jane	DOR 11	James	TAL 23
SELF, Singleton	FRE 70	Milly	DOR 63	Jane	BCI 536
SELICK, Thos.	D.C. 154	Samuel	DOR 64	John	ANN 390
SELL, Henry	FRE 197	SEPHUS, Joseph	TAL 50	John	CLN 111
Jacob	FRE 148	William (Negro)	TAL 45	John	KEN 121
Peter	FRE 203	SEPRIS, Phillip	BCI 357	John	TAL 24
SELLERS, Abraham	BCI 249	SEPTOR, Elizabeth	FRE 151	John of Jas.	TAL 26
George	BAL 159	John	FRE 147	John R.	CAL 67
Henry D.	QUE 38	SERGINT, Robert	CEC 146	Joseph	TAL 11
Jacob	BAL 159	SERIDENSTRICKER,		Lambert	KEN 118
John	BAL 140	Elizh.	BCI 178	Lydia	ANN 286
John	BCI 530	SERIGIN, John	BCI 354	Mark	TAL 21
Peter	BAL 164	SERRA, Agostine	D.C. 124	Marke	TAL 14
Susan	D.C. 170	John	D.C. 119	Nancy	ANN 299
William	FRE 81	SERRELL, Alex.	QUE 4	R.	BCI 377
SELLEY, Obadiah (?)		Archibald	DOR 3	Rihd.	BCI 477
	FRE 175	SERRIN, Hetty	D.C. 8	Samuel	DOR 3
SELLMAN, Mary	BCI 66	SERVECK, Danl.	BCI 334	Samuel	TAL 5
Susannah	ANN 276	SERVER, George	BCI 190	Thomas	BCI 29
Walter	ANN 362	Jane	BCI 299	Thomas	TAL 32
William	ANN 362	SERVERSON, Hance		Thos.	BCI 532
SELLSNON, Anne Elizabeth			KEN 122	Vachel	ANN 284
	ANN 261	SERVEYAOR, Charles		Vachel	ANN 287
SELMAN, Rachael	BAL 55		WAS 138	William	CLN 105
Sarah	BCI 516	SESSFORD, John	D.C. 79	William	DOR 65
SELMON, Gaseia	FRE 76	SESSLER, John	FRE 149	William	TAL 9
Gasua?	FRE 76	SETH, Charles	QUE 28	William R.	CAL 67
Jason	BAL 145	Herculees	CLN 96	SEWMALT, Henry	BAL 20
William	FRE 76	Jacob	QUE 32	John	BAL 20
SELSOM, Daniel	FRE 128	James	TAL 27	SEWMAN, Isaac	FRE 95
SEMANS, James	QUE 17	James G.	CLN 91	SEXON, Charles	BCI 72
John	QUE 19	John	TAL 21	SEXTON, Thomas	D.C. 14
Richd.	QUE 13	Susan	TAL 10	SEYBERT, David	ALL 8A
SEMERE, Peter	DOR 55	Wm.	QUE 6	SEYBERY, Abraham	WAS 97
Robert	DOR 55	SETON, Elizabeth M.-		SEYFORT, F. H.	BCI 445
SEMETRY, Hager	BCI 215	Principal of the		SEYMORE, Jonathan	TAL 38
SEMINARY-St. MARYS		Sisters of Charity		Levin, Ovsr.	TAL 2
	FRE 153		FRE 153	Richard	KEN 102
SEMMERS, Peter	WAS 140	SETTELL, Michael	WAS 74	William	TAL 37
SEMMES, Edward	D.C. 3	SETTER, Mathias	BCI 181	SEYMOUR, Henry	TAL 20
George	PRI 228	SETTLER, Abram	BCI 348	John	TAL 21
James	D.C. 55	SEUMALT, Phillip	BCI 31	Nancy	TAL 21
Joseph	CHA 191	SEVEAR, Vachel	ANN 398	Nicholas	TAL 21
Joseph	D.C. 27	SEVERN, Jesse	MON 165	Thomas	TAL 51
Josseph	SAI 88	SEVERSON, John	CEC 167	William	TAL 23
Lucy	D.C. 53	Samuel	CEC 167	SEYSTER, Jacob	ALL 29
Raphel	D.C. 29	Thomas	CEC 128	Jonathan	ALL 26
Richard	D.C. 6	SEWAL, Charles	CHA 218	Michael	ALL 29
Richard T.	CHA 190	SEWALL, Edward	CEC 128	SHA, Elijah	D.C. 42
Sampson	D.C. 49	Frances	CEC 167	SHAAFF, Mary (?)	D.C. 61
William E. B.	BCI 157	James	CEC 145	SHAALS, --- (Mrs.) (?)	
SEMMS, Benedict J.	(I.?)	Maria	D.C. 74		D.C. 47
	PRI 232	Mary	SAI 65	SHAATS, --- (Mrs.) (?)	
SEMONES, Chs.	QUE 14	Peter	D.C. 121		D.C. 47
SEMUIR, Clarissa	D.C. 192	Robert	D.C. 105	SHACKELS, --- (Mrs.)	
SENCELL, Peter	WAS 84	SEWARD, George	QUE 19		BCI 407
SENDORF, Joseph	D.C. 73	Jas.	QUE 10	SHACKLEFORD, John	
SENEY, David	QUE 11	John	KEN 101		D.C. 178
Sophia	BCI 260	John (Revd.)	DOR 45	SHAD, Samuel	WAS 137
SENNETT, Margt.	QUE 17	Levin	CLN 111	SHADE, Henry	BAL 146
Soln.	QUE 17	Thos.	QUE 15	John	BAL 146
SENSE, Adam	FRE 181	William	QUE 32	John	BCI 428
Mary	FRE 200	SEWEL, Francis	CHA 206	John	BCI 528
Peter	FRE 180	Henry	CHA 221	SHADOWS, Elizabeth	D.C. 14
SENSENEY, Jacob	BCI 259	Mary	CHA 207	SHADRICK, John	SAI 63
Jacob	FRE 200	Thomas	KEN 117	John, Junr.	SAI 63
Peter	FRE 202	SEWELL, Benjamin	ANN 393	Thomas	SAI 63
SENSENY, Christian	FRE 176	Charles S.	HAR 8	SHADSHER, Casper	WAS 103
SENSY, Eliza	BCI 12	Charlottee	TAL 9	SHADWEEL, Sesex	FRE 228A
SENTMYER, John	BAL 63	Clement	D.C. 213	SHADWELL, Reubin	FRE 74
		Elisha	ANN 332		

SHAEFER, Elizabeth	FRE 186	SHANE (continued),		SHARP (continued),	
Frederick	FRE 187	Henery (?)	BAL 79	Richd.	QUE 9
Jacob	FRE 188	Joseph	BCI 373	Robert	BCI 144
John	FRE 189	SHANEBARGER, Peter		William	CEC 146
SHAFER, Francis	WAS 145		WAS 126	SHARPE, Andrew	CLN 95
George	WAS 60	SHANEFIELD, Andrew		Horatia	CLN 98
John	BAL 228		WAS 101	John	TAL 5
John	FRE 86	Susan	WAS 101	Joshua	CLN 115
John	WAS 86	SHANER, Elizabeth	WAS 108	Rose	TAL 32
John, Senr.	FRE 131	John	FRE 168	Samuel	CLN 87
John, Junr.	FRE 131	SHANEY, Elizabeth	BCI 320	Thomas	TAL 5
Jonas	HAR 43	SHANK, Adam	WAS 90	SHARPER, William	CEC 146
Lenard	ANN 361	Adam	WAS 103	SHARPLESS, Aquilla	
Rosana	WAS 103	Andrew	WAS 102		ALL 3
William	CEC 146	Christian	FRE 226	John	TAL 21
SHAFFER, Abraham	BAL 163	Christian	WAS 97	Will.	D.C. 117
Andrew	BAL 139	Daniel	WAS 102	SHARPLEY, John	CEC 145
C. A.	BCI 355	George	FRE 226	SHARPS, David	ALL 4
Catharine	FRE 110	George	FRE 226	SHARRA, George	BCI 345
Daniel	FRE 154	George	FRE 227	SHARRAH, Joseph	FRE 147
David	BAL 155	George	WAS 118	SHARREN, John	FRE 196
Dorothy	FRE 105	Henry	WAS 102	SHARRER, Catherine	
Frederick	BAL 141	Henry	WAS 128		WAS 89
George	FRE 112	Henry	WAS 137	Joseph	BAL 156
George Mich.	BAL 154	Jacob	FRE 134	William	BAL 143
Henry	WAS 124A	Jacob	WAS 102	SHARRES, Joseph (?)	
Jacob	BAL 151	Jacob	WAS 103		BAL 156
Jacob	BAL 165	John	WAS 103	SHARRICK, Joseph	WAS 67
Jacob	FRE 112	Michael	FRE 227	SHARROD, Jacob	BCI 297
John	BAL 147	Michael	WAS 137	SHARTER, Edward (?)	
John	BAL 155	Peter	FRE 226		D.C. 32
John	BAL 160	Peter	WAS 117	SHARVEN, Thomas	WAS 82
John	BAL 164	Phebe	FRE 160	SHAUCK, Henry	BAL 158
John	FRE 109	Wm.	FRE 228A	John	BAL 158
John	FRE 112	SHANKLE, Jacob	FRE 115	SHAVELIRE, J.	BCI 216
John	FRE 115	SHANKLIN, Robert	BAL 242	SHAW, Ann	D.C. 107
John	FRE 162	SHANKS, --- (Captn.)		Archibald	BAL 214
Martain	BAL 154		BCI 80	Cathn.	BCI 180
Michael	BAL 140	John	FRE 162	Charles	SAI 95
Michael	BAL 151	John	FRE 225	Charlotte	ALL 13
Michael	BAL 154	John	SAI 96	Daniel	BAL 224
Michael	FRE 161	Joseph	D.C. 47	David	BAL 235
Moses	BAL 157	Thomas	SAI 96	Ellenor	D.C. 127
Nicholas	FRE 114	Wm.	BCI 479	Evan	PRI 183
Saml.	FRE 161	SHANNAN, Joseph	WAS 82	George	ALL 10A
SHAFFNER, Charles	WAS 117	SHANNER, Adam	BAL 156	Henery	BAL 79
John	WAS 116	SHANNON, Cordelia	D.C. 74	Henry	ALL 13
Mathias	WAS 60	George	HAR 23	Hugh	FRE 172
Michael	WAS 123	James	BCI 5	Isaiah	BCI 513
SHAFLEY, Jacob	KEN 104	Ns.	BCI 240	Jacob	WAS 106
SHAGHERCY, Patrick	BAL 51	Saml.	BCI 494	James	BAL 78
SHAINBAUGH, Lewis	ALL 31	Samuel	CEC 185	James	CLN 80
SHAKES, John	D.C. 175	SHANYBROOK, Casper		James	KEN 89
SHAKESPEAR, Jonathan			FRE 197	James	PRI 194
	BAL 178	SHAPES, Robert (?)	DOR 21	James L.	MON 164
SHALEBARGER, Elizabeth		SHAPPOTH, Elizabeth		Jane	D.C. 165
	WAS 100		BCI 39	John	ALL 13
SHALL, George	WAS 98	SHARAPS, Horatio	CAL 64	John	ANN 396
SHALLER, Christian	WAS 110	SHARE, Joseph	BCI 23	John	BCI 83
SHAMBAUGH, George	ALL 34	SHARER, --- (Widow)		John	BCI 243
SHAMBURG, Henry	BCI 477		FRE 171	John	CEC 166
John	BCI 375	Andrew	FRE 169	John	CHA 216
SHAMWELL, Joseph, Jr.		Jacob	FRE 181	John	MON 139
	SAI 97	William	FRE 183	Joshua	BAL 85
William	SAI 92	SHARESWOOD, William		Joshua	BAL 187
SHANA, George (?)	BCI 345		HAR 18	Joshua (at Coll.	
SHANABRUCH, Casper		William	HAR 28	HOWARD's Farm)	
	FRE 178	SHARKEY, R.	BCI 397		BAL 129
Joseph	FRE 178	SHARN, --- (Widow) (?)		Lemuel	D.C. 48
SHANAHAN, George	TAL 21		FRE 171	Levi	MON 154
James	TAL 5	SHARP, Benj.	D.C. 19	Lewis	BCI 534
Jessee	TAL 3	Henry	BCI 86	Mary	D.C. 12
SHANAMAN, --- (Mrs.)		James	BCI 95	Mary	D.C. 56
	BCI 410	James	HAR 60	Mary	KEN 94
SHANE, Daniel	BCI 254	John	CEC 145	Mathew	WAS 59
Francis	ANN 321	Josiah	PRI 183	Moses	FRE 202

SHAW (continued),		SHECKLES (continued),		SHEPARD, John	BCI 199
Neale H.	SAI 90	Enoch	ANN 269	Joseph	WAS 62
Nicholas	BCI 68	Francis	ANN 254	M.	BCI 339
Nicholas	HAR 61	Henry	D.C. 51	Thos. S.	BCI 354
Polly	PRI 197	John	ANN 264	SHEPHARD, Basil	ANN 393
Priscilla	CHA 216	John	D.C. 62	Elizabeth	CHA 197
Rezin	MON 154	John	MON 139	James	ANN 403
Richard	BAL 107	Richard	ANN 253	Mathew	WAS 147
Saml.	BCI 503	Samuel	D.C. 68	Michael	WAS 147
Samuel	BCI 80	SHEEHEE, John	DOR 51	William	FRE 176
Thomas	BAL 128	SHEEHY, Edmond	BCI 525	SHEPHARDS, Samuel	ANN 325
Thomas	FRE 100	Edwd.	D.C. 145	SHEPHART, Samuel	WAS 146
Thomas	PRI 183	SHEEL, Daniel (?)	FRE 218	SHEPHED, Simon	KEN 103
Thomas	WAS 59	SHEELY, Frederick	FRE 168	SHEPHERD, Abram	BAL 100
William	ALL 10A	John	FRE 145	Andrew	TAL 11
William	BAL 129	Peter	FRE 173	Anna	SOM 129
William	BAL 130	SHEER, Andrew	ANN 399	Christian	WAS 148
William	BAL 199	SHEERWOOD, Philip	BCI 79	Elisabeth?	FRE 126
William	DOR 49	SHEETS, Aaron	DOR 21	Elizabeth	FRE 126
William	WAS 133	George	FRE 147	George	WAS 147
William C.	BCI 272	Hannah	ANN 367	Jacob	WAS 148
William F.	CHA 201	SHEETZ, Adam	ALL 15	James	QUE 21
William S.	CHA 205	David	FRE 147	John	ALL 37
SHAWEN, Danl.	FRE 126	John	FRE 147	Joseph	D.C. 79
Joseph	FRE 133	SHEFFER, Jessee	TAL 11	Joseph	D.C. 178
SHAWER, Adam	BAL 138	Philip	FRE 132	Josias	BAL 78
SHAWKEY, Christian		SHEHAN, William (?)		Lawdowick?	D.C. 41
	WAS 98		TAL 52	Lowdowick	D.C. 41
SHAWL, Joseph	BAL 26	SHEHE, Joseph	BAL 178	Nathan	BAL 88
Samuel	BAL 27	SHEHEN, John	FRE 199	Paul	TAL 12
SHAWMON, David	WAS 87	SHEHY, Michael	CLN 85A	Sarah	D.C. 81
Peter	WAS 87	SHEILDS, Barnhart	WAS 110	Simon (?)	KEN 103
SHAWN, Chs.	QUE 11	SHEITZ, Daniel	WAS 99	Stephen	SOM 140
John	QUE 8	Henry	WAS 105	Solomon	FRE 176
Saml.	QUE 4	Martin	WAS 97	Thos.	MON 130
SHAWOOD, Philip	BCI 172	SHEKELL, Richard	HAR 7	SHEPPARD, George	DOR 61
SHAY, Thomas	HAR 23	William	HAR 7	Jacob	CLN 112
SHEAF, Maria	KEN 90	SHEKLY, Adam	WAS 96	John	D.C. 17
Perry	KEN 90	SHELBY, William	WAS 68	Joseph, Sr.	CLN 95
SHEAK, John	WAS 73	SHELDEN, Benjn.-Negro		Joseph, Jr.	CLN 86
SHEALER, Christopher			HAR 50	Philip	BCI 148
	WAS 103	SHELDON, James	BCI 143	Richard	BCI 463
John	WAS 62	John	BCI 143	Thomas	BCI 45
SHEALEY, George	BAL 218	William	BCI 2	SHEPPEARD, Lidia	BCI 286
SHEALS, Margt.	D.C. 88	SHELEY, Abraham	WAS 99	SHEPPERD, John	CEC 185
SHEARBERT, John	ANN 254	SHELHAMMER, George		SHERBERT, Benjamin	
SHEARER, Jane	CEC 146		ANN 319		ANN 279
John	WAS 86	SHELHOUSE, Peter	FRE 127	Edward	ANN 256
SHEARKEY, Hugh	BCI 512	SHELL, Conrod	BCI 115	Rezen	ANN 263
Michl.	BCI 517	SHELLCROUSE, Davd.		William	ANN 262
SHEARLY, John	FRE 85		D.C. 96	SHERBURNE, John	D.C. 75
SHEARRER, Daniel	BAL 160	SHELLER, Chris	BCI 182	Joseph	CHA 203
Jestena	BAL 163	SHELLMAN, William	FRE 94	Luke	CHA 204
SHEARS, Levin	DOR 34	SHELLOCK, Joseph	KEN 119	SHERCLIFF, Francis	ALL 38
SHEARWOOD, Hesiakiah		SHELLY, Peter	BCI 21	Melinda	ALL 38
	PRI 232	SHELMAN, Jacob	FRE 87	SHEREDINE, Asbury	HAR 62
Job	PRI 232	SHELTON, Fanny	SOM 129	James	HAR 39
Lewis	PRI 232	Fleet	WOR 153	John	BAL 208
SHEASE, George	WAS 101	Joshua	MON 135	SHERF, Christian	FRE 161
SHEATENHELM, George		Mary	FRE 84	SHERFIELD, John	D.C. 179
	FRE 78	Moses	D.C. 129	SHERFY, --- (Widow)	
Jacob	FRE 76A	Thomas	FRE 76A		FRE 181
SHEATHER, Mary	D.C. 190	SHEMWELL, James	SAI 88	SHERIDON, Richard	BCI 16
SHEATS, Dorothy	FRE 196	SHENELL, Sarah, widow		SHERIFF, Bennedick	PRI 194
Jacob	FRE 168		WOR 196	Joshua	PRI 236
John	FRE 77	SHENIN, Sarah (?)	KEN 101	Joshua, Junr.	PRI 236
William	FRE 73	SHENLEY, James	DOR 6	Levi	PRI 191A
SHEATZ, Jacob	WAS 138	SHENNECK, Jacob	BAL 210	Ruth	PRI 196
Joseph	WAS 138	SHENNINGTON, William		Samuel	PRI 197
SHEAVES, Rob G.	BCI 480		BCI 32	Thomas	PRI 182
SHECHTER, Henry	WAS 72	SHENTON, Charles	DOR 30	Thomas	PRI 235
Henry	WAS 72	Denard	DOR 28	SHERLOCK, Ralph	PRI 182
SHECKALLS, Benjamin		Dennis	DOR 30	William	PRI 203
	PRI 212	Margret	DOR 35	SHERM, John	FRE 145
SHECKELL, Richd.	D.C. 120	Rebeka	DOR 28	SHERMAN, Conrad	BAL 160
SHECKLES, Asa	MON 139	Thomas	DOR 30	Garner	D.C. 49
Caleb	CAL 64	William	DOR 30	Jacob	BAL 160

SHERMAN (continued),		
Jacob	FRE	186
Sarrah	BAL	139
William	DOR	53
William, Senr.	DOR	51
SHERMANDINE, Jas.		
	D.C.	160
SHERMENTINE, Elizabeth		
	SAI	65
Wm.	SAI	65
SHERMIZER, Jacob	CEC	145
SHERMON, Lydia	SAI	64
SHERON, Peter	D.C.	166
SHERONS, Peter-farm		
	D.C.	211
SHERR, Michael	BCI	321
SHERRAD, Mary A.	BCI	310
SHERRALS, Gloss	BCI	319
SHERREITZ, Catharine		
	FRE	186
SHERRIN, Robert	CLN	77
SHERRY, Charles	BCI	488
Peter	BCI	488
SHERWEERD, Sam.	BCI	350
SHERWOOD, --- (Mr.)		
	BCI	151
Charles	TAL	36
Elizabeth	TAL	11
Henry	TAL	46
Hugh	BCI	67
John	ALL	37
John W.	TAL	13
Pamelia	TAL	36
Richard	TAL	34
Richard	TAL	38
Richard, Jr.	TAL	36
Thomas	TAL	24
Thos.	D.C.	170
Thos.	D.C.	171
William	CLN	79
William	TAL	36
SHETRICK, Robert	WAS	149
SHEVERS, John	BCI	525
SHEW, Elizabeth	FRE	80
SHEWELL, Benjamin	HAR	42
Jane	HAR	62
William	WOR	189
SHEWEY, Christiana	WAS	73
SHIARMAN, Willimina		
	MON	175
SHIARMAR, Willimina (?)		
	MON	175
SHICKLES, Richard	D.C.	40
SHIELD, Saml.	BCI	333
SHIELDS, Ann	CEC	185
Chas.	D.C.	212
James	BCI	323
James	BCI	430
James	CEC	185
James	D.C.	88
Jane	KEN	104
John	D.C.	159
John	DOR	4
Loadman	CLN	89
Nancy	CEC	147
Nathan	TAL	46
Patrick	ANN	358
Solomon	BCI	47
Thos.	D.C.	167
William	D.C.	103
William	FRE	143
Wm.	BCI	509
SHIESLEY, Ludwig	FRE	169
SHIFLER, John	WAS	72
SHIHAN, William	TAL	52
SHIKEL, Dedrick	D.C.	201

SHILD, Sara	BCI	350
SHILES, Stephen	DOR	43
SHILFER, Nicholas	WAS	73
SHILLABER, Jonatn.		
	D.C.	160
SHILLINBURG, John		
	BCI	497
SHILLING, David	WAS	126
Frederick	WAS	95
John	WAS	126
Murry	BAL	8
Philip	WAS	126
SHILLINGSFORD, Mary		
	BCI	309
SHILT, Adam	FRE	190
SHILTNCK, Mary	FRE	132
SHIMELL, Henry	WAS	66
SHIMER, Jacob	ALL	12
James	ALL	12
SHIN, William	CEC	185
SHINGLE, Lawrence	FRE	155
Philip	WAS	109
Samuel	WAS	109
SHINGLEDECKER, Jacob		
	FRE	150
SHINGLER, John	FRE	77
SHININ, Sarah (?)	KEN	101
SHINLEY, James (?)	DOR	6
SHINNER (See also SKINNER),		
William (?)	DOR	7
William, Jr. (?)	DOR	7
SHINNICH, Solomon (?)		
	BAL	226
SHINNICK, Jacob	BCI	120
Solomon	BAL	226
SHIPER, Elisha (?)	BAL	153
SHIPHERD, Sutha	WOR	205
SHIPLEY, Adam	BAL	46
Adam	BAL	69
Adam, Junr.	BAL	49
Amon	BAL	46
Ann	BCI	499
Ann Maria	BAL	63
Benjamin	ANN	341
Benjamin	ANN	354
Calib	ANN	380
Denton	BAL	63
Edward	ANN	356
Eleanor	ANN	320
Elias	ANN	355
Eloysius	BAL	48
Eschael	BAL	49
Frederick	FRE	73
G. H.	BAL	65
Geo.	BCI	533
George	BAL	50
George	BAL	66
George O.	ANN	380
Greenbury	BAL	65
Grorae?	BAL	57
Henrietta	ANN	368
Henry	ANN	366
Hezakiah	BAL	65
Jesse	ANN	362
John	ANN	360
John	BAL	49
John	BAL	64
John	BAL	68
John	BAL	69
Johnza	ANN	358
Joshua (?)	BAL	79
Joshua	ANN	319
Leven	ANN	362
Lewis	BAL	61
Lloyd	MON	134

SHIPLEY (continued),		
Moses	BAL	62
Moses	BAL	69
Nathan	BAL	45
Nimrot	WAS	148
Peter	ANN	354
Peter	BAL	45
Peter	BAL	47
Peter	HAR	24
Precella	BAL	60
Rachael	BAL	63
Richard	BAL	50
Richard A.	ANN	328
Robert	ANN	355
Robert	BAL	4
Robert	BAL	41
Robert, of Adam	BAL	61
Saml.	FRE	129
Saml.	FRE	211
Talbott	FRE	74
Thomas	ANN	366
Thomas C.	FRE	74
Wm.	BCI	516
Zach	BCI	494
SHIPLY, Ezekiel	BAL	198
Loid	BCI	417
Vachel R.	BAL	7
SHIPMAN, Resin	D.C.	55
SHIRE, William	BAL	198
SHIRLEY, Joseph	WAS	90
Thomas	BAL	45
SHIRLOCK, Sarah	D.C.	90
SHIROCK, Samuel	BCI	34
SHIRRELL, Peter	BCI	519
SHIRTER, Thomas	PRI	187
SHITLER, John	FRE	220
SHIVER, Nathaniel	FRE	216
S.	BCI	399
SHIVERS, Arie	BCI	440
Eliheu P.	CAL	46
John	FRE	210
Joshua	FRE	212
Nicholas	FRE	219
Thomas	FRE	212
SHOAF, Jacob	FRE	124
SHOAFF, James	WAS	80
Mary	D.C.	61
SHOAFT, Jacob	WAS	79
SHOALS, --- (Mrs.)		
	D.C.	47
SHOAP, Jacob (?)	FRE	124
SHOATS, --- (Mrs.)		
	D.C.	47
SHOCHOCKLY, Peter		
	WOR	219
SHOCK, Elizth.	BCI	240
Hannah	BCI	297
Jacob	BAL	240
John	DOR	5
Michael	WAS	101
SHOCKEY, John	ALL	5
SHOCKLEY, Jonathan		
	SOM	134
Noble	SOM	111
SHOCKLY, Burton	WOR	218
Elijah	WOR	219
Elijah (Capt.)	WOR	203
James T.	WOR	203
John, of R.	WOR	213
Kiah	WOR	206
Nancy W.	WOR	205
Nelly-Wd.	WOR	216
Sollimon	WOR	217
William	WOR	213
SHOCKNEY, Rachel	BAL	8
SHOE, Jacob	BAL	152

SHOEBROOKS, James		SHORTER (continued),		SHRIVER (continued),	
	QUE 34	Moses	D.C.49	David	FRE 202
Mary	QUE 3	Oswell (?)	PRI 238	George (?)	FRE 73
SHOEMAKER, Abraham		Peter	ANN 390	Henry	WAS 110
	FRE 183	Peter	D.C.76	Isaac	FRE 186
Christian	FRE 132	Peter	WAS 121	Jacob	FRE 202
David	BAL 223	Saml.	D.C.116	John S.	BCI 483
David	D.C.80	Thomas (?)	PRI 187	SHRIVES, Joseph	BAL 50
David	D.C.91	Thomas	CHA 204	SHRODER, Henry	BCI 536
Edward	ANN 355	Will	D.C.116	SHROEDER, George	BCI 349
George	BCI 486	William	BCI 86	SHROTE, Catharine	BCI 476
Hammond	TAL 24	William	DOR 9	Henry	BCI 475
Henry	FRE 132	SHORTES, Roger	DOR 36	Mary	BCI 448
Hester	FRE 183	SHORTLE, Margaret		Mathias	BCI 475
John	FRE 169		D.C.196	SHROYER, Catharine	
Maris	BCI 341	SHORTO, Richd.	BCI 489		FRE 116
Mary	BAL 7	SHORTRIDGE, John		Frederick	FRE 190
Peter	FRE 204		BCI 135	SHRUPP, Mathias	FRE 159
Saml.	MON 164	SHORTROW, William		SHRYACK, John	BCI 130
William	FRE 169		BAL 187	SHRYER, John	ALL 29
SHOEMAN, Jacob	FRE 177	SHOTE, Nelly	BAL 195	SHUCK, Adam	BCI 293
SHOESTER, Margret		SHOTS, Philip	FRE 87	Daniel	WAS 102
	BAL 158	SHOTTEN, John	BCI 99	Jacob	D.C.149
SHOLLY, George	BCI 533	SHOUK, Jacob	CEC 185	SHUEY, John	WAS 72
SHOMAKER, Margaret		SHOUP, Baltzer	FRE 174	SHUFF, George	FRE 163
	FRE 227	Christian	WAS 107	James	FRE 162
Nicholas	FRE 221	Elizabeth	FRE 103	SHUGARD, William	WAS 117
SHOMAKIN, John	FRE 221	Martain	BAL 146	SHUK, Jacob	FRE 122
SHONAHAN, Deborah		SHOVER, Sophia	FRE 148	SHULER, Frederick	FRE 178
	DOR 62	SHOWCCHER, Martin (?)		James	BCI 184
SHONE, Adam	FRE 225		WAS 119	SHULL, John	FRE 196
SHOOK, Peter	FRE 111	SHOWECHER, Martin		John	FRE 202
Peter	FRE 112		WAS 119	Mary	FRE 194
SHOOLAY, Isaac	WAS 146	SHOWECKER, William		Michael	FRE 196
SHOP, Ann	BCI 169		WAS 107	Philip	FRE 196
SHOPES, Robert	DOR 21	SHOWERS, Samuel	WAS 62	SHULTY, Nicholas	WAS 120
SHORB, Andrew	BCI 453	SHOWMAN, Adam	WAS 68	SHULTZ, David	FRE 104
Conrad	FRE 173	David	WAS 65	George	FRE 104
Jacob	FRE 146	George	WAS 83	George P.	ALL 28
John, Senr.	FRE 170	Jacob	WAS 83	Henry	BAL 140
John, Junr.	FRE 145	John	WAS 68	Henry	BAL 152
SHORES, Edward	SOM 139	John	WAS 83	Henry	FRE 104
Esther	SOM 128	SHOWNS, Nicholas	D.C.188	John	FRE 144
Levin, Senr.	SOM 129	SHREAVES, John	D.C.39	John	WAS 125
Levin, Junr.	SOM 129	SHRECK, Wm.	BCI 192	John W.	FRE 117
Thomas	SOM 139	SHREVE, Anne	D.C.214	Marey	BCI 401
SHORT, Adam	CEC 146	Benjn.	D.C.214	Philip	BAL 152
David	CEC 147	Saml.	D.C.214	Samuel	BAL 166
Isaac	ANN 377	Thos.	D.C.199	SHUMAKER, John	WAS 150
Jacob	ANN 334	SHRIDER, Andrew	BCI 375	SHUMAN, George	WAS 115
John	ANN 285	Mary	BCI 338	Samuel	WAS 115
John	ANN 333	SHRIER, Jarry	BCI 336	Thomas	WAS 115
John	BCI 180	SHRIEVES, Hancock		SHUMATE, John	ALL 29
John	CEC 147		SOM 124	SHUNK, Daniel	FRE 176
John	CEC 147	SHRILOCK, Fanny	BCI 257	John	BCI 200
John, Senr.	ANN 337	SHRINER, Abraham		Joseph	FRE 171
John, Junr.	ANN 337		FRE 177	Peter (?)	FRE 226
Jonathin	CEC 146	George	FRE 169	Peter	FRE 171
Mary	TAL 46	George	FRE 173	SHUP, Abraham	WAS 139
William	CEC 147	Henry	FRE 181	Adam	WAS 89
SHORTEE, Oswell	PRI 238	Jacob	FRE 177	Peter	WAS 119
SHORTER, Ann	BCI 308	Michael	FRE 211	Susanah	WAS 89
Charles	ANN 390	Peter	FRE 169	SHUPP, Susannah	FRE 149
Charles	BCI 101	Peter	FRE 177	SHURE, Daniel	FRE 186
Charles	D.C.18	Peter	FRE 214	SHURES, Elias	MON 132
Charles	D.C.78	Phillip	FRE 183	SHURLEY, Richard	SAI 75
Clement	D.C.21	SHRIOCK, Eliza	BCI 484	SHUSTER, Saml.	D.C.138
Edward	D.C.32	SHRIVE, Benja.	CAL 54	SHUTT, August	BCI 187
Edwd.	D.C.78	Francis	CAL 47	George	WAS 74
Ellenor	D.C.83	Richd.	CAL 45	Jacob	BCI 485
Geo.	D.C.107	Richd., Junr.	CAL 48	John P.	BCI 508
Henretta	SAI 92	Samuel	CAL 47	SHUTTLE, Henry	D.C.52
Jane	D.C.107	SHRIVER, Abraham		SHUTTLEFOORD, Lewis	
Joseph	FRE 153		FRE 102		BCI 23
Letty	D.C.21	Andrew	FRE 194	SHYLOCK, John	D.C.30
Mary	D.C.86	Benjamin	FRE 175	SIBBY, Thos.	MON 175

SIBERT, Flora	MON 178A	SIMKINS, William	WAS 106	SIMMS (continued),		
Henry	WAS 134	SIMMANS, John	D.C.63	Edward	CHA 196	
Michael	WAS 133	SIMMENTON, Willm.	D.C.194	Francis	CHA 218	
Peter	WAS 106	SIMMERMAN (See also		George	D.C.189	
SIBLE, John H.	ANN 284	ZIMMERMAN),		George	PRI 226	
SIBLEY, James	PRI 183	--- (Mrs.)	BCI 406	Ignatius	CHA 191	
John	D.C.18	John	BAL 82	James	ANN 404	
William	PRI 196	SIMMERMON, George		James	CHA 203	
SICKLE, David	ALL 6		WAS 103	John	BCI 499	
Zachariah V.	ALL 6	SIMMERS, John	CEC 185	John	D.C.166	
SICKLES, Lewis V.	ALL 5A	Thomas	FRE 230	John	SAI 79	
SIDEL, Jacob	PRI 231	Thomas	FRE 234	Joseph	CHA 196	
SIDES, Andrew	BAL 87	SIMMES, Edward (?)	D.C.3	Mark	CHA 204	
Benjamin G.	ANN 358	Francis	SAI 88	Nancy-f.c.p.	HAR 11	
Savina	ANN 359	Thos.	D.C.168	Rebecca	PRI 238	
SIDESICKLE, Ann	BCI 160	SIMMONS, Aaron	CHA 194	Richard	PRI 229	
SIDLE, Daniel	WAS 134[A]	Abraham	KEN 124	Thomas	PRI 223	
George	WAS 134	Abram	MON 161	Willm.	D.C.166	
SIDNEY, George	CEC 167	Asberry	DOR 40	SIMON, Adam	FRE 115	
SIDWELL, Jesse	CEC 185	Basil	CAL 52	Charles	BCI 450	
Levi	CEC 185	Benjamine	CEC 127	Evan	BCI 78	
SIER, Beal	FRE 194	Benjn.	D.C.215	SIMOND, Math. W.	BCI 353	
John	BAL 157	Cornelias	WAS 69	SIMONEG, J. H.	BCI 479	
Nicodemus	FRE 194	Daniel	D.C.26	SIMONS, Andrew	FRE 198	
SIERS, Edward	ANN 324	David	CHA 196A	Ann	BCI 19	
Edward	ANN 324	Edward	DOR 30	Frederick; J.	ALL 25	
SIESS, Godfrey	FRE 154	Elisha	CEC 145	Jno.	KEN 123	
Jacob	FRE 154	George	FRE 75	SIMONSON, John	BCI 300	
Paul	FRE 154	George Y.	CAL 53A	SIMPCOE, William	CEC 166	
SIFERT, Henry	FRE 159	Isaac	ANN 262	SIMPERS, Benjamin	BAL 25	
John	FRE 158	Isaac	CAL 53A	Hannah	CEC 146	
SIFFERD, Christian	FRE 134	James	CEC 128	Isaac	CEC 147	
SIFTINGS, Samuel	BCI 89	James	D.C.132	Jacob	CEC 167	
SIFTON, Charles	FRE 142	James	FRE 81	Jemima	CEC 146	
Joseph	ALL 31	Jane	D.C.161	Jesse	CEC 146	
Richard	ANN 254	Jas., Senr.	FRE 122	John	CEC 167	
SIGH, Charles	DOR 39	Jenny	D.C.215	John, Jur.	CEC 166	
Edward	DOR 39	Jesse	PRI 202	Johnson	CEC 167	
Thomas	DOR 39	John (?)	D.C.63	March	CEC 146	
SIGLER, Adam	ALL 28	John	DOR 23	Nathaniel	CEC 147	
Grace	ALL 13	John	DOR 40	Richard	CEC 167	
Jacob	ALL 13	John	ANN 292	Ruben	CEC 146	
John	ALL 12	John H.	FRE 81	Ruben	CEC 147	
John	WAS 62	Joseph	ANN 389	Thomas	CEC 167	
Philip	ALL 11	Joseph	CEC 185	William	CEC 146	
Samuel	ALL 27	Joseph	KEN 91	William	CEC 146	
SIKES, John	BCI 156	Levin	DOR 56	SIMPKINS, Abel	ALL 30	
SILANCE, Richard	FRE 80	Mosses	DOR 23	Charles	SOM 141	
SILCOCK, Wm.	BCI 215	Richard	ANN 254	Dickeson	ALL 21	
SILCOX, Elias	KEN 122	Robert	D.C.12	John	ALL 5A	
Spencer	KEN 124	Saml.	BCI 196	William	ALL 29	
SILENCE, Enoch	SAI 68	Saml.	D.C.148	SIMPSAN, John	PRI 206	
John	D.C 43	Samuel	ANN 268	SIMPSON, Andrew	BCI 38	
Rebecca	D.C.186	Samuel	ALL 20A	Aga	BCI 429	
Rebuca?	D.C.186	Samuel	FRE 79A	Ann	CHA 202	
William	SAI 68	Solomon	KEN 123	Benjamin	PRI 221A	
SILIVANE, Abram	TAL 50	Thomas	ALL 7	Benjn.	D.C.198	
SILLHEART, George	WAS 108	Thomas	ANN 266	Bennedict	CHA 204	
SILLING, Andrew	WAS 59	Thomas	CEC 166	Catherine	CHA 222	
SILLIVEN, William	WOR 205	Thomas	DOR 44	Caty	FRE 219	
SILVER, Amos	HAR 19	Thomas	FRE 76	Charles	FRE 214	
Benjn.	HAR 19	Thos.	CAL 45	Daniel	CEC 166	
David	HAR 19	Thos.	D.C.215	Ebenezer	CEC 166	
Elexis	BCI 283	Will	D.C.105	Edward	DOR 45	
Garsham	HAR 19	William	ANN 265	Elijah	BCI 487	
William	HAR 70	William	BAL 173	Elizabeth	PRI 223	
SILVERS, Edward	WAS 125	William	BCI 95	Ezekiel	CAL 66A	
SILVERTHORN, Henry		William	FRE 192	Francis	CHA 224	
	BCI 505	William	HAR 28	Francis	MON 144	
SILVESTER, Joseph	BAL 115	William, of Chass.		George	CEC 166	
SILVEY, John	BAL 59		ANN 268	Gerrard	PRI 228	
SILVIAS, Francis	BCI 50	Zachariah	FRE 94	Gustavus	CHA 204	
SILVY, Loamy	TAL 45	SIMMS, Alexious	FRE 80	Harry	DOR 57	
William	FRE 151	Anthony	PRI 238	Henry	QUE 35	
SIM, Joseph W.	ANN 356	Anthony	SAI 82	Jacob, Jr.	DOR 52	
Thos. (Doc.)	D.C.14	Barshaba	D.C.189	James	CEC 185	
SIMINGTON, Peter	D.C.26	Bennet B.	CHA 192	James	D.C.11	

SIMPSON (continued),			SINCLAIR (continued),			SISSON, George	D.C.203
James	DOR	62	John	TAL	27	Martin	BCI 148
James	FRE	68	Peregrine	BCI	55	SISTERS OF CHARITY	
James R.	PRI	207	Perry	TAL	22		FRE 153
Jno.	D.C.113		Roberd	BCI	374	SITTLER, Danl.	BCI 508
John (?)	PRI	206	Robert	BCI	286	Jacob	BCI 513
John	BAL	93	Samuel	ANN	286	SITZ, George	WAS 95
John	BCI	9	Thomas	HAR	62	SITZLER, Phillip	BCI 320
John	CHA	222	William	BCI	115	SIX, George	FRE 168
John	D.C.46		William W.	BCI	91	Henry	FRE 177
John	PRI	217	SINCLAR, Susannah	BAL	85	John	FRE 168
John	TAL	4	SINCLARE, Francis	QUE	49	John	FRE 177
John	WAS	138	James	BAL	182	Leonard	FRE 177
Joseph	BAL	201	Pere	QUE	47	Phillip	FRE 168
Joseph	PRI	204	William	QUE	41	SIXE, Nathaniel	BAL 28
Josiah	D.C.79		SINCLEAR, Henry	SAI	94	SKEAR, John	CEC 146
Josias	D.C.71		John	BCI	474	SKEGGS, Rachel	KEN 108
Levin	TAL	11	SINCLORE, James	QUE	33	SKENIN, Sarah	KEN 101
Lewin	PRI	221A	SINDALL, Elizebeth	BAL	218	SKIDMORE, Ann	D.C.217
Lewis	D.C.117		John	BAL	225	Edwd.	D.C.217
Lewis	D.C.183		John	BCI	83	Gerard	D.C.191
Lloyd	PRI	203	Phillip	BAL	214	Jesse	D.C.191
Margt.	D.C.180		Solomon	BAL	110	SKILER, Ardel	TAL 38
Martin?	BCI	393	William	BAL	214	Obediah	TAL 38
Mary	ANN	383	SINE, Henry	ALL	4	SKILES, Elizabeth	FRE 199
Mary	CEC	166	SINEARD, John	BAL	215	SKILMAN, Robert	BCI 434
Mortin	BCI	393	SINGER, Eve	FRE	182	SKIMMINGS, Anthony	
Peter	TAL	3	Hannah	FRE	145		ALL 30
Reason	ALL	3	John	WAS	100	SKININ, Sarah (?)	KEN 101
Reason	FRE	218	Samuel	FRE	146	SKINNER (See also	
Sarah	DOR	54	SINGLETON, Anna	TAL	38	SHINNER),	
Sarrat	D.C.202		Elizth.	BCI	252	Andrew	TAL 6
Stephen	DOR	54	John	HAR	27	Ann	KEN 93
Tabby	DOR	56	William	HAR	22	Burdet	D.C.83
Thomas	MON	154	SINGO, Henny	QUE	29	Clement	CHA 191
Thomas	PRI	213	Phelix	QUE	40	Elisha	PRI 212
Tobias	D.C.107		SINIARD, John (?)	BAL	215	Eliza	DOR 12
Walter	FRE	113	SINK, George	FRE	173	Ewel	CHA 195
Water	BCI	173	William	WAS	62	Fordyce	CHA 195
William	FRE	160	SINKS, George	FRE	172	Gustavus	CHA 193
William	KEN	88	Joseph	FRE	172	Henry	TAL 9
Wm.	BCI	394	SINLEY, Alexr.	BCI	182	Henry, Jr.	TAL 9
SIMS, Andrew	BAL	218	SINN, David	PRI	218	Henry Smith	CAL 63
Ann	D.C.80		Henry	FRE	99	James	DOR 12
Charles	PRI	206	Philip	FRE	104	John	CHA 195
Delia	D.C.103		SINNERS, Elijah R.	BCI	45	John	QUE 34
Edward	KEN	108	SINNOTT, --- (Doctr.)			John	TAL 21
Hannah	ALL	29		BCI	459	John S.	BCI 443
Hannah, col'd.	BAL	214	SINTON (See also			Levin	TAL 7
Henry	D.C.115		LINTON),			Mary (Mrs.)	CAL 48
John	BCI	321	Joseph	BCI	239	Mordica	TAL 20
Joseph	BCI	305	Joseph	KEN	86	Phil	QUE 18
Mary C.	SOM	138	SINYARD, Abram	BAL	94	Quinton	CHA 193
Nancy	BCI	484	SIOUSSA, John	D.C.83		Richard	CLN 89
Nathl.	D.C.114		SIPE, John	BAL	222	Richard	QUE 26
Priscilla	ANN	273	Michl.	BCI	512	Richd.	CAL 49
Richd.	D.C.125		Michl.	BCI	516	Sarah (Mrs.)	CAL 48
Smith, Senr.	SOM	141	SIPHERT, Joseph	FRE	159	Silady	DOR 63
Smith, Junr.	SOM	141	SIPLEY, Joshua (?)	BAL	79	Silvester	CHA 194
Sud.	D.C.124		Thomas	BCI	63	Thomas	SOM 106
Thomas	ANN	305	SIPP, Henry	FRE	218	Thomas	TAL 12
Venus	PRI	204	SIRES, Alexander	ALL	30	Vickey	CHA 193
William	BCI	319	Benjamin	FRE	76	William	DOR 7
William	HAR	77	James	ALL	29	William	QUE 28
SIMSON, Achiles	ANN	378	SIRMAN, George	SOM	136	William	QUE 41
Benjamin	SOM	132	Isaac	SOM	136	William	TAL 21
SINCARD, John (?)	BAL	215	SISCO, James	CEC	128	William	TAL 45
SINCENER, Fred	BCI	481	SISK, Elizabeth	DOR	63	William, Jr.	DOR 7
SINCK, Leonard	BAL	44	Joseph	CLN	115	Willm.	D.C.202
SINCLAIR, Alexander			SISLER, George	ALL	5A	Zacharlah	D.C.32
	BCI	32	Samuel	ALL	5A	Zebulon	QUE 23
Caleb	CHA	207	SISSEL (See also CECIL,			SKIPER, Elisha	BAL 153
Charity	BAL	108	CIECILL, CISSALL,			SKIPPER, David	BAL 117
Elizabeth	BCI	161	CISSELL),			David	BCI 125
Isabella	BCI	81	William	ANN	335	John	BAL 29
John	BCI	268				SKIRVEN, Elizabeth	KEN 88

SMALLWOOD (continued),	**SMITH (continued),**	**SMITH (continued),**
Henry	PRI 218	Amelia	KEN 101	Daniel	ANN 259
Horace	D.C.55	Amos	HAR 56	Daniel	BCI 63
James	PRI 228	Andr.	BCI 480	Daniel	CLN 114
John	CHA 191	Andrew	BAL 189	Daniel	FRE 149
John	D.C.133	Andrew	DOR 8	Daniel	FRE 203
Joseph	ANN 383	Ann	BCI 223	Daniel	TAL 35
Judy	BCI 47	Ann	KEN 106	Daniel	WAS 126
Lewis	D.C.22	Ann	KEN 109	Daniel	WAS 137
Mary	BCI 480	Ann	KEN 118	Daniel	WOR 204
Mary	D.C.125	Anna	FRE 101	Daniel, Ovsr.	TAL 8
Nathaniel	PRI 218	Anne	ANN 359	Daniel (of Leond.)FRE 164
Rachel	TAL 38	Anne	WOR 193	Danl.	QUE 13
Ralph	BCI 120	Anthoney	WAS 109	Danl.	QUE 17
Richd. L.	CHA 214	Anthony	ANN 352	David	CLN 86
S. N.	D.C.112	Anthony	D.C.37	David	D.C.97
Samuel	CHA 212	Anthony-Negro HAR 80	David	FRE 229
Thomas M.	CHA 214	Aquilla	MON 165	David	WOR 156
Tome	PRI 195	Archabold	WOR 203	David M.	QUE 3
Walter B.	CHA 214	Archibald	CEC 166	Dennis A.	BAL 178
Will	FRE 183	Archibold	KEN 94	Diana	BCI 143
William	CLN 115	Arthur	BAL 223	Easter	SOM 156
Wm. T.	MON 161	Azariah	ANN 279	Edward	ANN 335
SMALLWOOD, Elizabeth		Baltzer	FRE 111	Edward	KEN 106A
	ANN 374	Barbary	FRE 142	Edward	WAS 124A
SMARR, George	ALL 2	Bartholomew	SAI 63	Edward-Negro	HAR 80
SMART, Jacob	DOR 12	Basil	ANN 310	Edwd.	D.C.190
Phillis	DOR 59	Basil	ANN 337	Eleanor	MON 132
Rachel	DOR 13	Basil	FRE 85	Elie	ANN 379
Zacheriah	D.C.30	Basil L.	BCI 2	Eliga	KEN 124
SMASHEY, James	WOR 178	Benjamin	CEC 128	Elijah	ANN 291
SMEA, John	FRE 190	Benjamin	SOM 141	Elijah	BCI 531
Peter	FRE 190	Benjamin	TAL 37	Eliz.	BCI 350
SMEACH, George	BAL 146	Benjamin M.	BCI 121	Eliz. H.	D.C.87
SMELSER, Henry	FRE 133	Benjamn. B.	BCI 309	Eliza	BCI 75
SMELTZ, John	FRE 156	Betsey	FRE 222	Eliza	D.C.96
SMELTZER, GeorgeFRE 201	Betsy	DOR 9	Eliza	QUE 13
Jacob	FRE 164	Brannock	CLN 110	Elizabeth	ALL 23
John	FRE 201	Bridget	CEC 185	Elizabeth	BCI 138
SMETZER, Michael FRE 201	C.	BCI 401	Elizabeth	FRE 83
SMICE, George	WAS 139	Caleb	CLN 105	Elizabeth	FRE 85
John	WAS 136	Catha.	BCI 531	Elizabeth	FRE 142
SMICK, Charles	BCI 95	Catharine	BCI 303	Elizabeth	HAR 7
SMIDDY, John	BCI 259	Cathn.	BCI 181	Elizabeth (Mrs.)	CAL 56
SMIDEGA, C.	BCI 367	Charles	BCI 185	Elwiley	SAI 55
SMIKE, John	FRE 223	Charles	CHA 224	Ely	BCI 530
John	FRE 225	Charles	D.C.146	Ely	HAR 39
SMILER, Margt.	D.C.111	Charles	DOR 53	Emory	QUE 3
SMILEY, --- (Mrs.)		Charles	FRE 149	Ephraim	BCI 89
	BCI 404	Charles	HAR 38	Epram	WAS 70
Isaac	BCI 131	Charles	KEN 115	Esther	BCI 297
Peter	FRE 141	Charles	QUE 31	Feilder B.	CAL 63
Robert	BCI 286	Charles	SAI 54	Ferdinan	BAL 209
W. R.	BCI 338	Charles	SOM 113	Fielder	PRI 237
SMILSON, Hez.	D.C.117	Charles	SOM 136	Frances	CEC 185
SMISH, Mathew (?)DOR 51	Charles	TAL 27	Frances	SOM 117
SMISNER, Samuel WAS 128	Charles-Negro HAR 49	Francis	CHA 207
SMITH, --- (?)	BCI 404	Charles, Overs.		Fred C.	BCI 346
--- (See SEGUIN			PRI 238	Frederick	BAL 140
& SMITH)		Charles S.	D.C.120	Frederick	FRE 179
--- (See SMITH &		Charles W.	CLN 99	Frederick	FRE 229
PEDINGER)		Chas.	D.C.108	Fredk.	FRE 224
--- (Major?)	KEN 93	Chas.	D.C.147	Geo.	BCI 190
--- (Mrs.)	D.C.56	Christian	ALL 38	Geo.	BCI 210
--- (Widaw)	BCI 410	Christian	FRE 220	Geo. C.	BCI 210
A. E. (Mrs.)	BCI 377	Christian	FRE 221	Geore	FRE 68
Abel	BAL 114	Christopher	MON 154	George	ALL 24
Abijah	D.C.123	Christopher	WAS 104	George	BAL 57
Abraham	D.C.44	Clayvell	WOR 204	George	BAL 196
Adam	BAL 185	Clement	CLN 110	George	BAL 228
Adam	BCI 7	Clement	D.C.56	George	CAL 64
Adam	FRE 223	Clement	PRI 208	George	FRE 80
Adam	FRE 225	Conrad	WAS 71	George	FRE 110
Affe	MON 159	Cornelius	CEC 185	George	FRE 146
Alexander	ALL 4	Cornelius	D.C.132	George	HAR 46
Alexander	BCI 38	Cyrus	BCI 306	George	QUE 38
Alexius	CHA 228	Dan	HAR 31	George	SOM 110

SMITH (continued),			SMITH (continued),			SMITH (continued),	
George	WAS 57		James	SOM 146		John	WAS 67
George	WAS 100		James	TAL 9		John	WAS 119
George	WAS 104		James	TAL 10		John	WAS 120
George	WAS 114		James	TAL 35		John, Senr.	ANN 259
George A.	CLN 104A		James	WAS 89		John, Senr.	ANN 283
George W.	CAL 66A		James	WAS 95		John, Senr.	ANN 401
H.	BCI 417		James	WOR 202		John, Senr.	BAL 54
Harry-Negro	HAR 65		James (Doct.)	BCI 270		John, Senr.	FRE 228
Henrey	BCI 402		James (H. Neck)	SOM 106		John, Senr.	WOR 172
Henry	ALL 23		James, Senr.	TAL 7		John, Jnr.	ANN 260
Henry	ANN 367		James L.	QUE 25		John, Junr.	BAL 56
Henry	ANN 369		James P.	BCI 309		John, Junr.	FRE 146
Henry	BAL 67		Jane	BCI 342		John, Junr.	FRE 228
Henry	D.C.79		Jane	D.C.83		John (of Andw.)	WOR 163
Henry	D.C.81		Janee E.	SAI 97		John (of Christ.)	
Henry	DOR 43		Jas.	D.C.115			FRE 142
Henry	DOR 54		Jas. (of John)	WOR 154		John (of Leonard)	
Henry	FRE 110		Jehu	HAR 37			FRE 164
Henry	FRE 130		Jeremiah	FRE 105		John E.	BCI 6
Henry	FRE 178		Jeremiah	SAI 54		John F.	D.C.211
Henry	WAS 72		Jerry	ANN 257		John H.	CHA 218
Herbert	FRE 169		Jerry	BCI 160		John H. M.	FRE 69
Holland	WOR 188		Jesse	BAL 185		John J.	BCI 358
Hopkins	TAL 11		Jesse	D.C.173		John M.	BCI 151
Horatio	ANN 311		Jessee	QUE 30		John T.	SOM 111
Hugh	D.C.183		Jno.	ANN 394		John W.	D.C.170
Hugh	HAR 78		Jno. Spear	BCI 171		John W.	PRI 207
Isaac	CAL 42		Job	BAL 179		John W.	PRI 215
Isaac	PRI 215		Job	BCI 497		Jonathan	WAS 132
Isaac	WAS 114		Job	SAI 56		Jos.	BCI 209
Isaac P.	WOR 169		Job, Sen.	BCI 210		Joseph	ALL 26
Isaah	WOR 202		Job J.	BCI 23		Joseph	ANN 271
Isabella	TAL 6		John?	DOR 37		Joseph	ANN 311
J.	BCI 398		John	ALL 4		Joseph	ANN 335
Jacob	ALL 4		John	ALL 24		Joseph	BAL 116
Jacob	BCI 343		John	ANN 288		Joseph	BAL 182
Jacob	BCI 517		John	ANN 328		Joseph	BCI 137
Jacob	FRE 111		John	BAL 11		Joseph	BCI 282
Jacob	FRE 144		John	BAL 37		Joseph	D.C.13
Jacob	FRE 176		John	BAL 109		Joseph	D.C.178
Jacob	FRE 179		John	BCI 20		Joseph	FRE 86
Jacob	FRE 203		John	BCI 21		Joseph	FRE 96
Jacob	FRE 216		John	BCI 28		Joseph	FRE 115
Jacob	MON 132		John	BCI 45		Joseph	FRE 146
Jacob	QUE 31		John	BCI 132		Joseph	FRE 225
Jacob	WAS 57		John	BCI 141		Joseph	HAR 21
Jacob	WAS 117		John	BCI 254		Joseph	HAR 22
Jacob	WOR 161		John	BCI 298		Joseph	KEN 91
Jacob G.	BCI 270		John	BCI 479		Joseph	QUE 24
Jahn	DOR 37		John	BCI 533		Joseph	SAI 91
James	ALL 28		John	CLN 96		Joseph	WAS 57
James	ANN 390		John	CEC 185		Joseph	WAS 135
James	BAL 69		John	D.C.33		Joseph	WAS 139
James	BAL 111		John	D.C.108		Joseph Sim	FRE 171
James	BCI 146		John	D.C.172		Joshua	BAL 54
James	BCI 182		John	D.C.216		Joshua	BAL 195
James	BCI 531		John	FRE 75		Joshua	HAR 64
James	CAL 51		John	FRE 111		Joshua, Junr.	BAL 56
James	CEC 146		John	FRE 125		Josiah	D.C.54
James	CEC 146		John	FRE 146		Josiah	SAI 65
James	D.C.35		John	FRE 156		Josuwa	WAS 101
James	D.C.94		John	FRE 222		Juliann	FRE 133
James	DOR 53		John	KEN 101		Justis	D.C.118
James	DOR 54		John	PRI 222		Kato	WAS 144
James	FRE 115		John	QUE 18		Kitty	D.C.18
James	FRE 143		John	QUE 41		Lakin	BAL 195
James	FRE 191		John	SAI 55		Larken H.	BAL 232
James	HAR 44		John	SAI 64		Leonard	FRE 85
James	KEN 109		John	SAI 94		Levin	CLN 94
James	KEN 121		John	SOM 128		Levin	DOR 57
James	PRI 215		John	SOM 139		Levina	BCI 527
James	PRI 237		John	SOM 151		Lewis	D.C.47
James	QUE 26		John	TAL 3		Lewis	SAI 56
James	QUE 34		John	WAS 58A		Lydia	PRI 203
James	SOM 134		John	WAS 61		Major	KEN 93

SMITH (continued),			SMITH (continued),			SMITH (continued),	
Marey	BCI	374	Perry	CLN	80	Sarah	HAR	78
Margaret	CHA	223	Perry	TAL	7	Sarah	SOM	110
Margaret	D.C.	159	Peter	BCI	224	Sarah	SOM	114
Margaretta	WAS	57	Peter	FRE	216	Sary	BCI	348
Margaretta	WAS	125	Peter	FRE	229	Serlathene	WAS	136
Margaretta	WAS	139	Peter	WAS	98	Seth	WOR	204
Margt.	BCI	224	Peter	WAS	117	Sidney	BCI	297
Marshill	WOR	206	Philamon M.	FRE	81	Simon	KEN	94
Martin	DOR	24	Philip	FRE	222	Soloman	DOR	30
Martin	FRE	114	Philip P.	ANN	354	Soloman	KEN	118
Martin	WAS	139	Pompery?	KEN	104	Solomon	FRE	203
Mary	ALL	28	Pompey	KEN	104	Solomon	FRE	221
Mary	BCI	70	Prince	D.C.	88	Solomon	FRE	227
Mary	BCI	79	Rachal	SAI	92	Sophia	BCI	324
Mary	BCI	91	Ralph	BAL	119	Stephen	BCI	95
Mary	BCI	431	Ralph	BCI	269	Stephen	KEN	89
Mary	BCI	518	Rebecca	CEC	185	Stephen	SAI	54
Mary	CLN	91	Rebecca	KEN	92	Stoughton	SOM	126
Mary	CEC	167	Rebecca (C.?)	CLN	96	Susan	WAS	60
Mary	D.C.	66	Rebeece	MON	178A	Susannah	BCI	209
Mary	D.C.	93	Richard	ANN	279	Tabby	D.C.	168
Mary	D.C.	199	Richard	BAL	55	Thomas	BAL	48
Mary	FRE	99	Richard	BCI	70	Thomas	BAL	196
Mary	FRE	105	Richard	D.C.	24	Thomas	BAL	247
Mary	FRE	131	Richard	D.C.	58	Thomas	BCI	69
Mary	FRE	201	Richard	DOR	57	Thomas	BCI	428
Mary	FRE	228	Richard	HAR	72	Thomas	BCI	465
Mary	KEN	104	Richard	PRI	187	Thomas	D.C.	6
Mary	SOM	139	Richard B.	CHA	228	Thomas	D.C.	9
Mary	WAS	139	Richard W.	BCI	28	Thomas	D.C.	28
Mary	WOR	186	Richd.	D.C.	74	Thomas	HAR	78
Mary-widow	WOR	188	Richd.	MON	175	Thomas	PRI	215
Mary Ann	FRE	111	Rob	BCI	480	Thomas	SAI	53A
Mathew	BCI	394	Robert	ANN	379	Thomas	TAL	31
Mathew	DOR	51	Robert	BCI	259	Thomas	WAS	97
Matthew	BCI	79	Robert	HAR	77	Thomas	WAS	138
Melinda	SAI	54	Robert	KEN	102	Thomas L., Ovsr.	TAL	6
Michael	WAS	134	Robert H.	CAL	64	Thomas P.	TAL	13
Michiel	KEN	116	Robt.	WOR	170	Thomas R.	BCI	47
Middleton	FRE	225	Rosanna	WAS	116	Thomas S.	CHA	208
Milby	WOR	187	S. H.	D.C.	137	Thomas S.	WOR	203
Modersa	DOR	36	Sabret	ANN	304	Thos.	BCI	334
Molly	CHA	200A	Sadaimon?	DOR	37	Thos.	D.C.	112
Mordecai	CAL	63	Salaimon	DOR	37	Thos.	D.C.	176
Mordecai F.	CAL	63	Sam.	BCI	358	Vernon	CHA	202
Mordieca	WOR	184	Saml.	BCI	498	Vincent	HAR	18
Moses	D.C.	207	Saml.	QUE	9	W. D.	BCI	188
Moses	TAL	4	Saml. (General)	BAL	249	Walter	BCI	222
Moses	TAL	32	Saml. P.	ALL	26	Walter	D.C.	48
Mosses	BCI	141	Saml. R.	BCI	535	Walter	PRI	203
Nancy	BCI	429	Saml. R.	WOR	180	Water, Junr.	CAL	50
Nancy	WOR	201	Samuel	BAL	127	Will.	D.C.	134
Nathan	BCI	35	Samuel	BAL	187	Will S.	D.C.	88
Nathan	BCI	129	Samuel	BAL	205	William	ANN	262
Nathan	KEN	88	Samuel	BAL	221	William	ANN	279
Nathan	KEN	94	Samuel	BCI	76	William	ANN	285
Nathaniel	ANN	260	Samuel	BCI	180	William	BAL	185
Nathaniel	HAR	26	Samuel	BCI	243	William	BCI	21
Nathl.	D.C.	92	Samuel	BCI	447	William	BCI	63
Nehemiah	DOR	19	Samuel	CHA	200A	William	BCI	144
Nicholas	BAL	181	Samuel	FRE	141	William	BCI	153
Nicholas	FRE	102	Samuel	FRE	219	William	BCI	302
Nicholas	KEN	114	Samuel	FRE	221	William	BCI	307
Nicholas	WAS	108	Samuel	HAR	40	William	CAL	60
Nichl.	BCI	482	Samuel	KEN	92	William	CAL	65
Nichs.	BCI	198	Samuel	SOM	156	William	CLN	96
Nick	PRI	196	Samuel	WAS	140	William	CEC	146
Obed	FRE	168	Samuel Lane	CAL	64	William	CEC	166
Oliver	KEN	115	Samuel R.	HAR	42	William	CEC	185
Paca	HAR	19	Sarah	BCI	441	William	CHA	193
Patrick	ANN	329	Sarah	CEC	185	William	D.C.	31
Patrick	BAL	247	Sarah	D.C.	88	William	D.C.	84
Patrick	PRI	228	Sarah	DOR	9	William	D.C.	106
Peggy	DOR	10	Sarah	FRE	109	William	D.C.	111
Pere	QUE	47	Sarah	HAR	27	William	FRE	192

SPALDING (continued),			SPAULDING, Basil	PRI 225	SPENCE (continued),		
Richard-oveser.			John	PRI 223	Joseph	TAL 3	
Robert BROOKE			Mary	PRI 239	Lemuel P.	WOR 171	
	SAI 81		Philip	PRI 235	Mary	WOR 171	
Robt.	CAL 51		SPAVING, Robert	BCI 313	Nancy	HAR 20	
Terecy	D.C.26		SPEAKE, --- (Mrs.)	D.C.87	Robert T.	BAL 189	
Thomas	SAI 80		Elizabeth	D.C.33	Thomas	CEC 146	
Zachariah	SAI 81		Francis R.	CHA 193	Thos. R. P., Doctr.		
SPANFORD, Samuel	BAL 111		Josiah	D.C.19		WOR 170	
SPANGLE, Francis	KEN 119		Lee M.	CHA 192	William	BCI 248	
SPANGLER, George	WAS 80		Mary	CHA 192	William	CEC 185	
George N.	FRE 72		Richard	CHA 192	Wm.	QUE 15	
Isaac	BCI 385		SPEAKER, John	FRE 159	SPENCER, --- (Madam) (?)		
SPANOGLE, George	PRI 230		SPEAKMAN, James	D.C.68		WAS 62	
SPARKES, Josiah, Senr.			George	D.C.152	Benja.	WOR 163	
	BAL 90		John	D.C.117	David	ALL 10A	
SPARKLIN, Azle	CLN 110		SPEALMAN, Elizabeth		Eleanor	TAL 21	
Delihay	CLN 110			FRE 106	Elizabeth	ALL 13	
Nancy	CLN 115		Jacob	ALL 22	Elizabeth	HAR 56	
Richard	CLN 115		Lawrence	ALL 23	Elizabeth (Mrs.)	CAL 42	
Samuel	CLN 110		Rudy	FRE 190	Elizabeth, Jr.	ALL 13	
SPARKS, A. W.	BCI 193		SPEAR, Barbara	BCI 271	Henry	TAL 37	
Abner	QUE 15		James	BIC 522	Hugh	TAL 20	
Daniel	QUE 30		Mary	BAL 111	Isaac	CHA 224	
Elijah	QUE 26		SPEARE, William	BCI 22	Isaac	KEN 101	
Elizabeth	QUE 35		SPEARMAN, Margret	KEN 115	Isaac	KEN 124	
Esther	QUE 2A		Wm.	KEN 116	Jacobb	BCI 34	
Henry	QUE 10		SPEARS, Martha	BCI 213	James	BAL 21	
Henry	QUE 36		Thomas	ANN 371	James	SAI 79	
Jances	QUE 2A		Wm.	BCI 491	Jesse	D.C.178	
John	QUE 14		SPECART, John	WAS 85	John	HAR 29	
John	QUE 30		SPECHT, Conrod	FRE 85	John	WAS 106	
John P.	QUE 8		SPECK, Adam	FRE 160	John, Senr.	WOR 162	
Joseph B.	QUE 2A		Elizabeth	WAS 137	John, Junr.	WOR 162	
Joshua	QUE 36		Martin	WAs 133	Jonathan	BCI 152	
Josiah, Junr.	BAL 85		Wm. A.	BCI 240	Lambert W.	TAL 6	
Julia	BAL 218		SPEDDEN, Elizabeth	BCI 116	Lisey	D.C.210	
Laban	BAL 241		Impsy	DOR 15	Lyddia	MON 132	
Levi	QUE 11		John	DOR 15	Mahlon	HAR 45	
Nathan	QUE 37		John, Sr.	DOR 14	Moses	ALL 13	
Rebecca	QUE 15		John of J. (1.?)	DOR 14	Nicholas	ANN 397	
Richard	TAL 5		Robert	DOR 15	Perry	TAL 19	
Riden	QUE 16		Robert Senr.	DOR 15	Phillis	TAL 37	
Risden	QUE 9		Vincent P.	DOR 15	Rebecca	D.C.90	
Robert	QUE 23		SPEDDING, Edward	TAL 6	Richard	KEN 89	
Sarah	CEC 127		John of R.	DOR 6	Richard	TAL 14	
Sarah	KEN 93		Ralph	DOR 6	Robert	ANN 269	
Sarah	QUE 15		Robert	TAL 10	Robert	BCI 126	
Sluyter	QUE 8		SPEEHEARD, Michael	WAS 67	Samuel	BCI 200	
Solm.	QUE 9		SPEEKS, R.	BCI 411	Sarah	D.C.90	
Stephen	BCI 122		SPEELMAN, David	WAS 60	Thomas	D.C.49	
Thomas	BAL 78		Jacob	WAS 72	William	FRE 87	
Walter	TAL 23		John	WAS 67	William	KEN 117	
William	CLN 81		John	WAS 73	Wm.	CAL 44	
William	QUE 33		John	WAS 87	SPENER, Chs.	QUE 18	
William	QUE 34		John	WAS 123	Phil.	QUE 18	
William	TAL 47		SPEER, George	KEN 118	SPENSER, Fredk.	BCI 57	
SPARKSMAN, George			SPEERMAN, William, j.		Robert	FRE 83A	
	WOR 158			KEN 120	SPEOSSARD, Peter	WAS 101	
SPARRAN, Thomas	BAL 247		SPEIGLER, Frederick		SPERRIER, Greenbury		
SPARROW, Anthony	BCI 158			WAS 110		FRE 210	
Ben	MON 160		John	WAS 93	SPICARD, David	ALL 4	
Fanny	DOR 50		Samuel	WAS 111	SPICER, Abraham	HAR 42	
Hezekiah	MON 161		Samuel	WAS 138	Jerimiah	DOR 24	
John	ANN 280		SPELBLING, Henry, of York		John	HAR 5	
John W.	D.C.21		(?)	SAI 80	Nancy	HAR 28	
Solomon	ANN 268		SPELLING, Henry, of York		Saml.	BCI 517	
Solomon	MON 161		(?)	SAI 80	Thomas	BAL 199	
Thomas	ANN 273		SPELLMAN, Benj.	D.C.5	Thos.	BCI 492	
Thos.	MON 135		SPENCE, Ambert	WOR 216	William	DOR 21	
Wm.	MON 160		Ann	CEC 167	SPICKNALL, James	CAL 60	
SPATES, Charles	MON 159		James	SOM 148	John	BCI 301	
Henrietta	MON 136		John	CEC 146	William	CAL 60	
Richd. P.	MON 136		John	CEC 146	SPIDDEN, Edward	BCI 367	
Wm.	MON 167		John	SOM 148	SPIDDIN, Levin T.	TAL 8A	
					SPIEDEN, Ann	D.C.123	

SPIERS, --- (Widaw)	BCI 407	SPRINGER, Abraham		STACKHOUSE (continued),			
John	ANN 346		CEC 185	John	CEc 147
SPIES, John P.	BCI 371	Christian	FRE 171	Silas	CEC 147
SPIKER, Adam	ALL 11	George	WAS 86	Stephen	ANN 358
Jacob	ALL 12	James	CEC 146	William	CEC 147
John	ALL 12	William	FRE 93	STAFFONER, John	FRE 229
Michael	ALL 18	SPRINGFIELD, Peter		STAFFOR, Catharine	BCI 2
SPIKNAIL, William H.			FRE 176	STAFFORD, Aron	BCI 32
	CAL 64	SPRINGLE, Daniel	BCI 196	Eben	CLN 97
SPIL, Philip	BCI 340	SPRINKLE, Henry	BAL 145	Elias	TAL 3
SPILLMAN, Peter	ALL 17	SPROLER, Wm.	BCI 228	Jas.	QUE 16
SPILMAN, --- (Mrs.)		SPROTSON, Samuel	CEC 185	Peter	CLN 96
	BCI 391	Thomas	CEC 185	William J.	BCI 62
Thos. F.	BCI 180	SPROULL, Frances	CEC 185	Wm.	BCI 227
SPINDLE, George	BAL 93	SPROUSE, Edward	TAL 33	STAGES, John	BCI 22
John	BAL 93	SPRUSBANK, Abram		STAGLE, Peter (?)	FRE 191
SPINER, Samuel	BCI 462		BCI 192	STAGNER, Jacob	FRE 190
SPINK, Edward, Senr.		SPRY, Caleb	QUE 8	Peter	FRE 190
	SAI 73A	Christ. R.	QUE 8	STAINS, John	BCI 29
George	SAI 73A	Christopher	KEN 115	Susannah	BCI 101
SPINKS, John	PRI 184	David	QUE 10	William	BCI 54
SPIRES, Peter	WOR 157	George	KEN 108	STAIR, Geo.	BCI 303
Thomas	BCI 36	George	QUE 13	STAIRES, Caleb	BAL 3
SPIRTZEL, John	BCI 321	George	QUE 17	STAIT, John	KEN 118
SPITSNAGLE, John	WAS 151	James	QUE 35	STAKE, Anthony (?)	WAS 79
SPITZENBERGER, Henry		Saml.	QUE 8	Catherine	WAS 119
	FRE 114	SPUNOGLE, Eleanor	MON 159	Elizabeth	HAR 9
SPITZNAGAL, Leonard?		SPURGIN, John	ALL 4	STALE, Joseph	BCI 463
	WAS 98	SPURIOR, Beal	BCI 272	STALEN, James (?)	TAL 47
Loonard	WAS 98	SPURRIEL, Thomas (?)		STALES, Lambt. (?)	QUE 3
SPITZNAUGLE, George			FRE 75	STALEY, Abaham	FRE 126
	WAS 96	SPURRIER, Allen	ANN 315	Catharine	FRE 111
SPIVES, Thomas (?)	BCI 36	Ann	ANN 318	Frederick	FRE 112
SPNCER, Able	BCI 210	Beall	BCI 91	Henry	FRE 226
SPOLDING, James	WAS 102	Denniss	ALL 16	Jacob	MON 132
SPONCELLER, Frederick		Elphias	BAL 67	John	FRE 112
	WAS 80	Henry	FRE 76	Joseph	FRE 112
SPONER, Chs. (?)	QUE 18	Jesse	ALL 23	Moses	FRE 112
SPONG, David	WAS 57	Joshua	ANN 370	Peter, Senr.	FRE 112
Mathias, Sen.	WAS 58	Joshua	FRE 75	Peter, Junr.	FRE 112
Mathias, Junr.	WAS 61	Thomas	FRE 75	STALINGS, John, of Benja.	
SPONSALER, John	FRE 106	William	ANN 316		CAL 60
SPONSELLER, Jacob	FRE 214	SPURRY, George	CLN 97	STALKER, John	ANN 389
Michael	FRE 140	SQUERRELL, Jacob	BAL 51	STALL, Andrew	BAL 217
SPONSLER, Adam	FRE 77	SQUIRES, George	ALL 22	Jacob	WAS 109
David	FRE 192	Joseph	ALL 17	Joseph (?)	BCI 463
Jacob	FRE 69	SRAWYER, Thomas	FRE 126	Michael	WAS 149
SPOON, Jacob	FRE 133	SRESS, Henry (?)	FRE 218	Reanna	BCI 97
SPOONER, Mary	D.C. 121	SRIAS, Thomas (?)	WAS 137	STALLCUP, Andrew	CEC 146
SPORT, Joseph	BCI 319	SRWAYER, Adam	FRE 132	John	CEC 147
SPOSELER, William	FRE 76A	STA--SBURY, Danl.		STALLING, Elizabeth	BAL 124
SPOTWOOD, Daniel	BCI 148		BCI 504	Isaac	BAL 117
SPRATT, James	D.C. 129	STABLEFORD, James W.		STALLINGS, Acquilla	BCI 152
Thos.	D.C. 100		CLN 86	Benjamin	FRE 117
SPRECKER, George	WAS 110	STABLER, Edwd.	D.C. 205	George	CAL 65
Philip, Senr.	WAS 110	James P.	MON 154	Jacob	HAR 23
Philip, Jun.	WAS 109	Thomas	MON 154	James	ANN 342
SPRIGG, Anthony	BCI 506	Willm.	D.C. 154	John	ANN 397
Ben	D.C. 100	STACH, Charles (?)		John	HAR 9
Daniel	WAS 119		DOR 12	Joshua	PRI 217
George	BCI 512	STACK, Charles	DOR 12	Lloyd	ALL 34
Henney	BCI 522	Charles	DOR 57	Margaret	ANN 401
James	MON 176	Cyrus	DOR 65	Perry Grynn	PRI 212
John	MON 129	George	WAS 78	Rebecca	ANN 391
Michael C.	ALL 14A	James	CLN 86	Saml.	BCI 487
Otho	FRE 79A	Joseph	CLN 115	Samuel	ALL 34
Saml.	MON 172	Levin	CLN 116	Sarah	D.C. 127
Samuel	PRI 205	Levin	DOR 51	Thomas	ALL 34
Thomas	BCI 228	Mary	CLN 114	William	CAL 43
Thos.	D.C. 80	Newton	DOR 57	Zachariah	BCI 92
William O.	WAS 95	Rachel	CLN 116	STALLINS, Charlot	ANN 276
SPRIGGS, Henry	FRE 112	Samuel	ANN 376	Edward	ANN 275
SPRIGS, Rachael	FRE 213	STACKERS, Solomon		James	ANN 270
SPRING, --- (Mrs.)	BCI 392		BCI 177	John	ANN 256
Abram	BCI 183	STACKHOUSE, David		Joseph	ANN 265
John	BCI 344		CEC 147	Thomas	ANN 274

STAYMOND, Peter	WAS 138	
STAYTON, Eleanor	D.C. 9	
STEADMAN, Samuel	PRI 185	
STEARE, Jacob	BAL 98	
STEED, William	QUE 8	
STEEL, Charles	PRI 216	
Chas.	D.C. 135	
Daniel (?)	FRE 218	
David	CEC 146	
Elizabeth	BCI 3	
Esther	CEC 185	
George	FRE 228	
Gerard	MON 166	
James	CLN 111	
James	CEC 146	
James	HAR 72	
John	FRE 219	
John	HAR 71	
John	WAS 139	
Levi	WAS 119	
Mary	DOR 3	
Mary (negro)	TAL 51	
Nancey	WAS 139	
Richd.	MON 161	
Robert	WAS 110	
This.?	BCI 529	
Thomas	CEC 185	
Thos.	BCI 529	
Thos.	D.C. 175	
Tom	PRI 187	
Whittington	WOR 185	
William	CEC 146	
STEELE, James	DOR 6	
John	DOR 6	
Rachel	D.C. 43	
Samuel	D.C. 59	
William	D.C. 58	
STEEN, James	D.C. 103	
Roseman	KEN 105	
STEEPLES, Charles	FRE 155	
STEER, Jacob	FRE 178	
STEEVER, George	BCI 202	
STEFFEE, Jacob	BAL 146	
John	BAL 145	
STEFFEY, Peter	FRE 190	
Peter	WAS 78	
STEFFY, Philip	WAS 79	
STEGER, Jacob	BCI 517	
STEIGERS, George	FRE 168	
John	FRE 172	
STEINBECK, John C.		
	BCI 380	
STEINER, Henry	FRE 102	
Henry, Senr.	FRE 94	
Henry, Junr.	FRE 95	
Jacob	FRE 94	
Jacob	FRE 96	
John	BCI 431	
John	D.C. 7	
Mary	FRE 117	
Stephen	FRE 94	
STEINMETZ, Michael	BCI 448	
STELL, John (?)	HAR 71	
STELLE, P. D.	D.C. 82	
STEM, David	FRE 202	
Jacob	FRE 199	
Martin	FRE 176	
Reuben	FRE 178	
STEMBEL, Frederick, Sr.		
	FRE 133	
Frederick, Jr.	FRE 134	
Henry	D.C. 50	
STEMBLE, Christian	WAS 121	
STEMBLER, John	BCI 477	
STEMMON, Mary	BAL 117	
STEMPLE, Antho. (?)	BCI 535	

STENE, Peter	BCI 535	
STENSON, John	QUE 8	
Thomas A. (?)	QUE 34	
Wm.	BCI 259	
STEPHEN, Jacob	WAS 73	
John	ANN 391	
Michael	BCI 146	
Richard H.	CEC 127	
STEPHENS, Charles	BCI 11	
Charles, Sr.	FRE 77	
Charles, Jr.	FRE 77	
David	BCI 199	
Jacob	CEC 128	
Jacob	HAR 30	
James	D..C14	
John	BCI 6	
John	BCI 37	
John	CEC 128	
John	SOM 101A	
John, of L.	DOR 50	
Joseph	FRE 82	
Resin	BAL 45	
Russel	D.C. 153	
Saml.	KEN 123	
Samuel	BAL 54	
Septomas	WAS 59	
Thomas	CEC 128	
Thomas R.	SAI 91	
William	BCI 40	
William	KEN 118	
STEPHENSON, Edward		
	BAL 54	
Ezekial	CEC 166	
George	BCI 11	
James	HAR 24	
John	BCI 427	
John	HAR 78	
Joshua	BCI 148	
Mary	D.C. 53	
Milby	D.C. 23	
Robt.	D.C. 172	
William	CEC 128	
William	HAR 24	
STEPHINS, Benjamin		
	FRE 77	
Ezekiel	FRE 77	
STEPHISON, Alexr.	BCI 170	
STEPHNS, John	FRE 68	
STEPLES, William	BAL 19	
STEPNEY, Peter-Negro		
	HAR 65	
Silena	D.C. 173	
STERENS, Rebecca (?)		
	WOR 196	
STERETT, Carles	BAL 188	
STERGEAN, Edwd.	BCI 193	
STERLING, Aron (Sen.)		
	SOM 144	
Aron (of A.)	SOM 151	
Aron (of John)	SOM 144	
Aron (of Tres.)	SOM 150	
Ephrim	SOM 149	
Ephrim	SOM 151	
Geo.	BCI 282	
George	SOM 144	
Henry, Senr.	SOM 149	
Henry (of E.)	SOM 150	
Henry (of H.)	SOM 151	
Isaac	SOM 149	
Isaac	SOM 150	
James	BCI 96	
James	SOM 144	
John	DOR 53	
John	SOM 150	
John (f.n.)	SOM 119	
John (of Tres.)	SOM 142A	

STERLING (continued),		
Michl.	BCI 537	
Shadrick	SOM 144	
Southy	SOM 151	
Southy	WOR 158	
Stephen	SOM 150	
Trevers (Senr.)	SOM 142A	
Trevers (of Trs.)	SOM 144	
Wm.	BCI 232	
STERNER, Adam	FRE 189	
Elizabeth	FRE 195	
Jonathan	FRE 189	
STERQUEL, Peter	BCI 183	
STERRET, --- (Mrs.)		
	BCI 395	
STERRETT, James	ANN 377	
Joseph	BCI 249	
Samuel	BCI 276	
STERRITT, Joseph	BAL 112	
STETT, Robt.	D.C. 165	
STEUART, Jaseph?	DOR 20	
Joseph	DOR 20	
STEVANS, William	CAL 64	
STEVENS, Abraham	BCI 509	
Ach	BCI 480	
Amos	DOR 28	
Artridge	TAL 25	
Azell	DOR 40	
Benjamin	TAL 14A	
Caleb	DOR 21	
Catoe	TAL 46	
Cesar	TAL 33	
Daniel	WOR 161	
David	BCI 353	
Edward	TAL 41	
Elizabeth	BCI 304	
Elizabeth	TAL 41	
George	BAL 161	
George	TAL 31	
George	TAL 40	
Horatio	FRE 213	
Isaac	ANN 390	
Jacob	ANN 354	
Jacob	KEN 86	
James	FRE 84	
James	FRE 86	
Jannetta R.	ANN 390	
Jas.	QUE 4	
John	CLN 109	
John	D.C. 106	
John	DOR 10	
John	FRE 84	
John	QUE 14	
John	TAL 13	
John, Jr.	TAL 41	
John D.	DOR 51	
John T.	KEN 95	
Jonathan	CLN 89	
Joseph	TAL 12	
Letty	SOM 128	
Levi	WOR 218	
Lyttleton	D.C. 90	
Mary	CLN 99	
Mathew	WAS 148	
Noah	CLN 97	
Peter	TAL 31	
Peter, Jr.	TAL 11	
Phillis	TAL 31	
Priscilla	SOM 135	
Ralph	DOR 6	
Rebecca	WOR 196	
Richard	ANN 277	
Richard	BCI 102	
Robert	D.C. 88	
Robert, Dr.	CLN 88	
Robinson	CLN 109	

STEVENS (continued),			STEWARD (continued),			STEWART (continued),		
Robt.	QUE	4	John	BCI	369	John A.	D.C.	143
Samuel	TAL	35	Mary	WAS	121	John C.	SOM	124
Samuel, Jr.	TAL	40	Rid.	BCI	386	John I.	DOR	12
Sarah	ANN	298	Robert	TAL	36	Joseph	BCI	509
Sarah	ANN	355	William	BCI	120	Joseph	BCI	523
Solomon (negro)	TAL	47	STEWART, --- (Doctor)			Joshua	ANN	331
Thomas	DOR	36	[his] Farm	BAL	241	Joshua	MON	178A
Thomas	DOR	58	--- (Mrs.)	D.C.	102	Julian	BCI	185
Thomas	TAL	33	Abraham	ANN	331	Levin	D.C.	32
Timothy	BCI	132	Alex.	D.C.	16	Madalia	D.C.	103
Timothy	BCI	135	Alexander	BCI	454	Mark	ALL	32
William	CLN	86	Alexr.	ANN	403	Mary	PRI	230
William	DOR	54	Ann	ANN	310	Merdeca	BCI	323
William	KEN	90	Ann	D.C.	14	Nancy	SOM	122
William	QUE	23	Ann	FRE	80	Nehemiah	CHA	194
William, Senr.	ANN	266	Archibald	BAL	179	Perry W.	TAL	49
William (of J.)	CLN	94	Benjamin	FRE	83A	Philip	BAL	224
William; W.T.	CLN	106	Benjn.	DOR	6	Philip	D.C.	108
STEVENSON, --- (Docter)			Calib	ANN	275	Phillis	ANN	301
	FRE	220	Charles	ANN	272	Rachel	BCI	507
--- (Mrs.)	PRI	187	Charles	ANN	298	Resin?	BAL	206
Basil D.	FRE	193	Charles	CHA	218	Rezin	BAL	206
Cath.	D.C.	77	Charles	MON	154	Rhoda	TAL	49
Charles	FRE	201	Charles (col'd)	BAL	217	Richard	ANN	309
Cosmo G.	BCI	197	Charlis?	CHA	218	Richard	CEC	185
Eliza	BCI	486	Chas.	D.C.	42	Robert	ANN	304
Elizabeth	BCI	270	Daniel	TAL	14	Robert	ANN	330
Elizabeth	FRE	194	Darky	TAL	50	Robert	BCI	114
Enoch	BCI	151	David	ANN	261	Robert	BCI	116
Harriet	WAS	145	David	ANN	273	Robert	SOM	109
Henry	BCI	507	David	D.C.	98	Roger	DOR	4
Henry	WOR	169	Dorsey	ANN	310	Samuel	D.C.	81
Hetty	WOR	184	Edmund	BCI	457	Sarah	D.C.	158
Isaiah	BCI	445	Edward	ANN	270	Sarah	SOM	134
Jemimah	FRE	187	Edward H.	ANN	261	Stephen	ANN	392
John	BCI	202	Edwd.	BCI	480	Thomas	ANN	330
Jonathan	WOR	159	Elenor	BCI	216	Thomas	BCI	157
Joseph	FRE	173	Eliza	D.C.	94	Thomas	D.C.	6
Joseph	HAR	31	Elizth.	D.C.	200	Thomas	DOR	7
Joseph	SOM	127	Ellenor	D.C.	108	Thos.	BCI	194
Joseph	WOR	159	Ezekiel	ANN	306	Trilas	KEN	92
Joshua	BAL	221	Ezekiel, of Dav.	ANN	298	W. A.	D.C.	85
Josiah	BAL	225	Fanny	D.C.	77	Walter	D.C.	71
Josiah	BCI	179	George	PRI	238	Walter	MON	176
Marshal	ANN	320	George C.	ANN	275	Will.	D.C.	79
Mathew	FRE	148	Henrietta	DOR	54	Will. H.	D.C.	72
Mich.	BCI	350	Henry	CHA	224	William	ANN	275
Nathan	BAL	223	Ignatius	CHA	218	William	BCI	113
Samuel	BCI	431	Isaac	CHA	217	William	CHA	216
Samuel	WOR	219	James	ANN	257	William	D.C.	21
Sarah	HAR	31	James	ANN	261	William	D.C.	52
Sater	BCI	274	James	ANN	375	William	DOR	36
Shedrick	BCI	398	James	BCI	126	William	FRE	116
Thomas	SOM	144	James	BCI	451	William	SOM	125
William	FRE	148	James	CHA	215	William P.	BCI	271
William P.?	WOR	212	James	D.C.	128	Willm.	D.C.	155
William R.	WOR	212	James	TAL	38	Wm.	BCI	177
Wm.	WOR	169	James (Doc.)	SOM	128	Wm.	BCI	480
STEVER, Adam	BCI	129	James (Doct.)	BCI	277	Wm.	MON	178A
Cathn.	BCI	184	James (Doctr.)			Wm. B.	D.C.	147
Elizabeth	BCI	120	(Farm)	BAL	129	Woolford	DOR	7
STEVINS, Peggy	WOR	181	James W.	DOR	4	Zachariah	ANN	297
Resin	FRE	209	Jarrett	SOM	138	STEWERT, Athel	TAL	48
STEVINSON, Hugh M.			Jas. M.	D.C.	166	John	WOR	187
	WOR	174	Jno. P.	MON	173	Samuel	DOR	10
John	WOR	179	John	ANN	264	STEWURT, James	BCI	321
John (Doctor)	WOR	153	John	BAL	127	STICKER, Elizabeth	FRE	228
Josias	FRE	173	John	BAL	189	STICKLE, Solomon	FRE	103
STEWARD, --- (Mrs.)			John	BCI	65	STICKNEY, Moses	D.C.	124
	BCI	358	John	BCI	119	STIDHAM, James	KEN	110
Adam	BCI	405	John	BCI	144	STIER, Margaret	FRE	68
David	WAS	134[A]	John	BCI	186	STIFF, Thomas	BCI	381
Elizabeth	WAS	123	John	BCI	428	STIFFLER, George	WAS	56
Henry	CEC	145	John	FRE	143	Jacob	WAS	86
J.	BCI	407	John	TAL	33	Sarah	WAS	82

STRONGWARE, Simon		STUMP (continued),		SUINITT, Mary	QUE 38		
	SOM 130	Samuel	BAL 83	SUIRE, Joseph	BCI 126		
STROOMAN, John	D.C.195	William	HAR 78	SUIT, Edward	PRI 194		
John	D.C.197	William	HAR 79	Horatio	PRI 193		
STROTH, James	D.C.9	STUMPT, Jos.	BCI 347	Jesse	PRI 182		
STROTHER, John	D.C.76	STUPES, Ephraim	CEC 146	Jesse	PRI 194		
STROUD, Mary	HAR 55	Ephraim	CEC 147	John	CHA 205		
Thomas	HAR 70	STUPHERD, Abram (?)		John H.	SAI 86A		
STROWL, Philip	WAS 126		BAL 100	John S.	PRI 203		
STRUMPHOWSER, George		STURGEON, Alexander		Nathaniel	PRI 193		
	WAs 132		CEC 166	Olliver B.	PRI 193		
STRUTOKOFF, Barney		Thomas	CEC 167	Philip	PRI 204		
	BCI 153	STURGES, Jos.	BCI 350	Samuel	SAI 90		
STRUTT, Charles	BAL 27	STURGESS, Martha	QUE 35	Walter	CHA 227		
STTOCKER, Bazel, Ovsr.		STURGIS, Christopher		William, Jun.	SAI 91		
	TAL 5		WOR 202	William B.	SAI 89		
STUART, Bennett	KEN 106	Harry	SOM 134	SUITER, Jacob	WAS 134[A]		
Charles	KEN 104	Henry	WOR 173	Peter	WAS 12		
Cloe	BCI 90	James	WOR 180	SUITOR, George	BCI 484		
Cuffee	KEN 120	Jane	WOR 186	SUKINS, Jesse	BAL 79		
Henry	KEN 116	Jesse	WOR 164	SULIVAN, Abraham	FRE 191		
Isaac	QUE 7	John, Senr.	WOR 179	Catharine	FRE 202		
James	QUE 25	Joshua	WOR 213	Daniel	FRE 202		
John	QUE 13	Leah	WOR 175	Jacob	FRE 193		
Margaret	D.C.35	Levi (of Richard)		Matthias	CEC 166		
Robert	WOR 211		WOR 174	SULIVANE, Ann E.	DOR 54		
Tho.	QUE 11	Levin, Senr.	WOR 157	Daniel	DOR 54		
William	CHA 214	Levin, Jnr.	WOR 155	Eliza	DOR 3		
William K.	QUE 26	Peter (of Levin)	WOR 175	Mary	DOR 39		
STUBBINS, Henery	BAL 95	Rachel	SOM 127	SULIVEN, Elizabeth	CEC 146		
Samuel	BAL 89	Richd., Senr.	WOR 180	John	BCI 373		
Thos.	BCI 508	Sally, Wd.	WOR 209	SULLAVIN, Henry	KEN 108		
STUBBLES, Jas.	QUE 16	Stephen, Esqr.	WOR 155	SULLEVEN, John	FRE 141		
STUBBS, Henry	CLN 108	Thos.	WOR 181	SULLIVAN, Conl.	MON 140		
Isaac	HAR 55	Titus	WOR 176	Cornelius	MON 155		
Richardson	CLN 108	William	SOM 135	Dennis	MON 154		
Richardson	CLN 113	Zadock, Esqr.	WOR 174	Eleanor	MON 154		
William	DOR 62	STURR, Jacob	WAS 123	Elizabeth	WAS 66		
STUBINS, Charles	BAL 27	STUTELEN, Levy	FRE 217	Florence	BCI 38		
Henry (?)	BAL 29	STUTELEY, William	QUE 30	James	ALL 30		
Henry	BAL 23	Wm.	QUE 18	James	BCI 97		
STUCHLEGER, John	WAS 94	STUTLER, Conrod (?)		James	MON 154		
STUCK, John	ALL 7		FRE 197	Jas.	BCI 167		
STUCKLEGER, John (?)		Elizabeth	FRE 103	Jemima	BAL 176		
	WAS 94	STVENSON, Wm. H.	FRE 220	Jesse	CAL 62		
STUDDER, Philip	WAS 136	STWART, Ann	ANN 315	John	ANN 320		
STUDDING, George	CEC 167	Joseph (?)	CEC 128	John	ANN 393		
STUDY, Ann	BCI 298	STYER, John	ALL 16	John	BCI 242		
John	FRE 195	STYERS, John	FRE 134	Margt.	BCI 215		
STUKELY, Mary	D.C.161	STYLES, Frideric	DOR 13	Michael	BCI 295		
STUL, Mary (?)	DOR 3	John	D.C.4	Michael	FRE 202		
STULL, Adam	FRE 114	John	D.C.24	William	HAR 70		
Christopher	FRE 224	Saml.	MON 166	SULLIVANE, Andrew	CLN 99		
George	FRE 114	STYLL, Thomas	CLN 88	Greenbury	CLN 116		
John	BAL 18	SUBER, Joseph	ANN 382	James	CLN 112		
John	FRE 114	SUCH, Danuel	BAL 23	John	CLN 115		
John	FRE 224	Jane	BAL 23	Peter	CLN 88		
John J. (I.?)	D.C.28	SUDDEN, John	BAL 125	Peter	CLN 111		
O. H. W.	WAS 115	SUDER, Jacob	BCI 334	Thomas	CLN 108		
STULLER, Conrod	FRE 197	SUDLER, Arthur	QUE 4	SULLIVEN, Joseph	ANN 277		
Henry	FRE 193	Ben	QUE 4	SULLIVIN, Morgan	ANN 268		
Uhlerick	FRE ±97	Ed	QUE 4	William	ANN 268		
STULLEY, William	BCI 459	Emery S.	SOM 151	SULSER, Jno., Senr.	FRE124		
STULTZ, Nicholas	FRE 222	Esther	SOM 151	John, Jr.	FRE 135		
STULZS, Henry	WAS 134[A]	Frederick	QUE 47	SULTZER, Peter	FRE 111		
STUMBOCK, Jacob	FRE 227	Mary A.	QUE 47	Sabastian	FRE 174		
STUMP, Anthoney	WAS 118	Nancy	QUE 20	SUMAN, Albert	FRE 128		
Cassandra	HAR 78	Thomas S.	SOM 146	Garrott	FRE 128		
Jim-f.c.p.	HAR 10	Tubman	SOM 123	SUMBY, Sampson	D.C.205		
John	ALL 34	William	SOM 146	SUMERS, Richard	WAS 118		
John	CEC 166	SUEL, Peter	SOM 106	SUMERVELL, Sophlah	SAI 94		
John W.	HAR 22	Ritchard	BAL 100	SUMERWELL, William	BAL 193		
Joseph	HAR 31	SUGARS, Edward	ANN 377	SUMES, Robt.	BCI 348		
Mary	FRE 226	Edward	BAL 207	SUMMERS, Andrew	WAS 140		
Reuben	HAR 28	George	ALL 13	Ann	BAL 2		
S.	BCI 336	SUIGAL, --- (Widaw)		Dawson	TAL 47		
			BCI 389				

TANY, Octo. C. (Doctr.)	CAL 59	TATMAN, Collin	CEC 147	TAYLOR (continued),	
		Jesse	CEC 128	Daniel	D.C.206
TANYHILL, John	CAL 65	John	CEC 128	Daniel	HAR 58
Mordecai	CAL 65	Joseph	ALL 33	David	BCI 453
Thomas	CAL 65	TATSAPAUGH, John		David	WAS 64
TANZEY, Arthur	FRE 69		D.C.176	David	WOR 162
TAPMAN, Jesse	WOR 158	Susanna	D.C.196	David	WOR 190
John	WOR 160	TATSEPAUGH, Elizth.		E. P.	D.C.151
Mathews	WOR 160		D.C.208	Edward	KEN 87
TAPP, Charlottie	BCI 457	TATTERSON, Alexr.		Edward	WOR 161
TARBOUR, David	D.C.207		D.C.211	Eleanor	HAR 27
TARBUTTON, Jas.	QUE 16	TATTLA, Robert	BCI 388	Eleonor	SAI 54
Saml.	QUE 12	TATTLE, --- (Mrs.)		Elhanah?	SAI 68
William	QUE 29		BCI 413	Elijah	D.C.193
William	TAL 49	TATUM, Stephen	BCI 122	Elizabeth	SOM 106
TARLTON, Edmund	SAI 67	TAULBURT, George T.		Elizth.	D.C.114
Elijah	SAI 65		PRI 235	Elizth.	D.C.214
Elizabeth	SAI 96	TAVERN, WASHINGN.		Elkanah	SAI 68
George	SAI 57		D.C.163	Fisher	SOM 118
George	SAI 96	TAVINS, John	D.C.212	Frederick	CEC 167
Margt.	D.C.148	TAWNEY, David	FRE 198	Geo.	BCI 377
Rhodolph	SAI 69	Frederick	FRE 204	George	BCI 149
Robert	SAI 66	George	ANN 350	George	HAR 8
Stephen	WAS 95	Jacob	FRE 186	George	HAR 23
Thomas	SAI 69	John	FRE 203	George	KEN 103
TARMAN, Fielder	PRI 215	Joseph, Jr.	FRE 220	George	SAI 57
James	BAL 127	TAWNEYHILL, Hanah		George	SOM 112
Philip	MON 164		WAS 65	George, Junr.	KEN 103
Saml.	MON 164	TAWS, Ezekiel	SOM 150	George (of Jon.)	WOR 155
TARR, --- (Major?)	WOR 169	Isaac	SOM 144	Hanna	BCI 405
Charles (of Jon)	WOR 160	William	SOM 150	Hannah	BCI 112
Jacob	BCI 191	TAWSAN, Jahn (?)	BCI 416	Hannah	D.C.7
Jeptha	WOR 162	TAWSON, James?	BAL 165	Hannah	HAR 20
John	QUE 48	Tames	BAL 165	Henry	FRE 126
John (of John)	WOR 160	TAY, John (?)	BCI 391	Henry, Sen.	KEN 93
Jonathan	TAL 22	Phillip	FRE 173	Henry, Junr.	KEN 88
Joshua	WOR 171	TAYLER, Ann	FRE 219	Hesekiah	BCI 125
Levi	WOR 173	Edward	BAL 159	Hesikiah	WOR 155
Levin S.	BCI 252	Jo	SOM 147	Hizekiah	PRI 214
Major	WOR 169	Joseph	BCI 304	Isaac	BAL 228
Margaret (of John)		Stephen	SOM 145	Isaac	BCI 78
	WOR 157	TAYLOE, John (?)	D.C.3	Isaac	CEC 147
Nancy (of Saml.)		TAYLOR (See also		Isaac	SOM 125
	WOR 161	SAYLOR),		Isaac	WOR 179
Peter	TAL 11	--- (?)	WOR 154	Isaac	WOR 209
Richard	TAL 22	--- (Col.) (See God-		Isaiah	HAR 18
Sophia	WOR 176	frey THOMAS (Col.		Jacob	CEC 147
William	TAL 11	TAYLOR)		Jacob	QUE 40
Wm., Senr.	WOR 180	A.	BCI 409	Jacob	WOR 161
TARRELL, Absolom	BCI 139	Abner	CEC 186	James	ANN 388
TARRIS, --- (Mrs.)	BCI 400	Abraham	BCI 98	James	BCI 103
TARRISFERRO, W. (?)		Abraham	HAR 20	James	BCI 182
	BCI 335	Alexa. (of Teacle)		James	FRE 147
TARTER, Hager	BCI 502		WOR 164	James	HAR 24
TARVIN, Ann	PRI 216	Alexander	PRI 206	James	HAR 24
John	PRI 213	Alice	TAL 4	James	WOR 169
Joseph	PRI 216	Ama	SOM 140	James M. (Doctr.)	CAL 46
TASKER, Danl.	MON 172	Andrew	PRI 215	James W.	WOR 189
Herculas	D.C.7	Ann	CEC 167	Jas., Senr.	WOR 160
Lydia	ANN 311	Anna	BCI 100	Jas. (of John)	WOR 160
Richard	ALL 3	Arther	WOR 190	Jehu	SOM 109
TASON, Joshua	BAL 92	Arthey	WOR 187	Jenifer	SAI 56
TASTET, Nichs.	D.C.86	Banja.	CAL 42	Jenifer S.	CLN 88
TATE, Alexr.	D.C.138	Basil	FRE 125	Jeremiah	CEC 147
Andrew	D.C.93	Benjamin	SOM 112	Jesse	HAR 6
Ben	QUE 5	Betsey	D.C.19	John	ANN 264
Elizabeth	BCI 65	Betsey D.	SOM 106	John	ANN 394
Francis	BCI 203	Caleb	PRI 203	John	BAL 86
James	HAR 55	Caleb	SAI 66	John	BCI 73
Jane	BCI 147	Cass	FRE 229	John	BCI 135
Joseph	QUE 31	Catharine	ALL 35	John	CLN 90
Maria	KEN 102	Catharine	KEN 91	John	CLN 106
Thomas	SOM 105	Charles	BAL 77	John	CEC 147
William P.	QUE 31	Charles	PRI 229	John	CEC 147
TATES, Charles (?)	FRE 123	Charlotte	D.C.3	John	CEC 148
TATHAM, Danl.	BCI 324	Corbin	HAR 58	John	CHA 196A

238

TAYLOR (continued),			TAYLOR (continued),			TEAL, Archible	BCI	30
John	D.C.	3	Sally	SOM	125	George	SAI	64
John	D.C.	6	Saml.	SOM	136	TEANER, John	FRE	213
John	D.C.	64	Samuel	ANN	278	John	QUE	39
John	D.C.	115	Samuel	BAL	215	TEAR, Barton	SAI	56
John	SOM	137	Samuel	BCI	394	TEARNAN, Patrick	BCI	271
John	WAS	88	Samuel	CEC	186	TEAS, Alex.	BCI	526
John	WOR	190	Samuel	HAR	7	Isaac (?)	SAI	64
John (Senr.)	SOM	108	Samuel	SOM	127	John	BCI	384
John (Junr.)	SOM	110	Samuel	WOR	185	TEBER, George	D.C.	206
John B.	BCI	124	Samuel, Capt.	WOR	217	TEBOLD, Jacob	BCI	320
John E.	BAL	217	Samuel (of Jirm)	WOR	211	TEE, Harry (?)	BAL	226
John T.	WOR	169	Sarah	ANN	285	James	SAI	67
Joseph	BAL	182	Sarah	BCI	49	Lamack	SAI	56
Joseph	BAL	248	Sarah	WOR	197	TEENER, George	BAL	69
Joseph	BCI	187	Simon	ALL	31	Phillip	BAL	69
Joseph	BCI	437	Solomon (f.n.)	SOM	118	TEFERBACH, Catharin		
Joseph	WOR	174	Step	KEN	115		FRE	203
Joshua	D.C.	167	Stephen	KEN	104	TELFER, John	D.C.	15
Josiah	D.C.	6	Stephen	SOM	109	Mathew	D.C.	35
Kendal	WOR	161	Stephen	WOR	155	TELKE, Telke	BCI	311
Lemuel G.	BCI	124	Stephen	WOR	216	TELLY, F.	BCI	376
Leven	BCI	30	Stephen (f.n.)	SOM	119	TEMPLE, Conrod	BAL	200
Levin	BCI	528	Susan	D.C.	55	Emory	QUE	19
Levin	WOR	190	Teacle (of Tiacle)			Isaac	HAR	76
Levin (Senr.)	SOM	104		WOR	163	Mathew	BCI	18
Levin (Jur.)	SOM	118	Tecle (of Kendal)			Samuel	HAR	77
Levin (of George)				WOR	161	William	HAR	40
	SOM	113	Thomas	BAL	200	Wm.	QUE	10
Levy	BCI	515	Thomas	BCI	14	TEMPLEMAN, Augustus		
Lucy	ANN	345	Thomas	CEC	167		BCI	57
Lydia	CEC	167	Thomas	CEC	168	John	ALL	12
Margl.	BCI	222	Thomas	CEC	186	TEMPLES, Joshua	QUE	16
Margt.?	BCI	222	Thomas	KEN	101	TENANT, Samuel	TAL	28
Mary	D.C.	146	Thomas	PRI	222	Thomas	BCI	40
Mary	D.C.	165	Thomas, sen.	D.C.	7	Thomas	BCI	246
Mary	MON	134	Thomas J. (I.?)	PRI	230	William	TAL	28
Mary	PRI	213	Thos.	D.C.	145	TENCH, Stan.	D.C.	127
Mary	SAI	65	Thos.	QUE	9	TENDER, N. Yd.	D.C.	133
Mary Ann	HAR	41	Thos.	QUE	10	TENESON, Absalom	SAI	57
Mary E.	ANN	392	Washington	CHA	201	Chas. C.	D.C.	158
Matthew	BCI	171	Wettha	WOR	171	TENLEY, Elizth.	D.C.	173
Matthias C.	SOM	123	William	ALL	17	Zenis	D.C.	207
Merren	WOR	190	William	ALL	25	TENLY, Henry	PRI	238
Moses	D.C.	132	William	ANN	388	Loyard	PRI	239
Nancy	D.C.	168	William	BAL	37	TENNANT, James	KEN	122
Nathan	QUE	19	William	BAL	233	TENNELLY, Sarah	D.C.	66
Nathaniel	PRI	218	William	CEC	147	TENNERSON, Edward		
Nicholas	BCI	159	William	CHA	226		SAI	78
Obediah	PRI	228	William	D.C.	20	John, overseer for		
Obediah	PRI	230	William	HAR	40	Wm. C. SOMMER-		
Paley?	WOR	185	William	KEN	105	VILL	SAI	76
Paran; Dr.	QUE	3	William	SOM	107	TENNETT, James	WAS	61
Patey	WOR	185	William	SOM	136	TENNFELEN, Richd.	FRE	126
Patsy	ANN	310	William	WOR	215	TENNISON, Absalom	CHA	204
Perry	BCI	19	William	WOR	216	George	CHA	204
Phiniston	BCI	88	William, Sen.	WOR	196	Joshua	D.C.	76
Pricy	BCI	29	William, Jun.	WOR	195	Saml.	D.C.	195
Rachel	ANN	346	William S.	BCI	16	Saml.	D.C.	197
Rachel	BAL	126	William W.	BCI	437	TENNY, Ann	D.C.	21
Rachel	QUE	40	Willm.	D.C.	190	TENSFIELD, Margarett		
Resin	D.C.	217	Wm.	BCI	184		BCI	298
Reuben	ALL	25	Wm. Gillet	WOR	174	TEPISH, John C.	BCI	141
Rhoda	PRI	211	Zeth	PRI	218	TEPPETT, Eli	SAI	90
Ricd.	D.C.	128	TAYMAN, John	PRI	206	TERMAIN, William	BAL	239
Richard	BAL	228	John	PRI	216	TERREL, James	BAL	85
Richard	BAL	234	Levi	PRI	217	TERRENCE, Jas.	D.C.	76
Richd.	D.C.	123	TAYMON, Elizabeth			TERRITT, W. H.	D.C.	117
Robert	CEC	148		ANN	288	TERRY, Benjamin	CEC	128
Robert	CEC	186	TEABAKER, John	BCI	59	Eli	CEC	167
Robert	CHA	189	TEACKLE, Littleton D.			Hosea	CEC	186
Robert	D.C.	32		SOM	128	Jacob	KEN	120
Robt.	BCI	168	TEAGUE, John	WOR	180	Michael	FRE	115
Robt. J. (I.?)	D.C.	199	Zeporah	WOR	171	Thompson-negro	CEC	128
Roger	ALL	25	TEAKLE, Joseph	DOR	39	William	ANN	401
Sacker	WOR	191	Leucreatia	TAL	12	William, Junr.	ANN	401

TESTER, Jacob (?)	FRE 127	THOMAS (continued)		THOMAS (continued),	
TEVIS, Benjamin	BCI 126	Edward	CHA 224	John	BCI 384
Joshua	BCI 442	Edward	SAI 70	John	BCI 519
THACKERY, John	CEC 167	Elizabeth	BCI 299	John	CLN 108
THAEME, H.	BCI 375	Elizabeth	FRE 86	John	D.C.31
THAMPSON, James	D.C.44	Elizabeth	MON 143	John	D.C.64
Susanna (?)	D.C.65	Elizabeth	QUE 41	John	D.C.79
THARNTON, Joseph	D.C.56	Elizh.	D.C.115	John	D.C.93
THARP, George	BCI 253	Elizth.	D.C.149	John	D.C.138
THARPE, Nancy	CLN 92	Ellis	ANN 298	John	D.C.167
THAW, John S.	D.C.37	Evan	BAL 177	John	DOR 12
Joseph	D.C.15	Gabrial	BCI 113	John	FRE 82
THAWLEY, Henry	CLN 78	Geo.	D.C.78	John	FRE 103
James	CLN 73	Geo.	D.C.106	John	FRE 123
John	CLN 73	Georg & E.	BCI 359	John	FRE 125
Samuel	CLN 73	George (See Thomas		John	FRE 127
Thomas	CLN 78	A. BOND (overseer		John	FRE 164
Weeden	CLN 80	for George THOMAS))		John	HAR 40
William	CLN 73	George	BAL 175	John	MON 155
THAYER, Stephen	ALL 3	George	D.C.201	John	QUE 6
THEBAN, Henry	BCI 118	George	FRE 85	John	QUE 37
THEKER, Walter	BCI 246	George	PRI 236	John	SOM 146
THEMSON, Thomas	BAL 26	George	SAI 98	John	WAS 108
THESIS, Froderick	D.C.24	George	WAS 73	John	WAS 125
THISTLE, Archibald		George S.	CHA 191	John, Sr.	DOR 14
	ALL 8A	George W.	KEN 101	John 3rd	MON 155
George	ALL 28	Godfrey (Col. TAY-		John A.	SAI 57
Thomas	ALL 28	LOR)	D.C.67	John B.	CHA 228
THOMAS, --- (?)	BCI 403	Henretta	SAI 55	John B.	PRI 213
---?	SAI 95	Henry	D.C.10	John C.	CEC 167
A. G. D.	BCI 510	Henry	DOR 49	John G.	TAL 47
Aaron	QUE 24	Henry	FRE 86	John H.	PRI 214
Abraham	BCI 133	Henry	FRE 102	John L.	BCI 158
Abraham	WAS 74	Henry	TAL 10	John R.	ANN 315
Abrm. J.	HAR 20	Henry	WAS 67	John W.	BCI 354
Alexander	ALL 6	Henry, of Gab.	FRE 82	Jonathan	CHA 222
Algernon	DOR 55	Hester	QUE 29	Joseph	BCI 62
Allen	ANN 322	Horace	DOR 63	Joseph	BCI 92
Andrew	CAL 67	Hugh	DOR 15	Joseph	BCI 393
Anthony	QUE 40	Hynson	QUE 7	Joseph	CEC 147
Archabald	FRE 82	Isaac	BCI 507	Joseph	D.C.108
Babinglon	DOR 14	Isaac	HAR 42	Joseph	DOR 20
Barten	BCI 24	Isaac	TAL 12	Joseph	FRE 84
Ben	MON 155	Isack	BAL 12	Joseph	MON 155
Benj.	WAS 146	Isaiah	BCI 220	Joseph	TAL 34
Benjamin	ANN 306	J. (I.?) V.	D.C.128	Joseph M.	FRE 69
Benjamin	BAL 164	Jacob	ALL 6	Joseph S.	KEN 91
Benjamin	BCI 92	Jacob	CEC 147	Joseph S.	SAI 64
Benjamin	SOM 148	Jacob	QUE 6	Joshua	DOR 16
Bladen	D.C.25	Jacob	WAS 103	Joshua	KEN 110
Brown	PRI 197	Jacob, Senr.	FRE 127	Josiah	FRE 125
Casandra	ANN 402	Jacob, Jr.	FRE 130	Kellay	WAS 149
Catharine	FRE 117	James (See John WIL-		Lambt.	BCI 186
Catherine	BCI 97	LIAMS, overseer		Lawry	D.C.5
Charles	BCI 38	for James THOMAS)		Leonard	FRE 86
Charles	BCI 425	James	BAL 66	Leven	FRE 82
Charles	BCI 500	James	BAL 130	Levi	SOM 148
Charles	FRE 79	James	D.C.22	Levin (negro)	TAL 23
Charles	SAI 97	James	D.C.211	Levin, Senr.	DOR 15
Clem.	D.C.100	James	FRE 142	Lewis	CEC 147
Conrad	WAS 70	James	HAR 76	Lucrea?	WAS 79
D. L.	BCI 186	James	KEN 104	Lucy	PRI 186
Daniel	FRE 80	James	SAI 94	Ludwick	WAS 74
Daniel	WAS 74	James, Sr.	DOR 14	Luerca?	WAS 79
David	BCI 167	James, of J. (I.?)		Mager	TAL 4
David	BCI 383		DOR 15	Margaret	KEN 90
David	BCI 535	James; R.P.	DOR 15	Margaret	SAI 53A
David	CHA 204	Jane	BCI 268	Margaretta	WAS 65
David	HAR 73	Jane A.	CEC 167	Margt.	QUE 7
David	WAS 71	Jared	D.C.31	Martha	KEN 90
Dianah	QUE 35	Jas.	DOR 11	Mary	BCI 133
Dianna	SAI 94	Jim (negro)	TAL 26	Mary	BCI 224
Dolly	TAL 10	John	ANN 301	Mary	CHA 204
Dorotha	QUE 37	John	BAL 95	Mary	D.C.14
E. (See Georg &		John	BAL 187	Mary	QUE 36
E. THOMAS)	BCI 359	John	BCI 266	Mary	SAI 64
Ebenezer	BAL 227			Mathew	BCI 387

THOMAS (continued),			THOMAS (continued),			THOMPSON (continued),		
Meelus?	QUE	49	Sterling	BCI	153	Bennett	SAI	77
Meetus	QUE	49	Susan	PRI	197	Bernard	HAR	43
Michael	FRE	86	Susan	QUE	30	Betsey?	PRI	207
Michael	FRE	117	Tamer	DOR	6	Betsey	KEN	117
Michael	WAS	66	Theodore	CEC	147	Catharine	FRE	144
Michael	WAS	72	Theodore	CEC	148	Catherine	BAL	187
Mitus (negro)	TAL	48	Tho.	QUE	15	Charles	CHA	228
Monacha	SAI	87	Thomas	BCI	308	Charles	D.C.	71
Mordecal	HAR	74	Thomas	DOR	58	Charles	DOR	40
Nancy	BCI	257	Thomas	SOM	148	Charles (of Wm.)	SAI	77
Nancy	BCI	530	Thomas	TAL	14A	Clement	MON	176
Nathan	ANN	285	Thomas E.	QUE	24	Colmore	PRI	226
Nathan	PRI	192	Thomas S.	CEC	167	Conrad	WAS	60
Nathaniel	CLN	80	Thos.	BCI	505	Craven P.	D.C.	144
Neal	PRI	191A	Tristram	QUE	18	Daniel	BAL	90
Nicholas	TAL	38	Tristram	TAL	10	Daniel	WAS	60
Notty	FRE	82	Vallentine	WAS	71	David	CHA	195
Owen	BCI	312	William	BAL	191	David H.	BCI	187
Patsy	D.C.	93	William	BCI	139	Dekar	CLN	110
Peggy	TAL	10	William	CEC	167	Draper	DOR	52
Peter	CLN	111	William	D.C.	5	Edward	BCI	91
Peter-Negro	HAR	65	William	DOR	12	Edward	CHA	220A
Philip	ANN	264	William	DOR	15	Eleanor	CHA	221
Philip	BCI	511	William	HAR	5	Elenor	D.C.	115
Philip	FRE	80	William	KEN	104	Elias	BCI	199
Philip P.	ANN	375	William	KEN	106	Eliza	MON	172
Philip W.	ANN	283	William	KEN	117	Elizabeth	BCI	59
Polly	DOR	14	William	MON	155	Elizabeth	MON	167
Price	CHA	225	William	PRI	193	Evan	MON	172
Priscilla	ANN	303	William	SAI	55	Fielder	ANN	373
Rachel	BCI	77	William	SAI	75	Francis	CHA	212
Rachel	QUE	39	William	SAI	91	Geo.	D.C.	106
Rebecca	CEC	147	William	SOM	148	George	CEC	186
Rhoda	CLN	91	William	TAL	35	George	SAI	96
Richard	BCI	84	William D.	QUE	41	George	TAL	50
Richard	D.C.	29	William R.	QUE	37	George F.	CLN	73
Richard	DOR	54	Wm.	BCI	333	Giles G.	CHA	207A
Richard	MON	155	Wm.	QUE	13	Hanson	CHA	207
Richard	TAL	13	Wm.	QUE	13	Hanson	PRI	226
Robert	ANN	269	Zachariah	CHA	201	Harriet	BCI	151
Robert	BCI	25	THOMPOSON, Stephen			Henny	SAI	81
Robert	CHA	212		PRI	229	Henry	ANN	393
Robert	CLN	91	THOMPSAN, Hugh	FRE	170	Henry	BAL	105
Robert	CLN	109	Jane	PRI	195	Henry	CHA	211
Robt.	D.C.	111	John	BCI	430	Henry	FRE	73
Robt.	QUE	4	Richd. (?)	D.C.	32	Henry	PRI	225
Roger	SAI	54	Stephen	BCI	460	Henry	SAI	91
S.	BCI	414	Thomas	BCI	460	Henry A. W.	SAI	93
Sally	SOM	148	THOMPSEN, Alex	BCI	376	Igns.	SAI	77
Saml.	BCI	495	John	BCI	376	Israel	ALL	3
Saml.	D.C.	100	Wm.	BCI	380	Israel	HAR	70
Saml.	QUE	6	THOMPSON, --- (Mrs.)			J. (I.?) P.	D.C.	194
Samuel	ALL	27		BCI	407	Jacob	BAL	63
Samuel	ANN	274	--- (Widaw)	BCI	388	James (?)	D.C.	44
Samuel	BCI	142	Abraham	CLN	94	James	BAL	125
Samuel	CEC	147	Abraham	CEC	128	James	CHA	208
Samuel	DOR	6	Alexander	BCI	9	James	D.C.	19
Samuel	FRE	84	Alexander	BCI	143	James	D.C.	22
Samuel	FRE	85	Alexr.	BCI	178	James	D.C.	52
Samuel	KEN	104	Allen	BCI	312	James	DOR	3
Samuel	QUE	24	Ann	BCI	82	James	DOR	52
Samuel	QUE	35	Ann	BCI	161	James	HAR	43
Samuel	TAL	14A	Ann	SAI	77	James	HAR	60
Samuel S.	FRE	84	Ann	SAI	89	James	WAS	88
Samuel W.	QUE	36	Annastasia	SAI	82	James, Junr.	HAR	61
Samuel W., Jr.	QUE	27	Anthoney	DOR	18	James of A.	CEC	186
Sarah	ANN	255	Anthony	CEC	186	James of J. (I.?)	CEC	186
Sarah	BCI	25	Anthony C.	TAL	27	James of Jno. B.	SAI	81
Sarah	QUE	25	Aquila	BCI	186	James (of Robt.)	SAI	74
Sarah	QUE	39	Archibald	HAR	63	James J. (I.?)	MON	172
Sarah M.	CEC	167	Barzelar	SAI	96	Jane	BCI	144
Sarrah	QUE	36	Basil	MON	178A	Jas.	D.C.	74
Simon	CLN	90	Belsey	PRI	207	Jas.	QUE	5
Singo (negro)	TAL	26	Benjamin	D.C.	54	Jenet	SAI	93
Solomon	ANN	285	Benjn.	D.C.	150	Jesse	SAI	87

TOWNSEND (continued),		TRAIL (continued),		TRAVRS (continued),	
Thomas	FRE 199	Hezekiah	MON 178A	Mathu	DOR 29
Thomas	TAL 20	James (?)	FRE 81	Robert?	DOR 32
Thomas, Jr.	TAL 20	James, Senr.	MON 171	Robrt	DOR 32
Thorogood	WOR 159	Nathan	ALL 38	Sarah	DOR 29
William	SOM 134	Nathan	MON 130	Thomas	DOR 24
Wm. (of Jno.)	WOR 161	Notley	MON 160	Vatchel (?)	DOR 29
Zadock, Senr.	WOR 180	Wm.	MON 132	William H.	DOR 30
TOWNSHEND, Ann	ANN 400	TRAINER, Joseph	BAL 8	TRAY, James	BCI 112
Daniel	CHA 228	TRAMMEL, Letty	D.C.171	TREADWAY, Asa H.	
Eleanor	PRI 218	Washg.	D.C.22		D.C.91
John	PRI 221A	TRANCLE, Lewis	BCI 315	TREADWELL, Stephen	
Saml. H.	PRI 216	TRANSCOMB, John	D.C.128		BAL 250
Singleton	PRI 218	TRAPNALL, Joseph	FRE 82	TREAKLE, Greenberry	
William	PRI 221A	TRAPNELL, Elizabeth			ANN 378
TOWNSLEY, James	HAR 45		BCI 95	Mary	ANN 379
TOWSAN, Rowley (?)		Elizabeth	BCI 120	Thomas	ANN 355
	BCI 458	TRAUCKELE, Daniel	WAS 109	TREAT, Richard	BCI 84
TOWSAND, Jacob T.		TRAVER, John	WAS 90	TREBOUT, Elizabeth	
	WAS 80	TRAVERES, John C.			BCI 55
TOWSON, Henry	BCI 146		DOR 24	TREDWAY, Aquila	HAR 26
James?	BAL 165	TRAVERS, Ann (?)	DOR 30	Edward	HAR 40
John	BCI 416	Benjamin	DOR 29	John	HAR 61
Joseph	BCI 266	Charles (?)	DOR 28	Thomas	HAR 78
Joshua	D.C.16	Devrx.	DOR 55	William	HAR 47
Nathan	D.C.73	Draper	DOR 35	TREDWELL, James	HAR 56
Philamon	BCI 210	E.	D.C.72	TREEMAN (See also	
Sarah	BCI 487	Geo.	D.C.116	FREEMAN, TRU-	
Tames?	BAL 165	Jacab?	DOR 23	MAN)	
Thomas	BCI 405	Jacob	D.C.72	Edward (?)	CAL 50
Thos.	BCI 481	Jacob	DOR 22	Eleanor	D.C.57
William	BAL 10	Jacob	DOR 23	John	MON 143
TOXEN, William	D.C.3	Jacob	DOR 23	TREESCOTT, Alexander (?)	
TOY, Alexander	BAL 61	John (?)	DOR 23		FRE 99
George	CEC 186	John (?)	DOR 28	TREGO, Thomas	CEC 186
Isaac	BCI 179	John, Senor (?)	DOR 28	TREGROE, Margaret	
John	BCI 391	John, of Mathew	DOR 29		DOR 56
Joseph	BCI 176	Levi C. (?)	DOR 25	TREHARN, Sally, Wd.	
TRACEY, Alice	HAR 63	Lewis	CHA 194		WOR 214
Barbary	WAS 126	Mathew? (?)	DOR 29	TREHEARN, Teackle	
Edward	HAR 63	Mathias (?)	DOR 23		SOM 125
James	BAL 244	Mathu (?)	DOR 29	TREMBLE, John	BCI 176
John	WAS 125	Robert?	DOR 29	TRENCHARD, Geo. O.	
Nathan W.	ALL 31	Robert? (?)	DOR 32		KEN 114
Pearce	BAL 113	Robrt	DOR 29	TRENKLE, Jacob	FRE 142
Philip	D.C.137	Robrt (?)	DOR 32	TRENT, Anthoney	SAI 78
Sarah	WOR 184	Sarah (?)	DOR 29	TRESS, Francis	BAL 193
Susanna	D.C.184	Susanah	BCI 122	TREW, Bartus	KEN 91
TRACY, Ann	PRI 230	Thomas (?)	DOR 24	Thomas W.	KEN 91
Elizabeth	FRE 201	Vatchel (?)	DOR 29	TREWETT, Peter	WOR 164
James	BAL 88	William	BCI 52	Samuel	CLN 74
James	BCI 501	William H. (?)	DOR 30	TRICE, Abraham	DOR 52
James	PRI 228	TRAVERSE, Charles		Clement	CLN 113
John	BAL 84		D.C.10	Cyrus	CLN 109
John	BCI 447	Charles	D.C.33	Ezekiel	CLN 109
John	FRE 73	Jabez	SOM 130	James B.	D.C.26
Jonathan (?)	BAL 14	James B.	DOR 45	Nancy	DOR 57
Joshua	BAL 87	John	D.C.23	William	DOR 51
Nicholas	BAL 208	Levin	DOR 58	TRICH, Henry	WAS 125
Peter	FRE 129	Nicholas	D.C.48	Jacob	WAS 126
William	BAL 155	Priscilla	SOM 114	TRICHET, Mary	BCI 136
Zachariah	BAL 87	Thos.	CAL 44	TRICK, William	WAS 107
TRADE, Littleton A.		Wm.	MON 141	TRICKELL, Frederick	
	WOR 156	TRAVIS, Boyl	FRE 85		WAS 112
TRADER, Henry	SOM 111	Jane	BCI 5	TRIDLE, Jacob	WAS 102
Joshua	WOR 203	John	HAR 39	Mary	D.C.184
Littleton A. (?)	WOR 156	Mary	BCI 30	TRIGEE, Jobe	DOR 19
Purnell	SOM 104	TRAVRS (See also		TRIGER, Arthur	DOR 19
Tecle A.	WOR 158	TRAVERS),		James	DOR 12
TRAGER, Sarah	HAR 23	Ann	DOR 30	Jobe (?)	DOR 19
William	HAR 19	Charles	DOR 28	Levin	DOR 21
TRAGO, John	HAR 20	John	DOR 23	Sally	DOR 22
TRAHEARN, Saml.		John	DOR 28	Thomas	DOR 19
(of Obediah)	WOR 170	John, Senor	DOR 28	Zachariah	DOR 11
TRAIL, Ashford	MON 160	Levi C.	DOR 25	TRIGERE, William	DOR 19
Edwd.	MON 131	Mathew?	DOR 29		

TUCKER (continued),		TUNNECLIFF, William		TURNER (continued),	
Richard	QUE 34		PRI 191A	John	D.C.98
Richd.	D.C.134	TUNNEY, Sarah	WAS 119	John	D.C.138
Rodney	WAS 65	TURBITT, Nicholas	FRE 98	John	HAR 63
Samuel	D.C.43	TURBUTT, Greenbury		John	KEN 109
Susan	QUE 47		TAL 9	John	KEN 119
Thomas	BAL 113	Samuel	TAL 38	John	PRI 182
Thomas	SAI 78	TURELL, Martin	BCI 459	John	SOM 114
Thos.	D.C.213	TURFLER, Joseph	BAL 53	John, ju.	KEN 119
William	ANN 269	TURILLEE, Phillip (?)		John L.	PRI 212
William	ANN 279		KEN 109	Jonathan	CHA 214
William	BCI 62	TURILLER, Phillip	KEN 109	Jos. R.	QUE 18
William	FRE 127	TURLEY, Simon	D.C.164	Joseph	CHA 217
William	HAR 24	TURNBAUGH, Jacob		Joseph	KEN 106A
William	MON 155		WAS 88	Joseph	KEN 121
William A.	BCI 90	Tetrick	BAL 99	Joseph	TAL 48
Wm.	CAL 48	TURNBOLD, Jabe	DOR 36	Joseph	TAL 52
Wm.	MON 136	Jobe?	DOR 36	Joseph, Jnr.	BCI 301
Zachariah	ANN 305	TURNBULL, --- (Mr.)		Joseph A.	PRI 212
Zachariah	ANN 305		BAL 243	Joshua	BCI 156
TUCKWORTH, Cathn.		John	BCI 535	Josiah	SAI 92
	BCI 193	Robt.	D.C.85	Kitty	CHA 227
TUDER, Joshua	BAL 120	Susan	D.C.79	Margaret	BCI 5
TUEL, Erasmus O. (?)		Wm.	MON 173	Margaret	BCI 112
	FRE 94	TURNEE, Ebinezer (?)		Mary	CHA 213
TUELL, James	D.C.117		KEN 109	Michael	BAL 183
Matthw.	D.C.117	John (?)	KEN 109	Nancy	CLN 111
TUFF, Synexoson	QUE 15	Rebeccah (?)	KEN 100	Nathan	BCI 36
TUGER, Zachariah (?)		William (?)	PRI 195	Oswald	D.C.114
	DOR 11	TURNER, --- (Mrs.)		Patk.	D.C.165
TUISTY, Stephen	KEN 106A		D.C.38	Pattey	BCI 533
TULEY, James	FRE 212	Abner	TAL 4	Rachael	D.C.192
TULL, Ananias	WOR 193	Abraham	PRI 195	Rachel	CLN 105
Benjn.	WOR 156	Alexander	D.C.9	Randolph	CHA 221
Betsy	SOM 153	Alexr.	BCI 315	Reason	PRI 202
Betsy (of Levin)	SOM 157	Amilka	CLN 96	Rebeccah	KEN 100
Edward	BCI 27	Andrew	HAR 60	Rebeccah	KEN 106A
Elsey	DOR 62	Asa	SOM 135	Richard	CAL 65
Jacob	SOM 123	Caleb	BCI 318	Richard	FRE 144
James	SOM 155	Charles	CHA 205	Richard	PRI 186
John	SOM 125	Charles	SAI 88	Richard	PRI 195
Joseph	WOR 159	Clement	CLN 106	Robert	BAL 107
Joshua	SOM 147	Daniel	HAR 44	Samuel	CAL 46
Levi	CLN 109	Didoe	TAL 9	Samuel	CHA 205
Levin	CLN 115	Ebinezer	KEN 109	Samuel	CHA 216
Levin	WOR 157	Edmond H.	WAS 79	Samuel	HAR 63
Levin	WOR 194	Edward	CLN 99	Samul	D.C.51
Levin (of Jacob)	SOM 124	Edward	CHA 227	Sarah	CAL 65
Nancy	SOM 149	Edward	QUE 27	Shadrach	PRI 182
Nicholas	SOM 133	Elenor	CAL 60	Thomas	ANN 255
Sally, Wd.	WOR 214	Ely	FRE 70	Thomas	CAL 62
Samuel	CAL 64	Ely	HAR 60	Thomas	CLN 111
Samuel	SOM 127	Garrettson	CLN 108	Thomas	CHA 204
Samuel	SOM 142A	Geo.	D.C.116	Thomas	HAR 5
Sarah	SOM 127	Geo. W.	KEN 124	Thomas W.	ANN 331
Soloman	WOR 164	George	CEC 147	Thos.	CAL 45
Stoughton	DOR 10	George	DOR 62	Thos.	D.C.36
Susan	WOR 160	George	SOM 150	Thos., Junr.	HAR 63
Thomas	DOR 60	George C.	CEC 186	Walter	WOR 156
Thomas	SOM 151	Henry	DOR 10	William	BAL 183
Wheatley	DOR 61	Henry	SAI 95	William	BCI 74
William	SOM 152	Henry	WOR 195	William	BCI 307
William	WOR 195	Isaac	FRE 95	William	CAL 63
William (of Benjn.)		Isaac	KEN 106A	William	CLN 74
	WOR 164	Jackson	WOR 210	William	CHA 228
TULLEY, Milley	SOM 106	Jacob	BCI 302	William	D.C.27
TULLY, Saml.	FRE 225	James	BAL 100	William	D.C.43
Stephen	SOM 105	James	BCI 295	William	HAR 8
TUMBLESON, Bennett		James	CLN 76	William	MON 155
	TAL 13	James	CHA 224	William	PRI 195
William	TAL 13	Jesse	SAI 88	William	SAI 96
TUMBLIN, John	CEC 128	Jessee	CLN 88	Wm.	BCI 535
TUMLINSON, Henry	MON 165	John	BCI 203	Wm.	KEN 121
TUNIS, Edward	DOR 13	John	CEC 167	TURNIER, Richard	CAL 60
Samuel	ANN 302	John	CHA 213	TURPIN, Elijah	WOR 181
		John	D.C.89	Hannah	SOM 145

		WAGNER, Catherine	D.C. 47	WALKER (continued),			
		Jacob	BCI 493	Chas.	BCI 321		
		Jacob	FRE 73	Chistepher	BAL 99		
		Phillip	BAL 41	Christianna	KEN 103		
		WAGONER, Christian		Cyrus	FRE 158		
			FRE 190	Daniel	BAL 99		
--- W ---		John	FRE 203	Daniel	BAL 165		
		Michael	FRE 193	Daniel	CHA 228		
WABLE, John	ALL 7	Michael	FRE 202	Daniel, Jr.	TAL 36		
WACHTER, George	FRE 116	WAILES, Dorothy	D.C. 114	David	D.C. 63		
Michael	FRE 116	William	SOM 117	David	D.C. 214		
Philip	FRE 115	WAIN, John	BCI 34	Dolly	KEN 103		
Samuel	FRE 114	WAINRIGHT, Bridgett		Dorney	BCI 500		
WACKTER, George	FRE 134		SOM 106	Edith	BCI 484		
WAD, Sarah	ANN 277	Cannon	SOM 116	Edward	FRE 71		
WADDELL, George	BCI 257	Hampleton	SOM 116	Eleanor	SOM 113		
Joseph	CLN 85A	James	TAL 11	Elender	SAI 89		
Thomas	CLN 106	John	SOM 115	Elijah	ANN 334		
William	CLN 108	Levin	SOM 114	Elisha	MON 171		
WADDLE, George	ALL 17	Nancy	SOM 114	Elizabeth	CEC 188		
George	FRE 162	Stephen	SOM 116	Elizabeth	D.C. 31		
Isaac	FRE 162	WAINWRIGHT, Joseph		Elizabeth	HAR 45		
James	FRE 163		SAI 94	Elizabeth	TAL 37		
John	BAL 114	Richard	SAI 92	Elizabeth	WAS 58		
WADE, Frances	BAL 92	Wm.	D.C. 46	Ellen	BCI 228		
Horatio	BAL 192	WAISS, Samuel	BAL 99	Fielder	D.C. 124		
Isabella	WAS 99	WAISTCOAT, James		Francis	BCI 83		
John	ANN 356		SOM 111	Francis	MON 142		
John	WAS 64	WAIT, Charles B. F.		Francis	PRI 204		
Larkin	BAL 59		WAS 147	Geo.	MON 141		
Lewis	WAS 83	Christian	BCI 71	George	BAL 158		
Manuel	ANN 317	WAITE, George W.	BAL 221	George	D.C. 16		
Nelson	BAL 241	James P.	BCI 131	George	HAR 19		
Robert	CHA 196	WAITES, William W.		George B.	FRE 85		
Robt. P.	MON 129		BCI 131	Hannah	FRE 127		
Sarah	CEC 187	WAITS, Joseph	BCI 82	Harry	KEN 104		
Zephaniah	D.C. 195	WAKELAND, Rebecca		Henny	QUE 32		
Zephaniah	D.C. 197		HAR 45	Henry	BCI 464		
WADLOW, Samuel	BAL 81	WALCOTT, Rob	BCI 494	Henry	FRE 104		
Solomon	HAR 79	WALDER, Henry	WAS 120	Isaac	ANN 311		
WADMAN, John	CLN 96	WALEA, Wm.	WOR 169	Isaac	MON 155		
Thomas, Sr.	CLN 92	WALER, James	BAL 131	J.	BCI 336		
Thomas, Jr.	CLN 86	WALERS, Samuel	DOR 8	Jacob	BCI 77		
William	CLN 97	WALES, Betsy, Wd.		James	D.C. 65		
WADSWORTH, Lydia			WOR 215	James	D.C 198		
	HAR 58	John	MON 131	James	D.C. 214		
Saml.	FRE 125	Jonathan	TAL 22	James	MON 131		
Thomas	BAL 90	Joseph	BCI 102	James	SAI 74		
William	BAL 203	Levin	BCI 66	Jerry	ANN 303		
William	FRE 110	Mable	TAL 26	Jessey	BAL 54		
WAELAND, Michael	BCI 72	Millburn	TAL 25	Jettson (?)	PRI 232		
WAESCHE, Frederick		WALFORD, John	BCI 17	John	BAL 55		
	BCI 266	WALINGSFORD, Joseph		John	BCI 482		
WAGERS, James	FRE 213		PRI 235	John	CLN 109		
WAGGAMAN, Henry P.		WALKE, Stephen	FRE 83	John	FRE 104		
	DOR 53	WALKEE, Benjamin (?)		John	FRE 213		
Sarah	DOR 13		PRI 226	John	HAR 25		
WAGGOMON, David		Benjamin	PRI 232	John	KEN 94		
	WAS 111	Jettson	PRI 232	John	MON 166		
WAGGONER, Christian		John (?)	PRI 240	John	PRI 192		
	FRE 219	Thomas	PRI 227	John	PRI 240		
Christopher, S.	ALL 34	Zackariah	PRI 236	John	QUE 45		
Christopher, J.	ALL 34	WALKER, --- (Mrs.)		John (Senr.)	SOM 111		
David	FRE 227		BCI 445	John, Junr.	FRE 104		
George	BCI 14	--- (Mrs.)	BCI 451	John B.	SAI 75		
Jacob	BAL 140	Ann	CEC 129	John D.	FRE 101		
John	CEC 149	Ann	CEC 188	John G.	BAL 2		
John	FRE 117	Arther	ANN 264	Joseph	BCI 507		
John	FRE 219	Benjamin (?)	PRI 232	Joseph	D.C. 73		
Mary	FRE 219	Benjamin	PRI 226	Levin	D.C. 185		
Upton	FRE 220	Benjn.	BCI 300	Marey E.	BCI 387		
Valentine	BCI 407	Betsey	D.C. 24	Margaret	BCI 133		
WAGGONIER, John	WAS 93	Charles	BAL 14	Mark	SOM 107		
John, Sen.	WAS 72	Charles	D.C. 83	Mary	BCI 502		
John, Jun.	WAS 72	Charlotte	BCI 322	Mary	FRE 183		
WAGLER, F. A.	D.C. 16	Charlotty	BAL 173	Mary	SOM 104		

WALKER (continued),			WALLACE (continued),			WALLING (continued),		
Mary Anne	ANN	373	James	HAR	47	Joseph, Junr.	FRE	100
Mathew	BCI	519	James	MON	166	WALLINGSFORD, Deborah		
Merry	CEC	148	John	DOR	31		PRI	192
Nancy	D.C.	176	John	MON	166	Joseph	PRI	194
Nancy	DOR	63	Joseph	BCI	438	Joseph	PRI	197
Nathan	PRI	182	Joseph	DOR	31	WALLIS, --- (?)	BCI	407
Rachael	PRI	186	Joseph M.	BCI	514	--- (Major?)	BCI	148
Sader T.	BCI	402	Juda	ANN	308	--- (Widow)	BCI	392
Saml. P.	BCI	526	Landswell?	DOR	7	Elizabeth	BCI	160
Samuel	BCI	186	Laudswell	DOR	7	Henry	KEN	120
Samuel D.	BCI	449	Mary	ANN	273	James	KEN	119
Simon	TAL	51	Mary	BCI	62	James	PRI	192
Spenser	SOM	108	Mathew	ALL	26	John	KEN	117
Tabitha	MON	155	Mathew	DOR	30	John, Jun.	BCI	386
Thomas (?)	PRI	227	Mathu	DOR	30	Major	BCI	148
Thomas	CLN	81	Nathan	ANN	302	Randall	HAR	75
Thomas	DOR	64	Nicy	DOR	45	S.	BCI	406
Thomas	FRE	79A	Rachel	SOM	152	Washington	PRI	192
Thomas	SOM	107	Richard	CHA	223	William	SOM	130
Thomas B.	HAR	59	Richard	D.C.	187	WALLOW, Judy	BAL	181
Thos. C.	BAL	3	Richard	SAI	65	WALLS, Benjamin	BCI	254
Vacheal	ANN	372	Robert	CEC	187	Daniel	CEC	149
Wesley	D.C.	63	Robert	DOR	60	George	TAL	11
William	BAL	47	Robert	MON	158A	Hester (?)	BCI	229
William	BCI	300	Saml.	D.C.	118	Jo W.	QUE	5
William	BCI	303	Sarah	CHA	204	John	BAL	183
William	CLN	108	Solomon	ANN	271	Saml.	QUE	15
William	CEC	187	Solomon	BCI	183	Susanna (?)	BAL	126
William	FRE	147	Thomas	BAL	218	Thomas (?)	BAL	226
William	FRE	171	Thomas	D.C.	41	Wm.	QUE	15
William	TAL	36	Thomas	PRI	228	WALLY, David	QUE	30
Wm.	MON	163	Uriah	BCI	83	Isaac	TAL	39
Zach.	D.C.	71	Valentine	ANN	303	Jerimiah?	TAL	50
Zach	D.C.	136	Will.	D.C.	88	Jerimioh	TAL	50
Zachariah	PRI	204	William	DOR	44	Nancy	QUE	28
Zackariah (?)	PRI	236	William	HAR	74	Willial	BCI	144
WALKINS, Caway (?)			William	KEN	109	WALMORE, George (?)		
	BCI	509	Wm. M.	BCI	515		BAL	94
John B.	PRI	206	WALLACK, Richd.	D.C.	95	WALMSLEY, Ann	CEC	129
WALL, Abraham	BAL	246	WALLAN, Mathu (?)	DOR	30	John	BCI	96
Elizh.	D.C.	128	WALLASE, Philip	BCI	272	Margaret	CEC	148
Geo.	BCI	394	WALLECE, Thomas	DOR	30	William	CEC	129
George	PRI	217	WALLEMS, A. W.	BCI	354	William	CEC	168
George-Negro	HAR	49	WALLER, Bazil	BCI	219	WALNUT, Hickman	ANN	273
Jacob	BCI	394	Elija	D.C.	179	WALSH, Hellena	BAL	47
James	BCI	55	Ephraim	WOR	204	Henry	BAL	67
Jane	PRI	217	Geo. B.	SOM	125	Henry	BCI	380
Jesse H. D.	PRI	183	George	SOM	111	Henry G.	BAL	65
John E.	BCI	229	Henry (?)	BCI	520	John	BCI	405
John T.	PRI	213	Henry	WAS	126	Mary	BAL	48
Levin	DOR	26	Jack (f.n.)	SOM	119	Peter	BCI	390
Margaret	DOR	5	Jacob	BCI	398	Resin H.	BAL	67
Michael	BCI	393	James (?)	BAL	131	Robert	BCI	267
Micheal?	DOR	23	James	BAL	115	WALSTON, Boaz, Esqr.		
Mickeal	DOR	23	James L.	SOM	101A		WOR	202
Patrick-Negro	HAR	80	John	BAL	24	Fanny	SOM	115
Susan	PRI	183	Joseph	BCI	491	George	SOM	153
Theodore	PRI	217	Nelson	SOM	140	Nemiah	SOM	152
Thos.	BCI	338	Rebecca	BCI	32	Peggy	SOM	152
William	BAL	43	Richard	SOM	101A	Sally, wd.	WOR	202
William	DOR	55	Sarah	BAL	19	Thomas	SOM	125
WALLACE, Brister	SOM	130	William, Senr.	SOM	122	WALSTROM, Peter	BCI	129
Caesar	BAL	128	William, Jun.	SOM	126	WALTEN, James	BCI	410
Cato	BAL	26	William L.	SOM	123	WALTER, Asa	SOM	115
Charles	SOM	129	Wm.	BCI	219	Charles	BCI	459
Deborah	MON	155	WALLERS, John	HAR	7	Daniel	SOM	114
Dolphin-Negro	HAR	79	WALLEY, Richard	CLN	97	Frances D.	SOM	108
Edward	ANN	301	WALLICE, James	WAS	86	George (of Benjamin)		
Edward	BCI	274	John	WAS	140		SOM	101A
Hetty	BCI	445	WALLICK, Ann	MON	140	George D.	SOM	115
James	ALL	5A	George	WAS	86	George W.	SOM	115
James	BCI	428	Mathias	WAS	101	Henry	BCI	520
James	CEC	149	WALLING, James	WAS	106	Jacob	BAL	160
James	DOR	30	John	FRE	99	Jacob	FRE	198
James	HAR	30	Joseph, Senr.	FRE	100	James	SOM	107

WALTER (continued)		WANTON, Phillp	D.C.198	WARD (continued),	
Jesse	SOM 103	WANWRIGHT, George		Matilda	D.C.88
John	BAL 160		WOR 206	Michael	D.C.86
John	BAL 209	WAPLE, Gerard	CHA 212	Patrick	ANN 381
Joseph	SOM 103	WARALL, J. C.	BCI 355	Patrick	BCI 151
Levin	SOM 109	WARBERTON, Thomas		Perry	CEC 149
Michael	FRE 191		CEC 149	Philip	KEN 93
Peter	FRE 175	WARD, Alex. C.	BCI 383	Philip	KEN 94
Robert	SOM 113	Amos	MON 173	Rachel	BCI 313
Walter	ALL 36	Asa	MON 177	Richard	ANN 281
William	SOM 114	Benjamin	HAR 19	Richard	HAR 73
WALTERS, Alexander		Betsey	D.C.20	Richard	HAR 75
	QUE 47	Ceasar	ANN 278	Richard	KEN 94
Benjamin	QUE 47	Cephas	ANN 254	Robert	ANN 281
Henry	BCI 473	Charles	BCI 525	Robert	BAL 43
Jacob-free	CAL 59	Charles	CEC 187	Robert	D.C.5
James (?)	MON 140	Eber.	D.C.118	Sally	SOM 126
James	ALL 38	Edwd.	BCI 524	Saml. & Co.	D.C.177
John	FRE 144	Eleanor	CHA 191	Samuel	ANN 281
Joseph T.	BAL 4	Eleanor	SOM 126	Samuel	ANN 331
Levin	QUE 2A	Elizabeth	BCI 282	Samuel	BAL 43
Nancy	MON 136	Elizabeth	BCI 311	Samuel	CEC 148
Philip	BCI 351	Ezekiel	SOM 144	Samuel	CHA 212
Samuel	ANN 353	Ezra	MON 174	Samuel	SOM 150
WALTHAM, Charlton		Francis	KEN 117	Sarah (?)	ANN 277
	HAR 7	George	KEN 119	Sarah	BCI 260
Charlton	HAR 8	George	MON 160	Sarah	WOR 161
Charlton	HAR 8	Hannah	SOM 150	Sophia	CHA 211
Charthom	BAL 114	Hariet	WOR 154	Sophia	SOM 150
John	BCI 367	Henry	ANN 315	Sotha	DOR 29
William	BCI 95	Henry	SOM 144	Stephen	SOM 125
WALTMAN, Henry	FRE 149	Henry	TAL 11	Stephen	SOM 146
Michael	FRE 157	Hezikiah	WOR 156	Stephen B.	PRI 218
WALTOM, Stephen	WOR 164	Ignatious P.	FRE 72	Thomas	BAL 7
WALTON, Cordelia-		Isaac	ALL 34	Thomas	SOM 142A
Negro	HAR 49	Isaac	SOM 146	Ulisses	D.C.51
Mary	BCI 30	Jacob	SOM 146	Walter	D.C.187
Nath.	BCI 213	Jacob	WAS 150	William	ALL 15
Thomas	BAL 233	James	ALL 16	William	ANN 281
Violetter	ANN 301	James	BCI 490	William	ANN 292
Wm.	WOR 164	James	HAR 77	William	BAL 44
WALTUM, Henry	SOM 124	James	SOM 126	William	BAL 208
WALTUS, James	MON 140	James	WAS 145	William	BCI 66
WALTZ, John	ALL 4	James W.	MON 155	William	BCI 429
Martin	FRE 86	Joanna E.	CHA 211	William	CEC 129
Rhinhart	FRE 229	John	ANN 261	William	CEC 149
Solomon	FRE 220	John	BAL 22	William	D.C.94
WALTZLER, Henry	FRE 224	John	BAL 43	William	SOM 146
WAMELING, Mary	BCI 307	John	BAL 53	William H.	BCI 36
WAMPLER, David	FRE 200	John	CHA 196	William H.	BCI 123
Frederick	FRE 154	John	D.C.14	WARDEN, William	HAR 76
John	FRE 186	John	D.C.187	WARDENBROOK, Samuel	
John L.	FRE 187	John	PRI 231		ANN 358
Leonard	BCI 502	John	SOM 149	WARDER, John	CHA 190
Ludwig	FRE 186	John, Senr.	BAL 43	Walter	CHA 194
Mary	FRE 209	John-col.	CEC 129	WARDIN, Ann	D.C.86
Philip E.	FRE 200	John-son John	CEC 129	WARDLE, William	BCI 440
WAMPS, Francis	ALL 36	John, of Robt.	ANN 281	WARE, Abraham	HAR 63
WAMSLEY, Isaac T.		John D.	CAL 60	Ann	D.C.74
	BAL 179	John P.	CEC 129	G.	BCI 388
John	BCI 134	John W.	FRE 71	Hugh	SOM 136
WANDERLY, Joseph		John W.	PRI 222	Isaiah	D.C.82
	FRE 144	Jonathn.	D.C.195	John	CHA 208
WANDLE, Mary	FRE 98	Jonathn.	D.C.197	Joyce	D.C.208
WANE, Ralph	BCI 37	Joseph	ANN 263	Nicholas	CHA 191
WANG, Warren (?)	PRI 238	Joseph	BAL 43	Peter	BAL 231
WANN, Edward	BAL 37	Joseph	D.C.76	Thomas	BAL 24
Horatio	BAL 43	Joseph	HAR 37	WAREHAM, John	HAR 18
John	BAL 60	Joseph	SOM 151	John	HAR 20
John	HAR 40	Leah, Wd.	WOR 217	John	HAR 26
John, Junr.	HAR 47	Levi (?)	WOR 154	WAREHIME, George	BAL 145
WANNALL, Thos.	D.C.73	Levi	SOM 150	Henry	BAL 160
WANNER, Jacob	WAS 107	Levin	SOM 142A	WAREND, Mary	BCI 217
John	WAS 107	Mary	DOR 46	WARENFELS, Peter	FRE 154
WANTLING, Jesse	BAL 81	Mary	SOM 149	WARES, Mary	D.C.20
Thomas	BAL 83	Mary (of Levi)	SOM 150		

WARFIELD, Achsah	ANN 357	WARFIELD (continued),		WARNER (continued),	
Alexander	FRE 80	William-[his] Slaves		William	BCI 209
Alexander	FRE 209	(See William &		William	CLN 81
Allen	ANN 296	George WARFIELDS		William	FRE 177
Allen	ANN 363	Slaves)	ANN 363	William W.	HAR 18
Amos	ANN 325	William & George-		WARNICK, John	ALL 2
Azel	ANN 368	[their] Slaves	ANN 363	Joseph	ALL 13
Bani	ANN 360	William W.	ANN 360	Joseph, Sen.	ALL 13
Basil	ANN 373	Wm. E.	DOR 55	Samuel	ALL 3
Benjamin	ANN 329	Zachariah	MON 156	William	ALL 12
Caleb	ANN 337	Zadock	FRE 218	WARNKEN, Henry	BCI 20
Calib	ANN 372	WARGMAN, Charles	BCI 270	WARREL, Chas.	BAL 5
Catharine	FRE 125	WARHAM, Abraham	KEN 89	WARREN, Ananias	WOR 190
Catherine	ANN 365	George	FRE 188	Ebenezer	WOR 185
Charles	BCI 382	Valentine	QUE 32	G. Washington	BCI 271
Charles D.	ANN 357	WARING, Basil	D.C.3	Isaac	WOR 184
Charles G.	ANN 333	Elizabeth M. (Mrs.)		John	CLN 110
Chars.	BCI 336		PRI 219	John	KEN 109
Daniel	ANN 367	Erasmus G.	PRI 203	Joseph	D.C.17
Deborah	ANN 291	Henry	D.C.56	Lucy	D.C.78
E.	BCI 376	Henry	PRI 202	Lydiea	WOR 186
Edward	ANN 362	Henry (Col.)	PRI 219	Nahum	D.C.112
Edwd.	MON 141	Macus S.	PRI 212	Pearcy	WOR 185
Elie G.	ANN 359	Richard M.	PRI 212	Robert	MON 155
Elizabeth	ANN 325	Susan	PRI 216	Saml.	KEN 116
Elizabeth	ANN 326	WARMAGIM, Jeremh.		Sarah P.	WOR 187
Elizabeth	WAS 64		BCI 171	Tamor	D.C.103
Ephram	ANN 362	WARMAN, Dennis	MON 138	Thomas	CLN 91
G. F. (Mrs.)	BAL 61	WARMSLEY, John	BAL 11	WARRENSFORD, Amelia	
George	ANN 358	John	KEN 120		D.C.95
George-[his] Slaves		Rachel	KEN 115	John	D.C.138
(See William &		WARNER, Aaron	HAR 77	WARRICK, Gay	BCI 117
George WARFIELDS		Abraham	BCI 26	Levin	SOM 156
Slaves)	ANN 363	Abraham	BCI 53	WARRING, Ann	SAI 90
George F.	BCI 440	Abraham	FRE 203	Edward G.	PRI 193
Greenberry	ANN 363	Andw. E.	BCI 249	Frank	PRI 182
Greenbury	ANN 371	Ann	KEN 119	Henry	MON 171
Gustavus	ANN 366	Anness	TAL 11	John	PRI 194
Henry R.	FRE 229	Asa	HAR 77	Marsham	PRI 193
Isaac	HAR 31	Aseph	HAR 76	Peter	SAI 97
James	ANN 291	Charlotte	BCI 224	Richard M.	PRI 194
John	ANN 325	Cuthbert	BCI 187	WARRINGS, --- (Miss)	
John	ANN 341	Elizabeth	WAS 116		PRI 195
John	DOR 15	Geo.	FRE 130	WARRINGTON, Ann	WOR 163
John H.	ANN 374	George	BCI 492	Richard W.	WOR 189
Joshua	ANN 364	George	FRE 200	WARROLL, Margt.	BCI 213
Lancelot	ANN 332	George	FRE 204	WARRUM, Isaac	BAL 207
Lloyd	ANN 371	George	FRE 229	WARTEN, Richard, Ovsr.	
Lot	TAL 10	George	WAS 66		TAL 37
Mary	ANN 342	George, Jr.	FRE 203	WARTERS, Bess	PRI 185
Mary	DOR 11	Henry	BCI 488	Hannah	ANN 376
Mashack	ANN 339	Jacob	BAL 185	Isaac	PRI 187
Nichls. D.	MON 134	Jacob	FRE 75	Jacob F.	PRI 187
Nicholas	WAS 60	Jane	BCI 198	Jacob H.	PRI 184
Peregrine	D.C.61	John	CLN 89	James	ANN 358
Peter	ANN 354	John	D.C.147	Kate	PRI 187
Philemond	ANN 365	John	FRE 82	Mary	PRI 185
Philemond D.	ANN 369	John	FRE 169	Mary	PRI 186
Philip	MON 156	John	FRE 209	Plummer	PRI 186
Richard	ANN 340	John	FRE 228A	Wilson	ANN 261
Richard	ANN 383	Jonathan	HAR 38	WARTHAN, Francis	FRE 78
Richard, of Jno.	ANN 340	Joseph	BCI 16	John	FRE 78
Robert	ANN 363	Julia	BCI 230	WARTHEN, Nicholas	FRE 122
Samuel	ANN 339	Letilia?	QUE 4	Thos.	FRE 135
Seth, Senr.	ANN 357	Margaret	BCI 94	WARTHIN, Thomas	D.C.112
Seth, Junr.	ANN 359	Marvel	CEC 187	Zephh.	D.C.112
Surratt D.	FRE 222	Melcher	BAL 164	WARTHINGTON, Nicholas	
Thomas	ANN 335	Michl.	BCI 488		ANN 372
Thomas	ANN 364	Nicholas	D.C.42	WARTON, Chs. H. W.	
Thomas W.	ANN 338	Overton C.	PRI [200]		MON 160
Thos.	D.C.132	Phillip	FRE 181	WARWICK, Ben	QUE 15
Tomas	FRE 222	Richard	CLN 85A	Dianna	BAL 246
Warner W.	ANN 365	Robert, Ovsr.	TAL 6	Henry	QUE 13
William	ANN 389	Saml.	D.C.162	Jonah	SOM 123
		Silas	HAR 77	Josiah	SOM 123
		Thomas	BCI 249	William R.	SOM 140

INDEX TO THE 1820 CENSUS OF MARYLAND AND WASHINGTON, D.C.

WASHBURD, Abraham		WATERS (continued),		WATKINS, Abel	HAR 56
	BCI 118	John	D.C.18	Allen	D.C.29
WASHBURN, James	SOM 138	John	D.C.57	Anne	ANN 262
Levi	D.C.11	John	SOM 112	Ascy T.	BCI 184
Reuben	SOM 134	Jonathan	ANN 392	Cassandra	MON 139
WASHINGN. TAVERN		Joseph	ANN 328	Charles	FRE 212
	D.C.163	Joseph	CHA 222	Daniel	ANN 261
WASHINGTON, Bailey		Joseph	WOR 174	Danl.	MON 139
	D.C.15	Joseph G.	BCI 370	Denton	FRE 79
Bershaba	WAS 145	Joshua	BCI 72	Elizabeth	CLN 113
Chs.	BCI 220	Joshua	SOM 153	Fyattee	ANN 320
George	PRI 219	Loyd	CHA 202	Gassaway	ANN 370
George C.	MON 165	Mary	BCI 530	Gaway	BCI 509
Lawrence	BCI 125	Mises-free	CAL 61	Henry	KEN 122
Nathaniel	SAI 86A	Nace-(C.W.?)	BCI 281	Horatio	WAS 108
Peter	D.C.118	Nancy	MON 173	Jane	D.C.101
R. P.	D.C.117	Nathan	PRI 181	Jeremh.	MON 172
Sarah	D.C.184	Nathl. M.	MON 178A	Jerm., Senr.	MON 141
Wm.	D.C.163	Nelly	DOR 56	John	ANN 275
WASHINGTON COTTON		Nichls.	MON 144	John	BAL 239
FACTORY	BAL 173	Peter	BCI 369	John	D.C.120
WASON, Levi	ANN 259	Peter	SOM 151	John	HAR 56
WASSAL, --- (Mrs.)		Peter	SOM 152	John, Junr.	HAR 56
	BCI 388	Plummer	MON 156	John B. (?)	PRI 206
WATCHMAN, John	BCI 311	Rachael	PRI 186	Jonathan	BAL 63
WATER, Joseph	FRE 218	Richad.	BCI 342	Jos.	MON 141
WATERMAN, Waren	BCI 147	Richard.	BCI 351	Joseph	ANN 253
WATERS, --- (?)	BCI 390	Richard	MON 156	Juda	D.C.189
--- (Widaw)	BCI 408	Richard	PRI 217	Leonard	MON 130
Aaron	BAL 107	Richard E.	SOM 152	Monson	CEC 187
Abraham	DOR 61	Richd.	BCI 171	Nichls. B.	MON 174
Acquillo	ANN 346	Richd. R.	MON 176	Nicholas	ANN 320
Adam	SOM 131	Robert	CLN 81	Nicholas	ANN 383
Adamson	MON 176	Samuel (?)	DOR 8	Nicholas	MON 139
Alexander	BAL 39	Samuel	PRI 181	Nicholas, of Thos.	
Alexander, Junr.		Samuel	SOM 137		ANN 289
	BAL 39	Seth	WAS 136	Nicholas G.	PRI 208
Alphred	MON 156	Silvia	CHA 222	Nicholas J. (I.?)	ANN 389
Aixd.	CAL 49	Somersett	MON 173	Rezin	ANN 085
Azel	MON 137	Stephen	BCI 449	Richard	ANN 253
Basil	MON 174	Susana	SOM 138	Richard G.	ANN 272
Benjamin	MON 156	Thede.	BCI 350	Richd.	MON 177
Benjn.	D.C.182	Thomas	ANN 332	Samuel C.	ANN 260
Charles	ANN 312	Thomas	MON 156	Thomas	ANN 338
Charles	DOR 11	Thomas G.	D.C.49	Thomas	CLN 112
Cibly	ANN 348	Thomas J. (I.?)	PRI 181	Thos.	MON 132
Deborah	D.C.21	Thos.	BCI 227	Thos.	MON 141
Dick	SOM 152	Thos.	MON 137	Thos.	MON 167
Dorothea	D.C.179	Will	SOM 152	William	ANN 261
Edward	ANN 346	William	ANN 330	William	BCI 465
Edward	BCI 160	William	BAL 39	Zach	BCI 534
Edward M.	SOM 145	William	BAL 229	WATLER, --- (?)	BCI 403
Elkanah	CHA 222	William	D.C.15	WATS, Barton	WAS 137
Fanny	BCI 258	William, Jun.	SOM 145	Nathan	BAL 28
Francis H.	SOM 151	William H.	SOM 151	WATSON, Abraham	WAS 135
Freborn G.	BCI 464	Zachr.	MON 174	Abram	CEC 168
Hagar	BCI 444	Zepheniah	CHA 223	Alex.	D.C.13
Hendley C.	CHA 224	Zephius	ANN 346	Benjamin	PRI 215
Henry B.	FRE 74	WATERSON, Jane	BCI 356	Benjamin S.	CAL 59
Henry G.	FRE 141	WATHAN, James	SAI 75	Benjn.	MON 142
Hezekiah	BCI 3	James H.	SAI 75	Charles	ANN 257
Horatio	FRE 98	WATHEN, Barton	CHA 200A	Charles	ANN 289
Howard	MON 178	Bennet	CHA 207	E.	BCI 396
Ignatius	MON 156	Daniel	CHA 222	Eason	DOR 43
Isaac	SOM 140	Francis	MON 172	Edward M. G.	FRE 69
Jacob	ANN 284	Gabl.	MON 134	Elizabeth	SAI 98
Jacob	BAL 4	Igns.	MON 142	Ezra (Capt.)	DOR 43
Jacob	BCI 532	John	CHA 207	Fielder	PRI 212
James	SOM 152	Joseph	CHA 204	George	ANN 286
James-ngro.	CEC 129	Martin	MON 133	Hezekiah, Sen.	PRI 213
Jas.	MON 174	Rebecka	CHA 206	Isaac	ANN 267
Jess	BCI 336	WATHIN, Leonard	MON 133	Isaac	CEC 168
Jim	PRI 181	WATKENS, Thomas	BCI 375	James	D.C.7
Job	D.C.17	Tobias	BCI 386	James	D.C.13
John	BCI 152	WATKIN, William	SAI 86A	James	D.C.111
John	BCI 501			James	HAR 59

255

WHITE (continued),		WHITE (continued),		WHITIM, William	CEC 129
John Campbell	BCI 252	Toby	HAR 11	WHITING, Carsille	D.C.182
John M.	SOM 138	Treacy	FRE 73	John	D.C.208
Johnathan	PRI 204	Ursula	MON 133	Unity	BCI 177
Jona	BCI 376	Walter, Sr.	FRE 70	WHITINGS, C.-farm	D.C.212
Jonathan	HAR 26	Walter, Jr.	FRE 70	WHITINGTON, James (of J.)	
Joseph	BAL 204	Walter D.	MON 142		SOM 151
Joseph	BCI 60	Walter K.	QUE 46	James (of Wm.)	SOM 146
Joseph	BCI 276	William	ALL 3	Sally	SOM 151
Joseph	D.C.42	William	ALL 4	Suthey	SOM 144
Joseph	SOM 110	William	BAL 236	WHITLE, Samuel	D.C.65
Joseph	WOR 216	William	BCI 120	WHITLER, Isaac	CHA 212
Joseph P.	BCI 15	William	BCI 320	WHITLEY, Lydia	CLN 81
Levi	CEC 187	William	TAL 10	WHITLICK, Sam.	CEC 129
Levi	QUE 48	William	WOR 169	WHITMAN, Jacob	WAS 77
Luke	WOR 197	William	WOR 210	WHITMER, Ann	WAS 111
Margaret	BCI 160	William, of Wm.	WOR 219	Benjamin, Jur.	FRE 173
Mary	ANN 372	William H.	PRI 222	Elizabeth	WAS 116
Mary	BAL 182	Wm. S.	WOR 169	George	FRE 169
Mary	BCI 19	WHITEACRE, Abel	CEC 187	John, Jun.	WAS 133
Mary	BCI 65	Jesse	CEC 187	WHITMON, George	FRE 150
Mary	D.C.148	WHITEFOOT, Thomas		WHITMORE, Benjamin (of G.)	
Mary	WOR 173		ANN 358		FRE 146
Milley	BCI 18	WHITEFORD, Ann	BAL 243	Benjamin of H. (A.?)	
Moses	ANN 303	Cunningham	HAR 70		FRE 146
Moses-f.c.p.	HAR 11	Daniel	HAR 74	Christian	FRE 145
Nancy	DOR 6	David	BCI 476	David	FRE 143
Nathan S.	MON 131	David, Senr.	BCI 477	Emmy	BCI 220
Nelson B. C.	SAI 96	Elizabeth	HAR 74	George	FRE 129
Orlando G.	ANN 363	Elizabeth	HAR 74	George	FRE 157
Osbourn	PRI 204	Hugh	HAR 74	George	PRI 229
Oswell	PRI 203	John	BAL 244	Henry	FRE 142
Otho	ANN 378	Michael	HAR 72	Henry, Jr.	FRE 160
Peter	SAI 55	Samuel	BAL 185	Jonas	FRE 146
Peter	SOM 126	Samuel	HAR 58	Nicholas	FRE 113
Peter	SOM 139	Thomas	BCI 76	WHITNEY, Daniel	BAL 209
Peter	WOR 210	William	HAR 75	Daniel	SOM 137
Phillip	WOR 196	WHITEHEAD, Edward		David	SOM 141
Priscilla	ANN 275		ANN 310	Elizh.	BCI 201
R.	BCI 373	Hezekiah	ANN 345	Henry P.	D.C.145
R.	BCI 406	John	ALL 28	Isaac	SOM 140
Resin	D.C.202	Lucy	ANN 332	Jared	D.C.33
Richard	ALL 6	Reason	ANN 345	Joseph G.	BCI 125
Richard	BAL 200	Richard	ANN 345	Margaret	SOM 140
Richd.	MON 167	Robert	ANN 378	Sarah	SOM 140
Robert	BCI 511	Samuel	ANN 345	Simon	BCI 451
Robert	D.C.23	WHITEHILL, Mary	FRE 214	WHITNY, Joseph	SOM 140
Robert	HAR 76	WHITEHOUSE, Mary	MON 166	WHITRIGHT, Philip	ANN 257
Rosanne	BCI 66	WHITELEATHER, Andrew		WHITSEL, George	CEC 148
Ruthy	ANN 345		BAL 154	WHITSON, David (?)	BCI 479
Saml. B.	MON 142	WHITELEY, Anthony		Joseph	HAR 38
Samuel	MON 155		CLN 111	WHITTEMORE, John	BCI 77
Samuel	MON 155	Barthula	CLN 75	WHITTEN, Nancy	FRE 97
Samuel	WAS 63	Byrng	CLN 112	WHITTENTON, Frank	
Shederick	FRE 77	Byrug?	CLN 112		BAL 118
Spencer	WOR 184	David	BCI 274	John	BCI 284
Stephen	BCI 102	Henry	CLN 99	WHITTER, Thomas	FRE 82
Stephen	BCI 159	William	CLN 109	WHITTINGTON, Benja.	
Stephen	BCI 319	William, Dr.	CLN 97		CAL 65
Stephen	WOR 158	WHITELOCK, Charles		Benjamin	CAL 61
Stephin	WOR 218		BCI 393	Benjamin	CAL 62
Thaddeus	MON 165	Charles	CEC 168	Betsy	BCI 293
Thomas (?)	DOR 60	Edward	CEC 168	Charles	ANN 269
Thomas	ALL 7	Elisha E.	SOM 137	Edward	CAL 58A
Thomas	ANN 391	James	SOM 139	Elizabeth	ANN 278
Thomas	BAL 36	John	CEC 168	Francis	ANN 268
Thomas	CEC 169	Moses	CEC 168	Henny	BCI 300
Thomas	CEC 187	Moses	CEC 188	Henry	CAL 52
Thomas	DOR 46	WHITELY, William	BAL 241	James	KEN 121
Thomas	PRI 226	WHITEMAN, George	BCI 485	John	CAL 63
Thomas	SOM 131	WHITEMORE, John	FRE 224	John	KEN 117
Thomas	SOM 154	WHITEN, Isaac	FRE 111	John	WOR 158
Thomas	WOR 202	Sarah	CHA 190	John A.	ANN 278
Thos.	BCI 523	WHITESIDE, James	MON 155	Joseph	ANN 290
Thos.	D.C.127	WHITHITE, Saml.	FRE 226	Matthias	SOM 111
Thos. C.	MON 166	WHITHNEY, Mary	WAS 116	Saml.	KEN 115

WHITTINGTON (continued),	WIGGINS (continued),	WILHAM (continued),
Samuel	ANN 269	Joseph	HAR 79	Wm.	BCI 219
Sarah	BCI 293	Sarah	D.C.103	WILHELM, George	BAL 162
Thomas	ANN 278	WIGHLEY, John	KEN 114	George	BCI 48
Thomas	CAL 64	WIGHT, Rezin	BCI 511	John	BAL 166
Thos., Dr.	QUE 7	Wm. J.	BCI 486	John	BCI 192
William	CAL 65	WIGHTT, C.	D.C.137	WILHIDE, Conrad	FRE 157
William	WOR 191	WIGLE, John	FRE 93	Frederick	FRE 158
William, Esqr.	WOR 219	WIKE, John	WAS 111	Frederick, Jr.	FRE 157
Wm.	WOR 170	WILAND, Nancy	ALL 9	Henry, of Fred.	FRE 160
WHITTLE, Jerrimiah	BAL 215	William	ALL 9	Henry of Jac.	FRE 163
John	FRE 129	WILBAR, Henry	D.C.200	Jacob	FRE 162
Nicholas	ANN 336	WILBURN, Benjn.	MON 136	Jacob, Jr.	FRE 162
Richd.	BCI 506	Resin	D.C.106	Jacob, of Fred.	FRE 163
Thos.	D.C.175	Robt.	D.C.134	John	FRE 158
WHOOLY, Geo.	BCI 494	William	MON 155	John, Jr.	FRE 158
WHOPPING, --- (Mr.)		Wm.	CAL 49	WILISON, John	WAS 63
(negro)	BAL 111	WILCOX, Chas. G.	D..C15	WILKERSON, Alexander	
WHORLY, Geo. (?)	BCI 494	Daniel	QUE 24		CHA 212
WHTTLE, Zachariah	PRI 197	Jacob	ANN 359	Danuel	BAL 10
WHY, John	BCI 513	John	ANN 368	Elizabeth (Miss)	CAL 50
Virlinda	ANN 377	John	D.C.209	Irving	WOR 193
WHYTE, Nancy	D.C.156	Joseph	CEC 148	James	SAI 80
WIANT, John	BAL 160	Mary	HAR 24	John B.	CHA 215
Peter	BCI 356	William	CEC 169	Nihey	WOR 193
WIATT, Edward	ALL 26	William	QUE 34	Nikey?	WOR 193
WICHARD, John	FRE 183	WILCOXEN, Jesse	D.C.133	Thomas	WAS 114
WICHELHAUSEN, J.		Thomas	PRI 183	Walter	CHA 213
	BCI 390	WILCOXON, Horatio	MON 131	Water	CHA 215
WICKEM, Joseph	FRE 215	Jesse	MON 174	WILKEY, Henry	BCI 450
WICKERSHAM, James		WILD, Henry	BCI 411	WILKINS, Betsey	KEN 119
	ANN 322	Lewis	BCI 24	Fanny	D.C.52
Mary Ann	BCI 75	WILDE, John	BCI 157	Henry	BAL 177
Susan	BCI 303	WILDER, Edward	SAI 95	Isaac	WOR 173
WICKERT, John	ALL 29	Rebecca	CHA 200A	James	QUE 31
WICKES, James	QUE 11	Sary	SAI 92	John	BAL 176
Joseph, Senr.	KEN 87	WILDERMAN, Elizabeth		John	SOM 145
Joseph, Jun.	KEN 91		BAL 176	John	WOR 172
Joseph 3d	KEN 85	WILDERS, Catherine	WAS 63	Jos.	BCI 351
Matthew	KEN 107	James	WAS 64	Mary	BCI 197
Samuel	KEN 87	WILDERSON, Charles		Mary	KEN 116
Samuel	KEN 107		BAL 14	Matthew	QUE 25
Simon	KEN 85	WILDEY, Thos.	BCI 181	Samuel	BAL 61
William	KEN 87	WILDGOOSE, Betsy	QUE 25	Sarah	BAL 62
WICKHAM, Stephen	BCI 226	WILDING, Ebenezar	BCI 17	Thomas	KEN 91
WICKHART, John	BAL 163	WILE, William	FRE 159	Thomas	SOM 151
WICKS, Edward	BAL 179	WILES, Jacob	WAS 149	William	BAL 48
Gabriel	BCI 307	Jas.	FRE 130	William, Jnr.	BCI 294
Lambert	KEN 116	Saml.	FRE 123	WILKINSON, Alice	CAL 66A
William	SOM 124	Thos.	FRE 127	Barbara (Mrs.)	CAL 67
WICKUM, Jacob	FRE 155	William	DOR 19	Christopher	QUE 32
John	FRE 155	William	HAR 29	David	BCI 516
WIDDOWS, Isaac	WAS 94	WILEY, Ann	BCI 68	Eleanor	CHA 224
John	WAS 104	David	HAR 61	Elizabeth	BAL 113
WIDERICK, George	FRE 114	Greenberry	BAL 78	John	BAL 113
WIDERMAN, George	BAL 177	Hiram	BCI 279	John	BCI 254
John	BAL 177	James	D.C.36	John	SAI 75
WIDGEON, Leu?	WOR 195	John	ALL 9	Joseph	BCI 284
Levi	WOR 195	John	WAS 138	Mary	BCI 10
WIDIGER, Isaac	BCI 408	Joshua	HAR 42	Newman B.	PRI 227
WIDOWS, John	WAS 94	Luke	BAL 219	Richd.	D.C.189
WIDRICK, Jacob	FRE 109	Mathew	HAR 61	Robert	CEC 169
WIEA, Isabella	BCI 307	Nancy-free	CAL 61	Robert B.	CAL 67
WIEGAND, Daniel	BCI 307	Nathan	CEC 187	Samuel	QUE 41
WIER, John	CEC 168	Nathaniel	HAR 70	Sarah	BCI 223
Mary	BCI 47	Robert	BCI 484	Shuble	BCI 12
Robert	CEC 168	Thomas	CEC 188	Thomas	BAL 113
WIGART, Andw.	BCI 255	Vincent	BAL 229	Thomas	BCI 86
Wm.	BCI 508	Vincent	CEC 187	Thomas	HAR 41
WIGFIELD, Jas.	D.C.134	William	CEC 188	Thos. H.	CAL 48
WIGGENS, Prince	KEN 109	WILFORD, Cornelius	WAS 103	William	QUE 27
WIGGINS, Ben.	QUE 9	Robert Y.	BCI 293	WILKS, Betsey	BCI 525
Charles	QUE 36	WILGUS, William	HAR 56	Charlot	WAS 106
Jno.	KEN 125	WILHAM, --- (Mrs.)	BCI 346	James	BCI 494
Jno.	QUE 10	John	ANN 331	John	WAS 106
John	HAR 72	William	ANN 331	Joseph	BCI 466

WILKS (continued),		
Thomas	BCI	318
Thomas	FRE	78A
WILL, George	D.C.	163
WILLABY, James	BAL	181
WILLAMSON, Janes	BCI	354
WILLARD, Salem	BCI	26
WILLCOTT, Jesse	BAL	246
WILLCOX, Nancy	DOR	51
WILLCOXEN, Thomas	PRI	239
WILLCUTT, John	TAL	3
WILLE, George	FRE	220
WILLEN, James	DOR	56
William	SOM	114
WILLET, Benjamin	CHA	214
Charles	CHA	213
George	CHA	213
John	CHA	213
Solomon	CHA	215
William	CHA	214
William (of James)	CHA	214
WILLETT, Benjn., Senr.		
	MON	139
Benjn., Junr.	MON	176
Burges	MON	159
John	BAL	111
John	MON	139
Joseph R.	PRI	191A
Ninian T.	PRI	194
Samuel	D.C.	31
Theodore	PRI	225
WILLEY, Capriel	DOR	42
Charles	HAR	19
Edward	DOR	33
Edward	DOR	37
Edward	DOR	41
Engelo	DOR	36
Engelo	DOR	37
Jabas	DOR	41
Jacob	DOR	37
John	BCI	118
Matthias	DOR	41
Newton	DOR	33
Nukes Thorinton	DOR	42
Paul McKuntire	DOR	42
Rachel	DOR	36
Rhoda	DOR	37
Richd.	D.C.	126
Robert?	DOR	33
Robrt	DOR	33
Samuel	DOR	36
Waitman	DOR	42
William	DOR	37
Zebulon	DOR	40
WILLHELAM, Henery	BAL	84
Hewery?	BAL	84
WILLHELM, John	BAL	84
John	BAL	153
WILLHIGHT, George	WAS	63
WILLIAINS, Ab?	WAS	106
Ale	WAS	106
All?	WAS	106
WILLIAM, Benjo.	BCI	333
Boroughs (?)	CHA	228
James	BCI	347
John	BCI	346
Johnsy	BAL	111
Thomas	SOM	146
W.	BCI	344
Zorobable	SOM	130
WILLIAMS, ---	ANN	389
--- (?)	BCI	383
--- (Widaw)	BCI	391
A. R.	BCI	392
Abba	ANN	335
Abner-Negro	HAR	79

WILLIAMS (continued),		
Abraham	BAL	124
Abraham	HAR	57
Abraham	HAR	63
Abram	CEC	168
Ailer	D.C.	208
Alexr.	D.C.	160
Alphred	MON	141
Amos	BCI	259
Andw.	BCI	184
Ann	BCI	81
Ann	FRE	214
Arnold	HAR	42
B.	BCI	369
Basil	D.C.	213
Benja.	BCI	522
Benja.	CAL	41A
Benja.	CAL	50
Benjamin	ANN	344
Benjamin	BAL	17
Benjamin	SAI	55
Benjamin	SOM	153
Benje.	BCI	477
Benjn.	BCI	199
Benjn.	MON	161
Bennet	BCI	171
Besee	BAL	99
Betey	SOM	147
Betsey	BCI	506
Betsy	BCI	457
Betty	SOM	126
Brook	D.C.	45
C.	BCI	415
Caleb	WOR	187
Cathn.	BCI	171
Ceaser	ANN	353
Charles	BAL	205
Charles	BCI	53
Charles	BCI	433
Charles	BCI	462
Charles-Negro	HAR	65
Cumbd. D.	BCI	259
Curtis	FRE	214
Daniel	BAL	124
David	ANN	359
David	BAL	199
David	BCI	150
Delelah	BCI	531
Dennis M.	PRI	198
Dianna	BCI	90
Dolly	D.C.	174
Edward	ANN	395
Edward	DOR	9
Edward	WAS	84
Edwards	BAL	5
Elie	WAS	146
Elisha	MON	136
Eliza	D.C.	186
Elizabeth	BAL	27
Elizabeth	BAL	99
Elizabeth	BCI	214
Elizabeth	BCI	434
Elizabeth	MON	164
Elizabeth	PRI	193
Elizabeth	WAS	107
Elizabeth F.	BCI	61
Elizth.	D.C.	207
Emmily	BCI	140
Ennion	BCI	180
Ephraim	BCI	98
Eunice	BCI	78
Evan	D.C.	186
Ezekiel	BCI	92
Fanny	BCI	496
Francis	BAL	205
Francis	BCI	102

WILLIAMS (continued),		
Francis	BCI	218
Francis	CAL	52
Francis	D,C.	192
Geo.	BCI	259
Geo.	BCI	320
Geo.	MON	140
George	BCI	30
George	BCI	99
George	BCI	121
George	BCI	142
George	TAL	34A
Giles	BCI	56
Griffin	CEC	168
Griffith	BCI	4
Hannah	BCI	535
Henny	BCI	322
Henry	ANN	300
Henry	BAL	205
Henry	BCI	434
Henry	CLN	85A
Henry	D.C.	150
Henry	D.C.	160
Henry	FRE	148
Henry	SOM	142A
Hezekiah	CHA	225
Hm. E.?	FRE	229
Isaac	MON	163
Isaac	SOM	112
Isaac	WOR	162
Isaac F.	SOM	132
Ishmeal	WOR	197
J.	BCI	367
J.	BCI	371
J.	BCI	399
Jacob	ANN	302
Jacob	BCI	185
Jacob	FRE	157
Jacob	FRE	204
Jacob	HAR	72
James	BAL	224
James	BCI	122
James	BCI	274
James	CLN	88
James	D.C.	41
James	D.C.	63
James	DOR	57
James	FRE	191
James	HAR	20
James	MON	136
James	SAI	74
James	SAI	91
James	TAL	8
James B.	QUE	28
Jane	TAL	4
Jas.	D.C.	101
Jas. R.	BCI	293
Jerh.	D.C.	41
Jesse	BCI	517
Jesse	CEC	168
Jno. M.	BCI	201
Jno. M.	MON	138
Jno. S.	MON	131
John	ANN	285
John	BAL	9
John	BAL	51
John	BAL	174
John	BCI	3
John	BCI	12
John	BCI	25
John	BCI	77
John	BCI	140
John	BCI	199
John	BCI	370
John	BCI	443
John	CLN	90

WILLIAMSON (continued),		
James	ANN	393
James	QUE	8
Jas.	FRE	135
Joanna	BCI	59
John	BCI	121
John	CLN	98
John	CEC	149
Peregrine	BCI	512
Samuel	CEC	168
Thomas	HAR	71
William	BCI	14
Zeporah	WOR	169
WILLIANS, Colmore	MON	136
WILLIARD, Andrew	FRE	157
Andrew, Jn.	FRE	157
Charles	FRE	157
Jacob	FRE	157
John	FRE	149
Lawrence	FRE	157
WILLIARFRITZ, Joseph		
	FRE	129
WILLIAS, Leven C.	(?)	
	WAS	117
Samuel	WAS	133
WILLIBY, John	DOR	5
WILLICE, Allen C.	CEC	129
WILLINER, Thomas	BCI	4
WILLING, Aaron	SOM	115
Chaplain	SOM	116
George	SOM	115
George M.	SOM	122
Isaiah	SOM	115
James	SOM	116
Josiah	BCI	177
Levi	DOR	33
Levin	SOM	115
Mary	PRI	204
Mary	SOM	115
Polly	SOM	124
Thomas	DOR	21
Tubman	SOM	116
William	SOM	115
Zacheus	SOM	115
WILLINGNYER, Caspr.		
	BCI	345
WILLINOR, Eleonor	SAI	65
WILLIOMS, John; Esqr.		
	DOR	18
WILLIS, Aaron	DOR	63
Ann	BCI	322
Arthur H.	DOR	10
Caesar	D.C.	190
Charles, Jr.	CLN	107
Cornelius	BCI	54
Edward (free negro)		
	SOM	118
Elijah	KEN	94
Elijah	WOR	179
Elijah	WOR	212
Elizabeth	CLN	114
Esther	CLN	110
Henry	FRE	228
Henry	TAL	11
James	DOR	55
John	BAL	92
John	DOR	51
John	KEN	105
John	TAL	38
Joseph	BAL	58
Joseph	CLN	115
Joshua	BCI	18
Lewis	CLN	110
Martin	BCI	456
Noah, Ovsr.	TAL	7
Peter	CLN	105

WILLIS (continued),		
Peter, Jr.	CLN	110
Philemon	TAL	38
Richard	CLN	115
Robt.	D.C.	194
Sameel	BAL	94
Short A.	CLN	96
Susan	KEN	104
Tempy (free negro)		
	SOM	118
Thomas	BCI	455
Thomas	CLN	112
Thomas, Sr.	CLN	105
Thomas, Jr.	CLN	105
William	CLN	113
William	FRE	93
William	TAL	47
William, Doctr.	BCI	265
Wm.	BCI	221
Wm.	BCI	415
WILLTSON, John	ALL	33
Joseph	CEC	149
Moses	ALL	33
Rachael	ALL	33
William	ALL	33
WILLISS, Nicholis	CAL	53A
WILLISTON, Ralph	PRI	201
WILLITT, Liddy	CAL	49
Tower	CAL	49
WILLKINS, Ann	KEN	102
Esther	KEN	110
Julyanna	KEN	100
WILLMER, Francis	KEN	87
James	KEN	105
John	KEN	109
Lameel?	KEN	104
Lanuel	KEN	104
Mary	KEN	101
William B.	KEN	95
WILLMORE, William	WOR	192
WILLOBY, John J.	BCI	483
WILLOCKS, William	CEC	187
WILLOUGHBEY, Martin		
	QUE	38
WILLOUGHBY, Andrew		
	CLN	110
Henry	CLN	88
Henry	CLN	107
John	CAL	43
Richard, Sr.	CLN	105
Richard, Jr.	CLN	104A
Sophia	CLN	114
Walker	TAL	2
William	CLN	109
WILLOURN, Phillip	WOR	192
WILLOWBY, Joseph	TAL	47
William	TAL	48
WILLS, Charles	CHA	213
Francis W.	BCI	266
John	BAL	193
John	CEC	148
John	D.C.	174
John B.	CHA	213
John B., Junr.	CHA	206
Joseph	BCI	309
Joseph J. (I.?)	CHA	210A
Mary Magdalen	FRE	145
Michael	FRE	94
Richard	BCI	282
Susan	BAL	13
William	HAR	29
William	PRI	207
WILLSAN, Henry	PRI	207
Priss	BCI	526
WILLSLAGER, Geo.	BCI	185

WILLSON, Aaron	CLN	94
Alexander	DOR	13
Alice	TAL	13
Ally	ALL	32
Amos	ALL	34
Christopher	CLN	73
Daniel	CLN	92
David	WAS	140
David T.	WAS	120
Edward	CLN	73
Edward	DOR	10
Eli	ALL	33
Elisha	CLN	89
Ezekiel	DOR	63
Flora	DOR	11
Frederick	KEN	108
George	CLN	88
George (Senr.)	SOM	101A
George D.	SOM	109
George W.	KEN	107
Hanner	FRE	215
Henry (?)	PRI	207
Henry	D.C.	4
Henry	D.C.	45
Isaac	D.C	55
Isaac	WAS	62
Isaac	WAS	134[A]
J. I.?) R.	D.C.	60
Jacob	WAS	65
James	ALL	36
James	CLN	75
James	CLN	89
James	D.C.	45
James	DOR	10
James	DOR	15
James	WAS	59
James	WAS	78
Jemima (free negro)		
	SOM	118
John	ALL	33
John	BCI	286
John	BCI	510
John	CLN	78
John	CLN	80
John	CLN	89
John	SOM	111
John	WAS	101
John of W.	ALL	33
Jonathan	CLN	108
Joseph	WAS	120
Lancelot	D.C.	64
Leah (free negro)	SOM	118
Levin	SOM	103
Lucy	DOR	21
Mary H.	SOM	111
Mitchel	SOM	108
Nathaniel K.	WAS	88
Noah	CLN	110
Norandin	D.C.	64
Otho	ALL	32
Peter	BCI	529
Peter	DOR	8
Saml.	BCI	497
Samuel	SOM	113
Sarah	CLN	91
Sarah	CLN	93
Solomon	CLN	88
Solomon	DOR	3
Solomon	KEN	106A
Thomas	CLN	72A
Thomas	D.C.	5
Thomas	D.C.	14
Thomas	D.C.	61
Thomas	KEN	108
Thomas	SOM	105
Thomas	WAS	60

ZOLLINGER (continued),		ZOUCK, Henry	BAL 153	ZUNBRUN, --- (Widow)		
John	BCI 367	ZUCK, Henry	WAS 61		FRE	168
Peter	FRE 150	Jacob	FRE 72	George	FRE	168
ZORN, Christian	BCI 152			Jacob	FRE	168
Sarah	BCI 200			John	FRE	175